Musica Naturalis

Rethinking Theory
Stephen G. Nichols and Victor E. Taylor, Series Editors

Musica Naturalis

*Speculative Music Theory and Poetics, from
Saint Augustine to the Late Middle Ages in France*

PHILIPP JESERICH

Translated by Michael J. Curley and Steven Rendall

Johns Hopkins University Press

Baltimore

This English edition has been translated from the original German publication: *Musica naturalis* (2008). © Franz Steiner Verlag, Stuttgart, Germany. All rights reserved.

The translation of this work was funded by Geisteswissenschaften International—Translation Funding for Work in the Humanities and Social Sciences from Germany, a joint initiative of the Fritz Thyssen Foundation, the German Federal Foreign Office, the collecting society VG WORT, and the Börsenverein des Deutschen Buchhandels (German Publishers & Booksellers Association).

Johns Hopkins University Press
2715 North Charles Street
Baltimore, Maryland 21218-4363
www.press.jhu.edu

Library of Congress Cataloging-in-Publication Data

Jeserich, Philipp.
　　[Musica naturalis. English]
　　Musica naturalis : speculative music theory and poetics, from Saint Augustine to the late Middle Ages in France / Philipp Jeserich ; translated by Michael J. Curley and Steven Rendall.
　　　　pages cm.— (Rethinking Theory)
　　Includes bibliographical references and index.
　　ISBN-13: 978-1-4214-1124-8 (hardcover : acid-free paper)
　　ISBN-10: 1-4214-1124-5 (hardcover : acid-free paper)
　　1. French poetry—to 1500—History and criticism. 2. Music theory—France—History—500–1400. I. Curley, Michael J., 1942– translator. II. Rendall, Steven, translator. III. title.
　　PQ211.J4713 2013
　　841'.109—dc23　　　2013013503

A catalog record for this book is available from the British Library.

*Καὶ μὴν καὶ μουσικὴ πᾶσα περὶ ἁρμονίαν ἔχουσα καὶ ῥυθμὸν
τὰ νοήματα, τὸν αὐτὸν τρόπον ἂν εἴη ὥσπερ ἐκεῖ ἡ περὶ τὸν
νοητὸν ῥυθμὸν ἔχουσα.*

Thus all music—since its thought is on melody and rhythm—
must be the earthly representation of the music there is
in the rhythm of the ideal realm.

Plotinus, *Enneads* V.9.11, 42
(Translated by Stephen MacKenna and B. S. Page)

CONTENTS

This study was first published in German in 2008. Its favorable reception suggested that it might be worthwhile to make it available to a broader international audience. I am pleased that it has been possible to do so with the translation and publication of this English edition.

This edition presents an abridged version of the original German text. The discussion of earlier scholarship had to be reduced; the extensive quotations from Latin sources regrettably could be given in English translation only. Where terminological issues are addressed, or where philological accuracy made giving the Latin original appear indispensable, extracts of the original Latin are inserted in the English text. Readers may wish to consult the German edition, where the Latin quotations are given in full.

The book began as a doctoral dissertation in literary studies. The area of research to which it seeks to contribute is the history of poetics. It takes as its starting point questions concerning the theory of poetry in the late Middle Ages in France and returns to them in conclusion. The answers it has to offer emerge from the opening up of a horizon of reflection in poetic theory that literary studies have up to this point recognized only partially. The central part of this study gives a broad presentation of the speculative branch of medieval music theory: Accounting for its philosophical, theological, and epistemological contexts and situating it within the broader developments of medieval learning, the study points out the relevance and vitality of speculative music theory as a discursive horizon of reflection on poetics from Late Antiquity down to the late fifteenth century in France.

In accordance with this interest, the study differs from investigations that focus on the relationship between the poetic text and the musical setting, and although in order to provide a broad analysis it takes musicological research into account, it does so selectively. The publication of this study in English is connected with the hope that it might serve to encourage literary scholars to engage in further and deeper examination of the sources in music theory discussed here.

The publication of this edition was suggested by Stephen G. Nichols, to whom I would like to offer my warmest thanks for his kind encouragement and support for the project. I also thank Joachim Küpper, who originally supervised my research, as well as the Börsenverein des Deutschen Buchhandels, which financed the translation. I am particularly indebted to the translators, Michael J. Curley and Steven Rendall, who have so diligently sought to meet the challenges of this project.

Part I

CHAPTER ONE

Trends in Recent Research on the Late Middle Ages

To JUDGE BY RECENT RESEARCH on the literature of the late Middle Ages in France, it seems that two phases can be distinguished.[1] The first is generally defined by means of temporal paraphrases such as "from Guillaume de Machaut to Charles d'Orléans,"[2] and is usually presented as being in the tradition of courtly literature. This vague profile[3] initially suggested a way of conceiving the continuity in Huizinga's famous metaphor of the "Autumn of the Middle Ages."[4] This conception seems to imply that the works concerned are an echo and conclusion of earlier ones, to which they can and must be related if one wants to deduce their own profile; and so this path was soon abandoned in favor of others. Instead, efforts were made to locate a new tradition nourished by the fractures in the old one, and to follow it out until the elements of an early modern conception of poetry emerged.[5] Jacqueline Cerquiglini identified, in the fourteenth century already, a newly emergent, "reflexive" mode of writing: "The fourteenth century sought to make writing its object, to reflect on the myths of its birth, and to substitute a reflexive practice of literature in French for an empirical one [. . .]."[6] Thus, it has been argued, a fundamental change in the self-conception of the poet and of poetry is introduced, a change that after 1400 led to the opening up of traditional forms, to the broadening of the thematic register, and increasingly to the "subjective" modeling of the lyrical "I."[7] This account has the indisputable advantage of responding to literary history's demand for consistency and meaning.[8] French poetry of the late Middle Ages is said to bear the signature of a process of differentiation in the course of which the practice of lyrical poetry freed itself from the formal, thematic, and performative constraints of the social order of late feudalism. The reflexivity of the specific processes and procedures of lyrical poetry, opening up the choice of form and subject, and the increasingly "subjective"-reflexive modeling of the lyrical "I," which can be interpreted either as a process of becoming conscious of the development or as a compensation for it, are supposed to be epiphenomenal to this process of differentiation itself.[9] Thus essential constituents of the poetic discourse of literary modernity go back to the fifteenth century, not only on the level of prominent individual characteristics but also on that of the founding structure of discourse.[10] However, the possibilities of integrating the work of the *Grands rhétoriqueurs*, conceived as a "second phase" within the French late Middle Ages, are limited: the more consistently literary historical modeling accentuates as "essential" characteristics of poetry "between Machaut and Charles d'Orléans" that are perceived as a proto-Renaissance or explicitly "modern," the more the work of the *rhétoriqueurs* falls into the problematic status of an interlude. The decades between 1450 and 1530 are assigned a traditional role here. Beginning with the Pléiade's insistence on the poet's "inspiration,"[11] the artful versification of the *rhétoriqueurs* fell first into contempt, then into oblivion. Pierre de Ronsard's trenchant comparison in the second preface to the *Franciade* of 1587 marks the highpoint of a polemic that had begun with Sebillet and Du Bellay: "There is as much difference between a poet and a versifier as between an old nag and a fine Neapolitan charger, or to compare them better, between a venerable prophet and a charlatan selling herbal remedies."[12] This polemic went on during the subsequent centuries. For seventeenth-century writers, the works of Chastellain, Molinet, or even Lemaire de Belges were not worth even the kind of polemic that had been mounted against the Pléiade. The great literary historians of the eighteenth century—Abbé Massieu, Abbé Goujet—agreed in flatly stating that the poets "who appeared during the reign of Charles VIII and Louis XII disfigured it [poetry] to such a point that it became almost unrecognizable. They achieved nothing of value by trying to do too well, and spoiled everything by over-refining it."[13] This critical hatchet job was repeated in the nineteenth century by Sainte-Beuve. His introduction to the first volume of an anthology of the masterpieces of French poetry edited by Eugène Crépet declared that the works of the *rhétoriqueurs* are soulless versifying and dead academicism: "The ingenious and the contrived replaced natural verve and fragmented the good vein into thousands of little artificial canals and scholastic compartments."[14] Anatole Montaiglon wrote the introduction to fifteenth-century verse for Crépet's anthology. In the sharpness of his judgment we can discern the assurance that comes from having the *communis opinio* on one's side:

> The whole uniquely pedantic and scholastic group of poets that crowned
> the end of the fifteenth century and remained official until the middle of

the reign of Francis I exhausted its strength in this puerile gymnastics; it would be impossible to expend more talent, more cleverness, more labor to say nothing or to say it as badly as possible. It is a school without a single master.[15]

In the great surveys of literary history that appeared in the early twentieth century we can still find similar, sometimes harsh invectives, for example in Henry Guy's influential *Histoire de la poésie au XVIe siècle* (1910), which nevertheless provides an informative overview, in Pierre Champion's *Histoire poétique du XVe siècle* (1923), and no less in Robert Bossuat's influential *Manuel bibliographique*.[16] René Doumic's popular *Histoire de la littérature française* (34th edition, 1916) seeks to consign poetry before 1500 to oblivion: in his view it should remain largely unpublished.[17]

Literary historiography tends to canonize whatever bears marks of the present.[18] This thesis is confirmed not only by the polemic extending over the centuries but especially by the revision of the judgment regarding the work of the *rhétoriqueurs* that began in the wake of the theoretical debates of the 1960s. Two pioneering articles by William L. Wiley and Pierre Jodogne stimulated new research on the *rhétoriqueurs'* poetics and poetry.[19] In addition to these scholarly works, a contribution published in 1967 by Albert-Marie Schmidt, a founding member of the *Ouvroir de Littérature Potentielle*, gained wide-ranging influence. His article, "L'Âge des rhétoriqueurs (1450–1530)," attributes to the *rhétoriqueurs'* poetry a conception of language and lyric that anticipates not only Baroque mannerism, but also modernism and surrealism, and indeed the most recent positions in poetics at the time.[20] In the last third of the twentieth century, such anachronistic readings of the *rhétoriqueurs'* poetics seem to have spawned the most productive branch of research on the *rhétoriqueurs*. Paul Zumthor's work was, partly in spite of his intentions, crucial in this regard. Zumthor's overall presentation, supplemented by several individual studies and an anthology,[21] appeared in 1978 under the title *Le Masque et la lumière. La Poétique des Grands rhétoriqueurs*.[22]

The study starts out by noting a continuity in the social context of poetic productivity: Just as for poetry between Guillaume de Machaut and Charles d'Orléans, for that written under Philip the Good and Charles the Bold in Burgundy, then under Margaret of Navarre, and finally under Charles VIII, Anne of Austria, Louis XII, and partly still under Francis I, the social integration of the producer and the product in courtly societies remained a historical *a priori*: "The social situation of the *rhétoriqueurs* is defined [. . .] by a relationship of subordination, more or less strict on the economic level, but always made official in accord with the titles used in some state apparatus. [. . .] his discourse was [. . .] important for social regulation: he confirmed, on the level of the dominant ideology, a hegemony."[23] Zumthor thus affiliates himself with the theses Daniel Poirion formulated on poetry between Guillaume de Machaut and Charles d'Orléans. Here, according to Poirion, the "perspective of fidelity to courtly values" remains dominant.[24] Poirion interprets the pronounced traditionalism of many texts written in that earlier phase of late Medieval French poetry as "the eminently poetic signification of a refusal, of a protest, of a revolt confronted by banal reality"[25] that strives to bridge the chasm opening up, in the course of a growing petrifaction of the formal and thematic registers, between ideal social norms and an increasingly deficient reality. For Poirion, until about 1450 poetry elevated courtly reality to a play of its ideals; its tendency to theatrical "representation"[26] corresponded to a playing out a "factitious chivalry" and a "general tendency to the spectacular" peculiar to late-feudalistic society.[27] Zumthor adopts this thesis[28] and argues that the poetry of the *rhétoriqueurs* had to be conceived on the basis of a structurally comparable but intensified problematics. Zumthor sees courtly life after 1450 as characterized by a generalized tendency toward "theatricalization,"[29] and precisely the "theatricalization" of the courtly order in the name of its preservation as an agent accelerating its further "hollowing-out": The performance of meaningless forms reduced to mere appearance transmitted no more than the empty shell of the forfeited self-evidence and plausibility of the order of the real. Zumthor thus locates the starting point of the *rhétoriqueurs'* poetry in the tension between a world that already bore the traits of early modern pluralization, on the one hand, and, on the other hand, in their task of encountering this pluralization through the "construction of an imaginary unity"[30] of the stratified, late feudal society:

> To accept or reject this world, such as it exists with its contradictions? The choice presented itself only superficially in these terms, at the level of the rhetorical surface of discourses. The *hors-texte* constitutes the given for which around the year 1500 the individual had no analytical criteria except for a few ancient, ineffective commonplaces. The contradictions were felt all the more intensely or even accepted. Whence, pushing matters to the extreme, we have two possible types of discourse. The first posits—or implies—that the world is good just as it is, that it subsists by virtue of a few religious, political, or simply worldly myths that still guarantee its fragile coherence, but also that it is empty. [. . .] The other discourse expands the referential contradictions, emphasizes them, integrates

them into its own mode, explodes in dislocations of every kind: it posits the upside-down world that is absurd insofar as it admits of no relationships other than aleatory ones. If we had to reduce what is only a dominant tendency to a simplistic formula, [. . .] this second discourse could be defined as Villon's; the first as the *rhétoriqueurs*'.[31]

If through its continuing "intercession" courtly poetry contributed to the continuation of the "fragile external coherence"[32] of the traditional order, then it had to be able to refer to what threatened this order: to the change in social structures, its symptoms. Zumthor considers its ability to do so as slight.[33] The literary text remains dependent on the staging of a "set of intellectual and discursive schemas that fulfill the social function of legitimating the order,"[34] which is not only decreasingly able to bridge the gap separating it from a deficient reality but actually deepens it through its theatrical elevation. Zumthor's ingenious argument now maintains that it was precisely the dynamics entailed that gave the poetic discourse of late Middle Ages its autonomy. The agent of the process was not, he claims, its own act of differentiation, but rather the increasingly heavy loss of extraliterary reference for which it could not compensate with its own means. Zumthor's example is Molinet's work:

> In the *Resource [du petit peuple]* Molinet shows himself to be passionately Burgundian and anti-French, but his discourse expresses this passion as an unconditional attachment to the aristocratic order, from which—as he sees it—truth and justice proceed when a virtuous prince rules. Without ever completely succeeding in doing so, the text tends to center on itself, to articulate an experience that is nothing other than itself. Its reference is thus established at the level of its totality rather than of its parts: like a light that it radiates, not like the lateral movement toward external objects that the word constantly "suspends." The literal meaning self-destructs insofar as another meaning is created as an always-incomplete metaphor of the former.[35]

A differentiation of an autonomous literary domain does not take place if the decreasing pressure to iterate the dominant discourse of legitimation opens up free areas, but on the contrary only if the tension between idealized norms and the deficient reality makes the conditions of this discourse's plausibility dwindle. Work with the signifier folds into work on the signifier: under the pressure of the oppressive order of the real, precisely in its phase of decline, the staged ideal "explodes," the liberated signifier remains behind as the medium of a "ludic," self-referential poetic praxis.[36] Zumthor understands this new availability of signifying material as a gain in poetic possibilities whose plumbing to the point of transgressing the linguistic primary code is elevated to a characteristic of the *rhétoriqueurs'* poetry: The "intentional exploitation of the possibilities offered by the linguistic system is sought,"[37] leading to a "deconstruction of the hereditary poetic language."[38] The new dynamics led to the "autonomy of the signifier" and the play of the "emancipated material":[39]

> The signifier, made available, demands its autonomy [. . .]. It cobbles itself
> together, full of sound and fury, multiplies itself, abounds, an infinity of
> surplus that is potential for the poet at the moment of writing and real
> and vertiginous for the reader urged to exhaust its suggestions . . . inex-
> haustible like everything useless. *Jonglerie* is a kind of "paragrammatic"
> semiotic practice.[40]

The process of "ludic ambiguization" first affects the prolongation of traditional conceptual orders and thus the iteration of the political discourse of power. To the unifying power of the old discourse of order, the *rhétoriqueurs'* work opposes the differential dynamics of the play of the signifier. Compensating this dynamics, according to Zumthor, an "*ordo* that substitutes for the disorder of appearances"[41] is formulated and provides instructions. A practice helps out where conceptual orders no longer offer orientation: "The technique that presides over it represents man's share amid chaos."[42] The poetry of the *Grands rhétoriqueurs* constitutes a universe of the disalienated signifier that is self-sufficient in its incompleteness:

> For them, the medieval artifact is no longer a simple fashioned object:
> beyond social pretexts, it posits itself as an anti-nature. [. . .] The disa-
> lienated signifier founds a universe that is peculiar to it. The poem only
> apparently reproduces a pre-existing cosmic order: it posits itself in and
> by itself. In that way the *rhétoriqueurs* escape the "medieval" civilization
> (if that expression is meaningful) on which they continue to be technically
> dependent.[43]

Zumthor's consistent willingness to entertain "big theses" inclines us to forgive him some inaccuracies.[44] The theoretical models dominant in the literary studies of the last decades allow us hardly any alternative to this indulgence: As Max Weber observed long ago, taking a distance on the material brings historical macrostructures and their processes more clearly into view but diminishes our ability to integrate contrary details.[45] However, objections can be made even at the chosen level of abstraction. Zumthor scarcely attempts to connect his theses (and their semiotic basis) with the fifteenth century's own metapoetic reflections. The repeated reference to the generally minor status of such reflections in his sprawling corpus is as unconvincing as a justification of the latter as is his reference to the limited conceptual range of the *Arts de seconde rhétorique* edited by Ernest Langlois[46] or the thesis, also repeated over and over, that the "intellectual apparatus" available to the *rhétoriqueurs* was "incapable of developing an adequate 'metalanguage.'"[47] This holds in particular because Zumthor devotes several chapters of his study to the identification of conceptual relationships that seem to fulfill such a reflective function. In the chapters on the "music, rhythm, and rhyme" complex,[48] Zumthor's study notes the "subordination of techniques, laboriously inventoried, to a general goal, which is to force language to engage in infinite numerical games,"[49] and cites as proof Molinet's definition of versification as "a kind of music called rhythmic (*richemique*), which contains a certain number of syllables with some suaveness of equisonance."[50] Zumthor then conceives composition founded on numerical orders as the practical implementation of a conception of the art of poetry based on *musica scientia*, calls Augustine's work known as *De musica* the most important reference for such a conception,[51] and emphasizes that the essential elements of the doctrine developed in this work were still valid for the *rhétoriqueurs*.[52] However, a few lines farther on, and without any mediation, he refers once again to the "disarticulation that they [the *rhétoriqueurs*] operate on signs, and the diversification of the processes of signification."[53] The reference to an emancipation of the signifier, of a "paragrammatic" semiotic practice as a characteristic of the *rhétoriqueurs'* poetics, stands in immediate juxtaposition to Zumthor's observations on numerical composition and on the recurrence of the terminology of musical theory in the context of discussions of poetics.

Zumthor avoids the need to clarify the relationship between the two results by referring to Eustache Deschamps's *Art de dictier* (1392). From Deschamps on, "music" stood only for "sounds as such":

> Between 1350 and 1450, a slow process gradually dissociated the terms of the equation. For the author of *De vulgari eloquentia*, poetry is *musica* because it is situated, within its own sphere, in the concert of cosmic rhythms: in the fifteenth century the powerful ethics that this conception implied faded away. Toward the end of the century, in his *Art de dictier*, Eustache Deschamps moved to a different level: that of sounds as such.[54]

Zumthor's work conveys the impression that the conception of poetry as a "paragrammatic" practice reflected in conceptions of a musicality of "sounds as such," which he sees as characteristic of the *rhétoriqueurs'* poetics, nourished the poetry of the late fifteenth century as much as it did the poetry of the late nineteenth and twentieth centuries in that comparison of poetics to absolute music for which the names Verlaine, Mallarmé, and Valéry stand.[55] The coincidence raises the question whether we have to do with a current in late Medieval poetry that actually has to be seen as a precursor of high modernist poetics—or, an alternative to be considered, whether Zumthor's semiotic account is in some fundamental respect based on anachronistic assumptions.

Although Zumthor's theses are far from uncontested, they continue to shape research on the *rhétoriqueurs* up to the present day. One reason could be that they allowed to homogenize the literary historical narrative that we presented at the outset: the poetics of the *rhétoriqueurs* no longer appears as an interlude with problematic status, but rather fits smoothly into the picture of a late Middle Ages that anticipates the "modern" in matters of poetic practice and metapoetic reflection. In the practice of research, this homogenization cleared the way for the successive antedating of the point at which we can assume the existence of an "autonomous," self-referential and self-sufficient poetic discourse. Thus Jacqueline Cerquiglini, for example, has tried to show that we have to assume that the art of poetry had an "autonomous value"[56] long before Machaut. She provides evidence for the broadening of the thematic dyad "armes et amours" by the addition of a third member, "art or letters," in the course of the fourteenth century, and interprets her findings as marks of a new self-reflexivity of literary discourse[57] and an increased importance of the "artistic" component of writing, which has to be considered early Humanistic—and culminates in the virtuoso craftsmanship of the *rhétoriqueurs*.[58] Correspondingly, Friedrich Wolfzettel emphasizes that "probably the most decisive [. . .] aspect of rhetorical poetics should be sought in the ideas of making and shaping and the concomitant category of work."[59]

At the center of the complex of theses summarized on the basis of exemplary contributions here stands the assessment of the artistry of the *rhétoriqueurs*, and of the "formalism" characteristic of their poetic art in particular. Its sources can be variously assessed.[60] Research seems to largely agree that such a formalism was alien to the Middle Ages. The conclusion drawn by Carol J. Harvey stands exemplary for the assessment of late Medieval French poetry current today:

> Shouldn't we ultimately refer, paradoxically, to the modernity of these poems of the Middle Ages? Modern in their own time, of course, through their break with the poetic code. But also modern in their open-ended

text, their play with sounds and words, their discourses that are simultaneously unequivocal and equivocal, with multiple meanings.[61]

A "sublimation in the experience of poetry,"[62] a "negative *mise en abyme* of traditional procedures,"[63] "an advanced consciousness of the value and resources of language"[64]—Friedrich Wolfzettel sums up the what appears to be a widely shared consensus:

> It is certainly not going too far to see [. . .] the poetics of the late medieval lyric in relation to the *Seconde Rhétorique* [. . .] as the beginning or at least a necessary preliminary stage of modern aesthetics. [. . .] Before the classical Renaissance of the Pléiade and its Neoplatonic influenced doctrine of inspiration and grace, and in contrast to it, the whole period of the *Seconde Rhétorique* represents the decisive transition to a poetics of work on language. [. . .] The disinhibited rhetoric of the late Middle Ages thus appears as a necessary stage on the way to the self-referentiality and autonomy of art in the modern age.[65]

The modernizing tradition of research, which Wolfzettel still subsumes under the categories of preparations, hints, and "preliminaries," culminates in Gisela Febel's study *Poesia ambigua oder Vom Alphabet zum Gedicht. Aspekte der Entwicklung der modernen französischen Lyrik bei den Grands rhétoriqueurs*.[66] Even though a few works had in the interim critically evaluated semiological interpretations of the *rhétoriqueurs*,[67] Febel repeats Zumthor's theses, developing and expanding them to appropriate the poetry of the late French Middle Ages for modernity and modernism. The systematic "work on form" does not show solely that their work is "undoubtedly modern-oriented."[68] Here Febel wants to see "in some sense" an "early modern figure of a linguistic turn."[69] Like Albert-Marie Schmidt, Febel sees modern verbal art as already present in the poetry of the late fifteenth century: in the proximity of their work to Paul Éluard's surrealism and to OULIPO, which like the *rhétoriqueurs* "mathematicizes textual structures," she discerns an "indication of the great modernity or possible currency of the *Grands rhétoriqueurs*"[70] and emphasizes the "uncanny modernity of the text" and even the "analogy of the *Grands rhétoriqueurs'* writing with the modern age."[71] Their "modern procedural poetics"[72] is supposed to point "beyond all historical difference to surprising similarities with the deconstructive procedures of late modernity described by de Man and others."[73] Through "typographical play, the invention of figural poems and riddles, the production of multiple readings, and therefore the exit of the indecipherability of the fourfold meaning of writing and the integration of an active reader,"[74] the *rhétoriqueurs'* poetry displays entirely new "liberties" in language use. Febel sees prominent examples of such a "liberation" of language in the displaying of homophonies and polysemies, in the breaking down of words into their syllables and individual letters. The "Latin language" is "deconstructed,"[75] then the "tradition of rhetoric,"[76] as the *rhétoriqueurs* turn away from the core Scholastic disciplines of the trivium of grammar, rhetoric, and dialectic, and feel themselves close to "other disciplines such as arithmetic, combinatorics, and music."[77] Now interpreting the turning of poets toward arithmetic and music as a turning away from the medieval heritage presupposes ignoring relevant parts of this heritage. This becomes important because Febel sees the orientation of text production toward arithmetic and music as "aspects" that "contribute to the construction of a modern poetics":[78]

> Combinatorics, musical concepts of harmony, and number become central to the new doctrine, [. . .] The work on the old paradigm, which may be heuristically called deconstructive, can perhaps be summed up as the process of making available figures and linguistic signs, as a release of signs and sounds from the inherited codes of the signifier-signified bonds, as a discovery (or uncovering) of the plenitude of the word [. . .]. In a second but actually parallel movement, there develops a poetics of procedure, a self-consciousness on the part of authors, an awareness of their novelty, a new relationship between poetry and music through the doctrine of numbers and combinatorics [. . .].[79]

This passage displays the constituents of the conceptual framework that suggests the conclusion that here we find an "autonomy" of the signifier and a "modern" procedural poetics: the connection of a formalism conceived on the basis of combinatorics and numerical composition with an anachronistic concept of harmony. Febel grounds her modernistic interpretation of late medieval formalism on the persistent use of the terminology of music theory in contexts of metapoetic reflection. Febel as well relies chiefly on two examples: Jean Molinet's already cited definition of lyric poetry as a kind of music called "rhythmic" and Eustache Deschamps's distinction between "musique naturele" and "musique artificiele" are central to her chapter on the "musicality" of the *rhétoriqueurs'* poetry. For Febel as well as for Zumthor, these references make plausible the application to the poetry of the late Middle Ages of theoretical elements taken from a modernistic poetics that systematically aligns poetry and absolute music. Deschamps's distinction between *musique naturele* and *musique artificiele* is understood to claim a "musicality" for lyrical poetry that is reduced "to sounds as such," to divide the recitation of a poem from its instrumental accompaniment and subsequently to attest, first, to the emancipation of verbal art from the performative framework on which its social integration depends, and second to its emancipation from the principle of reference in general. The *Art de dictier* will be summarized in the following pages taking this freighting of the work into account. The following report on research on the *Art de dictier* is intended to show in particular that the meaning assigned the work by scholarship on the late Middle Ages is the result of a tradition of reading Deschamps that aids and abets the tradition of research summarized up to this point.

CHAPTER TWO

Eustache Deschamps, *L'Art de Dictier*, 1392

Presentation and State of Research

Eustache Deschamps was born in Champagne around 1340.[1] The text that entered the canon under the title *Art de dictier* was written in November 1392, toward the end of a varied career in the service of the house of Valois-Orléans and probably at the behest and for the use of Philip II the Bold, Duke of Burgundy.[2] This work on the theory of poetry is the first of its kind in the French vernacular. It is extant in three manuscripts, the most recent of which is now preserved in the Bibliothèque de l'Arsenal in Paris. It was prepared in the eighteenth century for the lexicographer La Curne de Sainte-Palaye.[3] Its prototype is a complete transcript of Deschamps's works commissioned by Arnaud de Corbie on 581 parchment pages that were produced by the writing workshop of Raoul Tanguy, Paris, BNF f. fr. 840.[4] The third manuscript, Paris, BNF nouv. acqu. fr. 6221, has the same lacunae as fr. 840 and may go back to the same hyparchetype. Both manuscripts begin with the sentence "Ci commence l'art de dictier," hence the usual title given to this work. Both manuscripts conclude with the note "Ce fut fait le XXVe jour de novembre, l'an de grace de Nostre Seigneur, mil.ccc.iiiixx et douze," corresponding to the dating of the work in the second half of the year 1392. In the manuscript BNF f. fr. 840, the text consists of 27 pages on seven leaves.

Presentation

The text begins with these words: "Here begins the art of poetizing and making songs, ballads, *virelais*, and *rondeaus*."[5] The *chanson*, a term that in the late fourteenth century had become rather unspecific,[6] includes the *balade*, *virelais*, and *rondeau*. These are fixed forms in the tradition of Old French poetry,[7] song and dance forms that had already developed before

Machaut[8] and dominated the vernacular poetry of the late fourteenth and fifteenth centuries. Deschamps's discussion of these forms is preceded by a survey of the seven liberal arts:

> ENTRE LES VIJ ARS et sciences par lesquelles ce present monde est gouverne, et qui sont appellez ars liberaulx pour ce que anciennement nul se il n'estoit liberal, c'est a dire, fils de noble homme et astrait de noble lignie, n'osoit aprandre aucun d'iceuls ars; c'est assavoir: Grammaire, Logique, Rethorique, Geometrie, Aristmetique, Musique et Astronomie, lesquelz ars trouva, du tiers aige du monde et au temps de Habraham, Zozoastres, qui regnoit en Baterie [. . .], et par lesquelz aprandre et scavoir l'en peut venir a toute lettre science, et monter de la plus petite lettre jusquelz a la plus haulte.

> (AMONG THE SEVEN ARTS AND SCIENCES by which this world is guided today, namely, Grammar, Logic, Rhetoric, Geometry, Arithmetic, Music, and Astronomy, which are called "liberal" arts, because formerly, no one dared learn them unless he was "liberal," that is, the son of a nobleman and descended from a noble lineage, and which were founded by Zoroaster who reigned in Bactria, in the third age of the world, at the time of Abraham. By learning and understanding these, one can arrive at all knowledge and rise from the least letter up to the most exalted science.)[9]

The phrase "third age of the world" reflects the stratified concept that the Venerable Bede's *De temporum ratione* had defined: Deschamps is writing in the seventh and last age, which began with the birth of Jesus Christ.[10] The canon of the arts (which is traced back to Zoroaster, presented as Abraham's contemporary) is said to have been instituted in the third age of the world, which extends from the birth of Abraham to David. This canon corresponds to the one taught in faculties of arts. It should be noted that the brief inclusion of music as a discipline in the quadrivium corresponds to the oldest, most enduring curriculum in the faculties of arts in the Middle Ages, but that was not able to cope with the change resulting from the reception of Aristotle that began with the works of Adelard of Bath, Thierry of Chartres, John of Salisbury, and especially with Hugo of St. Victor's *Didascalion* (c. 1128).[11] This is noteworthy because Deschamps seems to have been familiar with the Aristotelian classification of the sciences.[12] With the exception of the section on music, the paragraphs devoted to the individual arts seem rather few. In accord with the tradition since Augustine's *De ordine*, grammar is identified as the basic linguistic discipline and thus the key to learning as such:

[E]st le premier et principal art gramaire, par lequel l'en vient et aprant
tous les autres ars par les figures des lettres de A, et B, C, que les enfans
aprannent premierement, et par lesquelz aprandre et scavoir l'en peut
venir a toute lettre science, et monter de la plus petite lettre jusquelz a la
plus haulte.

(The first and fundamental art is Grammar. Through Grammar, one can
learn all the other arts by means of the letters of the alphabet, which children learn first. By learning and understanding these, one can arrive at all
knowledge and rise from the least letter up to the most exalted science.)[13]

Dialectics, introduced as "logic," is dealt with by Deschamps in a single
sentence. It distinguishes the true from the false and makes one more adept
in dealing with words and fellow human beings:

Logique est apres une science d'arguer choses faintes et subtiles, coulou-
rees de faulx argumens, pour discerner et mieulx recognoistre la verite des
choses entre le faulx et le voir, et qui rent l'omme plus subtil en parole et
plus habille entre les autres.

(Then, Logic is a science of revealing matters feigned and crafty, tinged
with false arguments, in order to discern and better distinguish the truth
of matters, between the false and the true. It renders man more subtle of
speech and more adept among others.)[14]

If we were to read these lines in a seventeenth-century text, we would
be inclined to interpret them as barbs directed against the "worldly-wise"
rhetoric of the new sophists. However, the paragraph on rhetoric gives us
no reason to do so:

Rethorique est science de parler droictement, et a quatre parties en soy a
lui ramenees, toutes appliquees a son nom; car tout bon rethoricien doit
parler et dire ce qu'il veult monstrer saigement et briefment, substan-
cieusement et hardiement.

(Rhetoric is a science of speaking correctly, and includes four parts, all
components of its study. For every good rhetorician should speak and
say what he wants to demonstrate wisely, briefly, concisely, and forth-
rightly.)[15]

The discussions of the disciplines of the quadrivium are also brief, and
remain close to everyday practice. Geometry is introduced as an art of
craftsmen and builders.[16] Arithmetic is the art of all those who work with
numbers. Deschamps mentions its importance for traders, surveyors, and

money-changers, and also for measuring time and for astronomy.[17] The brief remarks on astronomy conflate, in the then common way, the astronomical and the astrological.[18] The section devoted to music, which concludes the overview and makes the transition to the didactic and exemplary part of the work, constitutes by itself about one-fifth of the *Art de dictier*. Here, too, we see the tendency toward the sketchy and undeveloped discerned by Deborah Sinnreich-Levy,[19] but the chapter on music is clearly distinguished from the foregoing ones by its length and conceptual depth. Its organization reminds us of treatises on the theory of music. The chapter is introduced by a paragraph on the *effectus musicae*, on the recreational and therapeutic powers of music:

> Musique est la derreniere science ainsis comme la medecine des vij arts; car quant le couraige et l'esperit des creatures ententives aux autres ars dessus declairez sont lassez et ennuyez de leurs labours, musique, par la doucour de sa science et la melodie de sa voix, leur chante par ses vj notes tiercoyees, quintes et doublees, ses chans delectables et plaisans, [. . .], tant que par sa melodie delectable les cuers et esperis de ceuls qui aux diz ars, par pensee, ymaginacion et labours de bras estoient travailliez, pesans et ennuiez, sont medicinez et recreez, et plus habiles apres a estudiez et labourez aux autres vj ars dessus nommez.

> (Music is thus the last science, the medicine of the seven arts. For when the hearts and spirits of creatures who understand the other aforementioned arts are weary and tired of their labors, music, by the sweetness of its science and the melody of its voice, sings its delightful and pleasing songs to them with its six notes in thirds, fifths, and octaves [. . .] until with its delightful melody the hearts and spirits of those who were fatigued, burdened, and bored in practicing the named arts through thought, imagination, and manual labor, are remedied and restored, and rendered more able thereafter to study and work on the other six arts named above.)[20]

This is followed by the often-cited statement, "Et est a scavoir que nous avons deux musiques, dont l'une est artficiele est l'autre est naturele" ("And it should be noted that we have two kinds of music, of which one is artificial and the other natural").[21] In view of the context, a distinction is made within music, a classification is established. Artificial music is based on the notes of the hexachord, which had been named using the initial syllables of the verses of Paul the Deacon's hymn to St. John ever since Guido of Arezzo (c. 992–1050) established his scale:

L'artificele [. . .] est appellee artificiele de son art, car par ses vj notes, qui
sont appellees us, re, my, fa, sol, la, l'en puet aprandre a chanter, acorder,
doubler, quintoier, tiercoier, tenir, deschanter, par figure de notes, par clefs
et par lignes, le plus rude homme du monde, ou au moins tant faire que,
suppose ore qu'il n'eust pas la voix habile pour chanter ou bien acorder,
scaroit il et pourroit congnoistre les accors ou discors avecques tout l'art
d'icelle science, [. . .].

(The artificial [. . .] is called artificial because of its art, for through its six
notes, which are called *us, re, my, fa, sol, la,* one can teach the most ignorant fellow in the world to sing, harmonize in doubles, fifths, and thirds,
sustaining the treble part, descant, using notation, by clefs and by lines, or
at least do well enough, supposing now that he had no voice capable of
singing or properly harmonizing, would know how and be able to recognize harmonies or discords with all the art of this science [. . .].)[22]

Artificial music is based on a learnable ability. Unlike natural music:

L'autre musique est appellee naturele pour ce qu'elle ne puet estre aprinse a nul, se son propre couraige naturelment ne s'i applique, et est une
musique de bouche en proferant paroules metrifiees, aucunefois en laiz,
autrefoiz en balades, autrefois en rondeaulx cengles et doubles, et en
chansons baladees, [. . .].

(The other music is called natural because it cannot be taught to anyone
unless his own inner feeling (*couraige*) is naturally inclined to it. It is an
oral music consisting in uttering measured words, sometimes in lays,
sometimes in balades, sometimes in single and double rondeaux and in
chansons baladées [. . .].)[23]

Most important for creating natural music is not the mastery of an art
but rather the musician's "couraige," which is "naturally inclined to it." Let
us emphasize this difficult remark, which requires philological elaboration.
Natural music is "measured discourse," and as such an "oral music." Let
this, too, be emphasized. The following, syntactically complicated sentence
justifies the conception of measured discourse as music:

Et ja soit ce que ceste musique naturele se face de volunte amoureuse a
la louenge des dames, et en autres manieres, selon les materes et le sente-
ment de ceuls qui en cest musique s'appliquent, et que les faiseurs d'icelle
ne saichent pas communement la musique artificiele ne donner chant par
art de notes a ce qu'ilz font, toutesvoies est appellee musique ceste science
naturele pour ce que les diz et chansons par eulx fait ou les livres metrifiez

se lisent de bouche, et proferent par voix non pas chantable, tant que les douces paroles ainsis faictes et recordees par voix plaisant aux escoutans qui les oyent, si que au puy s'amours anciennement et encores acoustumez en plusieurs villes et citez des pais et royaumes du monde.

(And even though this natural music originates from amorous desire in praise of women, and in other ways, according to the subjects chosen and the inclination of those who apply themselves to music; and even though those who make it usually do not know artificial music or how to give their lyrics an artful melody, nevertheless, this natural science is called always music because, the diz, chansons, and livres metrifiez that they compose are read out loud and uttered in a voice and not sung so long as the sweet words thus composed, recited aloud, are pleasing to the listeners who hear them, as it used to be at the *Puys d'amours* of old and as it is still the custom in several cities and countries and kingdoms of the world.)[24]

The key to the proper construction of this passage is the expression "ja soit que," that is, "and although it may be," and the complementary conjunction "toutesvoies," that is, "nevertheless." Deschamps refers to *fin' amor* as a possible occasion of poetry, emphasizes the poet's free choice of subjects, notes that the poet generally does not have to set his poem to a melody. But all this does not affect the "natural musicality" of poetry. The syntactical construction prevents it from being bound to particular contents and detaches it, as "music" in its own right, from instrumental accompaniment. *Metrical constraint*, as the musicality specific to the poem, the recitation, that is, the use of the *voice*, and also the poet's *inclination* for which learning and training cannot substitute, are joined in a complex that Deschamps calls a "natural science."

Both kinds of "music" are autonomous and can stand by themselves—"nevertheless, each of the two are pleasing to hear by themselves"[25]—yet they are bound together in a kind of complementarity that Deschamps conceives as a "conjunction of science" and also as *consonance*:

Et aussi ces deux musiques sont si consonans l'une aveques l'autre, que chascune puet bien estre appellee musique, pour la douceur tant du chant comme des paroles qui toutes sont prononcees et pointoyees par doucour de voix et ouverture de bouche; et est de ces deux ainsi comme un mariage en coniunction de science, par les chans qui sont plus anobliz et mieulx seans par la parole et faconde des diz qu'elle ne seroit seule de soi. Et semblablement les chansons natureles sont delectables et embellies par la melodie et les teneurs, trebles et contreteneurs du chant de la musique artificiele.

(And also these two kinds of music are so consonant with one another that each of them can well be called music, as much for the sweetness of the melody as for that of the words, which are all pronounced and made distinct by the sweetness of the voice and the opening of the mouth. It is as if these two were married in a conjunction of science, through melodies that are more noble and more appropriate through the words and eloquence of the poems than they would be by themselves. And similarly *chançons natureles* are delightful and embellished by melody, and the tenor, soprano, and contra-tenor parts of artificial music.)[26]

For the modern reader, the concept of "consonance" necessarily raises questions, because the definition of *musique naturele* specifies that the latter, in contrast to the song added to *musique artificiele*, does not consist in the singing of intervals but rather in metrical verse discourse. The use of the concept for the relation between the two kinds of music is nonetheless unequivocal.

The following "technical" part of the *Art de dictier* avoids so far as possible the specification of the usual subjects in short lyrical genres. The referential dimension of the text as a whole is taken up only when the identical or divergent meaning of a rhyming syllable is stipulated, or in an exceptional case in which, with a similar form, differences in the subject ground differences in the designation of the genre.[27] *Balade* and *sirventes*, *chanson royale* and *pastourelle*, *rondeau*, *virelai*, and *lai* are determined on formal grounds alone, by specification of those of their properties that can be determined by counting off. The introductory paragraph on the *balade* may serve as an example:

Et premierement est assavoir que il est balade de huit vers, dont la rubriche est pareille en ryme au vers antesequent, et toutefois que le derrain mot du primier vers de la balade est trois sillabes, il doit estre de xj piez, [. . .]. Et se le derrenier mot du second ver n'a que une ou deux sillabes, le dit ver sera de dix piez. Et se il y a aucun ver coppe qui soit de cinq piez, cellui qui vient apres doit estre de dix.

(And first one must know that it is a *balade* of eight verses, whose refrain is similar in rhyme to the next-to-last verse, and nevertheless [if] the last word of the first verse of the *balade* is three syllables, it has to be eleven feet, [. . .]. And if the last word of the second verse has only one or two syllables, that verse will have ten feet. And if there is any short verse that has five feet, the one that comes after it must have ten.)[28]

In addition to the formal specification of fixed forms based on numerical determinations, work on complex rhyme schemes already appears in

Deschamps.[29] The *Art de dictier*'s remarks are complemented by a large number of examples that Deschamps takes primarily from his own works. The text ends with a brief conclusion in which the author indicates that it is a didactic work commissioned by his employer.[30]

The following textual evidence emerges regarding Deschamps's concept of poetry: it is developed in a didactic manual, as the concluding dedication suggests. The degree to which the passages on theory are worked out must be assessed against this background. The seven liberal arts provide the organizational schema in which the remarks on the theory of versification are embedded. The systematic place of poetry within this schema is music as a quadrivial discipline, the discussion of which constitutes the theoretical treatise's main element. In the arrangement of the section on music and the developed parts on theory, for instance the reference to the *effectus musicae*, the genre pragmatics of the treatise on music shines through. Two genres are to be distinguished within quadrivial music: *musique artificiele*, which operates with the heptatonic scale, and *musique naturele*. The latter, versification, proceeds from a "natural inclination" different from the learnable art. It is *musique naturele* first of all insofar as it is measured discourse, that is, insofar as it has a numerically determined form, and secondly, insofar as it is presented orally. Both genres are "consonant."

State of Scholarship

If we set aside its pioneering role in the theoretical capacity of the French vernacular, down to the twentieth century Deschamps's *Art de dictier* remained either simply unknown or seen as a failed poetics. William Forrest Patterson, in his survey *Three Centuries of French Poetic Theory* (1935), was the first to highlight the text's importance.[31] He does not go beyond a brief commentary, but offers an initial clue to one of Deschamps's possible sources: Johannes de Garlandia's *Parisiana poetria*, written around 1220.[32] A polemical dismissal of the *Art de dictier* published by Georges Lote in 1949 attracted no attention,[33] so Patterson's account remained standard until a shift in research on Deschamps occurred that has persisted down to the present. Roger Dragonetti's study "'La poesie . . . ceste musique naturele.' Essai d'exégèse d'un passage de l'*Art de dictier* d'Eustache Deschamps"[34] has gone largely unchallenged in current research. Unlike Langlois and also unlike later research on the *rhétoriqueurs*, which assumes reception relationships, Dragonetti expressly distinguishes Deschamps's *Art de dictier* from the arts of second rhetoric in the fifteenth century. Whereas the latter concentrated on the "purely artistic," Dragonetti claims that Deschamps presented "a doctrine that goes beyond precisely the framework of pure technicity."[35] The "more" that is specific to the *Art de dictier* is supposed to be illuminated by the investigation of the tradition in which the text is inscribed. According to Dragonetti, Langlois's and Patterson's reference to Johannes de Garlandia's *Parisiana poetria* is misleading. Predecessors must be sought not in poetics but in the theory of music: the conception of poetry as *musique naturele* has to raise the question of what musicality means in the "musical speculation of the Middle Ages"[36] and what the relation between versification and this concept of musicality is.

Dragonetti points first to Boethius's *De institutione musica* as the fundamental work of medieval music theory. This work is not guided by musical practice, but rather continues the Pythagorean-Neoplatonic tradition of speculative metaphysics. Albrecht Riethmüller has aptly summarized the implications of this musical metaphysics:

> The object (*subjectum*) of speculative music theory [is] the grounding of music in an intelligible principle, that is, its object is viewed as music, and not—as moderns are used to thinking—exclusively music as sound (*musica sonora*); the domain into which it—also methodically—ultimately falls is the metaphysical domain. [. . .] *Grosso modo*, music as sound is only a continuation or imitation of music as a "harmony" running through all domains of the macro- and microcosm.[37]

According to Dragonetti, classifications such as Deschamps's *musique naturele/musique artificiele* distinction are to be related first of all to this complex.[38] Musical metaphysics teaches us not to reflect on music but rather to reflect in accord with it. Its goal is the reenactment of music as a "transcendent order" that is sometimes opened up by philosophical meditation, sometimes "through the intermediary of signs," which are to be construed as "symbols of musical transcendence." The capability addressed is thus the noetic:

> Theoretical treatises on medieval music teach us to think *in accord with* music, which is entirely different from reflecting *on* music. All the same, thinking in accord with music is conceivable only if thought itself always already belongs to *Music*, and if this *Music* itself is posited as a transcendent order whose meaning can be understood on two different levels: either by meditation, or by the mediation of signs, on the condition that the latter are understood as symbols of musical transcendence. [. . .] The sensory judgment made by the ear attentive to sounds should thus yield to the judgment of thought, because it alone proves truly capable of listening with precision to what passes through audible music.[39]

Dragonetti's sketch formulates essential considerations for the understanding of the *Art de dictier* and names the central determinants of the tradition. However, its implementation does not realize its possibilities. It begins by gauging the range of the concept of music in the medieval speculative tradition. *Qua numerus*, it also includes metrics and rhythmics; in addition, Deschamps's reference to music as a therapeutic agent presupposes familiarity with an important complex of traditional music theory, the doctrine of *ethos*.[40] But Dragonetti does not use these relationships as an opportunity to substantiate the connection of the *Art de dictier* with the medieval tradition by discovering its sources. This desideratum is whisked away by the statement that by the end of the fourteenth century, the conceptual foundation of this tradition has become "uncertain."[41] This "loss of certainty" is supposed to be symptomatic of the condition of speculative music theory at the end of the fourteenth century in general. Under the impact first of the reception of Aristotle, in the wake of which only concrete acoustic phenomena were still considered "music," the emphasis of reflection on music theory shifted from the speculative "superstructure" to the phenomenal substrate. Soon supported by theological-philosophical nominalism[42] a "triumphal movement of musical naturalism"[43] emerged which the "text of the *rhétoriqueur* (Deschamps) merely reflected."[44]

The proof for these theses is supposed to be a "rather cavalierly"[45] executed juxtaposition of Deschamps's definitions of the respective kinds of *musique* and Boethius's theory. The comparison schematically opposes one monolithic block called "musical naturalism," to an equally monolithic block called "speculative music theory." Dragonetti conceives music theory working on an Aristotelian basis since the thirteenth century as a conceptually homogeneous front struggling with one accord for the limitation to acoustic phenomena and against the speculative tradition based on Boethius. For Dragonetti, Roger Bacon (1214–1292/1294) was the first representative of radical philosophical criticism of the speculative concept of music in the Boethian tradition, while it was Johannes de Grocheo (c. 1255–c. 1320) who first took a position against the supposition of a cosmos ordered in harmony with musical proportions in music theory. The liquidation of the Boethian tradition in music theory reached its culmination with Adam of Fulda (c. 1445–1505).[46]

Dragonetti then argues that Deschamps drew from the music theory of the older tradition shaped by Boethius the concept of a possible consonance of *musique naturele* and *musique artificiele*, but his formulations remained unclear with respect to the concept of consonance involved.[47] For Dragonetti, Deschamps's formulations are symptomatic of the alleged decline of speculative music theory, which is also reflected in Deschamps's limitation to music perceivable through the senses.[48] It is supposed to be this reduction to phenomenal existence running counter to the tradition of speculative music theory that Deschamps—if not for the first time, at least in an original way—sought to depict in the distinction between *musique naturele* and *musique artificiele*.

As a classification, that is, terminologically, Dragonetti argues, this distinction remains true to the Boethian tradition.[49] Thus for Dragonetti the thesis that Deschamps distances himself from this tradition has to be proven by reviewing the history of the distinction in detail, a task that literary scholarship had thus far failed to perform.[50] The philologically necessary approach is indicated here.

Dragonetti then refers to Gerhart Pietzsch's *Klassifikation der Musik von Boetius bis Ugolino von Orvieto*,[51] a work that has remained a standard one on the subject, and implies that Pietzsch is tracing primarily the history of the distinction between *musique naturele* and *musique artificiele*, and that this distinction goes back to Boethius.[52] In fact, neither is the case. In Boethius's didactic writings on music neither the epitheton *artificialis* nor the epitheton *naturalis* is mentioned in connection with *musica*, in a classificatory or any other context. In the form it takes in Deschamps, the distinction is first found in the *Epistola de armonica institutione* composed by Regino of Prüm (c. 840–915). Pietzsch reconstructs not the history of this distinction but rather the *different* terminological vocabularies for the classification of music and their coevolution. Dragonetti's summary of *musica naturalis*, even though he seems to have taken into account Pietzsch's discussion of Regino's *Epistola*, reduces the heterogeneity of music-theory discourse to a linear history of decline:

> Applied to music, the term *naturalis* is first used to designate the universal
> harmony, a divinely inspired, transcendent music of which the human
> voice, apart from all art, increasingly becomes the privileged sign among
> theoreticians. The result of conceiving *musica naturalis* in humans on the
> basis of the natural instrument of the voice and not, as Boethius did, in
> the mode of a pure interiority, is that the term *naturalis* ends up designat-
> ing vocal music itself—for example, song and poetry in Roger Bacon, and
> poetry alone in Eustache Deschamps.[53]

Thus Deschamps's distinction would be situated terminologically in the tradition of Boethian music theory, but conceptually modeled on the musical naturalism that had been gaining ground since Aristotle had risen to become the dominant authority in music theory as well. The conclusions that Dragonetti draws from his sketch are extremely wide-ranging:

As transcendent music is increasingly conceived on the model of an acoustic form, it is music as art that is substituted for the order from which it originally received its direction. On the basis of this separation, music sets off down the path toward an adventure in which, left to its own signs and its autonomy, it was to be perpetually in search of its foundations.[54]

Music is then no longer considered a subordinate manifestation of an ontologically primary "transcendental" order, but is rather inscribed as a practice self-sufficient in its immanence. The distinction between *musique naturele* and *musique artificiele* "now serves only to mark a distinction within the domain of music perceptible through the senses."[55] As if that were not to say that poetry is still conceived as a part of music, Dragonetti concludes that there is an "autonomy of the poem" and a "double break":

> It remains that the poem marks a double break: first with the whole earlier lyric tradition in France, in which song resulted from a synthesis between words and melody, and then with the Boethian conception of music, since poetry has broken with the transcendence of its law. The consonance between music and poetry Eustache Deschamps sees as an artificial association when it is a matter of song regains its original unity in the natural music of rhythmical language, but on the basis of forgetting what previously constituted the truth of all music.[56]

The *Art de dictier* opposes rhythmic verse discourse as a self-empowered practice to the unity of recitation and instrumental accompaniment in performance and to the relation of versification as music to an ontologically prior "musical" order of being.

The reservations that Dragonetti's study necessarily attracts are immense. First, we must note the philologically precarious foundation of the argument, which seems traceable to an inadequate analysis of medieval music theory. The collocation *musica naturalis* does not occur in Boethius himself. The distinction found in Deschamps was introduced by Regino von Prüm in order to create a place for Christian choral music within the Boethian tradition and as a consistent expansion of the latter. The distinction became established and can be found until the late fifteenth century in the context of the "traditional" body of Boethian-Neoplatonic music theory.[57] Dragonetti's schematizing presentation of medieval music theory completely ignores the conservative Boethian musical literature that sought syntheses and continued to be produced in the late Middle Ages and the Renaissance, works like those of Engelbert of Admont (c. 1250–1331), Marchettus of Padua (born 1274), Johannes de Muris (1295–1331), Jacob of Liège (born c. 1260), or Ugolino of Orvieto (c. 1380–1452). Furthermore, it is questionable whether the works of the theoreticians that Dragonetti names as important actors in the decline of speculative music theory, Roger Bacon and Johannes de Grocheo, really prove his claims at all. At this point let us merely observe that Roger Bacon, who is generally associated with "Oxford Platonism," remained bound to the ontological foundations on which Boethius also built, that Johannes de Grocheo's work *De musica* is extant in only two manuscripts,[58] and that Adam of Fulda (c. 1445–1505) did not criticize the concept of the harmony of the spheres in itself, but rather delegated its further development to astronomy. In addition, and first of all, the problems that are raised by the relation of the text to the later tradition in medieval music theory remain unsolved. Dragonetti can no longer explain the conception of the relation between *musique naturele* and *musique artificiele* as "consonant" and the connection between the doctrine of ethos and music that includes poetry. His hypothesis that the original conditions of the plausibility of these connections has become obscure shifts the difficulties of his interpretive approach onto the author of the *Art de dictier*. Dragonetti does not go on to ask why Deschamps discusses the relation between poetry and music in the context of an overview of the seven liberal arts, which consequently does not conceive music, as the Aristotelian *ordo scientiarum* had suggested at least since Thomas, as a *scientia media*, even though the impact of Aristotelian-influenced music theory is assumed to be decisive. Finally, Dragonetti completely ignores older positions in poetics. For example, a glance at Johannes de Garlandia's *Parisiana poetria*, brought into the discussion by Langlois and Patterson, reveals that here "rhythmical" poetry is conceived and classified, in accord with genuine Boethian precepts, as *musica*; but Dragonetti does not mention this. His study does not achieve the goal of explaining Deschamps's reference to versification as *musique naturele* on the basis of its historical presuppositions in medieval music theory.

Nevertheless, scholarship has for the most part unreservedly adopted Dragonetti's view. His interpretation has become the standard reference for research on versification in the late fifteenth century, which has concluded, on the basis of the latter's formalism, on the one hand, and its relationships with music on the other, that it has a "modernist" profile. Thus as early as 1965 Kenneth Varty pushed Dragonetti's theses farther, arguing that the conception documented in the *Art de dictier* seemed "Verlaine-like."[59] However, Varty fails in his attempt to substantiate this claim by reference to the text. He blames this failure not on his own approach, but rather on Deschamps's alleged lack of ability as an author: "he wrote so badly."[60] For

Varty, the text itself is aporetic. On the one hand, poetry is conceived as a form of music, and, on the other hand, as a practice entirely independent of music: "It is music, and yet it is not. If he had defined poetry as a kind of rhetoric, he would not have been in this difficult position."[61] The alleged contradiction arises only because Varty does not see Deschamps's distinction as a distinction within music, and is completely unaware of the tradition of reflection on the theory of poetry within music theory. However, Varty concludes that Deschamps is incompetent, assuming that the description of poetry as music must have grounds other than systematic ones. For Varty, the author of the *Art de dictier* wanted to enhance the status of his lyrics by making them a form of music, since he himself was not capable of playing an instrument or singing.[62] Thus Varty's brief study shows in an exemplary way not the aporias in Deschamps's text, but rather the contradictions to which the interpretation established by Dragonetti leads. An excessively crude schematizing and abbreviating view of the history of medieval music theory leads to the Aristotelian, ostensibly empirical-phenomenological conception of music being applied as the only relevant one in the late Middle Ages. If Deschamps's distinction between *musique naturele* and *musique artificiele* is referred to this conception of music, then the conceptual coherence of the *Art de dictier* becomes difficult to understand.

This did not reduce the success of approaches to Deschamps's text based on Dragonetti's theses. Up to the present day, practically any scholarly work that discusses Deschamps's *Art de dictier* in general or the concept of *musica naturalis* and its implications in particular stays indebted to his arguments. Thematic investigations dominated Deschamps scholarship until the 1980s,[63] when the first monographs on the *Art de dictier* appeared.[64] In 1994 Deborah M. Sinnreich-Levi supplemented her 1987 dissertation with a critical edition of the text with an English translation and an analysis of the text.[65] Important contributions to research on the *Art de dictier* were published around the turn of the millennium. A number of articles and monographs has endeavored to develop new approaches and perspectives on Deschamps's work, without fundamentally questioning Dragonetti.[66] Accordingly, Dragonetti provides the argumentative basis for the modernizing readings of the works of the *rhétoriqueurs* summarized in the last chapter. Gisela Febel, to whose work we now return, joining our reviews of research on the *rhétoriqueurs'* poetics and on Deschamps's *Art de dictier*, sees metapoetic reflection using music theory concepts between Deschamps and the *rhétoriqueurs* as providing an important proof of her theses. Febel considers Deschamps's *Art de dictier*, which she interprets solely on the basis of Dragonetti's 1961 essay,[67] the first proof [*sic*] of a conception of "poetry as music" typical of "modern procedural poetics":

> The explicit recourse to the conception of poetry as music in Eustache Deschamps [. . .] makes it clear that the *ars* of music greatly influenced the principles of construction in the poetry of the *Grands rhétoriqueurs*. They were the first to succeed in transferring into poetic practice the initial steps Deschamps had taken toward a liberation of poetic discourse from the narrow connection with the *artes dictaminis*.[68]

By means of selected references to medieval music theory, Febel seeks to shed light on Deschamps's sources and models. Her observations on the connection between arithmetic, music, and poetry mention Augustine's *De musica*, Boethius's *Institutio arithmetica*, Isidore of Seville, the *Scolica enchiriadis*, anonymous illustrations of twelfth-century ideas about music, Guido of Arezzo, Johannes de Grocheo, and Johannes de Garlandia. Febel's overview alludes to the connection between arithmetic and music based on Pythagorean and Neoplatonic thought, but does not try to systematize these observations, and does not grasp the unity of the tradition she traces. In particular, she does not ask to what extent the reconstruction of this tradition might be able to contribute to a historically adequate understanding of the distinction between *musique artificiele* and *musique naturele* and its conceptual foundations—although she notes that the texts that mention this distinction come primarily from the "speculative branch"[69] of medieval music theory.

For now, we can sum up by saying that the scholarship represented up to this point proceeds in an unbalanced way. Deschamps's *Art de dictier* and the definition of poetry as *musique naturele* are, on the one hand, a reference point for a firmly established interpretive tradition that expends an immense amount of theory to appropriate in particular the poetics of the *rhétoriqueurs* as protomodern or modern. The conception of metrical discourse as a form of music has been praised as an anticipation of the high modernist poetics of the late nineteenth and early twentieth centuries. This freighting of the *Art de dictier* and the category of a *musique naturele* is not counterbalanced by any systematic analysis of its historical presuppositions. The success of Roger Dragonetti's study explains this lack of balance but leaves open the question as to why recent scholarship has not taken the obvious step across the disciplines. In the field of musicology, studies have been published since Dragonetti that not only examine the sources of Deschamps's classification of music, but also its relationship to the tradition of medieval music theory.

The Contributions of Musicology

Scholarship in musicology has systematically examined the history of musical theory in the Middle Ages, published many of its texts, and made this generally difficult field accessible. The already mentioned approaches go back to the 1920s. In 1929, Gerhard Pietzsch published his study on the classification of music from Boethius to Ugolino of Orvieto, which Dragonetti discusses only cursorily. Pietzsch shows that the distinction in Deschamps is found for the first time in Regino of Prüm's *Epistola de armonica institutione*, written around 900, and that it was introduced there in order to make a place for the Christian *cantus* in the framework of Boethian music theory.[70] Pietzsch expressly emphasizes that the text retains the conceptual context of the music theory drawn from Boethius, and especially the latter's speculative vanishing point.[71]

Michael Bernhard has devoted special studies to Regino's *Epistola* that offer, in addition to a survey of the text's transmission, a *stemma* and a commentary on the text, along with remarks on its reception history.[72] The verifiability of the distinction between *musica naturalis* and *musica artificialis* in Johannes Cotto (c. 1100), Johannes Aegidius Zamorensis (c. 1250–1300/1318), Jacob of Liège (born c. 1260), Hieronymus of Moravia (thirteenth century), Johannes de Muris (c. 1300–1350), Deschamps, and Adam of Fulda (1445–1505), who cites Regino by name, proves its enduring establishment in the discourse of music theory. Literary scholarship still has the task of questioning each of these references regarding their relation to thought on the theory of poetry. However, we can already note the continuity that can be discerned in these proofs: the theoreticians identified by scholarship on late medieval literature as warrantors for their interpretation of Deschamps are not mentioned in Bernhard's studies. It is the conservative strand of speculative music theory discourse adhering to Boethius that guarantees the receivability of the *musica naturalis/musica artificialis* distinction down to the fifteenth century. General surveys such as the collective work on the *Geschichte der Musiktheorie*,[73] which has been appearing since 1985 under the editorship of Frieder Zaminer and presents contributions by the most prominent scholars, also render schematizations, and first of all Dragonetti's, generally untenable. Michael Bernhard's studies on the survival of ancient Latin music theory and on technical musical literature in the Middle Ages[74] emphasize that the authority of speculative musical metaphysics after Boethius remained "intact in the late Middle Ages."[75] The classification of music into *musica naturalis* and *musica artificialis* has to be understood in relation to its models and presuppositions in Antiquity and the Middle Ages—not least since Carl Dahlhaus's survey of the change in music theory's subject area[76] and Albrecht Riethmüller's sketch of the history of the concept of music[77] suggest that we should be extremely cautious in absorbing medieval *musica* into interpretations that presuppose a concept of music reduced to purely auditory phenomena.

In addition, two studies devoted specially to the concept of a *musica naturalis* have broadened the frame of reference. Albrecht Riethmüller's article *"Musica naturalis"*[78] has pointed out that the distinction in question is already laid out in Aristides Quintilianus, and thus goes back, so far as its conceptual content is concerned, through the compiler of Greek music theory mentioned for instance by Martianus Capella, directly to its Pythagorean substrate. Calvin M. Bower's study "Natural and Artificial Music: The Origins of an Aesthetic Concept" proposes hypotheses regarding Regino of Prüm's immediate models and offers illuminating remarks on the conceptual context of their influence. Bower's detailed discussion leads first to the observation that the unity of the distinction is established by the concept of the *ordo entium*, so that a relationship of similarity is to be assumed that grounds, indirectly, the anagogic relevance of acoustic music: In the "musical" order of the acoustic work, the order of being as Creation is manifest.[79] Bower uses the Plotinian profile of the argument, which Egon Wellesz already noted in 1954,[80] as an occasion for seeking the sources of Regino of Prüm's distinction and its conceptual foundation in the influence, direct or mediated through Augustine, of Neoplatonism. Thus Regino's distinction can be traced back to the work of John Scotus Eriugena.[81] In fact, John Scotus Eriugena's *De divisione naturae* develops, as Werner Beierwaltes has observed,[82] approaches that are derived from Augustine's *De musica*—and thus from the work that Zumthor recognized as the most important reference for the definition of poetry as a kind of music called *richemique* in Jean Molinet's *Art de Rhétorique*. To judge by the possible sources, there seem to be relationships between Deschamps's *Art de dictier* and Jean Molinet's *Art de Rhétorique* that span the fifteenth century. But these relationships are of a wholly different kind than the ones literary scholarship has thus far assumed, and in accord with a different discursive field.

CHAPTER THREE

Desiderata in Research

"E"XCESSIVE" WORK on the signifying material to the point of transgressing the primary linguistic code, "exorbitance" in exhausting formal and rhyming technique possibilities; the self-reflexivity of these processes, the "autonomy" of lyrical discourse in distinction to instrumental accompaniment, to rhetoric, to the concept of *ordo*, or to social integration in general, if not in the fourteenth century, then in the fifteenth century at the latest; "the analogy of the écriture of the *Grands Rhétoriqueurs* to that of the present time"[1] up to the "early modern figure of a linguistic turn";[2] the constitution of a "modern procedural poetics" through the *rhétoriqueurs'* turning away from the "key Scholastic disciplines of the trivium of grammar, rhetoric, and dialectic" in favor of "the other disciplines, such as arithmetic, combinatorics, and music;"[3] a "new relationship between poetry and music by means of number theory and combinatorics";[4] and, as the central proof of the whole complex, nonliterary texts that reflect poetry in concepts that are drawn from music theory—the interpretive tradition thus summed up may seem conclusive to the present-day reader. The pillar of this interpretation is Roger Dragonetti's work. His conception of the *Art de dictier* operates with an outline of continuities and discontinuities on which the plausibility of the theses just summarized depends. These theses are *historically* plausible only if the following conditions are met: There must be no provable continuities between the older tradition's holistic conception of music and the late medieval French texts cited. To be able to provide a basis for the strong "autonomy hypothesis," the conception of poetry as music must be interpretable as a demand for the free availability of the phonetic, and work on sound units must imply a deliberate emancipation from meaning. The theses with which Dragonetti's study on Deschamps concluded offered this plausibility. Moreover, the discourse of music theory in the Middle Ages is deliberately schematized and simplified to the point that its history appears as a linear decline of speculative music theory. The highly schematized construct that understands the reception of Aristotle and

31

theological nominalism as triggers for the declared breaks is based on the assumption of the rapid and comprehensive establishment of a "triumphant movement of musical naturalism"[5] "that the *rhétoriqueur's* [Deschamps's] text merely reflects."[6] At the same time, it accepts the consequence that the option of *completely* deciphering the text is sacrificed to demands of the interpretive approach. Even if not to the same extent as interpretations of the *rhétoriqueurs* summarized here, these approaches to Deschamps's work recapitulate modernizing readings. Their status is problematic so long as the criterion of the value of an interpretive hypothesis is supposed to include, not only its possibility in the framework of the text's system of references and intertextual relations and its verifiability by the structure of the text,[7] but also its completeness. As modernizing readings, they also bestow interpretive options that cannot be reduced to the common denominator of what Nietzsche calls "present-day interests."[8] The discoveries made by musicological research raise the question whether literary scholarship's analysis of the traditional context involved might reveal interpretive options that could explicate Deschamps's text more or less completely. Such an explication challenged the tradition of research portrayed, but also made a shift in the methodological basis indispensable.

A broad front opposes modernizing readings. The idea of the *absolute* historicity of *every* act of understanding,[9] which was epoch-making at the time, was defended by Hans-Georg Gadamer against conceivable subjectivist interpretations.[10] Hans-Robert Jauß—though arguing in a rather "relativistic" way in comparison to Gadamer[11]—developed this idea into the formulation of a minimal consensus that "knowledge of a meaning in medieval literature [. . .] can be gained only by reflective passage through its alterity."[12] For Gadamer, and later for Jauß as well, this minimal consensus had an optimistic accent. Both assumed that understanding might encounter obstacles, but ultimately *always* remains possible—at the price, as Joachim Küpper has stressed,[13] of making the "reader's perspective an *a priori* condition of the process of understanding and relegating the structure of the text to the rank of a dependent variable."[14] This concession, which is acceptable only because of the inconceivability of the alternative—the text-objectivism that sought to treat the reader's understanding as the passive performance of a meaning inscribed in the text necessarily fails because of the polyvalence of the linguistic sign—has its systematic correlate in the conviction that text and reading are bound by a continuum: through "history," the coherence of a relation to tradition.[15] Only the *indebtedness of hermeneutics to a philosophy of history*, the assumption that the change in standpoint follows a logic that may be complex, still makes it possible to distinguish a "reasonable" reading of a text, especially one from the distant past, from naive or intentionally false readings. The abandonment of the metaphysical residue led to the breaching of this boundary: hermeneutics opened up to deconstruction.[16] The conclusion was not drawn—at least by Jauß himself. Instead, the resulting tension was shifted to the practice of reading texts: in its reception-aesthetics stage, the "postulated universality of hermeneutics" concealed a "partiality" for "what is affine to the present"[17]—for some authors, Petrarch, for the *Querelle des anciens et des modernes* (The Battle of the Books), and for certain lines of investigation, such as the concentration of the *lectura Dantis* on protomodern concepts of individuality in the well-known debate with Hugo Friedrich:[18]

> The privileged topics of discussion are text paradigms that can be easily subsumed under an image of tradition as the pre-history of modernity, [. . .] for all other texts [. . .] the merging of horizons always proceeds to the benefit of a present-day perspective.[19]

The fundamentally selective grip on tradition is less problematic. So long as the outlined methodological profile is limited by the restriction of its objects, it may be endorsed pragmatically in contradiction to the theoretically formulated claim to universality and in addition to a multitude of interests involved in knowledge that led beyond the portrayal of progress in the consciousness of freedom. Cases of *forced* modernization are harder to deflect onto the plurality of interpretations permitted by the text: readings in which the *dialogue* with the text, which is supposed to lead back to a deepened "self-understanding"[20] only after reflective passage through the alterity of the text, ends up being a *monologue*.

The danger of slipping into monologue is inherent in every discussion of texts. The danger is particularly great when literary study takes as its objects texts concerning which it is more difficult to make the univocal nature of the relation to tradition plausible than it is in the case of the works connected with the *Querelle des anciens et des modernes* or Petrarch. This holds especially for texts that date not from the period of what Yuri Lotman, in a striking phrase, called the age of the "aesthetics of contraposition," but rather from that of the "aesthetics of identity."[21] The *assumption* of a seamless continuum of meaning then easily becomes a corresponding *adjustment* of the material. The characteristic image of breaks or ruptures, with which the research summarized here operates, shows how such an adjustment can be constituted: the breaks in the relation to tradition are taken into account, but they are so positioned that the reader and the text always find themselves together on the "right" side, turned toward the present.

In the following pages we will explore alternative paths. In his dismissal of New Historicism entitled "Alter Wein in neuen Schläuchen,"[22] Jauß formulated the possible objections to an attempt at an understanding that itself confronts ruptures in tradition, which seeks to maintain alterity, and not be an assimilating reading per se. The New Historicism may raise the suspicion—like the archeology of discourse,[23] also rejected by Jauß—that here the long since theoretically abandoned project of reconstructing the past out of its fragments "as it really was,"[24] in Leopold von Ranke's famous words, is being revived. Küpper has emphasized that this criticism of the conceptual heart of the discourse-archeology approach misses the point: "[T]he metaphor of archeology [signifies] in Foucault not first of all an objective-reconstructive claim, but rather [is supposed] to transport another conception of the past than the one shaped by the philosophy of history."[25] To what appears—from the point of view of the developed present—to be hermeneutics' still linear conception of history archeology opposes the concept of sedimented strata that rest on one another and to that extent constitute a whole, whose connection can nonetheless range from the flowing transition of an extensive continuity to rupture. "History" so conceived is structured not by teleology, but rather by such ruptures—potentially contingently distributed and therefore to be made plausible on the basis of their preconditions. Accordingly, the point of the concept, which is crucial for the practice of literary study—and compatible with the initial assumptions of hermeneutics is: "Just as something new is a reaction to what precedes, so is it impossible to foresee, from the point of view of the preceding, what this something new will consist in."[26] The consequence, to concentrate on working out discursive strata and their relationships, to approach the text in question on the basis of its "epistemic" presuppositions, has been provided by Foucault with analytical instruments that themselves no longer require any introduction.[27] The outline proposed indicates how the following examination of scholarship on the late Middle Ages in general and on Deschamps in particular seeks to situate itself. Scholarship is aware of the *existence* of a tradition of theoretical reflection on poetry using musical concepts that draws on academic music theory, and has also noted, even though unspecifically, that Deschamps's *Art de dictier* is situated in this tradition. Nevertheless, the systematic working out, in the interests of literary scholarship, of the discourse of music theory that might shed light, for instance, on the possible sources and original implications of the *musique naturele/musique artificiele* distinction, remains to be achieved. Although the material is hardly fully developed, a consensus prevails regarding the question as to how the passages devoted to music in the *Art de dictier* are related to this material: they document a break with the older music theory dominated by Boethius under the aegis of the high Scholastic reception of Aristotle, theological nominalism, or both. The thesis infers unspecifically from developments in philosophy and theology to a music theory theoretically relevant to poetry, being based on a hardly tenable assessment of the evolution of discourses: the possibility of phase shifts between technical discourses that retain their operative distinctiveness—within certain limits—even under the Christian order of discourse is not considered. Similarly, homogeneity is attributed to medieval music theory that is hardly appropriate to the historical body of texts. Finally, it remains unexplained how the discourse in question constitutes verse as an object for reflection by music theory, which is exactly what the subsumption of verse under music implies, under medieval conditions, and which "literary aesthetic" implications this subsumption presents. The following study seeks to formulate answers to these questions, to escape the dangers of "monologic" modernizing, and thus, by consequence, to open up new ways of interpreting Deschamps's *Art de dictier*. My discussion will conclude with an attempt to revise the interpretive tradition on the work of Jean Molinet as a representative of the *rhétoriqueurs*.

My project takes the approaches and inquiries of earlier scholarship into account and seeks to integrate the references compiled. The point of departure is the finding presented from the side of musicology that first, the distinction found in Deschamps was appropriated from the discourse of *speculative* music theory, and second, the extension of this discourse should be assessed differently from the way it is assessed in current medieval scholarship: "In the Middle Ages, speculative music theory extends over more than a thousand years, from Augustine and Martianus Capella, Boethius and Cassiodorus, down to Johannes Tinctoris, who died in 1511."[28]

The "speculative" discourse of the Middle Ages is essentially the discourse of Christian theology. Correspondingly, I will attempt to situate the object of my investigation in the "analogical" episteme dominant from Christian late antiquity to the Renaissance and early modern period. The necessity of differentiating here among stages of development that open up differing horizons of world-modeling will be taken into account. The fourth chapter is devoted to the phase of constitution of the analogical episteme. Zumthor and Hüe have discerned in Augustine's *De musica* (c. 387–388) the most important reference for the subsumption of poetry under music; the discourse on poetry as music thus seems, under the conditions of the analogical discourse itself, to point back to this phase of constitution. The detailed presentation of Augustine's work in the fifth chapter seeks, on the one hand, to reconstruct the concept of music implied herein and its relevance for the discourse on verse, and, on the other, to show how this concept of music is to be situated in the context of the subjection of the pagan world of discourse to the order of "Christian discourse."

The textbooks of Boethius developed hegemonic influence in medieval music theory and operated on the same basis as Augustine's work on music. Moreover, only both works *together* completely opened up the field of Greek-pagan music theory, which led Ubaldo Pizzani to assume a text-genetic relationship between the two treatises: Boethius's *De institutione musica* is supposed to limit itself to those parts of the traditional doctrine that Augustine's *De musica* had not already discussed.[29] The medieval reception of both works saw this complementarity and conflated the two in accord with Boethian precepts. The presentation of Boethius's *Institutio musica* in my sixth chapter correspondingly concludes my remarks on Christian late antiquity. These two chapters will be rounded out by comments on the state of the sources and on reception history that will make it possible to offer an initial assessment of the scope of the concept of music developed by the *fondateurs de discursivité*[30] of medieval music theory.

When the specifics of the concept of music during the phase when the analogical discourse was being constituted have been explored and their implications for the discourse on verse examined, their existence in the subsequent developmental stages of the analogical episteme remain to be clarified. On the basis of treatises on music theory over ten centuries, not only the shaping and influence of the *musica naturalis / musica artificialis* distinction become comprehensible. The question whether the available sources can prove that the ruptures on which the research summarized depends actually exist still awaits critical testing. My seventh chapter, devoted to the sources, takes the differentiation of technical discourses into account: after asking in which periods the regulations of ways of talking about verse as music produced in the phase when the analogical discourse was being constituted remain functional, we will inquire into the question as to when and on what bases medieval theory of poetry sought to connect up with a "music theory" conceptualization of verse. With the question about reflection on the theory of poetry in contexts that decidedly belong to music theory, and the attempt to answer it with the help of a "description of discursive events as the horizon for seeking the unities that are formed in it"[31] worked out on the basis of sources in music theory itself, our study ventures onto largely virgin terrain. Whereas musicology has long devoted itself to the history of the theory of its subject, and the practical relationships between poetry and music in actual song have been worked out in detail, the development of the corpus of medieval music *theory* for literary studies remains in its early stages[32] and must be considered a desideratum of research with its own justification. The second part of our study grants a corresponding status, also quantitatively, to the interpretation of primary texts and to a reconstruction that takes into account the essential contexts of the concept of metrical discourse handed down by medieval music theory.

My working hypotheses may be formulated as follows: Eustache Deschamps's *Art de dictier* and the reference to poetic art as *musique naturele* document not a *break*, but rather a *continuity*. The text connects with a conception of poetry that had been traditional in music theory since late Christian antiquity and that had remained vital. The possibility of this connection is based on the alignment of speculative theory of music after 1300: it has not been abandoned, but—in order to ensure its consistency—continually and productively adapted to the evolving order of discourse. The conceptual foundations of this discourse (and of the conception of poetry situated here) are also the conceptual foundations of the analogical episteme. The conceptual unity and rigor of Deschamps's text is to be interpreted on the basis of this continuity. The insights gained in the course of our examination will enable us in conclusion to acquire a genuinely medieval perspective on the "formalism" of the *Grands rhétoriqueurs*.

Part II

CHAPTER FOUR

From Pagan Late Antiquity to the Christian Middle Ages

DRAWING ON AUGUSTINE AND BOETHIUS, scholarship on Deschamps traces the discussion of verse in the framework of medieval music theory back to the time in European cultural history when the historical formation that remained dominant for more than a thousand years was being constituted. The discourse of speculative music theory goes back still further, to the oldest strata of Western science. Mediated by Neoplatonism, in the Middle Ages it continued to be influential in the form reshaped in accord with Christian theology that it had taken on during its "colonization" by the *patres*. The following paragraphs sketch the context of this reshaping in order to provide an initial grounding of the horizon in which the theoretical texts to be reconstructed retain their plausibility.[1]

The central challenge of early Christian theory construction was the mission to the pagans. Its conceptual preparation, initially provided by the Apostle Paul of Tarsus (died c. 64), and then above all by Augustine (354–430), was carried out with respect to two essential problems. First, the new doctrine had to develop its Jewish substrate in such a way that it could be simultaneously appropriated and qualified as a preliminary stage that had been surpassed. Second, the Christian narrative of the God-creator found itself in opposition to the tradition of the "first," "Greek" enlightenment[2] that began in the fourth century BCE and had constituted and differentiated itself in opposition to myth, claiming to do away with the latter through consistent "rationalization." The consequences of this confrontation were dramatically momentous. The initial gain in reflexivity, which nourished Christian theology in part down to the twelfth century, led to further and increasing pressure for rationalization: "Ancient authors were at first used to provide means of argument for theology; but the heterogeneous medium immediately began to have a standardizing effect on the theoretical claim that developed its immanent rationality."[3] The possible consequences of clothing religious truths in the form of argumentative discourse were already recognized by Augustine. The domain of discourse equipped with dialectical means and arguing in the mode of logical deduction was limited to the existent, to Creation. Revealed statements were withdrawn from the domain of human reason. These statements, functioning as an axiomatics governed by the *auctoritas* of orthodox theology, are accessible only to faith. In order to appropriate the stock of ancient knowledge in accord with the standard of this distinction and to dissipate the tensions between the body of tradition and the Christian claim to superiority, theoretical elements appeared whose content and especially whose level of abstraction are relevant to the "literary-aesthetic" object of our investigation.

The discursive formation for the solution of these problems began to emerge with an argumentative figure in the Pauline tradition. The fifth chapter of Romans deals with the figure of Adam in Genesis and its relation to the Savior. According to Paul's formulation, which is varied in different ways, Adam, the father of mankind, is the "forma futuri" of Jesus:

> But death reigned from Adam unto Moses [. . .]; For if by the offence of
> one, many died: much more the grace of God and the gift, by the grace
> of one man, Jesus Christ, hath abounded unto many. [. . .] For if by one
> man's offence death reigned through one; much more they who receive
> abundance of grace and of the gift and of justice shall reign in life through
> one, Jesus Christ.[4]

The problem of mortality is conceptualized by recourse to a figure of argument in Roman law. Tertullian systematized this recourse and used it to communicate the doctrine to the Latin West[5] and thus to found a tradition that extends through Anselm of Canterbury's *Cur Deus homo* to early modern metaphysics of law. The figure of argument makes possible the absorption of Jewish teaching as a preliminary stage that has been transcended: the accentuation of the Fall into sin and its first cause, Adam, initially imposed by the interpretation of Jesus as a figure of divine salvation, allows the appropriation of the Old Testament narrative in accord with the schema of original rebellion and surrogate punishment and thus the conception of the new religion as a precise inversion of the same schema: as a *surrogate salvation*.

The institution of the "figural" *typos-antitypos* relationship, which can be shown not only in Paul but also and especially in the "Reflexionszitate" in Matthew,[6] offered, in addition to the option of incorporating the Jewish tradition, an argumentatively cogent formulation of the new doctrine. The possibility of relating the *figura* to the problems that emerged from the confrontation between the Christian religion of salvation and the pagan philosophical tradition was exploited by the acculturation thesis[7] concerning the origin of medieval figural discourse: Recourse to this schema is supposed to be due to the pressure of rationalization proceeding from the appropriation of Greek philosophy.

The new form of worship was partially subject to the form of argumentative discourse that has its origin in the debate culture of the Greek Polis: the laws of logic.[8] By appropriating the latter, early Christian theory construction became significantly more systematic;[9] the price to be paid is the anchoring of the gap between *fides* and *ratio* at the heart of dogma. The *figura* develops into a hermeneutics biased in favor of Christian doctrine: it relates two distinct, locally and temporally individualized complexes in accord with the standard of Christian teaching. Let us emphasize that the aspect under which the postulated relationship is produced can involve actions or persons, qualities or attributes, determinations that are content-related or purely formal, and can also be central or marginal to the phenomenon-complex. The criterion is not the adequate or complete "ascertainment" of the material observed, but rather the confirmation of an assumption that is posited as given and is indebted to the doctrinal content of the teaching:

> Figural conceptualization does not "seek" more or less evident analogies, but rather presupposes the analogical constitution of the material and explicates it on the basis of a feature that emerges only through the modeling itself and that may ultimately be constructed [. . .]. In comparison to the presupposed schema the material is reduced to relative insignificance: it functions illustratively.[10]

In its Pauline conception, the schema is already hierarchized. Neither *typos* nor *antitypos* is capable of being true in itself. The schema provides only for the truth of the observed "figural" relationship, and is to that extent always already more than merely heuristic in nature, insofar as it cannot be separated from doctrinal content. Determined according to the model of the announcement (which is incomplete and possibly faulty) and the fulfillment (which brings the truth to light), the form developed in time can appropriate not only the Jewish tradition but the *whole* heritage of the period *ante gratiam*. What is not compatible with the new teaching can be conceived as a stage of adumbration.

The underlying world picture is at first alien to the Greek substrate insofar as the latter's cyclical temporal structure[11] is opposed to the concept of a linear progression implied in this schema. It indicates not only the element of superiority but also a teleological process that in principle ends with the appearance of the age of fulfillment and still requires "only" the event that concludes time, the return of Christ.[12] The claim of the broadly conceived figural schema is correspondingly totalizing.

In an initial stage of expansion that served to secure the doctrine systematically, Origen made the New Testament available to allegorical reading. Augustine put this in the form that became standard for later developments.[13] In particular, the procedures for eliminating the elements that resist allegorical interpretation, whether on grounds of logic, morals, or simple comprehensibility, are taken directly from pagan allegorical myth interpretation.[14] To that extent allegorical Bible interpretation generalizes the approach to the appropriation of the *Old Testament* developed in Paul. The theory of fourfold meaning—literal, allegorical, moral, and anagogic— emerged as an attempt at systematizing interpretation: "Littera gesta docet, quid credas allegoria/Moralis quid agas, quo tendas anagogia" ("Literal [meaning] tells you facts, allegory what to believe, moral what to do, anagogia where you are going").[15]

The second stage of expansion builds on another passage in the Pauline tradition. From the monotheistic credo and the concept of the world as the creation of the one and only God, Paul infers that the ancients, with their discourses governed by competing paradigms, are also part of this Creation. Hence according to Paul even the pagans know as much as they can about God[16]—even if He has not revealed himself to them through the Word, as He did to the people of Israel. The assumption of a twofold revelation of the Creator, primarily in *scripture* and secondarily in Creation ("For the invisible things of him from the creation of the world are clearly seen, being understood by the things that are made, even his eternal power and Godhead"[17]) lays the foundations for the assimilation of *every* statement claiming relevance in accord with schemata that are shaped in advance by the revealed text. The figural interpretation of the Old Testament was elaborated in parallel in Patristic literature, thoroughly organized into a total reinterpretation of the Judaic tradition,[18] and finally more precisely conceived through the thesis of priority[19] borrowed from Alexandrine Judaism; it was particularly well-suited for popularization and pedagogy: the claim that pagan wisdom was directly dependent on the Old Testament, combined with the accusation of theft, allowed a reception of the ancient heritage that was more finely differentiated and at the same time more appropriative than the comparatively abstract notion of a common Creator. The most incisive image of this procedure is found in the interpretation of Deut. 21:11–13 offered by Jerome (347–420): As soon as the prisoner's (i.e., ancient wisdom's) hair has been shorn off, his nails cut, and his pagan clothing removed, one can take possession of him.[20]

The priority thesis acquires its power, which is visible in the conflict with the Neoplatonic schools of late Antiquity, from the possibility of building on debates that were conducted in the wake of the development of theistic positions within Neoplatonism itself. In the second century CE, the Neo-Pythagorean Numenios of Apamea maintained that Plato had learned from Pythagoras, who had himself acquired his knowledge from the barbarians of the East. Between the time of Plotinus and that of Iamblichus the conviction was established that the original wisdom had to be regained by returning to the "pure teachings" of the Orient.[21] By connecting its priority thesis with this narrative, Patristic literature succeeded in putting its own religion of revelation in the position of the doctrine sought and at the same time justified the reliance on Neoplatonism in the theological apparatus to be developed.[22]

The figural schema acquires its epoch-making universal applicability when it is made into a specifically Christian method of allegorical interpretation. Here the concept of "analogy," which is burdened with vagueness by the multiplicity of contexts in which it can be used, is supposed to guarantee at first only what Quintilian expresses in the catchy formula "aliud verbis, aliud sensu ostendit."[23] The signified is given the status of a signifier, that is, it has a "merely" referential function with regard to a secondary level of meaning described as the only "real" one capable of being true. Titus Flavius Clemens (c. 150–c. 205), known as Clement of Alexandria, explains how the idea—which had been current since Justin Martyr (c. 100–c. 165) and simply clothed in a striking metaphor by Jerome—was to be used: ancient wisdom conceals the truth behind "riddles and symbols, allegories and metaphors."[24]

Allegorical interpretation includes the typological-figural procedure insofar as both postulate a referential context that goes beyond the literal.[25] It becomes constitutive of an epoch through its connection with a preexisting inventory of secondary meanings that are different in content, through its claim to be a systematic, that is, a continuous operation that arrives solely at this inventory, and finally through its explicitly totalizing claim. This claim itself must be formulated neither too concretely nor too abstractly: texts are produced that fail to meet particular criteria or even all the criteria. The mark of the "Middle Ages," unified as an epoch by means of a heuristic makeshift, is that such texts are subordinated to other rules that correspond secondarily to the Christian order of discourse, are subjected to reservations regarding their relevance, or are, during the process of their reception, annotation, imitation and emulation, increasingly subordinated to the aforementioned formal principles or received with corresponding selectivity.

In Christian apologetics and Patristics, contributions that point not only gradually but also fundamentally beyond the Pauline basis emerged from the development of a problem that Paul was still incapable of foreseeing: the absence of the *parousia*.[26] The absorption of a "historical" time that proved to be unexpectedly prolonged was particularly explosive. Christian doctrines did not at first provide for it, but precluded its depreciation, since the highest possible level of earthly history had to be seen as having been already achieved with Jesus Christ's act of redemption, and the Passion had constituted all future time as an epoch *sub gratia*. The first solution that Augustine arrived at is marred by compromise: at best, the doctrine of predestination as the concept of a divine logic that is incomprehensible for humans but nonetheless given merely screens the problem. The essence and meaning of postincarnational history became a mystery of faith with the result that no binding, metaphysically guaranteed standards of action on the part of humans could be designated for this time. The concept was marginalized in the following centuries. The past solution, the complete absorption of postincarnational history, succeeded only after a new approach was adopted in the wake of fundamental reflection on the relationship between the Creator and time. For the Creator there was supposed to be no temporality at all:

> What is foreknowledge (*praescientia*) but knowledge of future events (*scientia futurorum*)? What is the future to God, who transcends all time? If knowledge grasps the things of God, they are not of the future, but of the present; for this reason, such awareness is not foreknowledge (*praescientia*), but only knowledge (*scientia*).[27]

Temporality has no truth value of its own; its only effect is to veil. The intensification of the concept seems at first to be in contradiction with the figural schema, which operates with finalities and not least, in the *typos/antitypos* schema, with temporal developments. The reason is the revision of the idea, which was already infected with doubt in John and Paul, that the *sub gratia* epoch could be understood as the *exact* counterpart, at a higher, salvation-history level, of the *ante legem* and *sub lege* epochs. Augustine rejects this idea, which could be put under pressure to justify itself by every event in postincarnational history, as too schematic. The theoretical element is replaced by the doctrine of the *civitates* that appear over the whole period of human history and may even be mingled and fight in the individual person.[28] From the beginning, all history is a battle between two realms: Here *amor sui*, *superbia*, and *luxuria* rule; there *caritas Dei*.[29] The transition, practiced even before Augustine, from the schemata veiled in the revelation texts to the modeling of posthistory is thus systematically guaranteed:

> The overcoming of the absence of the *parousia* comes at the cost of understanding all the respective history as a repetition of what has already occurred, whereby the question about the salvation-history meaning of an already fulfilled history that extends immeasurably but stands still *sub specie aeternitatis* remains unasked and probably must remain unasked.[30]

With Augustine's theoretical contribution the Christian view of history gained a literally homogeneous basis for the discourse about time vs. temporality. The primary difference between the two main epochs divided by the Passion of Christ remains, but their hierarchization begins: present history that takes place *sub gratia* actualizes configurations that in principle characterize of all times; the quality of postincarnational history as a "redeemed" era is blurred and first reappears in the Protestant recourse to the doctrine of predestination.

The goal of the recapitulated procedure is not to erase ancient pagan traditions but rather to integrate them into a Christian-oriented system of order, not to extinguish the established but rather to make it useful for the new doctrine. Thus we must speak not of an ancient pagan-Christian syncretism, but rather of a systematic subjection of ancient wisdom to the delimitations of a Christian discourse of order:

> In comparison to other forms of discourse that are known and/or have already been systematically described (*epistemai*), the defining characteristic of analogical discourse seems to be that it is a discourse of appropriation [. . .]. The discursive movement of orthodox analogism does not intend to constitute a specific model of reality by immediately resorting to the linguistic code, but instead "colonizes" already existing universes of discourse or even partial conceptual schemata that are preserved and handed on in this way, but are also deprived more or less rigorously of their immanent meaning.[31]

The Platonic-Neoplatonic ontology was handed down in much the same way. It was formative for Augustine's theory of Being, from the early writings in which he sought to work out and systematize Christian doctrine—for instance, *Contra Academicos* III.20.43: "for the time being, I trust in finding in the works of the Platonists a teaching that does not contradict our sacred doctrine"—to *De civitate Dei* VIII.9.10, where he endorses

Platonism from the standpoint of the elaborated Christian doctrine. In accord with what has been explained here, Augustine reads in the *Platonicorum libros* mentioned in *Confessiones* VII.9.13 not Platonism but rather the preliminary stages and annunciation of the doctrine of the *logos* in John: "You obtained for me [. . .] certain books of the Platonists [. . .], and there I read—not in these words, to be sure, but this very thing was commended strongly with many and manifold reasons—that in the beginning was the Word, and the Word was with God, and God was the Word."[32] Appropriated and reshaped in this way, Platonic ontology became the systematic foundation of Augustinian theology. Thoroughly "colonized" and reframed, Platonic-Neoplatonic ontology can retain its characteristic outline:

> Wherever Augustine speaks of worldly things, of their nature and order, their essence and existence, he is connected with a Platonist or Neoplatonist perspective; and because for him the ontological point of view that is here the relevant and sole essential one, into which everything that is to be said about nature and the natural world is integrated, his world view itself can be defined as Platonic. Augustinian ontology is Platonic ontology, [. . .]. Grounded in this way, Augustine's ontological conceptuality remains the same throughout his whole work, right down to his last writings.[33]

The major determinants of the Platonic doctrine of the two worlds can be found throughout Augustine's works, partly developed in his speculations on the Trinity. Being is characterized by the properties of timelessness and unity. This means that "esse ad manendum refertur" ("Being concerns that which remains") and correspondingly "esse autem aliquid, si manet, si constat" ("being is something if it remains, if it endures").[34] Being is opposed to changing existence, whose essential characteristics are *discrepantia, confusio, transitio, indigentia, mors*.[35] *This* world is characterized by the *potential* for change, not solely by *actual* coming into being and passing away: "Et si semper aliquid vivat, tamen si mutabilitatem patiatur, non proprie aeternum appellatur, quia non semper eiusmodi est" ("If something lives forever, and yet suffers change, it cannot rightly be called eternal, since it does not exist always in the same way").[36] As *non mutari, cum possit mutari* (something that does not change, but could change) it is distinguished from *prorsus non posse mutari* (something that cannot change), which is Being.[37] Change means falling away from Being or movement toward Being.[38] Consequently, to every existent corresponds an intelligible *natura* that is different from it.[39] Nature as the nature of an existent constitutes the latter's particular being, it consists in the *generalia bona* measure, form, order,[40] and in particular unity: "Omnis [. . .] forma ad unitatis regulam cogitur" ("Every [. . .] form is compelled toward the rule of unity").[41] What is crucial for our study is the appropriation of the Platonic tradition's ontology of number, which had already been broadened in Stoic doctrine. It was to provide conceptual guidance for the elaboration of thinking about the order of existents in terms of Creation, and for the formulation of a corresponding conception of form: "In tantum illis [*coelum, terra,* etc.] est esse, in quantum numerosa esse" ("Being is in those things [the sky, earth, etc.] only to the extent that they are ruled by numbers").[42] The standard passage cited since the beginning of the Christian appropriation of this number ontology is found in the *Liber sapientiae Salomonis* [*The Wisdom of Solomon*],[43] a potpourri of Jewish and Pythagorean-Platonic wisdom produced in Alexandria in the first century CE: "sed omnia in mensura et numero et pondere disposuisti" ("I have arranged all things with measure, and number, and weight") (11:21). Even before the conversion of the Platonic *mundus intelligibilis* into the essence of God in *De diversis quaestionibus octaginta tribus,*[44] the Platonic ideal numbers were absorbed into Christian doctrine as numbers *in mente divina.*[45] As *ratio sempiterna atque incommutabilis,*[46] these numbers connect with Christian creationism the Platonic doctrine of ideal numbers and the demiurge myth based on it in Plato's *Timaeus.*

By appropriating this ontology the figural schema acquires a "second dimension," and thus more "flexibility."[47] The "horizontal" unfolding in time is complemented from the outset by a "vertical" figural schema,[48] for which "in the domain of the senses a *figura* is always only an adumbration of the true, ideal *figura* conceived in the *mundus intelligibilis.*"[49] Worldly things "emblematize" Being in the beyond:

> Wherever Augustine speaks of the ideal existent, he conceives it directly as an attribute of the divine essence. In the distinction between sensible and intelligible Being, the *mundus intelligibilis* remains without its own content and is directly connected with the concept of God. [. . .] If for Plotinus the *kosmos noetos* was the world of noetic existents, then here Being is subsumed into the concept of God, omitting its worldly meaning, whereby the world of the existent in general is at the same time subordinated to the idea of divine kingship [. . .]. Where Augustine speaks of Being, he is speaking of God, in whose concept all the determinations that in the metaphysical tradition are peculiar to Being itself flow together.[50]

The "vertical" figural schema reduces the multiplicity of the phenomenal world discursively to the dimension of signs that refer to God the Creator, and thus, to use Dante's typological metaphor, to a plenitude of "impressions" made by the divine seal (*suggelo*)[51] on various materials. These may appear to be different, but are always only variants of one and the same signature with which the *divina sapientia* expresses itself in Creation. As a result, every "impression," every concrete element of Creation, is bound to every other through analogy. The point of reference remains Paul's assertion that the invisible nature of God becomes visible in the things that have been made.[52] Similarly, by supplementing the "horizontal" figural schema with the Platonic ontology of number, a form is acquired in which degrees of transparency are distinguishable: the more evident the form described by means of numerical harmonic relationships, the clearer the *signum*; the greater the anagogic capacity, the more transparent the sign as a *signum sacrum*, as a *signum Dei*. This is precisely where *De Musica* begins.

CHAPTER FIVE

Augustine, *De musica*

IN GENERAL, Augustine's attitude toward verbal art was shaped by his judgment regarding rhetoric, which was ambivalent: the partial justification of rhetorical polish when it serves to announce the truth of salvation corresponds to a condemnation when pleasing speech seeks to appeal to the senses. Plato's negative judgment of poets in the *Republic*, which Tertullian had already repeated, provided the theological basis for the precarious status of morally suspect profane literature. Apologetic passages elaborate the observation that the Bible is "enigmatic" and sometimes "dark" and thereby gains in beauty, as Augustine remarks in *De doctrina christiana* II.4.7–8. Significantly, the subject comes up in the context of the demand for an allegorical, that is, a unifying interpretation of the Bible: If we understand this statement as "aesthetic," then the question arises as to why a text that speaks the truth speaks in riddles. Correspondingly, *De doctrina christiana* IV.11.26 offers an interpretation that refers to didactics. Just as spices make food "tasty" for the eater, so rhetorical *ornatus* makes the text of revelation palatable for the reader. The argument is bound to this text; but in the Middle Ages, the passage was understood, as Ernst Robert Curtius has shown, as a justification for rhetorical amplification.[1] "Aesthetic" pleasure is seen as legitimate so long as it is regarded as deriving from a rhetorical amplification of the truth of salvation and is in the service of spreading Christian doctrine. Verbal art, which is here conceived on the basis of rhetoric, is thus legitimate only if it serves the glory of God and the propagation of the faith. This position was taken to be the Augustinian one in general, and in reflection on the theory of poetry and versification in the framework of disciplinary rhetoric it remained dominant throughout the period with which we are concerned here.

On the other hand, in research on literary history we find hardly any reference to the discussion of metrical verse discourse as a form of music developed in Augustine's early work entitled *De musica*. The subsumption of verse under music had been common since ancient Greek music theory.

Augustine's work provides the pagan models with Christian perspectives, but otherwise continues them largely unchanged.[2] Together with Boethius's textbook, *De musica* forms the "gateway" through which the ancient body of music theory made its way from Antiquity into the Christian Middle Ages.[3]

Augustine reconstructed this theory on the basis of its most elementary presuppositions. The reasons for doing so were due not only to economical demonstration, but also to the theory itself. My analysis takes this into account: staying close to the text, it follows the arc and emphases of the argument, but to some extent also its detours, in order to bring out the argumentative style peculiar to Patristic literature and its characteristic demands. My goal is not only to explicate the text but also to show how Christianity reshaped the materials appropriated from pagan music theory.

Introduction

De musica,[4] which was begun in Mediolanum, modern-day Milan,[5] while Augustine was preparing for his baptism in 387, and provisionally completed in Tagaste in North Africa toward the end of 388,[6] consists of six books. It is part of Augustine's early work, heavily influenced by Neoplatonism.[7] Book VI, at least, seems to have been subsequently reworked; Epistle 101.4 to Memorius suggests that the motive for this *retractio* was the increased Christian reshaping of the pagan materials dealt with in Books I through V[8] and the elaboration of the theological argument in Book VI.[9]

De musica is written as a didactic dialogue, a form that remained dominant in Augustine's work until his return to Tagaste. However, the generally marked personalization of the interlocutors in his early works is here replaced by an unspecified master and his disciple, and the dialogic modeling declines toward the end of the text.[10] The six books of *De musica* discuss "de rhythmo," and six further books "de melo" were planned, according to Epistle 101.3, but remained unwritten because of the burdens of Augustine's ecclesiastical duties.[11]

The distinction employed here opens up the field of ancient pagan music theory: *musica rhythmica* includes the partial domains of rhythm (*musica rhythmica*) and metrics (*musica metrica*), which is in fact discussed in *De musica*, while the subject of the unwritten books *de melo* would have been melodies and the theory of harmony. The distinction simplifies a three-part classification of the discipline of music, attested in a comparable form at least since Plato,[12] into *musica metrica*, *rhythmica*, and *harmonica*, in accord with which ancient Greek music theory distinguished between the "theoretical" and "practical" components of the discipline.[13] Augustine may have taken this triad, as well as his definition of music, which was soon to become common coin in the Middle Ages, from Marcus Terentius Varro's *Disciplinae*, which is today no longer extant;[14] regarding the reasons for the simplification we can now only speculate.[15]

Survey of the History of Scholarship

Compared with philological studies on Augustine, the scholarship devoted to *De musica* is relatively manageable. The discussion summarized below teaches us to attend to the aspects of the text that are important for a historically adequate understanding of the conceptual context.

The first studies of *De musica* appeared at the beginning of scholarly musicology in the late eighteenth century, and were marked from the outset by a negative judgment. The *Allgemeine Geschichte der Musik* written by Johann Nikolaus Forkel, who is now known chiefly as the author of the first biography of Bach, was published in two volumes in 1788 and 1801. It formulated a view of Augustine's work that was widely adopted by nineteenth-century writing on the history of music. For Forkel, the metrics developed in *De musica* is not "truly musical": "in this work there is little that is truly musical in the strict sense, except what is said in the first books about rhythm and related matters."[16] The criteria by which Forkel assesses the work are its proximity to musical practice and the concision of the analytical and descriptive terminology it offers for musical analysis. Forkel limits himself to noting the work's irrelevance to the history of music, but soon afterward the same criteria were overtly used to depreciate the text. François-Joseph Fétis's *Biographie universelle des musiciens et bibliographie générale de la musique*, published in 1837, calls *De musica* "a weak effort, not worthy of its author's talent."[17] The first attempts to revise this view, made at the beginning of the twentieth century, still employed the same criteria. In 1909 Wilhelm Scherer tried to draw from Augustine's work "points of view important not only for the history of thinking about music within the Church, but also for the aesthetic evaluation of music in general,"[18] and interpreted the text as evidence of early Christian Church music. Jean Huré's monograph, *Saint Augustin musicien. D'après le* De musica *et différentes pages de ses oeuvres, consacrées à la musique* (1924) is based on the same interest. It explicates the text by summarizing Books I and VI and providing a nearly literal translation of Books II through V, but surprises us by offering a polemical plea for the restitution of a *musica scientia* guided by Augustine.[19]

The first works that sought to interpret Augustine's work in its historical context appeared around 1930. Kathi Meyer-Baer's study reads *De musica* as an attempt to synthesize oriental practice and Greco-Latin music theory.[20] In the same year, Carlo del Grande and Gino Borghezio published works that also saw *De musica* as a work conceived with a synthetic intention, but assumed a merging of Hellenistic and Roman vocal practice and music theory appropriated from Greek sources.[21] The historical contextualization prepared the way for situating Augustine's work on music in the horizon of ancient *musica scientia,* which led to a fundamental reevaluation of the work in 1942. In a brief account of Book I of *De musica,* the anonymous author of a short article, "Pensées de Saint Augustin sur la musique,"[22] shows that it is precisely the separation of the practical execution of music from *musica scientia* that subtends the work's argument. Heinrich Hüschen adopted this thesis in 1949, identified the speculative perspective of *musica scientia,* and brought out for the first time the Christian-ethical interest in Augustine's dealing with music theory: Augustine recognizes "as valuable only music that contributes to the encouragement and deepening of the Christian religion and that thus corresponds to the tasks and goals of the Christian church."[23] The awareness of the "bridging function" that the work thus acquired was documented in the 1960s by Reinhold Hammerstein, who read *De musica* as a document of the "shift in emphasis from the ancient to the Christian conception of education and music,"[24] as well as by Günther Wille's standard work, *Musica Romana. Die Bedeutung der Musik im Leben der Römer.*[25]

In addition to works in the discipline of musicology, from the beginning of scholarly discussion of *De musica* there has been a branch of research that opposes the absorption of Augustine's work into studies on music by arguing that it is a textbook on rhythm and meter of only accidental relevance to musicology. Rudolf Westphal followed Alexandre J. H. Vincent's *Analyse du traité de métrique et de rhythmique de St. Augustin intitulé De musica,* published in 1849,[26] and took Augustine's work on music into account in collecting the fragments and theorems of Greek writers on rhythmics;[27] a year later H. Weil provided clarifications regarding the place of Augustine's text in the tradition of treatises on rhythmics and metrics.[28] August Wilhem Ambros's *Geschichte der Musik* observes that *De musica* contains nothing but "ancient metrics applied to music,"[29] Jacques-Marie de Crozals substantiates this view in a long study published in 1894,[30] and so does a monograph by Franco Amerio published in 1929.[31] Only after Amerio were metrics and rhythmics recognized as aspects of the conception of music in the pagan tradition that had become clear since Hüschen.

The bases for this recognition and hence for the merging of branches of research that had been separated since the middle of the nineteenth century led to a third approach that goes back to Heinz Edelstein's *Die Musikan-schauung Augustins nach seiner Schrift De musica* (1929).[32] This dissertation, written under the direction of Martin Heidegger, focused for the first time on the ontological-cosmological aspect of Augustine's music theory and recognized that *De musica* is inscribed within the Pythagorean-Platonic tradition. It insisted that in the Middle Ages, "in particular the ancient doctrine of the breadth of the concept of music, which extends beyond the acoustic to include all existents moving in an orderly way, was borrowed from Augustine."[33] According to Edelstein, *ordo* as the order of Being is manifest in the musical phenomenon, which includes not only acoustic but also nonacoustic "existents [. . .] that we are not accustomed to refer to as music."[34] The *musica disciplina* that figures in the canon of the *artes libe-rales* and that was the subject of Augustine's work is thus said to be no less than the preparation for the "recognition of the true."[35] Thus at the same time Edelstein's study, which Wilhelm Hoffmann supplemented in 1931 with an account of Augustine's conception of numbers,[36] paves the way for situating *De musica* in the educational canon of late Antiquity. Henry-Iré-née Marrou, in his book *Saint Augustin et la fin de la culture antique*, which appeared in 1938 and soon became a standard work,[37] and also Heinrich Hüschen and Solange Corbin sought to situate Augustine's work in this way.[38] In 1984, Ilsetraud Hadot was able to demonstrate the decisiveness of Augustine's work *De ordine* for the medieval conception of the educational program, within whose horizon *De musica* should also be understood.[39]

The relations to the Pythagorean-Platonic tradition demonstrated by Edelstein ultimately also affected scholarly theological and philosophical discussion of Augustine's work on music. In 1954 August Scharnagel first pointed out that according to Augustine's *De musica*, music is to be understood as an "embodiment and expression of Christian piety, as mediating between God and men,"[40] and another contribution to scholarship by Franco Amerio worked out the foundation of Augustine's work on music in the ontology of number. His study is the first detailed attempt to cope with its philosophical and theological implications, and starting from the question as to why the Christian Augustine turned so extensively to the ancient pagan discipline, it shows the anagogic relevance of the disciplines that Boethius later subsumed under the "quadrivium."[41] The number-ontology basis of music theory proves to be the conceptual foundation for the Christian-ethical functionalization of musical phenomena and education;[42] according to Amerio, the vagueness in the passages that are potentially relevant to practice can be explained by their basically metaphysical perspective: "At this point music merges with philosophy, and is no longer a science, but becomes itself philosophy and theology and mysticism, in which it is difficult to distinguish the points of articulation and to decide regarding the permanence or dissolution of this music in the higher speculative and practical activities."[43] Amerio's summary underscores the absorption of pagan wisdom as a result of Augustine's Christian theory construction regarding music: "St. Augustine has sought with undeniable brilliance to re-think and re-position pagan knowledge in such a way as to preserve or recuperate it within the new Christian cultural system."[44]

The 1960s were marked by the first summaries of scholarship up to that point. Carl Johan Perls's attempt to provide an overall account[45] presents the state of research and strongly emphasizes that Augustine's concept of music includes the art of poetry. Karl Gustav Fellerer sees in the ontological-cosmological dimension of the concept of music Augustine adapted for Christian theology the condition of its importance in the Middle Ages.[46] Edmund John Dehnert shows that the foundation of this concept of music in the ontology of number was the common basis for Augustine's and Boethius's writings on music;[47] in 1975 Adolf Nowak broadened the initial tracing of this ontology of number back to Plotinus and reframed it in the larger, Pythagorean-Neoplatonic context.[48] Tina Manferdini emphasizes the fundamentally religious character of an aesthetics that could be derived from Augustine's writing on music.[49] Thus the central determinants of Augustine's theory of music have been identified. From the 1960s on, the discussion of *De musica* has been conducted in the context of clearly delimited aspects and special questions. The most recent overall account, which discusses in detail the research only briefly summarized here and presents convincing textual analyses, was published by Adalbert Keller in 1993 under the title *Aurelius Augustinus und die Musik. Untersuchungen zu De musica im Kontext seines Schrifttums.*[50]

My summary presentation of scholarship shows that Augustine's work on music became clear insofar as research took into account the ontological-cosmological basis of the founding concept of music, its "holistic" (in the etymologically precise sense of the word) character, and its development in an equally "holistic" theory of music. From that time on, studies based on partial aspects, questions of musical practice, the relationship between musical practice and music theory or rhythmics and metrics came together in a coherent and complete interpretation of the text in which the relationship of each of these aspects to the founding ontology of number and the concept of *ordo*[51] became clear. This discovery guides the following studies as well, which will attend especially to the "literary-aesthetic" implications of Augustine's text on music. The latter have long been largely neglected in the relevant overviews of the theory of the beautiful and the artistic beautiful in the Middle Ages.[52]

Presentation
De musica, Book I. *Musica?*

The text begins *in medias res*, but on unexpected terminological terrain.
The *magister* asks his *discipulus* to define the metrical foot (*pes*) of the word
modus. The pupil makes use of his grammatical knowledge: the word has
two short syllables, and is thus a Pyrrhic foot with two quantities (*tempora*).
The teacher's second example, *bonus*, differs from *modus* with regard to its
meaning (*significatio*) and to its phonemic content (*litterarum sonus*), but
corresponds to it with respect to the *tempora* and their order, and thus with
respect to the *pes*. Things are different in the case of the third example: the
verb form *póne* and the adverb *poné* differ in accent (*acumen*). The grammatical terminology raises the question as to which discipline is concerned
with such differences. Drawing on his experience, the pupil replies: "I am
used to hearing these matters from the grammarians, and that is where I
learned them," but just to be sure, he adds: "but whether they are proper to
that art or are taken from elsewhere, I do not know."[53] A comparison that
anticipates the course of the investigation prepares the answer: "Now I ask
you this, if I twice strike a drum or a string as suddenly and quickly as we
pronounce the word *modus* or *bonus* would you recognize that those times
were the same?"[54] Although they are no longer talking about words but
rather about playing musical instruments, the pupil answers: "I would."[55]
He would also call such a beat a Pyrrhic foot, as the grammar teacher taught
it. Reflection on the bases of this terminological transfer leads to the true
subject of the didactic dialogue: its *designation* is the foot of two short beats
given by the grammarian, while the *object designated*, the *pulsus* itself, the
dimensio temporum specific to it, is a phenomenon that is also dealt with
in the linguistic domain of grammar, *but not exclusively or in a particularly
prominent way.*[56] Accordingly, the teacher concludes, there must be a *disciplina* that investigates not the designations but the phenomenon designated
itself.[57]

The *disciplina* referred to is music. Its definition, known from the tradition of Varro and probably transmitted by Censorinus,[58] becomes the starting point for the didactic dialogue, with the goal of testing it thoroughly:
"Musica est scientia bene modulandi" ("Music is the knowledge of modulating properly").[59] Book I, which lays the foundation for all that follows,
analyzes its components in order: *modulari*, the qualifying adverb *bene*,
and *scientia*.

Modulari is said to be the verbal derivative from *modus*, "measure" or "form." The quality of every successful work consists, the *magister* declares apodictically, in the preservation of the right measure. The right measure is the true object of *musica* as a discipline;[60] the word *modulari* in the definition thus designates what qualifies a movement (*motus*) as successful: "Therefore, modulation [*modulatio*] is not improperly called a certain skill in moving, or the means by which something is moved well. We cannot say that something is moved well if it does not keep its measure [*si modum non servat*]." In the following passages, "success" is defined in two respects. First, success involves movement in accord with *numerical measures*:

> Music is the knowledge of moving properly [*scientia bene movendi*]. This is so because whatever is harmoniously moved and has kept the measurements of times and intervals [*quidquid numerose servatis temporum atque intervallorum dimensionibus moveatur*] can already be said to move well (for it already delights, and for this reason not improperly is it already called modulation [*modulatio*]).[61]

This leads to the Pythagorean-Platonic conception of number, which the larger part of Book I discusses at length.[62]

In comparison the second determination of "success" is more weakly motivated and obviously indebted to the traditional context: the formative movement is "right" when it not only respects measure but is also appropriate to (congruent with) the life-world situation. The argument takes into account the musical ethos doctrine, devoted to the connection between *modi* and affective conditions, rather than the rhetorical criterion of *aptum*:[63]

> If someone, singing sweetly and dancing beautifully, acts wantonly when the situation demands seriousness, surely he does not use numerically harmonious modulation [*numerosa modulatio*] well, that is, the motion that is said to be good because it is numerically harmonious [*numerosa*], and bad when it is used inappropriately. To modulate is one thing, to modulate well is another. Modulation [*modulatio*] is thought to pertain to any singer, provided he does not err in the intervals of voice and sound; but good modulation [*modulatio*] pertains only to that liberal discipline, namely, music.[64]

The "right form" thus appears in a significant middle position that was decisive for the later functionalization of music theory in the Christian educational canon.[65] It is related both to the changing existent, insofar as it has to be "appropriate to the situation," and to the ground of Being, insofar as the numerical order of *musica rhythmica* refers to the latter.

Against the background of the precarious status of the arts in the context of the Platonic tradition, an urgent question arises: under what conditions does this *modulatio* appertain to the object of a *scientia bene modulandi* and thus legitimate a *musica scientia*? The demonstration uses the nightingale as an example. If the nightingale sings in the spring, it seems to "form" or "measure" rightly: its song (*cantus*) is rhythmical, and thus numerically ordered, it is pleasing (*suaviter*), and moreover appropriate for the season. However, the nightingale "forms" not on the basis of knowledge, but rather of instinct. All creatures that, guided by instinct, sing well (*bene cantant*), resemble it, but they are incapable of providing any information about the intervals sung (*intervalli acutarum graviumque vocum*) or measured rhythm (*numeri*). Like the products of virtuoso instrumentalists, dancers, or even poets, their works are unquestionably objects of *musica scientia*, but they do not bear witness to insight and reason, but are instead limited to the imitation of models.[66] In practice, *bene modulari* can be in accord with *scientia* without being "produced by *scientia*." There may be performers who practice an art on the basis of understanding, as the teacher expressly concedes, but practice does not necessarily presuppose understanding: "Nor do I affirm that all those who handle an instrument lack knowledge, but I say that not all of them have it."[67] A corresponding definition of poetry as right forming "based on instinct" is regularly found both in Augustine and Boethius and in medieval treatises on music by their successors. Consequently the foundation and legitimation of a *musica scientia* must definitely distance itself from practice, which it seems possible to reduce to *imitatio* and dexterity without this being either visually or audibly perceptible in the result.[68] Only the activity of the *intellectus* can be considered as *scientia*: "What do you think I mean but that whoever attributes knowledge to the mind alone denies it to irrational beings, and locates it neither in sense nor in memory [. . .], but only in the intellect?"[69] The *scientia modulandi* takes a *modulatio* as its object not with a view to a potential musical practice but rather exclusively for its own sake: "Therefore, it is now probable that knowledge of modulating [*scientia modulandi*] is the knowledge of moving well [*scientia bene movendi*], so that motion by itself is desired and therefore delights by itself [*per se ipse delectat*]."[70]

With *delectatio*, the definition introduces a new component into the context of reflection. The thesis that is perhaps most momentous for the later argumentation in *De musica* and its "aesthetic" implications remains implicit: the "rightly measured" is *eo ipso* pleasing. Number is the condition of possibility of moderation and thus of giving pleasure. What is pleasing is moved in accord with numerical measures. The foundation of music theory on arithmetic thus connects the question "about the possibility of giving delight" to "the question about the laws that govern numbers."[71]

The status and profile of the numerical order as such had at first been left undetermined; now they move toward the center of interest. The point of departure is a set of simple temporal distinctions borrowed from the system of quantifying metrics:

> M[agister].: [. . .] And I now ask you whether someone can run for a long time and quickly.
>
> D[iscipulus].: He can.
>
> M.: What about slowly and quickly?
>
> D.: Not at all.
>
> M.: Therefore, for a long time is one thing and slowly is another.
>
> D.: They are completely different.
>
> M.: Now I ask you what you think the contrary of long lasting is, just as quickness is the opposite of slowness?
>
> D.: No common term comes to mind. And so, I do not see any expression that I might oppose to long lasting, except not long lasting, [. . .].
>
> M.: You are right. When we speak in this way, we do not detract from the truth. [. . .] Let us, therefore, call these two contraries "for a long time" and "not for a long time" [*diu et non diu*].[72]

Diu and *non diu* refer, in relation to the definition of *musica*, to the (relatively)[73] different durations of two movements (*motus*). Their relationship may, the *magister* goes on, be conceived numerically: as ratios of natural numbers that are respectively equal (1:1, 2:2, 3:3 . . .) or unequal (1:2, 2:3, 3:4 . . .).[74] The theoretical prominence of this possibility follows from the monistic character of the young Augustine's Christian Neoplatonism. The priority given measure and limitation over immoderation and unlimitedness joins the Christian concept of the "good" (i.e., perfectly ordered) Creation, which was first "disturbed" by original sin, with the development of the categories of Being, likeness, and otherness in Plato's *Sophist*[75] and the Pythagorean privileging of the finite over the infinite dyad. The *magister* declares apodictically: "I think you also know that every measure and mode is correctly preferred to the immeasurable and the infinite [*omnem mensuram et modum immoderationi et infinitati recte anteponi*]."[76] The postulate has axiomatic validity for all further developments.

From this postulate follows first of all the priority, for the numerical description of measured movement, of simple, natural relationships that can be presented as a fraction of natural numbers. Such a *dimensio numerosa* combines different "movements" into a relationship that can be defined as a ratio:

> M.: Two movements, therefore, as we have said, which have some numerical relationship with one another [*habent aliquam numerosam dimensionem*], are preferable to those that have none.
>
> D.: That is clear and logical. For a certain movement and measure [*motus, atque mensura*] exists in numbers and joins them together [*quae in numeris est, sibimet copulat*], and the ones that lack this are surely not linked to one another by any ratio [*qua qui carent, non utique sibi aliqua ratione junguntur*].[77]

In the following, ratios that can be presented as fractions of natural numbers are called "rational," and those that cannot are called "irrational." This distinction is differentiated in accord with the principle of the priority of the simple and the equal. To the full satisfaction of the *magister*, the pupil systematizes as follows: The simpler a "rational" relationship, the greater its value. Ratios with the same number as dividend and divisor (1:1; 2:2; 3:3), *aequales*, are to be given precedence over those with unequal numbers (1:2, 2:3, 3:4 . . .), *inaequales*. For some of the *inaequales* one can say that both the dividend and the divisor are whole number multiples of their difference (2:4, 6:8, 9:12 . . .); these are called *connumerati*. The *inaequales* for which this does not hold are called *dinumerati*. The *connumerati* can be further divided into those in which no smaller number is contained (2:4) and those in which both numbers can be presented as whole number multiples of their difference (4:6, 6:8, 8:10 . . .). The former are called *complicati*, the latter, to designate the subset of *connumerati*, *sesquati* (diagram 1).

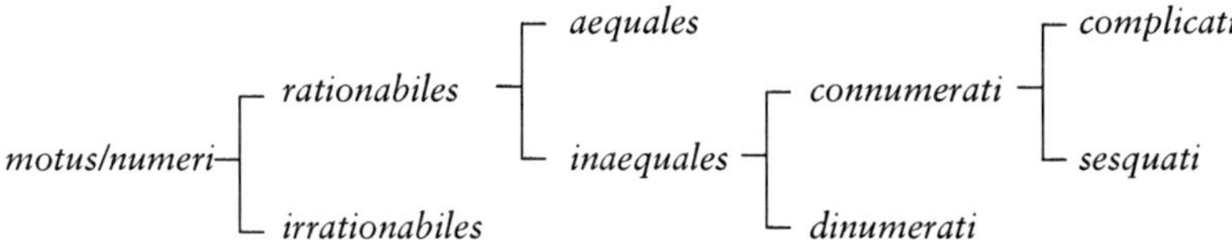

The didactic dialogue, which had begun from the relatively different duration of two syllabic quantities—from the difference between *diu* and *non diu*—has moved from the metrical phenomenon to the field of arithmetic. It is surveyed in accord with Euclid's *Elements*, with Nicomachus of Gerasa and Theon of Smyrna.[78] The argument first raises the problem that, as the *magister* notes in I.11.18, the terms of every proportion can be multiplied by any given number, and thus both of its components potentially strive toward the infinite. Here there is a threat of contradiction with the axiomatically introduced priority of the finite over the infinite. Accordingly there must be a *ratio* that provides the series moving toward infinity with measure (*modus*) and form (*forma*).[79] The regular return of the One, the *principium numerorum*, within the "infinite" progression of numbers, is assessed as an indication of the existence of such a *ratio*[80] that is presented as a "lex certa fixaque" and is moreover discernible in the series of numbers itself:

> Let us begin, therefore, this consideration of numbers from the beginning, as it appears, and let us see how much we can observe by the powers of our mind, and what is the reason [*ratio*] that, although a number may proceed to infinity, as we have said, men have made certain divisions in counting that bring them back to one [*a quibus ad unum rursus redeant*], the first of the numbers [*quod est principium numerorum*].[81]

The *ratio* that inscribes an order on the infinite progression of numbers is the decimal system:

> In counting we proceed from one to ten, and then come back to one; and if you want to multiply by ten, you progress in this fashion: ten, twenty, thirty, forty, all the way to one hundred; and counting by hundreds: one, two, three, four hundred; one thousand is the point from which you return. Why do we need to go further? You see the divisions I am discussing, the first rule of which demands starting at ten. For just as ten is ten times one, so one hundred contains ten tens, and a thousand has a hundred tens, and so on, as far as you want to go in divisions of this kind, which are determined by the number ten.[82]

Speaking of a *principium numerorum* presupposes that this *principium* is the beginning of something. The same goes for the end, *finis*; the two are connected by a middle, *medium*: "Ergo ut totum aliquid sit, principio et medio et fine constat." A "whole" has a beginning, a middle, and an end. The first number that meets this condition is the number three, which is the first "complete" or "perfect" number for precisely that reason.[83]

Now since there are even and uneven numbers, it must be possible to determine a first perfect number for each of the two classes of numbers. Thus if three is the first perfect uneven number, then four is the first perfect even number. Uneven numbers like three have an indivisible middle, while even numbers have a divisible middle. This leads back to the number one, because: "Individuum autem medium est unum, dividuum duo."[84] The number one is a "pure beginning" (*principium*), because it has neither middle nor end.[85] The number two, as the "second beginning," proceeds from the number one: thus one is the beginning *from which* all numbers are, and two is the beginning *through which* all numbers are:

> Now, this second beginning comes from that first one: the first comes from none, the second comes from the first; one and one make two, and thus they are both beginnings in the sense that all numbers come from one; but since they come about by combination and addition, the origin of combination and addition is correctly traced to the number two; hence, from that [*a quo*] first beginning all numbers derive, and through that [*per quod*] second beginning all numbers derive.[86]

The further explanation of the topic is assigned to arithmetic.[87] The *magister* strives to return to the narrower context of the investigation, but wants to develop the corresponding turnabout out of the reflection on arithmetic itself. A simple question introduces the turnabout: "Here let us come back to the work at hand as quickly as we can. And so, I ask, what does two added to one make?"[88] Three, the pupil replies, "Hence, these two beginnings of numbers added to one another make a complete and perfect number."[89] The sum of the two principles of the number series produces the first perfect number, which moreover also immediately follows them as a term in the series. A special *concordia* thus connects the two origins of the number series and the first perfect number—"Therefore, there is a great concord [*concordia*] among the first three numbers, for we say that no number can be interposed among one and two and three; but one and two make three"[90]—especially since this order is unique in the number series: "And you need to understand that this occurs in none of the remaining numbers: when you have noted any two joined to one another by order of counting, the one which is made of both follows them with no number intervening."[91] The theological connotations are nowhere made explicit.

The perceived *concordia* concludes a brief argument and opens up a new and longer one. First, it provides a foundation for the decimal system as the *ratio* of the otherwise infinite number series: ten, "the number that among all others is most strong"[92] is the sum of the numbers 1, 2, 3, and 4, of the two "original" and the first "perfect" numbers.[93] The derivation has thus reconstructed the Pythagorean *tetraktys*, generally emblematically represented as an equilateral triangle with ten points. The *concordia* is said to have an inherent, basic "tendency" to form the many into one—a unity that the pupil euphorically "admires" (*mirari*) and "loves" (*amare*), and which the *magister* moreover provides with ontological connotations that point beyond arithmetic. These connotations lead back to the rhythmical-metrical object. The reference is now to things (*res*), no longer exclusively to *numeri*:

M.: Do you not think it worth considering that as concord [*concordia*]
is more concentrated and connected, the more it tends toward unity
[*tanto magis in unitatem quamdam tendit*], and makes one thing out
of many [*et unum quiddam de pluribus efficit*]?

D.: I think that is quite true. I do not know why, but I marvel at and love
the unity that you commend.

M.: I much approve. But surely joining and binding of things best makes
something one [*quaelibet rerum copulatio atque connexio tunc maxime unum quiddam efficit*] when they fit the mean to the extreme and
the extreme to the mean [*cum et media extremis, et mediis extrema
consentiunt*].[94]

That which displays the property conceived with the verb *consentire*
tends toward *unitas*. This property is said then to be given, in the context
of number theory, when the middle terms correspond to the outer ones and
the outer terms to the middle ones. The derivation resorts to the first three
terms in the number series: In the series "1, 2, 3," the number two exceeds
the number one by the same amount as the number three exceeds the number two; this description names the one once, the two twice, the three once.
The *magister* now turns his attention to the sum of these factors:

M.: Hence, once, twice and once adds up to how many times?

D.: Four.

M.: Therefore, the number four rightly follows those three, and to it, indeed, the ordering is attributed according to that proportion.[95]

Furthermore, in the series 1, 2, 3, one and three are the outer terms and two
is the middle. If we now add up the outer terms, the result is equal to the
square of the middle term:

M.: Then, tell me, when we put together one, two and three, which is the
extreme and which the middle?

D.: One and three are the extremes, two the middle.

M.: Tell me, now, what do one and three make?

D.: Four.

M.: Well, two, the number in the middle, cannot be assigned to anything
but itself, can it? If that is so, tell me what twice two makes?)

D.: Four.

M.: So then, the middle agrees with the extremes, and the extreme with
the middle. If that is so, just as three excels as it comes after one and
two, since it consists of one and two, just so, four excels as it comes
after one and two and three, since four consists of one and three,

or twice two, which is an agreement by proportion [*proportione consensio*] of the extremes with the middle and the middle with the extremes. This is called ἀναλογία in Greek.[96]

The number four thus justifiably follows in the number series, since it is the *proportio* or ἀναλογία (from ἀνα λόγον—originally "according to the relationship") of these first three numbers. *Proportio* or ἀναλογία, terminologically a direct continuation of the metaphysics of music that leads from Archytas of Tarentum through Plato's *Timaeus* to Neoplatonism,[97] unify different terms and are therefore regarded as principles of the order so "beloved" by the pupil:

> Therefore, the number four rightly follows those three, and to it, indeed, the ordering is attributed according to that proportion [*ei quippe tribuitur ista proportione collatio*]. You should get used to recognizing how important that ordering is, since the unity that you said you love is caused by it alone in ordered things; the Greek name for this is ἀναλογία, which our authors call proportion. I'll use this term, if you agree [. . .].[98]

The "pulcherrimus progrediendi modus"[99] formed by the numbers 1, 2, 3, 4 bound "in closest friendship"[100] is identified as the true "ordering" element in *every* order. The unification of the different through *proportio* or ἀναλογία is, as a formal principle, valid beyond arithmetic: the transition from "pure" arithmology to music theory corresponds to the transition from number theory as such to the theory of numerical relationships.[101] If the order presented is named, it is the "highest conceivable": "non enim quidquam ordinatius fieri posse arbitror" ("I do not think that anything can be more orderly").[102] The comparative *ordinatius*, used with the negative indefinite pronoun *quidquid*, corresponds functionally to a superlative; the concept of *ordo* developed here thus opens the way to the concept, explained in *De ordine*, of an order of being that is the order of Creation.[103] Insofar as the "pulcherrimus"[104] *modus progrediendi* that underlies it is the "iustissima"[105] *progressio* itself, systematics and order connote the reducibility of *proportio* to the *unum principium* with the qualities "beauty" and "justness."

The results must still be related to the *motus* from which the didactic dialogue had abstracted, via *modulatio*, to the arithmetic way of arguing. This return to the concrete is allowed for by the previously parenthetical and apodictically introduced argument that *delectatio* indicates the existence of a measure and, indirectly, of numerical relationships, and does so, as is now emphasized, *independently* of a *rational understanding* of the numerical structure:

M.: [. . .] It is recognized that intervals in movements [*spatia in motibus*] alternate from single to double, either in the beat which is heard, or in the dancing which is seen; for will you not at least enjoy the rhythm that you feel [*saltem delecteris numerositate quam sentias*], even though you cannot declare what the numbers of its measure are [*non possis numeros ejus dimensionis edicere*]?

D.: It is just as you say. For those who know the numbers feel them in the beat and dancing, and easily declare what they are; and those who do not know them or cannot say what they are, do not deny that they take pleasure in them [*non negant tamen ex his se voluptate aliqua perfrui*].[106]

The presupposition is only that the "measured movement" is, for a human being, perceptible in time, "suited" to a human being's senses.[107] This premise grounds the choice of the "short measures" that please in verse and dancing as the point of departure and primary subject of the dialogue.[108] The metrical foot is music theory's privileged subject insofar as meter is a concrete manifestation of the numerical orders that are the subject of *musica disciplina* as *scientia*, and the one especially suited to human senses.

De musica, Books II–V. Feet, Meters, Rhythms

"Pay close attention, therefore, and now at last receive a sort of second exordium to our disputation"[109]—the second Book, "a veritable treatise on rhythmics and metrics,"[110] begins with these words. The goal is to appropriate the whole field of rhythmics and metrics, which had long been governed by grammar, for *musica scientia*. Whereas grammar, as "custos historiae,"[111] limits itself to guiding by means of *habitus* and unreflectively accepting traditional material,[112] *musica scientia* seeks to discover the "rationality" intrinsic to everything rightly measured[113] and thus also to rhythmics and metrics.[114] This is supposed to bring to light what is actually pleasing in a rightly measured verse, too.[115]

Accordingly, drawing the first distinction—*diu/non-diu*—implies the claim that the whole metrical system can be reformulated in arithmetic terms. All quantities, and thus also "short" and "long" defined in relation to one another, can be conceived as multiples of a short syllable which, defined as the "shortest temporal unit," is postulated as the functional equivalent of the number one as the *principium numerorum*. Augustine's conceptualization and philosophy of time in general proceed from this postulate.[116] Corresponding to the *prima progressio* from the number one to the number two, one long syllable is postulated to consist of two temporal units, and thus to sound twice as long as one short syllable. Thus, the *principle of unity* of the original difference *diu/non-diu* is the ἀναλογία or *proportio* 2:1.[117]

The passage establishes the transferability of the theorems developed arithmetically in Book I on the domain of *musica scientia*. Its subject is then developed successively from the quantitatively smallest unit of order, the individual short syllable, to the longest unit, rhythm.

Every metrical foot consists of two parts (*semi-pedes*) of at least one syllable each, *arsis* and *thesis*.[118] The master begins by noting that the ancients had called such a *collatio sonorum* a metrical foot when a *convenientia* could be observed. A *convenientia* occurs when *arsis* and *thesis* are joined in accord with a specific *numerositas* to form a *proportio*: "inter se aliqua numerositate conveniunt."[119] On this basis the repeated sequence can be differentiated internally, according to the number of syllables, or according to the distribution of the quantities within the sequence. The *discipulus* remembers the terms introduced for the classification of the *proportiones*: if a long syllable is joined with a short one to form a foot, and if the duration of a long syllable corresponds to twice that of a short syllable, then we have a construct in accord with the number genus (*genus numerorum*) of the *complicati*: the metrical foot corresponds to the *proportio* 2:1. If on the other hand two short or two long syllables are joined, as in the initial example—the word *modus*, a pyrrhic foot—then this construct (1:1 or 2:2) corresponds to the number genus of the *aequales*.[120]

If we can assume a sequence of two syllables, both of which can assume either "short" or "long" values, then there are four possible metrical feet, the shortest with two *tempora*, the longest with four (˘˘, ˘ –, – ˘, – –). This can also be conceived, as we might expect given the guiding binary distinction, in the progression developed in Book I, as the *discipulus* recognizes "cum magna animi voluptate."[121] From the discovery of the descriptive potential of this progression the *magister* deduces its normative valence: two times two possible quantities leads to four possible two-syllable feet each of which has at least two and at most four *tempora*. The number four is not exceeded in any passage, and correspondingly, the magister concludes normatively, the metrical foot also has to include a maximum of four syllables.[122]

In the following all possible distributions of short and long syllables are systematically listed. The inventory of all possible distributions, on the one hand,[123] and of all possible sequences of metrical feet on the other,[124] consequently resorts to the concepts and categories made available by the progression developed in Book I:[125] "[H]unc enim esse meliorem ordinem, vel potius hunc esse ordinem [. . .]" ("This is the better order, or rather, this

is *the* order, [. . .]").[126] At the end there is an inventory of the possible combinations of short and long in feet of two to four syllables, and in II.8.15
this inventory is related to the twenty-eight metrical feet that Latin poetry
took over from Greek poetry. This passage is one of the parts of the work
most widely known in the Middle Ages.

Just as a metrical foot consists of a variable number of syllables with
variably distributed quantities, so a verse consists of metrical feet of varying
kinds (*genus*) and numbers (*numerus*). Corresponding to the theorem of the
priority of equality and similarity[127] introduced in I.9.15, the construction
of a verse out of metrical feet of the same kind is considered as being both
"reasonable" and pleasing to the ear: "for the greatest equality [*summa
aequalitatis*] exists when feet of the same kind and name follow one another."[128] *Aequalitas* caresses the ear the most, so that one can say: the more
"equal," the more pleasant.

If different metrical feet were combined without jarring the ear, then the
impression of a pleasant sound would indicate the equality of the different
metrical feet with regard to a certain quality, namely their *numerositas*: "Do
you not agree that feet should be mixed with other feet when equality is
preserved [*aequalitate servata*]? For what can be more pleasing to the ear
than being soothed by variety but not deceived by equality [*cum et varietate
mulcentur, nec aequalitate fraudantur*]?"[129] Thus metrical feet that have the
same number of *tempora* can be sequenced as equal.[130] The pleasant sound
of the combination of different metrical feet follows from the phenomenon
of "ringing through," from the perceivability of *the equal within the different*. The fundamental "verse-aesthetic" relevance of this principle, even
over and beyond the arithmetic context of justification, is to be emphasized
as much as possible, just as is the fact that this principle formulates the
"musicality" of metrical discourse in general.

Thus the essential rules for the successive development of the greater
units of order have been formulated. Book III begins with general considerations on rhythm, meter, and verse that are taken from the tradition
since Aristoxenos of Tarentum[131] handed down by Aristides Quintilianus
and systematized and deepened in Books III, IV, and V. Different metrical
feet that have the same number of *tempora* can be combined in any quantity.[132] Such an infinite sequence of metrical feet is designated by the Greek
loan-word *rhythmus*, in order to avoid the polysemy of the Latin *numerus*,
which was already inherent in the Greek ῥυθμός.[133] If the infinite sequence
of "measured" feet itself receives a designated end as a measure and a repetitive basic structure, then we have a *metrum*. The *magister* infers, in
III.1.2, that every *metrum* is a rhythm, but not every rhythm is a *metrum*.[134]

The definition of measure as the criterion of distinction between meter and rhythm raises the question of the minimal and maximal length of a meter. The answer is provided by the contrast between meter and verse.

The definition of verse in II.7.14, generally conceived as the combination of a certain kind and a certain number of feet, proceeds from the question as to whether the negative-chiastic figure from III.1.2 can be repeated.[135] Meter is a rule-governed connection of feet (*legitima pedum connexio*). Since such a connection is possible only numerically (*numerose*), meter must also be a *numerus*, a rhythm. The sequence can contain an undetermined number of feet; however, then the result is a rhythm, but no longer a meter. If the number of feet is limited, the sequence becomes a meter. If the *metrum* is divided into two parts (*membra*), then it is called a verse.[136] The "harmonic" verse, the verse that especially pleases the ear, is one that can be divided symmetrically:

> Is not everything that is divided more beautiful if its parts agree in some equality [*si eorum partes aliqua parilitate concordent*], rather than being discordant and dissonant [*quam si discordes et dissonae sint*]? [. . .] Just as we find, therefore, that a foot is divided into two harmonious parts and delights the ear for that reason, if we find just such a meter, should we not justly prefer it to one lacking this regard?[137]

The part of the definition that serves to define the minimal and maximal length of a meter is the one that states that the verse consists of two parts (*membra*), not of two feet (*pedes*). The verse, like the *membrum*, must include several metrical feet. If, in accord with the preceding definition, a metrical foot consists of at least two *tempora*, then the shortest verse, consisting of two times two metrical feet, has eight *tempora*, and the longest has thirty-two (a maximum of four metrical feet with a maximum of four long syllables consisting of two *tempora* each). If verse and meter differ only in symmetrical divisibility, then the minimal and the maximal length determined for the verse must also hold for the meter.[138] Harmonic progression remains the principle of construction: "Especially in expanding the measure [*modum*], when the quaternary ratio [*quaternaria ratione*] has been preserved, it will join meter with verse, and verse with meter."[139] The exclusively formal line of argument, as well as the pupil's euphoric admiration, accentuate the point: "I understand and I approve. And I am delighted that in this fashion they have concord and agreement [*concordiam consensionemque*]."[140]

Now practice proves to be more refractory than the smooth derivation suggests. The constructive-synthetic layout of the argument makes it seem that every rhythm, every meter, can be resolved without restriction into metrical feet with the same number of *tempora*. Meters that are not regularly divisible into metrical feet may also be pleasing to the ear. The *magister* says reassuringly: "The judgment of our ears themselves [. . .] convinces us that it is meter both because it is more than a foot, and also it has a fixed ending. It would not sound with such sweet equality or be beaten with harmonious motion [*aut motu tam concinno plauderetur*], if it lacked harmony of numbers [*si non inesset in illo numerositas*], which can only truly be in this part of music."[141] The causal connection established at the outset between measure and *delectatio* makes the following reversal plausible: even an allegedly "incomplete" line has a pleasing sound, and must therefore have *aequalitas*, *motus concinnus*, and *numerositas*. The gap in the theoretical construction is closed by the introduction of *silentia*, which fill out the incomplete meter.[142] The solution strategy emphasizes that a meter is not desirable in itself; here, too, it is the *repetition of the same* that creates a pleasing effect. Only "whole" meters, possibly "rounded out" with pauses or "rests," are to be repeated "harmonically."

The scheme does not hesitate to contradict the customary practice of scansion. If they violate the laws of reason, it may be hard to teach the vulgar.[143] All the same, in case of doubt, one should trust not the ear, which is dominated by habit, and not the unreflective opinion of the multitude, but solely the "rational" set of regulations:

> For you know that in making verse it does not matter whether in this
> kind the anapest or the dactyl is put with the spondee: in measuring ratio-
> nally [*ad metiendum tamen rationabiliter*], which concerns the mind not
> the ear, this is sorted out by true and sure reason [*vera et certa ratione*],
> not by irrational opinion. We are not the first to notice this, but it was
> remarked long ago by well-established custom. [. . .] It is shameful fool-
> ishness that the authority of men is sought to strengthen reason, whereas
> nothing ought to be more excellent than the authority of reason and
> truth, which really is better than any man.[144]

The harsh tone already anticipates Book VI: the right of reason is to be established with regard to mere *habitus*, even in matters of regular scansion. What is at stake here is nothing less than the path to the knowledge of the "eternal nature of all things": "Thus the inveterate will of men and not the eternal reason of things [*aeterna rerum ratio*] must be considered when measuring verse."[145] The priority of arithmetic theory is in this sense absolutely valid. When it comes to a conflict, the established practice will be rejected as deficient, even if this requires a great deal of argumentation.

This may be illustrated by an example. Verses of six feet are considered the noblest, a convention that must be subjected to the test of reason (V.11.23). Traditionally, the Latin "heroic verse," the dactylic hexameter, is divided into two *membra* of five and seven half-feet, which seems to violate the rule of symmetry. The *magister* uses the set of tools that has been developed to refute this view and to defend the excellence of the *senarius* against the "poet's caprices."[146] His solution makes use of the foundation of geometry in arithmetic. A given length can be divided up randomly; the square of the length will correspond to the sum of the squares of their parts. With regard to time as well, we can speak of "length" (*temporis longitudo*), and thus also in the case of the verse. The verse has a certain length, its parts are the verse's *membra*. Augustine's "solution" begins with the "numeric" properties of the parts compared: by adding a "rest," the seven half-feet of the second hemistich could become eight half-feet, and thus enlarged to become four two-syllable feet. Hence, according to Augustine's definition of verse, this hemistich can be considered as a verse in its own right. Consequently, it can be divided, according to the rules of division introduced, into two parts of three and four half-feet. The sum of the squares of these numbers ($3^2 + 4^2$) is 25. The other hemistich of the six-foot verse, which consists of five half-feet could not be divided up in the same way, but the square of the number of its half-feet is also equal to 25. The joy produced by this discovery knows no bounds: "Not without cause, therefore, have verses of six feet been considered more famous and more noble, for one can hardly say how great a difference exists between their equality in unequal members [*inter illorum aequalitatem in membris imparibus*] and that of all others."[147] No matter how evident the difference between the hemistiches examined may seem, when seen against the background of the ontological priority of the "numerical structure," this evidence is reduced to—nothing. The schematizing reduction to the numerical-harmonic relationship effaces the differences perceived by the senses. Accordingly, concerning the system of metrics and rhythmics developed in *De musica*, which conceives the units of metrical order on the basis of the constitution of the human sensory apparatus as superb objectifications of the numeric order of Being and Creation, we can say that every regularly formed metrical foot, every verse, every meter, every rhythm, appears as a manifestation and objectification of the eternal *rerum ratio*;[148] pleasure is the sense-receptive counterpart of precisely these properties. The pleasure taken in a beautiful verse indicates that its metrical structure can be explained as the play of the same in the different, as a manifestation of the intelligible and ontologically primary numerical order. Book VI undertakes this explanation, leaving the sensory behind and taking as its subject the numerical order that is manifested in metrics:

Now, if you have nothing to say to contradict this, let this be the end of
the disputation, so that now, from what concerns the part of music that is
in numbers and time, from the sensible tracks, let us come with as much
wisdom as we can muster to the very den itself, which is free of all bodily
form [*ubi ab omni corpore aliena est*].[149]

De musica, Book VI. *Musica a corporeis ad incorporea*
Book VI, which was tackled only after Augustine's return to Tagaste, concludes *De musica* by carrying out the anagoge: "a corporeis ad incorporea
transeamus."[150] The music theory developed by systematically appropriating pagan materials is here given a genuinely Christian accent:

> One cannot really talk about sources for Book VI. While remaining faith-
> ful to the Pythagorean, Platonic, and Neoplatonic traditions, Augustine
> undertakes a general re-elaboration. Basing himself on the Christian faith,
> he arrives at an entirely original system.[151]

Books II to V extracted quantifying metrics from the domain of grammar
and reconstructed it, drawing on the definitions and theorems of arithmetic,
as part of *musica scientia*. The broadened procedure systematically privileges the formal components of lyric poetry, and in addition puts "sense of
form"[152] over affective effect: the secondary syntagmatic organization of
metrical discourse is not only granted priority over text semantics, but is la-
beled ontologically as "form" and transferred to the domain of theological
discourse. In this way the procedure used in Books I to V, that of clarifying
the verse by reference to the numerical determination of its form can be
made functional for the path *a corporeis ad incorporea* and thus ultimately
for the way to God:

> We thought it worthy of discussion so that young people, or men of any
> age whom God has endowed with good ability, might be torn away not
> hastily but by sure stages and by the light of reason from the senses of the
> flesh and from carnal letters [*sed quibusdam gradibus a sensibus carnis
> atque a carnalibus litteris*], to which it is difficult for them not to adhere,
> and so that they might adhere, through the love of unchanging truth, to
> the one God and Lord of all things who watches over human minds with
> no intervening nature [*nulla natura interposita*].[153]

This sketch contains *in nuce* the project of Book VI. First, it shows how
simply the concept of anagoge, Platonic in its structure, can be appropriated in practice-related contexts by replacing the world of Ideas with
the personal God.[154] Furthermore, it shows the status attributed to the

objects of *musica scientia* in the Christian order of discourse that was being constituted:

> Whoever reads these books will find that we have engaged with grammatical and poetic minds, not with the intention of staying with them, but with the necessity of moving through them [*sed iterandi necessitate versatos*]. When the reader has come to this book, if, as I hope and sincerely pray, God and Our Lord has guided our purpose and will, and has led us to our intended goal, the reader will know that it is not a worthless road in a worthless realm through which we (who are not very strong) now have preferred to walk with the weak of mind, rather than to cast headlong those with weaker wing through the open air.[155]

Poetry, grammar, and the disciplines are the stations on the way to a transcendent goal. Their objects are signs, like fingers, which point to the essential—and who would take the finger itself for what is signified? The possible claims of *musica scientia* are qualified, it is deprived of any right of its own, and it is put in the service of religious interests; when it is not, it is depreciated as childishness.[156]

Nonetheless, and significantly, a specific verse remains the starting point for Book VI: Ambrose's "Deus Creator omnium."[157] Using the verse's four iambs or twelve *tempora* and the method developed in Books I to V, the *magister* begins the explication of the causal relationship that is supposed to exist between numerical order and *delectatio*. The didactic dialogue begins again by attempting to provide an epistemological foundation for this relationship, and by inquiring into the ways of perceiving the sound of verse.

> You, therefore, my friend, who shares the reasoning process with me, tell me, if it pleases you, as we pass from corporeal things to incorporeal [*ut a corporeis ad incorporea transeamus*], and pronounce the verse *Deus creator omnium*, where do you think that the four iambs of which it consists and the twelve times are? Must we say that the numbers are only in the sound that is heard, or also in the sense of the hearer as related to the ears, or also in the act of reciting, or since the verse is recognized, also in our memory?[158]

In the perceived sound, in the sense of hearing, in performing the recitation, and in memory—the four iambs of which the verse consists "exist" in all these domains. These modes of being are discussed in succession.

Insofar as the sense of hearing makes it possible to perceive numerically ordered *motus*, or vibrations in the air, its constitution must be similar to that of what is perceived. The terms of the relation are the numerical order of the rhythm to be heard, on the one hand, and the "ipsius sensus numerous" ("number of the sense itself")[159] on the other hand. The *magister* begins by inferring from this two distinct modes of existence for the *numeri* underlying the rhythmic: first, they "exist" as a potential of the sense of hearing, even when no sensory stimulus is provided. Insofar as this potential is realized only in the experience of sound, that is, insofar as it begins with sound but ceases with the latter's end, it follows that, second, the *numeri* of the perceived sound exist independently of any concrete auditory experience.[160] Furthermore, humans can silently imagine tones and melodies, and the pulse-beat and breathing are undoubtedly rhythmical in nature. *Imaginatio*, *respiratio*, and *pulsus* are reduced to a common "operatio animi"[161] founded on specific *numeri*. These numbers are also granted an existence independent of the first kinds of *numeri* mentioned.[162] *Memoria* also has specific *numeri*;[163] finally, a fifth category of numbers is considered to underlay a "naturalis vis judicari,"[164] which "latently" causes numerical orders to be found pleasing.[165] The assumption of these *numeri iudiciales* combines the "Pythagorean-Platonic tradition with Plotinus's turn inward toward the soul as 'inner form.'"[166] Attempts to hierarchize these categories of numbers that differ in their mode of existence fill the largest part of Book VI of *De musica*. A first attempt ends with a provisional solution and the insight that the procedure used falls short. A second attempt takes this into account and develops the analogical interpretation as a transition from the knowing subject's self-thematization to the transcendental conditions of knowledge in general. Both attempts remain guided by the specific verse as an example.

The first attempt starts from the observation that there can be no doubt regarding the absolute priority of the *iudiciales*, and that the other categories of numbers are to be ordered in accord with the principle of causality: Cause has priority over effect.[167] All productive *numeri* that underlie performative acts accordingly have priority over receptive *numeri*; the *numeri* of the memory are assigned the lowest rank. The first approach to the problem thus leads to a hierarchy with the *iudiciales* at the summit, the active *numeri* in a still unclear order in the middle, and remembered *numeri* at the bottom.

The principle of causality now requires that the numbers governing sound be given priority over those in the power of hearing. Since the latter are considered as belonging to the *anima*, this contradicts, as the *discipulus* interjects, the fundamental priority of everything spiritual over the corporal-material.[168] There is a threat that the *anima* will be subjected to the effects of the body. Augustine's theory of knowledge, a statement of which concludes the first attempt, can be seen as a defense against this danger. This is introduced by positive attitude toward the body specific to the theological context. Instead of deploring the body's power one may instead marvel at the fact that it can affect the soul—a possibility that would perhaps never have been granted without the fall into sin and the subjection of the body to the law of death. Thus the body has a beauty of its own (*pulchritudo sui generis*) that acts like an adornment in relation to the *dignitas animae*:

> One should marvel that the body can do anything in the soul. Perhaps it would not be able to do so if the body, which the soul used to animate and govern with no trouble and the greatest ease, had not been changed for the worse by the first sin, and been subjected to corruption and death; nevertheless, the body has its own kind of beauty and by this alone it commends the dignity of the soul, of which neither wound nor illness deserved to be without the honor of some elegance.[169]

This positive attitude toward the body is possible because while the Savior has redeemed the human race's sin (*peccatum*), the *consequences* of the Fall nonetheless persist, even *sub gratia*.[170] The original corruption of mankind continues to operate insofar as the body is able to affect the soul. It is the fundamental depreciation of this affection that has become obsolete with Christ's act of redemption.[171] Whereas the reasoning of Books I to V is largely Neoplatonist, here the Christian Augustine defines himself.

The respective truth content (*veritas*) becomes the criterion for evaluating both spiritual and bodily matters; the unity of the criterion of value accounts for the unity of the numerical foundation of both sensory and rational knowledge. A tree seen with the eyes is *in corpore facta*, but nevertheless superior in "truth" to a tree dreamed of *in anima*.[172] The *numeri* of pleasant-sounding rhythm are substantially *numeri*, and only accidentally corporal or spiritual.[173] The question initially posed, which leads to the problem of the causal priority of the corporal-material over the spiritual, is thus withdrawn as unnecessary for the establishment of a hierarchy. The danger it had concealed is not thereby warded off, but rather circumvented: the law of causality does not grant the body priority over the spiritual, but simply grants one class of *numeri* priority over another: "Why do we hesitate, therefore, to prefer sounding and corporeal numbers [*sonantes numeros atque corporeos*] to those that arise from them, although they arise in the soul, which is better then the body? We prefer numbers to numbers, or creating things to created ones, not the body to the soul."[174]

The sense impressions that are among the objects of *musica scientia* can thus be discussed without regard to a priori value judgments. To this end the argument begins again with the relation between numerical order and *delectatio* and now certifies that the latter has an ethical relevance.

Concerning the body, it can be said that: "For bodies are better to the extent that they are more harmonious [*numerosiora*] through such numbers."[175] Concerning the soul, the "musical" *numeri* are an occasion to turn toward the "divine numbers of wisdom": "Indeed, the soul becomes better by lacking those numbers that it receives through the body, when it turns away from the carnal senses and is transformed by the divine numbers of Wisdom [*et divinis sapientiae numeris reformatur*]."[176] As Augustine, continuing Plotinus's expansion of the doctrine of the beautiful into an ethics, explains,[177] the move toward the "inner" numerical structure of the soul consummates the ethical and religious life of men: "After delight has been restored to the numbers of reason [*in rationis numeros restituta*], our whole life is turned toward God, giving numbers of health to the body [*dans corpori numeros sanitatis*], while not receiving happiness from it; this will happen after the exterior man has been destroyed and his alteration for the better has taken place."[178] The insight into the numerical structure of creation, which *De musica* consistently develops out of the work on the metrical form of the verse, leads directly to the vision of the truth of salvation. Augustine refers to Eccles. 7:26: "Indeed, it is said in Scripture: I turned my mind to know and to search out and to seek wisdom and the sum of things [*ut scirem et considerarem et quaererem sapientiam et numerum*]."[179] Referring to metrical discourse as *musica* thus accentuates its *anagogic potential* and its *ethical valence*.

This accentuation is central for the "literary aesthetics" that can be extrapolated from *De musica* and is at the same time bound to the conceptual context that it develops. Accordingly, we will first round out the presentation of the latter. For the narrower context, the problem of hierarchization, the ethical functionalization of the *numeri* active in performance and reception is without gain. Only a shift in the argumentative level allows this problem to be solved, in a sudden attack, so to speak. The *magister* begins again by noting that sense perception affects and changes the body. Affections of the body can "correspond" (*congruere*) to the soul or not, and their own activity can consequently unsettle it or not. Correspondence produces a feeling of pleasure (*voluptas*), noncorrespondence produces a feeling of lack. The latter is experienced as *dolor* or *labor*. The soul accommodates this alleged influence of the bodily, but is in no way "subjected" to it. On the other hand, as *instrumenta corporis* the senses are in the service of the will and thus of the soul: the soul attends to the stimulus felt by the body and then makes use of its *instrumenta* in full self-mastery. "I think that the soul, when it senses, reflects these actions in the responses of the body, but does not feel them"—the soul "suffers" (*pati*) nothing at all. It acts fundamentally arbitrarily.[180] Reprehensible behavior, the self-diminishment of the soul, always presupposes an active decision of the will to turn toward the sensuous *qua sensuous*:

When the soul experiences something through its own actions, the experience comes from itself; but clearly while it accommodates itself to the body it is less itself on that account, for the body is always less than the soul. When the soul has turned, therefore, from its Lord to its servant, it is wanting by necessity; likewise, when it has turned from its servant to its Lord, it advances by necessity, and it offers to its servant a very easy life, one with little trouble and toil, to which no attention is turned because of its most lofty tranquility; this is like the condition of the body that health gives to it: [. . .].[181]

The syntactical parallelism emphasizes the parting of the ways: on the one hand, the adherence to the sensuous, on the other, the stoic concept of *tranquilitas animi*[182] interpreted in a Christian manner; here *uti*, there *frui*.[183] The heard numbers of metrical discourse have anagogic relevance since the theory of perception outlined suggests that "seeing through" the verse to reveal the numerical constituents of its form reduces the soul's activity to executing the *ratio* and thus to sheer self-reference.[184] The problem that had forced Augustine to write the epistemological excursus is not actually solved, but rather spirited away: his theory of cognition makes irrelevant the objections to the consequences of a hierarchization of the *numeri* in accord with the principle of causality. In concluding the first "attempt" he emphasizes that sensible, sounding *numeri* occupy the last rank, even after the *recordabiles*. The perceiving *numeri occursores* come next, than the actively producing *progressores*. Both, as "active" in cognition, are given priority over remembered *numeri*. The first rank is occupied by the *numeri iudiciales*.[185]

With respect to each of these *numeri* Augustine raises the question of their mortality, their perishability or imperishability in time (IV.7.17) The *recordabiles* are forgotten, all others vanish instantly. In contrast, the *iudiciales* do not vanish and are not "forgotten." They are an enduring possession of all humans and an element of the *hominis natura*. All the same, they seem not to be entirely relieved of temporality. Their failure to grasp rhythms that measure ultra-long periods of time is incompatible with the predicate of immortality.[186] This limit to their capacity is explained by reference to the proportion between the macrocosm and the microcosm:

Why are they not able to do so? It is because a sense of places and times has been granted to every sentient creature in its own kind in proportion to the universe [*proportione universitatis*], so that as its body is great in proportion to the body of the universe, of which it is a part, and its age is great in proportion to the age of the universe, of which it is a part, just so its sense is suited to its action, which it pursues in proportion to the motion of the universe, of which it is a part.[187]

The cognitive potential of the *numeri iudiciales* corresponds to the place of man in the order of creation. Its relative deficiency is a consequence of human mortality; its relative superiority consists in its "ordering" power over the various *numeri* of the body. This superiority is documented by its origin in God as the *auctor omnis convenientiae atque concordiae*:

> For the progressing numbers [*progressores*] are modified with the hidden agreement of the judicial ones [*iudiciales*] when they seek some numerically ordered operation in the body [*in corpore numerosam operationem appetunt*]. For whether walking with unequal step, or striking with unequal intervals of blows, or eating or drinking with unequal motions of the jaws, or finally, scraping with unequal motions of the nails, and without listing many other such operations, that which restrains us and protects us from unequal motions when we look to do something with the members of the body, and silently requires some equality, that is the judicial number of some kind that implies that God is the creator of living things [*quod conditorem animalis insinuat Deum*]. Surely it is proper to think that He is the author of all harmony and concord [*auctorem omnis convenientiae atque concordiae*].[188]

Thus *all* the categories of numbers presented up to this point prove to be ontologically inferior. It is precisely this discovery that generates the anagoge: it raises the question as to whether there is any ontologically prior category of numbers that does not have the defect of *mortalitas*, and to that extent "transcends" the other five *generi numerorum*.[189] This question is the subject of the *pars secunda* of Book VI.

Ambrose's verse "Deus Creator omnium" remains the starting point for all of Augustine's considerations. Perceived with the *numeri occursores*, remembered and recognized with the *recordabiles*, recited with the *progressores*, and distinguished with the *iudiciales*, depending on whether they produce pleasure or displeasure, enjoyment or nonenjoyment, the verse still remains without "evaluation" (*aestimatio*). The latter is a process of assessment (*aestimare ratione*) that is exclusively intellectual and far from any sensual delectation (*delectare sensu*):

> I think that when the verse we have proposed, *God Creator of all things*, is sung we hear it with the metrical [*occursoribus*] numbers, recognize

it with the remembered [*recordabilibus*] ones, recite it with the advancing ones [*progressoribus*], are delighted by the judicial ones [*iudiciales*], evaluate it with I know not what others, and that concerning this delight, which is like a judgment of the judicial numbers, we get another more certain judgment according to the more hidden ones. Do you think it is one and the same thing to be delighted by sense and to evaluate with reason [*unum atque idem videtur delectari sensu, et aestimare ratione*]?[190]

This *aestimatio* must be based on a category of numbers that is peculiar to it and that makes necessary the review of the classification of numbers previously elaborated (VI.6.16).[191] The new numbers that are the condition of *aestimatio ratione* are to be called *numeri iudiciales*, while the former *iudiciales* are now to be called *sensuales*, because their *iudicium* has its primary object in the senses. The *sonantes* are termed *corporales*, because in that way dance and other measured movements such as pantomime can be more clearly included along with metrical discourse. The new classification is thus as follows: (1) *numeri iudiciales*, (2) *numeri sensuales*, (3) *numeri progressores*, (4) *numeri occursores*, (5) *numeri recordabiles*, (6) *numeri corporales*.[192] Taking into account the reshaped horizon resulting from the introduction of *aestimatio* and the revision of the *generi numerorum*, the considerations on *musica rhythmica* are now recapitulated and subjected to renewed testing by the power of reason (*vis potentiaque rationis*).[193] Summing up, Augustine declares that in Book I, reason recognized the conception of a free movement in order and beauty as the *definiens* of right forming (I.2.3), determined the difference of quantities and proved capable of distinguishing it from the tempo of the recitation (I.7.13), while in Books II to V it undertook to divide up time into metrical feet, rhythms, and verses. Finally, he suggests, it is also reason that distinguished numbers that are bound to the body from those that pertain to reason alone (VI.1.2ff.).[194] *The repetition of the same* as the cause of "aesthetic" pleasure is recapitulated and reformulated with greater emphasis on its "poetic" relevance: "What is it that we love in sensible harmonious numbers [*quod in sensibili numerositate diligimus*]? Anything other than *a certain equality and intervals equally measured* [*aliud praeter parilitatem quamdam et aequaliter dimensa intervalla*]?"[195]

The anagogic interpretation begins with the *relationship of similarity* between a concrete relation of equality, for instance between metrical feet of the same measure, and equality itself as a predicate of the personal God. The projection of the principle of equivalence from the paradigmatic axis of selection onto the syntagmatic axis of combination, *redundant sequencing* as a repetition of the same *in time*, points to the ideal, *atemporal* One and the Same that is identical with the principle and "essence" of number (*numerositas*): "[N]ihil enim est horum sensibilium, quod nobis non aequalitate aut similitudine placeat. *Ubi autem aequalitas aut similitudo, ibi numerositas*; nihil est quippe tam aequale aut simile quam unum et unum" ("For there is nothing in these sensible things that does not please us with equality and similarity. *Where there is equality or similarity, however, there is harmony of numbers* (*numerositas*); indeed, nothing is as equal and similar as one and one").[196] The argument's level of abstraction is crucial: like unity, equality, and symmetry, *order as such* is traced back to forms of *numerositas* as its ontological precondition. Insofar as it has a created form, *everything* that exists seems to be bound to the Creator. As a form of order, the created form is a priori beautiful. This holds especially for all *numerically* constituted entities, for numbers and their relationships, for metrical feet, verses, meters, rhythms:

> Number, however, begins at one, and is beautiful in respect to equality and similarity [*et aequalitate ac similitudine pulcher*], and is joined by order [*et ordine copulatur*]. For this reason, whoever claims that there is no nature that does not seek unity so that it might be what it is, and try to be like itself as far as it can, and possess its own order as its security, either in place or time or in the body with some measure, he must claim that all things have been made and established [*facta atque condita*], whatever they are and however great they are, from one principle and that they are linked through a form equal to it and similar to the riches of His goodness [*ab uno principio per aequalem illi ac similem speciem divitiis bonitatis ejus*], by which they joined together, as one and one from one, by a most precious charity, as I have said.[197]

Similarly, through "the goodness of divine love" and through a "common origin," everything created stands in a relationship of order that can be described as "sameness" or "similarity," as *aequalitas* or *similitudo*, and can be gradated. Order as such refers "figurally," as it were, to the One and the Same. This holds for every harmonic relationship based on numbers and particularly for every rhythmic-metric order:

> Whence comes this mode of progression [*progressionis modus*], therefore, from the first to the fourth? Whence the equality of parts, which are found in length, width and height? Whence the "correlationality" [*correlationalitas*] (for thus I have preferred to call analogy) whereby the ratio that length has to an indivisible point, width has to length, and height has

to width? Whence do they come, I ask, unless from that most lofty and eternal preeminence of numbers [*illo summo atque aeterno principatu numerorum*], and from similarity, equality and order [*et similitudinis et aequalitatis et ordinis*]? But if you take these things away from earth, there will be nothing.[198]

Here the claim of *musica scientia* is not only broadened, in that on the basis of the doctrine developed in Books I to V *every* form of order founded on redundancies now becomes plausible as an object. In the context, what is crucial is that the conceptual heart of Augustine's theory of music is detached from quantifying metrics. The move toward abstraction is systematically a move forward on the path *a corporeis ad incorporea*. In a historical perspective, it increases the adaptability of the theoretical elements propounded in *De musica* to the evolution of the metrical system—which was for Augustine already foreseeable. The doctrine can, while generally maintaining theoretical consistency, include metrical systems based on dynamic accentuation or syllable counting, so long as these can be presented as being founded on processes of numerical ordering and phenomena of redundancy.

The sixth book ends with emphases on this metaphysics of order that stress its wide scope and sharpen the Christian-ethical character of the whole. The specification of the ethical points breaks the ground. Attending to numerical orders situates the soul in the "rational harmony" of Creation and heals the body of the temptations of *lascivitas*:

> But when the mind has been raised up to spiritual things and remains focused there, even the impulse of this intimacy is broken and, after being repressed for a while, it dies out. For it was greater when we followed it; it is surely less when we restrain it, but is not entirely negated, and thus in certain backward steps away from every lustful movement in which there is a defect in the essence of the soul, and after delight has been restored to the numbers of reason [*delectatione in rationis numeros restituta*], our whole life is turned toward God, giving numbers of health to the body [*dans corpori numeros sanitatis*], [. . .].[199]

This process of healing allows the Christian, after overcoming *curiositas*[200] (VI.13.39) and *superbia*[201] (VI.13.40), to integrate all *numeri* and thereby achieve a truly human life, a life in *caritas Dei*:[202] In Christian life in *caritas* all *numeri*, even those of the body, retain their own law, their own right as inherently different. As "imitations" of the eternal *numeri*; nevertheless, in accord with the criterion of their *perfectio*, they are part of a hierarchically organized whole, of *harmonia*.[203] The right to exist is not questioned for any level of this hierarchy; each one is "beautiful" in itself. Each one appears as posited in accord with divine *providentia* as part of this "consonance," and is to be "used" as a stage on the way to the vision of the pinnacle of the hierarchy:

> What sullies the soul, however, is not evil, since even the body is a creature of God and is adorned with its own beauty, though it is inferior [*et specie sua quamvis infima decoratur*], but on account of the dignity of the soul the body is scorned, just as the dignity of gold fades when mixed with even the purest silver. For this reason then, whatever numbers have been made from our mortality [*quicumque de nostra quoque poenali mortalitate numeri facti sunt*], which is our punishment, let us not alienate them from the working of divine providence [*a fabricatione divinae providentiae*], since they are beautiful in their own kind, yet let us not love them so that we might be blessed by enjoying such things. For we shall do without these things because they are temporal, and like a plank in the waves, neither reject them as burdensome, nor embrace them as secure, but use them well [*sed bene utendo carebimus*].[204]

Distancing or indifference with regard to the all-inclusive order is impossible, not even plausible: "he who does not love the laws is made subject to them."[205] The sinner, too, is subject to this order, displays divine *numeri*, and in this particular respect is even "beautiful."[206] In the numerical harmonic relationships the *motus vitalis* guided by God himself reaches deep into the depths of Hell, and incorporates the whole of Creation, down to the falling of leaves and the number of hairs on a man's head, in a system of numerical correspondences:

> Likewise, a vital motion [*vitalis motus*] precedes and modifies those numbers that work in the intervals of time; it serves the Lord of all things, has no separate temporal intervals, but works by a power that manages time; over this power the rational and intellectual numbers [*rationales et intellectuales numeri*] of the blessed and saintly souls, receiving the law of God with no interposition of nature, transmit down to the earthly and infernal judgments that law, without which a leaf does not fall from a tree and by which our hairs have been numbered.[207]

Properly measured verse makes this all-inclusive order concrete, accessible to the senses, and therefore has an anagogic quality.[208] As a concretion of the *ordo entium* particularly adapted to the human senses, the form of properly measured verse is a *figura* of the *summa, inconcussa incommutabilis, aeterna aequalitas,* of the *carmen universitatis:*

What things are superior, if not those in which the highest, unshaken, unchangeable, eternal equality resides [*illa quibus summa, inconcussa, incommutabilis, aeterna manet aequalitas*], where there is no time, because there is no change, and from which times are fashioned, and situated and modified, in imitation of eternity, while the rotation of the heaven returns to the same place, and calls back the celestial bodies to the same place, and through days, months, years, and periods of years, and other orbits of the stars, obeys the laws of equality and unity and order [*legibus aequalitatis et unitatis et ordinationis obtemperat*]? The orbits thus link with a harmonious [*numerosa*] succession of their times things subject to celestial things, as though to the song of the universe [*carmini universitatis*].[209]

The form of the verse is patterned according to an order that is also manifested in the cyclical course of the heavenly bodies, of the days, months, and years—a relationship that Augustine's treatise on music does not elaborate, but that was to become, after Boethius, a central determinant of reflection on the theory of music under the conditions of the analogical order of discourse. In its quality as music, the verse makes the order of Creation, understood as numerical, accessible to sense experience. Correspondingly, the *delectatio* produced by measured form is given a positive ethical value. If man occupies the place assigned to him between the inferior bodily entities and the superior divine ones, then *delectatio* orients the soul toward the highest good, toward *beatitudo*:

> Let us not look askance, therefore, at things inferior to us, but with the help of our Lord and God let us locate ourselves between those things that are beneath and those that are above us, so that we are not offended by inferior things, but take pleasure in superior things alone. *Pleasure is like a weight to the soul. Pleasure, therefore, orients the soul* [*Delectatio quippe quasi pondus est animae. Delectatio ergo ordinat animam*].[210]

The level of abstraction of this "musical theory of poetry"—whose starting point is not a specific form, but rather form and order per se—has far-reaching consequences. The form of the verse is the actual subject of the argument; its execution is consequently formalistic and, following from its arithmetic premises and to that extent without regard to the ongoing polemic against profane poetry and actors,[211] *systematically indifferent to the content*. Its pertinence for a discourse meant to be all-inclusive is based precisely on this. A manifestation in the sense summarized, that is, one with all metaphysical references, is already given when the verse displays *any order at all* that can be understood as a specific redundancy. Every verse is thus subjected to the argument worked out in Books I and VI, and every verse is functionalized for the Christian order of discourse. At the same time every verse acquires dignity as anagogically relevant. A manifestation of the *ordo entium* is always already present when order can be discerned at all, because the Christian doctrine of *ordo* monopolizes the concept of order. Outside the *ordo* there is—nothing. Perhaps this is one of the points of the example with which Augustine began Book VI: *Deus creator omnium.*[212]

De musica and *De ordine*

The *Retractationes*, which date from 426–427, testify to the context in which Augustine's work on music was earlier conceived and worked out. Positioned as one in a series of *disciplinarum libros*, *De musica* was produced in the course of the appropriation of the canon of late antique education and its adaptation to a Christian function:

> At the very time when I was about to receive baptism in Milan, I tried to write *The Books of the Disciplines*, consulting those who were with me and who were not averse to studies of this kind; I wanted to attain or to lead others to attain as by sure steps the noncorporeal through the corporeal [*per corporalia cupiens ad incorporalia quibusdam quasi passibus certis vel pervenire vel ducere*]. Of these books, however, I was only able to complete the book *On Grammar*, which later went missing from our library, and the six books of *On Music*, up to the part called *rhythm*. I wrote those six books, however, after being baptized and after returning to Africa from Italy, having in fact only begun the book on that discipline in Milan. On the other five disciplines, likewise begun in Milan—on dialectic, rhetoric, geometry, arithmetic, and philosophy—only the beginnings remained, and even those I lost; I think that they can be obtained from other people.[213]

The explanation of the canon of the liberal arts presupposed here by the reference to the Greek concept of "general education" or ἐγκύκλιος παιδεία,[214] along with the placing of Latin music theory in its traditional disciplinary continuity,[215] situates *De musica* in its historical context. Regarding the medieval extension of the educational program and the place of music in it, however, this contextualization seems insufficient. The canon of the seven liberal arts may first be found in its medieval form in Martianus Capella, and may have become accepted following Cassiodorus;[216] Ilsetraud Hadot has been able to show that Augustine's *De ordine* played an important role in the stabilization and long-term success of the form of the canon found in Martianus Capella. Only after Augustine had elaborated it into a unified course of education claiming systematic necessity and a consistent theological goal was the course for teaching and studying, which until Late Antiquity had remained fixed only in its guidelines, consolidated and elevated to the status of an authoritative *ordo scientarum*.[217] Christian medieval discussion of music theory in the framework of the *artes liberales*—and thus indirectly the reflection on poetics in the framework of this music theory—stands in a relationship of conditionality, which is to be specified on a case-by-case basis, to the foundation of the canon in *De ordine*. Augustine conceives the study of the *artes* as a preparation for theology, and thus sets a speculative goal for each individual discipline. This gives the traditional canon a new legitimacy, but at the same time further strengthens the already pronounced emphasis that this canon puts on the theoretical components of an area of study. In the case of the theory of music including metrical discourse, this emphasis begins with the concept of *ordo*, which is Pythagorean-Platonic in its outline, but is now conceived in a Christian-theological way and referentially broadened. Both concern the "literary-aesthetic" implications of *De musica*; moreover, the concept of *ordo* in general will remain central for our whole study.[218]

Adolf Dyroff once called the didactic dialogue *De ordine* "a first confession":[219] composed in the late autumn or winter of 386, this work is at the heart of Augustine's early writing. It is presented as a "record" of a dialogue that took place over several days, in which, in addition to the *magister* Augustine, the friends Trygetius and Licentius participate, along with Monica, Augustine's mother. The initial question is formulated in the dedicatory epistle to Zenobius, which relates the partially meandering discussion to a consistent problem. There seems to be a gap between the assumption, inherent in Christian belief, of an order comprehending all existents, on the one hand, and the contingency and purposelessness of reality as experienced by humans. God appears to be too weak to set human affairs in order as well, or else is himself responsible for the evil that results from the rule of the accidental and the disordered.[220] How can the existence of a divine order be made evident when sense experience contradicts its existence? How can the existence of evil in a divinely ordered world be justified?

The dialogue begins with the most urgent question, the problem of theodicy. The *magister* defines the concept of *ordo* as an all-encompassing complex formed by the whole of the existing causal relationships, neither good nor bad in itself:

It seems to me that order is neither good nor bad. I ask this: what do you think is contrary to order? Nothing, he says. For how is anything able to

be contrary to that which has seized and taken the whole? For what will
be contrary to order must be beyond order. But I see nothing beyond order. One must conclude, therefore, that there is nothing contrary to order.
[. . .] I understand that no one errs without a cause. But a series of causes
is contained within order. Error itself not only arises from a cause, but
even gives rise to something else of which it is the cause. For this reason,
since it is not beyond order, it cannot be contrary to order.[221]

The causal order includes no value distinctions. God, who is all good,
loves good and evil in different ways: he "loves [the fact that] he loves
good and does not love evil." Both good and evil are thus connected with
the unitary foundation of divine *diligere* that founds *ordo* as the order of
being and value. The *pulchritudo* peculiar to this causal order is based on
the "harmony" of opposites that *De musica* derives from the relation of all
existence to God as the ground of Being:[222]

> God does not love evil, he said, for no other reason than that it is not
> of the nature of order that God love evil. He loves order greatly since
> through it he does not love evil. Are things truly evil which can be not
> in order, although God does not love them? For it is of the very order of
> evils that they are not loved by God. Does the order of things—that God
> loves good and does not love evil—seem insignificant to you? In this way,
> evil, which God does not love, is not outside of order, nevertheless He
> loves order itself. He loves this very thing: to love good and not to love
> evil. This is a matter of great order and of divine arrangement. This order
> and arrangement, since they preserve the symmetry of the universe by this
> distinction, make it necessary that evil exist. *In such a way, as though by
> antitheses* in some manner, *that is, by contraries*, which we find pleasing
> even in oratory, *the beauty of all things is at once figured* [*ex antithetis
> quodammodo, quod nobis etiam in oratione iucundum est, ex contrariis,
> omnium simul rerum pulchritudo figuratur*].[223]

Order gives "to each his own," and in this respect, it is "just." However,
this first consequence initially only intensifies the gap that appears at the
beginning of the discussion, that between the metaphysics of order and the
experience of contingency, especially since the latter seems to bear exclusively on human life.[224] Against the background of the order of Creation,
which is "harmonic" and purposeful down to the most insignificant detail,
the *inconstantia* of human existence stands out all the more sharply: "But
this point is even more replete with questions: that the parts of a flea are arranged and assigned roles admirably, while human life is tossed and turned

by the fickleness of countless disturbances."[225] The bridging of the gap is achieved by means of the image of a mosaic: the discrepancy between the dogmatic claim of order and the experienced reality constructed through sense-perception is conceived as the difference between two perspectives on the same phenomenon:

> Having agreed on this, if someone turns his eye closely to examine an inlaid pavement and sees nothing beyond the border of one small tile, he might blame the artisan for being ignorant of arrangement and composition; for this reason he thinks the variety of small stones has been disturbed, because the mosaic, coming together in the form of integral beauty, cannot be at once discerned and inspected. Something like this happens to less erudite men, who are not able to understand and consider the universal harmony and concord of things [*universam rerum coaptationem atque concentum*] with their weak intellects: if something offends them, because it is too large for their understanding, they think that there is some great flaw in things. [. . .] Thus, when the mind has come back to itself, it recognizes what the beauty of the universe [*pulchritudo universitatis*] is; the word universe assuredly takes its name from "one." To see that beauty, therefore, is not permitted to the soul that goes forth toward many things, and follows avidly after poverty, which he does not know can be avoided only by aloofness from the multitude.[226]

The overall image, the *coaptatio*, escapes the observer, whose view is limited to the contour of the individual tessera. The view of the whole organized in accord with the law of causality, the *contemplatio mundi*, is promised to the person who turns to God. The point of all the rest is the development of this difference into a program of education: The inquiry into the divine final cause of the order of events conceived as causally unified promises to lead to the achievement of a total perspective as *sapientia* and *contemplatio mundi*.[227]

In principle, it must be possible for everyone to gain this view of *ordo*, since rationality is said to be a quality of the order of Being and at the same time a capability of every human being. However, the *magister* limits this possibility to "a few healthy people."[228] The majority need to be prepared for it. For this purpose, Augustine appropriates the study of the *artes*:

> If you care about order, I say, you must go back to those verses. For instruction in the liberal disciplines, when modest and concise, produces devotees who are more alert, more determined, and more prepared to embrace truth, so that they more keenly seek, more steadfastly strive for,

> and finally, more sweetly embrace, Licentius, what is called the blessed
> life [*beata vita*].[229]

Education "cleanses the mind," develops the "divine seeds," even among
"less educated" persons of "limited intelligence."[230] Only it must be ensured
that the *ratio* arrives at the correct results in accord with Christian doctrine:
its conclusions must not contradict the authorities. This is guaranteed by
reference to the *conditio peccatoris*, the "sinful self-estrangement of the
individual":[231] The account in Genesis makes possible the *practical* devaluation of man's rational faculty while *theoretically* maintaining its ability
to attain a view of the order of Being: fallen *ratio* requires guidance by the
theological authority, which interprets the revealed text. It is no accident
that Anselm of Canterbury's *crede, ut intelligas* is already found in Augustine.[232]

Clinging to the sensible, to the created existent, is viewed as "sinful self-
estrangement." Contemplation, concentration on the "inner," the intelligible, Being, the Creator, lead to the "true self": "Whoever would know
himself needs a great habit of withdrawing from the senses, and gathering
his mind into himself and keeping it within himself."[233] The concept must
seem self-contradictory to the modern reader, who will tend to consider
the inner core of his "self" as unique in the strongest sense.[234] In contrast,
Augustine's argument is based on stressing *ratio*, which knows its origin
and ideal model in God, as the human being's "true self."[235] The limitation of the individual *ratio*'s potential by reference to the individual's "self-
estrangement," which also allows Christian education to be garbed in the
semantics of salvation and care,[236] is confirmed by the authority of revelation over its *ratio*, without having to abandon the claim to the rationality
of the doctrine itself. The production of right understanding is left to the
Christian, and difficulties are blamed on his deficiency. This is masked by
stressing that the achievement of this insight is possible and held compatible
with the doctrine's claim to rationality by the argument that although the
priority of reason is "objective," the priority of authority is "temporal."[237]

The theoretical apparatus makes it possible to consider the specific content of education secondary with regard to a concept of education that
reduces the concrete material to be taught to the medium of a specific "practice of the self."[238] Here, education is identity construction that involves an
actualization of preexisting schemata ("obedience to a system of rules,"[239]
as Foucault puts it): "especially if you choose the better way, ready yourself
for and place yourself in that very order about which I am writing to you."[240]
Salvation in the beyond is promised for obedience, while disobedience

may lead to the loss of salvation: "If we hold fast to order in life, it will lead us to God, and if we do not hold fast to it in life, we shall not come to God."[241] The ideal conduct of life and the educational program complement each other as a reenactment and coperformance of the path to God conceived by divine *ordo*, which offers insight into the order of Creation and thus also the dissolution of the contradiction, formulated at the outset, between the assertion of order and the experience of contingency:

> This discipline is the very law of God, which abides always with Him fixed and unshaken, as though written upon wise souls, so that they know that they live so much better and so much more sublimely to the extent that they contemplate it more perfectly by knowing, and guard it more diligently by living. For those who want to know it, therefore, this discipline commands that a twin order be followed: one part concerns life, the other concerns learning [*cuius una pars vitae, altera eruditionis est*].[242]

The *magister* does not identify the execution of this project methodologically as "analysis," but rather distinguishes two elements in the individual's *ratio* that are brought together only in the result of the analytical procedure. As a heuristic strategy, the *ratio* guides, much like the arithmetic foundation in Book I of *De musica*, the quest for the *universa universorum principium* ("what is beyond all things, what the beginning of all things is").[243] It follows the *signa* of the past and present workings of divine reason and reconstructs the way in which it has pleased the latter to manifest itself:

> Whoever has entered without any hesitation follows the precepts of the best life, through which, when he has been made docile, then at last he will learn: how much reason was contained in those things that he followed before wisdom; what reason itself is, now that he is strong and able he follows and understands after the cradle of authority; what intellect is, in which all things exist, or rather which is all things; and beyond all things, what the beginning of all things is. [. . .] Authority is partly divine, and partly human. But the true, firm, and highest is that which is called divine. [. . .] That authority, therefore, is called divine that not only in sensible signs transcends every human faculty, but also urges man along, and shows him how far it has lowered itself on his account, and orders that he not be bound by the senses, to which those things appear wondrous, but rather that he fly upward toward the intellect [. . .].[244]

The following outline of the doctrine of "signatures" resumes with regard to the anagogic potential of the pleasing sensory stimulus, whose rationale we have followed in *De musica*.[245] Signs of this kind are said to be found primarily in the realm of auditory and visual perception, and especially in those that are pleasing for the ear or the eye.[246] As in *De musica*, the pleasing effect of a sensory stimulus can be traced back to the ordered structure inherent in it: to the sense of sight, *congruentia partium* appears as beautiful, to the sense of hearing, *numerositas rationalis* of the composition appears as *suaviter*.[247] Here as well, *pulchritudo* is consequently traced back to *modulatio*: "In the pleasure of those senses, therefore, we must admit that in what pertains to reason [*id ad rationem pertinere fateamur*] there is a certain measure and modulation [*quaedam dimensio atque modulatio*]."[248] And here too *carmina* are used as an example: "This is broadly obvious and is spread through nearly all the arts and works of mankind. Now in songs, in which likewise we say that there is reason [*ratio*] pertaining to the pleasure of the ears, who does not feel that measure is the maker of all this sweetness [*quis non sentiat dimensionem esse totius huius suavitatis opificem*]?"[249] *De ordine* confirms our reconstruction of the argument beginning from the formal qualities of the concrete verbal artwork still more explicitly than *De musica* itself. Form and content may be *independent of each other rationabiliter*, "pleasing" independently of each other, and, with all the metaphysical implications, "beautiful": "When we hear those lines then: *Why does the winter sun hasten to sink in the ocean, / and what delay holds back the late nights?* we praise the meter and the meaning in different ways, nor do we mean the same thing when we say: it produces sound reasonably [*rationabiliter sonat*], and it was spoken reasonably [*rationabiliter dictum*]."[250]

De ordine explains that *rationabilitas*, which produces *delectatio* and in so doing invites us to anagogically ascend toward the *intelligibilia*, is only one of the rational's three "modes of appearance": "Now there are three kinds of things in which that 'rational' appears. One is in deeds directed towards some end, the other in speaking, and the third in enjoyment."[251] The first of these modes of appearance urges us to act prudently, the second to teach rightly, the third to engage in *beate contemplari*: "The first warns us to do nothing randomly, the second to teach correctly [*recte docere*], and the last to contemplate happily [*beate contemplari*]."[252] Making clear the connection of rightly measured verse with its numerical foundation in *musica scientia* appears as an exemplary *recte docere*: right teaching has to make clear the connection between the object of the domain taught with its numerical, and in this sense "rational," foundation.

After the existent has been traced analytically to the *universa universorum principium* as the ground of Being, Reason, which appears in personified form in the *magister*'s monologue, undertakes the deductive reconstruction of the order of Being from this *principium*.[253] Movement along the path to the contemplation of the order of Being presupposes an adequate medium, language, and, in order to preserve the "words of absent speakers," writing. Thus Ratio distinguishes first among consonants, vowels, and semivowels, delimits syllables, creates word classes.[254] However, language remains useless so long as it lacks designatable objects, so long as the indefinite *multitudo rerum* has not been developed by order and limitation, by counting: "It could have done none of these things, however, if the multitude of things [*multitudo rerum*] seemed to open to infinity with no determined limit. Therefore, the usefulness of numbering [*utilitas numerandi*] was noticed because of its great necessity."[255] Language itself is not an exception to this rule: Ratio, pondering on numbers and measured magnitudes, determines the quantities, declares that the relationship of long to short syllables may correspond to the *proportio* 2:1, and conceives the whole system in "fixed rules": "Not unmindful, then, of numbers and measurement [*numerorum et dimensionis*], it directed the mind to the various pauses of voices and syllables, and then ascertained that some intervals of time were double and others were simple, through which the long and the short syllables were extended. It took note, too, of these things and arranged them in fixed rules [*in regulas certas*]."[256] With the establishment of the mutually complementary realms of word and number as the media of all further reflective activity, Ratio thereby "completes," *nota bene*, grammar.[257] Ratio then turns reflexively in upon itself, investigates its "resources" and "tools," and thus establishes dialectic. In the latter "reason shows itself to itself": it distinguishes the true from the false, teaches us how to teach, teaches how to learn what is taught, knows what knowing means.[258] Since in general human beings do not pursue truth on their own, but instead give priority to their own "feelings" and "habits," Ratio indicates a particular "capacity" for teaching these deviants: rhetoric.[259] Grammar, dialectic, and rhetoric, the disciplines later consolidated as the *artes sermonicales*, *logicae*, or *verbales* of the *trivium*,[260] are assigned the function of *recte docere*. They are instruments with their own meaning and justification but without any independent claim to truth.

In contrast, the disciplines that Boethius calls the *quadruvium* [*sic*] and that were later called *artes reales*[261] lead to *beate contemplari*. The strong weighting of the *artes* based on numbers in the Platonic tradition of the *communis mathematica scientia* breaks with the "essentially literary culture founded on grammar and rhetoric and tending to realize the ideal type of the orator"[262] current in Augustine's day. *Contemplatio* comes to be understood as turned toward God, but not as a mythical-instantaneous experience of the vision of God, but rather as a way of life in which *sapientia* and life in *caritas Dei* mutually condition and supplement each other. The path to its realization passes through stages that "support," as it were, the turning away from the sensory and the ascent (*anagoge*) toward God:

> Then reason wanted to hasten to the most blessed contemplation of divine things [*rerum divinarum beatissimam contemplationem*]. Lest it not fall from on high, however, it looked for steps, and built for itself a pathway through its possessions and order. It longed for the beauty that it could observe alone and simple without using the eyes. But since it was impeded by the senses, for a while it turned its eyes toward them as they clamored to have truth for themselves and called reason back with insistent din as it was hasting to go on to other things.[263]

The stage model allows not only gains in systematization but also the Christian appropriation of the ancient part of ἐγκύκλιος παιδεία that leads to θεωρία, the "contemplation" of the supreme good. This central section of *De ordine* begins, as is emphasized, with *musica et poetica*,[264] music and the art of poetry.

The sense of hearing, the *magister* says, makes use of words. But Ratio knows the difference "between the sound and what it is a sign of" (*inter sonum et id cuius signum esset*): the ear does recognize the sound,[265] but this is no more than raw material so long as it is not connected by a temporal measure and performed in a properly measured mixture of accents.[266] Grammar, which is responsible for the medium of language in general and for naming (*vocare*) in particular, designates these "measures" as metrical feet and accents.[267] Not grammar, the *custos historiae*, but rather *ratio* develops out of these elements the formal units of order discussed in *De musica*—and "thus produces (*genere*) poets":

> And because in words themselves it was easy to observe the shorts and longs of syllables scattered in almost equal number in discourse, it tried to arrange those feet in a fixed order, and to conjoin them. And having followed the sense of hearing at first, it marked divisions on the measures, which it called pauses and members. And lest the series of feet moved on further than its investigation could sustain, it set up a limit whereby it was reversed, and called it verse because of that word. What was not limited to a fixed end, however, but ran rationally with arranged feet, it called rhythms, which in Latin can be called nothing other than number. Out of this poets were born. When it saw their great importance not only with regard to sounds but also to words and things, it honored them greatly, and gave them power over whatever rational lies they desired.[268]

The numerical quality of the formal structure has such weight that even the representation of "facts of reason in deceptive pictures produced by the imagination" does not reduce the value of poetry. The numerical order that is manifest in meter, rhythm, and melody is "divine and eternal":

> On this step, therefore, it realized that, whether in rhythms or in modulation itself numbers ruled and brought everything about [*intellegebat regnare numeros totumque perficere*]. Reason examined most diligently what they might be, and found them to be divine and eternal [*reperiebat divinos et sempiternos*], especially because with their help it had formed everything mentioned above [*ipsis auxiliantibus omnia superiora contexuerat*].[269]

The other disciplines of the later quadrivium are discussed in a comparable way. Each of them serves "partly life [*partim ad usum vitae*], partly knowledge and *contemplatio* [*partim ad cognitionem rerum contemplationemque*]."[270] Every discipline based on numbers can be included in a Christian educational program as an introduction to the vision of God, because work on practical and sensible objects can gradually be redeemed in favor of pure arithmology.[271] Objects of a discipline that are primary in the curriculum, sensible, and in this respect suitable *ad usum vitae,* thus gain legitimacy as possible starting points on the way toward the vision of God. The price to be paid is the reduction of these objects to "shadows and traces" of the "true" numerical order:

> In all these disciplines, therefore, everything presented itself to reason as numerically based [*numerosa*], and yet was more clearly evident in those dimensions that, as reason thought about and considered them within itself, appeared most true. In sense experience, it rather found shadows and traces of them [*umbras earum potius atque vestigia recolebat*].[272]

With the acquisition of insight into the numerical order, the distinction between *ratio* as the knowing subject and rational order as an object of knowledge collapses. Becoming self-conscious, *ratio* recognizes itself as the "eternal number" through which everything is counted:

> It investigated all things diligently, and perceived that it was indeed capable of much, and that whatever it could accomplish, it was able to do so because of numbers [*quidquid posset, numeris posse*]. A miracle influenced it, and it began to suspect that it was that very number itself by which all things are numbered [*suspicari coepit seipsam fortasse numerum esse eum ipsum quo cuncta numerarentur*], or if not, that this number, nevertheless, was where it labored to arrive.[273]

Reason, present to itself, develops the totality of the subject matters delegated to the individual disciplines in their relationship to the numerical order, and thus indirectly the absolute ontological prevalence of number: anyone who has attempted to describe the octave or to survey the field will be able to assess the potential of number—and at the same time see that the numerical entity is not exhausted by any of its manifestations and uses. Each of the traditional disciplines thus retains its contour, objects, and methods, but is put in the service of helping the individual reason become conscious of its numerical nature. The endpoint and real goal of the whole educational program are the "origin of all things, which itself no longer has an origin," and the vision of the true God.[274]

Here we see clearly how the colonization of pagan knowledge by the Christian order of discourse in Augustine contrasts with the older, abrupt repudiation formulated, for instance, by Tertullian.[275] Differentiation and polemics are replaced by appropriation and "colonization," by integrating the *artes* in general and the *quadrivium* in particular as a propaedeutics for theology:

> Now in music, in geometry, in the motions of the stars, in the requirements of numbers [*in numerorum necessitatibus*], order reigns in such a way that if one wanted to see its source, as it were, and its innermost court, he would find it in these disciplines or he would be led without error through these to it. For such learning, if one uses it moderately (for there is nothing to be feared in this matter except excess), nourishes the soldier of philosophy or even the general, so that he flies where he will, and attains and leads others to attain that highest goal, beyond which he neither can, nor should, nor desires to seek to know.[276]

The doctrine set forth in *De ordine* strongly emphasizes rationality, sometimes as a property of Christian doctrine itself, and sometimes as a faculty to be cultivated by the Christian. The rational development of the order of Being is superior to mere belief, but it is this development that first joins genuine selfhood and the vision of God with "ethicalness" and "perfect life": "For the soul gradually leads itself to good habits and the best life not by faith alone but by trustworthy reason."[277] The theological conception of *ordo* includes the order of Being and Creation, the order of teaching and knowledge, and finally the order of life in *caritas Dei*. The promise of *beatitudo* combines the theological, the epistemological-didactic, and the practical-ethical levels of the argument.

According to the *Confessions*, the position of Augustine's early work regarding the possibility and essence of *beatitudo* originally developed out of Cicero's *Hortensius*:[278] happiness beyond all vain striving for fame and riches in the world of change is to be sought beyond *sensibilia*, in the realm of *intelligibilia*.[279] Working out such a doctrine in accord with the model of Neoplatonic ontology thus leads Augustine to a strict disjunction between *beatitudo* and ephemeral *sensibilia*.[280] Consequently, *beatitudo* coincides with the accomplishments of *ratio* or *intellectus*.[281] This connection, combined with the argument's foundation in number ontology, is genuinely Pythagorean. The influence of this doctrine, which may have emerged from that of Iamblichus,[282] is made explicit in the concluding words of *De Ordine*. Alypius remarks: "What then? Was not that venerable and nearly divine discipline, which Pythagoras rightly possessed and which was proven to be his, disclosed to us by you today for our eyes?"[283] And Augustine, the *magister*, answers: "I accept that gladly, I reply."[284]

A Summary: *Aequalitas numerosa*

It is characteristic of the properties of premodern theories of the beautiful and the creation of artworks to be completely unaffected by the controversies regarding the way their objects should be conceived that have marked discussion of the "aesthetic" ever since Alexander Gottlieb Baumgarten. In the young Augustine's Neoplatonic framework, the "beauty" of the beautiful object is an objective quality of the latter, and to that extent not subject to the individual observer's varying assessments:[285] "Because of its intelligibility, the 'beautiful existent' makes possible a judgment that implies the claim that what it says *is* really so, as it says it: neither appearance, nor mere consciousness."[286] The question regarding the condition of the possibility of such a judgment is answered within the Neoplatonic frame of reference through the doctrine of *μέθεξις,* methexis: the phenomenal beautiful is beautiful through participation, through the partial realization of the idea of the beautiful. "Omne pulchrum pulchritudine [pulchrum]" ("every beautiful thing is beautiful because of beauty") is analogous to "omne aeternum aeternitate aeternum est [. . .] et omne bonum bonitate" ("every eternal thing is eternal because of eternity [. . .] and every good thing is good because of goodness").[287] The idea of beauty thus guarantees, in varying degrees of participation,[288] the being-beautiful of all existents. It further guarantees that the thus objectively beautiful is posited as such by the creative freedom of that which is absolute beauty, since the existent as a whole is the product of the divinity creating *ex nihilo*: In specific Christian contradistinction from Plato and pretheistic Neoplatonism, beauty according to Augustine is not one idea among others, even if according to the *Symposium* it is the noblest one, but rather, as an idea in the *mens divina*, a predication of the personal divinity itself. We seem likely to arrive at greater clarity if, in attempting to situate *De musica* conclusively and synoptically in the context of this paradigmatic metaphysical and ontological foundation of the beautiful, we start from the most general questions: In what way can the beautiful be distinguished from other predicates of the existent in itself?

The most general reason for being-beautiful is *form*, in the familiar spatial metaphorics: *inner* and *outer* form shaped in accord with the idea.[289] In Latin, it is common to speak of *species* or *forma*; *De musica* uses *modus* and, above all in Book VI, *ordo*. Divine *creatio* posits the existent as self-identical (*finitum*) and distinct from others (*definitum*); the created *species intelligibilis* is at the same time the foundation of existence and a constituent of concrete outer form.[290] Every formed existent is part of the order of Creation (*ordo entium*) insofar as the *species intelligibilis* comprises the set of all possible relations to other existents and to the ground of Being. This includes its relation to its origin and possible goal or end; both coincide in God as the common, form-determining origin (*forma omnium*).[291] On this level of abstraction, for the immanent observer "form" coincides with "beauty":[292] beauty is implied by the concept and by the being of form,[293] and *to that extent* it is an objective quality of every beautiful existent. It is no accident that the Latin *speciosus* and *formosus* can be interpreted not only as meaning "having shape or form," but also as meaning "having a beautiful shape or form."

In Augustine's work, beauty as an implication of form is specified by means of the concepts of *similitudo, convenientia, congruentia, correspondentia, harmonia*, and, at first with restrictions, *aequalitas*.[294] Each of these concepts stems from the semantic field of *relationality* and designates a relationship between at least two elements, thus assuming a state of plurality.[295] The plural existent is characterized by the dissimilarity of its elements and by its origin: *regio dissimilitudinis* (reign of difference).[296] However, the tendency is toward its origin: "[O]mnia in unum tendunt" ("All things tend towards the One").[297] The *tendentia in unum* prevails over disparate plurality, and especially over the ontological *tendere ad nihilum* and the ethical *tendere ad inertiam*. Judgments about the presence of *aequalitas, similitudo, congruentia*, or *convenientia* concern first of all the object-quality of the beautiful existent: only the relationality of its parts qualifiable with these concepts constitutes an existent object—as "unity in plurality"[298]—as a whole:

> In the primary sense of the concept, the beautiful itself belongs to one of
> the highest ideas in the existent, and thus to the ideas in which everything

existent participates in a greater or a lesser degree, and its specific characteristic or specific potential is the preservation of a "proportion" and the accommodation and reconciliation of opposites into a harmonious (complex) order.[299]

As an ontologically prior form, this relational order is to be distinguished from its material manifestation in the concrete object. "Beauty" as a quality appertains to form. The "inner," intelligible relationality is the necessary condition of "outer," sensible beauty.[300] The former is characterized by a higher degree of beauty because the relationality constitutive of beauty is present unaffected by the resistance of the material.

For understanding the extension of the prevailing concept of music into late Antiquity and the Middle Ages it is of central importance to grasp the relationality constitutive of form and thus of beauty in *De musica* and throughout Augustine's work[301] as a numerical relationship, as a relation between natural numbers: "[F]ormas habent, quia numeros habent: adime illis haec, nihil erunt" ("They have forms because they have numbers; separate them and there will be nothing").[302] Accordingly, the "ontologically conceived identity and difference [of numbers] constitutes the qualitative identity and difference of the existent itself";[303] "numbers are conceived as conceptual principles that constitute Being."[304] Here we must remember that Augustinian arithmology takes as its starting point a conception of number entirely different from that of modern arithmetic. It develops first in connection with the outlined ontology and out of the union of mathematical and metaphysical thinking in the Pythagorean-Neoplatonic tradition:

> By "number," the ancient Platonists understood the particular possibilities of the synthesis of unity and plurality and the particular relationships of order and structure developed in this synthesis that constitute a whole out of parts.[305]

It is above all Book I of *De musica* that establishes the relation to this tradition. It draws on the writings of Euclid and Theon of Smyrna, and especially on the Ἀριθμητικὴ εἰσαγωγή, the "Introduction to Arithmetics" of Nicomachus of Gerasa (c. 60–c. 120 CE).[306] The latter work, which was transmitted by Porphyry and Iamblichus, used as a textbook in the Neoplatonic schools of Athens and Alexandria, and much commented upon,[307] is among the most influential Neoplatonic sources. It was originally supplemented and expanded by a now-lost work on "theological arithmetic" that we must assume had an influence on the number-ontology foundation of the concept of form and relationality in *De musica*.[308]

The educational material made useful for Neoplatonism by Nicomachus points back through Plotinus's differentiated number ontology to the time of the "self-development of Greek thought from Homer to the Sophists and Socrates" that Wilhelm Nestle described as the "first Enlightenment" in European cultural history.[309] The line of tradition runs less through the decidedly Pythagorean educational system of Philolaus of Croton (470–390 BCE) and his pupils than through the appropriation of Pythagorean educational elements in Plato's middle dialogues. It is based on two mythical narratives that remain associated with the name of Pythagoras of Samos (born c. 570 BCE): "Pythagoras on the monochord" and "Pythagoras in the smithy."[310] Whether one should avoid the concept of "discovery" and ascribe instead the "analogical connection of metaphysics, mathematics, and music characteristic of the Pythagorean approach," to an "original 'intuition'"[311] or, like Johannes Lohmann, undertake a philologically precise reconstruction of the shift in the meaning of $\mu\acute{\alpha}\vartheta\eta\mu\alpha$ (originally "that which is learnt" or "lesson") between Homer and Pythagoras, we will not attempt to decide here.[312] Aristotle's *Metaphysics*, which is, along with Eudemus of Rhodes, the most important source on this connection, reports that the reference to number as not only the "origin" ($\dot{\alpha}\rho\chi\acute{\eta}$) but also as the "essence" ($o\dot{v}\varsigma\acute{\iota}\alpha$) of all things goes back to Pythagoras of Samos:

> Contemporaneously with these philosophers and before them, the so-called Pythagoreans, who were the first to take up mathematics, not only advanced this study, but also having been brought up in it they thought its principles were the principles of all things. Since of these principles numbers are by nature the first, and in numbers they seemed to see many resemblances to the things that exist and come into being—more than in fire and earth and water (such and such a modification of numbers being justice, another being soul and reason, another being opportunity—and similarly almost all other things being numerically expressible); since, again, they saw that the modifications and the ratios of the musical scales were expressible in numbers;—since, then, all other things seemed in their whole nature to be modeled on numbers, and numbers seemed to be the first things in the whole of nature, they supposed the elements of numbers to be the elements of all things, and the whole heaven to be a musical scale and a number.[313]

The importance of what Aristotle sums up here is seen less in his criticism than in the way early Pythagoreanism distinguished itself from the pre-Socratics' theory of the elements. With the reference to number as the "essence of the world [. . .] for the first time something that is not a thing, such as water, is seen as the essence of the world; instead, in number, something ideal is raised to the rank of the essence of the world."[314] For precisely that reason, in Iamblichus's *De Vita Pythagorica* Pythagoras is still considered the founder of all philosophy,[315] and Augustine, who in *De Civitate Dei* VIII.4 contrasts the Pythagorean-cosmological approach with the Socratic-ethical approach and conceives Plato's work as a development of both, also recognizes in it the condition of possibility of all "theory." Thus were first laid the operative foundations for the "spiritualistic structural realism"[316] that was to characterize cosmological outlines of the ontological contexture down to modern times. Plato built on them and conceived number as a "form-giving principle," as determining (πέρας) everything that is materially undetermined (ἄπειρον). The *Statesman* and the *Philebus* document the appropriation of the Pythagorean doctrine of ideal numbers; the *Euthyde-mus* aligns pure arithmetic with dialectical philosophy;[317] the *Phaedo* distinguishes numbers perceptible through the senses from actually ideal numbers;[318] the former are related to the latter as beautiful things are related to the beautiful.[319] Sensible numbers are subject to change and passing away, while ideal numbers are eternal and immutable. Knowing them is an act of "recollection" (ἀνάμνησις).[320]

Plotinus follows the Platonic theory of ideal numbers and puts it into the form that influenced Augustine. First, Plotinus notes that "[t]he authentic number is the one that is observed in the Ideas and helps to produce them, but its highest level is the number that is in the existent, is joined to it, and precedes existing things. And in it existing things have their foundation, source, root, and ultimate ground."[321] Second, Plotinus seeks to synthesize Platonic and Aristotelian doctrine in the area of number theory by means of a four-part classification of numbers.[322] He calls "essential" the numbers that the Pythagorean tradition and thus also Nicomachus of Gerasa subsumed under the "first tetractys,"[323] the numbers one, two, three, and four, supplemented by ten.[324] From these are distinguished the "monadic" or "quantitative" numbers, which emerge through the accumulation of units: the quantitative number ten, representing ten units, is said to be essential in a different way from the "essential" number ten.[325] Third, sensible things have a numerically structured order based on numbers with a specific mode of being: if ten dancers dance a roundelay, then this roundelay must be characterized by a structure that excludes the possibility of it being danced by nine or eleven dancers. "For that reason the number ten *qua* Idea is related to the ten of this roundelay danced as beauty *qua* Idea is related to the beauty manifesting itself in this roundelay danced here and now."[326] Fourth, a number that once again has a specific mode of being operates as an "affection of the soul"[327] in humans' numerical capability.[328] In order to mediate between Platonic and Aristotelian doctrine, a classification is introduced that combines the numbers operating in the human capability with the ideal numbers viewed in the act of recollection. Let us set aside the pertinence of the attempted synthesis, given the criticism of the theory of ideal numbers in Aristotle's *Metaphysics*. What we need to note here is that from the intellectual perspective of Neoplatonism, which since Plotinus had opened up to Eastern religious doctrines, taken on a theistic form, and thus become capable of being joined to the Jewish revealed religion,[329] it is only a small step to Augustine's classification of the modes of being of numbers into *numeri judicales, sensuales, progressores, occursores, recordabiles,* and *corporales* in *De musica* VI.9.24. The conception of the order of Being as a continuum of numbers and their relationships is part of the Pythagorean-Platonic substrate of Augustine's early writings. Augustine develops this conception for the Christian order of discourse by referring to *Liber sapientiae* 11:21, "sed omnia in mensura et numero et pondere disposuisti." The survey develops the precise position in the system occupied by this statement: the *creator omnium*'s act of creation, the Judeo-Christian doctrine of a creation *ex nihilo*, is placed, as the foundation of harmonic numerical relationships, at the center of pagan teaching.

The level of abstraction on which the colonization of pagan theory takes place allows the Christian appropriation and refunctionalization of the complex without essential modifications of its conceptual substance. Established as *scientia*, guided methodologically, and guaranteed by the corrective of *auctoritas*, the reflection on the determinants of form in general—the intelligible principles of relationality, which can be conceived as rational numbers and in accord with the categories of *aequalitas, similitudo, congruentia,* or *convenientia*—are seen as leading to the vision of the *ordo entium*. The order of Creation as an intelligible order of numbers and numerical relationships sets the ontological conditions of form as such, the conditions of beauty as a quality of any form whatever, the conditions of determining identification and delimiting distinction, and thus the epistemic conditions of knowledge of all the aforementioned. Every form of *modus* and productive *modulari* is inherent in the order of Creation itself[330] and thus so is *musica scientia* as *scientia bene modulandi*. If only form is rationally conceivable, if the existent is possible and knowable only as formed, if the form of any existent consists in "inner," "numerical" relationality, which is as such already "beautiful," and if, finally, the *principium numerorum* is the number "out of which" all numbers are produced, then the *principium numerorum* is the *principium* of all form and all beauty. All potential and actually realized forms, as well as their "objective" (in the sense of derived) beauty are posited by God. Only against the background of this doctrine can the theory of metrical discourse set forth in Augustine's treatise on music be completely developed. Two aspects are particularly relevant for "literary aesthetics."

If the beautiful appearing in time is beautiful qua participation in the supratemporal and invariant Idea of Beauty in God, if it refers to this Idea in God and metrical discourse displays this quality of reference in an especially sensible way, if the possibility of describing numerically the intelligible relationality constituting the beautiful object allows the construction of this reference to the accessible path *a corporeis ad incorporea*, then the sensible beauty at least of verse is anagogically relevant. The argument preformed in Plato's *Phaedrus*[331] privileges the beauty of the *form* of metrical discourse as the starting point of the anamnetic return of thought to the ground of Being: as a guide and invitation to the *regressio a temporalibus ad aeterna* or, according to *De musica*, to the *itinerarium a corporeis ad incorporea*. In addition to its anamnetic relevance, what is crucial here is the increased legitimacy that the concept promises to provide for verse as *musica*. The latter is indebted and bound to the Neoplatonic substrate of Augustine's early writings.[332]

Thus doubts about the influence and relevance of the theory set forth in *De musica* in general and of the ontology of the beautiful in particular beyond Augustine's early work may arise. After the lost early work *De pulchro et apto* and *De musica*, Augustine made no further systematic statements about questions of the beautiful; the theory of the beautiful that can be extrapolated from his main works even appears to distance itself from the Neoplatonic concepts in the early writings. It emphasizes not only Plato in opposition to his interpreter Plotinus, but also the beautiful as an effect in opposition to the beautiful as an objective quality of the beautiful object, and thus the systematic importance of Christian doctrine and especially the dogma of original sin.[333] The quoted *retractatio* of the work on music, which castigates its overt Pythagoreanism, allows for that and led to the work's exclusion from the canon of the *theological* faculties. Outside theological discussions, however, this rejection of the work on music had little effect. Historicizing periodizations such as early work, main phase, late work are largely alien to the medieval recipient. The gap perceived by the modern reader between the long stretches of genuinely Neoplatonic argumentation in Augustine's early work and the critical reduction of the Neoplatonic substrate in his main and late work was not seen in this form by the Middle Ages. The prestige of *auctoritas* and, generally speaking, the absence of thinking in terms of historical processes and change bridge the gap that separates Augustine's early work from his main work. Medieval reception of Augustine's work can consequently conflate his theory of metrical discourse as *musica* with Boethius's theory of music, which is also based on the Pythagorean-Neoplatonic tradition. The result is a homogeneous, Christian-accented doctrine that covers the whole field of music theory in the Pythagorean-Neoplatonic tradition. Within this doctrine, the Augustinian conception of an anagogically relevant and therefore legitimate lyrical poetry as *musica* remains plausible. The following chapters reconstruct in detail the process of this conflation and the continuity of the resulting theory down to the late Middle Ages; this chapter will conclude with observations on the state of the sources and on the reception history of Augustine's theory of music in particular. *De musica* becomes the reference point for a concept of metrical discourse that can claim legitimacy for verse insofar as it is *musica*—and precisely with systematic disregard of content and in opposition to the restriction, due to the potentially objectionable effect, to which it might be subjected from a theological perspective and with reference to Augustine's main work.

The second emphasis relevant to "literary aesthetics" that is posited by the doctrine set forth in *De musica* is based on the postulated connection between numerical order and prereflective, sensory pleasure (*delectatio*). Pleasure in the beautiful indicates that the pleasing object has a numerical order: "pulchra *numero* placent."[334] This argument also begins with number as determining the relationality conceived as the form of a whole and consequently presupposes at least a two-part form: Augustine's analysis defines the verse, the example not chosen accidentally and discussed in great detail, as a meter divisible into precisely two *membra* of a determinate number of quantities. Thus the verse appears as the manifestation of a form that can be defined as ἀναλογία or *proportio* out of the multitude of *aequales* (n:n).

Everything sensible that is pleasing displays a similarity or equality, all similarity or equality being based on a specific *numerositas*: "Nihil [. . .] est horum sensibilium, quod nobis non aequalitate aut similitudine placeat. Ubi autem aequalitas aut similitudo, ibi numerositas" ("There is nothing in these sensible things that does not please us with equality and similarity. Where there is equality or similarity, however, there is harmony of numbers").[335] The question raised at the beginning of this resume—how can the beautiful be differentiated from other predicates of the existent by the latter itself?—is thus answered. Something that is objectively beautiful and at the same time pleasing is numerically measured, and as a result its form displays *similitudo* or *aequalitas*:

Since the numerical structure determines the inner orderliness, every individual existent's enduring self-agreement or equality with itself (*aequalitas
numerosa*), and since this structure of being founds the inner, intelligible
shape or form of an existent as well as its outer shape or form, it also has
aesthetic meaning: it addresses directly the "capacity for aesthetic judgment," it is the reason why the existent can be experienced and qualified
as beautiful and as a manifestation of the inner structure arouses agreement—pleasure.[336]

Insofar as in the case of verse this *aequalitas* designates the equality of isometric units succeeding one another in time, equality "in equal measures
of measured intervals (*parilitatem quamdam et aequaliter dimensa intervalla*),"[337] what is pleasing here is equivalence in the sense of repetition,
that is, of recurrence or, as Jean Cohen puts it, "determined redundancy."[338]

The conceivable impression that the whole argumentative complex leads
to or explicitly pleads for highly redundant and for that reason semantically
poor verse is mistaken—and not only because the *varietas* prized in the
Middle Ages is of a kind different from that the modern reader is inclined to
demand. The emphasis of the abstract argumentation based on relationality
and number is, as the "defense" of the *senarius* shows, on broadening the
extension of the term *aequalitas*. What is sought is the systematic description of *the order of possible variations*, with the goal of subjecting the differentiated body of phenomena, which seems to the initial sense impression
to be disparate, to the postulated primacy of the equal and the one, to the
theory of the objectively beautiful, and thus indirectly to the theological
concept of order:

> Since here [in *De musica*)] tracing of form, shape, and beauty back to
> simple numbers and numerical relationships does not [mean] a tracing
> back to sterile, ever-identical, dogmatically canonized, and moreover
> simple numerical proportions, but rather a tracing back to numerical
> principles that are in fact simple, but lead, through the observation of the
> differentiations they make possible, to the methodologically organized con-
> struction of increasingly complex numerical structures. This means that this
> numerical understanding enables us to repeatedly discover new, multiform
> relationships of measure, but on the other hand never leads to mere arbi-
> trariness, meaningless accident, or indeed chaotic undecidability.[339]

Arbogast Schmitt rightly emphasizes the constructive option that Augustinian theory opened up. The inventory of all possible metrical feet undertaken
in *De musica* was based on a clearly delimited interest. The definition of the

relationship between a long and a short syllable in accord with the *proportio* 2:1, the determination of the total number of the quantities of a metrical foot, the description of the distribution of quantities within the metrical foot, and finally the determination of the minimal and maximal length of the units of metrical order, *membrum, versus, metrum,* und *rhythmus,* and their conception as sequences of a certain number of *pedes* forms a manageable set of inventoried building blocks (metrical feet, possibly *semi-pedes,* and *silentiae*) and extremely elementary rules of combination.

Sequences consist of a minimal number of x and a maximal number of y elements. Depending in each case on the form of construction, particular parts have to correspond with respect to the amount of their quantities. In addition, the distribution of the quantities is not regulated. A *membrum* defined by the kind of verse and the requirement of symmetry can be produced by a variety of different combinations of metrical feet. Deviations, "stretching" redundancy by combining a definite amount of quantities by using different metrical feet or different combinations of the latter, do not erode the principle, but instead increase its valence. Only if one takes the level of the argument's abstraction into account are the "aesthetic" implications of the assignment to particular redundancy opened up:

> Equality as an essential element of symmetry [is] not identifiable with a
> "uniformity" promoting boredom; instead, it is a rationality integrated
> into a unity by equivalent, rationally constituted and rationally conceiv-
> able "magnitude."[340]

This "constructive rationality" can be appreciated as joy in recognizing the same, in the repetitive, as joy in the *sense of form*. In the latter, *delectatio* and the anagogic functionalization of metrical discourse as *musica* merge.

De musica teaches in addition the systematic disregard of the referential dimension of versified language, without making assertions about the status of reference as such. In particular, the concept of the "musicality" of verse developed in *De musica* does not stand in contradiction to referentiality. Primary meanings are disregarded in favor of a system of secondary meanings whose *level of abstraction* is unlocked only when the tradition of reflection on the theory of poetry in music theory is developed on the basis of the contexts elaborated up to this point. The conception of metrical discourse as *musica* goes far beyond the general observation that the "hierarchy of super-linguistic equivalences"[341] that is generated from its rhythmical-metrical-prosodic structure and is constitutive of lyric allows "the semantics of the word to recede, in the verse, into the background."[342] The theory of verse as *musica* conceives equivalence as a specific relationality of linguistic elements qualified by *aequalitas* or *similitudo*. The set of such relations constitutes, insofar as the arithmetical describability of the position of all the elements and the set of their relations is presupposed, the lyrical work's form. In this sense, every form describes not only the "set of the relations connecting the elements of a system with one another," but also includes "all the relational connections isomorphic with them."[343] This grounds the applicability of the theory appropriated by Augustine to all metrical systems that can be reconstructed from the principle of equivalence or determined redundancy.

The historically specific profile of this theory follows from the relation between this concept of form and the theological concept of order indebted to Neoplatonism that constitutes "musical" form as a "sign of truth." The continuity of this relation, which under the Christian order of discourse was always already invoked in addressing a phenomenon "music," is the key argument of our further reasoning.

With regard to a few of the scholarly theses summed up in part I, we can in conclusion emphasize in particular a few implications of the theory of metrical discourse as *musica* laid out in *De musica*. From the foundation of the doctrine of the *ordo entium* in the theory of ideal numbers seen from a Christian perspective and the associated ontology, on the one hand, and the development of lyrical poetry from the concept of form indebted to this ontology, on the other hand, it follows that the set of possible lyric forms is always already determined, every conceivable verse already "created." The "combining" rationality reproduces, detects, discovers, but never creates anything new. *De musica* offers no aesthetics of production: the concept simply denies human beings any originary creativity.[344] Human activity remains limited to the realization of possibilities that are inherent in the order of Creation. This is one reason why the Middle Ages did not make a fundamental distinction between the arts, between artwork and handicraft in the narrowest sense. *De musica* conducts the argument very explicitly using the example of the poet: "May I ask if you think that the rhythmical or metrical art, which those who make verses employ, has some numbers that they use to fashion verse [*aliquos numeros, secundum quos fabricant versus*]?"[345] Ephemeral numbers, like those of a verse, presuppose enduring numbers (*manentibus numeris*).[346] The enduring *numeri* used by the *versificator* can be forgotten by the latter, but recalled at any time, for instance in philosophical conversation.[347] Maieutics could bring to consciousness the enduring *numeri* used by the *versificator* even if they were never before known: "Why, therefore, should we believe that what is eternal and unchangeable is given to the soul, if it does not come from an eternal and unchangeable

God?"[348] Every work, every actual creation of form or order presupposes a capability affine to the origin of order as such, in the case of the poet the capability based on the *numeri iudiciales*: "They are the order-templates, as it were, for musical works, which are created with the help of the ephemeral numbers within the matter."[349] Thus in the finely worked poem the *versificator* translates into contingent matter forms that were previously divinely created in their entirety.[350]

On grounds of systematic rigor already, the disqualification of human *ars* allows of no exception. The concepts of *similitudo* and *aequalitas*, on which Augustine's theory of the sensible beautiful is based, are conceived in hierarchically structured oppositions and are introduced axiomatically: "You will resolve this easily if you understand that equality and similarity are superior to inequality and dissimilarity."[351] Everything existent exists qua participation in the ground of Being: participation as a concept admitting of degrees makes it possible to naturalize real distinctions as "in accord with the order of Creation" and thus to justify them.[352]

Both *aequalitas* and *similitudo* are related to the concept of participation, but they refer to different aspects of the latter.[353] *Aequalitas* designates the positive limiting value of *similitudo*; inequality is given if equality must be denied, regardless of the possible *similitudo* of individual aspects or parts. Thus *similitudo* is a form of *inaequalitas*, and *dissimilitudo* is its positive limiting value. *Dissimilitudo* thus negates *aequalitas* not only with respect to a whole, but also with respect to any part of the latter. Under the ontological contexture based on the concept of participation, *inaequalitas* is only conceivable as unequal participation in Being. *Dissimilitudo* negates absolutely such a participation for one of the components placed in relationship and thus its existence. Accordingly, neither *dissimilitudo* nor *aequalitas* appear in the creaturely-existent in the strict sense. Everything that *is* resembles everything else in at least this respect: "Indeed, true equality and likeness, and true and primary unity is perceived neither by the eye of the body nor by any such sense, but by the intellect [*mente intellecta*]."[354] Consequently, a given similarity can be conceived both as a *signum sacrum* and as a reference to other existents: "*aequalitas* and *similitudo* [are] the reason why the knowing human mind can on the one hand discover the relatedness of the many and on the other hand get lost in the multitude of things."[355] The doctrine can encounter this through the distinction between *uti* and *frui*,[356] but it must forestall the suspicion that the "misunderstanding" of the *similitudines* is to be ascribed to Creation itself. *De musica* does this by means of the abstract structure of the concepts *similitudo* and *aequalitas*, through their foundation in the concept of form, which refers

to numerical relationships. The more abstract the structure, the more similarities and equalities will ensue, the more completely the concept of order
comprehends the set of all existents, the more Creation is grasped without
exception in its quality referring to the divine, and the more necessarily
must any *frui* be blamed on the deficiency of the one who has failed to take
the right path.

The question regarding the provenance of *similitudo, aequalitas,* and
the sensible *ordo*—"Whence do they come, I ask, unless from that most
lofty and eternal preeminence of numbers, and from similarity, equality,
and order [*nisi ab illo summa atque aeterno principatur numerorum et similitudinis et aequalitatis et ordinis*]?"[357]—must thus be named rhetorical.
Augustine's theory allows for *no* form whatsoever of the order of *similitudo*
and *aequalitas* that is *not* connected by a structural homology with the
ordo entium and is consequently not of potential anagogic relevance.[358]
The differently cited expositions on the role of evil and vice in the *carmen
universitatis* are to be understood in this context. The whole theory is ef-
fectively immunized against deviation and contradiction; every "false note"
is conveniently assimilated as contributing to the "harmony" of the overall
structure.

Under these auspices, art in general and verse in particular are programmatically *not* autonomous, while at the same time being relevant *only for
that reason*. Against this background, what is surprising is less the continuing interest, also with respect to the Middle Ages, in ferreting out instances
of "subversion" or refuges of artistic "autonomy." It is surprising that these
were considered something particularly worth discussing, and their absence
problematic or at least deplorable. It should be emphasized that the ontology of the beautiful, the exclusive occupation of the ground of being of
every kind of beauty by the divinity and the consequent anagogic relevance
of "fine" art had an initially *liberating* effect with regard to the depreciation of the arts stemming from Plato and in addition contained indirectly *a
positive assessment of artistic work*.[359]

The execution of the anagoge—the passing on from the theory set forth
in Books I to V concerning numerical orders in concrete rhythms and meters
to the vision of the order of Being and Creation in Book VI—can completely
disregard the contents of the verse in question. The argument in itself is also
valid without restriction for verses that present something heterodox.[360]
Form and content can be *independent* of one another *rationaliter, De ordine* explains, and *De musica* emphasizes more than once the ontological
priority of number with regard to the mutable and the arbitrariness of the
word subjected to humans. The numerical order constitutive of verse (and

its "musicality") is, in accord with its Being, an incomplete imitation of the order of ideal numbers *in mente divina*. As *De musica* stresses, among these imitations the measured order of verse is particularly prominent, since it is "com-mensurate" with human senses. The positive assessment of the "technical" components of artistic creation (*ars*) does not involve the *creatio* of concrete subject matter that could be distinguished by its content and mode of representation[361] or "new" forms. The theory excludes the possibility of absolutely "new" forms, and it is only for that reason that the form manifested in verse is of any interest at all: the positive assessment of metrical discourse as *musica* conceives the work as a sensible "concretization of reality in general."[362]

The Augustinian theory of "poetry as music" is totalizing. It succeeds in relating to the one God of the Christian revelation not just a random bit of metrical discourse, but metrical discourse in general and thus the blossomings of the pagan tradition so present to Augustine. To that extent it contributes to the preparation of the "colonizing" order of discourse in the sense of chapter 4 above. A piece of verse that could not be conceived in the categories provided in *De musica* and thus resisted on its own being subjected to the regulative principles of the Christian world-shaping discourse, would have to forego any specific redundancy, any order or form of the kind described. Such lyric poems were first accepted with the writers of free verse and then with the avant-garde movements of the twentieth century, without ever becoming completely dominant in practice.[363] The arithmetical conceivability of metrical form or equivalence allows "the semantics of the word in the verse to recede into the background"[364] an option for anagogic relevance that has become meaningless for modernity. The conception of metrical discourse as *musica* implies the disqualification of the work with regard to the "originality" of its form, but at the same time and on the same basis the valorization of precisely this form as a vivid concretization of the *ordo entium*. For poetics, the Augustinian theory remains available for development and productive so long as the underlying metrics, whether quantitative, musically or dynamically accented, syllable-counting or rhyming, starts from the construction of specific redundancies, *aequalitates* and *similitudines*.

State of the Sources and Influence

The manifold influence of Augustine's *De musica* has been studied extensively. Consequently, the discussion in the following pages is limited to a sketch of the state of the sources and the most important contexts in which Augustine's text has been influential.

Augustine's authority made *De musica* one of the most often copied treatises of medieval music theory. The general inventory of the extant manuscripts of Augustine's works undertaken by the Vienna Academy of Sciences already lists more than one hundred copies of *De musica,* showing that down to the fifteenth century the text remained influential throughout Latin Europe, the present-day Benelux countries, Germany, and the British Isles. Not only was it present in library collections, but new copies were regularly produced all over western Europe. Most of the extant copies are in the British Isles or in Italy; both regions indicate that toward the late Middle Ages there was an increasingly broad distribution of the text.[365] The volume of the inventory devoted to France has not yet been published, and scholarship must thus rely on the work that Patrick Le Bœuf published in 1986 under the title *La tradition manuscrite du De musica de Saint Augustin.* Le Bœuf's survey, which makes no claim to be exhaustive, lists twenty-two manuscripts in France that prove a continuous engagement with the text from the ninth to the fifteenth century.[366]

The stemma drawn up by Le Bœuf allows us to formulate credible hypotheses regarding the range of the text's distribution.[367] The earliest copies can be localized in the Corbie-Metz-Laon-Soissons area, the cradle of the Carolingian dynasty. The relationships between the Carolingians and Tours, held by the Capetians, are well known. The relationship of the manuscripts Tours 286 and Angers 486 to the manuscript stemming from Corbie, Paris, BNF lat. 133275, locates the origins of the manuscript tradition of *De musica* in the milieu of Charlemagne's court library, to which we will later be able to trace the spread of Boethius's *De institutione musica* as well. From the twelfth century on, the presence of the work in the great educational institutions of Paris was solidified and maintained at a comparable level well into the fourteenth and fifteenth centuries, though we cannot observe a similar increase in the number of copies as in the British Isles or in Italy.

The peculiarities of manuscript tradition suggest that we should consult the extant complementary catalogs in order to complete the picture by inferring possible lost manuscripts, while recognizing that the results of these sources generally require interpretation. In this respect we can once again refer to Le Bœuf's work.[368] The catalog listings confirm the hypothesis that copies of Augustine's work on music spread from the Carolingian collection. In the ninth century the work is already attested in all the essential centers of the eastern Frankish realm, although no manuscripts from these regions are extant. The Western tradition, which soon diversifies, is similarly proven by manuscripts and catalogs; around the middle of the twelfth century *De musica* reached Bec-Hellouin and possibly from there made its way to England.

The work was acquired by Cluny, and in the thirteenth century by the Cistercians, the cathedral school in Chartres, the Augustinian canons, and the Franciscans. It was widely found in educational institutions; finally, the catalog listing also confirms a further increase in the number of copies in Italy and England in the fourteenth and fifteenth centuries.

In addition to the complete copies and extracts, there are also many excerpts and abridgments for study and teaching, as well as a large number of composite manuscripts that can illustrate the prestige as well as the ongoing practical relevance of the text.[369] An epitome, entitled *Praecepta artis musicae collecta ex libris sex Aurelii Augustini de musica*[370] and produced in the ninth century at the latest, edits the work as a *textbook on metrics*. This epitome was still being copied in the fifteenth century.[371] Finally, the ongoing currency of the work is proven by excerpts and extracts,[372] abundant marginal and interlinear glosses,[373] and independent collections of glosses.[374]

The temporal extension and intensity of the influence exercised by *De musica* as a reference for the conception of verse as music rests on the authority of the work in essentially three contexts: in music theory, in number theory, and in number symbolism, and, in close association with the latter, in the framework of the premodern "aesthetics of proportion."[375] The generally satisfactory state of research allows us to develop these connections by means of a few brief remarks.

De musica's influence on music theory[376] follows from its pioneering role in appropriating pagan music theory for the Christian order of discourse. Greek Patristics had already sought to give a Christian interpretation to Pythagorean-Platonic number and music theory, the doctrine of the cosmos as harmony. Théodore Gérold has defended the thesis that Clement of Alexandria's *Protreptikos* and *Stromates* prove the influence of Pythagorean-Platonic ethical theory in music;[377] according to him, Methodius of Olympus (died c. 311), Basil the Great (329–379), and then in the West, Ambrose, were entirely under the influence of Pythagorean cosmology and its musical-harmonic imagery.[378] But Augustine was the first to develop the theory for Christian doctrine systematically and in the framework of a treatise specifically on music. The work's resulting prominence, enhanced by its author's authority, is reflected in the rapid, ubiquitous spread of striking quotations and definitions, on the one hand, and in diffuse references to Augustine and alleged quotations of the authority on the other.[379] This makes it harder to prove direct references to the text. The oldest verifiable reference to knowledge of the work is found in Cassiodorus's *Institutiones divinarum et saecularium litterarum* II.5.2; Aldhelm's *De metris et aenigmatibus ac pedum regulis*, written toward the end of the seventh century, mentions *De musica* as an example of a work composed in dialogue form.[380] Hrabanus Maurus draws on Cassiodorus and Augustine,[381] while John Scotus Eriugena's *Periphyseon* refers, in I.39 and III.36, to Book VI of *De musica*; the text, which seems to have been a source for Regino of Prüm's *Epistola de armonica institutione* and the distinction between *musica naturalis* and *musica artificialis*, develops the "musical" register of Pythagorean-Platonic cosmology into its most impressive form in the early Middle Ages. Knowledge of Augustine's work can also be proven by the treatment of "numerose canere" in the *Scolica enchiriadis*,[382] which in turn influenced chapter XV of Guido of Arezzo's (c. 992–1050) *Micrologus*, which is devoted to the same subject.[383] The first chapter of Petrus de Sancto Dionysio's *Tractatus de musica*, composed in 1321, cites the definition of sound as a form of movement from *De musica* II.3.3;[384] Jacob of Liège's *Speculum musicae* cites Book VI of *De musica* extensively to illustrate the concepts of *musica mundana* and *musica humana* drawn from Boethius's *De institutione musica*.[385] In this connection, Augustine's *De musica* is still relevant in the fifteenth century, as in Ugolino of Orvieto's (c. 1380–1457) *Declaratio musicae disciplinae*.[386]

In Augustine's work the appropriation of pagan-antique music theory is flanked—corresponding to the importance that the report in the *Confessiones* attaches to psalmody[387]— by observations on early Christian musical practice that contributed to the anchoring of vocal practice in the liturgy.[388] These commentaries have developed their own history of influence. Thus the *Scolica enchiriadis* II.263 ff. cites *De ordine* II.14.41 and II.15.42 on the discussion of the essence of the *numerus*; Johannes Tinctoris's *Liber de natura et proprietate tonorum* and his *Complexus effectuum musicae* cite the *Confessiones*;[389] Adam of Fulda also quotes from Augustine's *Epistolae* on the definition and effect of music.[390]

Both complexes, the appropriation of the metaphysically oriented inventory of pagan-antique theory and the establishment of musical practice in the liturgy, make Augustine's statements on music, along with those of Boethius, the most influential reference for Christian and late antique music theory. Here the limits of theoretical development in the following centuries are set:

> Saint Augustine is unquestionably the one who gave the basic outline of the way music and musical thought entered the domain of the Christian Church and became an organic part of the life of the growing Christian community. He defined the inclusion of *musica sonora* within the divine concept and justified its practice in agreement with Christian theology.[391]

A single example chosen for its prominence can illustrate this. In 1954 William G. Waite put forward the thesis that Augustine's *De musica* should be seen as the theoretical foundation of the isorhythm of Pérotin's École de Notre Dame and the *ars nova*.[392] Waite's thesis, which has in the meantime been qualified but not fundamentally challenged,[393] is directly relevant to the context of our investigation. The papal bull *Docta sanctorum patrum* (1322), which will be discussed later, prohibits the practice of the *ars nova* in churches. It moved into the courtyards, where Guillaume de Machaut established himself as its most advanced representative.

The example illustrates the continuing influence developed by *De musica* despite the later distancing from the Pythagorean-Platonic tradition, and despite the strongly Bible-centered, verbally oriented profile of Augustine's main theological works, which deliberately distinguish themselves from the assimilated ancient corpus. The main theological works prefer to reduce the function of the study of the *artes* to the understanding of the Bible.[394] The argument on which Augustine's arithmology is based, which *De musica* and *De ordine* develop, and *De libero arbitrio* makes explicit, remains valid over and beyond the early work: the insight into the numerical order of Being corresponds to the view of truth designated by *sapientia*.[395] Moreover, the connection between *musica* and arithmology—and thus also the valorizing of the arithmetically describable form of verse as anagogically relevant—is not retracted in the main works. *De doctrina christiana* justifies the argument anew: sometimes by reference to the Bible,[396] and sometimes by absorbing Platonic wisdom by means of the priority thesis. According to *De Civitate Dei* VIII.11, Plato must have drawn on Jeremiah and Moses.

The currency of the association of arithmology with *sapientia* even in Augustine's main and late works is shown not least by a multitude of number-symbolism interpretations that became major references for medieval number theory and number symbolism. Thus *De trinitate* 4.2.2 explains that the mystery of the Redemption consists in the fact that through the death of Christ the twofold death of men is discharged; the corporal death (one) and the spiritual death (two). The "consonance" of the two is described by the *proportio* 1:2, which corresponds to the complete consonance, the interval of the octave. The redemption "rings," as it were, in the octave. The importance of *De musica* for medieval number symbolism can be considered as largely worked out. Since Vincent Foster Hopper's path-breaking study on *Medieval Number Symbolism*[397] there has been a consensus that "the whole Middle Ages is based, in number symbolism almost more than in other areas, completely on the Augustinian tradition."[398] Hincmar of Rheims already regards procedures based on Augustine as self-evident, while Alcuin integrates them into the figural schema.[399] As Heinz Meyer's overview shows,[400] down to the late Middle Ages, there were no major interruptions of the conception of number symbolism undertaken by Augustine, and in the fifteenth century this conception actually acquired a new currency. This can be proven by Luca Pacioli's *Summa de arithmetica* (1494), along with other *rara arithmetica* that David Eugene Amith collected and annotated.[401] Ernst Hellgardt has also shown that Augustine's *De musica* influenced numerical composition located beyond the nexus of poetics and music theory or indifferent to the latter; Karl Langosch has also proven this influence using examples from Goliardic poetry.[402] Examples from the Old French poetic tradition, such as the Eulalia sequence,[403] would not be difficult to provide.

The impact of Augustinian arithmology on number theory and number symbolism is inseparable from its significance for the general theory of the beautiful. Edgar de Bruyne's *Études d'esthétique médiévale* has demonstrated the persistent influence that *De musica* retained in High and Late Scholasticism; in his now classic work on Gothic cathedrals, Otto von Simson called Augustine's work "the most influential aesthetic treatise of the Christian Middle Ages."[404] In the context of our studies we can limit ourselves to naming the most important receivers of the theory developed in *De musica*. We have already mentioned John Scotus Eriugena (810–877),[405] but the High Middle Ages also remains true to the late antique, "holistically" conceived theory of music: "The Romanesque and even the Gothic periods add nothing new to the musical view of the world,"[406] as de Bruyne generously sums it up, and more precisely: this model of the world was shaped by the "Augustinian aesthetics" taken from *De musica* and Boethius. Hugo of St. Victor (c. 1097–1141) who was the first after John Scotus Eriugena to devote a relevant section of his wide-ranging work to the problem of the beautiful,[407] his student Richard, and also the School of Chartres remained faithful to "an essentially musical aesthetics"[408] based on Augustine's formalistic theory of the beautiful.[409] In the work of Alexander of Hales (died 1245), the mediation of the ternary relationship *modus-species-ordo* based on arithmology is central to thinking about the beautiful, with the Biblical reference from *Liber sapientiae* 11:21. Alexander's *Summa universae theologiae* quotes Augustine alone forty-three times.[410] Via Augustine's early writings, Robert Grosseteste (1175–1253) also stands in the Pythagorean-Neoplatonic tradition,[411] seeking to link the stronger, "visual" conception of the beautiful based on the metaphysics of light and *claritas* with the auditive, rational, number-based conception of the Pythagorean-Platonic tradition. He succeeds in doing so by interpreting *claritas* as an epiphenomenon of the perfect *consonantia* of form with itself: "It is called good in itself or beautiful in itself because it gives itself to all in such a way that to each thing it adapts beauty, that is, a clear and distinct consonance [*consonantiam manifestam et dilucidam*] [. . .] of itself to itself and of the parts of the self to one another, to itself and to that which is outside the self [*sui ad se et suorum ad invicem et ad se et ad ea quae exterius*]."[412] De Bruyne summarizes: "The system is still Augustinianism:"[413] measure determines beautiful form, measures can be described as relationships between natural numbers or proportions. The repetition of the same proportions creates harmonies: "They follow the continuous and discrete measures of beings; their proportions and proportionality are the harmonies and concordances of beings [*proportionalitas ex quibus se habentibus ad invicem sunt entium harmoniae et concordiae*]."[414] The beautiful refers to God, leads—through *delectatio*[415]—to him.[416]

Grosseteste's reflection on the beautiful shares the implications concerning the form of the work that we have recognized as constitutive for the subsumption of verse under music. The most beautiful kind of repetition is the repetition of the same: "Let us remember that *all beauty, that is, all 'concord,'* derives from one of these fundamental proportionalities, repeated identically in a whole, no matter what magnitudes are related [. . .]."[417] Here as well, it is obvious that "Grosseteste remains fundamentally faithful to the Bishop of Hippo."[418] Finally, this also bears on the status of the arts: for Augustine, a properly measured verse is a concrete manifestation of the *ordo entium*, graphic and suited to the human senses. Robert Grosseteste makes use of a comparison. The form created by the artist is like the image of an object in shadows as seen in a lighted mirror; it is more visible than the "real" object itself: "When a likeness or exemplar is of a clearer essence than the object of which it is the image, knowledge of the thing is nobler, clearer and more suitable as a likeness or exemplar." De Bruyne asks rhetorically: "Must we take this to mean that even the same cubist structure of the universe or the mathematical framework of a melody gives us clearer, more distinct and more noble knowledge than the experience of concrete things?"[419]

After Robert Grosseteste, the *doctor seraphicus* Bonaventure (1221–1274) took his cue from Augustine: "Saint Bonaventure chose as his teacher of aesthetics the Saint Augustine of the philosophy of music. [. . .] the whole of Bonaventure's aesthetics gravitates around the principle drawn from Book VI of *De musica*."[420] Bonaventure recapitulates Augustine's number genera according to *De musica* and *De vera religione* and supplements them with a number category that determines the production of numerical orders, the *numeri artificiales*.[421] According to Bonaventure as well, everything that exists is beautiful, insofar as it has form.[422] The beauty of form and its enjoyment follows from measure and presupposes a relation describable as measure qua *aequalitas* of the parts, qua *convenientia*,[423] the latter being a proportion, which is itself ultimately number:

> Since all things are beautiful, therefore, and are in some way delightful, both beauty and delight are not without proportion, and proportion is first in numbers, it is necessary that all things be numerically harmonious [*necesse est omnia esse numerosa*]. For this reason, number is the principal pattern in the mind of the Creator [*numerus est praecipuum in animo Conditoris exemplar*].[424]

Insofar as number makes proportion possible, it makes *delectatio* possible, since: "Every delightful thing exists by reason of proportionality [*ratione proportionalitatis*]."[425] The observation of the proportional structure of a beautiful object corresponds to the "contemplative" observation of *sensibilia* with a view to their Creator.[426] God's creation coincides with the institution of the numerical and thus also beautiful order;[427] the promised insight into the order of Creation through the ascent "per sensibilia [. . .] ad intelligibilia" ("through the objects of sense [. . .] toward intelligible ones")[428] to the vision of God corresponds to the vision of the utmost *aequalitas* and consequently to the highest *delectatio*.[429] The order of Creation is manifest in "musical" proportions. Bonaventure follows Augustine even in conceiving *pulchritudo* as *aequalitas numerosa*,[430] and thus also in conceiving the beautiful as a concrete manifestation of the *ordo entium*, as the reflection of the same in the different: "[P]*ulchritudo* consistit in *ordine*" ("*Beauty* consists in *order*").[431] Bonaventure also takes the beautiful to be a sign referring to the Creator and emphasizes the anagogic relevance of beautiful form for the ascent *per signa ad signata*.

It might be objected that reference to the survival of *De musica* in the mysticism of the Augustinian canons and the Franciscans is hardly to be taken as proof of its continuing relevance and wide influence. In fact, its influence declined after 1300. The continuing concern with the work proven by the manuscript tradition may have been nourished by the ongoing interest in Neoplatonic material. Despite the Aristotelian reorientation of Scholastic theology, *De divinis nominibus*, a work by Pseudo-Dionysius the Areopagite based on Proclus, remained until the late Middle Ages the standard treatise on the essence of the beautiful. Thus the early work of the Cologne Doctor of the Church Albert the Great (c. 1200–1280) is dominated by the commentary on *De divinis nominibus*, in which Augustine's

De musica is regularly cited in support.[432] The symbolic interpretation of numerical relationships, which takes on great importance in the work of Albert the Great and also shapes his statements on music, is based on Augustine.[433] Even his late work devoted to a complete commentary on the *corpus aristotelicum* always cites *De musica* when music is the subject, for example in the commentary on Aristotle's *Politics*. Albert the Great's two most important pupils, Ulrich of Strasburg (c. 1220–1272) and Thomas Aquinas (c. 1225–1274), take as their point of departure the same sources as their teacher: the Neoplatonic-influenced texts that were the sources for Augustine's early writings, those of Pseudo-Dionysius the Areopagite, Plato's *Timaeus*, Aristotle's *Nicomachean Ethics*, Cicero, and Seneca.[434] They further develop these sources, but in a different direction. Ulrich takes from Robert Grosseteste the merger of the aesthetics of *claritas* and the aesthetics of form, which is Augustinian in its approach, in a differentiated system of consonances and proportions.[435] Thomas Aquinas was influenced by Aristotle's arguments against Pythagoreanism and Platonism, but nonetheless did not systematically ignore Neoplatonic theoretical writings. Precisely those parts of Neoplatonic doctrine that underlie the speculative theory of music that includes metrical discourse as *musica* retain their contour. These remarks will be elaborated in a later chapter. However, here they may help clarify the influence of the theory of music whose key assumptions are Neoplatonic in general and of Augustine's *De musica* in particular on the Aristotle-dominated thought of the later Middle Ages. The theory acquired from Augustine underlies the music theory of Adam of Fulda, Franchino Gafori, Johannes Cochlaeus, Martin Agricola, Zarlino, Andreas Ornitoparchus, Glareanus, and Thomas Morley. Ficino's *Theologia Platonica* teaches the active character of sense perception with constant reference to Book VI of *De musica*, Francisco Salinas's *De musica libri septem* (1577) again makes use of *De musica* in dealing with metrics, and the same goes for Nicolas Bergier's *La Musique speculative* (c. 1600). Evidence for the knowledge of Augustine's work is found in Johannes Tinctoris, Cornelius Agrippa of Nettesheim, Luther, and Calvin.[436] In the seventeenth century Athanasius Kircher still refers to Augustine's view of music in the chapter "Symphonismus Coelorum" of his *Musurgia universalis*.

CHAPTER SIX

Boethius, *De institutione arithmetica* and *De institutione musica*

AUGUSTINE'S *De musica* was never completed. After six books on *musica rhythmica*, the parts *de melo* fell victim to the burdens of his ecclesiastical duties.[1] Boethius's textbook entitled *De institutione musica* was composed around 500, a century after Augustine's work. It limits itself to questions concerning melody and the theory of consonance,[2] the contents of *musica harmonica*, although a remark in *De Intitutione musica* I.34 shows an awareness that only a part of late antique *musica scientia* was thus covered:

> That person is a musician [*musicus*] who has the ability to judge according to speculation or reason [*secundum speculationem rationemve*] that has been set forth and is suited to music concerning modes and rhythms and kinds of songs, mixed forms, and all kinds, about which there will be a later explanation, and the songs of the poets [*de poetarum carminibus*].[3]

According to Boethius, the objects of the *musicus* are musical rhythms, *modi* (*doricus, lydius, phyrgius*, etc.), *genera* (*diatonicum, chromaticum, enharmonicum*), *permixtiones* or chords, and finally *carmina poetarum*. Thus Boethius himself seems to have deliberately not dealt with certain areas of *musica scientia*—precisely those areas with which Augustine's *De musica* had dealt.[4] Both works limit themselves to certain areas of pagan music theory, and taken together they offer a complete, nonoverlapping account of the speculative theory of music founded on Pythagorean-Neoplatonic bases.

From this complementarity Ubaldo Pizzani concluded that there is a genetic relationship between the two texts: for him, Boethius conceived his textbook as a continuation of Augustine's.[5] Pizzani's thesis cannot be verified because of the lack of explicit proofs in Boethius's text. Nonetheless, it reflects the conception current in the Middle Ages. Boethius's and Augustine's writings on music were read as parts of a common whole,[6] and in the fourteenth century they were still being bound together in a single codex.[7]

This merging explains, first of all, why a large number of epitomes of Augustine and manuscript copies of his work are limited to the treatment of rhythmics and metrics in Books II–V of *De musica*, whereas Book I, which provides an introduction to number theory, no longer receives much attention. In Boethius's work, *De institutione musica* stands alongside his *De insitutione arithmetica*. By the ninth century the latter work, which draws on the same Neoplatonic sources as Book I of Augustine's *De musica*, had become the standard textbook on arithmetic in the quadrivium. The abbreviation offered by Augustine was made obsolete by Boethius's detailed account, and as a result replaced the former in pedagogical practice. The *Institutio arithmetica*, the *Institutio musica* on *musica harmonica*, and Augustine's *De musica* on *musica metrica* complemented each other in an account of *musica scientia* that was founded and sufficient for pedagogical needs. Augustine's theory was absorbed into the conceptual context of Boethian music theory and secured a systematic place in it for verse. Music theory and pedagogical practice unified the whole complex in accord with Boethius's concepts: "Boethius' treatise [*De institutione musica*] established the framework for the analysis of music throughout the Middle Ages and Renaissance, and Augustine's work was adapted to fit the popular pattern."[8]

The context of our investigation suggests that we should take this reception history into account in discussing Boethius's theory. We will inquire not only into the latter's conceptual outline, but also into which qualities it made available to the gradual unification of the body of late antique music theory. Answers to both questions can be found by delving deeper into the Pythagorean substrate of late antique theory, from which the systematics of Boethius's work, its particular conceptual scope, the connection between arithmetic and *musica harmonica*, and finally the connection between *musica harmonica* and *rhythmica* or *metrica* developed. The section begins by situating the textbook in Boethius's work as a whole, which brings out aspects of his extensive oeuvre that are relevant for our "continuity thesis," and closes with an overview of the state of the sources and the reception history. Since the following chapters deal specifically with the continuity of the speculative metaphysics of music on Boethian foundations down to the late Middle Ages and the systematic place of verse in this metaphysics, here we will limit ourselves to the textbook's significance for the medieval educational system. This will make possible an initial assessment of the extent of its dissemination that will serve as the starting point for the following detailed studies.

Boethius's Music Theory in Context
Biographical Matters and the *Consolatio philosophiae*

The contexts relevant to the influence of Boethius's music theory include first of all his biography,[9] although dates for the life of Anitius Manlius Severinus Boethius are few and disputed in detail. Even the year of his birth must remain open, though a date between 475 and 477 is assumed. In addition, we can only speculate regarding his education.[10] Around 506, Boethius began to have close relationships with Theodoric, and in 510 he became consul; in 523, as *magister officiorum* he became the highest official in the imperial administration. One year later he was arrested for unexplained reasons and finally executed, without having been given an opportunity to defend himself. His death in Pavia is one of the few certain facts we have concerning him; tradition says he died on 23 October 525. According to a life edited by Rudolf Peiper, shortly after his death, Boethius was already being venerated by the *provinciales*.[11] The extent of the cult remained limited,[12] but Boethius nonetheless finally entered the *Acta sanctorum* for the month of May.[13] Although he is not mentioned in the *Martyrologium Romanum* or the *Bibliotheca Hagiographica Latina*, on 15 December 1883 Pope Leo XIII confirmed his veneration as a martyr in the diocese of Pavia and set 23 October as his holiday.[14]

The significance of the biographical data is connected with the success of the *Consolatio*. Put to death at the behest of a Roman emperor who seemed to the Middle Ages an opponent of the Catholic religion, Boethius acquired soon after his execution the halo of the martyr. His book of consolation was read as a devotional work and a document of his martyrdom.[15] The reception history of the work has been exhaustively studied.[16] Assessments regarding it are full of superlatives: in bibliophiles' catalogs, the *Consolatio* is said to be "the most beloved textbook of the Middle Ages,"[17] "the bedside book of medieval humanism."[18] Ferdinand Sassen clearly underscored the text's importance: "Apart from the Holy Scripture, no book so strongly shaped the whole culture of this period as the *Consolatio*."[19] Over four hundred manuscripts are extant.[20] In the ninth century the *Consolatio philosophiae* had already become a standard school text.[21] The commentary tradition begun in the ninth century by John Scotus Eriugena, extends to around 1500,[22] and the number of studies that have examined the reception history in Middle Latin and vernacular literatures is now almost overwhelming.[23] The oldest translation, by the Anglo-Saxon King Alfred (848–899), was produced in the late ninth century;[24] the series of translations into French, "by far the richest and most complex"[25] in the area of European vernaculars, began around 1230. Twelve distinct translations had appeared before the first printing in 1471.[26]

The reception history of the *Consolatio philosophiae* is one of the contexts relevant to the continuity of Boethian music theory, and not only because it vouches for the authority of the author and for more than a millennium made the work known to every Central European with an elementary education. David S. Chamberlain has devoted an extensive study to the music theory content of the *Consolatio philosophiae* that relates the *itinerarium mentis ad Deum* described here to the anagogic potential of *musicae*. Chamberlain's conclusion goes too far: "Indeed, the work [the *Consolatio philosophiae*] may be said to have a main theme that is musical and to embody a more complete philosophy of music than *De [institutione] musica* itself."[27] However, this exaggeration does not diminish the pertinence of three essential observations based on careful textual study. Philosophia hosts Musica and Rhetorica at her fireside[28] and comments on *metra* as refreshing *musica*.[29] The *ordo* concept, on which Philosophia bases the *cura* applied to the *lethargicus*,[30] is illustrated by examples that can be classified as manifestations of the "musical" order of the cosmos discussed in *De institutione musica*.[31] Thus the text as a whole, independently of hypostatized textual relationships or authorial intentions, can be read as an explanation and illustration of the anagogic potential of various *musicae*. Finally, the "philosophical" terminology used in the *Consolatio* bears the mark of music theory. These discoveries suggest a relationship between the *Consolatio philosophiae* and *De institutione musica*, but conceptually they seem not to go beyond the propaedeutic that will be described extensively in the following chapter. Accordingly, for the discussion of the *Consolatio* in detail we refer to the work of Chamberlain as well as that of Henry Chadwick, who complemented the former's observations in 1981.[32] In any case, for the proof of our continuity thesis it is significant that the *Consolatio philosophiae* may have contributed to the dissemination of Boethian music theory and that its spread and reception history, precisely in France and down into the late Middle Ages, support our working hypothesis at least as supplementary evidence.

Commentaries, Translations, *Opuscula sacra*

The *Consolatio philosophiae* concludes an opus in which the literary played a minor role. An adequate access to the historical situation and to the profile of Boethius's work may be offered less by the *Consolatio* than by his assessment of the situation of learning in his days. "Aliud est autem uti ratione, vel habet rationem" ("It is one thing to have reason, another to use it"),[33] we read in the commentary on Porphyry, as if these lines were applicable to the situation of quadrivial education in the early sixth century. The old canon of the ἐγκύκλιος παιδεία had gradually been replaced by the ideal of the rhetorician.[34] The Latin West had good textbooks for rhetoric and grammar,[35] but introductions to the quadrivial disciplines were largely lacking. A generation before Boethius, Books VI–IX of Martianus Cappella's *De nuptiis Philologiae et Mercurii* sought to make the quadrivial disciplines available in a form agreeable to Latin readers, but these were precisely not suitable for acquiring a solid education in mathematics. In addition to the Neoplatonic sources on arithmetic and music that had already been exploited by Augustine, Macrobius's commentary on Cicero's *Somnium Scipionis* offered Platonic ideas about astronomy; Calcidius wrote his difficult commentary on the *Timaeus* in the fourth century. These texts, which presupposed that readers already had wide-ranging knowledge, led to the development of an enormous body of commentaries. Some of these study aids proved very successful: Ficino found Theon of Smyrna's *Expositio doctrinarum mathematicarum ad legendum Platonem utilium*[36] so helpful that he translated it into Latin in 1463. However, on the whole these commentaries were hardly adequate to make up for the lack of introductions suitable for teaching. A comparable impression seems to have inspired Boethius's wide-ranging writings. Around 500 he began work on texts that were devoted less to technical discussion than to the representation of the generally accepted core of each discipline. In parallel, translations and commentaries on the most important didactic works in the tradition appeared.[37] Brief discussions of these texts will be presented in subject groups and in order to situate Boethian music theory in their context.

Between 500 and 505 Boethius began to produce a series of translations, commentaries, and didactic writings, at first on dialectics. The significance of these works for Scholastic methodology has been generally accepted by scholars since Martin Grabmann's epoch-making study.[38] First came a commentary in dialogue form on Porphyry's Εἰσαγωγή,[39] the introduction to logic most widely used in the Neoplatonic schools, which was available in Marius Victorinus's translation. In 508 or 509 this work was supplemented by Boethius's own translation of Porphyry's text as well as by an expanded version of the commentary in five books addressed to advanced students.[40] Between 507 and 509 Boethius produced, in addition to a translation of *De interpretatione*, two commentaries on this text in two and six books, respectively.[41] In 510, the year he was elected Consul, Boethius completed the translation of Aristotle's *Categories* and commented on the work following Porphyry.[42] A commentary on Aristotle's *Topics* mentions translations of this text as well as of the *Analytica priora* and *posteriora*. These have now been lost.[43] There followed the treatises *Introductio ad Syllogismos categoricos, De Syllogismo categorico, De Syllogismo hypothetico,* and *De divisione,* all explanations of Aristotelian logic.[44] Older editions of his work also include, as translations by Boethius, the last four parts of Aristotle's *Organon.* On 19 March 1255, the Paris faculty of arts included these allegedly Boethian translations in its curriculum along with the *Topics,*[45] thus making them, together with the *Categories* and *De interpretatione,* part of the foundation for the study of theology. This attribution has since been refuted,[46] but it nevertheless testifies to Boethius's importance for the reception of Aristotle after 1230 and as a commentator in general.[47]

Boethius's commentaries offer in part acute, Platonizing ways of reading Aristotle's works.[48] This is important for the later course of our investigation, and especially for the chapter devoted to Thomas Aquinas. The synthetic interest that leads to these ways of reading is made explicit in a passage from the commentary on *De interpretatione.* The goal is supposed to be the complete translation of the work of Plato and Aristotle, motivated by the intention, known since the early Augustine, of finally resolving with the differences between the two works: "When all this is accomplished, for my part, I shall not disdain to gather together the opinions of Plato and Aristotle into one accord in some way, and demonstrate in these writings that they did not disagree in all things, as many do, but agreed on most things, especially those relating to philosophy."[49]

Putting matters in a Neoplatonic perspective led to controversies regarding Boethius's religious belief. These were made obsolete by Hermann Usener's discovery of a previously unknown fragment of Cassiodorus in 1877.[50] The text designates Boethius as the author of a *liber de Sancta Trinitate,* of *capita quaedam dogmatica* and a *liber contra Nestorium.* The text consists of five Christian theological studies whose authors had been a matter of debate before Usener's discovery, and that were then brought together as Boethius's *Opuscula sacra.*[51] From the ninth century on, these short texts—they total, depending on the edition, barely 130 pages—enjoyed, as Max Manitius has noted, an "almost canonical respect."[52] The first treatise, titled *Quomodo Trinitas unus Deus ac non tres Dei* or *De Trinitate,* a letter to his father-in-law Symmachus, provides an introduction to the doctrine of the Trinity and offers a sketch of dialectic-theological methodology that bears an Aristotelian stamp and concludes with critical remarks on Arianism. The treatise *Utrum Pater et Filius et Spiritus Sanctus de divinitate substantialiter praedicentur*, which is also only a few pages long, and the longer text *Quomodo substantiae in eo quod sint bonae sint cum non sint substantialia bonae*, called *De hebdomadibus*, both deal with a Trinitarian subject. *De fide catholica* provides a compressed summary of Christian doctrine, supplemented by brief surveys of Biblical and Church history as well as the most serious heresies. Finally, *Contra Eutychen et Nestorium* deals with a christological subject and develops the definition of the *persona* qua its "naturae rationalibus individua substantia" ("individual substance of a rational nature")[53] that was to remain mandatory for the semantic inventory of Scholasticism.

For the reception history of the *Opuscula* we must emphasize a fundamental tension that is important for our later argument. Consistently following Aristotelian method and consistently using Aristotelian terminology, Boethius's theological studies present a Neoplatonic ontology and metaphysics that is interpreted in a consistently Christian way: "The influence of Aristotle is limited here [in the *Opuscula sacra*] entirely to the formal tools of construction that the Stagirite's logical tools put at his [Boethius's] disposal. The true content of the theological writings is purely Augustinian, or, if one will, Neoplatonic."[54] Thus, to name only a few examples, Boethius consistently uses the terminology made available by Aristotelian metaphysics, but nonetheless ignores the proofs of God developed in the *Physics* and *Metaphysics*. In the Trinitarian theory the substantiality of God is conceived Neoplatonically as "transsubstantiality": "nam substantia in illo non est vere substantia, sed ultra substantiam" ("for substance in Him is not truly substance, but is beyond substance").[55] In other passages God is opposed, as "pure form" to formed matter, which clearly overstretches the Aristotelian ἐνέργεια/δύναμις dichotomy.[56] In the *Opuscula sacra*, where their ontological difference is to be explained, the relation between Creator and Creation is always described using the words *fluere* or *defluere*. The verbs connote the Neoplatonic concept of emanation, especially since Boethius conceives the being of the created with respect to the being of the Creator as an *esse per partitionem* or *esse participatum*. In the reception history of the *Opuscula sacra*, the tension seen in these examples is transformed into a work program that from Lanfranc (died 1089) and Anselm of Canterbury onward becomes the project of High Scholasticism itself. This work program can be discerned in the proem of the treatise *De trinitate*, where it is formulated with explicit reference to Augustine:[57] the goal is to achieve a complete, rational reconstruction of the *ordo entium* systematically covering the *whole* of Creation. The methodological preparation for this project has also been traced back to Boethius.[58] The treatise *De hebdomadibus* is devoted in general to ontological considerations within the Neoplatonic horizon, but it was influential chiefly as a methodological work. The opuscule seeks to offer terms and rules of inference that are to serve as the foundation for an axiomatic method developed on a mathematical paradigm for resolving philosophical-theological problems: "As is customary in mathematics and other disciplines, I have set forth the terms and rules by which I shall prove everything that follows."[59] In Christian theology, until the twelfth century the treatise was considered paradigmatic for the theological instrumentalization of philosophical ontology, for the reconciliation of philosophical *ratio* and Christian *fides*. Stimulated by the terms and rules developed in *De hebdomadibus*, Alain de Lille (1128–1203), whose *Regulae* or *Maximae theologiae* refer expressly to Boethius's *liber regularium*,[60] and Nicholas of Amiens's *Ars fidei catholicae* set out to produce a complete axiomatic elaboration of Scholastic theological method.[61] Consequently, the argument sketched out in *De hebdomadibus* became "definitive for Scholasticism."[62]

Thomas Aquinas's commentary *Expositio de libri de hebdomadibus* and *Super de Trinitate*, written between 1257 and 1259, applied the possibilities of methodological rigor and stringency opened up by Boethius's works to the *Opuscula* themselves. But even Thomas does not completely resolve the aforementioned tension between the inventory of Aristotelian concepts and methods, on the one hand, and the Neoplatonic ontology on the other. In parts of the theological doctrine this tension remains inscribed in the work of the *doctor angelicus* as well as in the Aristotelianism of the High and Late Middle Ages as a whole. As a consequence of the reception history of the *Opuscula sacra*, this tension will become an important reference point for our discussion of the scholarly opinion summarized in part I, namely that in the course of the thirteenth-century reception of Aristotle there was a "break" in the speculative theory of music.

The Propaedeutics

Boethius's propaedeutics are among his early works. Their composition is related to the desperate situation of quadrivial education at the beginning of the sixth century that we summarized at the outset. In the preface to *De institutione arithmetica*, which takes the form of a dedication to Symmachus, Boethius states his intention to write introductions to each of the mathematical disciplines that were canonical since Archytas of Tarentum[63] (428–347 BCE): propaedeutics to arithmetic, music, geometry, and astronomy. A letter by Cassiodorus written around 507 suggests that in that year Boethius had already completed this project.[64] However, only the work on arithmetic and part of that on music are extant. A work on geometry is proven by Cassiodorus, but no copy of it has been preserved. We know nothing about a work on astronomy.[65] The arguments presented to provide the foundation and to set the goals for the canon (here summed up for the first time using the metaphor of the *quadruvium*) correspond to those familiar from Augustine. Boethius also assigns *beate contemplari* and *inspectio veritatis* as the goals of quadrivial education.[66] Education in the quadrivial disciplines is supposed to ascend through "levels" toward the vision of the *intelligibilia* with the "mind's eye":

> This is the quadrivium [*quadruvium*], where they must go whose more excellent mind, while shaped in the senses that we have created, is sent on toward the more certain things of the intelligence [*ad intelligentiae certiora perducitur*]. There are certain levels and stages of progression by which the mind can ascend and move forward, so that these disciplines might illuminate once again the mind's eye, which, as Plato says, is more worthy to be nurtured and preserved than many bodily eyes. Truth can be found and investigated by the light of that eye alone, which, I say, has been overwhelmed and deprived by the bodily senses.[67]

However, unlike Augustine in *De ordine*, Boethius does not conceive the quadrivial disciplines primarily on the basis of the order of teaching and studying the *artes liberales*, but rather in a general classification of the sciences.[68] The latter is close to the one that in Aristotle's *Metaphysics* leads to the distinction of theology as "the highest science."[69] *Philosophia speculativa* is distinguished from *philosophia practica*; the former is further differentiated into *physica, mathematica,* and *theologia*; the latter into *moralis, oeconomica,* and *politica.* The quadrivial disciplines, as mathematical and in accord with the indicated goals of *beate contemplari* and *inspectio veritatis*, are subsumed under *philosophia speculativa.* However, regarding music in particular, *De institutione musica* I.1 provides a complement that must be emphasized: "It follows that although there are four disciplines of mathematics, and the three others also investigate truth, music is connected not only to speculation but also to morality [*musica vero non modo speculationi, verum etiam moralitati coniuncta sit*]."[70] The assignment of music theory to *philosophia speculativa* is complemented by the reference to its "moral" dimension; between *philosophia speculativa* and *philosophia practica, musica scientia* is conceived as an "ethically determined science of numbers."[71] The reconstruction of Boethius's theory should take this situation of *musica* between *inspectio veritatis* and ethical relevance as its point of departure and should also lead back to it.

De institutione arithmetica

According to the chronology established since Brandt,[72] *De institutione ar-ithmetica* is the first introductory textbook that Boethius took up and completed. It is a free, partly expanded translation of Nicomachus of Gerasa's Ἀριθμητικὴ εἰσαγωγή.[73] The presentation is to be understood as the foundation of quadrivial knowledge seen as the path to *scientia* itself, and situates itself explicitly in the Pythagorean tradition.[74] Boethius also begins with fundamental observations concerning the classification of numbers; we recapitulate these only insofar as they make the relation to Augustine clear and are indispensable for understanding Boethius's later remarks.

Like Augustine, Boethius assumes that the infinite is inaccessible to knowledge: "Nothing that is infinite can be gathered together by knowledge or comprehended by the mind [*vel scientia potest colligi vel mente comprehendi*], but reason itself takes up the subject, wherein it can employ the searching skill of truth [*in quibus possit indagatricem veritatis exercere sollertiam*]."[75] Thus the numerically based sciences of the quadrivium first prepare the way for the *indagatarix veritatis* and construct, on the basis of arithmetic, steps toward the vision of the true.[76] The "ascent" reveals, as Boethius puts it, echoing *Timaeus* 32–36,[77] the activity of *natura* as the *fabricator mundi*[78] that creates "numerorum ratione":[79]

> Which of these disciplines must we learn first, if not the one that occupies the first place and plays the role of a mother in a kind of way? This is arithmetic. It is prior to all other disciplines because God, the creator of the great mass of this world, considered it first as the exemplar of his thought [*huius mundanae molis conditor deus primam suae habuit ratiocinationis exemplar*], and in its pattern He established all things with reason, as does a builder, using the numbers of an assigned order to find concord [*ad hanc cuncta constituit quaecumque fabricante ratione per numeros adsignati ordinis inuenere concordiam*].[80]

The question for Boethian doctrine is thus also the possibility of comprehending a posited order of creation in accord with numerical relationships *in mente divina*:

> Everything that has been constructed from the primordial nature of things appears to have been formed by virtue of numbers [*numerorum videntur ratione formata*]. Numbers served as the principal exemplar in the mind of the Creator [*principale in animo conditoris exemplar*]. The multiplicity of the four elements was obtained from this source, and from it came the changes of the seasons, the motion of the stars, and the rotation of the heavens.[81]

According to this order of numbers, everything existent is connected through a common origin: "These are the elements of which numbers are composed: even and odd. Although they are disparate and contrary, nevertheless, because of divine power they flow from one begetting [*ex una tamen genitura profluunt*], and are united in one composition and one modulation [*in unam compositionem modulationemque iunguntur*]."[82] Boethius's definition of number borrowed from Nicomachus should be situated before this conception of the order of creation as numerical *modulatio*: "Numerus est unitatum collectio vel quantitatis acervus ex unitatibus profusus" ("Number is a collection of unities or a mass of quantity consisting of unities").[83]

Number, as the principle of unity of a discrete multitude, is the form, the numerical existent the set of its manifest variations. In Boethius as well, and with the familiar arguments, the number one is designated as the generator and principle of all numbers in their natural order (*naturali dispositione*), and correspondingly, equality is designated as the principle of every *proportio*: "Just as unity and plurality form the basis [*principium*] of numbers, so equality forms the basis of proportions."[84] As the principle of the numerical order constructed by the Creator, the number one has a distinctive *natura*, the *natura eiusdem*. The latter is distinguished, probably following Plato's *Sophist* and Pythagorean sources,[85] from a part of the created numerical order that cannot be reduced to the One, an Other that is qua *privatio* differing:

> They say that the substances of everything consist in that which is of its
> own proper habit, and which cannot be altered in any way. This is the
> nature that has assigned substance to variable motion. They call that
> the first immutable nature of one and the same substance [*illam primam
> inmutabilem naturam unius eiusdemque substantiae vocant*]. And there
> is another [*hanc vero alterius*], which, clearly following after that first
> immutable [nature], is a second, which without doubt concerns unity and
> duality, and this number, following after one, has been turned into another number.[86]

Natura eiusdem (μονάς) has absolute, objective, temporal and qualitative priority over *natura alterius* (δυάς). Creation as a whole is a "harmonic merging" of both in *amicitia*.[87]

De institutione arithmetica also designates the numbers one through four as the generators of the series of numbers developing out of the *unum principium*. In accord with the Pythagorean-Greek and Judeo-Christian traditions, the sum of these numbers, ten, is considered the perfect number. To the numbers one through four correspond the primary arithmetic proportions 1:1, 1:2, 2:3, 3:4, summed up in the "harmonic" proportion 6:8:9:12. This constitutes Creation as harmony and an "ordered whole." It is not for nothing that here Boethius already refers to music:

> It remains now to discuss the greatest and perfect harmony [*maxima per-fectaque harmonia*] which, comprised of three intervals, has great power in the orderly structure of musical compositions, and in speculation about questions concerning nature [*in speculatione naturalium quaestionum*]. Nothing more perfect in medial proportions of this sort has been found which, produced in three intervals, contributes to the nature and substance of a most perfect body.[88]

De institutione arithmetica derives from the distinction of *naturae* elementary classes of numbers and a classification of elementary geometrical forms. Uneven numbers and equilateral geometrical figures exhibit the *natura eiusdem* of identity, while even numbers and figures *parte altera longiores* exhibit the *natura alterius* of duality and inequality:

> Therefore, since it is the nature of tetragons that they arise out of odd numbers, and are participants in unity, that is, of its immutable substance, they are equal to all their parts, because angles to angles, sides to sides, and length to length are equal. It must be said that numbers are participants in this kind of nature and of immutable substance [*numeros eiusdem naturae atque inmutabilis substantiae participes*], and that those numbers that equality creates longer in one part, are of another substance [*alterius dicimus esse substantiae*].[89]

Despite the workings of two *naturae*, Creation is considered a "harmonic whole." Thus in the numerical order it must be possible to designate a principle that relates each of the groups of numbers and figures to each other and puts them into an all-inclusive order: "Therefore, although they are contrary, nevertheless they are mixed together in a sort of friendship and kinship [*amicitiam cognationemque*], and they produce one body of number out of the idea and governance of that unity."[90] The derivation of the principle begins with quadratic numbers. *Natura eiusdem* is inherent in them because they can be constructed by adding up the quantity of uneven numbers that corresponds to the square, counted from the number one as the *principium numerorum*: $1+3=4=2^2$; $1+3+5=9=3^2$; $1+3+5+7=16=4^2$, and so on. As even or equal numbers, they are at the same time elements of the dyadic series. The squares and right-angled figures *partes altera longiores* are consequently considered ontologically prior, since they—the following connection is crucial—can be seen as the result of the merging of series following from the opposite principles: from the principle of identity follow the quadratic figures (2×2, 3×3, 4×4, etc.), the quadratic numbers (4, 9, 16, etc.), and equal proportions (2/2, 3/3, 4/4, etc.); from the principle of alterity the figures *per altera longiores* (1×2, 2×3, 3×4), even numbers that are not quadratic numbers (2; 6; 12), unequal proportions (1/2, 2/3, 3/4, etc.). From the relating and simplification of the series developed out of the principles of identity and alterity, beginning with the numbers for unity (1) and duality (2), follow the primary proportions, the relationships that tradition called *proportio dupla, sesquialtera, sesquitertia*, and so on (diagram 2):[91]

$$\left.\begin{cases} 1 \quad 4 \quad 9 \quad 16 \\ \qquad\qquad\qquad [\ldots] \\ 2 \quad 6 \quad 12 \quad 20 \end{cases}\right\} = 1/2;\ 2/3;\ 3/4;\ 4/5;\ [\ldots]$$

The same series is produced in inverted form if the arithmetic presentation of quadratics and right-angled *partes altera longiores* are related to one another (diagram 3):

$$\left.\begin{cases} 4 \quad 9 \quad 16 \quad 25 \\ \qquad\qquad\qquad [\ldots] \\ 2 \quad 6 \quad 12 \quad 20 \end{cases}\right\} = 2/1;\ 3/2;\ 4/3;\ 5/4;\ [\ldots]$$

By ordering the constructed rational numbers according to their amount, the two series can be brought together in a sequence. Here the numbers that correspond to the area of the quadratics alternate with the numbers that correspond to the area of nonequilateral rectangles: 1, 2, 4, 9, 12, 16, 20, etc. If these are ordered in regular 3-tuples the result is a series of regular proportions. Each element of this series can be again reduced to elementary proportions constructed from the numbers 1 to 4, with the value of 1 (diagrams 4.1, 4.2, 4.3):

$$\begin{cases} 1 \\ 2 \\ 4 \end{cases} = 1/2 : 2/4 = 1 \qquad \begin{cases} 4 \\ 6 \\ 9 \end{cases} = 4/6 : 6/9 = 1 \qquad \begin{cases} 9 \\ 12 \\ 16 \end{cases} = 9/12 : 12/16 = 1$$

These proportions are not specific elements in the numerical order, but rather elements in the numerical order as such, the result of putting the original series in regular relationships, a "mixture" of *natura eiusdem* and *natura alterius,* of identity and difference, unity and plurality, immobility and mobility. Correspondingly, "every ratio of forms arises from squares and figures longer on one side."[92] *Amicitia* is the principle of this relation, whose ontological quality is underscored: "thus we see a certain consensus of those numbers and a friendship in producing other parts of numbers, so that not without reason in this does it seem that *in all things* [*in omnibus rebus*] the nature of things has drawn on the type of number [*a numeri specie natura rerum sumpsisse videatur*]."[93]

The all-inclusive order that governs existence can consequently be conceived as an order of proportions. It is the essence of proportion (*proportionalitas*) that it can bring together in *concordia* constituents of this world that are contrary qua *natura* and yet similar qua numerosity and in their relation to the Creator, as emanations of the transcendent One. As indicated in our preface, Boethius's arithmetical discourse is an "analogical discourse" par excellence; *proportio* stands for Greek ἀναλογία (ἀνὰ λόγον, "according to the relationship"):

> Therefore, proportionality is the adoption and collection [*adsumptio ad unum atque collectio*] into one of twos or threes or any ratios whatever. Let us define it in a common way: proportionality is a similar relationship existing between two or more ratios, even if they have been composed not of the same but of different quantities. [. . .] Proportion is a certain relationship of two terms to one another, a kind of cohesion [*continentia*], as it were. The accommodation of these things brings about something that is proportional. Proportionality arises out of joined ratios.[94]

The ἀναλογίαι *convenientia, aemulatio, analogia,* and *sympathia* classified by Foucault[95] presuppose the ontological foundation that the Christian order of discourse acquired by colonizing the Neoplatonic number ontology. Conceiving the signified-signifier relations qua "similarity," using etymology as a means to reconstruct "original," nonarbitrary signified-signifier relations is pertinent only on this condition and only at the next step.[96]

As examples of the manifestations of the "proportional" order produced from the "same" and the "different," Boethius mentions, like Augustine, the syllables in the word and the tones in the harmonic interval:

> [Let us examine] the elements of things out of which [that is, odd and even] all things are composed, and into whose dissolution all things are

turned again. The elements of a speaking voice are the letters (from them comes the progressive linking of syllables, which is brought back to its end in the same terms). Similarly, sound possesses the same power in music.[97]

Moreover, in the textbook on arithmetic Boethius demonstrates not only the anagogic but also the ethical implications of his number theory. Anyone who clings to the *multitude* of numbers, yields to *pravitas humana*, becomes a slave of the many, overlooks the *order* of numbers that proceeds from the One, refers to it, and leads to it: "Human error separates what is by nature simple and undivided, and converts it from the true and perfect into the false and imperfect."[98] The *Consolatio philosophiae* explains the argument: III.9 tells of the striving for power, fame, honor, or joy, which must fail so long as it lacks the insight that all the worldly goods for which we strive are based on a single *substantia* that is the one and only worthwhile goal. The corresponding terminology marks the complementarity of the concepts: "Human baseness divides what is one and simple by nature, and while attempting to obtain a part of a thing that has no parts, it gets neither a part, which is nothing, nor the thing itself, which it least desires."[99] A person who becomes a slave of the worldly many fails to recognize that the One created the many. The path to this insight is shown by arithmetic, through the proof of the general reducibility of all numbers to the One as the *unum principium* of the "proportional" *ordo entium*. It is no accident that this idea aroused the interest of the Scholastics more than any other part of the work. The most famous commentary, *Scholium ad Boethii Arithmeticam*[100] by Gerbert of Aurillac (c. 950–1003) was known as the *saltus Gerberti* and remained a standard reference until the late Middle Ages.

The conceptual relationship between *De institutione arithmetica* and *De institutione musica* is so close that the two treatises can be seen as a single work.[101] The textbook on arithmetic concludes with an attempt to construct a classification of proportions, that is, an inventory of proportionalities (diagram 5).

To that end Boethius surveys his most important authorities—the Pythagoreans, Plato, Aristotle—and hits upon the familiar triad that had already been introduced by Archytas of Tarentum: "It is admitted and known by the ancients that in the philosophy of Pythagoras, or Plato, or Aristotle there were three ways to knowledge: arithmetic, geometry and harmonics."[102] According to Boethius, further, "nameless" proportionalities were added until finally ten were named, out of respect for the Pythagorean esteem for the number ten.[103] After each of these proportionalities has been discussed

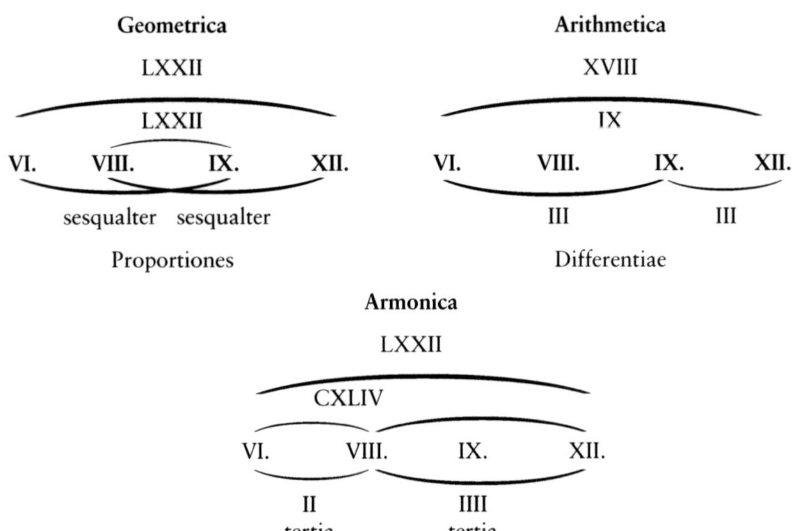

Geometric, arithmetic, and harmonic *proportionalitas* according to *De institutione arithmetica* II.54, p. 172

briefly once again, four charts conclude *De institutione arithmetica*. First, a schematic representation of the three proportionalities corresponding to the explanation given by Archytas. The fourth chart already includes the object of the next textbook: a schematic representation of the consonants proceeding from the "harmonic" proportion 6:8:9:12, including the Greek and Latin designations of the intervals (diagram 6).

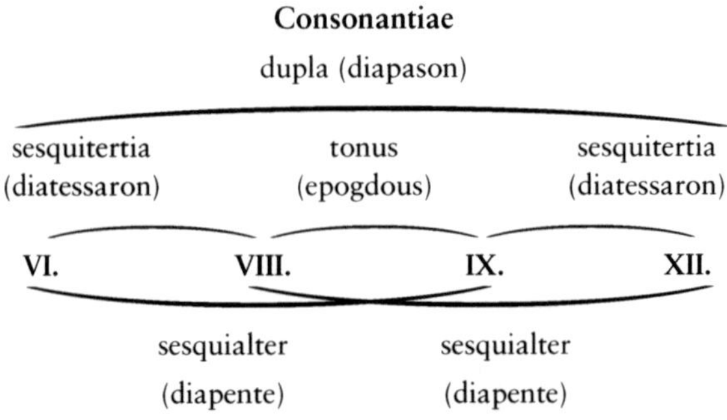

Consonant intervals according to *De Institutione arithmetica* II.54, p. 172

The relation between the two charts is crucial for our investigation. First of all, "consonance" is a technical term in arithmetic. "Consonance" can be said to exist wherever the corresponding numerical relationships are present—independently of whether the statement refers to acoustic or other phenomena. The concept of consonance in speculative music theory is initially conceived purely arithmetically. It potentially refers to *any* referent, so long as it is, as a "discrete" or "discontinuous" multitude, quantifiable.

The number of extant manuscripts, more than two hundred, indicates the importance and influence of the *Institutio arithmetica*.[104] Ample glosses testify to the widespread use of the texts in teaching and study.[105] The work's influence is clear wherever its author appears as a personification of *arithmetica*—for instance, as Émile Mâle suggested, on the west portal of the Chartres cathedral, or still in 1503 in Gregorius Reisch's *Margarita philosophica*.[106] The significance of the *Institutio arithmetica* for teaching and study survived the important transformations and further developments of arithmetic. Bede and Alcuin, Hrabanus Maurus (c. 780–856), and the "computist" Helpericus (ninth century) owe their arithmetical knowledge to Boethius's work and develop its influence; we have already mentioned Gerbert of Aurillac's *Scholium ad Boethii Arithmeticam*. The introduction of Arabic mathematics in the eleventh and twelfth centuries made supplements indispensable, but the work remained unchallenged as a textbook down into the thirteenth century. Thus prominent thinkers such as Alexander Neckam, Albert the Great, Thomas Aquinas, Bonaventure, Roger Bacon, and Robert Grosseteste in particular relied on Boethius's authority when dealing with mathematical questions: "[F]or the teaching of the first of the quadrivial arithmetic, the Boethian *De Institutione Arithmetica* appears to have maintained its position as a basic text, and this was the case despite the fact that in the thirteenth century there were available for the study of arithmetic, in its various practical as well as other aspects, a wealth of materials both old and new."[107] A glance at the material reveals the reasons for this: the *Algorismus* of Johannes de Sacrobosco (c. 1195–1256), which replaced *De institutione arithmetica* as the most widespread textbook and after its first printing in 1488 remained in use until the end of the sixteenth century,[108] presented itself as a simplified summary and cautious supplement to Boethius's text, especially regarding the use of Arab numerals. The latter greatly simplified practical calculation, but left the conception of the function of arithmetic in the disciplinary canon untouched. The orientation of the quadrivium as an *itinerarium mentis ad Deum*, the distinction of the quadrivial disciplines as propaedeutics to philosophy were retained, as is shown by an anonymous commentary on Johannes de Sacrobosco's *Tractatus de Sphaera* (c. 1230) that is based on Boethius:

Note that among all the disciplines of the quadrivium those are especially
to be sought that best lead to wisdom. Boethius made this clear in the first
book of his Arithmetic, where he says that there are four parts that reveal
themselves, that is, the quadrivium, because lacking them one cannot find
the truth, and without contemplation on them, one cannot acquire the
contemplation of truth [*non potest habere speculationem veritatis*]. And
elsewhere he says. "No one is ready for philosophy who is ignorant of
these four disciplines."[109]

The "analogical" orientation of the complex and the "holistic" claim
of Boethian arithmology, which is crucial for the continuity of music
theory, largely remain intact down to the late Middle Ages. Examples
could be multiplied. Michael Masi has summarized the situation this way:
"[T]he Boethian mathematics enjoyed an extraordinary increase in popu-
larity and influence between 1200 and 1600."[110] Such findings feed the previously mentioned doubts regarding the nature of the ruptures with which
the research summarized in part I operates. In chapters seven to nine, our
presentation of the developments in the thirteenth, fourteenth, and fifteenth
centuries will confirm these doubts: in the discourse of music theory, we
cannot speak of a general and complete dissolution of the foundations of
late antique music theory in the wake of the reception of Aristotle.

De institutione musica

The treatise *De institutione musica* was composed immediately after the
textbook on arithmetic. As Calvin S. Bowers's study of the sources has
shown, it is primarily a compilation and is "wholly Pythagorean."[111] The
outline of the appropriated texts remains largely recognizable: Books I to IV
follow Nicomachus of Gerasa, Book V, on consonance and the appreciation
of consonance, the only one completed among what appear to have been
three additional books on Nicomachus, follows Ptolemy.[112] Its fidelity to its
sources makes the *Institutio musica* the most important mediation between
the music theory of pagan Antiquity and Late Antiquity, on the one hand,
and the Christian Middle Ages on the other.[113]

Augustine dealt with the number ontology tradition primarily in the interest of colonizing it and putting it in the service of Christian theology.
Boethius's *Institutio musica* develops the Pythagorean tradition's concept
of music not only on sounder arithmetic bases, but also in direct connection with the historical presuppositions of this concept. *Musica harmonica*
was suited for this: since the fourth century BCE, the arithmetic description
of the symphonic intervals, the fourth (3/4), the fifth (2/3), and the octave

(1/2) had been seen as the achievement of Pythagoras of Samos. It is the historical and systematic starting point for Pythagorean doctrine.[114] What is tradition-founding and central for the understanding of the theory is not the description itself, but rather the fact that all the intervals mentioned can be derived from the "harmonic" proportion 6:8:9:12. We have already examined its construction in *De institutione arithmetica* from the first four natural numbers. The proportion includes the two possibilities of dividing the octave (6/12 = 1/2) into the fourth (6/8 = 3/4) and the fifth (8/12 = 2/3), as well as the difference between them, the whole tone (8/9). Nicomachus of Gerasa calls them the "first" *tetraktys* preceding even the number series one to four, the "source of consonances" (diagram 7):[115]

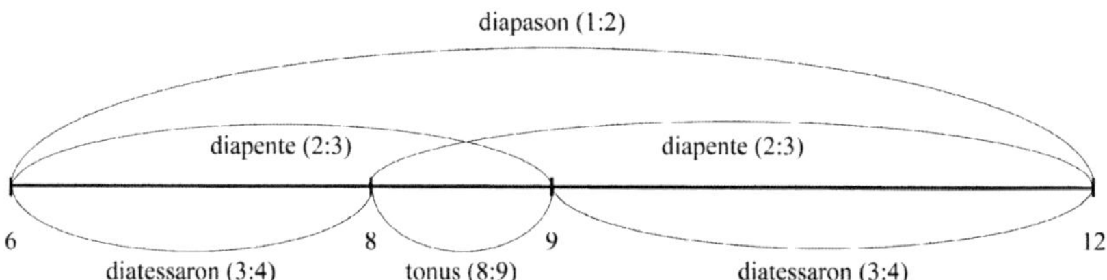

The symphonic intervals, the framing intervals of Greek harmonics, can be completed to form a heptatonic scale using the relative tones gained by further division of the symphonic intervals.[116] There are two possible ways of deriving the relative tones of each scale, each of them historically chosen by one of the early Pythagorean schools.[117] The "acousmatics" shortened the string of the monochord by ear until the desired tone was heard. The result could be determined by measuring the length of the string. This inductive procedure made it possible to match rational numbers with the harmonic intervals only for the framework tones. In opposition to the latter was the postulate of the "mathematicians," that the proportions that could be derived from the first *tetraktys* also had to make possible the deduction of the relative tones: if each interval corresponds to a fraction of two positive natural numbers that can ultimately be simplified to a fraction of the form $(n+1)/n$, then the relative tones of the scale can be derived by a dichotomic division of the framing intervals: as intervals lying as close as possible to the precise division of the framing tones relative to the *tetraktys*. The result is a "dichotomic pyramid" that is still presented in Nicomachus of Gerasa's brief Ἐγχειρίδιον, his Introduction to Harmonics (diagram 8).

Not all the intervals determined in this way are used in the practical performance of music. However, this does not limit the validity of the proce-

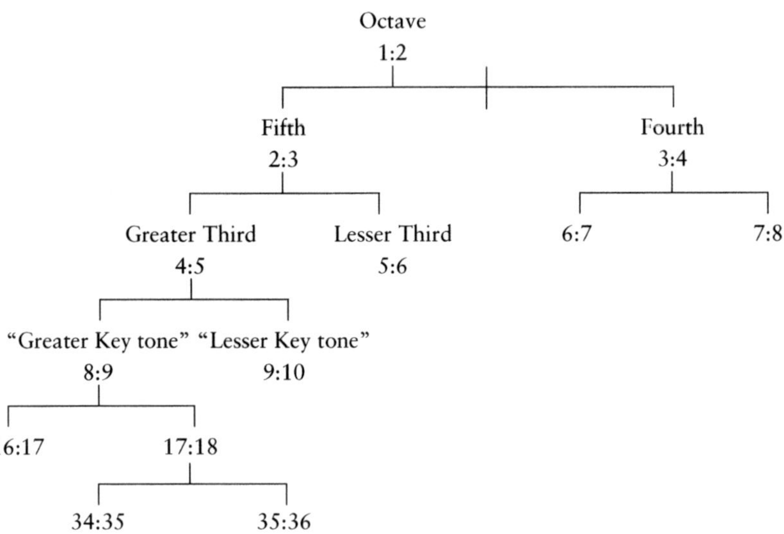

dure. From the musician's point of view, the choice of certain relative tones founds the *genos* of the scale produced; from the mathematician's point of view, this choice is contingent: the dichotomic division can be repeated *ad infinitum.* It is interrupted only by a *convention of use*—and can correspondingly be resumed later on, for instance, in the fourteenth century, when Philippe de Vitry was concerned about the interest in new *genera*.[118]

For the differentiation of Pythagorean doctrine and its significance for the history of science in general and in music theory in particular, it is crucial that this progression, which can be extended linearly, no longer needs to be connected back to the monochord and thus to sense experience: its elements can be acquired noetically. The fractions produced from the *tetraktys,* which correspond to the four framing intervals, constitute an enumerable, infinite series (*stoichos*): 1/2, 2/3, 3/4, 4/5, etc. Terminological studies, for instance those carried out by Hermann Koller and Johannes Lohmann, have suggested that we should see in the inductive and deductive methods of philosophy analogical constructions that correspond to the "acousmatic" and the "mathematical" models for deriving the relative tones of the scale:

> This procedure of acoustic deduction very strongly influenced the whole philosophical method of the sophists and especially of Plato. Following the Pythagorean mathematicians, they created the dichotomy of linguistic concepts and constructed the basic concepts of logic, for as its name

indicates, *logikè techné* is first of all the "art of determining the *logoi*," numerical relationships. Thus the first work that dealt with *logikè techné* or canon (Democritus) was entitled "The Doctrine of Relationships or Canon" (monochord). But the acousmatic, empirical orientation also had an effect on the incipient science, because the inductive procedure was guided precisely by the acoustic method, in which the finger was moved along the bridge of the monochord until the tone sought was determined by ear, whereupon the value was measured. The terminology of the inductive procedure clearly shows that it was determined in the acousmatic's workshop. Both these procedures used by the Pythagoreans served as models for the construction of other sciences in the second half of the fifth century BCE. For the Greeks, rationality was first of all numerosity.[119]

The multiplicity of the hypotheses regarding the origin of these methods suggests that we should be cautious in evaluating Koller's wide-ranging theses, but one must grant a high degree of plausibility to the philologically precise reconstructions that Koller and Lohmann have presented.[120] Plato, for instance, proves the connection. The much commented-upon methodological reflection in *Philebus* 16b–20a[121] understands the arithmetic description of a rhythmic-metrical phenomenon as paradigmatic for the "rational" conception of a phenomenon as such:

> But when you have grasped, my dear friend, the number and nature of the intervals formed by high pitch and low pitch in sound, and the notes that bound those intervals, and all the systems of notes that result from them, the systems which we have learned, conformably to the teaching of the men of old days who discerned them, to call "scales," and when, further, you have grasped certain corresponding features of the performer's bodily movements, features that must, so we are told, be numerically determined and be called "figures" and "measures," bearing in mind all the time that this is always the right way to deal with the one-and-many problem—only then, when you have grasped all this, have you gained real understanding, and whatever be the "one" that you have selected for investigating, that is the way to get insight about it.[122]

For a tradition reaching from the Pythagoreans through Plato down to late antiquity, this heuristics conceived as the "vision" of the numerical harmonic foundations of the cosmos coincides with "science" as such. The young Augustine "colonized" it for Christian doctrine by equating *mens divina* and *mundus intelligibilis*. Whether the procedure became, in the form that Philolaus gave it, the foundation for an "investigative logic for natural science" that "first made a rational domination of the world possible at all"[123] must remain undecided here. However, it is certain that if Cicero's *Tusculanes*,[124] like Boethius's *De institutione arithmetica*[125] and *De institutione musica*,[126] trace philosophy back to Pythagoras, this method is seen as paradigmatically philosophical. Both follow Plato's *Laws*:

> No son of man will ever come to a settled fear of God until he has grasped the two truths we are now affirming, the soul's dateless anteriority to all things generable, her immortality and sovereignty over the world of bodies, and moreover that presence among the heavenly bodies of a mind of all things of which we have spoken so often already. He must also possess the requisite preliminary sciences, perceive the links which connect them with music, and apply his knowledge meetly to his moral and legal behavior, [. . .].[127]

This background shows precisely what claim is made when dialectic is called, as it repeatedly is in Plato's work, the "most important art of the muses."[128] First of all, the unification of arithmetic, geometry, stereometry, and astronomy as mathematical sciences by recourse to theoretical elements that are taken from the work on the monochord, and then the projection of the "harmonic" order of the proportions as "cosmos" already demonstrable in the earliest Pythagorean speculation and developed out of the *tetraktys*, create the foundation for measuring the *ordo entium* in accord with the model of the noetically produced progression.[129] Aristotle, though critical of Pythagorean number theory, also adhered to this view.[130] The proposition, handed down in Aristotle's *Metaphysics* as a Pythagorean doctrine, that "the measure is always homogeneous with the thing measured,"[131] includes the subject of knowledge and the object of knowledge in a rational—that is, numerical—continuum generated by the aforementioned progression. The proportions summed up in the first *tetraktys* constitute the cosmos itself and are at the same time axioms of its deductive reconstruction. The proportions underlying consonant intervals are the "foundations of music and thus of the world itself in the Pythagorean sense."[132]

Despite Platonism's and Christianity's depreciation of this world, which is subject to change, the dependency of the whole theory on musical acoustics lends the concept a significant advantage in clearness and plausibility. To the proportions as the basal elements of the numerical-harmonic order corresponds, with the symphonic interval, a form perceptible by the senses. The arithmetically based abstract "science" and the simplest music represent a relation of mutual confirmation that provides the latter with relevance, the former with increased plausibility and clarity.

It was not for nothing that not only metrics, rhythmics, and harmonics, but also other arts sought early on to associate themselves with this science. In the second half of the fifth century BCE, Polykleitos was the first to compose a work on the fine arts entitled *Kanon* based on the procedure acquired from the monochord. It took as its starting point the measures derived from the body to determine the regular proportions of the human frame and relate them to the numerical-harmonic order of the cosmos.[133] This concept gained its widest influence through the textbook on architecture put together by Marcus Vitruvius Pollio (first century BCE),[134] which was never forgotten during the Middle Ages and was also cited in music-theory contexts.[135] However, it was in music theory that the Pythagorean doctrine remained most transparent with regard to its historical sources, most true to them, and most decisive for further developments. Boethius put it into the form that remained standard for over a thousand years.

Following Augustine and in accord with *multitudo ad aliquid* defined as the object of music as a quadrivial science, Boethius defines acoustic phenomena as *motus:*[136] Sound presupposes the vibration of the air that carries it to the ear.[137] Augustine develops *musica rhythmica* from the length of syllables. For the harmonics discussed by Boethius, the rapidity of the vibration or frequency, to be defined in terms of *tarditas* and *velocitas,* is an existent that is numerical in a comparable way.[138] Here too we can say: whatever displays *numerositas* is numerical *by nature* and potentially transparent with respect to the numerical order.

Two *different* tones generate an interval that can be consonant or dissonant.[139] Thus in music, "consonance is a mixture of high and low sound [*acuti soni gravisque mixtura*] falling agreeably and uniformly [*suaviter uniformiterque*] on the ears."[140] Following the model of the monochord, each interval can be related to a numerical value that corresponds to the quotient of the frequency of the tones constituting the interval. An interval is consonant or sounds *suavis* when the *proportio* is derived from the "first" *tetraktys* 6:8:9:12 and can hence be "reduced" to *aequalitas* and *unum:* "For consonance is the concord of voices different from one another but brought together into one [*dissimilium inter se vocum in unum redacta concordia*]."[141] For this too holds: "Just as unity is the origin of plurality and number [*unitas pluralitatis numerique principium*], so equality is the origin of proportions [*ita aequalitas proportionum*]."[142] Hearing in the consonance of tones of unequal pitches the *proportiones* manifested as *consonantiae* is actually perceiving the sensible realization of the "inseparable *unity* through which both numbers are constituted."[143] In accord with the speculative orientation of Boethius's textbook, the object of *musica scientia* is determined not as pleasant melody or euphonious harmony per se, but rather as the "transparency" of the *proportiones* with respect to this unity. Its goal is the understanding of a given interval structure: "Just as in seeing it is not enough for learned men to see colors and forms, unless they investigate also what their nature [*proprietas*] is, so it is not enough for songs [*cantilenis musicis*] to be enjoyed unless we also learn the ratio of voices by which they have been brought together [*nisi etiam quali inter se conjunctae sint vocum proportione discatur*]."[144] This sentence should be read as the explanation of the place of music in the educational program of quadrivial studies.[145] For Boethius, only someone who devotes himself to *musica*, not for the sake of concrete works, but rather for that of the vision of the *aeternae rationes* is a true *musicus*: "That person is a musician [*musicus*] who with due reason claims knowledge of singing not in service to performance but by command of speculation [*non servitio operis sed imperio speculationis*]."[146]

The goal of the *Institutio musica* is to derive from arithmetic the whole subject matter of *musica harmonica*. An exhaustive examination of the text would take us too far away from the context of our investigation. However, every limitation to an "excerpt" presupposes the modular nature of a theory that includes unity, systematic closure, and the necessity of its conceptual relationships among its most essential characteristics. Considering the degree of consistency and rigor of the theory, separating and differentiating individual parts must be artificial and cannot do justice to the object. The remedy seems to be to follow the historical material not only conceptually, but also in terms of representation. Speculative music theory in the Pythagorean tradition takes as its starting point structural homologies between the "musical" work and the cosmos. The structural homology indicates a common ground in Being: both the interval structure of a melody and the order of Creation stand in a relationship of subordination to the ideal numerical order *in mente divina*, a relationship that must be specified in each case. Augustine's theory of music had attached this model of a multilevel cosmos to the theological concept of order. In contrast, Boethius's *De institutione musica* reconstructs the multilevel model of the cosmos as a genuinely music-theoretical, tripartite classification that underscores the possibility of perceiving through the senses the one numerical order in the multiplicity of its manifestations.

Boethius distinguishes three *genera musicae* that are bound together by *similitudo* and organized hierarchically according to their individual fullness of being and *perfectio*: "There are three kinds of music. The first concerns the world [*prima quidem mundana est*], the second concerns humans [*secunda vero humana*], and the third has been established in certain instruments [*tertia, quae in quibusdam constituta est instrumentis*]."[147] Although conceptual analogies can be found earlier, especially in Aristides Quintilianus,[148] the classification of *musica* into *mundana, humana,* and *instrumentalis* must be attributed to the Greek glosses in the sources used by Boethius or to Boethius himself.[149] The triad classifies the perceptible manifestations of an order that is ontologically prior and eternal, intelligible, numerical-harmonic, proportional-relational, and to that extent "musical." None of the *musicae,* not even *musica mundana,* is the ideal "musical" order itself: "In this classification, it is a question only of the *concrete forms* most characteristic of *harmony as such.*"[150]

The elaborations concerning the *genera,* which are on the whole brief, are devoted primarily to *musica mundana.* Before Boethius, a similar denomination is found in Macrobius[151] and in Favonius Eulogius,[152] while Aristides Quintilianus describes the *genus* as ἁρμονία τοῦ κόσμου.[153] *Musica mundana* includes the revolutions of the stars, the "harmonic" construction of the elements and cyclical natural phenomena, such as the course of the seasons: "To begin, the first kind of music, the one concerned with the world [*quae est mundana*], is to be sought particularly in those things that are seen in the sky, in the conjuncture of elements, or in the variety of the seasons."[154] Contrary to what might be expected, *musica mundana* is believed to possess acoustic reality: The revolution of the stars produces a sound that is not heard only because its omnipresence has dulled our hearing.[155]

The category of *musica mundana* is essential for the emphasis on clarity in Boethius's music theory to which we have referred. Its broadening in medieval treatises on music to include other cyclical natural phenomena, for instance the tides, underscores the intuitiveness of the concept. It combines the theological hypothesis of an *ordo entium* constituted by numbers with the experiential reality of agrarian-oriented societies and subjects this reality to a "musical" and as such consequently theocentric interpretation.

Directly related to *musica mundana* is *musica instrumentalis,* which is discussed by Aristides Quintilianus as ἁρμονία ἐν ὀργάνοις.[156] The concept has been the subject of controversial debates. Fritz Reckow polemically opposed older accounts that sought to see *musica instrumentalis* primarily as factually audible music. The brief phrase "quae in quibusdam constituta est instrumentis" ("which has been established in certain instruments")[157] is supposed to "be taken seriously" as referring to "a *musica*" that is "inherent" in specific instruments, firmly established, "available."[158] There is much to be said for the notion that the concept of *musica instrumentalis* includes both. Thus the ethical relevance of *musica instrumentalis,* which remains to be discussed, presupposes a sound that can be heard and affect the mind. In contrast, Boethius's explanation of the individual *musicae*'s relationships of similarity using the examples of the tones of the scale and the construction of instruments can be read in accord with Reckow: The seven tones of the scale correspond to the *ordo coelestis*, the paths of the heavenly bodies from Saturn to the moon;[159] Terpander's seven-sided lyre reproduces this connection,[160] and Mercury, who constructed the first instrument, had put four strings on his lute in accord with the four elements.[161] The symbolic relations do not replace the foundation of the doctrine in Pythagorean-Neoplatonic number ontology, but complement it. The significance of *musica instrumentalis* is derived exclusively from such analogical structures, whether these are simple symbolic relations of the kind indicated or based on the insight that in the concrete work of music, the numerical-harmonic constituents of the *ordo entium* become manifest.[162] Since every "musical" work displays specific *numerositates*, and every manifest *numerositas* presupposes the development of the number series out of the distinction between *natura eiusdem* and *natura alterius*, all melodic and harmonic intervals are perceptible concrete forms of the single Creation as the "harmonic" coincidence of both *naturae*:

> A clear, simple, perfect, fundamental melody is constituted by a series of sounds, some of which, being self-identical, repeat one another, while others follow one another in the regular intervals of the octave, the fifth, and the fourth. Thus the two sounds of the octave constitute a delectable harmony because one represents unity, the other duality; the former is defined by itself, the latter inaugurates an infinite series; the latter reminds us of something male, stable, permanent, while the latter has a feminine, fluent, changing character. But both of them are related to one another in a beautiful whole that constitutes a unity, thanks to the simplest proportion.[163]

In a form that is easy to grasp, transparent, and spontaneously available to the senses, the concrete work makes manifest the ordered structure of Creation discernible in the law of the numerical progression. We must repeatedly emphasize the ontological priority of numbers and their relationships. The work of music does not make the order of Creation manifest when or because it is "musical" in nature. Rather, *it is only because it makes the order of Creation manifest that the concrete work is music at all.*

With respect to this discovery of the formalistic and "intellectualistic" character of the whole scheme de Bruyne has emphasized that:

> Boethius's aesthetics has a mathematical, scientific, positivist appearance. Whereas Theon of Smyrna and Nicomachus of Gerasa, among the pagans, and Saint Augustine and other Church Fathers emphasize the alle-

gorical significance of numbers and proportions, Boethius attends only to
their mathematical and formal properties. Along with Vitruvius, he is the
main theoretician of pure formalism, an admirer of clear, simple, harmonious structure, the first apologist of "symphonic" beauty."[164]

Nonetheless, de Bruyne underestimates the value that Boethius assigns
throughout to the perceptible concrete forms of the numerical-harmonic
order. Likewise, his theory of music consequently argues arithmetically *and*
consistently from the evidence of the perceptible, insofar as the reference
to the plenitude of the manifestations of the numerical-harmonic order
must not interrupt the arithmetically prepared argumentation. The point
of the whole theory is that analogical discourse levels out differences to arrive at a kind of "abstract"/clear-concrete continuum that is hierarchically
differentiated but uninterrupted. The order of ideal numbers, the *musica
mundana*, and the concrete works of *musica instrumentalis* constitute a
closed and ordered system of relationships of (imperfect) imitation. The
trust in the power of discourse characteristic of Boethius's theory, and the
consequent reliance on phenomena in the conviction that they are reduc-
ible to the *unum principium*, provides scope and power for the "holistic"
claim of Boethian music theory. The consequent emphasis on the sensible
manifestations of the numerical-harmonic order even beyond human works
provides the theory, if not with increased theoretical pithiness, at least with
an increased plausibility, clarity, and power to discursively shape the world.

In accord with its ontological formulation, Boethius's theory is necessarily totalizing and unifying. Here as well truth and beauty coincide, and
as "aesthetic experience" and "knowledge of the truth" cannot plausibly
be separated. Here, too, each of these activities tending to lead to concern
with the work for its own sake drifts toward sinful deviancy insofar as it
interrupts the ascent from the created world to the vision of the Creator.

Boethius's theory also considers the "musical" work anagogically relevant, and his theory also demands the devaluation of the artist's work that
results from the merger of Neoplatonic ontology and the doctrine of creation as the price to be paid for this anagogical relevance. Accordingly, the
true *musicus* is sharply distinguished from practitioners. The latter practice
music as an art for the sake of concrete works, contingent manifestations of
the ideal numerical-harmonic order. The former engages in music as *scientia*
and has in view order itself, as necessary and eternal:

> That person is a musician who with due reason claims knowledge of
> singing not in service to the performance but by command of speculation
> [*non servitio operis sed imperio speculationis*]. We see this in constructing

buildings and waging wars, notably in the opposing terms of the vocabulary for these activities. For buildings are inscribed with and triumphs preceded by the names of those by whose command and reason they were ordained, not of those by whose labor and service they were completed. Therefore, there are three kinds of people engaged in musical art. One is concerned with instruments [*quod instrumentis agitur*], the second composes songs [*fingit carmina*], and the third judges instrumental performance and song [*instrumentorum opus carmenque diiudicat*].[165]

Among the practitioners Boethius explicitly mentions not only instrumentalists and critics but also poets, and provides a systematic place in *musica instrumentalis* for the *carmina*. Augustine had discussed verse in detail; Boethius's textbook accordingly limits itself to the place of poetry and poets in the classification of the *musicae*. The poet creates, we still read, less on a solid theoretical foundation than out of "natural instinct": "The second category of those who concern themselves with music is that of the poets, who are led to music not so much by speculation and reason, but by some natural instinct [*quod non potius speculatione ac ratione, quam naturali quodam instinctu fertur ad carmen*]."[166] The argument is also found in Augustine.

Boethius does not explicitly state which kind of knowledge the poet uses "out of natural instinct." The theoretical context identifies "consonant proportions" as the constituents and common feature of everything "musical"—proportions that can be derived from the *tetraktys*. In *musica harmonica* they are manifest in the "harmonic" consonance of tones. Starting from the same arithmetic foundations, in *De musica* Augustine reconstructs metrics on the basis of the *tetraktys*. Whereas Boethius sees in *musica harmonica* a "consonance," Augustine sees in it a relationality characterized by *aequalitas* and *similitudo*. In verse, in *musica rhythmica*, the repetition of isorhythmic units and a determined redundancy or equivalence corresponds to the sequencing of consonant melodic or harmonic intervals in *musica harmonica*. These principles are the ones that the practitioners of a given kind of *musica* use "out of natural instinct": "natural musicality" in *musica harmonica*, "a sense of form"[167] in verse.

Consonance and the appreciation of consonance provide the transition to the third component of Boethius's triad, *musica humana*, which is defined in Aristides Quintilianus as ἁρμονία τῆς ψυχῆς.[168] It designates, borrowing a word from Gerbert of Aurillac, the "sound of the spheres in the microcosm": the "harmonic" *coaptatio* or *temperatio*, so far as possible, of parts that are in themselves disparate. The human being, as a being composed of body and soul, is conceived as "relational in himself." The concept of the "proportional" coincidence of his aptitudes and capacities constitutes the human being as a whole and gives the musical concept of *harmonia* ethical relevance. Body and soul conform "musically," and so do individual *facultates* of the soul, such as *sensibilia* and the rational abilities, the organs and the elements, for instance in metabolism, and finally the members of the body:

> What mixes that incorporeal liveliness of reason with the body, if not some precise joining together [*coaptatio*], and combination, as it were, of low and high pitches bringing about nearly one consonance [*consonantiam*]? What but this unites the parts of the soul itself, wherein, as it pleased Aristotle, the rational has been united to the irrational? What combines the elements of the body, or keeps the parts of the body together with unwavering unity?[169]

The concept as a whole may have been borrowed from Calcidius's commentary on the *Timaeus*.[170] Boethius sees the hypotheses regarding the nature of the *corpus*, the *anima*, and their relationship to each other as the foundation, qua *similitudo*, for the psyche's susceptibility to music. *Musica mundana, instrumentalis*, and the human being must all be similarly constituted, so that the effect of music on human beings is to be explained as "sympathetic": "I have said these things so that there can be no doubt that the condition of our soul and body appears to be established by the very proportions [*proportionibus*] by which a later discussion will show that harmonic modulations [*armonicas modulations*] are joined together and united."[171] In this way the ancient pagan doctrine of *ethos*[172] and the ethical emphasis of the theory as a whole can be integrated and justified.

Thus my qualification of Boethius's music theory as "holistic" (in the literal, etymological sense of the term) becomes clear: the triad *musica mundana/humana/instrumentalis* binds the cosmos, human beings, and the concrete manifestations of the relational, "rational," and numerical-harmonic order together in a continuum. This continuum can be described as musical and in its extent coincides with Augustine's *ordo entium*.

On the whole, it seeks to attain the vision of the *intelligibilia*. Statements regarding the beautiful or harmonic consonance pursue a clearly delimited objective: if their object is a *musica* that consists of sounds and can be perceived by the senses, this object is discussed relative to an interest in knowledge for which the sensible is always only the occasion, never the final goal—whether it is a matter of measured discourse in a poem or of instrumental music.[173] Augustine had begun precisely here and conceived the possibility of discerning through the pleasant stimulation of the senses its numerical structure as a "call of God," and that is just how Boethius was to be read over the following centuries:

> Wherever you turn, she speaks to you through the vestiges which she imprinted on her works, and she calls you back within yourself as you are slipping into external things through their very forms, so that you understand that what delights you in the body and seduces you through the bodily senses is based on numbers [*numerosum*]. You seek the cause of this, and come back to yourself, and realize that you cannot either approve or disapprove of what you come in contact with through the senses of the body, unless you possess certain laws of beauty to which you refer whatever beautiful things you feel outside yourself [*nisi apud te habeas quasdam pulchritudinis leges ad quas referas quaeque pulchra sentis exterius*].[174]

Boethius concludes chapter I.1 of his work on music—a chapter that is conceived as a preface and is almost entirely devoted to the ethical and psychagogic power of music—with the formulation of the speculative objective of knowledge. This reflects the special status of music that was emphasized in Boethius's classification of the sciences cited at the outset: *musica disciplina* does not pursue a speculative interest alone, but is also the only one of the quadrivial disciplines to pursue the practical-ethical goal of morality.[175] *De institutione musica* approaches these goals by means of two lines of argument that are at first conducted in parallel and then finally merged. This arrangement of the future standard work of medieval music theory, for which Augustine's *De musica* showed the way in a comparable fashion, is important for my broader argument because *both* levels of Boethius's reasoning advocate the "holistic" claim of the theory as a whole: The conception of "enharmonic" music as an actualization of the *ordo entium* is the *condition of the plausibility* of the somatic-physiological, psychological and ethical-moral concept of "salutary" *musica*. The interrelation of speculative interest on the one hand, and of the practical-ethical emphasis on the other hand, are *necessary* within the theory. Neither of the two components is plausible unrelated to the *whole* of the theory, even if this reference remained implicit.

The previously mentioned levels of argumentation condition one another and are developed in consistent relation to one another. Their respective starting points only partly indicate this relationship. On the one hand there is the question of the psychagogic-ethical or, in a broader sense, the "therapeutic" power of music, which according to Boethius affects not only the moral but also the psychic *conditio* of human beings.[176] On the other hand, there is the question of the *vis harmonica,* of the nature of the ability to appreciate consonance.[177]

Like Ptolemy, Boethius views the appreciation of consonance as a process in which the pleasure of the senses—in Augustine *delectatio,* in Boethius, partly *delectatio* but usually *gaudium*—and the cognitive performance of reason complement each other.[178] Senses and reason are seen as initially susceptible to music independently of each other, and to that extent in their own ways as *instrumenta* of the ("rational") *vis harmonica.*[179] The senses open up the material to the judgment of reason: sensual pleasure, even though it is a confused mode of perception, "indicates" consonance and achieves an approximate assessment. Reason refines the sense impression, perceives the *integritas* and *veritas* of consonance, determines its species, that is, the *proportio* on which the interval is based, and if necessary, adjusts the judgment previously suggested by sense impression:

> For sense observes something confused but that is proximate to that which it is. Reason evaluates the whole, and inquires into the profoundest differences. Thus, sense discovers confused things that are, nevertheless, close to the truth, but receives their wholeness through reason. Reason itself discerns wholeness [*invenit integritatem*], yet receives a confused and proximate likeness to truth. For sense comprehends nothing about wholeness, but arrives only at an approximation, while reason judges.[180]

For Boethius as well, sensual pleasure in consonance is, if not the systematic, at least the practical starting point for reason's anagogic ascent toward the *imperium speculationis.* The same holds for the doctrine of *ethos*: its development out of the theory of the three *musicae* begins with the question of the grounds for sensual pleasure. *Gaudium* is said to be the result of a *coaptatio* of two numerical-harmonic structures. One of them is the structure of the acoustic work, and the other is the affective disposition of the receiver conceived as a specific relation between the rational and irrational parts of the soul:

> When we hear what has been conjoined aptly and suitably in sound based on what has been joined and suitably fit together within us, and take delight in this, we also recognize that we ourselves have been composed in the same likeness. Likeness is a friend, but unlikeness is hateful and hostile.[181]

This *coaptatio* is at first unconscious and prereflexive, but it determines both receptive and productive dispositions. The "lascivious mind," in Boethius's example, is particularly affected by "lascivious" *musica instrumentalis* and will tend to compose it.[182] The basis for the sense of pleasure in the *coaptatio* of *musica* and individual states of mind, of *musica instrumentalis* and *musica humana,* leads to the conclusion that music modally corresponding to an affective disposition increases that disposition, while other *modi* could lead to qualitative changes.[183] Thus suitable *musica* could succeed in moderating and even governing the irrational parts of the soul:

> Is it not also clear that the spirits of fighting men in battle are inflamed by the sound of the trumpets? If it is likely that one can be roused out of a calm state of mind into fury and rage, there is no doubt that a temperate mode can restrain the rage or excessive desire of the troubled mind.[184]

If it is a matter of the closer definition of the *modi* that could serve to moderate the affects, then Boethius repeats the conservative position with regard to music that Plato puts forward in the *Republic* and also in the *Laws.* It has to be "plain, simple, and manly": "For this reason, Plato thinks that when music is arranged in the best way and is chastely composed it is a great guardian of the republic in so far as it is modest, simple, manly, and not effeminate, savage, or inconstant."[185] Here, music theory's speculative objective and reflection on the ethical relevance of music, the "inner" harmony of human beings and the order of the cosmos come together in a way that remained influential down to the late Middle Ages.[186]

The demand for *simplicitas* with respect to the moderation of the affects and thus in the practical-ethical horizon is based explicitly[187] on the same foundations as the analysis of the *musicus,* on Nicomachus's arithmology. The consonances recommended as *modesta ac simplex* are precisely the ones that correspond to the simplest *proportiones,* to the plainest, least refined *gaudium,* and are at the same time the most comprehensible to reason: "This first, agreeable consonance, whose quality sense more clearly grasps, should be considered the greatest."[188] The simplest relationships are the simple to double (1/2, the octave), triple and quadruple, to simple plus its half (*proportio sesquialtera,* 2/3, the fifth) and to the simple plus its third (*proportio sesquitertia,* 3/4, the fourth).[189] The discussion of the music that is most likely to contribute to "harmonic" *musica humana* leads back to the simplest consonances—to the framing intervals of Greek harmonics, and especially to the consonances that are most transparent with respect to their *numerositas* and thus also the most useful for the anagogic ascent to the vision of the *intelligibilia.* The ethical, the speculative, and the "aesthetic" dimension of Boethius's theory potentially to be extrapolated coincide in the demand for *simplicitas.*

Thus if we take the extent and conceptual range of the theory into account, the closure and homogeneity of the whole theoretical apparatus are remarkable. Boethius's classification of *musicae* into *musica mundana, humana,* and *instrumentalis* makes explicit the "holistic" claim of Pythagorean-Neoplatonic number theory. It foresees systematic places for the areas of ancient pagan music theory that Boethius himself does not discuss—such as lyric poetry seen as *musica metrica* or *rhythmica*—but which Augustine had already dealt with. Boethius's derivation of the speculative theoretical elements from arithmology is concise, however, his classification consequently sharpens the ability of the abstract theory to integrate phenomena that are vivid and part of everyday experience. The category of *musica mundana* may have contributed decisively to the success of the theory.

Boethius too conceives the "musical" work as a sensible manifestation of the *ordo entium.* Here as well the conception of a phenomenon as "musical" emphasizes first a formal property (*numerositas*) and then its anagogic relevance. Correspondingly, Boethius's music theory provides the "musical work," whether it concerns melodies, harmonies, or metrical discourse, with legitimacy and relevance. For here too we can say that insofar as sensual pleasure (*gaudium* or *delectatio*) indicates simple consonance, the latter counts as affect-moderating, and is at the same time at its most transparent with regard to the *proportio* describing the consonance. Sensual pleasure, the moderation of the affects as a contribution to ethical life, and the *contemplatio* of the numerical-harmonic *ordo entium* as the living out of the theoretical way of life or as *caritas Dei* are not mutually contradictory.

In the following chapters, we will discuss the reception history of the work through studies of exemplary texts and investigate its relevance to the poetic theory of the Middle Ages. The following paragraphs that conclude this chapter will therefore be limited to laying the foundation for these further studies. A survey of the significance of *De institutione musica* for medieval educational institutions seeks to provide a preliminary assessment of the distribution and availability of the text.

Both of Boethius's texts, *De institutione arithmetica* and *De institutione musica,* developed their influence with the Carolingian reform and the collection of manuscripts on which it was essentially based. "Quis saltem poterit seriem enumerare librorum,/quos tua de multis copulat sententia terris?" ("Who then could enumerate the list of books,/that your judgment brought together from many lands?")[190]—these verses come from a dedicatory poem addressed to Charlemagne that was placed at the front of a now lost codex of Wigbod's interpretation of the Octateuch. The texts to which they allude presumably already included *De institutione musica. De institutione arithmetica* was probably first brought back to the continent by the *scoti peregrinantes* and spread from there;[191] in contrast, the work on music reached the Carolingian court in the course of the previously mentioned collection of manuscripts, as Michael Bernhardt has argued.[192] It spread from an archetype copied there,[193] first in France and then, as an integral part of the Carolingian *philosophia naturalis*,[194] to the educational institutions of northwest Europe.[195] This spread took place in the conjunction which, according to Bernhard Bischoff, should already be assumed for the archetype in Charlemagne's court library: in a codex including among other texts Augustine's *De musica* and Cassiodorus's *Institutiones*.[196] Without the systematics Boethius made possible the rise of music theory in the ninth and tenth centuries is inconceivable.[197]

Currently, the oldest inventory evidence comes from Reginbert's Reichenau book catalog, which mentions among the monastery's acquisitions between 835 and 842 "libri quinque de musica" by Boethius.[198] In the following centuries, no work on music theory was copied as often as *De institutione musica*. The exhaustive documentation of the extensive transmission of texts allows us to rely on the research accomplished: Calvin M. Bower's inventory of the manuscripts up to 1500 lists 137 copies, sixteen excerpts of various kinds, six independent commentaries, and sixteen further manuscripts that are connected with the manuscript tradition of *De institutio musica*.[199] Here I will mention only two examples. The cathedral school of Orléans had a copy dating from the tenth century.[200] The Paris manuscript, BNF lat. 18514, a fourteenth-century copy that had been in the Collège de Navarre in the interim and to which had been added extensive glosses regarding the arithmetical basis of the theory, contains a presentation of Pythagoras in fol. 84. It proves that the tradition in which Boethius's work is inscribed was clearly discernible.[201]

Starting in the ninth century, excerpts and glosses on *De institutione musica* develop their own, distinct tradition.[202] In addition to glosses, commentaries unaccompanied by the primary text were produced and widely distributed.[203] Marie-Elizabeth Duchez has claimed that John Scotus Eriugena was the first medieval writer to rely extensively on Boethius's work. Bernhard has pointed out two quotations from Boethius's text in Amalarius of Metz's *Liber officialis*, the first version of which dates from around 823 and thus might have been written earlier than John Scotus Eriugena's commentary on Martianus Capella.[204] Thus we can tentatively assume that 823 is the year of the oldest documented proof of reception.

The dissemination and reception of *De institutione musica* coincides with the updating of the educational canon whose systematization under Christian auspices we have followed in Augustine's *De ordine*. Its realization seems at first in danger of failing: the accumulating mass of text proves

to be difficult to interpret, since its context is unclear and its presuppositions unknown.[205] Seeming plausibilities like the statements regarding the
distinction between *artes* and *disciplinae*[206] that are to be found in Isidore
of Seville's *Etymologiae* and that later became common everywhere, exist
alongside classifications of the sciences that are full of content but irreducible to one another, and moreover have a wider scope than the traditional
canon of the *septem artes*.[207] For its own part, each classification bears
witness to curricular models and must have had a corrosive retroactive
effect on the updated canon, especially since at first textbooks (*textus*) for
teaching the canon of the *septem artes*—or any other canon—were lacking.
Martianus Capella's *De nuptiis Philologiae et Mercurii* may be "impossible
for a modern reader to enjoy," as Curtius put it.[208] However, after 800 the
text had the advantage of devoting, after the comparatively short framing
discussion in the first two chapters, one chapter to each *ars* and thus providing disciplinary studies with elementary material in a prestructured framework. Its impact in this function is shown not only by the ample glosses on
the oldest manuscripts[209] and by the commentaries produced as early as the
ninth century by an anonymous author,[210] by John Scotus Eriugena, and
by Remigius of Auxerre.[211] Evidence for the influence of this text on the
practice of teaching is found primarily in a rich manuscript tradition that includes, according to Claudio Leonardi's inventory, 241 copies.[212] The books
of Martianus Cappella's work were soon taken out of their context and
supplemented by other, thematically appropriate educational writings. The
codex Ivrea 84 may serve as an example in our context: The richly glossed
ninth book of *De nuptiis Philologiae et Mercurii* is here found together with
Augustine's *De musica* and Boethius's *De institutione musica*.[213] *De nuptiis
Philologiae et Mercurii* sets up an organizational grid that guides the updating of the *studii*. Only when late antique propaedeutics became widespread
did the deficiencies of Martianus Capella's text become conspicuous. Its
overview then appeared, "compared to Boethius's thoroughly developed
musical system," to be a "superficial introduction."[214]

The reception of Boethius in music theory, to which the next chapter is
devoted, takes as its starting point this organizational grid and the adoption of the corresponding introductory textbooks in teaching. After 800,
Boethius rose to become the "most influential teacher of the medieval musician."[215] His text became a "standard work" that provided guidance "everywhere from the ninth century on."[216] With a few and transitory restrictions it remained authoritative in the practice of teaching until the end of
the Middle Ages, and to some extent even later. At Oxford University it was
the only textbook on music that was ever obligatory, and was mentioned in

the university's statutes even in the nineteenth century.[217] The influence of the textbooks on arithmetic and music was so wide-ranging that scholars have been able to assert that they enjoyed a hegemonic validity: "two subjects [were] dominated for centuries by Boethius's writings: arithmetic and music."[218] *De institutione musica* acquired a "dominant authority"[219] and was "throughout medieval times and much later [. . .] the standard text for schools and universities."[220]

Boethius was the chief authority in the musical education of the early Christian centers, for example in Reichenau, the workshops of Berno and Hermann of Reichenau (Hermannus Contractus), and in St. Gall, where the Irish monk Moengal taught Boethius's writings.[221] With the development of the educational system and the incipient differentiation between basic and secondary, "academic" education, elementary curricula emerged that also included training in the quadrivial disciplines. Arithmetic was introduced using Johannes de Sacrobosco's brief *Algorismus*,[222] an abridged version of Euclid's *Elementa* was in use as a textbook of geometry,[223] and elementary astronomy included a knowledge of *computus* and of the *Tractatus de sphaera*, also by Sacrobosco.[224] If a *textus* for music is also mentioned, then it is Boethius's work.[225] In important studies, Max Haas has sought to reconstitute the profile of this elementary music education and its chief pedagogical goals.[226] The broad scope and richness in material of these studies enable us to rely on them and to endorse Haas's own summary:

> In the Middle Ages, musical education was of secondary importance from
> the point of view of the history of science, because in terms of its function
> its primary relevance was to the history of education and social history.
> When children were taught music, they were not taught what music is,
> but rather music was used to teach them what the world is. To be more
> precise: If children appropriated world-pictures in the course of their
> socialization, the *ars musica* was not the superordinate model, but rather
> the model that made the first factors of order accessible in such a way
> that sense experience and understanding are mutually related on the basis
> of everyday activities.[227]

Thus according to Haas *musica* performs what must be called a cognitive schematizing according to and in terms of analogical discourse. The condition of this function is the emphasis on clarity and vividness that we have underscored in the classification of music into *musica mundana, humana,* and *instrumentalis.* Boethius's textbook laid not only the historical[228] but also the individual-cognitive, "epistemic" foundations for the continuity that is the subject of this book.

The institutions of higher education, the monastery and cathedral schools, and finally the universities, could begin here without interruption. After a temporary decline in the study of *musica speculativa* in the tenth century, which should be seen in relation to the Cluniac and Cistercian reforms, it was taught primarily in the cathedral schools. Chartres and Rheims, where Gerbert of Aurillac taught using Boethius's introductory texts,[229] may serve as examples. The collection of *quaestiones* for the licentiate examination at the University of Paris extant in the Barcelona manuscript Ripoll 109, which was produced between 1230 and 1245, is based primarily on Boethius.[230] A decline of academic music education in the late thirteenth century must be noted, but it was of limited scope.[231] For example, Johannes de Grocheo's work *De musica*, which flatly denied the existence of a *musica mundana* and *humana*, and which Roger Dragonetti and Gisela Febel cite as proof of their theses, had, according to Nan Cooke Carpenter, "little influence upon writers of musical treatises in the following centuries."[232] Eva Hirtler also emphasizes this with regard to the late Middle Ages: "For centuries, Johannes de Grocheo's was the only direct criticism [of the Neoplatonic concept of music]."[233]

The often-cited abridgment of the parts of the *Institutio musica* prescribed for students to Books I and II[234] does not prove the decline of the "holistic" concept of music; instead, it is precisely these parts of the work that contain the arithmetic introduction, the *musica mundana/humana/instrumentalis* triad that primarily underlies the "holistic" nature of Boethius's theory, the comments on poetry, and the passages on the psychagogic potential of music. The abbreviations may be due to the changed requirements of teaching and the changed practice of the *ars nova* which could finally no longer be reduced to the late antique body of theory, but the construction of a sharp break in speculative music theory around 1300 nevertheless goes too far. The *ars nova* of the thirteenth and fourteenth centuries increased the authority not only of Augustine's *De musica* but also, once again, that of Boethius's theory of music: "with the *ars nova*, music once again became truly a specialty of the Masters of Arts who were interested in mathematics. [. . .] around 1320, this led to a renewal of interest in Boethius's *De musica* [*sic*]."[235] Abridgments of Boethius such as the *Musica speculativa* and *Arithmetica speculativa* by Johannes de Muris (c. 1290–1350), who taught at the Sorbonne toward the end of the first half of the fourteenth century, took into account the changed needs of teaching and once again led to an "unending diffusion of his [Boethius's] doctrine at home and abroad."[236] Precisely in France, "the musical capital of Europe until the mid-fifteenth century,"[237] "theorists in the fourteenth century continued to discuss both *musica theoretica* and *musica practica*, basing their speculative discussions upon Boethius and other authorities."[238] As Bernhard's summary indicates—and we should underscore this—the influence of Boethius's textbooks remained "uninterrupted even in the late Middle Ages."[239] The multiplicity of new copies made in the fourteenth and fifteenth centuries, partly already under the influence of Renaissance humanism, primarily but not exclusively in Italy, proves the currency and conventionality of the *Institutio musica*.[240] If examples of the continuity of the textbooks on music theory during the centuries generally lumped together as the late Middle Ages were required here, we could cite the anonymous *Quatuor principalia*, Ugolino of Orvieto, Person Gobelinus, Johannes Hothbys's *Excitatio*, Johannes Legrense, Ramos de Pareja, Adam of Fulda, Johannes Tinctoris, or Franchino Gafori's *Theorice musiche*, which appeared in 1495, shortly after Molinet's *Art de rhétorique*.

CHAPTER SEVEN

Speculative Music Theory in the Boethian Tradition, 500–1500

BOETHIUS'S TRIAD, *musica mundana/humana/instrumentalis* proved to be unusually stable. Until the late Middle Ages, its metaphysical foundation remained the authoritative limit of the evolution of music theory discourse. The primacy of theory remained central: every numerical harmonic relationship, every *proportionalitas* is ontologically prior to any manifest proportion. Insofar as the *proportionalitates* are accessible to the developing *ratio* or the vision of the *intellectus*, but not to the fallible senses, the *eruditus vir* engaging in speculative theory of music becomes the paradigmatic *musicus*.

From this it follows, first, that our central questions cannot be answered solely by means of arguments that are based on instrumental practice, the developments of poetry alone, or both actual relationships. Music theory concepts such as the Boethian triad *musica mundana/humana/instrumentalis* or the distinction between *musica naturalis* and *musica artificialis* are, according to their claims, equally indifferent to practice—and especially to changes in practice. Arguments of the type "poetry and instrumental accompaniment part ways at such-and-such a point in time" may be accurate, but they say little or nothing about the pertinence or conceptual content of a distinction like the one in question here at a specific point in time. This holds true so long as the use of this distinction can be related to the discourse of speculative music theory.

Down to the fourteenth and fifteenth centuries, treatises on music theory are inscribed in this discourse. To prove this and to counter the schematizations worked out at the beginning, the following sections sketch the evolution of this discourse from late antiquity down to the fifteenth century, down to the age of late medieval poetry in France. With respect to the research presented in part I and the working hypotheses formulated there, the goal of this reconstruction remains first of all to prove a continuity of the discourse of speculative music theory down to the late fourteenth and fifteenth centuries, on the one hand, and, on the other, to prove that the distinction cited by Deschamps in 1392 is rooted in precisely this strand of the discourse. With respect to the multitude of texts that are in question and in view of the risk of expanding the analysis to panoramic dimensions, for the choice of crucial evidence we will rely on the preparatory work done by musicologists and the sketches of the reception history of works thus far presented in this connection. In considering the corpus so constituted we will be asking three questions: Do the texts concerned establish, through explicit references to the Boethian triad or otherwise, a connection with the "holistic" concept of music? Which *genera musicae* are distinguished? And finally, does the treatise on music in question provide a systematic place for verbal art? The chapter begins with an overview of the possible competing paradigms in late antique music theory and closes with a section on the relation between the Aristotelian reorientation of the order of discourse and speculative music theory.

The Initial Situation in Late Antiquity: Competing Paradigms?

Augustine's *De musica* and Boethius's propaedeutics stand monolithically in the music theory discourse of late antiquity, but they do not stand there alone. Research has revealed a larger number of late antique contributions to the discussion of music theory. These have remained partly without influence. This is true, for instance, of chapter I.10 in Quintilian's *Institutiones oratoriae*.[1] Although terminological overlaps between Quintilian's rhetoric and music scholarship on voice training might have offered opportunities for making connections,[2] Quintilian's work was first cited again in the *Complexus effectuum musicum* written by the Flemish Renaissance music theoretician Johannes Tinctoris (c. 1435–1511). Censorinus's work *De die natali*, written around 238, and the *Fragmentum Censorini* that were bound together with it[3] briefly aroused interest, presumably initially on the basis of a fourth-century uncial codex,[4] and then disappeared from the debate. Favonius Eulogius's commentary on the *Somnium Scipionis*[5] and Fulgentius's *Mitologiae*[6] can also be mentioned here. In addition to these soon-to-be-forgotten works there are texts that are relevant to music theory and remained influential during the following centuries. They raise the question whether we have to assume from the outset a differentiation of medieval music theory that is opposed to the hegemony of the speculative music theory shaped by Pythagoreanism and Neoplatonism. A few brief remarks on the texts and their reception history will allow us to set aside these doubts.

Calcidius, Macrobius, Martianus Capella

Among the texts that remained relevant to reflection on music theory over the long term was first of all the translation of part of the *Timaeus* (17a–53c) that was made by the Christian Calicidius around 321.[7] A more comprehensive commentary interpreting Plato's dialogue Neoplatonically supplements the text.[8] For centuries, this translation, which is extant in about 150 manuscripts,[9] remained the only text of Plato's that was available in Latin. Thus we should always assume that references to the *Timaeus* were based on acquaintance with this text. The proofs of reception referring to the commentary in the context of music theory make the relevance of the text for *musica scientia* as a whole seem rather slim. *Musica enchiriadis* and *Scolica enchiriadis* refer to the *Timaeus* as their source for the elementary doctrine,[10] the author of the organ pipe measure produced in the entourage of Gerbert of Aurillac, usually named after its incipit *Rogatus*, mentions Calcidius's work,[11] Aribo Scholasticus's *De musica* (c. 1070) quotes it verbatim,[12] and Engelbert of Admont (c. 1250–1331) mentions Calcidius's commentary in connection with *musica mundana*.[13]

The commentary on the *Somnium Scipionis* that Macrobius wrote around 400 was far more relevant for music theory. This text became an important source of quadrivial knowledge for the following centuries; its manuscript tradition alone counts 230 copies, plus various excerpts and commentaries.[14] At first, Macrobius was read by earlier medieval Irish astronomers and cosmologists; examples are offered by the commentaries on Martianus Capella by Martin of Laon and John Scotus Eriugena.[15] Macrobius's remarks on the harmony of the spheres were adopted by Gottfried of St. Victor and Bartholomaeus Anglicus; Vincent of Beauvais's *Speculum doctrinale* cites in XVI.24 the Pythagoras legend from this text.[16] The first work on music theory that cites Macrobius is Regino of Prüm's *Epistola de armonica instituitione*;[17] to determine the pipe measure, Aribo Scholasticus refers to the formula that Macrobius provided for calculating the area of a circle.[18] This formula is also found in Bartolomé Ramos de Pareja's *Musica practica* of 1492.[19] The *Musica manualis* attributed to John Wylde quotes Macrobius at length on the *effectus musicae* and on the determination of intervals;[20] Marchettus of Padua shows an awareness of the text at the beginning of his *Lucidarium*;[21] Jacob of Liège cites Macrobius in the framework of his remarks on *musica mundana* (I.13) and on the metaphysics of number (VI.62), Johannes Tinctoris refers to the theory of intervals in his *Liber de arte contrapuncti*;[22] moreover, Macrobius is mentioned by Engelbert of Admont, Ugolino of Orvieto, and Johannes Hothby.[23] The evidence shows that the text remained a reference for the Pythagorean-Platonic heritage in music theory down to the late Middle Ages and the Renaissance. In addition to a brief but often-copied theory of intervals, Macrobius's commentary on the *Somnium Scipionis* provided, along with Calcidius's annotated translation of the *Timaeus*, standard references for three concepts developed in the *Timaeus*: for the relational essence of matter, which could be formulated in numerical relationships, for its "harmonic" basis in the world-soul, and finally for the demiurge, the creator-god. Furthermore, cosmological considerations are of interest: the movements of the celestial bodies, the circular paths of the planets, the apparent counter-revolution of the fixed stars, the immobility of the Earth.

We have already noted the importance of Martianus Capella's allegorical narrative *De nuptiis Philologiae et Mercurii*, presumably composed in Carthage or Rome before 439. On the occasion of the event mentioned in the title, a group of revelers has gathered (lib. I–II). To entertain them, personifications of the *septem artes liberales* appear and present their arts (lib. III–IX). *Musica disciplina* is the subject of Book IX and is largely presented following Aristides Quintilianus.[24] The first section (921–929) presents the *effectus musicae*, while the third section (930–938) defines and classifies music. The book closes with the presentation of harmonics and rhythmics (939–994). The focus of the work can be determined from the quantitative relationships. The representation of the ancient pedagogical material remains rather limited. It is based on the presentation of arithmetic in Book VII, which takes its cue from Nicomachus of Gerasa, and is introduced by Varro's definition of music, which was also cited by Augustine.[25] Martianus Capella distinguishes among material, productive, and perceptive kinds of music. "Material" music is distinguished, like *musica instrumentalis* in Boethius, and includes, as in Augustine and also in Boethius, the music of *verba*. Musica (the personification of music) says:

> Before that, Lasus, a man from the city of Hermione, taught music to mortals, and only three kinds of music were known: ὑλικόν [matter], ἀπεργαστικόν [practice], and ἐξγγελτικόν [*sic*] [exposition], which is also ἑρμηνευτικόν [interpretation]. Ὑλικόν is that which sounds together out of continuous and similar things, such as sound, numbers, and words. Of these, harmony [*harmonica*] concerns melody, rhythm [*rhythmica*] concerns numbers, and metrics [*metrica*] concerns words.[26]

The distinction among *musica harmonica*, *rhythmica*, and *metrica*, which we have already discussed in connection with their consolidation in Augustine, is limited to audible music. The *harmoniae* have nevertheless already been set forth in the book on arithmetic, and elaborated on the basis of the Neoplatonic number ontology.[27] Astronomia also refers explicitly to Pythagoras and the cosmology of the *Timaeus*.[28] Rhythmics and melodics are rooted in the numerical order,[29] and rhythmics is developed, in a way similar to Augustine's, on the basis of the quantity of syllables, their *numerositas,* and number genera. Metrical feet are also situated in the numerical order.[30] Martianus Capella transmits, in condensed but complete form, the central determinants of the Pythagorean-Neoplatonic conception of metrical discourse as *musica*.[31] The work does not merely offer no resistance to the discourse of "holistic" music theory that was developed out of Boethius's *De institutione musica*. The unification of the discourse of music theory that began in the ninth century was to integrate Martianus Capella's classification of the *musicae* as a differentiation of *musica instrumentalis* and thus strengthen and confirm the systematic place of verse in Boethius's classification. Thus Martianus Capella's work does not provide evidence of the competing paradigms within late antique music theory, either. The diffusion of his work over the following centuries[32] proves instead the availability of the Pythagorean-Neoplatonic conception of metrical discourse as *musica* so long as the work was read.

The essential point concerning the influence of the work in the context of music theory has already been stated in connection with the reception of Boethius's *Institutio musica*. The importance of Martianus Capella for music theory declined as Boethius's propaedeutics gained acceptance. Up to the twelfth century, Book IX is still found in composite manuscripts.[33] To the extent that Martianus Capella's account of music had to exist alongside the textbooks composed by Augustine and especially Boethius, which were more detailed and fully compatible in content, interest was limited to the first two books, which were used as sources of mythological material. Thus Martianus Capella is encountered partly in the glosses on Boethius; the *Scolica enchiriadis* cites a definition of tone from Remigius's commentary on *De nuptiis Philologiae et Mercurii*;[34] in explaining the Greek terms for the tones Hucbald of Saint-Amand even prefers Martianus Capella's more detailed explanation to Boethius's brief one.[35] Regino of Prüm borrows from Martianus Capella the connection between the muses and the planets;[36] Engelbert of Admont still mentions him, but only in connection with his commentator Remigius.[37] Finally, he is found again in Johannes Tinctoris.

This brief survey shows why the sources provided no resistance to Boethian music theory. Martianus Capella, Macrobius, and Calcidius shared the conceptual foundation on which Augustine and Boethius also built.

The integration of their works into the Boethian theory that was becoming dominant, imposed itself and thus supported and increased that concept's authority.

Cassiodorus and Isidore of Seville

Flavius Magnus Aurelius Cassiodorus (485/87–c. 580) wrote his *Institutiones divinarum et saecularium litterarum* after 540, in the second part of his life, which he devoted to a monkish existence after an eminently political early life that in many respects resembled that of Boethius.[38] As a writer, Cassiodorus is a sophisticated dilettante on the Roman patrician model, but not a speculative thinker. His work is in many respects symptomatic of the path taken by the disciplines in the sixth century. Boethius concludes the living pagan tradition; Cassiodorus is already leaving it behind with what is ultimately a brief survey against the background of Christian doctrine. At the turn of the seventh century, Isidore of Seville presses one more time for preservation and collection, and then the Roman south ceases for a long time to play a role in the discussion of music theory.

Cassiodorus's *Institutiones divinarum et saecularium litterarum* was written as a textbook for a community of monks. The work draws on the connection between the *ordo entium*, the *ordo discendi*, and life *in caritas Dei* that was given conceptual grounding in Augustine's *De ordine*. On the educational program formulated in the latter work, Cassiodorus's *Institutiones* work out presentations of the disciplines that provide at least a fully fledged overview suitable as a *textus*. The Christian significance of the educational program and the use of studies as an *itinerarium mentis ad Deum* are emphasized. This can already be discerned in the structure of the work: Book I is devoted to clerical studies, introduces the reader to the study of the Bible and the most important conciliar decisions (I.1–11), offers arrangements of the scriptures according to Jerome, Augustine, and the Septuagint (I.12–14), communicates the corresponding reading competence (I.15–17), and finally summarizes spiritual and practical rules for life in the monastery of Vivarium (I.18–33). Book II is the first to be devoted to the secular sciences. Music is dealt with in chapter II.V, as the second quadrivial science after arithmetic. In Cassiodorus's work, the considerations presented here conclude a concern with music that began when he was serving as Theodoric's *quaestor*. The *Variae* preserve a lengthy *digressio* on the theory of music; his commentary on the Psalms, *Expositio in psalterium* also makes statements regarding music.

The letter that has come down to us as *Variae* II.40 was addressed to Boethius. Interested in the Neoplatonic, speculative concept of music,[39] the text provides a brief sketch of the disciplines that can be seen as an abbreviation of Varro and that concentrates on the *effectus musicae*. The following lengthy quotation offers an impression:

> That we may pass beyond such matters following the example of the wise Ithacan, let us speak of the psaltery fallen from heaven, which a man who was celebrated throughout the world composed and modulated in such a way for the welfare of the soul, so that through these hymns the wounds of the mind might be healed and the unique grace of God be sought. [. . .] Although many instruments of delight have been found, none have been discovered more effective in moving the mind than the attractive resounding of the concave cithara. For this reason we think that cord is so named in music because it easily moves our hearts [*corda*], [. . .]. The harmony of heaven cannot be explained adequately by human speech, which reason alone gave to the mind, but nature did not reveal to the ears. They say that we should believe that heavenly beatitude enjoys those delights that neither have an end nor grow weak with interruption. Moreover, they assert that beings above us dwell in that very perception, that celestial beings enjoy such delights, and that beings absorbed in such contemplations are perpetually encompassed by blessed delights. They considered the subject well if they had located the cause of heavenly beatitude not in sounds, but in their creator, where joy without end truly exists, eternity remains always without weariness, and only the contemplation of God produces happiness that cannot be surpassed. This sight truly offers eternal life, and amasses joys.[40]

The effort to grasp the *effectus musicae* as a consequence of "harmonic" sound impression, and to put it in an anagogic perspective is clear. The *musicus* is promised the *beatitudo contemplationis* in God.

To the assessment of the anagogic relevance of music corresponds a reference that has been seen as a possible source for the distinction between *musica naturalis* and *musica artificialis* that was introduced by Regino of Prüm and later cited by Deschamps. Cassiodorus underscores that the *effectus musicae* are called forth only by *musica artificialis* or *manualis*: "All of these things appear to have been brought about by human study through manual music [*humano studio per manualem musicam*]. [. . .] Usefully, it was discovered that artificial music [*artificialem musicam*], that is music discovered by the experiments of musicians on various instruments, was contained in fifteen modes."[41] It is opposed to the *naturalis rhythmus* that is peculiar to the "inspired voice." It is conceived here, as in Augustine, on the basis of the metrical foot. Thus in the brief *digressio* Cassiodorus already connects metrical discourse based on feet with *naturalis rhythmus*: "A natural rhythm [*naturalis rhythmus*] is known to be ascribed to the living voice [*animatae voci*]. The voice preserves a lovely melody when it is silent at the right time, when it speaks fittingly, and when with calm voice it walks along the path of intonation on musical feet."[42] Pietzsch proposed that here we can find the "seeds for the classification of music built on similar foundations by Regino of Prüm"[43] that is echoed in Deschamps, but did not pursue the question as to where Cassiodorus's *Institutiones* got this opposition. Hermann Abert has suggested that Cassiodorus also made use of Aristides Quintilianus. Albrecht Riethmüller accordingly suggested that the latter's work on music might be seen as the source of the *musica naturalis/ musica artificialis* distinction.[44] In fact, there seems to be a connection. In Aristides Quintilianus as well, the Pythagorean tradition's concept of music is dominant:

> Only the aforesaid, music, is extended through all matter—so to speak—and reaches through all time, adorning the soul with the beauties of harmonia and composing the body with proper rhythms, suitable for children because of the good things deriving from melody and for those advancing in age because it transmits the beauties of measured diction and, simply, of discourse as a whole. But for those still older, it explains both the nature of numbers and the variety of proportions; it gradually reveals the harmoniai that are, through these, in all bodies; and most important and most perfect and concering a thing difficult for all men to comprehend, it is able to supply the ratios of the soul—the soul of each person seperately and, as well, even the soul of the universe. The divine argument of the wise man, Panaceus the Pythagorean, confirms my view: he says that it is the business of music not only to organize the parts of the sound one to another, but also to assemble and harmoniously join together everything as has a nature.[45]

Aristides Quintilianus classifies music as follows:

> Of the whole art of music, one certain part is called theoretical, the other, practical. The theoretical is what discerns the technical rules of the art and the main categories and their parts and, moreover, examines its beginnings from on high, its natural causes, and its consonance with things as they are. The practical is what operates in accord with these technical rules and pursues its object—which, of course, is also called the educational. The theoretical is divided into the natural and the technical. Of these, with respect to the natural, the one part is the arithmetic and the

other part has the same name as the class itself—the natural, which discourses about things as they are; and with respect to the technical, there are three parts: harmonic, rhythmic, and metric. The practical is parted into the application of the aforesaid categories and their expression. With respect to the application, the parts are melic composition, rhythmic composition, and poesy; [. . .].[46]

Here, number theory and the metaphysics of music are "natural music"; "technical" or "artificial music" are the parts that Augustine (rhythmics, metrics) and Boethius (harmonics) discussed. Cassiodorus remains close to it, but emphasizes metrical discourse as a "music of the voice," insofar as it is produced by the "inspired instrument" created by God himself. What has been created by human hands is a mere imitation of this marvelous "instrument." Not only the distinction itself but also the argument on which it is based have exact analogues in Regino; the relationship to Cassiodorus's *Variae* suggested by Abert and again by Riethmüller is accordingly quite clear. A tradition proceeding from an archetype in the abbey of Lorsch and ultimately consisting of more than a hundred manuscripts makes a direct connection conceivable.[47]

While the *Variae* still discuss metrical discourse including music with regard to a secular audience,[48] the writings after 540 are devoted to the community of monks at Vivarium. In the preface to the *Institutiones* already, the unconditional priority of theology with respect to secular *scientiae* is made clear.[49] The new status of the disciplines can be discerned in the conception of Varro's definition of *musica* in the fifth chapter of Book II. The passage shifts the accent from the arithmetical frame of reference to the practical and ethical implications of *musica*, without thereby shifting the music-metaphysics perspective of the theoretical apparatus. The *ordo entium* to be seen in the numerical order is now discussed less ontologically, with respect to its existence and knowability, than anthropologically and ethically, with a view to the Christian's practical life:

The discipline of music is spread through every act of our life on the following grounds: if we first obey the commands of the Creator, and we serve with pure mind the rules set up by Him. Whatever we say, or whatever moves us within by the beating of the pulse in our veins, is shown to be associated through musical rhythms with the powers of harmony [*per musicos rithmos armoniae virtutibus probatur esse sociatum*]. Music is the knowledge of modulating properly [*scientia bene modulandi*]. If we conduct ourselves properly, we show ourselves to be associated with this discipline. When we do evil, however, we have no music. Heaven and earth and all things in them are pervaded with heavenly stewardship and are not without music. Pythagoras shows that this world was founded and can be governed through music [*mundum per musicam conditum et gubernari posse*].[50]

Music is everything that happens in accord with the will of the Creator, from the pulsing of the blood to decent speech. The numerical harmonic relationships that underlie every correct *modulatio* appear as emanations of the divine will. It is education in *musica scientia* that communicates this insight: "whatever in heavenly or earthly matters fittingly occurs according to the disposition of the Author is not exempt from this discipline of music."[51]

The classification of music presented in the *Institutiones* is limited to those *musicae* that Aristides Quintilianus had listed as "technical": "there are three parts to music: harmonic [*armonica*]-rhythmic [*rithmica*]-metric [*metrica*]."[52] Metrical discourse remains a part of *musica*; the classification includes precisely the areas covered by Augustine's and Boethius's textbooks taken together. The object of *scientia harmonica* is levels of pitch—"Harmonics is music which distinguishes in sounds between high and low."[53] Rhythmics is conceived on the model of the word: it investigates the "flow of words" in order to determine whether the "sound fits well or poorly into the whole" of the text in question: "The rhythmic part is that which determines whether in the flowing together of words the sound produced holds together well or badly."[54] *Metrica*, finally, is concerned with the measurement of syllables and includes, as examples show, the established metrical system: "The metrical part is that which recognizes the measure of different meters [*mensuram diversorum metrorum*] with plausible reason, as in the heroic, the iamb, and the elegiac."[55] Karl Borinski has argued that these passages can be read as an "aesthetics" of metrical discourse.[56] This may be correct within limits, but it presupposes that the passages in Cassiodorus are read in the context set forth here. The remarks on the *numerositas* of metrical discourse provide the conceptual foundation for all the elements of Cassiodorus's theory of music that might be considered relevant from a literary-aesthetic point of view. This *numerositas* is the "musical" quality par excellence of measured verse, in line with the general definition given in *Institutiones* II.3.21: "Music is the discipline that is concerned with numbers [*quae de numerus loquitur*]."[57] Cassiodorus offers no resistance to the spread and establishment of Boethian music theory,[58] which seems to have been no longer available in Vivarium.

The effort made in the *Insitutiones* to expedite in the interest of the Christian order of discourse the speculative emphasis inherent in pagan music theory has remained decisive for what has been called since Martin Grabmann the "pre-Scholastic."[59] The text became, especially in the early Middle Ages, a much-read and widely distributed textbook expanded by interpolations.[60] The chapter on music, which has come down to us separately in several manuscripts,[61] "although it claims to be only an introduction for a specific purpose, became a guide for the early Middle Ages."[62] Alcuin made use of the *Institutiones* for his *Dialogus de dialectica*, Hrabanus Maurus for his work *De institutione clericorum*. Around 900 traces are found in the *Quaestiones grammaticae* attributed to Gottschalk of Orbais and in an *Ars geometrica*. In the Munich codex 2599, produced around 1200, a series of images showing the personified *artes* along with their teachers, depicts Cassiodorus together with Geometria.[63] Despite the massive aftereffects, Cassiodorus influenced music theory only in the early Middle Ages. There is probably direct knowledge of the *Institutiones* in Aurelianus Reomensis.[64] Regino of Prüm made use of it: "Cassiodorus affirms that there are fifteen tones in secular literature," we read in one passage.[65] Renate Federhofer-Königs showed direct knowledge of Cassiodorus in a manuscript from Graz dating from the fourteenth century,[66] and Walter Odington's *Summa de speculatione musicae* draws directly on the *Institutiones*.[67]

Cassiodorus's *Institutiones* owe their influence largely to the *Etymologiae* of Isidore of Seville (c. 560–636). Karl Schmidt collected the great number of quotations and paraphrases of Cassiodorus relating to music in a concordance.[68] The Romanic Isidore, archbishop of Seville from 600 on, leader of the synod of Seville in 619 and of that of Toledo in 633, is considered the last of the Western Fathers of the Church. Clement VIII canonized him in 1598, and in 1722 Innocent XIII raised him to the rank of a Doctor of the Church. The *Etymologiae* are extant in more than a hundred copies scattered all over Europe.[69] No account of the work or its author can dispense with a reference to the fact that Isidore's work, along with those of Augustine, Boethius, and Cassiodorus, exercised the most long-lasting influence on the Middle Ages. The passages devoted to the *artes*, which are drawn from a large number of sources,[70] influenced all the sciences. As a complete text as well as in the form of excerpts made as late as the fifteenth and sixteenth centuries, the *Etymologiae* remained useful as an introduction to the study of the *artes*.[71]

The *Etymologiae* provide first of all evidence concerning musical practice in the early Middle Ages, especially regarding early liturgical chanting that is of interest.[72] The work systematizes and organizes the doctrine handed down in music theory, gives it its own accent, but hardly expands the body of theory. The passages on music take Cassiodorus as their point of departure, weaving in didactic material from other discussions, clearly arrange the latter and strengthen, by means of a chapter that reworks Martianus Capella, *De musicis numeris* (III.23), the number-theory foundation of the tradition.[73] The account is far from having the exceptional transparency and insight into the extension of the numerical harmonic order on which Boethius's textbooks are based, but it does offer a pertinent summary of Pythagorean-Neoplatonic doctrine. Music or "musicality," derived etymologically in the usual way from the muses,[74] is considered to be a quality of the order of Creation arrayed in numbers. Combining the Boethian definition of the object of music as *multitudo ad aliquid* with Cassiodorus's model, Isidore offers this definition of music: "Music is the discipline that speaks of numbers related to something [*quae de numeris loquitur qui ad aliquid sunt*]."[75] Isidore adds:

> Therefore, without Music no discipline can be perfected, for there is nothing without Music. It is said that the world itself is composed of a certain harmony of sounds [*mundus quadam harmonia sonorum fertur esse compositus*], and that the heavens themselves turn according to a modulation of harmony [*sub harmoniae modulatione revolvi*]. Music moves the emotions, and it beckons the senses to a different condition.[76]

The levels on which the numerical harmonic order is manifested as *musica mundana* and *musica humana* in Boethius are conceptually present in Isidore as well. The systematic place of the Boethian *musica instrumentalis* is filled by the three *partes musicae* that Cassiodorus had discussed. Thus according to Isidore music also includes metrical discourse:[77]

> Music has three parts: harmonic, rhythmic, and metric. The harmonic part distinguishes between high and low sounds. The rhythmic part concerns the impressions made by words, and whether sound accords well or badly. The metric part recognizes the measure of various meters with a credible formula to be, for example, heroic, iambic, elegiac, and so on.[78]

There follows the distinction of three *naturae soni*, which is found in comparable form in Augustine:

> It is well known that every sound, which is the material of songs, has a triform nature. The first is the harmonic [*harmonica*], which concerns the singing voice. The second is the organic [*organica*], which concerns blowing. The third is rhythmic [*rhythmica*], which counts numbers with the plucking of the fingers.[79]

In order to show their complementarity, both classifications have to be related to the definition of music as *disciplina quae de numeris loquitur*. The *partes musicae* point to various ways of manifesting the numerical harmonic order, various forms of *numerositas* that can but need not be realized acoustically. The distinction between the *naturae soni* distinguishes the modes of concretely producing sounds. The *natura* of vocal sounds is called *harmonica*: "The first division of music, which is called harmonic, that is, the modulation of the voice [*modulatio vocis*], has to do with comedies, tragedies, choral song, or anyone who sings with his own voice."[80] The term *organica* covers all the instruments that produce sound by means of a stream of air or the vibration of air columns;[81] percussion instruments and those that are plucked with a plectrum produce a sound "of rhythmical nature."

In contrast to the relatively weak impact of the parts dedicated to theory of music, given the wide diffusion of more developed didactic material such as Boethius's works, other passages had a broad influence. Isidore systematically sets pagan mythological references alongside Christian ones, as when he juxtaposes the Biblical Tubal with Pythagoras as the inventors of the *ars musica*.[82] He recapitulates Augustine's statements regarding the Bible's mystical numbers and number symbolism, and thus contributes to the significance of *De musica*. Moreover, the *Etymologiae* discuss the *effectus musicae* in the context of medicine, which plays a prominent role in Isidore's educational system as "second philosophy" or "philosophy of the body."[83] The relation between the pulse and numerical harmonic order, the broadening of the ethos doctrine into a "physiological" foundation achieved the status of a model and was repeatedly cited from the *Etymologiae*.[84] The striking sentences "it is said that the world itself is composed of a certain harmony of sounds"[85] and "whatever we say, or whatever pulsation of the veins moves us inwardly, is shown to be associated through musical rhythms with the powers of harmony,"[86] which establish the relation to the harmony of the spheres and *musica humana*, are found verbatim down to the late Middle Ages,[87] the latter in Hrabanus Maurus,[88] Pseudo-Aristotle,[89] and Marchettus of Padua,[90] the former also in Hrabanus Maurus,[91] Giraldus Cambrensis,[92] Vincent of Beauvais,[93] Pseudo-Aristotle,[94] and Simon Tunstede.[95] The establishment of Boethius's *Institutio musica* soon pushed Isidore's remarks into the background. It was primarily the encyclopedists seeking brief accounts who drew on Isidore. Thus the *Etymologiae* provided a central source on music theory for Hrabanus Maurus, for Hugo of St. Victor's *Didascalion*, and also for Dominicus Gundissalinus, Bartholomaeus Anglicus, Michael Scotus, Vincent of Beauvais, and, noteworthily, for Roger Bacon.[96] For professional writers, the *Etymologiae* offered a few useful introductory *topoi*, but it was seldom analyzed *in extenso*. Aurelianus Reomensis drew from Isidore a large part of the knowledge communicated at the beginning of his *Musica disciplina*, but remains an exception in this regard. Since Isidore himself draws on Cassiodorus, it is often impossible to decide which of the two was the source. The use of Isidore can first be determined with certainty in Johannes Aegidius Zamorensis, who quotes from several books of the *Etymologiae* and marks his borrowings by adding "ut dicit Isidorus" ("as Isidore says") and similar phrases. Walter Odington's *Summa de speculatione musicae* shows that he had made a thorough study of the *Etymologiae*; a whole chapter of his work (V.7) introduces liturgical terms borrowed from Isidore.[97] Marchettus of Padua refers expressly to him; Jacob of Liège's *Speculum musicae* offers a series of excerpts (chap. II–VII). Some passages, mostly on definition, etymology, and the origins of music, are still used by Ugolino of Orvieto[98] and Johannes Tinctoris in his *Complexus effectuum musices*.[99]

The "holistic" conception of music dominates the late antique sources. Each of the texts cited refers explicitly to the Pythagorean-Neoplatonic concept of music. Everything concerning the essence of music that the Christian Middle Ages was able to draw from its late antique *auctoritates* implicitly presupposes this conception. The classifications of music offered are inconsistent, yet they agree in conceiving metrical discourse as music.

The Church Fathers' genuine contribution to music theory was limited to Christian vocal music, to psalmody and the hymnody practiced in the countries of the eastern Mediterranean. No attempt was made to mediate between theory and Christian practice. The depreciation of practice in favor of music theory speculation, which can be considered a basic trait of late antique music theory, did not seek such a mediation:

> How closely related to Neoplatonism Christianity was from the start is
> most clearly shown by the observation of their mutual aesthetics of music.
> Both share the conviction that all sensory stimulation in art is without
> value, only the Greeks see the sensory-beautiful as the lowest level of
> knowledge, whereas the Christians see the lack of value as so great that
> it is pernicious. But the Church Fathers' tendency to interpret the ele-
> ments and factors of music symbolically also finds parallels among the
> Neopythagoreans and Neoplatonists. In the allegorizing tendencies espe-
> cially, and in number symbolism, the two orientations are very close to
> the Jewish-Greek views of Philo. From Neopythagoreanism, the Church
> Fathers took the idea that music exercises its power throughout the uni-
> verse. Thus we can say with confidence that the foundations of the early
> Christian aesthetics of music, as well as three-quarters of its details, were
> taken over from Neopythagoreanism.[100]

To sum up, the Christian "colonization" of the body of pagan theory was accomplished early on: "In its main lines, the Church Fathers' aesthetics of music [. . .] was already completed in the West during the time of Augustine, and in the East during that of Basil [the Great], that is, in the fourth and fifth centuries."[101]

Discussion of music theory resumed in the eight and early ninth centuries, in northwestern Europe. The merging of pagan antique theory and Christian practice now became of primary interest: "The analysis and organization of the choral repertory, on the one hand, and the understanding of the mathematically founded order of the tonal system on the other, along with the harmonization of these two contrary basic positions, constituted the problem of music theory up to the end of the millennium."[102] The new reception and establishment of Boethian music theory took place at this time:[103] The arithmetical description of music replaced the provisional notation of choral music, which had been guided by grammar, and revived the Pythagorean-Platonic tradition's concept of music based on the ontology of number.[104] This transition can be clarified by works from the time such as Hrabanus Maurus's *De universo* (esp. lib. XVIII) and *De institutione clericorum* (II.47–51),[105] which draws on those of Cassiodorus, Isidore, and Augustine,[106] the poems of Theodulf of Orléans (750/760–821)[107] or the Reichenau Benedictine Walahfrid Strabo[108] (d. 849), to whose *Visio Wettini* we owe the earliest literary representation of the afterlife.[109] However, to discuss it would lead us too far away from our investigation, and I shall therefore continue my account with texts that concern the previously mentioned merging. The guiding question we have formulated remains valid: does the text establish a connection, through explicit reference to the Boethian triad or otherwise, with the speculative conception of music? Which *genera musicae* are distinguished? And finally: does the treatise on music in question provide a systematic place for verbal art, for *carmina*?

Pagan and Late Antique Theory, Early Medieval Christian Practice: Synthetic Approaches in Aurelianus Reomensis and Regino of Prüm

Psalmody and Christian choral music steadily developed from the sixth century onward. Its place in the liturgy was so quickly established that the conciliar decision of Clovesho in 747 had to provide textbooks sent from Rome. This decision, which urged the development of musical notation,[110] revaluated Christian musical practice in such a way that the quadrivial music theory had to give way sooner or later. The sharp increase in the production of music theory that began in the ninth century took place at the time when the textualization of the allelulia melisma laid the foundations for the hymn and the sequence. It was not for nothing that the foundations for an important branch of medieval poetry were laid here.[111]

Boethius's *Institutio musica*, which became more widespread in the wake of the Carolingian reform, transmitted education in music theory at a high level, was able to grasp the musical development theoretically, and was easily connected with the Platonizing theology of early Scholasticism. However, it provided no systematic place for Christian *musica vocalis*. Isidore's remarks on music theory, which are guided by Cassiodorus, could not coexist with Boethius's *Institutio musica*, but they covered Christian practice. In the ninth century problem-oriented syntheses emerged, the most important of which are the subject of this section.

In arrangement and content, Aurelianus Reomensis's *Musica disciplina* is exemplary of the emerging solutions. It was written around 850 in the monastery of St. Jean in Réomé.[112] It is, along with *Alia musica* and *Musica* and *Scolica enchiriadis*, the earliest medieval work on music theory that bears the mark of careful study of Boethius,[113] and in this respect it is "almost entirely a florilegium."[114] The text repudiates the Patristic condemnation of musical practice,[115] compiles Biblical and pagan-mythological material for the development and use of music, and in its first part, chapters I to VII, offers a general theory of music. Starting from the Augustinian definition of music,[116] Boethius, Cassiodorus, and Isidore are evaluated here. The second, more comprehensive part provides the first detailed theory of ecclesiastical modes.[117] Whereas this second part takes contemporary teaching into account, the first part completely follows the authorities. The eclectic compilation leads to very redundant chapters that always give the same answers, conceived in varying conceptual material depending on the authority cited, to the same questions. In this respect the text is representative of early Scholasticism.[118]

The whole of music theory is comprehended in the Boethian triad, which is referred to in chapters III through VI: "Three kinds of music are known to exist. The first concerns the world [*mundana*], the second concerns humans [*humana*], and the third has been established in certain instruments [*quae quibusdam constat instrumentis*]."[119] The explication of the *genera* follows Boethius, in part word-for-word. In accord with the general tendency increasingly to infiltrate Christian elements into pagan material or material indifferent to the order of discourse, theological considerations are set alongside Boethius's arguments for the acoustic, even if not audible, reality of *musica mundana*:

Cosmic music [*musica mundana*] can be seen especially in things in the heavens or on earth, and that appear in the variety of elements and seasons. The philosophers claim that the heavens revolve. How can it be that the swiftly moving mechanism of the heavens is impelled through a silent and quiet course? And if its sound does not reach our ears, we acknowledge that a certain harmony of modulation [*harmonia modulationis*] exists in the heavens, especially since the Lord says to Job: Who puts to sleep the music of the heavens?[120]

The emphasis on analogical relationships given through the senses, which we have underscored as characteristic of the Boethian triad, makes it easier to integrate references that are drawn from the scriptures. Thus a Bible quotation is supposed to justify the idea that for the explication of the concept *musica humana*, "homo" and "microscosmos" are to be understood as synonyms, which is at best a simplifying interpretation of these terms: "Human music [*musica humana*] abounds fully in the microcosm, that is, in the small world, as the philosophers call mankind. *Micros* is Greek; in Latin it means *small*; *cosmos* means *world*. Mankind is therefore called the small world, [. . .]."[121] The conceptual substance of the idea remains unaffected by this. The explanation of *musica humana* remains true to Boethius.[122] *Musica instrumentalis* is given significantly less attention:

> The third kind of music is established in certain instruments [*musica quae in quibusdam consistit instrumentis*], such as organs, citharas, lyres, and many others. Instrumental music has been separated from the science and the understanding of music, and is performed by a stretching, as with strings, or by the breath, as with flutes; some instruments are moved by water, as the organ; or by percussion, as in those instruments which are struck over a rounded base. Each produces different sounds.[123]

Now Aurelianus Reomensis adds a further distinction, taken from Cassiodorus. Here we see the merging and unification of variously accentuated classifications of late antique provenance on Boethian models to which we have already referred several times:

> Up to this point we have discussed the genres of music, and have asserted that there are three kinds of music, the first concerning the world [*mundana*], the second concerning humans [*humana*], and the third, as established in certain instruments [*quae in multis constat instrumentis*]. Now, however, let us take note of the parts of human music, as best we can, with the help of the Creator. There are three parts to human music: harmonic [*harmonica*], rhythmic [*rhythmica*], and metric [*metrica*].[124]

This passage conceives Cassiodorus's classification, presumably taken from Isidore, as a differentiation not of *musica instrumentalis*, but rather of *musica humana*. This does not correspond to the doctrine of the authorities, who were known to the author, as the first part of the treatise sufficiently proves, and must have at first been jarring. Pietzsch suggested that the passage quoted might best be understood as a conjecture on the part of later *scriptores* who had adapted the text to more recent classifications, for example that of Nicolaus de Capua.[125] Pietzsch quotes the *Musica disciplina* in Gerbert's edition,[126] whose text was based on a fifteenth century manuscript; the argument might thus have been plausible. However, it is not correct. The edition produced by Lawrence Gushee, whose collation includes the oldest known manuscripts of the treatise (Valenciennes, Bibl. mun. 148, c. 900 and Pommersfelden, Bibl. der Grafen Schönborn-Wiesentheid 2805, the part cited dating from the tenth century[127]), confirms the version of the text given by Gerbert. We thus note that first, Aurelianus Reomensis understands the terms *musica harmonica-rithmica-metrica*, which he borrowed from Cassiodorus's *Institutiones* by way of Isidore, as a differentiation of musica humana and so accentuates the latter. The question about the argument to be assessed may be postponed for the moment.

Aurelianus Reomensis's treatise proves that in the ninth century music theory started up again as a speculative science founded on metaphysics of number, was carried on by means of Boethian concepts, which despite the infiltration of Christian material retained their contour. The priority of the Christian truth of salvation was secured by an argument that very frequently appears in Renaissance poetics, but which had never fallen into oblivion in the Middle Ages, either:[128] Aurelianus justifies the appropriation and continuation of the pagan substrate of Boethian metaphysics of music by arguing that God "inspired" Pythagoras.[129] The foundation of the theory in the ontology of number remains intact, including its systematic place in the quadrivium and the Boethian definition of *musica scientia* as the science of the *multitudo ad aliquid*.[130] "Musical activity" now appears to be a divine commandment, and moreover covered by Biblical authority. Two quotations from the Apocalypse of St. John are said to prove that human music is pleasing to God. It imitates the choir of angels and makes the world harmony ring out in praise of its Creator:

> We read that even the heavenly citizens are distinguished by the tokens
> of this art, as we read in the Apocalypse: "They have the harps of God."
> And elsewhere: "As the harpists harp on their harps." We can conclude
> from this that the office of singing is pleasing to God if it is accomplished

with an attentive mind; for in this we imitate the chorus of angels, who are said to sing the praises of God without interruption. Assuredly, the structure of this world and its natural coherence contains a certain harmonic agreement. If you examine how other things rejoice together [. . .], you will understand that every created thing is linked together in a marvelous harmony and is adapted to itself [*omnis creatura harmonia sociata, sibi conveniat*].[131]

Man is enabled to make music by the capacity of his body, his own "instrument," which must be "tuned" by a *sobria mens*, a sober-minded temperament. The corporal and ethical constitution of the singer is seen as a factor that determines the quality of his song. For that reason the conception of Cassiodorus's classification *musica harmonica-rithmica-metrica* is plausible as a differentiation of *musica humana* within the text:

Even man himself will not doubt that he is ready-made for this discipline by a great aptitude. For he knows that he has everything generally associated with this art. In his throat he has a reed for singing; in his breast he has a harp, equipped as it were with strings in the fibers of his lung; risings and fallings are in the flowing changes of the veins and the pulse. The serious mind will easily apply all these things to itself.[132]

Distinctions are also drawn among musical instruments, which are man-made, and the divinely created human body, the "instrument" of choral chant. The ethical disposition of the singer, reproduced in *musica humana*, corresponds to the "tuning" of this instrument. The increased Christian penetration of Boethian music theory in the wake of its reappropriation in the ninth century thus adds ethical accents that give a Christian twist to the antique pagan anthropological residues of the music theory inspired by Neoplatonism. The argument inaugurated by Cassiodorus, which resembles Regino of Prüm's generally more complex solution, works at the same time toward a merger of Christian choral practice and late antique pagan music theory.

Thus the recourse to Cassiodorus also ensures metrical discourse a systematic place in the classification of *musicae*. The object of *musica harmonica* is levels of pitch.[133] *Musica metrica* and *rithmica* deal with the principles of the sequencing of syllables and words. Aurelianus's concept of *musica rithmica* is noteworthy. As an example, he cites the verse that Augustine had also cited in Book VI of *De musica*, and understands quantifying metrics as *musica metrica*. Verses that are metrical in accord with the principle of syllable count are called *musica rithmica*:

The rhythmic part of music [*rithmica*] investigates the association of words, and whether sounds fit together well or badly. Rhythm seems to be similar to meter, which is a composition of words according to certain measures [*modulata verborum compositio*], examined not by the system of meters, but sorted by the number of syllables and by the judgment of the ears. This applies to most Ambrosian hymns. Thus, "Eternal King, Lord, and Creator of all things" looks to have been composed in iambic meter, but it does not follow the law of poetic meter, but is drawn out according to a rhythmic measure [*rithmica modulatione*]. Whoever has a scintilla of knowledge about metrics can follow our argument on this topic. Meter is quantity with modulation [*ratio cum modulatione*], whereas rhythm is modulation without quantity [*modulatio sine ratione*], and is divided into a number of syllables.[134]

This passage not only proves that the relationships between music theory and verse qua *numerositas* remain transparent, but also illustrates the vitality of these proofs, insofar as the late antique framework, which is here Augustinian, is understood conceptually and applied to more recent metrical developments. Aurelianus's way of proceeding testifies to his awareness that he is now operating in the framework of the musical theory of poetry. The model from which Aurelianus draws the following passages on rhythmics is the chapter "De rithmo" in the Venerable Bede's (c. 673–735) *De arte metrica*.[135] This work, whose author, a Benedictine best known for his *Historia ecclesiastica gentis Anglorum*, is a brief synthesis of theoretical texts from pagan late antiquity eclectically assembled for the use of Christian readers.[136] Bede recapitulates the foundations of quantifying metrics[137] and offers this definition: "A foot is a fixed measure of syllables and times [*syllabarum et temporum certa dinumeratio*]. It is called a foot because we use it like a one-foot ruler to measure verse."[138] The construction of the usual *versus* on the basis of two- three-, and four-syllable feet, including the determination of their quantities is dealt with briefly. The remarks correspond to the common lore presented in detail in Augustine's *De musica*. The difficulties begin with the discussion of dactylic hexameter and pentameter. Some of Bede's examples, all taken from Christian works, revive traditional verse measures in the distribution of quantities. For example, the following verse from Ambrose:

   · – | · – | · – | · –

Jam sur - git ho - ra ter - ti - a

Bede descibes this verse as iambic tetrameter,[139] and thus as a verse consisting of two symmetrical *membra* composed of two feet parsed through the *proportio* 1:2. However, other examples, which are also taken from Ambrose's work, cannot be parsed in this way:

＿　＿　＿　＿　·　·　·

Rex ae - ter - ne do - mi - ne

＿　＿　·　＿　·　＿　·　＿

Re - rum cre - a - tor om - ni - um[140]

The discrepancies with the system of classical metrics are not great; for instance, the long syllable at the beginning of the second verse appears as a variation on iambic tetrameter.[141] In contrast, other deviations, such as counting *do-* and *-ne* as syllables, were seen in the system of quantifying metrics as *lapsus*. The relatively recent rhyming versification, probably first established in the Latin West by Semitic Christians,[142] is correspondingly summed up in a chapter of its own under the rubric "De Rithmo."[143] It brings *rithmus* into the traditional system as a syllable-counting metrics, in accord with the Augustinian dictum that every *metrum* is a *rithmus* but not every *rithmus* is a *metrum*:

> Rhythm is similar to meter. It is the measured arrangement of words
> [*verborum modulata conpositio*], not according to the rules of meter, but
> evaluated by the judgment of the ears according to the number of syl-
> lables, as we see in the songs of the vernacular poets. Rhythm can exist by
> itself without meter, but meter cannot exist without rhythm.[144]

Bede conceives the verse defined by the number of syllables as a *rithmus*, without ever referring to music theory. His description of syllable-counting metrics, which is considered the first of its kind since Marius Victorinus, nonetheless retains not only terminologically the option of connecting with the discourse of speculative music theory. Bede conceives countability and thus *numerositas* as the specific quality of a verse constructed in accord with syllable-counting metrics. The latter must therefore be conceived, in accord with the Pythagorean-Neoplatonic bases of the discourse of speculative music theory, per se as *musica*. Long before Alberic of Monte Cassino's treatise on rhythmics, to be discussed later, or Johannes de Garlandia's poetics reconnected with music theory from the side of poetics, this conclusion had been drawn by early music theoreticians like Aurelianus Reomensis. With *musica metrica* and *musica rithmica*, with the "reshuffled" categories of Cassiodorus, either the older quantifying and the new syllable-counting metrics were conceived as *musica*. The view of Cassiodorus's distinction as a differentiation of the Boethian *musica humana* relates both forms of metrical discourse to the speculative conception of music; among Aurelianus

Reomensis's original contributions is to have privileged verse as a form of music that man produces by means of his "natural instrument," his created body.

An argument close to that of Aurelianus Reomensis is found in the text that introduced into the discourse of music theory the distinction between *musica naturalis* and *musica artificialis*. History owes to the Benedictine monk Regino of Prüm (c. 840–915), in addition to the *Epistola de armonica institutione*, a universal chronicle from the birth of Christ to 906/908, a manual of ecclesiastical rules for episcopal parish inspection visits and synodal court procedure, and one of our most important sources for the legal history of manoralism, the Prüm rent-roll for 893.[145] The *Epistola*,[146] "for the most part a compendium of traditional music theory,"[147] was written after 899 to meet practical needs. The cultivation of music in the Archbishopric of Trier was stagnant, and the *Tonarius* and the *Epistola* were intended to provide help.[148] The merging of speculative music theory with choral and instrumental practice was not the treatise's true goal, but it was nevertheless one of its results.

The epistle begins with a reference to the deficient cultivation of music in Trier, chapters 2 and 3 are concerned with tonal material, chapter 4 defines the *tonus* and then differentiates between church modes, the *toni naturalis musicae*, and the five whole tones and two half-tones, the *toni artificialis musicae*. The fifth chapter offers the distinction *musica naturalis/musica artificialis* as a means of classifying music, and chapters 6 to 8 are devoted to various definitions: first an etymology of the word *musica* is given, then come passages defining *vox* and *sonus* as well as *consonantia* and *dissonantia*. Chapter 9 states the numerical relationships that underlie the various *consonantiae*, and chapter 10 broadens these remarks in the direction of more fundamental arithmetical considerations on the genera of numerical relationships. The following chapters offer a historical overview and a detailed description of the metaphysics of music: chapter 12 recounts the Pythagorean basis of a mathematically founded theory of music, chapter 13 discusses music in the canon of the *septem artes liberales*, and chapter 14 introduces the Greek technical terminology. Chapters 15 and 16 return to consonances and scale tones on the basis of the terminology that has been introduced in the foregoing chapters, then chapter 17 aligns the seven notes with the seven planets, while chapter 18 offers remarks on the difference between the theoretician and the practitioner of music. The work ends with a chapter on mnemotechnic verses (chapter 19) and a conclusion (chapter 20). Regino's *Epistola* introduces the distinction between *musica naturalis* and *musica artificialis* that has been so frequently discussed in research on lyric poetry of the late Middle Ages in France, so this text will accordingly be discussed in greater detail.

The *Epistola* testifies to the intensive study of the late antique sources of music theory.[149] Boethius's textbooks are the standard reference; 69 of the 138 borrowings identified by Bernhard in Regino's text are to Boethius's *De institutione musica*. Of those, 66 are verbatim quotations. The number, form, and integration of these quotations into the argument prove a substantial and precise knowledge of the textbook that gives Regino's *Epistola*, along with Aurelianus's *Musica disciplina* and the *Musica enchiriadis*, a pioneering status in the reception of Boethius. In addition to Boethius's text, Regino's most important source is Macrobius's commentary on the *Somnium Scipionis*. In presenting this text we have already referred to the central status held, methodologically, by the metaphysics of number and, thematically, by the harmony of the spheres. Remigius of Auxerre's commentary on Martianus Capella seems to have been available to Regino in one of the widely distributed abridgments. The enumeration of the planets and the muses associated with them in chapter 17 is taken directly from Martianus's work. The *Epistola* itself testifies, as has already been said, to the knowledge of Cassiodorus's *Institutiones*; however, the borrowings from the chapters on music are limited to the differentiation of *musica artificialis*, for which Regino adopts the three categories of the *tensibile*, *inflatile*, and *percussibile*. Connections that are just as minimal can be shown with Fulgentius's *Mitologiae*, from which the epistle takes, largely verbatim, the saga of Orpheus and Eurydice in the tenth chapter of Book III. Connections with Aurelianus's *Musica disciplina* are probable on the basis of the often identical sources of both works, but hard to prove.[150]

The real contribution to music theory made by Regino of Prüm's *Epistola* consists primarily in the introduction of the well-known distinction. The remark "Inveniuntur vero in naturali musica, id est, in cantilena [. . .]" ("Now, in natural music, that is in song, there are found [. . .]") occurs incidentally in relation to *tonus* and *modi*.[151] A few lines farther on, it is conceded that explanation is necessary. The comment testifies to an awareness of the innovativeness of the category:

> And because mention has been made already concerning natural and artificial music [*de naturali et artificiali musica*], the less skillful musician may ask: what is the difference between natural and artificial music? We respond to this that every modulation of harmonic arrangement is one and the same in the sounds of consonances [*omnis harmonicae institutionis modulatio una eademque sit in consonantiarum sonis*], nevertheless, there

is natural and artificial music. Thus, natural music is that which produces sound with no musical instrument, no touch of the fingers, no human striking or touch, but breathed upon by God [*naturalis itaque musica est, quae nullo instrumento musico, nullo tactu digitorum, nullo humano impulsu aut tactu resonat, sed divinus adspirata sola natura docente dulces modulatur modos*], and with nature alone as teacher, it measures out [*modulatur*] sweet modes. This music comes about in the motion of the heavens or in the human voice. Some add a third kind that is made by irrational creatures with sound or voice.[152]

Musica naturalis and *artificialis* are *musica* qua consonance; the latter is common to both. Consonance in accord with Boethius and, with reference to his textbook on arithmetic, is attributed to the presence of a *proportio*:[153] "Consonance is thus defined: consonance is the concord of voices different from one another but brought together into one [*dissimilium inter se vocum in unum redacta concordia*]. [. . .] There are numbers that create consonances."[154] God is said to have revealed them first of all to Pythagoras: "One should know that the often-mentioned consonances in no way were invented by the human mind, but they were revealed to Pythagoras by a certain divine agreement [*divino quodam nutu*]."[155] The works of the human voice and the movements of the spheres are conceived as manifestations of *musica naturalis*. Regino situates the connection, which has its condition of plausibility first of all in the conception of all acoustic phenomena as forms of *motus*, explicitly in the Pythagorean tradition:

> That music exists in the motion of the heavens is perceived by the Pythagoreans according to the following argument. They ask: how can it come about that the swiftly moving mechanism of the heavens is impelled by a silent and quiet course? Although that sound does not reach our ears, it cannot be that such very swift motion lacks sound, especially when the courses of the stars are linked together with such great fitness and convenience that nothing linked together and connected in this fashion can be known. For some are carried along in a high orbit and others in a low orbit, and thus, all of them are turned with equal impulse, so that through various unequal orbits a fixed order of courses is established. Therefore, it is argued that in the motion of the heavens there is a fixed order of modulation. [. . .] Some motions are swift, while others are slow. If motion is slow or variable it produces low sounds, if rapid and compact it must produce high sounds. No sound exists in things without motion. Therefore, musicians define sound as follows: sound is an indissoluble striking

of the air that reaches the ear [*sonus est percussio aëris indissoluta usque ad auditum*].[156]

Consequently, the following sections align each interval with a planet sphere, according to the rapidity of the heavenly body's rotation.[157] The ninth planet sphere, that of the Earth, makes no sound, since it remains unmoved at the center of the cosmos. The *Epistola* specifically emphasizes that in addition to the Pythagorean tradition, Cicero, Macrobius, and Boethius, the *praedicatores* of the Christian religion also support this doctrine: "not only the pagan philosophers, but also the robust preachers of the Christian faith agree about this harmony of the heavens [*coelesti harmonia*]."[158]

The subsumption of the music of the spheres and the *cantilena* under a common category is based on the absence of a man-made instrument. In the music of the spheres and vocal music, the Creation itself resounds, *divinus adspirata*.[159] The series of negations ("[n]aturalis itaque musica est, quae nullo instrumento musico, nullo tactu digitorum, nullo humano impulsu aut tactu resonat") adds a strong rhetorical accent here. The voice is a natural human capability, it is God's work, like the harmony of the spheres, the course of the seasons, the tides. Here the "world soul" sounds, as the sections on *musica naturalis* close: "Justly, therefore, does music capture everything that lives, since the heavenly soul [*coelestis anima*], by which the universe is animated, took its beginning from music [*originem sumsit ex musica*], as Plato and his followers were pleased to note."[160] The argument is familiar to us from Cassiodorus's *Variae*; the relations between Regino and Cassiodorus suggested by Abert and Riethmüller are thus supported by not only the terminological but also the conceptual nearness of the texts.

Musica artificialis is the music that humans imitate from the model of *musica naturalis* and by means of "artificial instruments of sound"[161] that are not created by God: "That music is called artificial [*artificialis musica*] that was conceived and invented by human art and ingenuity, and is based in certain instruments [*in quibusdam consistit instrumentis*]."[162] Conceptually, it corresponds to the greatest extent to Boethius's *musica instrumentalis*.[163] Regino also notes the possibility that the musical "work" has an anagogic function. *Musica artificialis* is seen as "illustrative material" for acquiring *musica scientia*, insofar as it provides a concrete form of abstract numerical harmonic relationships, knowledge of which must be gained "through the sensible":

> Anyone wishing to learn about this art should know that although natural music takes great precedence over artificial music, no one can know the power of natural music except through artificial music. Therefore,

although our disquisition began with natural music, it must finish with artificial music, so that we may demonstrate invisible things through visible
things [*ut per rem visibilem invisibilem demonstrare valeamus*].[164]

This argument, which goes far beyond the goals of a practice-oriented didactic treatise, led Calvin M. Bower to propose that it is indebted to older
sources that do not belong primarily to the domain of music theory. Egon
Wellesz had already expressed the view that the *musica naturalis/musica
artificialis* distinction indicates not only "a reflection of Neoplatonic ideas"
but also "a noticeable parallel with Byzantine musical theory as it had developed under the influence of Gnostic and Plotinian ideas."[165] Drawing on
these suggestions, Bower argues that Regino's distinction goes back conceptually to John Scotus Eriugena (810–886), and through him to Pseudo-
Dionysius the Areopagite.[166]

First, Bower is able to show that Regino's *Epistola* and *Tonarius* quote
extensively and verbatim from John Scotus Eriugena's commentary on Martianus Capella and Remigius of Auxerre.[167] In both texts the concept of
musica artificialis is used in a way comparable to the way it is used in Regino's *Epistola*. Although in these commentaries *musica artificialis* is distinguished, not from a *musica naturalis* but rather from a *musica coelestis*,[168]
it is again conceived, as in Regino, as structurally analogous to the latter.
Thus Remigius of Auxerre: "True music is always in the heavens [*musica
enim vera semper in caelo est*], in the motion of the celestial spheres and
in the motion of the seven planets; what is on earth is artificial music, and
has been made in imitation of heavenly music [*illa vero quae in terra est
artificialis est et ad similitudinem illam factam*]."[169] Bower is able to provide
further evidence for this proposed direct relationship of reception.[170]

The same does not hold without qualification for the concept of a *musica
naturalis*. Bower can show the initially not very specific distinction between
artificialis and *naturalis* in John Scotus Eriugena's *Expositiones in ierarchiam coelestem*, a presentation of Pseudo-Dionysius the Areopagite's *De
divinis nominibus*. John Scotus Eriugena comments on the remarks on the
relationship between sensible beauty and the idea of beauty as follows:

> Material lights [*materialia lumina*], whether the kind that has been set in
> heavenly space by nature [*naturaliter*], or the kind that is made on earth
> through human agency [*humano artificio efficiuntur*], are images of the
> intelligible lights [*imagines sunt intelligibilium luminum*], and above all
> of true light itself, which illuminates every man coming into the world,
> and which burns forever and inextinguishably in the minds of angels and
> man.[171]

The passage based on the Platonic and Neoplatonic metaphorics of light sums up two lower ontological levels as *naturalis* on the one hand, as *artificialis* on the other: the luminous being of the *intelligibilia* is manifest in the "natural" light to be seen in the harmony of the heavenly bodies, and equally manifest, although in a different way, in the "artificial" light of man-made goods. The same passage represents the path toward the vision of the *intelligibilia*, a path that John Scotus Eriugena calls *disciplinae liberales* or *naturales*:

> [Dionysius the Areopagite] calls those sacred disciplines διεξοδιχάς, that is, passages through, for to the enlightened those are ways through and level ground, or pathways through which we follow the way of knowledge. Using a more common interpretation, we can think of διεξοδιχάς as disciplines that flow along. For just as many waters flow and run together out of various sources into one river bed, so too, are the natural and liberal disciplines [*naturales et liberales disciplinae*] united in one and the same significance of internal contemplation as the highest source of all wisdom, Jesus Christ.[172]

The *disciplinae liberales* or *naturales* lead to the vision of intelligible truths on the ontological level designated with the epithet *naturalis*. They lead, as in Augustine's *De ordine*, to the vision of the order of Creation. The origin of this order is the Creator or, precisely, the trinitarian *persona* of Christ associated with the λόγος. Just as the term *naturalis* can be predicated of the group of the *disciplinae* or *artes*, so, according to Bower, it can also be predicated of each of the individual arts: "The term naturalis might well be applied to any of the liberal arts: *astronomia naturalis, geometria naturalis,* or *musica naturalis*; for each of these arts leads to knowledge of some aspect of the natural, or physical world."[173] Proofs are provided by the commentary on Boethius's *Consolatio* attributed to John Scotus Eriugena, which uses the same terms in explaining the relationship of imitation between the different realms of being:

> Because we have made mention of this sensible world, let us consider what its function is, whence, and in what manner it was made. All work is either the work of God [*opus Dei*], the work of nature [*opus naturae*], or the work of a craftsman imitating nature [*artificis imitantis naturam*]. The work of God is like the νους, that is, the divine mind, the word of the Father, the world, the world-soul, and the chaos that once existed, that is, the confusion of the elements, which is called ὕλη. The work of nature is double: when something arises out of planted seeds, as when men come

from men and trees from trees, or when something arises from itself, as when some trees rise from the ground on their own without any seed. The work of a craftsman imitating nature is like an image of something else [*statua alicuius*].[174]

The central argument of the passage concerns the classification of *sensibilia* in accord with their Creator. It corresponds to Regino's arguments for the subsumption of the movements of the stars and the sounds of the voice under the category *musica naturalis*. John Scotus Eriugena distinguishes between God's Creation, the works of created Nature, which grow qua progeniture, and the works based on *ars*, which imitate those of Nature. The ontological hierarchy implies a hierarchy of the respective ground of being:

> [T]he sensible world is twofold, the natural and the artificial, the artificial being an imitation of the natural world, just as the natural world was created in imitation of images in the mind of God. In other words, the visible natural world imitates the invisible world in the intellect of God, while the creations of man, the artifices, imitate the visible world of nature, and each of these two lower orders is ontologically dependent upon the highest order.[175]

Here we need to take the context of John Scotus Eriugena's argument into account. It presupposes the concept of beauty as *aequalitas numerosa* that we have summarized in discussing Augustine's work on music. A passage from *De divisione naturae* on the beauty of the universe brings together the most important elements:

> Thus, the beauty of the entire created universe, of like and unlike things, was established with admirable harmony [*marabili quadam harmonia constituta est*] out of different kinds and various forms, and different orders of substances and accidents, but drawn together into an inexpressible unity [*in unitatem quandam ineffabilem compacta*]. Just as melody in music [*organicum melos*] is formed out of different qualities and quantities of sound, when they are heard individually and separately, they are greatly isolated from one another by differences of tension and proportions of release. Yet, when they are adapted to one another according to sure and rational rules in the art of music [*secundum certas rationabilesque artis musicae regulas*] in individual tropes, they yield a certain natural sweetness. Thus, the harmony of the universe [*universitatis concordia*] has been attained according to the uniform will of the Creator out of different subdivisions of one nature, which are dissonant when viewed individually.[176]

Since Ernst Ludwig Waeltner's refutation, the thesis initially proposed in musicology by Hugo Riemann and rather critically summarized by Jacques Handschin, namely that this representation of the *organicum melos* is the first mention of polyphonic music,[177] has been considered outdated.[178] But Waeltner's account, which considers the passage to be a "comparison"[179] of the universe and the *organicum melos*, does not apply either. Creation and *organicum melos* share, in the sufficiently discussed way, the same numerical structure. This is why John Scotus Eriugena resorts to "musical" terminology. Developing the possibilities opened up by the integration of the Neoplatonic, numerically grounded concept of harmony and *Liber sapientiae* 11:21,[180] the passage from *De divisione naturae* offers an order based on the structural homology of numerical orders, as it were a "metonymic" account of the order of the universe conceived as *harmonia*. In accord with its numerical structure, music is the most plausible and immediately "rational," and yet nonetheless sensible manifestation of this "cosmic" harmony. The explanatory value of the metonymy is based thereon.[181] The argument exploits the possibility of extrapolating a theory of the sensible beautiful out of Augustine's work on music. Werner Beierwaltes has made the essential points in his article, the "Idea of Harmony in the Early Middle Ages." He clarified the concept of harmony found in John Scotus Eriugena by reference to his Neoplatonic assumptions, put it in his Pythagorean-Neoplatonic and early medieval Christian context and, against the background of the older discussion already described, inquired into its relevance for music theory.[182] He underscores especially the continuity of the relation between the order of Creation and music, of numerical structure, order, measure, and beauty, which founds the anagogic relevance of the "musical" phenomenon:

> In Eriugena's view, *music* is to be understood as an analogy with the harmony of the world. Because it is determined by created numerical relationships and the possibility of taking the concrete form of a harmony of notes, it can conversely also open up and further the universal harmony on which it is itself based.[183]

Regino's argument that dealing with *musica artificialis* could contribute to the understanding of the *musica naturalis* that also includes *musica mundana* has a true model in John Scotus Eriugena's remarks. It refers, via his illustration of the *pulchritudo universalis* as "musical," to the concept formulated in Augustine:

> The basis of the harmony (the *honestissima concordia* or *conveniens adunatio*) that is identical with beauty and appears as such, is thus not

the perceptible sound of instruments, for instance, but rather the rational (i.e., being itself "ratio" [λόγος] and accessible only to it) *relationships* or *connections* through which the different and contradictory [. . .] are brought together and exist together as a unity: [. . .] These *internal*, intelligible relationships are constitutive for *sense* experience of worldly harmony as well as for the harmony of the "musicum modulamen," and "*appear*" in this dimension (analogously to the concept of "theophany").[184]

On the basis of his findings, Beierwaltes recommends that Handschin's theses be reconsidered against the background of the demonstrated connection between John Scotus Eriugena and Augustine's *De musica*, but did not extend his remarks beyond the author of *De divisione naturae*. The possibility of establishing a connection with Bower's argument concerning Regino is, however, obvious. John Scotus Eriugena defines *musica* as the discipline that illuminates the *harmonia* of the order of Creation: "Music is the discipline that discerns through the light of reason the harmony of all things [*omnium harmoniam rationis lumine dignoscens*], whether they are in motion or in a knowable state, and with natural proportions."[185] Accordingly, education in the *disciplinae*, in whose framework this music theory finds its place, is the presupposition for any higher knowledge. The *disciplina naturalis* "reflects the process of nature itself, for rational thought and nature proceed according to the same dialectical processes: division and analytic."[186] Division differentiates the *essentia* into *genera*, *genera* into *species*, *species* into individuals, individuals into their *partes*; analysis combines the parts into whole entities, and these into *species*, *species* into *genera*, *genera* into *essentiae*—the end of one of the processes is the beginning of the other. In this, the process of reasoning as guided by the disciplines proceeds in analogy to the natural itself, which proceeds out of the unity of its descent and returns back to it:

> The end of all motion is its beginning; it terminates in no other end but its beginning, from which it begins to be moved, and toward which it always desires to return, to stop, and rest there. This can be understood not only from the parts of the world, but also from the whole world itself. For its end is its beginning, which it seeks, and having found it, it comes to rest. Its substance does not perish, but it returns to the conditions [*rationes*] out of which it set forth.[187]

In the following John Scotus Eriugena explains how the principle of cyclical movement works in the *disciplinae naturales*. Grammar begins with the letters from which everything written takes its departure, and into which analysis breaks it down again; rhetoric begins with a question, on which the whole argument is based and to which it leads back; dialectic begins with the *essentia*, from which all forms develop and to which they are reduced; arithmetic begins with the number one, out of which all numbers develop and to which they are traced back; geometry begins with the point, out of which all figures are developed and into which they are all resolved again.[188] Music begins with the *tonus*: "Does not music begin from its beginning, which we call [*tonum*]? And does it not move around harmonies [*symphonias*], whether simple or complex, which repeat its tone, that is, its beginning, because it subsists with all it strength and power in tone?"[189] Bower shows that by the word *tonus* the text refers to the concept that is commonly called *modus* (a conceptual vagueness that was usual at the time) and that the reference to *modus* corresponds exactly to the argument in Regino of Prüm's *Epistola de armonica institutione*:

> Thus, natural music is that which produces sound with no musical instrument, no touch of the fingers, no human striking or touch, but breathed upon by God, and with nature alone as teacher it measures out the modes [*divinus adspirata sola natura docente dulces modulatur modos*]. This music comes about in the motion of the heavens or in the human voice. Some add a third kind that is made by irrational creatures with sound or voice.[190]

The *modus* sung with the voice, man's divinely created instrument, is thus supposed to correspond, with respect to its cyclical "movement" through the scale defined by a given *modus*—in Middle Latin, a term for the mode or key and the interval, and also a rhythm concept of the *ars antiqua* and the *ars nova*[191]—to the *motus coeli*. The argument broadens the theologically motivated conception of the voice, which may have been borrowed from Cassiodorus, as a "natural instrument" by giving it a consistently "musical" and thus to that extent, within the domain of the late antique body of theory, more consistent dimension of meaning.

Regino's complex distinction thus becomes clear against the background of the speculative music theory of Late Antiquity and the efforts made by thinkers such as John Scotus Eriugena to build on the same foundations. It provides a systematic place for *musica vocalis* and extracts Christian choral chant from the general devaluation of the practice of music, without endangering the conceptual rigor of the discourse of speulative music theory itself. Correspondingly, Hammerstein sums up: "This is fundamentally the ancient doctrine that is merely using other terms. The Boethian conception ultimately underlies it."[192]

However, precisely the observation that the conceptual rigor of the Boethian theory is preserved raises the question of the fate of *musica humana*. We have already emphasized in this connection the functional significance of this medial element of Boethius's triad for the whole of his music theory. In fact, the concept is also found in the *Epistola*, in the paragraphs devoted to the doctrine of ethos.[193] By convention, modes are classified according to their affective character and named after the archaic Greek tribes these affective characters are associated with. Regino extends the usual classification to include a differentiation in accord with the individual's age, but otherwise repeats the thesis that certain *modi* correspond to certain affective conditions.[194] The explanations of the distinction *musica naturalis/musica artificialis* leave no doubt that it covers the domain of the *musicae* in a totalizing way: at the same time, the use of the concept of *musica humana* as well shows that Regino's distinction emerges from a conscious debate with the Boethian triad. Conveying both classifications can be described as a metonymic reduction: *musica humana,* which in Boethius means, to grossly oversimplify, the "harmonic" *coaptatio* sometimes of the body and soul, sometimes of the parts of the soul, appears here sometimes as the condition of the possibility of its product, regular song, and sometimes as an effect of music.[195] It determines the ability to sing: Only those are capable of choral chanting whose *musica humana* is in harmony with Christian doctrine, whose body and soul are in accord.[196] A similar argumentative structure—only the good man can be a good orator—is familiar from the treatises on rhetoric in the tradition of Cicero and Quintilian. In music theory, Engelbert of Admont was to argue this way, although in this particular regard, on Aristotelian bases.[197] *Musica humana* thus remains the mediating part of *musica mundana* and of a musical practice, but insofar as the special case of choral chant becomes central and is combined with *musica mundana* to form *musica naturalis*, it is deprived of the special worth that Boethius had attributed to it. Ethical questions have come to be monopolized by the theological discourse; remains and residues of pagan anthropology are progressively reduced. For the music theory presented here as a whole, this reduction is of minor relevance. The traditional body of theory's conceptual cohesion remains intact.

Regino's suggestion to adapt the traditional system of classification to include Christian vocal practice is in itself largely convincing.[198] The constitution of the voice as an "instrument" created by God himself might also have clearly strained the late antique body of theory, but it could build on the theorem of the priority of *causa* over *effectus* and thus expect a certain consistency and hence connectibility within the discursive landscape of the

Middle Ages. The eminent promotion of what Deschamps called "musique de bouche" ("mouth music"),[199] a direct consequence of Regino's classification, nonetheless remains bound—and this must be strongly emphasized—to precisely this theocentric constitution of the Christian order of discourse. It is based on a "shortcut" on the way to be followed, qua tracing the analogical references, from the phenomenon to its final cause: the absence of a man-made instrument. The "musicality" of verse is not discussed in Regino's *Epistola de armonica institutione,* in accord with the reason for the textbook, and brought back in only in the course of the reception of its distinction.

Beyond the *musica naturalis/musica artificialis* distinction, the influence of the text, given its general conformity to the Boethian basis, is limited to secondary aspects that we need not discuss in our survey: the subsumption of the sounds of the creature without reason under *musica naturalis* and the defining disassociation of *vox* and *sonus,* which goes its own way. The reception history of the text can be explained only by the success of the *musica naturalis/musica artificialis* distinction. Its adoption in some of the central works on music theory in the High Middle Ages clearly indicates that Regino's way of integrating Christian vocal music into the traditional body of theory was regarded as plausible. Johannes Cotto's *De musica,* written around 1100 and one of the most widely disseminated treatises on music theory between 1100 and 1400, transmits Regino's distinction;[200] it is found again in a modified form in Johannes de Muris's *Musica speculativa secundum Boethium* of 1323,[201] which was written hardly seventy years before Deschamps's *Art de dictier.* Although the latest manuscripts of the *Epistola de armonica institutione* date from the twelfth century,[202] at the end of the fifteenth century Adam of Fulda seems to quote the work directly.[203] In the interest of our hypothesis of continuity, we will pursue further the path indicated by these texts.

Speculative Music Theory in the Boethian Tradition up to 1250

Over the following centuries, the music theory established in the ninth century on Boethian grounds underwent modifications, some of which were important. This theory could not fail to be affected by the general evolution of the order of discourse toward a unified Scholastic method, usually provisionally outlined by reference to Anselm of Canterbury (d. 1109), Peter Abelard (d. 1142), and the Aristotelianism that was then establishing itself, the highpoints of Christian Platonisms[204] in the School of Chartres or around the Augustinian canons abbey founded by William of Champeaux

(d. 1121), the reorientation and completion of Scholastic theory construction on Aristotelian foundations in the course of the thirteenth century, and finally the outbreak of epistemologically pessimistic nominalism. Accordingly, what is at issue here is not the coevolution of discourses assumed and generally traced back to Aristotelianism and nominalism by research on the late Middle Ages, but rather the modes of this coevolution. Following Dragonetti, the research summarized in part I presupposes an erosion of the Neoplatonic concept of music that begins, if not simultaneously, at least very close in time to these developments: the nominalistic argument exerts influence through the work of William of Ockham (c. 1285–1349/50), which was written after 1330.[205] Deschamps's text was written in 1392. In the following, we maintain on the contrary that the discourse of speculative music theory was less spontaneously devalued by the Aristotelian challenge than research on the Late Middle Ages tends to assume. Moreover, the discourse of music theory reacted by attempting to address the arising problem of discrepant theoretical approaches to "musical" phenomena by the production of integrative models. In the course of the fourteenth century, most treatises on music theory still argued conservatively, continuing the Neoplatonic conception of music even where the Aristotelian arguments against music as *scientia mathematica* were known—partly at the price of creating contradictory bodies of theory and lines of argument. In the discourse of speculative music theory, little attention was paid to the nominalistic argument. We will prove these claims by using selected passages from the work of Johannes Cotto (Afflighemensis) (c. 1100), Aribo Scholasticus (end of the eleventh century), Jerome of Moravia (c. 1250), Johannes Aegidius Zamorensis (c. 1250–1300/1318), Engelbert of Admont (c. 1250–1331), Marchettus of Padua (b. 1274), Johannes de Muris (1295–before 1360), Jacob of Liège (b. 1260), Ugolino of Orvieto (c. 1380–1452), and Adam of Fulda (c. 1445–1505), and also draw on texts on scientific theory and didactic materials.

The late antique system of the *artes*, including the place and concept of *musica scientia*, remained largely stable down to the work of the School of Chartres. William of Conche's (c. 1090–after 1154) commentary, *Glosae super Platonem*, preceded by a potent *Accessus ad Timaeum*,[206] formulates a brief overview of the scientific theory of his time. Philosophy is divided into *practica* and *theorica*; *ethica, echonomica*, and *politica* belong to *philosophia practica*.[207] *Philosophia theorica* includes *theologia, mathematica*, and *phisica*; *philosophia mathematica* includes the quadrivial disciplines.[208] Only music is given its own, comparatively more extensive paragraph, in which three *species musicae* are distinguished: "There are three kinds of music: instrumental [*instrumentalis*], cosmic [*mundana*], and human [*humana*]. There are three types of instrumental music: melic [*melica*], metric [*metrica*], and rhythmic [*rithmica*]. There are three kinds of melic music: diatonic, enharmonic, and chromatic."[209] The individual classemes are familiar; the expression *musica melica* (instead of *harmonica*) is found here for the first time and spread during the thirteenth century under the influence of texts transmitted by Arab writers. The Boethian triad continued to be taken for granted, as was the subsumption under music of metrical discourse as *musica metrica* or *rithmica*. The textbooks that took this *ordo scientiarum* into account are compiled in Thierry of Chartres's (c. 1085–1156) *Heptateuchon*,[210] an important source for the beginning reception of Aristotle, which already lists the whole *Organon* with the sole exception of the *Analytica posteriora*. Thierry's prologue[211] allows us to prove the hegemonic validity of the Boethian propaedeutics for the quadrivial disciplines.[212] Alain of Lille's (1120–1202) *Anticlaudianus*, written a generation later, bears witness to this hegemony. This work, which borrows both its structure and its goals from Martianus Capella's *De nuptiis Philologiae et Mercurii*, seeks to provide an encyclopedic inventory of the knowledge of its time. The seven liberal arts appear as *septem sorores*, as seven maidenly sisters who make a brief survey of the objects of "their" arts. Music is dealt with here in the familiar ways. In addition to its *effectus*, its cosmological implications are summarized, and three species distinguished:

> Music marks off the months, establishes the seasons of the year,
> Limits variations, binds the elements together, links the planets,
> Moves the stars, and alters their location. Music weaves together
> The parts of the human body, and sets in order the little cosmos,
> And adorns him with the appearance of the greater world.
> Thus, the pigmy deserves to be little brother to the giant,
> And the lesser being to be portrayed in the image of the greater.
> Music unites the parts of the soul, [. . .]
> [. . .], and regulates pitches,
> And number marks out their intervals.[213]

With the completion of the Aristotelian *Organon*, first the reception of the *Topics*, the *Elenchus*, and the *Analytics*, and then with the appropriation of Aristotle's complete works, Jewish-Arab and later Neoplatonic sources, the shift in the High Middle Ages's epistemology begins. On this subject, we can refer to general overviews.[214] During the transition from Early to High Scholasticism the Augustinian canons' abbey of St. Victor near Paris, led by its abbot, Hugo of St. Victor (c. 1097–1141), experienced its heyday. The propaedeutic and encyclopedic works that were produced there are among the most important between Anselm of Canterbury and the great *summae* of High Scholasticism.[215] The *Eruditionis didascaliae libri VII*, usually known as the *Didascalion* and composed around 1128, is considered the most important "work on epistemology produced by Early Scholasticism"[216] and "enjoyed," as Weisheipl puts it, a "continuous circulation from the time it was written."[217] The encyclopedically arranged introduction to philosophy and theology is based on the Augustinian instrumentalization of secular knowledge for the acquisition of insight into the order of being that leads to the *vita beata*.[218] The classification of secular sciences proposed here, taken from Radulfus Arden's *Speculum universale*, is "one of the most influential of medieval classifications of knowledge."[219] *Philosophia* is divided, in accord with a combination of Stoic and Boethian-Aristotelian distinctions, into "theorica (id est speculativa), practica (id est, ethica, moralis), mechanica, logica." *Philosophia practica* is further divided into ethics, economics, and politics, while *philosophia theorica* is further divided into "theologia, mathematica, physica," and *mathematica* into "arithmetica, musica, geometria, astronomia."[220] The quadrivium remains the path to the *secreta sapientiae* of Creation, to the vision of the "laws of order and harmony in the macro- and microcosm as God's good Creation."[221] The classification of the *musicae* is based on Boethius, but merges the expansions of his classification up to that point in a subtle classification of the manifestations of the numerical harmonic order. Because of the elaborate, detailed nature of the passages concerned, Hugo's classification will be presented in the form of a diagram (diagrams 9 and 10).[222]

The classification rests on the Pythagorean-Neoplatonic foundation that had been the basis of music theory since late antiquity and includes the whole of the area covered by the Boethian triad. In "music of the elements" we note in particular the differentiation that reminds us of *Liber sapientiae* 11:21. Unlike Aurelianus Reomensis and Regino of Prüm, the "music of the voice" is classified not under *musica humana* but rather under *musica instrumentalis*. However, the music of the voice is differentiated depending on the *instrumentum* producing the sound. It accordingly combines chants (*cantilenae*) and song (*carmina*), that is, verse. Correspondingly, poetry falls under music, and poets under musicians, as an addition, a quotation from Boethius's *De insitutione musica* I.34, emphasizes once again: "There are also three kinds of music: one that composes songs [*carmina fingit*], another that involves instruments, a third that judges instrumental works and song."[223]

musica

musica mundana		musica humana		musica instrumentalis	
elementis	numero pondere mensura	corpore	vegetatione humoribus operatione	pulsu	tympanis chordis
planetis	situ motu naturae	anima	virtutibus potentiis	flatu	tibils organis
temporibus	diebus mensibus annis	connexu utriusque	est quaedam naturalis amicita	voce	carminibus cantilenis

music

world music		human music		instrumental music	
elements	number weight measure	body	vegetation humors works	striking	drums strings
planets	location movement nature	soul	abilities powers	breath	flutes organ
seasons	days months years	uniting both	is a certain natural friendship	voice	songs chants

Musica scientia according to Hugo of St. Victor, *Didascalion* II.12, col. 756a–757b

The classification of *musica instrumentalis* in accord with the ways of producing sound and the clear emphasis on the voice that we have already seen in the works of Aurelianus Reomensis and Regino of Prüm does not contradict, either for these authors or for Hugo of St. Victor, the "holistic" concept of music based on the Boethian tradition. The same holds for contemporary treatises on music, even if they are conceived as manuals remaining close to practice. Three examples, the writings on music by Johannes Cotto, Jerome of Moravia, and Aribo Scholasticus, may be used to prove this.

Johannes Cotto's *De musica*[224] written around 1100, is a critical appropriation of Guido of Arrezo's *Micrologus* in line with tradition.[225] It became one of the most widely read writings on music theory in the Middle Ages, and was still being regularly copied after 1400.[226] The work largely avoids the usual preface on the phenomenon of music in the horizon of its cosmological implications, on classificatory or etymological questions. Cotto discusses the usefulness of a knowledge of music theory for clerics, briefly aligns music with the canon of the *artes*, offers a few statements on the origin of music, and then begins *in medias res* with a passage "How many musical instruments are there."[227] The few introductory words that are nonetheless found here thus take on the appearance of the fundamental and elementary. The classification of the *musicae* it presents is thus instructive in our context. Though very briefly, the Boethian triad and Regino's distinction are both mentioned. The presentation proves the substantial penetration of Regino's argument:

> It is known that there are two kinds of instruments for all sounds [*instrumenta omnium sonorum*]: natural and artificial. The natural is divided into the cosmic and the human [*naturale aliud mundanum aliud humanum*]. According to the philosophers, the natural instrument is a harmonious dissonance of celestial motion, which is rightly called harmony [*harmonia*]. I call the spaces of the throat, which we call the windpipe, a natural instrument, for they are naturally suited [*naturaliter aptae*] to take in and breathe out air, and from this action sound is produced. [. . .] An instrument is called artificial because it is suited to producing artificial sound, that is, sound not produced by means of nature [*non per naturam, sed per artificium ad reddendum sonitum adaptatur*].[228]

The accent Johannes Cotto puts on sound and the ways of producing it also does not contradict the "holistic" layout of the concept of music. The quantifiability of acoustic phenomena, the foundation of consonances in the system of proportions and their reducibility to the Pythagorean *tetraktys* make every "musical" acoustic phenomenon appear to be constituted in a way analogous to the numerical harmonic order of Creation, so long as the conception of *musica* as *scientia mathematica* is taken for granted.[229] Accordingly, verse, as "rationally ordered" by numbers, is to that extent *musica*. This is suggested by an interesting remark that closes the passage on the *potentiae musicae*: A lack of educational material must not lead the practician to neglect practice. He can—nota bene—teach himself by studying the poet's verses: "Although new compositions in the church are not necessary now, we can nevertheless exercise our talents in singing the rhythms and the mournful verses of the poets [*in rhythmis, & lugubribus versibus poetarum*]."[230]

Although the relation between Johannes Cotto and Regino is obvious, neither he nor Boethius are mentioned explicitly. The distinction must have become, along with the Boethian triad, part of the common classificatory stock, which can be adopted, as Johannes Cotto does, but also modified, for example with regard to the body of phenomena in question. The first possibility is further illustrated by Jerome of Moravia, the second by Aribo Scholasticus.

Jerome of Moravia's *Tractatus de musica*, an extensive work of compilation, was produced in Paris between 1272 and 1304.[231] Of the twenty-eight chapters assembling disparate doctrines with the goal of presenting a broad panorama of the music theory of its time, only three, chapters 24, 25, and 28, offer independent achievements by the writer. The other sections rely on repeating verbatim or paraphrasing older sources, the central thread of the argument following Boethius. The treatise begins with the connection between *motus, proportio,* and *consonantia,* along with a description of the processes of evaluating consonance according to Boethius, conceives *musica* in accord with Boethius's definition as the science of the *multitudo ad aliquid* and establishes in detail the relation with the Pythagorean-Neoplatonic theory of numbers following *De institutione arithmetica.*[232] On the classification of music, Jerome presents the approaches of Boethius, Cassiodorus, Isidore, and now also Al-Farabi. Thus the triad *musica mundana/humana/ intrumentalis* is mentioned several times, quoted from different theoreticians referring to Boethius, differentiated, and proven with examples of the respective manifestation of the numerical harmonic order.[233] In chapter 9, *De sujecto musice,* it is cited from Johannes Cotto's *De musica*—along with the distinctions drawn by Regino:

> The subject of music is sound itself, but separated into kinds [*discretus*]. According to Johannes: "there are two kinds of instruments for making sound: natural and artificial [*naturale scilicet et artificiale*]. The natural kind comprises the human [*humana*] and the cosmic [*mundana*]. Natural sound is a harmonious consonance of celestial motion [*caelestis volubilitas concors consonantia*], which is rightly called harmony. We call the spaces in the throat, which we term the windpipe, a natural instrument of man [*naturale autem instrumentum humanum*], for they are naturally suited to take in and breathe out air, and from this action they naturally

produce sound. An instrument is called artificial because it is suited to producing artificial sound, that is, sound not produced by means of nature [*non per naturam, sed per artificium ad reddendum sonum adaptatur*]."[234]

It is then explained, following Boethius's *De institutione musica* I.34, who is to be considered a "musician":

> Therefore, while there are three kinds of men who deal with music, the instrumentalist, the poet, and the musician, Boethius teaches us what to think about the musician at the end of the first book of his work on music, saying: "There are three kinds of people engaged in musical art. One is concerned with instruments, the second composes songs [*fingit carmina*], and the third judges instrumental performance and song."[235]

Jerome of Moravia offers an extensively documented panorama of the music theory of his time. It is dominated by Boethius's speculative concept of music and its foundations in the ontology of number. For our purposes here, panoramas of this kind are instructive in the same way as concisely composed theoretical texts, and the lack of coherent argumentation and structured presentation, which cannot be wholly denied, should not be allowed to deceive us regarding the diffusion and massive reception of such compilations. They leave no doubt as to the currency and dominance of the speculative substrate in music theory. This holds true down to the late Middle Ages: As Christian Meyer has shown, Jerome of Moravia's treatise remained a widely used textbook down to the fifteenth century.[236]

In accord with the hegemony of the speculative concept of music, at the end of the eleventh century we find an assessment of the possibilities that the totalizing structure of the concept opens up. This can be shown by asking how Regino of Prüm's *musica naturalis/musica artificialis* distinction was used. The Benedictine Aribo Scholasticus[237] was a theoretician "familiar with the most recent technical literature. He had a critical attitude toward contemporary scholarship, was schooled in Neo-Pythagorean and Neoplatonic ways of thought as well as in Christian theology," and rose to become toward the end of the eleventh century "one of the most important representatives of medieval music symbolism."[238] Between 1068 and 1078, he produced his treatise *De musica*,[239] which is extant in thirteen manuscripts.[240] This clairvoyant work adopts Regino's *musica naturalis/musica artificialis* distinction and formulates a consequence that has to be drawn from the privileging of the voice as an *instrumentum*, on the one hand, and from the totalizing structure of the discourse of speculative music theory, on the other hand. Aribo starts out from a simple observation. The histrions unanimously condemned in Christian-late antique music theory sing, as Boethius acknowledged regarding poets, out of "natural instinct."[241] They use proper sound materials, and bring their melodies "back to the keynote," just as Regino had said about *musica naturalis*:[242]

> Although art does not discover something first and nature later, a certain wise man claims that what came forth from the womb of the mother rough and course, nevertheless became nicely polished through art. For art is said to derive from strict rules [*ab arctis regulis*], to which it must adhere and conform. We can conclude in particular that music is quite closely related to and natural in us by the fact that histrions [*histriones*], completely wanting in knowledge of the art of music, blamelessly sing secular odes that in no way violate the various positions of tones and semitones, and that properly return to the final pitch. Therefore, Plato discusses the birth of the soul plausibly, if not truly, and says that it has been shaped according to musical proportions.[243]

Regino had also already formulated the argument concerning the practical priority of *musica naturalis*: "natural music by far precedes artificial music."[244] But he had also seen vocal music as being exclusively Christian choral music. Aribo in contrast uses the *musica naturalis/musica artificialis* distinction to differentiate between dilettantes and singers educated in music theory. The histrions are counted among the lay people. They produce good music out of *iocunditas*. The argument follows the Boethian doctrine of ethos, whose point Aribo clearly discerns: "Anyone can understand that music is ethical, that is, moral, because [. . .] it confers its benefits without the perception of art [*sua confert beneficia sine artis perceptione*]."[245] The histrion's music is well-measured, uses proper sound material, and is in addition appropriate in terms of mood. But it is limited, Aribo says rather theoretically, to the intervals *sesquitertia*, *sesquialtera*, and *sesquioctava*, to the fourth, the fifth, and the octave, the perfect consonances contained in the "first *tetraktys*."[246] Aribo sees these as being in "natural" *similitudo* to the elated mood of *iocunditas*, whose suitable expression requires no education in music theory. He therefore considers the music of histrions as *musica naturalis*. In contrast, someone who can complete these frame intervals—by dichotomic division[247]—to form a heptatonic scale, who combines his practical abilities with a substantial understanding of its theoretical foundations is practicing *musica artificialis*:

> Histrions and other such musicians are such by nature, not by art. The musician by art is one who understands clearly the natural composition of all forms: diatessaron, diapente, diapason; he recognizes through reason

the servile disposition of the tropes of nature; he evaluates efficiently the operation of the principal chords; he retains in memory the appropriateness of the tropes, which consist of six chords.[248]

Aribo reads Regino accurately. The *Epistola de armonica institutione* had ascribed the intervals *diatessaron*, *diapente*, and *diapason* solely to *musica artificialis*.[249] Aribo's appropriation of Regino's distinction runs the risk, like Deschamps's *Art de dictier*, of being read from a modern point of view as an apology for the lay person and his "art."[250] In actuality, Aribo's treatise realizes the potential that the colonization of the numerically based, Neoplatonic concept of music had opened up to the Christian order of discourse: the devaluation of *everything* created to the benefit of the Creator, the conception of *every* form of order as a *signum* referring to this Creator, its reduction to a sensible manifestation and reification of the one *ordo*.[251] The lay person corresponds here to the verse from Virgil that Augustine cites in *De musica*. Its profane content does not diminish the anagogic potential of the verse; this potential is an intrinsic quality of its form. Analogously, Aribo's argument is not, or no more than secondarily, a discourse *pro arte*, but rather an explanation of the systematic place of every kind of music *as music* within the Christian order of discourse in general and in speculative music theory in particular: it is the realization of a God-given potential.

The expansion of the argument that Aribo's treatise demonstrates can be proven in various contexts, including those that research on the late Middle Ages has assumed to be distant models for the practice of the *rhétoriqueurs*. In connection with the work of Jean Molinet, Paul Zumthor observed: "Minstrelsy [*jonglerie*] belongs to a 'paragrammatic' semiotic practice."[252] Molinet's work is thus situated in a certain tradition that Zumthor's work on minstrelsy had helped us discern and understand.[253] In the work of the *joculatores*, which was in verse, Zumthor notes, with a generalizing intention, the following:

> Also, in this respect the minstrels represent, in our view, the tip of the iceberg that reveals a universal essence. From Latin to the vernacular languages, from the literate cleric to the itinerant entertainer, the same tendency traverses and animates eight or ten centuries of poetry. Language, transformed by the magic of verse, is founded less on a "reality," on an external model governing the ordinary perception of facts, than on itself.[254]

We want to contrast this conception, which seems to conceive the poetic discourse of the Middle Ages as self-referential per se, with an illustration, a

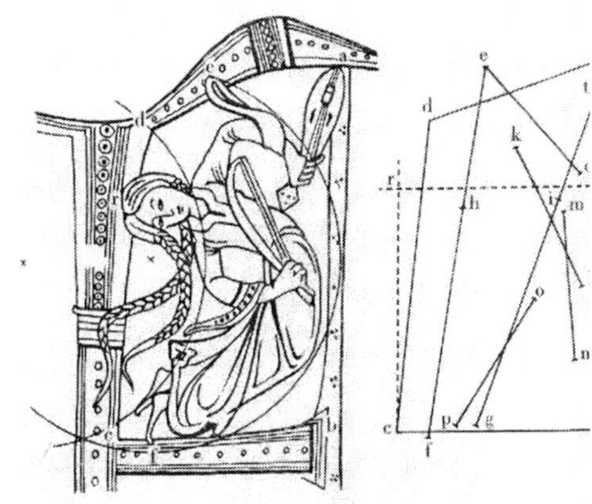

Initial from the Montiramey breviary, late twelfth or early thirteenth century, BNF lat. 796, fol. 212v. Sketch after Waesberghe 1967 (reproduction by courtesy of Bärenreiter Verlag, Kassel, Germany)

miniature from the well-known Montiramey breviary, a late twelfth or early thirteenth century manuscript now in the French national library.[255] The female minstrel swinging her braids, depicted in a striking pose and in detail by an artist from the school of Cluny, decorates the letter F. The figure is clearly framed, the head, braids, and flying left sleeve overflow the frame, as do the lute and the toes of her right foot. Joseph Smits van Waesberghe, who was the first to pay attention to this illustration,[256] discerned a puncture in the parchment under the head. At the same level, at left next to the downstroke of the F, a red dot can be seen. Both markings remain from the use of a circle that aided in the construction of the figure, as the drawing below shows. Two circles predetermine the form of the image, even if the swinging of the robe obscures the rhythm of the drawing. Something surprising is revealed if the most prominent points in the drawing are connected with lines, as is shown in the sketch. The point r locates the part in the girl's hair, point e the tip of the high-flying sleeve, point f the tips of the toes on the right foot. The line a–i indicates the length of the lute, the line a–t the length from the bridge to the end of the tailpiece, the line e–q the length from the extreme tip of the sleeve to the hand on the neck of the lute, etc.

Waesberghe has measured the corresponding lengths and found the following relationships: ig : ai = kl : eh = 3:2; ai : ti = 4:3; ai = eh = kl = op = eq = mn = ½ de; ai : de = 1:2. The relationships in length correspond to those of the Pythagorean *tetraktys*. The verse of the female minstrel playing the lute may really be, as Zumthor maintains, a self-referential play with words. But as the construction of the image suggests, to the twelfth-century illustrator the minstrel's playing—her *musica vulgaris*, as it was beginning to be called in the High Middle Ages[257]—seems to be no more and no less than a manifestation of the one and only *musica*.

The Reception of Aristotle I. *Musica disciplina* in a Collection of *Quaestiones* Provided by the Paris Faculty of Arts around 1250 (Ms. Barcelona, Ripoll 109)

The consequences of the reception of the complete Aristotelian *Organon* for Early Scholastic realism have been studied exhaustively.[258] We can limit ourselves here to brief remarks in connection with the introduction to the analogical order of discourse in Chapter II.1, which will help situate the following discussion.

With the appropriation of Aristotelian hylomorphism,[259] the Christian order of discourse reached its highest degree of systematization. The consequences of the perfection achieved are familiar. They led to the "self-destabilization" of the theological order of discourse and ultimately to the epistemological pessimism of the nominalists. The decree published on 7 March 1277 by the bishop of Paris, Etienne Tempier (d. 1279), states that the initial assumption of the Scholastic will to systematization, the assumption that Creation is similar to the Creator, ordered toward him and stable and fixed in this order, necessarily leads to the consequence that God must be conceived as an entity bound to its creation—and that therefore the predicate *omnipotentia* must be denied him.[260] Among the 219 incriminated theses are two central lessons of St. Thomas Aquinas, in particular his theory of individuation.

Thomas applied the Aristotelian set of tools to the conceptualization of the relationship of the Creator and his Creation, whereas Patristics had worked with Paul's concept of the Creator revealed in Creation.[261] The argument Thomas uses as a leitmotif in the *Summa theologiae* is strikingly expressed in I, qu. 9, art. 1 ad 2: There is nothing that was not created by God, and therefore nothing that is not itself related to him by a relationship of similarity. The degree of this similarity varies according to the distance from the "unmoved mover":

Nothing can exist which does not come from divine wisdom by way of a certain imitation [*quod non procedat a divina sapientia per quandam imitationem*], just as from the first effective and formal principle; so, too, works of art come from the wisdom of the artist. Therefore, in as much as likeness to divine wisdom comes in degrees from the highest of things, which more fully participate in its likeness, down to the lowest of things, which participate less [*similitudo divinae sapientiae gradatim procedit a supremis, quae magis participant de eius similitudine, usque ad infima rerum, quae minus participant*], there is said to be a certain procession and motion of divine wisdom into a thing: just as when we say that the sun reaches the earth, when a ray of its light strikes the earth.[262]

In this system, the individuating principle is matter.[263] Through the separation of the analogical principle (qua relation to the Creator) from the individuating principle (qua materiality), individual characteristics—of the individual, the species, the genus—are reduced to secondary characteristics. Primary importance is given to analogical relationships, to the "signature" of God. The conception of the existing plurality as a product of the matricial multiplication of identical forms of being reduces everything individual to its exemplary quality. Only through this quality does it acquire a relative dignity, for instance, as an object of knowledge.[264] *Sub specie aeternitatis*, the infinite plenitude of historical individuals is reduced to a few, hierarchically differentiated classes. In contrast to the equally "totalizing" concept of order in early, Neoplatonically conceived stages of the development of analogical discourse, the Thomistic doctrine of individuation leads to a harmonization of relational connections that so thoroughly suppresses the concept of opposition that the theory loses sight of the world: "On its most developed level, this discourse's model of the world no longer shapes the world, but now refers back largely to its own principles."[265] The two paradigms are not in a relationship of opposition but rather in one of complementarity: the incipient new hylomorphic-metaphysical Thomism holds fast, on dogmatic grounds, to the Augustinian concept of order. Although it turns partially against its Neoplatonic basis, Thomism adheres to the traditional doctrine by preserving its conceptual points and systematic implications. As in the following we aim for statements regarding the status of Neoplatonic elements beyond the reception of Aristotle, and therefore regarding the profile of analogical discourse in the later Middle Ages, this aspect of Thomism will have to be taken into account. As will be shown in the following chapters, this is crucial for discerning and understanding basic continuities in the discourse of speculative music theory.

From the beginnings of the reception of Aristotle to the complete development of Scholastic Aristotelianism, more than a hundred years went by. Around 1125 the school of translators established by Archbishop Raymond of Toledo began its work; around 1150 we can prove a familiarity with the whole of the Aristotelian *Organon* in the work of Johannes Gundissalinus, who had translated Al-Farabi's *De scientiis* into Latin.[266] However, Albert the Great was the first to address the revision and reorientation of the fund of theological theory building guided by Aristotle, which Thomas's hylomorphist metaphysics was to complete. The extensive diffusion of the new doctrine was ensured by the establishment of the *corpus aristotelicum* in educational institutions. The regulations issued by the Paris faculty of arts on 19 March 1255 made the study of the two *Analytics* and the *Topics*, conceived as *logica nova*, obligatory for prospective theologians.[267] In addition to the *Categories* and *De interpretatione* in Boethius's translation and with his commentary, that is, in addition to basic logical concepts, Aristotelian methodology and epistemology were now to be studied as well. The consequences for the concept of the quadrivial sciences, which was very closely connected with Neoplatonic ontology of number and thus for speculative music theory are foreseeable.[268] Since a discovery made by Martin Grabmann in 1927, these consequences can be reconstructed by reference to a document that allows us to determine precisely the effects of the reception of Aristotle on the discussion of music theory and the doctrine of *musica scientia*.

Between 1230 and 1240/45, an unknown compiler put together a collection of *quaestiones* that sums up the knowledge required for baccalaureate or licentiate examination at the University of Paris's faculty of arts. The text, which is extant in the manuscript Barcelona, Ripoll 190,[269] is ordered by disciplines. Each section is preceded by a brief introduction designating the objects of the *scientia* concerned and the standard textbook. For music, Boethius's *Institutio musica* is recommended[270] and adduced for the introductory classification of *musica* in accord with the familiar triad:

> Music consists of discrete movable quantity [*de quantitate discreta mobili est musica*], for it consists of sound, or of number determined by proportion in sonority [*contractus numerus in proportione sonoritatis*]. It is divided into three parts. One is instrumental [*instrumentalis*], another cosmic [*mundana*], another human [*humana*]. Instrumental music is that which explores the sound of flutes, drums, and instruments of that sort. Cosmic music is perceived in the sonority of the parts of the world, and especially the greatest of the super-celestial bodies. The philosophers

maintained that sweet-sounding harmony is found in the lower celestial bodies, which perhaps is not heard by us because of the great distance between us and those bodies. Human music is perceived in the modulated raising and lowering of the voice, as seen in various kinds of songs.[271]

The conspicuous accentuation of concrete acoustic phenomena must not contradict the speculative aims of music theory as we have followed. The relationship of mutual confirmation of the sense experience of consonance and the speculative system allows shifts of accent of this kind. It is not the traditional range of the objects of music theory discourse that causes problems, but rather the shift of its epistemological framework in the wake of the reception of Aristotle. The form of *quaestio* that was being established made this apparent.

The *quaestio* formulates or quotes theses, confronts them with objections (*objectiones*), and usually concludes with arguments beginning with the phrase *sed contra* that refute the objections and confirm the initial theses or, if necessary, modify them. In the *objectiones* it is usual to cite authorities, whether that of the *Scriptures* or that of the Doctors of the Church. The form tends to *harmonize* the authorities and the initial thesis. If necessary, differences are conjured away by greatly broadening the interpretive framework or by introducing or differentiating conceptual distinctions. In the case of speculative music theory, these efforts to harmonize discrepant bodies of theory fail: the Aristotelian contributions often explicitly contradict the authorities. The conflict—which indirectly contributes to strengthening dialectic at the expense of *artes* and *auctoritates*—is based on the Aristotelian criticism of the Pythagorean-Platonic concept of number in the *Physics* and *Metaphysics*. Additionally, Aristotelian contributions to "musical" subjects in a stricter sense are taken into account, for example regarding the difference between *sonus* and *vox* according to *De anima* II.8 (419b–421a) and the work *De sensu et sensato*, I (437a) and VII (448a–b), on the concept of the harmony of the spheres according to *De caelo et mundo* II.9 (290b–291a), and finally on *vox* and *harmonia* according to chapter 11 (898b–906a) and chapter 19 (917b–923a) of the *Problemata*—a text that is spurious but nonetheless quickly gained wide distribution through Peter of Abano's commentary of 1303.[272] The collection of *quaestiones* designates emerging contradictions and develops solutions on Aristotelian bases without opening up to question the whole of the body of theory established on Boethian principles.[273]

The collection of *quaestiones* defines the object of *musica scientia* not as Boethius does, that is, as *multitudo ad aliquid*, but rather as *quantitas discreta mobilis*.[274] This changes the relation between music and arithmetic: according to Boethius, the object of the latter is *multitudo per se*, that of the former *multitudo ad aliquid*; the collection of *quaestiones* conceives numbers operating in music through the predicate of "mobility." This specification follows initially from the effort to unify the conception of the quadrivium according to Boethius himself. The relationship between arithmetic and music is aligned, presumably under the influence of Aristotle's *Physics*,[275] with that between geometry (*magnitudo immobilis*) and astronomy (*magnitudo mobilis*).[276]

Insofar as sound is defined as *quantitas discreta mobilis*, the definition may be related to Boethius's (and Augustine's) definition of *motus* as the *causa efficiens* of sound and remains coherent within the Boethian body of theory, although referring to *quantitas* instead of *multitudo* gives it an Aristotelian appeal.[277] It conceives the subject of *musica scientia* as number "determined by" *sonus*: "Music consists of discrete movable quantity [*de quantitate discreta mobili est musica*], for it consists of sound, or of number determined by proportion in sonority [*contractus numerus in proportione sonoritatis*]."[278] For *musica instrumentalis* and, as we have seen by following the development from Cassiodorus to Johannes Cotto, *musica humana*, this new view is unproblematic. For the concept of *musica mundana*, whose plausibility essentially consisted in the possibility of integrating lifeworld phenomena that are "ordered" and to that extent display *numerositas*, this definition leads to an accentuation of its most "implausible" aspect: the music of the spheres as an actual acoustic phenomenon. This, however, is not the goal of the operation. Instead, it is an argumentative concession that serves a goal that is not exactly Aristotelian: subsuming all three of the Boethian *genera musicae* under the definition of music as *quantitas discreta mobilis* preserves the possibility of conceiving *musica scientia, within* the Aristotelian horizon, as a mathematical science:

> Sound is defined as determined number, as number related to sound, and thus is declared to be a specification of number and, consequently, a subject of mathematics. The otherwise imperative alignment with the objects of physics in the sense of Aristotle's *Physics* is thus avoided.[279]

The term "proportion" used in the definition reveals the motive for avoiding this alignment: the argument seeks to maintain the possibility of understanding acoustic music as a manifestation of the numerical harmonic order of *proportiones*. However, as a result of the attempt to keep *musica scientia* within the mathematical sciences by concentrating on sound conceived as a specification of *numerus*, the systematic place of *proportio* in music theory becomes unclear. If the objects of *musica scientia* are, on the one hand, *quantitates discretae mobiles*, and, on the other, "harmonic" proportions as the bases of consonances, then it is concerned with relations between numbers, on the one hand, and with relations between numbers and sounds, on the other. Both cases once again require that the classification of *musica scientia* among the mathematical sciences be justified: proportions as relations between numbers are the object of arithmetic, and only arithmetic, while proportions as relations among numbers and sounds are not an object of mathematical science. The solution offered by the collection of *quaestiones* is exemplary of how the Pythagorean-Neoplatonic and Aristotelian doctrines are tentatively reconciled in speculative music theory after 1250.

In Boethius's *De institutione arithmetica* number is discussed *ad numerum*; however, number put in a relationship, so goes the objection, is merely identical with number "determined" by sound. According to this argument, *musica scientia* is simply superfluous, since the bases of the doctrine of consonances were already dealt with in Book II of the textbook on arithmetic:

> Since in the second book of *On Arithmetic* number is determined on the basis of the commensurability of its proportion [*secundum aptitudinem sue proportionis*], but number in proportion is the same as one determined by sonority [*numerus proportionatus idem est quod contractus in sonoritate*]. It is in such sound that music consists. Thus, it appears that the discipline of music is superfluous, when we determine that sound is considered in this way in the second book of *On Arithmetic*.[280]

The objection's *recusatio*, which is largely based on the theory of logical subordination derived from Aristotle's *Posterior Analytics* I.7,[281] starts from the argument's weakest premise: the simple equation of number related *ad numerum* and number in proportion determined by sound. The rebuttal weaves in here a hierarchical differentiation typical of analogical discourse in its hylomorphistic level of development. The term *numerus contractus in proportione sonoritatis* contains several determinations that are related to one another as *genus proximum* and *differentia specifica*. The *genus* is the *numerus contractus*, while *species* are, on the one hand, numbers in sound, and, on the other hand, *nota bene*, numbers present as proportions "in things," that is, as formal determinants: "First we must say that determined number in general is in particular number determined by sound, then again it is number in things according to the commensurability of their proportion [*quoniam determinatum est de numero contracto generaliter ad numerum sonorum et ad numerum, qui est in rebus secundum aptitudinem sue proportionis*]."[282] This distinction of the generic *numerus contractus* from its specifications provides the basis for a distinction between two disciplines: the object of one of them is the *numerus contractus* in general, while the object of the other is the *numerus contractus in sonum*. Both stand in a relation of the general to the particular, in accord with the relation between their objects:

> Because of this, another special form of knowledge [*alia scientia specialis*] was able to come about, which treated numbers in general [*in qua determinetur de numeris generaliter*], not only those determined by proportion in sonority [*non specialiter contractis ad proportionem sonoritatis*]. These two forms of knowledge are distinguished, therefore, as general and specific [. . .].[283]

As the fifth *quaestio* explains, this process of relating the two disciplines dealing with the *numerus contractus* presupposes that they have a common substance. Aristotle maintained that "mathematical" definitions defined "abstracts." But, the objection already mentioned claims, *musica scientia* deals with number determined by the relationship to something concrete, and is hence not a mathematical science: "Likewise, although all of mathematics concerns abstract things [*sit de rebus abstractis*], music is about determined number [*de numero contracto*]. Therefore, it seems that music is not a mathematical form of knowledge [*non sit scientia mathematica*]."[284] The *recusatio* of the objection resorts to a Neoplatonic argument:[285] the relationship of the *numeri* that are the object of *musica scientia* to sound does not indicate the determination of the *numeri* as such, but rather the self-limitation of *musica scientia* to a "more concrete" partial aspect of the substantially one *numerus*:

> [I]t must be said that a determination of number in sonority [*contractio numeri in sonoritate*] is not incompatible with abstraction. A number is said to be determined if related to sonority, not because it may be determined by some special matter [*contrahatur ad aliquam materiam specialem*], but because it is determined by more particular occurrences [*contrahitur ad passiones specialiores*] than the occurrences of numbers established by arithmetic.[286]

Number is posited Neoplatonically as *genus*, and what exists materially, like the concretely realized sound, is conceived as an ontologically secondary manifestation on the basis of numbers specified by a *differentia specifica* (here, *contractio*). Thus the assumption of different substances, which would otherwise be imperative in the Aristotelian framework, can be avoided. The systematic consequence is a differentiation of levels of the greatest incisiveness. While the object of *musica scientia* is defined as *numerus contractus in proportione sonoritatis*, and thus as specifically but not generically different from the object of arithmetic, the Neoplatonic tradition's generic concept of number and therefore the option of a "holistic" projection of music theory as a form of world-shaping discourse is maintained, without having to give up the proximity to phenomenal existence that follows from the concentration on acoustical phenomena inspired by Aristotle. The "harmonic" numerical order is thus no longer designated as ontologically prior, as it is in the Platonic tradition. However, it is still designated, in line with the Aristotelian conception of the mathematical, as a form of perceiving the sensible capable of having truth-value.[287]

The differentiation of levels is understood as a domain-specific abstraction. The condition of its possibility is the assumption of a plural *natura* of number *in unam substantiam*: qua nature, the *numerus* is *both* an abstraction *and* a concrete sound. Arithmetic and music abstract from the object of the respective other science, but deal with the substantially identical *numerus*:

> We might express this differently and say that number has a dual nature
> [*duplicem habet naturam*]. It has one nature according to which it draws
> from a numerical thing [*abstrahit a re numerali*]. Arithmetic has to do
> with this kind of nature, in which number is determined according to its
> different combinations in abstraction [*de numero secundum diversas sui
> conbinationes in abstractione*]. Number has a second nature according
> to which it draws from every number on its way to sonority [*ab omni
> numero in via sonoritatis*]. Thus, it is clear that one need not exclude the
> other.[288]

The impression that the relationship between the Neoplatonic concept of number in theory of music and Aristotelian epistemology was synthetic *from the outset*, an impression that must be expressly emphasized against the background of the scholarly theses on the late Middle Ages portrayed in part I of this work, has two significant consequences in our context. In the passage cited from the collection of *quaestiones* at the beginning, the recourse to the Boethian triad already shows that the differentiation of two *naturae* in one substance not only leaves intact the relation between arithmetic and music theory. It also preserves the possibility of conceiving acoustic musical works as sensible realizations of a numerical harmonic order that stands in a relationship (which must now be determined anew) to the order of Creation. The second consequence is, correspondingly, that the relation between generic number and consonant sounds is still singled out as a type of formal determination of a created world-element. This is proven not least by the placing of music in the framework of *philosophia naturalis*, which includes the quadrivial disciplines along with *physica* or *scientia naturalis inferior*.[289] The Aristotelian revision of the Boethian tradition in music theory requires that its foundations in number ontology be discarded. However, neither this nor the more consistent emphasis on acoustic phenomena deprives the speculative concept of music of its bases. The generic concept of number, and especially its conception as *form* (as opposed to matter) left the Boethian triad of *musica mundana, humana,* and *instrumentalis* an explanatory potential that entailed, at the beginning of the fourteenth century already, "renewed interest in Boethius."[290] As a result, it is not consistently Aristotelian contributions limiting themselves to sound as such that became dominant in the following centuries, but rather attempts to synthesize Neoplatonic and Aristotelian elements on increasingly complex levels. Such attempts could, as we will later show, count on the backing of Thomism.

This also concerns the theory of metrical discourse as *musica,* and is applied to it in the collection of *quaestiones*. The ninth *quaestio* raises the question in what respect poetry can be understood as music—a proof of the self-evidence and currency of this understanding, as the collection of *quaestiones* is a textbook of the most general kind, intended to prepare students for an examination. Despite the reevaluation of the ontological quality of number, the answer given in this *quaestio* is in accord with the previously described tradition. The argument distinguishes metrical constraint as form constituted by *numerositas* from content left to the discretion of the poet. Whereas this content is posited as arbitrary, disqualified as "not capable of being known scientifically," and assigned to the domain of rhetoric, metrics is "of musical nature." The work on form constituted by *numerositas* and this work alone is, as metrics, attributed to *musica*:

> Moreover, one is accustomed to ask whether poetics is to be classified as
> music. It would seem so, since such knowledge concerns the measuring
> out of feet into meters according to numbers. And it must be said that
> the poetic art, according to the material with which it is concerned, deals
> with something by means of knowledge. It concerns stories and fictions
> [*de fabulis et fictis*], and thus is no object of scientific knowledge; nor can
> it be subordinated differently by reference to number, that is, according to
> *the measure seen in verses, since these are by nature musical* [*hec sint de
> natura musice*]. According to what is expressed in stories and fictions, in
> every consideration of the beautiful, poetic art has to be classified prop
> erly under rhetoric.[291]

Although reoriented in an Aristotelian way, this music theory includes metrical discourse as music, and thus distinguishes its form by contrast to its content, which is subject to arbitrariness. It does not, as we want to emphasize, proceed exclusively from the acoustic quality of the spoken word.

The continuing vitality of the conception of metrical discourse as music is not the only factor decisive for the further outlining of our continuity thesis. The question as to what consequences this conception has for the status of metrical writing is also crucial. From the structural homology of the form of metrical discourse, on the one hand, and the *ordo entium* established in numerical relationships, on the other, Augustinus's *De musica* had derived the special anagogic relevance of this form. The reception of Aristotle puts this conclusion in question. The collection of *quaestiones* shows, however, that this need not lead to the erasure of traditional theoretical elements, but may instead encourage their functionally equivalent replacement while retaining the conceptual points. Above all, the fact that key propositions of Christian dogma were and remained set in Platonizing concepts limited the possibilities for theology to switch over completely to Aristotelian premises. A reconstruction of the tradition in question here must take that into account and, as a consequence, strive for more differentiated explanations than the schematic accounts provided by the tradition of scholarship outlined at the outset suggest. We will seek to consolidate these theses by examining Thomas Aquinas's statements on music, his concept of *ordo*, and his theory of the beautiful, in order to understand the context of the collection of *quaestiones* and provide a solid foundation for the following presentation of exemplary writings on music theory from the thirteenth, fourteenth, and fifteenth centuries.

The Reception of Aristotle II: Thomas Aquinas's Positions

The importance of music and music theory in Aquinas's wide-ranging work is rather slight; the scope, depth, and degree of systematization of his scattered statements on these subjects[292] are limited. For us, Aquinas's work is significant as the consummation of High Scholastic system-building on Aristotelian bases. His writings allow us to inquire into the continuities and discontinuities of theoretical elements crucial for music theory in the Boethian tradition in general, and for the subsumption of metrical discourse under music in particular.[293]

The reception of Aristotle's *Metaphysics* put into effect the critique of Pythagorean and Platonic ideal number theory presented in Books 13 and 14. Central concepts of the Neoplatonic tradition in music theory, right down to the attempt at synthesis presented in the collection of *quaestiones*, were thereby made obsolete. As an example, we will cite only the most pertinent paragraph from Thomas's commentary:

If we say, however, that sensible things are *ratios* [*rationes*], that is, proportions of numbers [*proportiones numerorum*], and that on this basis numbers are the causes of these sensible things, as we observe in *harmonies* [*symphoniis*], that is, in musical consonances, since numbers are said to be the causes of consonances to the extent that numerical proportions, which are applied to sounds, produce consonances, it is clear that one must posit in addition to those numbers in sensible things some one general number to which numerical proportions are applied [*oportebat praeter ipsos numeros in sensibilibus ponere aliquod unum secundum genus, cui applicantur proportiones numerales*]. Thus, the proportions in particular of those things, which are the proportions of that general number, constitute sensible things. And likewise, sounds are found in consonances in addition to numerical proportions. If, however, that to which the numerical proportion is applied in sensible things is matter, it is obvious that we must say that those separate numbers that are species represent a proportional relationship of some one thing to another [*ipsi numeri separati qui sunt species, sint proportiones alicuius unius, scilicet ad aliquod aliud*]. One must declare that this man, who is Callias or Socrates, is similar to the ideal man, who is called *autosanthropos*, that is, man as man. If Callias is not only a number, but rather is a ratio or proportion in the number of elements, particularly of fire, earth, water, and air, that ideal man will be a ratio or proportion in the numbers of certain things; the ideal man will not be a number because of his substance. It follows from this that there will be no number *in addition to those*, that is, in addition to numbered things [*ex quo sequitur, quod nullus numerus erit* praeter ea, *id est praeter res numeratas*]. For if the number of species is separate in the highest degree, and is not separate from things, but is a certain proportion of numbered things, no other number will now be separate. This contradicts the Platonists.[294]

No "ideal" number precedes the multitude of numbered elements of the world—the residues of Neoplatonic number theory in the distinction between two *naturae* in a single generic number are thereby erased. In accord with this position, sounds were soon examined in the framework of lectures on the *Physics* and in connection with chapter II.8 of Aristotle's *De anima*.[295] And yet *musica scientia* was not considered one of the physical sciences. In his commentary on Boethius's *De trinitate*, Aquinas notes that as a science of quantities, mathematics does not simply disregard matter. It does abstract from the *materia sensibilis*, but generic quantity is to be assigned to *materia intelligibilis*.[296] Movement (*motus*) as the *causa efficiens* of acoustic phenomena does not fall under the genus of quantity but "participates" in the *natura quantitatis*:

> By its very nature motion does not have to do with the category of quantity [*non pertinet ad genus quantitatis*], but it partakes somewhat in the nature of quantity from another source [*participat aliquid de natura quantitatis aliunde*], according to which the division of motion is derived either from the division of space or from the division of some mobile thing; therefore, it is not the mathematician's task to consider motion, and yet, mathematical principles can be applied to motion [*principia mathematica ad motum applicari possunt*].[297]

Thomas classifies *scientiae* according to the way in which they deal with *res naturalia, res mathematica,* or the application of the latter to the former. He describes sciences such as *musica* or *astrologia,* whose object is "applied" quantities, as *scientia media*:

> Therefore, while the principles of mathematics are applicable to natural things, the reverse is not true, because physics is based on a mathematical supposition, but the reverse is not true [. . .]. Thus, there are three levels of knowledge concerned with natural and mathematical things. Some of these are purely natural, and consider the properties of natural things. Physics, agriculture, and other sciences belong to this level. Others are purely mathematical, and concern quantities absolutely, such as geometry, which treats of magnitude, and arithmetic, which treats of number. Still others are intermediate, and apply mathematical principles to natural things [*mediae, quae principia mathematica ad res naturales applicant*]. Music, astrology, and other sciences belong to this level. These show a greater affinity to mathematics, however, because in their view what is physical is material, as it were, whereas what is mathematical is formal, as it were [*id quod est physicum est quasi materiale, quod autem est mathematicum est quasi formale*]. Thus, music considers sounds, not as sounds per se, but because they relate to proportional numbers. The same is true in other levels of knowledge. Hence, they demonstrate their conclusions about natural things, but through the medium of mathematics.[298]

Thus along with the Neoplatonic concept of number, the situation of music in the canon of the mathematical sciences belongs to the past. The Aristotelian reorientation unsettles the systematic heart of traditional music theory. And yet scholarship has shown that neither the new Aristotelian approach in general nor the criticism of number ontology or the speculative orientation of the quadrivial sciences in particular led Christian theology to abandon these Neoplatonic elements altogether.[299] We can pursue here neither the Neoplatonic continuities in Aquinas's work *in toto* nor the consequences of the reception of Aristotle for Neoplatonic music theory as a whole. The guiding question for the following sections can only be which Neoplatonic theoretical elements persisted within Thomism in such a way that after the decline of Christian Platonism there continued to be ways to hook up with the Boethian concept of music and to conceive metrical discourse as "music" in terms of this concept. We will take as our starting point the working concepts of the Pythagorean-Neoplatonic tradition in which its "holistic" nature is concentrated: *proportio, consonantia*, and *harmonia*.

Thomas's concept of *proportio* provides the basis for all continuities to be shown in the following. It is developed in his commentary on Boethius's *De trinitate*, where Thomas seeks to dissolve the previously mentioned tension between Neoplatonic and Aristotelian elements that is characteristic of Boethius's opuscule. Thomas does so by extending the notion's reference beyond numerical relationships. *Proportio* is initially defined as "habitudo duorum ad invicem convenientium in aliquo, secundum quod conveniunt aut differunt" ("the relation between two things agreeing with one another in something in respect of which they agree or differ").[300] In this, *habitudo* or *relatio* (Thomas uses the two terms as synonyms),[301] two *modi* are distinguished:

> Things may agree in one way in the same genus of quantity or quality, as in the relation of one surface to another, or of one number to another, in as much as one exceeds the other or is equal to it, or as heat is related to heat, and thus in no way can there be proportion between God and creature, since they do not agree in any genus [*non conveniant in aliquo genere*]. In another way things can be understood to agree when they come together in some order [*in aliquo ordine conveniunt*], and thus proportion can be observed between matter and form, between maker and made, and so on, and such proportion is required between the knowing power and the knowable, since the knowable is a sort of act of the knowing power. And thus, there is even a proportion of creature to God, as the thing caused to its cause, and the knower to the knowable.[302]

The term *proportio* is used to designate not only the relation between quantities or proportions, but the relation of qualities as well. The relations between quantities or proportions include geometric, arithmetic, and "harmonic" proportions. Thus "numerical proportions applied to sounds [. . .] constitute musical consonances."[303] Furthermore, a *proportio* exists between entities that "come together in some order": between matter and form, potential and act, subject of knowledge and object of knowledge, and even between Creator and creature. Each of these manifestations is important for Thomas's further argument, and mine as well. The new breadth of the concept of *proportio* marked out by this definition can be illustrated by reference to a passage from the *Summa theologiae*. Taking as his point of departure a passage in Rom. 13:1 that we have already discussed in connection with the constitution of the Christian order of discourse, Thomas explains his conception of the order of Being and Creation. Following Aristotle, he argues on the basis of the principle of causality:

> The causality of God, however, who is the first agent, extends itself to all beings, not only as to the principles of species [*principia speciei*], but even as to the individual principles [*individualia principia*], and not only of incorruptible things, but also of corruptible ones as well. Thus, it is necessary that everything that has being in any way has been ordained by God to exist for some end, as the apostle said in Romans 13: Those powers that are, are ordained of God.[304]

As we have shown, Thomas's concept of *proportio* includes the relationship *causati ad causam* ("the caused to the cause"). So, according to Thomas as well, the order of Being and Creation is a "proportional" order. Insofar as the *causalitas Dei* concerns absolutely all existents, this concept of order is once again constituted "holistically."[305]

The *proportiones* mentioned by Thomas include the *numeri ad numerum* relationships and ultimately the order of these proportions itself. Thus the basis of the Neoplatonic concept of *ordo* in number ontology is elided, but the theorems derived from it remain intact so long as they do not necessarily presuppose this ontological basis and can be harmonized with the broadened concept of *proportio*.[306] Conceptually, the ontological interpretation of relationality discussed in Aristotle's *Categories* seems to underlie the whole complex.[307] The numerical harmonic order as an order deducible from the *tetraktys*, as proportional relationships that also include the *numerus contractus in proportione sonoritatis* as the object of *musica scientia* and with the latter metrical discourse, becomes one proportional order among others. However, it remains an element of a relational system within the created existent that points to the Creator. Speaking of the Thomistic system's tendency to "harmonize" finds its systematic justification here. At the same time, the argument's Neoplatonic appeal, notable at the latest when Thomistic thinking about *ordo* becomes the subject of discussion, is based on this broad conception of *proportio*. For example, in de Bruyne's summary:

In each sphere of existence, harmony appears under one form or another,
as a type in individuals and as a principle of symmetry in organisms, as
a module of proportions in edifices: what is called "commensuratio" in
pure magnitudes appears as "convenientia" in qualities, as "coaptatio" in
substances, as "concordia, amicitia, communio" in social consciousnesses.
Everywhere, the suitable proportions are the expression of the requirements of nature as such, and consequently of the ideal conceived by God;
everywhere they are an element of total beauty.[308]

This summary brings us to the concepts of *harmonia* and *consonantia*,
which are likewise not erased as residues of the old doctrine, but rather
harmonized with the expanded concept of *proportio*. They lead toward the
Thomistic doctrine of the beautiful, the discussion of which will conclude
our survey of Neoplatonic residues in Thomism.

Initially, the numerical relationships deduced from the first *tetraktys* and
then, usually supplemented by the epithet *musicalis* or *musicae*, the consonant interval[309] are called *consonantia*. Thus the concept's primary meaning
is clear. Its harmonization with the broadened concept of *proportio* leads to
the interchangeability of these terms, "proportio sive consonantia,"[310] and
finally to the expansion of the term *consonantia*'s reference to all *proportiones* based on accordance *in aliquo ordine*. In this use, the concept ranges
from the "ordered" arrangement of the man-made work—"One whole consists in the consonance of order [*consonantia ordinis*], as is the case with an
army, another in the consonance of composition [*consonantia compositio-
nis*], as is the case with a house; the same reasoning applies to both"[311]—via
the *consonantia naturalis* of the order of creation[312] to the relationship of the
divine *personae* in speculation about the Trinity. Consider for instance the
following proposition, and especially the preposition *per*: "Dicit enim Hi-
larius, in libro de Synod., quod pater et filius et spiritus sanctus sunt quidem
per substantiam tria, *per* consonantiam vero unum" ("In his book *On the
Synods*, Hilary says that the Father and the Son and the Holy Spirit are
three by substance, but one by consonance").[313] *Proportio* and *consonantia*
may have been reconceived according to the Aristotelian frame of reference.
The concept of order they span nevertheless remains in tune with the musical register. Thus discourse about the *consonantia* of the order of Creation
can eventuate in the commentary on Pseudo-Dionysius the Areopagite's *De
divinis nominibus* without a distancing word:

First, he says that *because of* the aforesaid simple nature there is *a single
and indissoluble association of all things* [*una et indissolubiis complexio
omnium*], *by which* all things agree in one universal order [*secundum*

scilicet quod omnia conveniunt in uno ordine universi] which remains indissoluble. For this reason, in the same universe a certain harmony, that is, a proportioned concord [*proportionata concordia*], is caused by God; this is what Dionysius says, adding: *perfect consonance is harmonized [et concordatur consonantia perfecta*]. Harmony is nothing but concordant consonance [*concors consonantia*].[314]

The significance of the concept of *harmonia* for music theory is also clear to Thomas: "Harmony is caused in sound by a due proportion of numbers [*ex debita proportione numerorum*]."[315] This concept is also adapted to the new and broadened concept of *proportio*: "harmony is a due order and proportion [*debitum ordinem et proportionem*]."[316] The key sentence formulates the consequence: "Harmony is nothing but concordant consonance [*concors consonantia*]."[317] The relation produced between *consonantia* and *harmonia* extends the synonymic series: *proportio, consonantia, harmonia.* The differences of the concepts in the Neoplatonic tradition are clear, but the harmonizing tendency invested in Thomas's concept of *proportio* gradually levels out these differentiations.

Thomas's theory of the beautiful must also be seen against the background of this tendency to harmonize. It is developed essentially in the commentary on Pseudo-Dionysius's *De divinis nominibus* and also, despite the modifications summarized below,[318] largely in accord with this work: "Thomas borrows his *whole* theory of the *pulchrum* from Dionysius, with the exception of the relationship of the beautiful to knowledge."[319]

The relation of the concept of harmony to the broadened conception of *proportio* makes it possible—just as does the number-continuum in Neoplatonic doctrine—to broaden its reference. Thus, to begin with, it includes other sense impressions: "Proportions in sound are called harmonies, and by a certain likeness [*per quandam similitudinem*], proportions fittingly are called harmonies of all things [*quarumcumque rerum harmoniae*]."[320] This broadening brings *proportio* closer to Augustine's concept of form, insofar as it designates a specific relationality of the parts of a whole. In this intensified form, proportionality as "objective determination" or "ratio pulchritudinis"[321] becomes central to Thomas's conception of the beautiful. The latter has three components. Two of these remain loyal to the tradition shaped by Neoplatonism. The third component, initially developed in the *Summa theologiae*, broadens the Neoplatonic doctrine by assuming a "subjective" aspect in the determination of the beautiful, conditional on the perceiving consciousness. The history of aesthetic theory generally views this as Thomas's genuine contribution.[322]

An object that makes a pleasing impression is called "beautiful": "A beautiful thing is one whose apprehension pleases."[323] The conception worked out in the discussion of the *Nicomachean Ethics* emphasizes a form of enjoyment that is viewed as irreducible to bodily pleasure and as purposeless, but completely immanent:[324] self-sufficient contemplation of beautiful form in its harmonic guise, "convenientiam sui [. . .] in pulchritudine secundum seipsam" ("its agreement [. . .] with itself in beauty").[325] Still, it must be emphasized that according to Thomas, this genuinely "aesthetic" pleasure presupposes qualities of the object contemplated that can be reduced neither to the immanence nor to the attitude of the observer. These qualities alone provide the aesthetic experience with an occasion and an object, and to that extent are prior to it. Thomas himself notes, with the terseness occasionally characteristic of his argumentation: "Therefore, a thing is not beautiful because we love it; rather we love it because it is beautiful and good."[326] We see here why Dyroff came to contrast Thomas's conception with modern "empathy theories": "They include the opposed point of view insofar as they do not postulate a shift from the subjective to the objective, but rather a shift from the objective to the subjective."[327]

Thomas's explanations of the *objective* determinations of the beautiful largely agree with the older body of theory. The first determination is the ontological conception of the *pulchrum* as a transcendental,[328] which shares in the existent qua *participatio*. The validity and scope of the Platonic doctrine of participation is thus restricted and at the same time "affirmed and adopted in its most important objectives."[329] Even according to the Aristotelian Thomas, everything that is beautiful is beautiful only qua *participatio* in the beautiful as such in God:

> [Dionysius the Pseudo-Areopagite] says first that God, who is the super-substantial beautiful thing [*supersubstantiale pulchrum*], is called beauty because He gives beauty to all created beings according to the particular nature of each [*omnibus entibus creatis dat pulchritudinem, secundum proprietatem uniuscuiusque*]; [. . .] He says first, therefore, that in the first cause, that is, in God, the beautiful and beauty cannot be separated, [*in causa prima, scilicet Deo non sunt dividenda pulchrum et pulchritudo*] [. . .] He says that in beings the beautiful and beauty are distinguished as participant and participation [*in existentibus, pulchrum et pulchritudo distinguuntur secundum participans et participatum*]. Thus, a thing is called beautiful that shares in beauty [*ita quod pulchrum dicitur hoc quod participat pulchritudinem*], whereas beauty is a sharing in the first cause that creates all beautiful things. For the beauty of a creature is only a like-

ness that has shared in divine beauty [*similitudo divinae pulchritudinis in rebus participata*].[330]

God is the original ground of everything beautiful, and is expressed as the beauty of the creature in Creation, which is beautiful insofar as it resembles Him. Beautiful things point to God, because everything beautiful is beautiful qua *imitatio Dei*: "For all things were made to imitate divine beauty, each in its own way [*ut divinam pulchritudinem qualitercumque imitentur*]. Thirdly, He is the exemplary cause, since everything is patterned after divine beauty [*omnia distinguuntur secundum pulchrum divinum*]."[331]

For our reconstruction of the Augustinian theory of the beautiful within music theory, including metrical discourse considered as *musica*, two aspects turned out to be crucial: the doctrine of participation and the conception of beauty as an intrinsic quality of form. Thomas's conception of beauty and the beautiful seems to conform to these elements of the Augustinian tradition as well. This is suggested by the well-known tripartite definition of the objective conditions of the beautiful in the *Summa theologiae*, qu. 8, a. 8: "Three things are required for beauty: first, integrity, or perfection [*intregritas, sive perfectio*], for things lacking something are ugly on this account; then, due proportion, or consonance [*debita proportio, sive consonantia*]; and finally, clarity [*claritas*], for things that have a bright color are said to be beautiful."[332] *Integritas sive perfectio* is to be conceived as material determination. The example given suggests that *integritas* should be understood as "completeness," as "appropriate magnitude,"[333] and as a reference to the metaphysical presuppositions of the *perfectio* that Thomas briefly summarizes in the following definition: "Perfect is called what does not lack anything, according to the measure of its perfection [*secundum modum suae perfectionis*]."[334] At first, *claritas* seems to refer back to Pseudo-Dionysius the Areopagite's metaphorics of light and the "qualitative" aesthetics based on it, which connects the anagogic relevance of the beautiful not with form, but rather, in a comparable way, with the quality peculiar to precious stones, the gold of the pictorial background, or saturated primary colors. The Abbot Suger of St. Denis's (1081–1151) famous description is the most engaging example:

> Thus, now and then, when, because of my pleasure in the beauty of the house of God, the multicolored beauty of gems called me away from external cares, and respectful meditation, transporting me away from material things to immaterial ones [*de materialibus ad immaterialia transferendo*], persuaded me to apply myself to the variety of the holy virtues, then I seem to see myself staying as it were in some far-off region of the

earth, neither entirely in the filth of the earth, nor entirely in the purity of
heaven, and able to be transported by the gift of God from this inferior
place to that superior one in an anagogical fashion [*anagogico more*].[335]

Throughout the Middle Ages, the "aesthetic of proportion" was accompanied by the sensitivity to *suavitas coloris* documented here.[336] Thomas's
conception of *claritas* seems to attempt to reconcile the two approaches: the
quality of *claritas* peculiar to the beautiful object is conceived as a formal
determination, as the "shining through of form" in its manifestation:[337]

> Clarity is a feature of beauty, as has been said. Every form, however,
> through which a thing has existence is a partaking of divine clarity [*omnis
> autem forma, per quam res habet esse, est participatio quaedam divinae
> claritatis*]. And he adds that individual things are beautiful according to
> their own nature, that is, according to their own form [*singula sunt pul-
> chra secundum propriam rationem, idest secundum propriam formam*].
> Thus, it is obvious that the existence of all things comes from divine
> beauty.[338]

De Bruyne comments:

> "Clarity" designates a formal quality whose pure perception is a source
> of aesthetic joy. [. . .] The metaphysical value of clarity is identical with a
> certain transparency of the form in the colors of the body or in the radi-
> ance of the mind. Hence clarity is, still more than proportion, expressive
> of the organizing principle that is called the substantial form.[339]

Obviously, here the relevant metaphysical conception of form is not the
Neoplatonic one; but both of them posit a similar thing. The grounding of
beauty in the "shining-through of form" accentuates the aspects of a given
object revelatory of its ontologically prior form, pattern, or type, as opposed to the deviant or "individual" marks of the concrete manifestation.
Both concepts are variants of an "aesthetic of identity."[340] The more obvious form is in this sense, the more the object produced resembles the type,
the more beautiful the object. Likewise, according to the hylomorphistic
theory of individuation, "beauty" as a quality is characteristic of all existence. As a quality, it varies in degree with the "shining-through of form":

> As for the objective characteristics of the Beautiful, they are obviously
> analogically present in forms. Since they qualify form as such, they are
> not absent from any object, while at the same time appearing to differing
> degrees in things. The more perfect they are, the more they radiate the
> "Beautiful."[341]

This understanding of *claritas* also makes clear the inner connection of the criterion with the third, "objective" condition of the beautiful. The reference to *proportio sive consonantia* supplies the criterion according to which the individual object's degree of beauty can be determined. If one wanted to identify (against the text's explicit interests) the implications of the Thomistic theory that are relevant to production and reception aesthetics, this would be where to start. Among the previously mentioned "objective" conditions of beauty, only the aspect of form designated by *proportio sive consonantia* and understood as the condition of the object's beautiful appearence falls within the scope of artistic creation. First of all, *proportio* is the appropriate relationship of the parts forming a whole, "pulchritudo [consistit] in debita proportione membrorum" ("beauty consists in a due proportion of parts"),[342] a specific "balance" accessible to the senses and to that extent equivalent to the Augustinian category of correct measurement, which refers to numerical relationships. If a form is "balanced" in this sense, then it is at the same time, Thomas assumes, the form corresponding to the *dispositio naturae* of the object and thus the perfect realization of the type: "If members are taken to be the hand, the foot, and so on, their disposition according to nature is beauty [*earum dispositio naturae conveniens, est pulchritudo*]."[343] Both implications of *proportio sive consonantia* situate the trans-individual form of the individual object in the order of proportions pointing to God. Significantly, Thomas expresses the complex's "holistic" implications with the concept *consonantia*:

> God is the cause of consonance in things [*causa consonantiae in rebus*].
> But there is a two-fold aspect to consonance. First, in the way that
> creatures are oriented toward God [*secundum ordinem creaturarum ad
> Deum*]. He [Dionysius] touches on this when he says that God is the
> cause of consonance, *as calling all things to Himself* [*causa consonantiae,
> sicut vocans omnia ad seipsum*], [. . .] Second, consonance is in things,
> according to their arrangement to one another [*ordinationem earum ad
> invicem*]. He [Dionysius] touches on this when he says in the same place
> that He gathers all things into all things [*congregat omnia in omnibus*].[344]

Deus est causa consonantiae, sicut vocans omnia ad seipsum—this turn of phrase could also have been found in Augustine's work on music. Here as well, Thomas accentuates the foundation of the *ordo entium* in the principle of causality and adds a doctrine of grace to the genuinely Platonic concept of the anagogic.[345] Nevertheless, the referential character of the beautiful existent remains transparent and vital and at the same time bound to formal determinations of this existent.

Thomas's conception of the subjective perception of the beautiful also grants the latter's anagogic relevance a rank unexpectedly high in the Aristotelian framework. The subjective experience of the beautiful begins with *delectatio*, which is prereflectively indicated by the *debita harmonia* of the beautiful object: "The soul takes pleasure in all harmonious things [*in omnibus harmonizatis*], and it is offended by things that are without due harmony in sounds as well as in colors [. . .]."[346] Sensual enjoyment indicates the *similitudo*—already introduced as a form of *proportio*—of the subject of knowledge and the object of knowledge: "Beauty consists in due proportion [*debita proportione*], because sense takes pleasure in duly proportioned things, as it does in things similar to it, for sense is a kind of reason, as is every cognitive faculty."[347] This *similitudo* triggers *appetitus*,[348] appetitive striving. The specific quality of the "objectively" beautiful sight or sound is that desire comes to rest in its contemplation:

> What calms the appetite when it is seen or known pertains to the nature
> of beauty [*ad rationem pulchri*]. Those senses that particularly concern
> the beautiful are to the highest degree cognitive, that is, sight and hearing,
> for they are in service to reason. For we say that visible things and sounds
> are beautiful.[349]

This "calming" of the *appetitus* grounds the fundamentally positive ethical valence of the beautiful. As its systematic basis, Thomas introduces the substantial unity of *pulchrum* and *bonum*: since according to Aristotle's *Nicomachean Ethics* the good is "that at which all things aim,"[350] it is part of the essence of the good that striving comes to rest in its possession. Insofar as the beautiful and the good are *substantially identical*, the good and the beautiful are the—exclusive[351]—objects of appetitive striving, though in accord with different *rationes*. The beautiful addresses the *vis cognoscitiva*, sense knowledge, and is thus a principle of form, whereas the good is essentially a principle of purpose.[352] In desiring the beautiful, humans are desiring the good with the senses. Here aspects of the Thomistic theory that have previously been discussed separately come together:

> The beautiful and the good are the same thing fundamentally, because
> they are based on the same thing, namely, form [*super eandem rem fundantur, scilicet super formam*]. Because of this, the good is praised as
> beautiful. But the two differ when looked at rationally. For the good has
> to do properly with appetite, since the good is what all things long for.
> Therefore, good has the aspect of an end, [. . .]. The beautiful, however,
> concerns the cognitive faculty, for beautiful things are those that please

when seen. Therefore, beauty consists in due proportion [*in debita pro-portione*], [. . .].[353]

De Bruyne tends to put strong emphasis on the continuities, but his summary is nevertheless substantially appropriate:

> The mind does not project its harmony onto things and does not create beauty. It does not receive passively the objective harmony of the form and does not undergo beauty. It recognizes the pre-established harmony between the structure of the subject and that of the object and finds itself immersed *in a completely musical world*: that is what constitutes aesthetic joy.[354]

Ultimately, Thomas also makes the experience of the beautiful functional for the path toward God. The contemplation of the beautiful in balanced proportion refines the cognitive faculty and contributes to the *perfectio intellectus*. It is no accident that Peter of Auvergne, Thomas's pupil, who completed his preceptor's commentary on Aristotle's *Politics* (which had been broken off after *liber 3, lectio 6*),[355] made this consequence explicit by using the example of music:

> One should know that the sound of musical harmony is apprehended first by the sense of hearing. And when it moves that sense with proportion [*proportionaliter*], and through reason [*secundum mediam rationem*], by which it was composed, it causes pleasure. [. . .] Beyond this, in the intention of the harmonious sounds the intellect considers the nature and cause of proportion [*in intentione soni harmoniaci intellectus considerat rationem et causam proportionis*], as though it were something intelligible in itself, and in which a certain perfection of the intellect [*perfectio intellectus*] can be found.[356]

The *perfectio intellectus* produces *felicitas* and at the same time leads toward the highest: whatever serves the *intellectus* promotes (theoretical) knowledge of the true as (practical) prudence, as the Christian's steadfast pursuit of the right path:

> Happiness [*felicitas*] is a human operation in regard to the intellect. Within the intellect one must consider the speculative [*speculativum*], whose end is knowledge of the truth [*cognitio veritatis*], and the practical, whose end is action. Accordingly, a double happiness is assigned to man. The speculative one is an operation of man according to the perfect contemplative faculty, which is wisdom. The other is practical, which is a perfection of man according to his perfect practical faculty, which is prudence.[357]

Correspondingly, perfect beauty is—according to the principle: "It is natural for man to arrive at intelligible things through the senses [*per sensibilia ad intelligibilia veniat*]"[358]—the beauty of the contemplative life consisting in the exercise of rationality: "Hence, in the contemplative life [*vita contemplativa*], which consists in the exercise of reason [*in actu rationis*], beauty is found in itself and essentially [*per se et essentialiter invenitur pulchritudo*]."[359]

The Thomistic theory of the beautiful remains essentially Neoplatonic. All the theoretical elements important in the context of our investigation are continued in Thomas and confirmed in their systematic connection. The old doctrine is incorporated into an outline of a "proportional" order that is essentially rooted in the hylomorphistic theory of individuation (*proportio* of matter and form), and is broadened by the greater weight given to the subjective perception of the beautiful, but thereby alone hardly distinguishes itself from Neoplatonic theory. The Aristotelian reorientation in general and the qualification of the concept of the anagogic in particular reduced the experience that the beautiful can communicate to the experience of the whole of the *immanent* order. The function of referring to the Creator is nonetheless all the more strongly emphasized. In fact, differences exist less in the theory of the beautiful than in the assessment and instrumentalization of beautiful works, in the assessment of artificial beauty. Whereas Augustine's *De musica* had not only provided a theoretical grounding for the way the profane work can be instrumentalized and subordinated to the conceptual articles of the Christian order of discourse, but also performed it, Thomas's theory of the beautiful has striking gaps in precisely this area.

Questions regarding the status of artificial beauty in the Middle Ages are fundamentally confronted with the problem of delimiting its object. The modern privileging of the "fine" arts has no medieval equivalent. They were not differentiated from crafts. Thomas exemplifies this in a paradigmatic way. His criteria for the judgment of "artistic" activity are expediency and general morality. He distinguishes between arts assessed in terms of their *utilitas*, crafts in the narrower sense, and arts connected with *delectatio*, with the beautiful. He approves of any art or craft that seeks to produce something beautiful, whose performance and product does not contradict morality—which is not vicious, which is beneficial or even necessary for life, and is instructive for laypeople or praises God.[360] Even beauty that is sought "for its own sake" but with a practical interest is not rejected so long as it is sought moderately and not in base desire. Thus concerning women's finery he writes: "Sober and moderate ornaments are not forbidden for women, but only those that are superfluous, immodest, and unchaste."[361] It is offensive to feign what is not the case, but it is permissible to conceal what is offensive—for example in matters of beauty: "It is one thing to pretend to have beauty that one does not possess, and another thing to hide wickedness."[362]

Beauty that is sought for the sake of pure pleasure, for example the artistic beauty in the work of actors and *joculatores*, Thomas considers as *ludus*, as play in the service of the human community: "Play is necessary to the intercourse of human life, and therefore, even the work of actors, which aims to bring comfort to men, is not in itself forbidden."[363] The category includes the multitude of profane and trivial pleasures in which all strata of medieval societies indulged and to which we may owe more than one outstanding "art work." In its (intentional) purposelessness alone, the playful deserves no verdict, as long as it fosters (by effect) a righteous life. Thus the ethical valence of the activity seeking the beautiful for the sake of pleasure must be judged on a case-by-case basis.

To begin with, in accord with its effect of fostering righteous life, the beautiful is useful as refreshment and calming of the exhausted mind and body.[364] The body can be refreshed by rest, and this must also be possible for the *anima*: "Just as bodily rest dispels weariness of the body, it is also proper that weariness of the soul is dispelled by rest of the soul."[365] Its *refocillatio* (refocusing) is provided by the pleasure, *delectatio*, that arises when the *intellectus* temporarily yields to the passions: "The soul's rest is pleasure, as was stated above, when it is driven by the passions."[366] Thomas's comment cleverly leads from the restorative effect of artistic beauty to its risks. Beyond the rule "the aforesaid pleasure should not be sought in any wicked or injurious deeds or words"[367] stands the Aristotelian notion of *virtus* as a habit rationally directed toward the morally right.[368] The beautiful object, by intention created and sought for its own sake, is meant to contribute to the consolidation of this habit by effect. This is the case when a work of art is "appropriate" to a given life-world context, "appropriateness" being here what Augustine's *De musica* had discussed as the desideratum of *decentia* as *congruentia* of *modulatio* and a given affective situation.[369] Thomas, whose quotation of Augustine's work on music is not accidental here,[370] repeats the argument, using the example of representation through movement: "It is obvious that there is moral virtue concerned with the direction of these movements. The direction of these movements, however, is observed in two ways. One concerns suitability to the person. The other concerns suitability to other persons, affairs, or places."[371]

Thomas sees the required *convenientia* not as founded in numerical relationships, but nonetheless as *proportio*, in accord with the definition of its further *modi* as "convenientia [. . .] in aliquo ordine."[372] According to

Thomas as well, "appropriateness" remains subsumed under and determined by the system of *proportiones* that relates the "ontological order" and the "ethical order"[373] to one another. So long as the "artist," obeying the Aristotelian imperative of keeping μεσότης, deviates from the right measure neither by *defectio* nor by *excessus*, so long as the "playful" quest for the beautiful for its own sake has as its goal to refresh the mind, sets a good example, and consoles the suffering, and thus so long as "art" conforms to the "proportional" *ordo*, there is nothing sinful about it: "In so far as austerity is a virtue, it does not exclude all pleasures, but only those that are superfluous and lacking order."[374] Thomas gives as his example the actors whom Augustine so severely criticized:

> Therefore, the occupation of actors, which is directed at bringing comfort to men, is not forbidden in itself, nor are actors in a state of sin, as long as they use play moderately, that is, they do not use any forbidden language or actions in their play, and that they do not engage in play in unsuitable matters and times.[375]

For the visual arts, this implies a moderate imitative realism: "We understand that a certain image is said to be beautiful when it perfectly represents its subject [*si perfecte repraesentat rem*], even if this subject is wicked."[376] As far as music is concerned, Thomas demands that it adhere to the simple ways that Plato, Aristotle, and also Boethius had seen as moderating. In addition to Aristotle's discussion in Book 8 of the *Politics*, Thomas knew the exposition of the musical ethos theory and the *effectus musicae* in Boethius's *De institutione muica* I.1:

> The praise of the voice is necessary so as to arouse the love of man for God. For this reason, whatever is useful to this end is fittingly assumed into divine praises. It is obvious that according to diverse melodies of sounds the souls of men are disposed in different ways, as the philosopher makes clear in the seventh book of the *Politics*, and as Boethius makes clear in the prologue to his work on music.[377]

Thomas's position with regard to verse is not very differentiated and does not differ from his brief remarks on verbal art in general. Poetry makes use of metaphorical discourse "propter repraesentationem," that is, for the sake of the pleasure taken in imitation itself. In that respect it is opposed to the Bible and theology, which make use of figural discourse "propter necessitatem et utilitatem" ("out of necessity and utility").[378] Accordingly, poetry is not rejected, so long as it is committed to truth: "Poeticae artis est veritatem rerum aliquibus similitudinibus fictis designare" ("It is the nature of the poetic art to indicate the truth of things with certain crafted comparisons").[379] Thomas thus judges poetry according to the use of figural discourse. The consequences are plumbed by Dante in a well-known letter dedicating his *Paradiso* to Cangrande della Scala:[380] here a truth-dimension is claimed for his work, which is straightforwardly assigned to the *modus tractandi* of the fictive. The argument given is that the poem can be interpreted, in accord with the theory of fourfold meaning, on the model of Biblical hermeneutics.[381]

Dante's claim can serve to make our account more precise. It draws attention to an imbalance that characterizes Thomas's theory of the beautiful. His conception of the beautiful in the arts, for which he argues on ethical and "functional" grounds, stands in a disproportional relationship to the theory of the beautiful as such and its special relevance, even if not for anagogic interpretation, at least for the training of the *intellectus* and the experience of the "immanent" *ordo entium* as a whole. Thomas's theory of the beautiful lacks a positive assessment of the work that exploits the spiritual potential of the beautiful not only in the sense of *decorum* and *ornatus*, but also in the sense and in the service of Christian doctrine itself. The *Commedia* may be read as an answer to the question as to what form such a work must take, and it is not for nothing that Dante also conceives verse as discourse bound by the rules of rhetoric, on the one hand, and, those of music, on the other.[382] Yet there are other possible answers, limited by the determinants that can be extrapolated from Thomas's concept of the beautiful. The most important determinations are *integritas sive perfectio, claritas* as the "shining through of form," and *proportio sive consonantia* as formal determinations, the "aesthetic" experience of the whole of the *ordo* as a consequence of these three "objective" determinants of the beauty of the work in question, and thus, maybe implicitly, the reference to their Creator as the "causa consonantiae et claritatis in omnibus."[383] To these we must add the nascent work's consistent ethical accentuation according to the "moral order," which is an expression of the reverence and respect man pays to the Creator.

One might ask whether the conceptual lacuna thus outlined in Thomas Aquinas's theory of the beautiful, which owes so much to the Neoplatonic tradition, is one of the initial conditions for the renewal of music theory based on Boethius after 1300—the renewal that seeks to adapt Boethius's speculative conception to the Aristotelian parameters and thus to develop it in a new and different way. The increasing differentiation between theory and practice, which is one consequence of this renewal under Aristotelian premises, is beyond all question. Nevertheless, treatises close to practice repeatedly cite the Boethian triad *musica mundana/humana/instrumentalis*, with which the *musica naturalis/artificialis* distinction also remains associated. The "holistic" emphasis of Boethius's music theory remains plausible and attractive. Our presentation of Thomas's positions allows us to formulate hypotheses regarding the grounds for this. The new Aristotelianism does erase Neoplatonic epistemology's foundation in number ontology. Nonetheless, by reconceptualizing the Augustinian *ordo* as an immanent system of "proportional" orders that also continue to be formulated in "musical" registers, it creates the conditions of plausibility for further developments of speculative music theory based on Boethius: "All things are associated in one universal order [*in uno ordine universi*], which remains indissoluble. For this reason, in the same universe a certain harmony [*harmonia*], that is, a proportioned concord [*proportionata concordia*], is caused by God."[384] Boethius's classification of music according to the manifestations of the ontologically prior numerical order in "determined redundancies" can be linked, precisely through the limitation to forms of this order's *manifestations*, to Aristotelian-Thomistic immanentism. This is true particularly because the numerical order is not simply disclaimed but incorporated into the order of *proportiones*. It remains so even in theological discourse, where the Boethian distinction of *musica mundana, musica humana,* and *musica instrumentals* continues to serve as a particularly clear and therefore privileged classification of the concrete manifestations of this order. In the Dominicans' orthodox Scholastic Thomism, Cardinal Thomas Cajetan's (1469–1534) *De nominum analogia* still stresses Thomas's theory of proportions in this way.[385] The Boethian triad is thus suitable not solely as a model of the "proportional" *ordo entium*. Insofar as the interval structure was viewed by all Christian and most pagan *auctoritates* as an exemplary manifestation of a "harmonic" proportional *form*, music can fill the lacuna in the Thomistic theory of the beautiful that we have discerned: music provides and communicates the experience of the *whole* of the immanent "proportional" order of Being related to the Creator and pointing to the Creator. The Thomistic theory offers the option of making such connections, niches of plausibility and legitimacy that allow the adaptation of the discourse of speculative music theory in the Neoplatonic tradition to the new immanentism.[386] It did not necessarily result in ruptures.

Speculative Music Theory in the Boethian Tradition up to 1500

There is no question that after 1250 medieval music theory tended increasingly to emphasize practice at the expense of metaphysical speculation.[387]

However, that does not necessarily imply that this shift in emphasis led to the repression of speculative music theory and is thus to be interpreted as a break in the sense of the scholarly view summarized in part I. The distinction between shifts in emphasis taking place within the boundaries of the plausibility of the body of theory, that is, the evolution of the discourse itself, and the breakdown of the discursive series is crucial. The findings of musicological research—"speculative music theory never completely succumbed, either in the late Middle Ages or afterward, very much like Pythagoreanism as a world-view (and many times often in connection with the latter)"[388]—suggests, like our argument taking into account the evolution of the analogical order of discourse, not breaks, but rather shifts of the specified kind. In the framework of the Thomistic model of *ordo* based on an extended concept of *proportio*, Boethian music theory remains, along with the initial *musica mundana/humana/instrumentalis* triad, open to further development. If it were asked what parameters beyond the reconstructed systematics contributed to this continuity, many examples could be cited. We could mention John XXII's banning of the *ars nova* from the churches in 1323/24, which formulated, drawing on Boethius's ethos doctrine, reservations concerning the new music in the extravagantis *Docta sanctorum patrum*:

> But some followers of the new school, while they occupy themselves in measuring beats, focus on new notes, prefer to compose their own rather than sing the ancient songs. Church hymns are sung in semibreves and minims, and they are shot through with brief notes. These musicians interrupt their melodies with hockets, polish them with descants, sometimes stuff them with a third voice, and motets in the vernacular. Thus, sometimes they scorn the foundation of the antiphon and the gradual, and ignore the foundation on which they are building. They do not even know the tones that they ignore. [. . .] The voices run but do not rest. They intoxicate rather than soothe the ears. They feign with gestures what they perform. In this way, devotion, which ought to be sought, is scorned, and indecencies, which ought to be avoided, are displayed. Boethius did not speak in vain when he said that the lewd mind takes pleasure in lewd modes, or by frequently hearing them, it becomes weak and shatters.[389]

We might also mention university teaching. Between 1289 and 1292, the Sorbonne's library was divided into two parts, a student library called the *libraria magna* or *communis*, which contained the most important works for everyday study, and the *parva libraria*, with the stored holdings.[390] In 1290 these holdings include 1017 volumes, but the catalog has been lost.

A catalog for 1338 is extant: the *parva libraria*'s stacks contained—along with two manuscripts *de cantu organico*, a *Musica* by Guido Augensis and another by an unknown Milo—three copies of Boethius's *Institutio musica*.[391] The students' library had Jerome of Moravia's *Tractatus de musica*, which we have discussed, two commentaries *de musica*, the first of which was presumably a commentary on Boethius, while the second has an incipit that points in the same direction, "Musice tria sunt genera," and also a copy of Augustine's *De musica*. The function of studies in music theory seem to remain unchanged, as these textbooks suggest.[392] An *Accessus philosophorum* produced between 1230 and 1240 vividly formulates this pedagogical goal of developing a Being-in-the world specific to analogical discourse:

> The final cause or the utility [*causa finalis uel utilitas*] of music, according to theory, is to inform the human intellect about recognizing the causes and reasons out of which all of its harmonies are composed [*informatio intellectus humani in cognitione causarum et rationum omnis eius ex quo armonie componuntur*]. Utility comes out of this informing of our intellect in respect to all things [*rei uniuerse*], since the substance of all things consists in harmonic agreement [*substantia rei uniuerse consistat in compositione armonica*], a known agreement, and the nature of harmonic consonances, and we are thereby led to a recognition of all being [*cognitionem esse uniuersi*].[393]

The finding that from the reception of Aristotle we cannot draw the sweeping conclusion that there was an interruption of speculative music theory in the Boethian tradition holds even for the allegedly most aggressive proponents of the *via nova*, for instance for Roger Bacon (c. 1219–1292/94). Roger Dragonetti cited Bacon's remarks on music as proof of his hypothesis concerning Deschamps's *Art de dictier*. Hence a few comments on Bacon's conception of music should introduce the following section on speculative music theory and its relations to verse after 1250.

The first impression made by the text seems to validate Dragonetti's reference. The statement in Bacon's *Opus tertium* (c. 1267), to the effect that the subject of disciplinary music is sound, "according to all authors, music in truth concerns sound"[394] need not, as the reference to authorities already indicates, be directed against the body of tradition. But where Bacon compares the Boethian theory, taken as representative of "the Pythagoreans," with that of Aristotle, cited primarily from *De caelo* and *De anima*, his judgment is unequivocal: "[N]ulla est musica mundana" ("There is no cosmic music").[395] This statement fits perfectly into the—basically justified—description of Roger Bacon as an early empiricist.[396] Nevertheless, this view of the Franciscan masks not only Bacon's tireless efforts on behalf of the hegemony of the theologically dominated order of discourse but also his studies on magic. It misleads us into seeing Bacon as writing polemics against *musica speculativa* as a whole. The passage cited argues not against the numerical harmonic order of the movement of the heavenly spheres, but rather, with Aristotle, against the thesis that this movement produces a real sound. The reduction of the object of music to acoustic phenomena, in support of which Dragonetti cites Bacon, is contradicted in the same paragraph by the inclusion of "parts of music [. . .], that are concerned with the visible."[397] The conceivable argument that this *musica circa visibile* is limited to the created multiplicity and thus to the objects of *physica* contradicts Bacon's point. In connection with the examples of *musica circa visibile* given— "gestures, springing, jumping, applauding, choruses, and all manner of flexing the body"[398]—Bacon cites the discussion of applause in Augustine's *De musica* II.13.24.[399] Augustine is the leading authority for the theory of the beautiful that was put forward by Thomas of York, Robert Grosseteste, and Roger Bacon: "The Oxford Franciscans remain faithful to his [Augustine's] teaching, and it is music that they place at the foundation of their aesthetics: Roger Bacon provides the most remarkable testimony to this fact."[400] Bacon considers "musical" not only sound and movement phenomena but also, explicitly, meter. For Bacon, who closely follows Augustine's *De musica* here, the common quality of these phenomena is a "proportional order" indicated through sensual pleasure: "For gestures are designed for song, instruments, meter, similar movements, and suitable formations, [. . .] when all of these conform to fitting proportions [*proportionibus convenientibus*], perfect sensible delight occurs in the two senses."[401] The connection of pleasure with *proportio* evokes a conception of form that—in accord with the systematic reference to Boethius and Augustine, especially in the passages cited from the *Opus tertium*—refers to numerical relationships and thus to the mathematical sciences.

The central importance of the mathematical sciences in Bacon's theory is determined by two factors. Only *mathematica*, which Bacon follows Aristotle in conceiving, along with *philosophia divina* and *naturalis*, as "modus philosophiae essentialis,"[402] leads to the truth. It is the model and measure of every other *scientia*, even the other *modi philosophiae essentialis* and logic: "Every science requires mathematics."[403] The strong emphasis on mathematics is owed to the second factor. Bacon earned a place in the history of science for the power he attributed to the mathematical method when it was combined with the methods of empirical verification, with *scientia experimentalis*.[404] Even before Bacon the possibility of verifying the dogma by reference to Creation was not denied, and it was not an accident that in the phase of constituting the Christian order of discourse the Creation was conceived as a "second revelation."[405] However, "misunderstandings" were forestalled by the systematic priority of the revealed text and, in the course of history, by the authorities. With regard to the latter's teaching, reference to the Creation was assigned at most an illustrative function. Bacon recognizes the unconditional authority of the Biblical revelation, but rejects the proof *per auctoritatem*: The fathers and doctors of the Church did not receive the revelation themselves, but arrived at their dogmas by interpretation. Their theses thus require verification. The latter is made possible by the Creation. The authorities' doctrine is thus subjected to the condition of experimental verification: "What is approved through authorities is determined with more certainty by experience."[406] Here the empirical-mathematical method does not serve solely to test the dogmas derived from the revealed text. It also opens up its own path leading "through Creation to the Creator": "the entire course of philosophy consists in the idea that through the knowledge of His creature, the Creator may be known."[407]

However, in Bacon's work this claim, though certainly wide-ranging, is located in a theological context that remains extremely close to the tradition. Bacon, who because of his merging of mathematics and empirical science is regularly claimed to have been the founder of "modern" science,[408] remains thoroughly a theologian with respect to his epistemological interests. The world-modeling discourse his works stand for remains theocentrically constituted. Within its conceptual framework, two assumptions are to be made to ensure the validity, independent of time or place, of scientific propositions arrived at through induction: God has expressed himself in his Creation, and the act of Creation is concluded. The quadrivial sciences retain their priority insofar as they identify objects or propositions to be verified by *scientia experimentalis*, and insofar as only they can identify *causae propter quid*: "Mathematics perfects natural sciences by giving a true explanation of natural phenomena, and regulates them by determining the utility and validity of experimentation in each branch of natural science."[409] According to Bacon's doctrine, the propositions derived in accord with empirical-mathematical methods are precisely *not* conceived as elements of a constructive-rationalist model such as Descartes formulated in an epoch-making way.[410] They are seen as the keys to the *secreta aeterna* of Creation and the Creator, and thus as the foundation and starting point for theological system construction based on the mathematical sciences as the privileged *modus philosophiae essentialis*. Mathematics is still metaphysically grounded as "the gate and key to all sciences" deduced directly from the *principium mundi*: "Mathematics is the gate and key to these sciences [*harum scientiarum porta et clavis*], which the saints from the beginning of the world discovered."[411] In opposition to an increasingly dominant Aristotelianism, "Oxford Platonism"[412] retained Augustinian characteristics: "Unconsciously and inevitably these masters [Grosseteste and Bacon] expounded the [Aristotelian] text in the light of the traditional, living Platonism, derived from St. Augustine and confirmed by twelfth-century translations of Arabian philosophers."[413]

The vulnerability of the system sketched to the question regarding the relationship between the predication of omnipotence and the propositions that Bacon calls *lex communes naturae* (common laws of nature) or *lex naturae universalis*[414] (universal laws of nature) underscores the roots of the doctrine in the analogical discourse of the Middle Ages. Claiming Bacon's works as references for a concept of *musica* limited to "sounds as such" thus falls short, underestimates the abstract nature of Christian-Neoplatonic thinking about music. What appears to be an abandonment of the Pythagoreans and a statement in favor of Aristotelianism so far as acoustic music is concerned proves to be, through "the utilization of a superordinate movement, a binding proportion," a "statement in favor of number metaphysics. Here our author shows himself to be a Platonist, guided, if not by Plato himself, then at least by Augustine's Christian interpretation of Plato."[415]

The orientation of *scientia mathematica* toward the *principium mundi* constitutes Bacon's empirical approach as a mere *instrumentum* of a "revealing" science, interrogating the numerical-harmonically organized Creation about its originator. This leads to "both a didactic and an ontological centering on mathematics, in fact on the quadrivium."[416] Accordingly, in Bacon's work, *musica* comes up when the relation of an act or a discipline to the order of Creation is established or is to be emphasized. This has consequences for the conception and instrumentalization of poetics. The disciplines of the trivium are conceived as propaedeutics, logic, and grammar are conceived as "accidental" *modi* of philosophy.[417] Rhetoric and poetics are subordinated to logic, insofar as the latter prepares *argumenta*, and at the same time connected in their *usus* with *philosophia moralis*:

> It is right that rhetoric, which is concerned with composing arguments and teaching us to argue, is a branch of logic, and that its use is part of moral philosophy. Similarly, poetry has two parts: composing a poetic argument, and using it. The first is part of logic, while the second is part of moral philosophy.[418]

The connection with *philosophia moralis* is explained by the argument
that poetry is supposed to illustrate in verbal form what *philosophia moralis* advises us to do.[419] Thus the *argumentum poëticum* is seen as a *species*
of the *argumentum rhetoricum* and determined in its content as the one that
leads toward the worship of God in words and deeds.[420] It looks as though
poetry, far from being subsumed under music, is assigned to rhetoric, and in
addition to logic; in any case, to the trivium and not to music as a quadrivial
discipline.

In fact, Bacon conceives the trivium as the *usus* of the knowledge first
acquired in the quadrivial disciplines as insight into the *natura* and *proprietas* of the subjects in question,[421] and thus postulates a factual relation
between the trivial and quadrivial disciplines in the explanation of which
musica plays a central role. His remarks on grammar, which closely follow
Augustine's *De musica*, make this clear. The pupil is taught the qualities of
the voice in general, of prose, rhythm, and meter in particular, but only *per
viam narrationis* ("by means of narration"), not *per causas, nec per rationes*
("not through causes or reasons"). It is incumbent on music to consider the
natura and *proprietas* of both prose and rhythmical-metrical constraint:

> And although the grammatical part provides boys with matter that con-
> cerns the nature of speech in prosody, meter, and rhythm, nevertheless,
> it does this in a puerile fashion, and through narration [*per viam narra-
> tionis*], not through causes or reasons [*non per causas, nec per rationes*].
> For another science has the task of providing the causes of these things,
> especially the science that has to consider fully the nature of tones. Music
> alone, whose kinds and parts are many, does this.[422]

Music as a mathematical science and quadrivial discipline thus appears
as the "comprehensively founding science"[423] for reflection on the formal
aspects of the verbal, whose status Bacon enhances to the point of proposing
that "Grammar depends causally on music."[424] The same holds for rhetoric,
in the framework of which *philosophia musicae* can be useful for preaching.[425] The causal connection with music establishes the conception of rhetoric on the basis of the goal of the transmission of knowledge and concern
for salvation. Its function is also limited to the transmission of insights that
have been gained in the quadrivial disciplines and prepared by logic. This
transmission benefits from the formal amplification of discourse through
decorum and *ornatus*, the nature and reasons of which are objects of music:
"As for the elegance, adornment, and sweetness of an argument, neither
the logician nor the grammarian can assign causes and nature to them,
but only the musician."[426] The *musicus* thus monopolizes the systematic

description of and reflection on the formal composition of discourse. The "musical" quality founded on *numerositas* provides the basis for the latter's beauty: "Aesthetics itself is reduced to mathematics, poetry deriving all its beauty and enchanting power from rhythm, that is, from music, which is ultimately based on number."[427]

The reduction of logic to the function of preparing the insights gained in the quadrivial disciplines to make them easier to understand corresponds to the consequent conception of grammar and rhetoric on the basis of their goals, on the one hand, and on the other, of the quadrivial disciplines as the site of the acquisition of knowledge. This function is also seen as dependent on the guidelines provided by *musica*. Here we may emphasize the verb *mendicare*, "beg": "the entire utility of logic springs from a comparison of all logical arguments to arguments of this sort; therefore, since they depend on musical arguments, logic must beg the power of music [*necesse est logicam mendicare potestatem musicae*]."[428] As in the case of grammar, the dependency of logic on music is causal in nature.[429] In the case of logic, this dependency exists in two ways. First, insofar as the goal of logic is the argumentative formulation of knowledge in such a way that it promotes virtue and future happiness, one of the objectives of logic is to take into account the purposeful presentation of the argument. Accordingly, here the same arguments hold as in the case of grammar and rhetoric, and thus rhetoric and poetics are subordinated to logic. Second, the dependency of the logical procedure of proof on *musica* is based on the notion that its principle (*principium*), the theory of categories presented in Aristotle's *Posterior Analytics*, is developed out of the category of quantity and that the latter is the object of mathematical science.[430] This thesis illustrates the number-theory foundation of his doctrine. The "holistic" implications of the mathematical sciences and with them of *musica* are the dominants in his theory, no matter how strongly developed are its empirical components. The form of metrical discourse remains connected with the numerical order and located in the mathematical sciences so far as the scientific elaboration of its *natura* and *proprietas* is concerned. Against the background of tradition, the question of the acoustic reality of *musica mundana*, for example, is an important but not decisive one for the implications of Bacon's concept of music as a whole. Bacon's theory does not prove Dragonetti's hypothesis of a break, but supports instead our working hypothesis of a continuity of the Christian-Neoplatonic concept of music. With its empirical components, Roger Bacon's work shows how pronounced the adaptability of the Christian order of discourse is, so long as the founding concept of *ordo* can be considered plausible. Even Bacon's sketch of a theory, which is characterized by an unprecedented openness to the empirical, does not see reference to concrete sound as the object of *musica* as an abandonment of the discourse of speculative music theory, but rather as a shift in emphasis within this discourse. The order of numbers and numerical relationships continues to merge mathematical speculation and concrete sense phenomena in mutual confirmation. The discourse of music theory can adapt to the shift in parameters and retain its world-modeling quality so long as it can render plausible the connectibility of the "musical" phenomenon—the harmonic intervals, isorhythmic units, every particular redundancy—with a preexisting, superordinate system establishing, on various levels up to the highest principle of unity as such, the unity of discrete multitudes. This order of Being can, as in the case of Roger Bacon appealing to Augustine, still be seen as numerical-harmonic, but it can also be conceived differently, as Thomas Aquinas shows. What is crucial for the whole context is only that it be possible to describe the "measured" phenomenon as a concrete and preeminent manifestation of this order of Being.

In treatises on music after 1250, synthetic attempts of this kind are to be encountered everywhere. If we wanted to take examples from the context of Oxford Platonism, then we could mention the passages on music in *De ortu scientarium*, a work by the Dominican Richard Kilwardby (c. 1215–1279).[431] We draw our examples from the continent in order to demonstrate the continuity of the discourse of speculative theory of music precisely where Aristotelianism gained hegemonic validity within a few decades.

The *De musica* written by the Benedictine monk Engelbert of Admont (c. 1250–1331),[432] who had studied between 1271 and 1285 in Prague and with the Aristotelians in Padua,[433] shows the synthetic argument with exemplary clarity. This work offers a systematic introduction to music theory. It opens with a chapter entitled "Quid sit musica generaliter," followed by a section called "De triplici musica." Even the Aristotelian Engelbert begins with the words "According to Boethius, Book 1, chapter 2, music has three parts,"[434] and then pits the Boethian-Platonic position against the Aristotelian one:

Cosmic music [*musica mundana*] consists in and is considered in the proportions of motions, the magnitude of celestial bodies, their distances in space, and their positions and motions. Plato took great pains to discuss and explore musical harmony in the *Timaeus*, as did his followers, defenders, and commentators, such as Chalcidius on the *Timaeus*, Macrobius on the *Dream of Scipio*, and Remigius on Martianus Capella. Although Aristotle in the second book of *On the Heavens and the Earth*

demolished with plain reasoning and denied the claim that the heavenly
bodies produced sound, nevertheless, he did not deny other proportions
of motions [*proporciones motuum*], the magnitude of those very bodies,
and the distances and spaces between them.[435]

The composition already makes the question regarding the sound of the
harmony of the spheres seem secondary. The conception of the course of
the heavenly bodies as a form of music is based on the "proportional" order
that is manifested in this movement, and not at all on in its acoustic quality.
The often-cited thirteenth-century criticism of the concept of the harmony
of the spheres laid out in Aristotle's *De caelo* affects only an accidental
characteristic of the latter. It can be sacrificed without necessarily putting
up for negotiation the idea of the "musical" order of Creation as a whole.

The criticism made by the opponents of the traditional body of music
theory in the Aristotelian camp hardly goes beyond the argument formulated by Engelbert. The same holds for Arabian influences,[436] as can be
shown by the works of Al-Hasan Al-Katib or Al-Farabi,[437] whose *De scientiis* contains a chapter on music that sums up his monumental *Kitab
al-musiqa al-kabir*, which remained, because of the defects of Gundissalinus's inadequate translation,[438] unknown to the Latin Middle Ages.[439] The
"holistic" implications of the concept of music remain so stable that in the
fourteenth century, writing in music theory puts forward downright orthodox Pythagorean-Neoplatonic positions. In order to show not only the
continuity of the speculative concept of music but also the heterogeneous
constitution of the conceptions in detail, and thus to challenge the schematizing conceptions described in part I, we present the following examples in
chronological order.

First, the *Ars musica* written by Johannes Aegidius Zamorensis (c.
1250–1300/1318) adheres, in explicit accord with the Platonic paradigm
and against Aristotelian positions, to a conception of the principle of the
"coherence" of the *artes* as established by arithmetic (as *cunctarum mater*,
"mother of all") and music:

> Then, too, Plato commended music, saying that just as Arithmetic is the
> mother of all arts [*cunctarum mater est artium*], so also, Music is her sis-
> ter. In Plato's view, no science is considered complete without the melodic
> art, no matter how distinguished it is. In the arts of Grammar it appears
> in consonance and dissonance of letters in orthography, and in the con-
> sonance of feet in the art of meter. In Logic it is found in the consonance
> and dissonance of propositions in the art of syllogisms. In Rhetoric it is
> found in consonance and dissonance of rhythms and such. Thus, not only

in these, but also in all celestial bodies that exist, especially in elemental and mixed ones, a most beautiful melody comes forth in accord with divinely ordained musical consonances and dissonances [*secundum consonantias & dissonantias musicales divinitus ordinatas*].[440]

The text assigns metrics to grammar, rhythmics to rhetoric; however, the discussion of "musicality" fundamentally implies a connection with an ordering principle that is as such the object of the mathematical sciences founded on arithmetic. This is taken into account by Johannes Aegidius Zamorensis's differentiation of the *musicae*, which once again proves the establishment of the distinction introduced by Regino of Prüm. He distinguishes four "species sive modi [musicae]," aspects or modes of music: "One is cosmic [*mundana*], another is human [*humana*], another is the music of the spheres [*coelestis*], and the last is instrumental or artificial [*instrumentalis seu artificialis*]."[441] The *musica coelestis* is seen as *musica*, "wherein they describe the heavens as revolving within circles according to harmonic modulation [*sub harmonica modulatione*]."[442] *Musica mundana* includes the harmony of the elements and cyclical natural phenomena.[443] The definition of *musica humana* corresponds to the traditional view, and the differentiation of *musica instrumentalis* seems to follow Regino:

> Some instrumental music is living, because it is produced by a living instrument; another kind is dead, for it is produced by a dead instrument. This appears in the viella, the cithara, the organ, and other such instruments, which will be discussed at the end of this work. According to other writers, skill in music relies on two kinds of instruments: natural and artificial [*naturali & artificiali*]. The human voice is shaped by a natural instrument, such as the arteries, the tongue, the palate, the lips, and the lungs. [. . .] An artificial instrument produces artificial sound, as is the case with the cithara, organs, the viellas, and other musical instruments, which are produced by craft, rather than by nature; as we see, they produce an artificial sound, not a natural one [*quae fiunt artificio, non natura, & artificiosum, non naturalem, ut vidimus, reddunt sonum*].[444]

The distinction between "natural" and "artificial" instruments simplifies Regino's conception of a *musica naturalis*, which included the "balanced" *musica humana* as the precondition for harmonic chant, into a physiological description of the vocal and respiratory apparatuses. At the same time, Regino's binary distinction enters into a very much more differentiated classification system than the *Epistola de armonica institutione* had offered. The conception of the *musica naturalis-musica artificialis* distinction as a differentiation of *musica instrumentalis* takes into account the systematic extension, already found in Jerome of Moravia, of the category of *musica naturalis* to all products of the human voice. The latter, as a divinely created, animate and "natural" instrument is still distinguished from the inanimate, man-made instrument. The analogical connection between *musica instrumentalis*, although now differentiated according to Regino's distinction, *musica humana, mundana,* and *coelestis* remains just as intact as the common foundation of these *musicae* in the numerical order. The latter, for its part, remains "as such" the object of arithmetic, its sensible-concrete manifestations the object of music.

In addition to the speculative conception of music, the Neoplatonic-Neopythagorean foundation and the classificatory inventory of the tradition, the possibility of conceiving the work as a concrete manifestation of the *ordo entium* also remains—including the analytic and generative possibilities inherent in number theory. Here we take as an example the work of Marchettus of Padua (c. 1274–c. 1319), whose innovations in harmony, notation, and the system of modes became central for the *ars nova*.[445] This theoretician left, in addition to the *Pomerium in arte musicae mensuratae* and a *Brevis compilatio in arte musicae mensuratae* summarizing it, a comprehensive *Lucidarium musicae planae* that may have been written around 1317.[446] The traditional Pythagorean-Neoplatonic doctrine, along with its implications founded in number theory—"music is a science that consists of proportional numbers, quantities, measures, conjunctions, and consonances"[447]—provides here the foundation, not only for a summary of the tradition, but also for new theory construction: "In Marchetto's treatises, indeed—which survey the entire field of music theory as their author conceived it—Pythagoreanism serves not only as the basis of the theories of rhythm and tuning but also of counterpoint and modal doctrine."[448] A detailed presentation could prove that the Boethian tradition was still alive around 1320, but that would take us too far away from the focus of our investigation.[449] Here we will limit ourselves to a brief reference to the "holistic" implications of the theory presented and its conceptual foundations. Marchettus sees, with reference to Pythagoras, Boethius, and Isidore of Seville, the *principium mundi* that rules the world, the body, and the soul as musical:

> According to Isidore, no science can be complete without music, for nothing is gathered together without it [*nihil enim sine ea legitur*]. [. . .] Hence, Pythagoras used to say that this world is founded on music [*per musicam conditum esse*], and can be governed by it, since even whatever

is moved internally by pulsations of the veins is shown to be associated
with the power of harmony through musical rhythms [*per musicos rhyth-
mos harmoniae virtutibus probatur associatum*].[450]

The numerical harmonic order is established by God and as such is an object of arithmetic.[451] The same holds for the system of harmonic proportions
and consonances, as Marchettus notes regarding the interval of the fourth:
"the consonance of the dyatessaron by divine disposition [*divina dispositione*] rejoices in the number four so much that it has four parts, and comes
about by fourfold division [. . .]."[452] The divine disposition is deduced, in
accord with the Pythagorean-Neoplatonic basis of the doctrine, from the
order of the first *tetraktys*. Marchettus clarifies the implications of the numbers subsumed under the *tetraktys* by using the example of the number
four. The examples he offers range from the four seasons through the four
cardinal directions, the four elements, and the four bodily fluids of humoral
pathology to the number-symbolism implications of the four gospels.[453] The
pulchritudo specific to the *ars musica* follows from its analogical relation
to this world-guiding *musica universalis* founded in the numerical order:

> More beautiful among the arts is music, about which Remigius says: The
> vastness of music takes in all living and inanimate things [*magnitudo mu-
> sices capit omne quod vivit, & quod non vivit*]. The singing of the angels,
> archangels, saints, and all who say "sanctus, sanctus, sanctus" before
> God ceaselessly proclaim music. [. . .] Among the trees [of the arts] mu-
> sic is admirable. Her branches are beautifully proportioned by numbers;
> her flowers are varieties of consonances; her fruits are sweet harmonies
> brought to maturity by those very consonances. About this Bernard says:
> There is one, universal music, whose vastness, by the will of God selects
> and moves continuously all things [*una est musica universalis cuius mag-
> nitudo nutu divino caput movet continue omnia*] that have been moved
> in the heavens, and that exist on earth, in the sea, in the voice of men and
> animals, through the growth of bodies, and through years, days, and sea-
> sons.[454]

From the numerical order, Marchettus does not construct solely the traditional body of ideas; he broadens the latter on the model of the noetic
procedure of the Pythagorean "mathematicians."[455] On the same bases and
with the same "holistic" claim, in his *Pomerium in arte musicae menuratae*
he also reconstructs the whole of rhythmics.[456] The vitality of traditional
concepts of music on Neoplatonic bases in the fourteenth century is thus
unquestionable. The fundamental breaks that the scholars whose work was

summarized in part I tended to assume, do not exist, especially since conservative treatises like that of Marchettus of Padua were extremely influential. Jan F. Herlinger has studied the influence of the *Lucidarium* and concluded that the text "was indeed one of the most influential treatises of the Middle Ages."[457]

Even such treatises reflect the attractiveness of the "holistic" implications of music theory in the Boethian tradition that try to avoid introducing into music as a quadrivial discipline the metaphysical implications handed down with Boethius, astronomical considerations, the seasons, or the harmony of the elements. The works of Johannes de Muris (c. 1295–before 1360) testify to this. This mathematician, astronomer, and theoretician of music was active around 1320 as a *magister* at the Sorbonne's faculty of arts, where he advocated the "[a]*rtes liberales* [as] the starting point and foundation of any scientific work."[458] His mathematical writings, which include, in addition to his chief work *Quadripartium opus numerorum* (completed in 1343) an *Arithmetica speculativa* that adheres closely to Boethius,[459] were influential for centuries as textbooks for the quadrivial disciplines,[460] and lay the conceptual foundation for his writings on music theory. Between 1323 and 1325 he produced two versions of a *Musica speculativa secundum Boethium*[461] generally regarded as a faithful abridgment of Boethius.[462] Its transmission in forty-eight manuscripts and three early printed versions proves its broad distribution.[463] Moreover, we should assume that from 1323 on, this work was used as a textbook in the faculty of arts.[464] Together with the works of Philippe de Vitry and the treatise *De numeris harmonicus* authored by Levi ben Gerson (also known as Gersonides or Leo Hebraeus, 1288–1344), Johannes de Muris's mathematical and music theory works founded the *ars nova*'s leading school of theoreticians and also a pedagogical tradition that was dominant in France over the following centuries.[465] Here too we will present only the passages essential for the connection between the musical and a "holistic" order founded on numerical relationships.

Johannes de Muris's works are permeated by the effort to guarantee the unity of the quadrivial disciplines and along with it, that of music theory as a *scientia mathematica*. In his view, in the recent past the textbooks of Boethius and other writers had been too little read, "and it happens that they are abhorred as unintelligible or exceedingly difficult."[466] He opposed this obnubilation of authority. At the beginning of the long version of *Musica speculativa*, we read: "Since music concerns sound as related to numbers [*de sono relato ad numeros*], it is necessary for music to consider two things: number and sound."[467] Conceiving the acoustic phenomenon as *motus* and thus as quantifiable retains the option of relating it, qua *proportio*, to the *proportiones generales numerorum*: "Since it has been shown that music consists of sounds, which are proportional to one another in some way according to the number of motions found in them, reviewing the general proportions of numbers [*proportiones generales numerorum*] is not without profit."[468] Johannes de Muris, who with his *Fractiones* of 1324 and the previously mentioned *Opus quadripartium numerorum* also contributed works considered important in the history of mathematics, developed his own classification of *proportiones*,[469] which enjoyed a certain influence in the *musica mensurabilis* of the following centuries. The introduction of this new classification into *musica scientia* is justified with the arguments that were to grant to the acoustic sense impression, the tone as a "physical" phenomenon, the weight that they were to have after the scientific developments of the twelfth and thirteenth century.[470] The priority of the noetic is nonetheless retained:

> The most distinguished Pythagoras, who excelled in the most subtle investigation into numerical proportions, did not want to put faith in the judgment of the ears where consonances were concerned: [. . .] it is the role of reason, not the ear, to distinguish among numerical proportions [*numerorum proportionibus discernere*]: [. . .]; and yet, one is not at all willing to deprive hearing of the judgment of consonances, because if there were no hearing, there would be no ratio in sounds at all; but first, there is a way to maintain a certain middle course: hearing becomes a sort of servant to the office of consonances or harmonies [*de consonantiis vel harmoniarum officio*], a judge of the intellect, and the ear weighs what is divided and diminished; from this the intellect organizes a universal and complete science [*scientia universalis et completa*] on the basis of the ear's first recognition.[471]

The sense of hearing as *famulus,* as slave or servant, on the basis of whose impressions the *ratio* can undertake its *opus* of *numerorum proportionibus discernere* (discerning the proportions of numbers), and the *intellectus* can advance toward *scientia universalis et completa*—the conception follows Boethius's *De institutione musica* V.2. Johannes de Muris explains the discovery of the relations between proportions and consonances by recourse to the legend of the forge;[472] the proportional relationships formulated in the first *tetraktys* are referred to as "the principles of this art."[473] These principles are established by God as the author of nature: "It was not man, but the author of nature [*auctor naturae*] who created consonances in things [*consonantias fecit in rebus*]."[474] The conception of harmonic intervals as sensible realizations of a numerical harmonic order that coincides with the order of Being and Creation remains intact, and along with it the special status of quadrivial music among the arts. Thus in Johannes de Muris's *Quaestiones super partes musicae* we read:

> What is music? Music is the mistress art of the arts [*ars artium domina*], containing in herself the beginnings of all methods [*omnium principia methodorum*] on the first level of certitude, confirmed in the nature of all things, remarkably internalized proportionally, delightful to the intellect, loved by the ear. Music gladdens the downcast, rewards the eager, thwarts the envious, comforts the weak, keeps awake the vigilant, awakens the sleepers, nourishes love, honors its possessor, if music, which was established at last for the praise of God, has pursued its just goal.[475]

The double emphasis here is important. It underscores not only that *musica* includes within itself the methodological *principia* of all other arts and confirms their value through the *natura rerum omnium*, through music as a sensible, immanently regulative principle. This principle is closely connected as well to the *effectus musicae* systematized in the musical doctrine of ethos and with the latter, to the ethical power of music in a Christian sense. This connection, which had been inscribed in the discourse of speculative music theory ever since its phase of constitution, remains intact in the fourteenth century. It even seems to count as an essential lesson, though the *Quaestiones super partes musicae* collect basic elements of music theory and central definitions in very abridged form.

Thus we must attribute special weight to the fact that the distinction between *musica naturalis* and *musica artificialis*, quoted a few decades later by Eustache Deschamps, is found in the *Summa musicae* by this important fourteenth-century teacher.[476] Johannes de Muris strengthens the Boethian substrate of Regino's distinction, using *musica instrumentalis* and *musica artificialis* as synonyms. *Musica naturalis* includes both *musica mundana* and *musica humana*: "Some music is natural [*naturalis*], some is instrumental [*instrumentalis*]. Some natural music is human [*humana*], and some is cosmic [*mundana*]."[477] In Johannes de Muris, the *instrumenta*, whose products are viewed as *musica artificialis*, also include the human voice. The latter appears, in what may be a concession to Regino, as the most noble *instrumentum* that produces sounds (*soni*) as well as words:

> Many kinds of musical instruments are artificial [*artificialis*]. They can be divided into three sorts, and are called stringed, bored, and bowel-like. [. . .] These produce sounds that vary according to their different materials and shapes. Among the other musical instruments, the most worthy

and universal is that of the human voice [*instrumentum vocis humanae est dignissimum et universalis*], because it brings forth both sound and words, whereas the others produce sound alone but no voice.[478]

The synthetically structured sketches of the fourteenth century culminated around 1330 in the *Speculum musicae* of Jacob of Liège (c. 1260–after 1330).[479] This work, which is considered the most comprehensive text on music theory produced in the Middle Ages, offers a monumental musical encyclopedia in 521 chapters in seven books that "absorbs all the recognizable earlier trends and combines them into a large, unified system:"[480] "a work whose author knows everything about the evolution of music theory from Greco-Roman Antiquity down to his own time."[481] In the only complete extant manuscript (Paris, BNF lat. 7207) the *Speculum musicae* runs to 293 sheets or 586 pages, densely covered with words, of which hardly any escape abbreviation, sometimes by several syllables. My discussion of this work here, which cannot do justice to its full breadth, is not intended solely to provide still another proof of the continuity of the speculative concept of music. The *Speculum musicae* reflects this continuity itself in the sense of an evolution of the discourse that we have opposed to the break-hypothesis proposed by the scholarship summarized in part I, and thus it allows us to back these components of our working hypothesis with historical material as well. Ultimately, Jacob of Liège uses the opportunity to continue the speculative concept of music under the new parameters that we have identified in Thomas Aquinas's work: Jan A. Aertsen has called the doctrine of the *Speculum musicae* a "metamusic"[482] related to the *ens numeratum* that takes into account the reorientation of Scholastic theology carried out since Aquinas.

The *Speculum musicae* describes the contexts of its production in a way that is familiar to us from the work of Johannes de Muris. The study of the ancients, chapter II.56 tells us, has been replaced by that of the commentators on it and contemporary music theorists, and the old authorities' doctrine has been distorted to the point of being unrecognizable. Only contact with Boethius's *De institutio musica* brought clarity to the author and thus became the occasion for revising contemporary theory on Boethian bases.[483] Boethius's doctrine of numbers and proportions provides the firm foundation to which contemporary theory, seen as disparate and inadequately grounded, can be related back not only in the prospective interest of the coherence of *musica scientia*, but also as a way of reestablishing it. The argument implies the continuity thesis in far more trenchant form than it is defended here: the *Speculum musicae* sees reflection on music theory since Boethius as a gradual growth (*crescere*) and extension (*augere, augmentare, adinvenire, superaedificare*) of knowledge about music and the possibilities in practice. This growth and expansion are, however, no more than elaborations on principles (*principia, fundamenta, aliquod universale*) that had already been discovered and formulated in an exemplary way in late Antiquity:

> Since [Boethius] treated consonances and musical tones pre-eminently, did he not also lay the foundations upon which later musicians established themselves? They constructed new modalities and reached new conclusions. Since their demonstrations were enriched, knowledge grew through these modalities, and passed from incomplete to complete through the scholarship of learned men. Art that is achieved through experimentation and practice is no little thing. It is a great thing to have discovered the foundations of knowledge [*scientiae fundamenta*], the principles of knowledge [*scientiae principia*]; even if the number of these discoveries is small, their strength and power is great: one had discovered something universal [*aliquod universale*], the principle of art and science [*principium artis atque scientiae*].[484]

The combination of proximity to practice and the desire for system, of a close connection to the texts on which the discourse is based and the striving to exhaust the conceptual possibilities set out here is characteristic of the *Speculum musicae*. It is inherent in the recapitulated conceptualization of the evolution of the discourse.

The work formulates a far-reaching claim that exhausts the implications of the speculative conception of music. The object of *musica scientia* is seen as simply everything that exists, insofar as it is *numeratum*:

> Music's objective, however, generally understood, concerns number in things, not considered absolutely, but in relation to something [*numerum rerum quarumcumque non absolute, sed ad aliquid*] [. . .] so that it might apply itself to beings compared to one another, and to consider them in any condition compared to one another. Accordingly, as metaphysics extends itself to every being, in so far as the reason for being in general is found in every being, so too, music extends itself to each numbered thing for that reason [*musica ad omne ens numeratum sub illa ratione*] [. . .] And since, according to the philosopher, there are three branches of knowledge concerned with all being, dialectics, sophistics, and metaphysics, which we call philosophy, music was added to these, [. . .]. Music, however, applies itself to every thing that is numbered [*musica applicat se ad rem omnem numeratam*].[485]

Here music theory arrives at the claim to have "the same universality as philosophy"[486] and infringes on theology's area of competence insofar as the all-inclusive "musical" order even includes the *proportio* of the Creator and the Creation:[487] "For music [. . .] objectively extends itself nearly to all things [*quasi ad omnia se extendit*], to God and to creatures, incorporeal and corporeal, heavenly and human, to theoretical and practical modes of knowing."[488]

The founding of the argument in number theory, which does not need to be explained again here, corresponds to the genuine Boethian tradition in music theory.[489] Apart from that, the systematic and terminological parallels with Aquinas's doctrine of proportions are obvious:

> Music is not only generally concerned with number in sounds, or with number in sounds compared to one another, but with the number of things compared with one another at the same time, just as among those things a certain appearance of proportion, concord, order or connection can be observed [*prout inter illas attendi potest quaedam habitudo cuiusdam proportionis, concordiae, ordinis vel connexionis*], so that the appearance concerned can be understood through harmonic modulation generally considered [*per harmonicam modulationem generaliter sumptam*], as has been said. Nor does music consider number in things absolutely, but rather as among plural and distinct things that have been compared at the same time, when the appearance of a certain connection, order, proportion, or concord is found [*habitudo cuiusdam connectionis, ordinis, proportionis vel concordiae*], whether those things are sonorous, human or terrestrial, corporal or spiritual, celestial or super-celestial.[490]

Around 1330 the conception of these *habitudines, ordines, connectiones,* and *concordiae,* going far beyond the acoustic phenomenon as grounded in numerical relationships, was still justified by reference to the well-known verse from *Liber sapientiae* 11:21:

> [A]s is clear in Boethius, harmonic modulation does not alone proclaim modulation of sounds [*harmonica modulatio non sola sonorum dicat modulationem*]. At another time, he asks, what besides harmony links together four different elements and contrary powers [. . .] so that they come together in one body or one instrument? That harmony, however, does not come about out of a mixture of sounds, but out of a suitable place for and proportion of those very qualities [*ex convenienti situ et proportione qualitatum ipsorum*]. Isidore claims that this world is said to be established by a certain harmony. Likewise, according to Isidore, music

extends itself to everything [*musica extendit se ad omnia*], since nothing exists without it. Therefore, it extends itself to transcendent and divine things [*ad res dilatat se transcendentes et divinas*], if indeed God creates all things through numbers, weight and measure [*Deus omnia fecit in numero, pondere et mensura*], for all things that come forth from the primal origin of things have been formed according to numbers [*ratione numerorum formata sunt*].[491]

Jacob of Liège maintains the Boethian triad *musica mundana/humana/instrumentalis*, but modifies it by making use of the option that we have developed in the last section on the basis of its Thomistic presuppositions: "According to Boethius, music is divided into cosmic [*mundana*], human [*humana*], and instrumental or sonorous [*instrumentalem vel sonoram*], and all of these treat natural things [*naturalibus*]."[492] The following chapter provides each of these *musicae* with explanations that speak for a thousand years of music theory in Latin Western Europe.[493] The claim of the *Speculum musicae*, which points beyond the interests of the Boethian triad, leads to the introduction of a fourth *species musicae*. It designates the ideal principles of the "musical" *ordo entium*, the numerical harmony *in mente divina*, as *musica coelestis vel divina*: "It seems that another species of music can be added to these, which can be called celestial or divine [*coelestis vel divina*]. This concerns things apart from motion and sensible matter, and is related to being and the intellect, transcendent things [*res transcendentes*] that pertain to metaphysics and divine knowledge."[494] The reference to metaphysics or theology is systematic: Jacob of Liège seeks to take into account the Aristotelian *ordo scientiarum*, associating *musica coelestis vel divina* with *metaphysica*, *musica mundana* and *humana* with *physica*, and *musica instrumentalis*, in accord with Thomas Acquinas, with *physica* and *mathematica*.[495] However, precisely these associations foreground the "holistic" nature of the music theory sketched out, which emphasizes the *integration* of increasingly differentiated disciplines:

> Now, it seems that harmonic modulation [*harmonica modulatio*], as regards music in general, ought not to be limited to natural and corporeal things, which is the concern of cosmic and human music [*mundanam et humanam musicam*], sounds and voices, or instrumental music [*musica instrumentalis*]. It ought to consider the motor intelligences of the world, even the first mover [*intelligentias orbium motrices, etiam ad primum motorem*], [. . .]. Proportion is required even between the mover and the moved, [. . .]. [496]

The conception interprets the cosmology borrowed from Aristotle's *Phys-ics* in accord with the Neoplatonic, "musical" schemata that had already influenced Thomas Aquinas's concept of *ordo*. This interpretation is meant to ground *musica scientia*'s "metaphysical" assertions:

> It will belong to another kind of music to examine proportion, order, and concord [*proportionem, ordinem, concordiam*], which those sepa-rate motors possess among themselves, and to the motor that is utterly prime, and to those things that it moves. And perhaps, if Boethius in particular had followed up on his discussion of cosmic music, he would have come to the subject of the motor of the celestial orbs. Aristotle took this path through the topic of motion to attain an awareness of separate substances. What is the inconvenience if we extend harmonic modulation as generally understood, not only to corporeal, natural things, and sub-stantial numbered things, but even to metaphysical things [*ad metaphysi-cales*]? Among alternately numbered and compared things an appearance of some connection, order, concord, or proportion [*quaedam habitudo cuiusdam connexionis, ordinis, concordiae vel proportionis*] is observed, so that harmonic modulation might be included under three rather than two branches of theoretical philosophy, [. . .].)[497]

The Boethian classification of the *musicae* is merged with Aristotelian cos-mology by dint of the *motus*; its foundation in number theory is integrated into this conception as a theory of the formal determinants of these *motus*. *Musica scientia* takes as its object the "proportional" and in that sense "mu-sical" order of the cosmic *motus*. Insofar as the latter includes all realms from that of the unmoved mover to that of the most insignificant part of the world and the purview of *musica scientia* includes this whole completely and with regard to the Creator, it approaches theology as a discipline claim-ing to integrate all of the individual sciences *sub ratione*, as segmentary disciplines with a limited scope. Aquinas's *Summa theologiae* had used this argument to distinguish theology from the individual sciences, granted the latter a certain measure of freedom in the production of knowledge and methodology,[498] and yet at the same time confirmed the hegemonic claim of the order of discourse monopolized by theology:

> Nothing prevents those inferior powers or conditions from being distrib-uted around materials that commonly fall under one power or condition, since the superior power or condition regards the object under a more universal formal reckoning [*sub universaliori ratione formali*]. Just as the object of ordinary sense is sensible, because it incorporates the visible and

the audible, so also the common sense, although it is one power, extends itself to all the objects of the five senses. Similarly, sacred doctrine, being one, can consider under one reckoning things that are treated in different philosophical disciplines [*in diversis scientiis philosophicis*], in so far as they are divinely revealed things, so that it might be a sort of division of divine science, which among all of them has the character of being one and simple [*quae est una et simplex omnium*].[499]

The "rapprochement" carried out by Jacob of Liège never becomes a competition; the theologically guided order of discourse is never put in question in the *Speculum musicae*.[500] It remains, although worked out concisely, a complementarity. In the fourteenth century, it demonstrates the vitality and, through the exhaustion of the possibilities inherent in the concept, the hegemony of the Christian-Neoplatonic, speculative conception of music.

This is also shown by the remarks on *musica instrumentalis*. It remains, despite some concessions to the musical practice of the High Middle Ages,[501] conceived as an ontologically subordinate "imitation." The differentiation according to the *instrumentum* deriving from Regino of Prüm makes it possible to formulate this hierarchy: "[. . .] naturalia instrumenta perfectiora artificialibus. Ars enim naturam imitatur [. . .]" ("natural instruments are more perfect than artificial ones. For art imitates nature [. . .]").[502] Both of these are further differentiated. A "first division of instrumental music"[503] distinguishes between *musica plana* and *musica mensurabilis*, while a "second division of instrumental music"[504] is introduced with reference to Isidore's *Etymologiae*:

In the third book of the *Etymologies*, Isidore divides music into harmonic, rhythmic, and metric [*harmonicam, rythmicam, et metricam*]. Harmonics distinguishes between high and low pitch in sounds. Rhythm concerns the stress of words, and whether their sound accords well or badly, so as to produce a good or bad sound. Rhythm also seems to consider the harmony of words [*verborum consonantiam*], [mildness], and word-play [*allusionem*], especially at the end of words. If it does not pay heed to the value of time in the syllables of words [*in dictionum syllabis temporis non attendat valorem*], whether short or long, which is the concern of metrics, nevertheless, it does consider the number of syllables [*numerum attendit syllabarum*]. Metrics distinguishes the measure of time in different meters, whether the meter is a dactyl, an iamb, a choriamb, and so on, as the meters are called, either according to the feet out of which they are constructed, their subject matter, or their inventors.[505]

It is obvious that the comment on *musica metrica* is a theoretical element drawn from tradition that is still oriented by the system of quantifying metrics, but once again its vitality is just as obvious. The remarks on *musica rhythmica* seem to describe syllable-counting and end-rhyming metrics. They testify to the power of speculative music theory in general and of the *Speculum musicae* in particular to assimilate not only Latin quantitative and "rhythmical" verse, but also contemporary French verse in an age that is already that of Guillaume de Machaut (1300/1305–1377) and Eustache Deschamps (1345–1404). Verse, both quantitative and syllabic, is seen as "musical," and not only in the sense that everything existing as *numeratum* falls under the category of *musica*. Verse is highlighted as one of the manifestations of the "musical" order of being that is marked by a special evidence and for that reason should be explicitly classified and emphasized as *musica*.

Jacob of Liège's *Speculum musicae* had hardly any impact. In our context, it illustrates the vitality and productivity of a discourse whose central theoretical elements were derived from the tradition of Christian-Neoplatonic speculative music theory. Jacob of Liège shows not only that we can hardly speak of breaks or a rupture in the Pythagorean-Neoplatonic tradition, but also that a generation before Deschamps the discourse of speculative music theory was preparing the furthest development of its implications.

This discourse continued to be current down to the time of the *Grands rhétoriqueurs*. The status of *musica practica* continued to rise, while the systematic coherence of the theoretical elements that connected the acoustic work with the concept of the "holistic" order declined. Nevertheless the connection was never lost, and continued without interruption into Neoplatonic and Neopythagorean positions in the sixteenth and seventeenth centuries. The speculative branch of music theory, in which questions of classification like that raised by Deschamps are situated, takes thirteenth- and fourteenth-century debates in theology and the theory of science into account, but does not therefore oppose the old authorities. Two final examples, presented only briefly here, are intended to prove this and to extend our reconstruction to the end of the fifteenth century.

Ugolino of Orvieto (c. 1380–1452)[506] had participated in the Council of Constance in 1412, as Forli's delegate. In 1425 he was elevated to archdeacon in Constance, and in 1429 he was elected *canonicus* in Ferrara, and served as archpriest there from 1431 to 1448. In 1448 he joined, as a vicar, the service of Cardinal Pietro Barbo, the later Pope Paul II, whom he served as papal secretary until his death. In the course of this extremely successful ecclesiastical career he produced the ambitious *Declaratio musicae disciplinae* in five books. We will limit ourselves to passages that "frame" the practical parts of the work in Books I to III and set for these the familiar speculative aim.

A proem introduces the work and promises the rationally governed soul, the developed *intellectus*, insight into the divine workings and along with it the *beatitudo* of the vision of God: "If the soul is governed by reason, it understands God with the operation of the intellect, and delights in His will."[507] Ugolino von Orvieto takes as his point of departure the concept of Creation as a second revelation: all knowledge begins with sensation, and by abstraction from the sensible plurality insight into what binds it together can be gained.[508] So long as believers and the curious do not "fall short" of the claim to knowledge, in accord with Aquinas's warning,[509] the *conditor omnium* is also revealed in the Creation. We will leave it to Ugolino of Orvieto to describe again the order of Creation and what is promised to those who gain insight into its origin and principle:

> In the celestial hierarchy the separate substances perpetually stand near divine majesty, in order to praise it in its infinite goodness. These substances, knowing the boundless exaltedness of such great majesty in the manner of creatures, and understanding the infinity of its wisdom, endlessly proclaim with its own incredible sweetness of mildness in celestial music of marvelous harmony [*caelesti musica mirabilis harmoniae*], and with repeated sweetness: Sanctus, Sanctus, Sanctus. Indeed, celestial music [*musica coelestis*] is the beginning of all cosmic music [*omnis mundanae*], the source of all human and instrumental music [*omnis humanae ac instrumentalis initium et origo*], and the origin of proportion in every melody, the conjunction of all consonances, the agreement of all voices, the sweet and uniform mixture, if this can be said, of all harmonies of low and high pitch; out of the uniform desire of all things through accented and unaccented, that is, through the greater and lesser intellection of one praise, arises the same concord, the highest delight of one for another; in the celestial hierarchy there is no disagreement or disharmony.[510]

The *caelestis musica* as *principium* of *musica mundana*, *initium* and *origo* of *musica humana* and *instrumentalis*, as the harmony of all harmonies and disharmonies, which points to the one and only *conditor*—toward the middle of the fifteenth century, the "holistic" conception of music has been adapted to the broadened Thomistic concept of *proportio*, but its extension has not been curtailed. It seems more alive than ever. We should note the proximity to the Boethian model itself in the domains where the thirteenth century had introduced and established modifications, for instance in the question of the acoustic reality of *musica mundana*, whose existence the author of the *Declaratio* assumes.[511] What is especially note-worthy is the substantial theological and ethical filling-out and development of the concept drawn from Boethius, which proves the vitality of the dis-course. The introductory passage on *musica humana* can give us an idea of this:

> Human music [*humana musica*], which everyone recognizes within him-self by observing, harmonizes [*concordat*] with its shout of joy the parts of the soul, that is, its powers, so that the possible intellect in particular may retain the species perceived by sense, and render it as an act of the in-telligence [*in intelligentiae actum reducat*]. The material and mortal body might be linked to the immaterial and immortal soul by a distance reach-ing to infinity, were it not connected by the musical harmony [*musica harmonia*] of its sweetness. For by means of its harmony music causes contrary operations of bodies to agree together, since the body serves the ruling soul as an instrument of musical concord, and through musical harmony it joins together the mixed parts and elements of the body.[512]

The passages cited may suffice as proofs for the argument in favor of continuity. The discussion of *musica* continues to appeal to a "musical" order of being; the *musicus* is directed to its actualization, whether in the form of a speculative vision or in that of performing the work. *Both* are modi of one and the same activity: "But music is first the condition existing in the mind of the musician that directs him to explore what is knowable in music [*ad speculandum scibilia musicae*], and this concerns speculative music [*musicam speculativam*]. A second condition exists in the mind of the musician directing him to perform musical works [. . .])."[513]

The *Musica* of Adam of Fulda (c. 1445–1505)[514] appeared in 1490, in the year the author took up a position as Frederick the Wise's musical conduc-tor and a professorship in Wittenberg. Jean Molinet's *Art de rhétorique* was produced at the same time. Adam of Fulda was a contemporary of Josquin Desprez and had already put into practice Johannes Tinctoris's innovations in composition theory, he shows everywhere his precise knowledge of the music of the early Renaissance. His work is not that of a theorist primarily guided by the existing body of texts, and that is why it is of special relevance as a proof of our continuity thesis. For Adam of Fulda, music is still "one of the quadrivial [arts]"[515] and moreover, he presents it, with a reference Plato, as the "the art of arts, the science of sciences."[516] The theory and practice of music may be corrupt, as Adam of Fulda complains at length, but it still maintains contact with the ancients: "O, if Boethius were alive

[. . .]."[517] The first of the four parts of the work deals, in accord with the traditional *genera*, "with authorities and also the usefulness and description of the art [of music]."[518] Regarding the *auctoritates*, it is first said that the author draws "from Boethius's book on music";[519] the series of authorities that are later mentioned in the text reflects the pagan Greek as well as the Judeo-Christian roots of the discourse, and ranks Regino of Prüm among the most important authorities:

> But since music is the best, why are we not permitted to imitate it, as the holy fathers and prophets eagerly did in order to praise God? We have in the old law Moses and his sister Miriam, Joshua, the son of Nun, King David, and many musicians among the prophets, whom it would be tedious to list. In our own dispensation, indeed, we have the most holy Popes Gregory and John, holy Jerome, among others, blessed Bernard, Isidore, Boethius, Odo, Berno, Guido, Hucbald, Regino, Otto, Notker, King Robert of France, Herman, the nephew of the Emperor Henry, and many others, whom I pass over for the sake of brevity. Among the gentile philosophers there is Pythagoras, Xerxes, Aristoxenus, Archytas, Philolaus, Ptolemy, Annicius, Linus of Thebes, Mercury, Orpheus, Amphion, and many others, whom it would be difficult to enumerate.[520]

The synopsis, which does not distinguish between myth and history and cares little about chronology, does not mention Augustine, but Adam of Fulda nonetheless seems to know his *De musica* as well:

> This is the definition of music: Music is the art that teaches how to form voices, and to accentuate with correct proportion those that have been formed through sound; or it is a liberal science that truly and regularly manages the capacity for singing. As Isidore says in the first book of his *Etymologies* music is a sort of science of the muses; or music comes from the musical instrument the musa, and is applied to all the others, or it is from madusica, that is, from the said melody of that kind, which exists only in the required consonance of voices. But Augustine says to Jerome: music is the science of sense, or the sense of modulating well [*scientia sensus, sensusve bene modulandi*] for warning of a great thing, even to mortals who have rational souls through the generosity of God. Virgil appears to mention this in the *Bucolics*, where he says: *The beginning of the Muses is from Jove; all things are full of Jove.*[521]

The passage seems to imply the narrowing of the concept of music to vocal music, and in fact this is the main subject of the work. Nevertheless, Adam of Fulda's short introduction also does not forego relating *musica*, conceived here according to Regino of Prüm's modification of the Boethian triad, to the cosmic order:

> Music is of two sorts: natural and artificial [*naturalis & artificialis*]. Natural music is cosmic or human [*mundana & humana*]. Cosmic music concerns the resonances of the super-celestial bodies on account of the motion of the spheres, where it is thought there will be the greatest concord. Mathematicians [*mathematici*] study this kind of music. Human music exists in the body and the soul, in spirits and the connection of members, for man lives as long as there is harmony; when its proportion is broken, he dies. Natural philosophers [*physici*] study this kind of music.[522]

In Adam of Fulda as well, the differentiation and increasing segmentation of disciplinary discourses is taken into account. The *mathematici* devote themselves to *musica mundana*, the *physici* devote themselves to *musica humana*, and therefore are assigned competences in the traditional ethos doctrine as well.[523] The unity of the one order comprehending the totality of the objects of different disciplinary discourses, and thus guaranteeing the unity of Creation as established through analogical relationships, continues to be conceived in accord with the speculative concept of music. Correspondingly, *musica artificialis*, which for Adam of Fulda includes *musica instrumentalis* and *musica vocalis*, continues to be conceived according to this concept: "Artificial: musicians follow this kind of music. It is either instrumental or vocal. Instrumental music is sound brought about by different instruments, [. . .]."[524] *Musica vocalis* is divided into *musica vocalis usualis*, which includes the everyday language of humans as well as the sounds made by animals, and *musica vocalis regulata* in the narrow musical sense. The latter is further differentiated. It seems as though here the limitation of the concept of music to chant is taken into account, but a few pages later Adam of Fulda's *Musica* once again proves faithful to his most important authority: "Three kinds relate to music; one deals with instruments [*instrumentis agitur*]; the other makes songs [*fingit carmina*]; the third judges both [*utrumque diiudicat*]."[525] The quotation from Boethius's *De institutione musica* I.34 alone would be interesting, but not very significant for our continuity thesis. However, it is the object of specific comment. Adam of Fulda sees that the *poeta* is meant, and repeats Boethius's critical argument. The poet creates "his" music by instinct, and is thus to be excluded from the group of those who devote themselves to speculative music theory: "Second, he who makes songs belongs among the poets, and he is to be set apart from those who are brought to song by speculation and reason, rather than by natural instinct [*potius speculatione ac ratione, quam naturali quodam instinctu fertur ad carmen*].”[526] The argument has remained the same since the year 400: the poet creates his work out of “natural” instinct—possibly, like the instrumentalist, without insight into *musica scientia*. And yet his product, metrical discourse, is musical in nature and manifests the “musical” *ordo entium*.

Examples proving the continuity of the discourse of speculative music theory could be multiplied. Again and again we encounter the old authorities. When Franchino Gafori’s *Theorica musice* appeared in 1492, shortly after Molinet’s *Art de rhétorique*, speculative arithmetic was largely replaced by the secular and commercial arithmetic of the fifteenth century, such as it is also found in Deschamps.[527] But the authorities of late Antiquity remain relevant: Boethius above all, Augustine’s *De musica*, Cassiodorus’s *Institutiones*, Isidore’s *Etymologiae*, Aristides Quintilianus, Calcidius’s commentary on the *Timaeus*, Macrobius’s commentary on the *Somnium Scipionis*—the sources of the *Theorica musice*, which Walter Kreyszig has identified,[528] speak for themselves. With respect to the theory and practice of composition in the fifteenth century as a whole and in particular in Gafori, Margaret V. Sandresky has spoken of the “continuing concept of the Platonic-Pythagorean system.”[529] A synthetic impulse that preserves the world-modeling quality of *musica* remains dominant—even and as well in theoretical texts that seek to deal with practical innovations.[530] The fact that some of the post-Boethian extensions of the inventory of music theory terminology—including Regino’s—were unstable does not change this finding. Instead, it testifies to the vitality of a discourse that emphasizes over and over the conceptual core of the traditional doctrine by trying to adapt to theoretical and practical innovations, to integrate them, not least terminologically. It is precisely the terminological dynamic to be found on the levels of differentiation subordinate to the primary triad *musica mundana/ humana/instrumentalis* that shows and underscores the discourse of speculative music theory’s capacity for adaptation and accommodation: where *musica* is discussed with a theoretical intention—and in the discursive context reconstructed up to this point, which tends to keep *musica theoretica* and *musica practica* closely connected at least in didactic and educational contexts,[531] this does not necessarily mean more than that questions regarding the origin, classification, or effect of music are raised—the Christian-Neoplatonic, speculative concept of music is invoked. This concept goes through phases of expansion and reduction, and sometimes both at the same time: Thomism supersedes the Neoplatonic doctrine of ideal numbers and thus reduces the ontological foundation of the traditional doctrine, but it broadens, for the purpose of iterating the Augustinian doctrine of *ordo*, the concept of *proportio*, conceived under which elements of traditional number theory can continue to exist. The conceptual core of the theory remains comparatively stable.

The context of our investigation does not allow us to formulate hypotheses regarding the reasons for this continuity. We might consider the quality characteristic of the traditional body of theory to be productively and convincingly merging an extremely wide-ranging and differentiated realm of objects—abstract numerical speculation, the Christian doctrine of Creation, the harmonic interval and the vivid, cyclical natural phenomenon, the movement of the stars, the tides, the seasons, humoral pathology, even the dance of the muses—in a homogeneous and analogically closed context of "mythical" plasticity. Peripatetically oriented High Scholasticism apparently had little to oppose to the doctrine's vividness and proximity to the realities of life in societies ultimately shaped by agrarian concerns.[532] If even Aristotelianism is not implemented throughout, it is hardly surprising that the nominalistic argument, which is repeatedly brought into the debate by the scholarship summarized in part I, is acknowledged in music theory contexts, but does not lead to the implosion of the traditional body of theory.[533] Down to the late Middle Ages, we may state a continuity of at least a speculative branch within music theory. It is this largely Neopythagorean and Neoplatonic branch that includes verse as *musica*. This continuity is to be seen against the background, but given independantly of development in adjacent disciplinary contexts, such as theology or the theory of science. Disciplinary discourses, even under the hegemony exerted by the Christian order of discourse, evolve if not independently, then at least largely out of phase. Both findings contradict the initial assumptions made by the scholarship summarized in part I regarding the poetry of the late French Middle Ages in general and Eustache Deschamps's *Art de dictier* in particular.

CHAPTER EIGHT

Speculative Music Theory and Poetics

THE "CONTINUITY" thesis formulated provisionally at the outset can now be considered proven. It remains to do a "cross-check." The discourse of speculative music theory approaches verse as music from late Antiquity down through the late Middle Ages. Thus the option of connecting reflection on verse with the speculative concept of music has been demonstrated, but not whether this option was exploited by poetics as well.

After Horace's *Epistula ad pisones de arte poetica* no determined effort to write a poetics was made for a thousand years.[1] Its subject matter merged into the disciplines of the trivium. In addition to their continuing role in music theory, which represented only a secondary strand of reflection on the theory of poetry, since Ennius metrics and rhythmics had had a place in rhetoric,[2] and for the rest established themselves in the area of grammar, despite Augustine's invectives against the *custos historiae*. Pertinent accounts include Quintilian's remarks in *Institutiones oratoriae* IX.4.45, Sergius's commentary of Donatus, *Explanationes in artem Donati*, Maximus Victorinus's *Ars Palaemonis de metrica institutione*, Atilius Fortunatianus's *Ars metrica*, Terentianus Maurus's *De metris*, Mallius Theodorus's *De metris*, Audax's *Excerpta*, and the Venerable Bede's *De arte metrica*. The disciplinary anchoring of metrics and rhythmics in the trivium is of a kind completely different from that of *musica metrica* and *rhythmica*. The relation of the disciplines of the trivium to the *ordo entium* is, as *De ordine* explains, generally genetic in kind and thus not specifically distinguished.

The precarious situation of poetics among the three *artes* of the trivium was not resolved later on,[3] but pragmatically suspended by teaching poetics in conjunction with the disciplines of grammar and rhetoric. In the late twelfth and thirteenth centuries, this convention broke down. Comprehensive poetics that were clearly emancipated from grammar emerged: Matthew of Vendôme's *Ars versificatoria* (c. 1175), Geoffrey of Vinsauf's *Poetria nova* (1208–1213) and *Documentum de modo et arte dictandi et versificandi* (after 1213), Gervais of Melkley's *Ars versificaria* (c. 1215), Johannes de Garlandia's *Parisiana poetria* (c. 1220), and Eberhard the German's *Laborintus* (after 1213, before 1280).[4] Douglas Kelly has described the object of these new poetics appropriately as "the future poem";[5] James J. Murphy views the common character of these writings, in accord with the didactic presentation of their content, as "preceptive."[6] Underlying their emergence were multiple influences that conditioned in various ways and to various extents the shape of the individual work. A description of three of these influences will help us understand and determine the degree of representativeness of our example, which must then be discussed in detail. We will provide a brief, introductory summary of the changes in the constitution of disciplinary grammar on the level of the didactic material and the epistemological interests pursued; then we will discuss at greater length the proliferation of treatises on "literary" rhythmics. This will lead us directly to our example, Johannes de Garlandia's *Parisiana poetria*.

Until 1200, the teaching of grammar was dominated by Donatus's *Artes minor* and *maior*, Priscian's *Institutio grammaticae* and its minute analysis of the first twelve verses of the *Aeneid*, the *Partitiones duodecim versum Aeneidios principium*. Priscian, Donatus, and their commentaries served as *textus*, as textbooks in elementary as well as higher education; for the most part, more recent contributions to theory construction were developed and discussed not in the form of independent treatises but rather in commentaries on one of these works. The first new textbooks to establish themselves were the *Doctrinale* of Alexander of Villedieu (c. 1170–1250)[7] and the *Graecismus* of Eberhard of Béthune (c. 1200). It eventually came to a qualification and marginalization of the old textbooks, and with the expectable temporal delay, they were replaced in university teaching.[8] For example, in Paris Priscian's *Institutiones* was replaced by the *Doctrinale* in 1366.[9] In a parallel way, the application of dialectic methods to the subject area of the *ars grammatica* pushes aside the doctrine of Donatus and Priscian, who retain relevance only for elementary education.[10] The application of the Aristotelian *logica nova* to grammar as the fundamental verbal discipline leads to gains in abstraction and complexity: questions like "What is a *nomen*?" are replaced by questions such as "How does a *nomen* designate what it designates?" A new trend in grammatical theory construction emerges that takes shape in the works of Martin of Dacia, Siger of Courtrai, Johannes of Dacia, Thomas of Erfurt, Boethius of Dacia, and Michael of Marbais. Contemporaries called it *grammatica speculativa*.[11] The title of Martin of Dacia's *De modis significandi*, written toward the end of the thirteenth century, summarizes the new interests in a catch-phrase.[12] Robert H. Robins has summarized the constructive principle of the works of these *modistae*, using the example of Siger of Courtrai:

> He [Siger of Courtrai] begins with an account of the semantic functioning of words, a general theory of meaning, based on scholastic philosophy. To understand his grammatical method, and it is typical of the period, we must understand his semantics, which also is, in general, common ground to the Modistae as a group and itself depends on scholastic metaphysics of the time. Things, according to this scheme, possess as existents various qualities or modes of being (*modi essendi*). The mind apprehends these by the active modes of understanding (*modi intelligendi activi*), to which there correspond the passive modes of understanding (*modi intelligendi passivi*), the qualities of things as apprehended by the mind. In language the mind confers on vocal noises (*voces*) the active modes of signification (*modi significandi activi*), in virtue of which they become words (*dictiones*) and parts of speech (*partes orationis*), and signify the qualities of things; these are now represented by the passive modes of signification (*modi significandi passivi*), the qualities of things as signified by words.[13]

The path-breaking reorientation of disciplinary grammar carried out by the *modistae* between 1275 and 1325[14] remained influential down to the late Middle Ages and Renaissance. Erasmus of Rotterdam still made reference to a late representative of this school, Michael of Marbais.[15] The price paid for this reorientation is a significantly higher level of abstraction and an increased degree of complexity in grammatic theory. Precisely these factors are operative in the differentiation of poetics. The refocusing of technical grammatical discourse on questions of propositional logic and linguistic theory deprives the situation of poetics in grammar of its conditions of plausibility. The older tradition had generally practiced disciplinary grammar as an art of declaiming and speaking properly and could derive its authority from the subject of linguistic correctness. Hugo of St. Victor's *Didascalion* still offers this definition: "grammar is the knowledge of speaking without fault [*scientia loquendi sine vitio*]."[16] The discourse practiced by the *modistae* no longer offers this possibility. The resulting gains in knowledge in the areas of propositional logic and general linguistic theory may have made it possible to inquire into the "how" of writing with new precision,[17] and may consequently also had a stimulating effect on the new poetics. But the development we have described also resulted in the loss of the self-evident normative-prescriptive value that once followed from the orientation of the discipline toward linguistic correctness. The six comprehensive poetics that emerged in the course of a century reflected both of these outcomes: the reconstitution of grammar as a science in the new sense led to the liberation of poetics and to the necessity of compensating for the loss of grounding that this liberation initially signified. The destabilization of the old authorities and the reorientation of the epistemological interests pursued in grammar thus influenced the differentiation of poetics. The actual form taken by the new poetics was shaped by a third factor: the theoretical concern with speech rhythms that began to emerge in the twelfth and thirteenth centuries.[18]

The development of a "rhythmic" poetry in Latin has been the subject of great controversy in scholarship; a summary of the discussion would exceed the bounds of what is possible here. Even before Augustine Marius Victorinus had defined "rhythm" in poetry by counting syllables: "What appears to be like meter? Rhythm. What is rhythm? A modulated composition of words [*verborum modulata compositio*] not according to metrical computation [*non metrica ratione*], but considered through numerical scansion judged by the ears [*numeros scansione ad judicium aurium examinata*], like the songs of the popular poets."[19] This definition can be connected in an exemplary way with our concept of determined redundancy: Borinksi sees the central element of the definition as consisting in the "general idea of agreement (of 'accented syllables' and concluding cadences: 'similiter desinens' = ὁμοιοτελευτόν)."[20] In *De Civitate Dei* IV.24 Augustine had noted that African speakers of Latin had lost their sense of the quantification of the idiom, and thus is might seem plausible to hypothesize that quantitative verse found a plausible successor in "rhythmical" verse, soon defined as "a counted number of syllables with final consonance," initially in Latin, and then in its Romance variants.[21] However, the early Latin *rhythmus* presents itself less homogeneously than these hypotheses suggest. In late Antiquity and the early Middle Ages, syllable-counting, dynamically accented verse is found sometimes without rhyme, sometimes with end-rhyme, and sometimes with end-rhyme in increments of as many as several rhyming syllables that have been connected with the development of the refrain.[22] Concerning "rhythmical" verse with end-rhymes, to which we will return later, Wilhelm Meyer first suggested that dynamically accented meter spread to the Latin West with Semitic Christians, in the course of the third and fourth centuries.[23] Meyer had to concede that rhyme is practically absent precisely from Old Testament poetry, and his thesis was thus able to shed light on the provenance of "rhythmical" verse, but not on that of end-rhyme. Eduard Norden saw this as a reason to reject Meyer's hypothesis *in toto* and, like Borinski, to derive end-rhyme from the figure of *Homoioteleuton* and thus from ancient art-prose.[24] Karl Georg Kuhn recognized the weakness of this hypothesis: "The linguistic shaping of the old Church's prayers, which were on the whole simple and natural" was now derived "from the most highly developed art form of ancient discourse and from its refined, almost mannerist feeling for language."[25] Kuhn argues for a reevaluation of Meyer's theses and demonstrates formal relationships between rhymed Christian hymns since the third and fourth centuries and Jewish synagogal poetry since the first century. However, whether the reception of this Jewish Piyyut poetry presupposed, as Albrecht Dihle thought,[26] Greek accentuated metrics, and thus that the latter must be seen, as our reconstruction of the history of music theory suggests as well, as the true inspiration of early "rhythmical" verse in Latin, remains an open question. The same goes for the value of the fact noted in passing by Norden,[27] namely that rhyme appears in incantations and "magical" contexts as well as in pagan-cultish contexts, as Frederic Raby has shown.[28]

The earliest medieval source texts providing evidence of rhythmical poetry with end-rhymes are found in Ireland. From there, it seems to have passed to England and then back to the continent.[29] It is no accident that in the early eighth century the Venerable Bede's *De arte metrica* provides the first definition of *rhythmus* in the medieval sense. This is the passage that Aurelianus Reomensis inserts into his treatise on music around 850:

> Rhythm appears to be similar to meter. It is a modulated composition of words [*verborum modulata conpositio*], not according to metrical reckoning, but considered by the number of syllables for the judgment of the ears, as are the songs of the popular poets. Rhythm can exist without meter, but meter cannot exist without rhythm. The subject can be defined more clearly as follows: meter is computation with modulation [*metrum est ratio cum modulatione*]; rhythm is modulation without computation [*rithmus modulatio sine ratione*].[30]

The definition of "rhythmical" verse on the basis of the number of syllables was initially only one of several ways to model quantification. In France as in Italy, attempts to model quantitative verse qua identification of word-accent with the Latin quantitative *ictus*,[31] were dominant, while in the Iberian peninsula the verse was initially defined by the number of words.[32] The question as to whether the systematic difference between "metrical" and "rhythmical" verse in Latin and in the vernaculars led directly to the separation and to the independent development of each or remained guided by "metrical" verse, continues to be debated.[33]

In the eleventh and twelfth centuries, "rhythmical" verse with end-rhymes, which was at first scorned as inferior,[34] spread in liturgical and para-liturgical contexts.[35] Alongside early polyphony[36] there emerged a treatise-literature devoted, with theoretical intentions, to the disciplining and notation of speech rhythms that remained productive well into the thirteenth century. Its centers lay in France, in Paris, Chartres, Orléans, Blois, Tours, Laon, and Reims.[37] For our further argument, it is crucial to distinguish between the value of this development for "rhythmical" verse as verse (though it was for the most part sung)[38] that was considered an imitation or at least a continuation of ancient, quantitative metrics, on the one hand, and for voice-leading in polyphony, on the other, and then to consider both aspects in their complementarity.[39]

The *De rithmis* Alberic of Monte Cassino (d. 1088) is considered the starting point for the treatise literature on speech rhythms.[40] This work, which is indebted to Bede's *De arte metrica*,[41] discusses rhythmical verse without any apologetic introduction[42] and thus accounts for the reevaluation of "rhythmical" verse construction. In addition, the work testifies to the emancipation of "rhythmical" verse construction from the model of quantitative verse:

> There are some rhythms in which only the number of syllables is considered, without any consideration of their length or brevity. There are others with a fixed and determined number of syllables in which one attends to length and brevity as well. To put it more clearly: rhythms and meters are equivalent [*rithmi pariter sunt et metra*].[43]

Here we see reflected the difference in principle that separates quantitative and "rhythmical" metrics. "Rhythmical" verse does not require quantification, and the syllable-counting principle can stand by itself. Likewise, the author is aware that "rhythmical" verse long remained oriented toward the quantitative, and that in a given "rhythmical" verse, the distribution of the quantities may even be completely regular. Such a verse could be viewed both as "rhythmical" and as quantitative. However, the examples of the "rhythmical" verse-type offered by Alberic correct the first impression. The rules of quantification may appear to be observed in the individual case, but in fact the examples discussed are "rhythmical verses" whose common ground with quantitative verse is reduced to the accent on the *penultima*. The discussion of the twelve-syllable verse can serve as an example:

> The twelve-syllable rhythm is the one that consists of twelve syllables to a fixed line. This kind of rhythm uses a two-fold computation in its composition. For, sometimes it is arranged such that the first part of each line consists of five syllables, the penultimate being long by the accent; the

last part of the line is composed of seven syllables, the penultimate being made short by the accent.[44]

Even where the two metrical systems seem to coincide, the compositional principle is that of "rhythmical" metrics. However, the possibility of this coincidence indicates the structural comparability of the two metrical systems: "[A]ll rhythmic verse employs syllable count as its main structural feature,"[45] Margot E. Fassler notes, and Murphy says more pointedly: "The whole emphasis is upon the mathematical structure of lines."[46] The constructive principle of *rhythmus* is the countability of syllables and thus a specific *numerositas* that is to be grasped functionally as the "form" of the verse. As Zumthor remarks: "It is a matter of a structuring number, of a proportionality constitutive of structure, of 'number' qua source or explanation of unity."[47] "Rhythmical" and quantitative verses thus differ in their base, but not in their definition by numerical determinations and not in their emphasis on the isometric construction of repeatable units. If one wanted to locate "rhythmical" verse in the system presented in Augustine's *De musica*, it would correspond conceptually to the *metrum*. The structural homology accordingly retains the option of relating metrical discourse of whatever type, through the connection with the numerical order, both to the musical practice developing in parallel and also, without relevant restrictions with regard to the Augustinian foundation, to the "holistic" conception of music. The crucial importance of the first books of Augustine's *De musica* for the rhythmical coordination of singing voices, which has been underscored in relation to early polyphony,[48] is to be seen in this context and holds both for the development of "rhythmical" verse and the possibilty of reflecting it theoretically in terms provided by music theory. Fassler has strikingly emphasized the complementarity of these developments: "The total penetration of the poetic and musical arts by the rhythmical style described by Alberic of Monte Cassino was the most significant single event of the twelfth century *in either of these realms*."[49] John Stevens has provided an authoritative description of the parallel developments in musical practice and "rhythmical" poetry and thus emphasized the "holistic" conception of music as the conceptual foundation of the development, although in his study the accent is on words *to* music (i.e., song), not on words *as* music.[50] In view of his works, in the following we will limit ourselves to a few examples that will allow us to present a simplified account of the development and make the transition to Johannes de Garlandia's *Parisiana poetria*.

A generation after Alberic, Thomas of Capua (before 1185–1239) clarified the systematic place of considerations on speech rhythms in his widely distributed *Ars dictandi*. This work identified three *genera* of discourse: "Three kinds of writing have been defined by the ancients: prose, as in Cassiodorus; meter, as in Virgil; and rhythm, as in [Hugh] Primas."[51] The following explanation already includes end-rhyme as well: "[Prose] proceeds with long and harmonious flow, free of metrical law; [meter] is accompanied by a number of feet and sounds, and by scansion; [rhythm] is constructed by the number of syllables and by the consonances of words [*sillabarum numero et vocum consonantiis*]," and more precisely, "Rhythm comes from 'fissure' (*rima*), either because it is the boundary or the separation of rhythms, because in addition to a given computation of syllables it is distinguished by a final consonance [*quia sub certa computatione sillibarum cum finali consonantia distinguitor*], and thus it is set within bounds."[52] Here the musical term *consonantia* is encountered as a designation of the effect that sometimes results from isorhythm, that is, from the repetition of the unit defined by a given number of syllables, and sometimes, as *consonantia finalis*, from end-rhyme. Both the concept of "rhythmical" verse documented here and the terminological formulation of the effect based on isorhythm/isometry as *consonantia* established themselves. This is proven by the treatise literature that emerged in the course of the thirteenth century. Giovanni Mari has edited the most important texts. The first treatise, written in the twelfth century,[53] *De rithmico dictamine*, offers this definition: "Rhythm is a rhyming [*consonans*] equality of syllables assembled under a given number [*sub certo numero comprehensarum*]."[54] What is crucial with respect to Alberic of Monte Cassino is the broadening of the frame of reference to the repetition of larger rhythmical units. The "sub certo numero comprehendere" refers to the grouping of verses into *clausulae* that have to contain at least two and at most five verses. Precise rules are also given for the number of syllables to be included in each verse: it has to be, of course, at least four and at most sixteen syllables long.[55] The *Regulae rithmis*, also from the twelfth century, shares the definition of rhythm given in the treatise *De rithmico dictamine*;[56] the third treatise published by Mari, which appeared around 1250, offers a more detailed definition: "First, rhythm is defined as follows: Rhythm is the utterance of syllables assembled by a given number [*certo numero comprehensa*], and it derives from the Greek *ritmos*, which means 'number' in Latin, or consonance in rhythm, wherein syllables are counted."[57] The fourth treatise, which Friedrich Zarncke dates to the late twelfth century,[58] puts special emphasis on the numerical order: "Rhythm is a harmonious [*congrua*], consonant [*consona*] arrangement of utterances, uninterruptedly produced by uniformity of syllables [*sillabarum aequalitate*]. Rhythm comes from the Greek *rithmos*, meaning number, since it must be composed according to a fixed rule of numbers. Number must be considered in rhythm first in the lines, and next in the syllables and consonances [*in sillabis et consonanciis*]."[59] In the seventh treatise, written about 1400, the description of end-rhyme referred to as "consonance" becomes obvious: "Consonance [*consonantia*] is the equality of final letters at the end of words [*equalis convenentia [sic] in fine dictionum secundum finalem litterarum*]. Rhythm comes from the Greek *rithmos*, which in Latin is 'number.' Rhythm, therefore, is number."[60]

The treatises on rhythmics prove the establishment of end-rhyme as a substantial characteristic of "rhythmical" verse.[61] Most notably, we can sum up by noting that each of the treatises cited emphasizes *numerositas*. Brunetto Latini (c. 1230–1294), Dante's putative teacher, who wrote his encyclopedic work *Li livres dou Tresor* in French and thus was the first ever to produce an encyclopedia in a vernacular language, formulates this concisely: "[Q]ui bien voudra rimer, il li convient conter totes les silabes de ses diz en tel maniere que li vers soient acordables en nombre [. . .]" ("Whoever wants to rhyme must count all the syllables of his poems in such a way that the verses are in agreement in number").[62] Thus the possibility of connecting "rhythmical" poetry with end-rhyme with the discourse of speculative music theory is given. This holds in particular since the primary musical meaning of the concept *consonantia* is still kept in mind and both the isometry realized in the form of syllable-counting and end-rhyme can be conceived as forms of equivalence, of "determined redundancy." Finally, *numerositas* offers, precisely because the concept is not very specific, a multiplicity of ways of making use of this possible connection. The conceptual relationships are so extensive that a late fourteenth-century treatise on rhythmics views rhythmical end-rhyme poetry as an *imitatio* of music harmonies in the medium of language. The *Tractatus de rithmis vel rithmorum magistri Tybini*[63] has come down to us in a Seitenstetten codex: "according to writers on rhetoric, the art of rhythm was patterned after musical consonance [*ars rithmicalis facta est ad similitudinem consonantie musicalis*]."[64] Insofar as it is verbal, rhythmical poetry presupposes grammar, and is thus, according to Nikolaus from Dybin in Bulgaria, a "genus secunde rhetorice scientie," "a sort of second rhetorical science."[65] Just as the *ars rithmica* is modeled on musical consonance, the *ars rhetorica* is modeled on *musica*:

> I strongly agree, however, that the art of rhetoric was patterned after music. For, just as in music, consonance is not expanded to more [. . .] than eight tones, and is diminished only to four, because consonance made from one tone is not raised further, except to the diapason, that is, to the

eighth tone, nor is it diminished further, except to the diatessaron, that is, to the fourth tone. Those who write about rhythm do much the same; one rhyme ought not to stand further from the other than eight syllables, or less than four. And the aforementioned rules demand that.[66]

However grounded the statements regarding the theory of intervals themselves may be in detail, the argument presupposes a conception of the "rhythmical" based on combinations of equivalence and variation. The "rhythmical" verse is conceived as a temporal unit regularly partitioned by a fixed number of syllables. The phonemic group situated in the same syllable in successive verses is repeated at the same temporal intervals; what comes in between varies. The relation to the theory of musical intervals produces a parallel between scale intervals and the ordinal numbers of the syllables, counted from the beginning of the verse: to the harmonic interval of the octave, the eighth tone of the heptatonic scale, corresponds the repetition of a phonemic group in the eighth syllable, for instance in end-rhyming *octosyllabic* couplets. The modern reader will tend to assume that the choice of the reference unit is arbitrary, and in fact it must be conceded to the monism of the whole approach that the actual choice of the reference unit is hardly relevant so long as such units are combined in a clearly numerically specified way. As long as numerical specification, a numerical order, can be discerned, this excludes arbitrariness. The proof of a numerical order in a given phenomenon and the attribution of this phenomenon to the objects of music theory coincide; the "musicality" of the "rhythmically" measured verse is founded on the latter's *numerositas* and does not necessarily imply any further specifications, and in particular any assertions regarding sound.

The text can be considered representative in the way it relates verse to *musica*. Scholarship has determined that "from the thirteenth century [. . .] to the fifteenth century, from which the Seitenstetten codex comes, the harmonic theory of rhythmical proportions" also "had an almost dogmatic validity in the furthest circles of the grammatical world."[67] Borinski already clearly saw the motives for the association of "literary" rhythmics with music, which does not require the reference to practice—the fact that, for instance, "rhythmical" verse was generally sung. These motives are worth our attention, not least because Mari has already related Eustache Deschamps's *Art de dictier* with the treatises on rhythmics that he analyzed:[68]

> How then did scholars arrive at such a strongly crystallized, special, and apparently dogmatic theory on the basis of the very general ancient elements outlined at the beginning? Well, first of all again, I believe, from

the Middle Ages' general need for commandments and prohibitions, for precise demarcation of the boundaries of what was allowed and what not. Then in the thirteenth century came the rise of mensural music. The harmonic intervals became the bearers of a firm, unalterable order in the consonance of voices, a kind of mathematical predestination precisely in the extremely fleeting material of the human voice. The Pythagorean *musica mundana* seemed to be revealed in *musica instrumentalis*. Rhythmics immediately remembered its ancient connection with music theory and also began to calculate harmonically.[69]

Borinski's view needs to be supplemented by recognizing that the "memory" that "rhythmical" poetry belonged to music never disappeared in genuine music theory. However, the aim of the analyzed treatise literature on "literary" rhythmics is aptly described. The conception of "literary" rhythmics and the horizon of its reflection offer the option of connecting up with the speculative conception of music. This option was used by a text that older research on the late Middle Ages already considered one of Deschamps's possible sources: Johannes de Garlandia's *Parisiana poetria*.

Johannes Anglicus or Johannes de Garlandia (c. 1195–after 1272) studied at Oxford and came in 1220 to Paris. During the strike at the University of Paris between 1229 and 1232, he lived in Toulouse.[70] After his return to Paris, he taught until his death in the monastery school in the rue de Garlande, the so-called "Clos de Garlande."[71] The Englishman was the author of literary works, for instance the widely read *De mysteriis ecclesiae* and an *Epithalamium Mariae virginis*, but he is considered a central figure in teaching at the University of Paris in the thirteenth century chiefly because of his propaedeutic works. At the beginning of the sixteenth century, these propaedeutics were still in use all over Europe, and were printed early on in Cologne and on the lower Rhine, in Antwerp and Deventer.[72] This is particularly true of *De arte prosayca, metrica et rithmica*, better known, after the *incipit*, as *Parisiana poetria*. This work, which was written in 1220,[73] already attracted the attention of contemporaries and was widely used as a textbook in higher education. Hugo of Trimberg (before 1235–after 1313) recommended it in his *Registrum multorum auctorum* (c. 1280),[74] a collection of recommended textbooks for students. About eighty manuscripts of Johannes de Garlandia's work are extant.[75]

The context suggests that we should at least raise in an introductory way one of the open questions in research on Johannes de Garlandia. It has been debated whether the author of the *Parisiana poetria* is identical with the music theoretician of the same name, similar birth and death dates, and same place of activity.[76] In the theory of intervals, the theory of consonance, and notation, the works of the *musicus* met with a success in no way inferior to that of the writings of the grammarian. Today they are still regarded as among the most important sources on the music theory of the thirteenth century: "[They] bespeak a man who, far from being a traditionalist, is an exponent of the most advanced developments in contemporary polyphony."[77] Two works are attributed to the music theoretician Johannes de Garlandia, an *Introductio musice plane*, which Edmond de Coussemaker has edited on the basis of a manuscript from St. Dié,[78] and an *Introductio de musica mensurabili*[79] that makes explicit references to Pérotin, among others, and must have appeared shortly after 1250.[80] It was attributed to Johannes around 1275 by Jerome of Moravia.[81] William Waite argues for the identity of the two theoreticians,[82] and was contradicted by Erich Reimer in the commentary section of his 1972 edition of the *Introductio de musica mensurabili*[83] and by Rudolf Rasch in his 1969 study on the theory of notation.[84] Research currently tends to assume that two different people were involved, although the work of the grammarian Johannes de Garlandia shows that he had knowledge of music theory. In the didactic poem *De triumphis ecclesiae* the presentation of the *scientiae* as taught in Toulouse is in this respect explicit. The verses on music are influenced by the Aristotelian *ordo scientiarum*, but operate with classifications long familiar from the tradition. For the sake of the *arbor scientiarum* represented here as a rose tree, we cite the passage in context:

> The pruning hook [*falx*] attacks the briar patch, learning cuts
> The branches and the thistles, and enlivens the roses.
> Knowledge divides and leafs into eloquence, a branch;
> He who understands it advances, and commands eloquence.
> Eloquence has three branches, which it tends in order:
> Grammar, logic, and the thyme of rhetoric.
> Thence wisdom brings forth speculation,
> And the branch whose name will be practical science.
> Practical science produces the branch called ethics,
> Whose divided limb flowers with a triple frond.
> Ethics prepares these for the city, the house, and the self in turn,
> For the wise man ought to be circumspect about himself.
> Speculation produces the heavenly word, yielding to natural science,
> And mathematics, and it flourishes with a triple frond.
> Mathematics enumerates, measures, harmonizes [*consonat*],
> Studies the stars, and enables us to learn about the individual ones.

I praise the divine sciences, and I offer natural science
To those who have grown old in secrets.
Music links all [*cuncta ligat*], the cosmic [*mundana*], and the human, but then
Instrumental music [*instrumentalis*] divides into three parts;
Metric [*metrica*] joins itself to melody [*melica*], and rhythmic [*rhythmica*]
  to metric,
But the path of sweet melody is divided into three ways.
It gives enharmonics for study and for various dances,
And a ready chromatic, and diatonic for trumpets.
Diatonic music thrived in Toulouse when we came there,
And the warlike crowd was amazed at the modes of melody.
Orpheus moved the woods with modulation of his harp,
And Amphion made the stones rise up with his lyre.[85]

Regarding the veiled allusion in the image of the pruning hook (*falx*) we can only speculate. From the main trunk of *sapientia* a low limb, eloquence, sticks out, and then branches out into the theoretical or speculative sciences, on the one hand, and the practical sciences, on the other. Following tradition, the theoretical sciences branch into the physical, mathematical, and theological sciences. The quadrivial *artes* fall under the mathematical sciences; here only music is further differentiated. It is classified in accord with the Boethian triad, whose "holistic" implication strongly accentuates the phrase "musica cuncta ligat" at the beginning of the verse. Cassiodorus's further differentiation of *musica instrumentalis* provides systematic places for quantitative metrics (*musica metrica*) and syllable-counting metrics (*musica rhythmica*). The early branching off of *eloquentia*, along with the sciences of the trivium viewed as propaedeutic to philosophy, corresponds to their situation according to Boethius[86] and underscores the traditional honor granted to the quadrivium. The profile of this *ordo scientiarum* may be explained by the source of the passage, which was probably William of Conche's commentary on the *Timaeus*. We have discussed his remarks on music earlier. Here, too, the classification of the sciences is depicted in the image of the *arbor scientiae*. The knowledge of the *Timaeus* shown in the prologue of the *Epithalamium* attributed to the grammarian Johannes de Garlandia[87] makes familiarity with William of Conche's commentary seem possible, especially since Johannes de Garlandia's poetic sketch uses not the traditional term *musica harmonica* but rather *musica melica*, which William's commentary on the *Timaeus* had introduced.[88]

According to Traugott Lawler, the intellectual environment of the School of Chartres alluded to in connection with this commentary is the broader context in which the *Parisiana poetria* was produced. The work documents university teaching in Paris around 1220 and may have been conceived, as the *incipit*—"Parisiana iubar diffundit gloria, clerus/Crescit, Apolineas fons iaculatur aquas" ("Parisian glory spreads splendor abroad, the clergy/Thrives, the fountain breaks forth with the waters of Apollo")[89] suggests, as a manual for it.[90] The text, which has been handed down in six manuscripts,[91] is impressive first of all by the breadth of its scope: "[I]t is the only thorough attempt we have to gather three distinct areas of the medieval arts of discourse (*ars poetica, ars rhythmica, ars dictaminis*) under a single series of rules."[92] Johannes de Garlandia's presentation of the three *dictamen* is indebted to the *Rhetorica ad Herennium*, Horace's poetics, and Geoffrey of Vinsauf's *Poetria nova* and *Documentum de modo et arte dictandi et versificandi*.[93] The work seeks systematics and consistent classification throughout. It conceives the sequence prose-meter-rhythm as increasing in formal specification.[94] Concerning rhythmics, the *Parisiana poetria* recognizes the latter as a bridge between grammar and music and establishes, with a concise precision that indicates that the possibility of this reference is taken for granted, the connection with the "holistic" conception of music. "Rhymed verse [*rithmica*] is a branch of the art of music [*species artis musicae*],"[95] and moreover, "music is divided into cosmic [*mundana*], which concerns proportion in the sounds of the elements, and human [*humana*], which concerns proportion and concord of the humors, and instrumental [*instrumentalis*], which concerns instrumental concord [*concordia instrumentali*]."[96] The explicit connection established between "literary" rhythmics and the speculative music theory shaped by Boethius in one of the most influential poetics of the High Middle Ages must be underscored and emphasized as important evidence in the overall context of our argument.

The categories of the Boethian triad are briefly presented in the following pages. Here *musica instrumentalis* is differentiated (as it had already been in *De triumphis ecclesiae?*), following William of Conches, into *musica melica, metrica*, and *rithmica*. In accord with the previously cited treatises on rhythmics, isometric verses with end-rhymes are considered *musica rithmica*: "Rhythmics is the art that teaches us how to make rhyme [*rithmum facere*]. Rhyme [*rithmus*] is described as follows: rhyme is the harmony of words with similar endings [*consonancia dictionum in fine similium*], arranged around a fixed number of syllables [*sub certo numero*], but without metrical feet."[97] The following passage explicates each individual term:

"Consonance" [*consonancia*] stands for the genre. For, music is the consonance of things and sounds [*rerum et uocum consonancia*], or "discordant concord" [*discordia concors*] or "concordant discord" [*concordia discors*]. "Words with similar endings" shows its difference from melody. "Around a fixed number of syllables" indicates that rhyme consists of syllables, few or many. "Without metrical feet" shows its difference from the art of metrical poetry [*artis metrice*]. "Arranged" indicates that the rhyming of words ought to occur in order [*ordinate debent cadere*].[98]

Musica melica, *metrica*, and *rithmica* are assigned as species to the generic category of "consonancia." *Musica rithmica* is distinguished from the quantitative *metrica* by reference to syllable-count, and from *melica* by reference to end-rhyme, whose origin the author presumes to be found in the figure of speech *similiter desinens* (ὁμοιοτελευτόν).[99] The phrase *consonancia rerum et vocum* accentuates the frame of reference of speculative music theory as we have reconstructed it up to this point. The specification by the ancient Pythagorean terms "concordia discors and discordia concors"[100] accounts for the unity of the different Many, for the vision of the whole, which we have determined to be the point of the discourse described, from the Greek models through Augustine's concept of *ordo* and Aquinas's broadening of the reference of the concept of *proportio*. As in the treatises on literary rhythmics that we have discussed, the musical concept of consonance, to be realized in verse as determined redundancy or equivalence, is in Johannes de Garlandia the defining concept of his theory of "rhythmical" poetry.

The *ordinatio* of "rhythmical" verse that the passage quoted from Johannes de Garlandia's *Parisiana poetria* mentions in conclusion makes the transition to arithmology, which here as well provides the conceptual foundation for any discourse on music. "Rhythmical" verse is related to the order of *proportiones* and thus to the musical theory of intervals. Here we will quote the whole paragraph entitled *De Consonanciis et Proporcionibus Rithmorum*:

> Rhyming consonances [*consonancie rithmales*] keep to the proportion of sexqualtera (3:2) and sexquitertia (4:3); and these proportions occur in music: in two, or double one, as between one and two, where there is a double proportion; in three, as between two and three, where there is a sexqualtera proportion; in four, as between three and four, where there is a sexquitertia proportion. In the discantus and organum there happens to be rhyme [*consonanciam*] in the second and third, and the fourth and fifth; and this is like the dyapente, which consists of five tones, or like the dyatessaron, which consists of four tones, or like the diapason, which is a consonance of several of these, for it includes the dyapente and the dyatessaron.[101]

The mention of *discantus* and *organum*, the counter- or parallel voice leading in early polyphony, establishes relationships with contemporary music theory; both concepts are closely associated with the name of the music theorist Johannes de Garlandia.[102] On the one hand, intervals between rhyming phonemic groups are equated with the respective arithmetical proportions underlying them, and on the other hand, in a way similar to the previously cited treatise on rhythmics by Nikolaus of Dybin, they are also equated with the number of a given scale degree, counted from the key tone. In practice, this equation is conducted in a strikingly simple way, as an example may show. In the paragraph *De Nominibus et Consonantia Rithmorum*, rhyme schemes are classified according to the position of the first appearance of a variation, as determined by counting:

> Likewise, rhyme [*rithmus*] is said to be distrophic, tristrophic, tetrastrophic, and pentastrophic. Distrophic rhyme has variation in consonance in the second line of a couplet; tristrophic rhyme has it in the third line, tetrastrophic rhythm has it in the fourth line; pentastrophic rhythm has it in the fifth line. Composite rhyme goes no further than this, unless many of them arise from the same consonance [*consonancia*].[103]

The *Parisiana poetria* offers the following example of the *pentastrophos*, preceded by the explanation "it [an iambic line] is added as a fifth line, like a diapente [*ad similitudinem diapente*], as follows:"[104]

Eua mundum deformauit,
Aue mundum reformauit,
Munda mundum emundauit,
Pia nefas expiauit,
Via uiris inuia.

(Eve deformed the world,
"Ave" reformed it, making it pure,
A pure one cleansed the world,
A pious woman expiated sin,
A pathless path for men.)[105]

The variation in rhyme in the fifth line corresponds to the fifth degree of the heptatonic scale, the *diapente* or quint. Again, the parallel seems artificial—it could be argued in the same way that the quint resembles a row of four apples and one pear. The modern reader will find the comparison farcical and want to point out the difference in complexity between the speculative music theory founded on *numerositas* described in such detail in chapters 5 and 6a, on the one hand, and this attempt to fit the "rhythmical" poetry of the twelfth and thirteenth centuries into the system of speculative music theory on the other. Both objections disregard the monism of the reconstructed theory. Here too we have to emphasize that from the perspective of this body of theory, absolutely every order conceivable as based on *numerositas* is significant and refers, as Johannes de Garlandia explains by citing the Boethian triad, to music as a "holistic" principle. Johannes de Garlandia's argument is plausible under epistemic conditions that consider every *numerositas* as *res significans*—even if the material substrate is very banal.[106]

Thus, the following conclusion seems justified: "[I]ndeed, in the thirteenth century and in Paris, the concept of rhythm as it belongs to the poetic tradition became again part of the art of music."[107] It is crucial to take the implications of this merger into account. "Crosschecking" with the treatise literature on "literary" rhythmics and Johannes de Garlandia's *Parisiana poetria* proves that not only does the discourse of speculative music theory include metrical discourse as *musica*, but that poetics also uses the options thus provided. An example contemporary with Johannes de Garlandia reminds us of the implications of this connection. A poem of request and praise that Henry of Avranches sent to Emperor Friedrich II at the beginning of the thirteenth century begins with a comparison of poetry and prose. Whereas prose informs us only about the arbitrariness of human needs, poetry bears the attributes of the divine world-order mentioned in *Liber sapientiae* 11:21. Metrical discourse is the "creative" discourse of God:

> There are two modes: prose and meter, which embrace everything
> That man utters or writes. Human will brings forth prose
> Without weight and without measure;
> But meter is a divine kind of speech [*species divina loquendi*].
> Surely God made the world with number [*numero*], measure [*mensura*],
> And weight [*pondere*], and the quintessence shines brightly in those three,
> In such a manner speaks the law given to Moses, every prophetic speech,
> And the Gospel, and precise words
> Express the beautiful; for that mode of speaking measures [*metitur modus*],
> And weighs [*ponderat*] and numbers [*numerat*] sounds and their duration.
> The man Adonius and his wife Sapha passed it on
> From Hebrew to the Greeks, and the Greeks passed it on to the Latins.[108]

CHAPTER NINE

Instead of a Summary

Speculative Music Theory and Poetics in the French Vernacular. Évrart de Conty's *Échecs amoureux* and *Glose*

THE WORKING HYPOTHESIS formulated at the end of the first part of this study asserted the existence of a continuity reaching from the time of the constitution of the Christian order of discourse to the late Middle Ages, to which should be related not only erudite texts in Latin but also Eustache Deschamps's *Art de dictier*, a work written in French and moreover indebted to the courtly context in which it was produced. Dragonetti's suggestion that the sources of Deschamps's distinction between *musique naturele* and *musique artificiele* were to be sought in the discourse of medieval music theory inevitably led scholars to concentrate on Latin texts. Although this hardly requires any special justification in view of the unchallenged dominance of Latin in the fourteenth and fifteenth centuries in all the domains of knowledge relevant to our reconstruction, a sufficiently differentiated reference written in the French language and coming from a courtly environment may help dispel possible reservations regarding our continuity thesis. The didactic poem entitled *Échecs amoureux* enables us to provide this reference and at the same time formulate the promised summary. This work, which breaks off after 30,060 rhymed octosyllabic verses,[1] was initially dated to the decade following 1370; more recent research suggests a later date. The author has been identified as Évrart de Conty, *maître régent* of the faculty of medicine at the University of Paris between 1353 and 1405, Charles V's personal physician, and presumably also the author of a comprehensive prose commentary on his own work.[2]

The *Échecs amoureux* is extant in two manuscripts.[3] The manuscript Venice, Biblioteca Nazionale Marciana, Fr. App. 23 is incomplete at the beginning and the end, and includes no more than half of the other extant copy, the manuscript Oc. 66, which is in the Saxon State Library in Dresden but now illegible because of war damage. Parts of this manuscript were published before 1945 and thus preserved for scholarship,[4] including the sections on music (fol. 130d–137a), which Hermann Abert had transcribed and published in 1904.[5] Against the background of our account up to this point, which has anticipated the detailed commentary, and in order to let the text itself offer a concluding resume of the speculative music theory handed down to the late Middle Ages in France, we will limit ourselves here to a presentation of the passages in the seventh part that are relevant to our context. Here Pallas Athena is dealing with the education of children. The reference to the recreational effect of music introduces a presentation of the quadrivial disciplines that is based on Boethius, Cassiodorus, Macrobius's commentary on the *Somnium Scipionis,* and Martianus Capella.[6] Three functions and qualities of music are discussed:

> la premiere est ce qu'elle donne,
> comme j'ay dit, a la personne,
> recreacion et repos,
> et ce vault a nostre propos,
> car au voir dire, elle tient lieu
> d'excellent et de noble jeu,
> et qui tous aultrez jeux excede
> pour donner confort et remede
> et plaisant consolacion
> contre la perturbation,
> la sollicitude et la paine,
> qui puet estre en la vie humaine.

> (the first is what it gives,
> as I've said, to the person,
> recreation and rest,
> and that counts here,
> because in truth it offers
> excellent and noble play
> and exceeds all other amusements
> in giving comfort and remedy
> and pleasant consolation
> for the perturbation,
> the care and pain,
> that may occur in human life.)[7]

This passage, which presumably alludes the music of *metra* in Boethius's *Consolatio philosophiae*,[8] introduces the presentation of the central argument of the *ethos* doctrine, the sympathetic effect of music that Boethius discussed in *De instititutione musica* I.1, using the example of the *lascivus*:

> aussy te dy-je de musique
> que sa doulceur, quant on l'applicque
> a celle tristesse excellente
> qu'elle l'enforcist et augmente
> et que la personne en empire,
> et pour ce veulent aucun dire,
> que musique fait le cuer lie,
> plus joyeux et plus esveillie
> et le triste plus triste aussy,
> quant la tristesse est excessive

> (I also tell you about music,
> that its sweetness when applied
> to that overwhelming sadness
> increases and augments it
> and the person suffers more
> so some people say
> that music gladdens the heart,
> makes it more joyous and gay,
> and the sad heart sadder too,
> when sadness is excessive.)[9]

This argument about the evocation, strengthening, or diminishing of an affective disposition through suitably modulated music had been a topos of music theory speculation since ancient Pythagoreanism. At first it was discussed in a political-social context (as it is here as well, as the third function of music),[10] but by Augustine's time at the latest it had been exploited in a Christian-ethical way as well, and with Boethius it became a common concept in medieval music theory. The *Échecs amoureux* merge the doctrine with the courtly concept of virtue that had emerged through the melding of Christian ethics and the moral codes of a warrior class in the figure of the *miles christianus*.[11] Consequently, the positive effects of the musical phenomenon are emphasized not only with respect to the Christian concern for salvation, but also with respect to pride, desire for battle, compassion, and pity:

> que veulx tu plus? par ce sot il
> et ceulx qui ont l'engien soubtil

composer diversez chansons
et plusieurs manierez de tons
et qui ont diverses mesures
et aussy vertus et natures
d'encliner les cuers des personnes
a pluiseurs [*sic*] fins masles ou bonnes.
car aucun chant ont tel mesure
qu'il enclinent l'omme a luxure
et a fole concupiscence
pour leur doulce et mole influence;
li aultre par leur asprete
enclinent leurs cuers a fierte
et font desirer la bataille;
lu aultre aussy sont de tel taille
qu'il font de leur condicion
encliner a compassion
et leurs cuers mouvoir a pite
et li aultre ont propriete
aussy d'encliner a vertu
et a bien [. . .].

(What more do you want? Because he knew
and those who have subtle minds
to compose various songs
and several kinds of voices
and who have diverse rhythms
and also virtues and natures
to incline people's hearts
to several ends bad or good.
For some songs have such rhythm
that they incline man to lustfulness
and mad concupiscence
by their sweet and soft influence;
the others, by their fierceness
incline their hearts to pride
and make them desire battle;
the other [songs] are also such
that they make [people] naturally
inclined to compassion
and moves their hearts to pity

and others have the property
of inclining as well to virtue
and to good [. . .])[12]

The *Échecs amoureux* expands the traditional *ethos* doctrine by referring
to music's "medical" relevance, which will be found in Deschamps as well.[13]
This doctrine is tailored to a specific milieu, without the conceptual connection traditionally emphasizing the moderation of the affects being sacrificed:

briefment musique a tel puissance
qu'elle refraint les passions,
les folles inclinacions
et les mauvaises voulentes,
dont li cuers puet estre tentes,
et au contraire le retrait
par son melodieux attrait
qui ainsy comme je t'expose
a bonnez pensees dispose
et a bon propos l'ame humaine

(in short, music has such power
that it moderates the passions,
mad inclinations
and evil desires
by which hearts may be tempted,
and on the contrary the detachment
produced by its melodious attraction,
as I am explaining to you,
disposes the human soul to good thoughts
and good intentions.)[14]

The second complex, which is dealt with after the ethical power of music
and before its functions in the political context, underscores the provenance
of the music theory presented, sets the continuity of the discourse of speculative music theory before our eyes, and sums up the latter's most important theoretical elements. Speculative music theory is initially introduced as
mental exercise and intellectual pleasure:

Musique vault secondement
pour employer l'entendement
en belle speculacion
et de grant delectacion.

car musique intellectuelle
est si dilettable et si belle
a ceulx qui la savent entendre
[. . .]
quel contemplacion puet estre,
biaulx amiz, ou monde terrestre
plus belle ne plus delittable
a l'entendement raisonnable,
qui veult soubtilletes apprendre,
qu'en bien la nature comprendre
et la maniere de chansons
et la proporcion des sons,
dont les consonanciez viennent,
et quelx nombres y appartiennent?

(secondly, music is valuable
to employ the intellect
in fine speculation
and great delectation.
for intellectual music
is so delightful and beautiful
for those who know how to listen to it
[. . .]
what contemplation can be,
good friends, in the terrestrial world,
more beautiful or more delightful
to the reasonable intellect,
that wants to learn subtleties,
to understand nature rightly
and the manner of songs
and the proportion of sounds,
from which consonances come,
and what numbers belong to them?)[15]

Then the text recapitulates Pythagoras's discovery of the three framing intervals of the Greek theory of harmony, the derivation of "harmonic proportions" in arithmetic, the description of harmonic intervals in accord with these proportions, and the theory of mensuration. For our continuity thesis and for the purposes of a conclusion, what is important is that here, in a French text contemporary with Deschamps, the discussion of music invokes the horizon of speculative music theory (*musique intellectuelle*), whose object is the understanding of the "natural" order (*la nature comprendre*). This understanding coincides with the understanding of composition (*la maniere de chansons*) and its numerical harmonic bases (*quelx nombres y appartiennent*), and thus presupposes the structural homology of the musical work and the *ordo entium* revealed in nature. The pleasure (*delectation*) to be derived from "intellectual" involvement with music arises, according to the discussion of *delectatio* in Augustine or of *gaudium* in Boethius, from the understanding of this order. Here the methodological model is musical analysis. Any opposition that might be constructed between joy and pleasure, on the one hand, and musical speculation, on the other, disregards the historical evidence. Even the courtly instrumentalization of *musique intellectuelle*, the emphasis on *delectation* is an emphasis that leaves the consistency of the traditional doctrine and its speculative aims untouched. The point of distinguishing a "musical" phenomenon and attending to it is to arrive at the experience of the *whole* of the order of creation. Thus after discussing the numerical-proportional bases of acoustic music, which are explained using the forge legend, Pallas Athena makes the transition to *musica mundana*. The elements of the sublunar world, *lez chosez du monde*, are integrated into a "harmonic" order:

> Qui considere aussy comment
> le ciel et li quattre element
> et les mistionz et les chosez
> qui sont dedans le ciel enclosez,
> meismes les choses parfaittez
> selon les anchiiens sont faittez
> par proporcion armonique,
> comme li accort de musique
> dont j'ay fait devant mencion,
> il y a contemplacion
> sans faille aussi tres delittable
> et c'est ce qu'aucun bien nottable
> appellent musique mondaine.
> et ce n'est pas parole vaine,
> ains le dient pour ce qu'il samble
> que lez chosez du monde ensamble,
> quant a ses parties nottablez,
> sont aussy comme concordablez
> et consonanz sanz nul descort,
> comme li musical accort.

(Also whoever considers how
the heavens and the four elements
and mixtures and things
that are enclosed within the heavens,
even perfect things
according to the ancients are made
by harmonic proportion,
there is contemplation
also delightful without fault
and that's what some very notable people
call cosmic music.
and that is not an empty word,
for they say it because it seems
that the things of the world taken together,
as for its notable parts,
are also as if capable of concord
and consonance with no discord
like musical harmony.)[16]

The provenance of the doctrine developed here is obvious. In the following discussion of the harmony and "musicality" of the movement of the spheres it becomes still clearer:

briefment li anchiien disoient
que li ciel qui ainsy toirnoient
entour la terre nuit et jour
continuelment sanz sejour
et lez estoilles ensement
nays cellez du firmament
et toutez leurs proprietes,
leurs vertus et leurz quantites
et leurs distancez de la terre,
qui est belle chose a enquerre,
et meismez leur mouvement
sont ordonnez trez subtilment
par ceste musical mesure
qui moult est plaisant a nature.

(In short, the ancients said
that the heavens that revolve
around the earth night and day

continually, without stopping
and the stars, also
not hidden by the firmament
and all their properties,
their virtues and their quantities
and their distances from the earth,
such a fine thing to inquire into,
and even their movement
are very subtly ordered
by this musical measure
that is very pleasing to nature.)[17]

The *musical mesure* refers to the constant measure, the regular repetition of cyclical natural phenomena, and hypostatizes a unifying principle of the natural order. As the following passage in the *Échecs amoureux* proves, this is considered the Creator's seal and signature. This has two consequences that contributed to the function of the model in the courtly context. The religious interest in highlighting harmonic-proportional, "musical" orders in this world is retained. At the same time such orders, if found or manifested in works of art, gain legitimacy as indirectly founded in God's act of creation. Numbers and their relationships provide the medium of the foundation of order; in the phrase *divine mesure* one can hear an echo of the familiar phrase from the *Liber sapientiae* 11:21. We leave the relevant passages in their context:

c'est chose a croire raisonnable
a ceulx qui ont soubtil engien,
car il appartient aussy bien
comme chilz dieux sur tous premiers
soit sur tous tres soubtilz ouvriers,
trez bonz tres puissanz trez parfaiz
que chilz mondez aussi fu faiz
trez beaulx et tres bien ordonnez
et tres bien proporcionnez,
ad fin comme il est convenable
que *l'oeuvre a l'ouvrier soit samblable.*
Et certainement si est il,
car chilz qui a l'engien soubtil et qui bien la beaulte espreuve
du naturel monde, il le treuve
de fachon tres esmerveillable
et de beaulte incorrompable.

Et *c'est voir par especial*
de la beaulte celestial
dont il s'ensieult au dire voir
qu'il ne doit rienz au ciel avoir
sanz raison fait de n'aventure,
ainz doit par divine mesure
comme oevre d'ouvrier tres parfait
tout quant qu'il y a estre fait
tres bien et tres parfaittement,
et pour ce c'on voit clerement
les proporcions musicaulx
estre sur toutez efficaulx
et de la plus grande excellence,
comme moustre l'experience
en plusieurs cas evidemment,
il doit sembler generalment
que *le ciel et toutes les choses*
qui sont en sa nature encloses
doivent toutez estre ordonneez
faittez et proporcionneez
par la musical ordonnance
dont je te fay cy remambrance.

(It's a reasonable thing to believe
for those who have subtle minds,
for it is fitting as well,
since these gods above all
are especially very subtle workers,
very good, very powerful, very perfect,
that this world was also made
very beautiful and well-ordered
and very well proportioned,
so that it is fitting
that *the work resemble the worker.*
And certainly it is so,
for he who has a subtle mind
and feels well the beauty
of the natural world, finds it
very marvelous in fashion
and of incorruptible beauty.

And *it is to see especially*
by the celestial beauty
from which it follows in truth
that there must be nothing in the heavens
made without reason or by accident,
and thus by divine measure [it] must be
like the work of a very perfect worker
insofar as it has been made
very well and very perfectly
and because we see clearly
the musical proportions
being more efficacious than any
and of the greatest excellence,
as experience shows us
clearly in several cases
that *the heavens and all things*
that are included in its nature
must all be ordered
made and proportioned
by the musical ordering
of which I remind you here.[18]

Seen against the background of our explanations, the insistent reference to the beauty of the perfect, "proportional" order hardly requires further comment. The condition of plausibility and the point of prenominalist Scholastic theology, the concept of a God expressing himself in his Creation, which constitutes the former as the latter's *imago*, is explicitly formulated in this absolutely not theological context. The "holistic" concept of music vividly interpreting the *proportio* of the Creator and Creation is to be understood as the embodiment of this concept:

[. . .] touttes les nottablez chosez
qui sont en ce grant monde enclosez,
quel part qu'ellez soient poseez,
ou hault ou bas, sont composeez
par droite mesure armonique,
comme sont li son de musique
qui sont ensamble consonant
et que c'est chose appartenant
a l'ordonnance dessus dite,
ou nature moult se delitte,

comme en chose tres prouffitable
et qui est et ferme et estable.
car l'ordre du monde terrestre
sieut l'ordre du monde celestre [. . .].

([. . .] all the remarkable things
that are enclosed in this great world,
wherever they are placed,
whether high or low, are composed
by correct harmonic measure,
as are the sounds of music
which are in consonance with each other
and it is something belonging
to the above-mentioned order,
in which nature takes much pleasure,
as in something very beneficial
and that is firm and stable.
for the order of the terrestrial world
follows the order of the celestial world [. . .])[19]

The theoretical elements that are important for the model's implications
for the status of the "musical" arts remain functional and clear as well. The
thirteenth century's arguments against the acoustic quality of the harmony
of the spheres are integrated, but the thesis of a structural homology of the
"artificial" ordering of the work and the ordering of Being central to the
whole doctrine is maintained. Thus the argument of the *similitudo* of the two,
the assumption that the "musical" form of a given work has in itself a referential quality, and finally the instrumentalization of prereflective pleasure
as an indication of this *similitudo* are systematically justified:

Ainsy doit il estre entendu,
que li ciel, [. . .]
font par leurs divers mouvements
sonz et melodieux accors,
non pas teulx que les sonnans cors
c'on oist en cest monde terrestre,
car ce ne puest par raison estre,
ains est chose a dire trop rude
maiz sanz plus par similitude
pour les proporcions samblables
qui sont ou ciel ymaginables

aux proporcions de musique
qui font lez accors que j'explique,
si ques la musique celestre,
qui bien considere son estre,
au nombre sans plus se rapporte
qui moult l'entendement conforte
et se puet dire ensement
que tout aussy samblablement
que la musical melodie
est plaisans a la humaine vie
et gracieuse et aggreable
pour la meslee concordable
de divers sons oys ensamble.

(Thus it must be understood,
that the heavens, [. . .]
make by their diverse movements
sounds and melodious harmonies,
not those [made] by the sounding horns
one hears in this terrestrial world,
for that cannot be by reason,
thus a thing too hard to say
but simply by similitude
for the similar proportions
that can be seen in the heavens
in the proportion of music
that make the harmonies I am explaining,
like the celestial music,
whoever well considers its being
refers simply to number
which greatly comforts the mind
and thus it can be said
in just the same way
that musical melody
is pleasing to human life
and gracious and agreeable
because of the harmonizable mixture
of diverse sounds heard together.)[20]

From the *similitudo* of "heavenly" and acoustic music the text first infers
that the latter is pleasing to God,[21] and then emphasizes the "production

aesthetics" implications of this doctrine. The reference to the muses is supposed to be seen as an allegory of the paradigmatic nature of the harmony of the spheres for any "reproduced" order of work: the corresponding passage is entitled "Comment ceste celeste musique est, ce samble, segnefie par les muses que li poete anchiien mettoient au ciel" ("How this celestial music is, it seems, signified by the muses that the ancient poets put in the heavens").[22] The conceptualization of the "musical" phenomenon or work as a concrete manifestation of the order of Being and Creation, the idea that the theoretically oriented concern with the "musical" object of the vision of the whole guides and introduces this order seems not to have lost its pervasiveness between Augustine and 1400. The actuality of speculative music theory is evident precisely in this text, which is indebted not to a "scientific" context of use but rather to an attempt to produce an *aemulatio* of the *Roman de la rose*. Only the question as to how metrical discourse is situated with respect to the concept of music remains open.

This is discussed in the extensive prose commentary on the *Échecs amoureux* that Evrart de Conty or one of his pupils probably wrote between 1398 and 1414.[23] The text, which is extant in six manuscripts,[24] is thought to be the first French commentary on a work that was itself written in French, and also the first to consider such a work as equal in value to classical literature.[25] The prose commentary begins by stating the problem that initiated its compilation. The *Échecs amoureux* compiles a selection from the cultural stock on the model of a medieval encyclopedia. The selection itself seems to have proven viable, the prose commentary limits itself to amplifications. However, the presentation of the material in rhyming octosyllabic couplets seems soon to have been viewed as a hindrance to its reception. The occasion and declared goal of the commentary is the transposition of the content presented in the *Échecs amoureux* into easy-to-read prose, and the augmentation of its accessibility by abandoning of the allegorical mode of presentation:

> Ce livre present fu fait et ordonné principalment a l'instance d'un autre fait en rime nagueres et de nouvel venu a congnoissance qui est intitulé Des Eschez amoureux et Des Eschez d'Amours aussy comme pour desclairer aucunes choses que la rime contient qui semblent estre obscures et estranges de premiere face. Et pour ce fu il fait en prose, pour ce que prose est plus clere a entendre par raison que n'est rime.

> (The present book was made and commissioned principally on the occasion of another earlier made in rhyme and newly come to light, which is entitled Des Eschez amoureux and also Des Eschez d'Amours, in order

to make clear certain things that the rhyme contains that seem at first obscure and strange. And for that reason it was made in prose, because prose is easier to understand by reason than rhyme is.)[26]

In the fifteenth and sixteenth centuries the commentary was considered an important work and had a rich reception history, only parts of which have been studied. The continuing success of the commentary may be attributed to the fact that the text does not limit itself to a simplification in form but provides the content presented in the *Échecs amoureux* with extensive supplements. The general arrangement and aim of the commentary increases its validity as evidence for our working thesis, since it can be assumed that the material supplied for the further substantiation of the lore presented in the *Échecs amoureux* was chosen because it was widely accepted or a matter of general consensus.

The section devoted to music is situated in the context of a mythological excursus.[27] It seeks to clarify the allegorical personifications appearing in the *Échecs amoureux* with respect to their function in the text and to explain them by situating them in the mythological pantheon. Venus, Juno, Pallas Athena, Paris, and Mercury provide the occasion for an extensive discussion, largely taken from Pierre Bersuire's (c. 1290–1362) *De formis figurisque deorum*, of the sixteen most important deities of the ancient pantheon. This expands into an overview of the traditional cosmological, philosophical-theological, practical-ethical, and political knowledge, and includes, in the context of a discussion of Apollo and the muses, a survey of the seven liberal arts. The latter is characterized by consistent *moralization*. Each section consists of a (more extensive) presentation of the most important contents of the respective *ars* and a (less extensive) presentation of its moral aspects and of the possibilities of applying it psychologically or psychagogically. The discussion of music in chapters 20 to 48 is provided, in a way true to the model of the *Échecs amoureux*, with supplements taken chiefly from Boethius's textbook, "almost the sole source of this study."[28] Contemporary musical practice is occasionally mentioned, along with more recent developments in theory, but on the whole does not find its way into the work. Thus it seems that around 1400 the speculative conception of music in the Boethian tradition was still considered the essential one for disciplinary music theory.

The material provided as a complement to the *Échecs amoureux* confirms this impression—for instance, the passage in chapter 32, in which *musica rhythmica* is the subject. Joseph Mettlich showed that the *Glose* draws on Johannes de Garlandia's *Parisiana poetria*.[29] Rhymed verse with a fixed number of syllables is said to be structured in accord with "musical" proportions. The argument, which is based on the theory of proportions presented in Boethius's *De institutione arithmetica*, starts, as does the Augustinian theory of verse, from the conception of the relation of long to short syllables in the proportion 2:1 and the principle of symmetrical distribution: the *proportio* verse-*membrum* corresponds to the *proportio* 2:1 and thus is said to be structurally homologous with the traditional perfect interval, diapason/octave. On this basis a theory of verse is developed that formalizes the length of the verse, the number of syllables, and the position of the caesura according to the rules of the Pythagorean theory of proportions. Mettlich has aptly described the procedure: "For him [the author of the *Glose*], the verse line is a sounding string—a monochord whose length is determined by the number of syllables."[30] The connection with speculative music theory is constituted by the classification borrowed from Cassiodorus, conceived as a differentiation of the Boethian *musica instrumentalis*. *Musique es mettres* and *musique es rimes* are also *musique instrumental*:[31]

> L'autre musique instrumental [*sic*], qui est la droite propre et la vraie musique, a es chans et es sons dont nous usons son lieu principalment, soient chans exercez par nostre voix humaine ou par aucuns instrumens faiz par l'art ou par engin humain, [. . .]. Ceste musique instrumental a aussy lieu et peut estre trouvee es mettres et es rimes. Nous devons doncques savoir que les musicaulx nombres et les proporcions dont les consonancies se deppendent n'ont pas lieu seulement es melodies et es chans de nostre voix humaine [. . .], ains ont lieu es paroles, [. . .]. Et par especial ceste musique a lieu es mettres et es rimes. Pour quoy nous devons considerer que les mettres et les rimes sont une maniere de parole nombrees et mesurees de certaine mesure [. . .].

> (The other instrumental music, which is genuine and true music, occurs mainly in songs and sounds that we use, whether songs produced by our human voice or by instruments made by art or by human intelligence [. . .]. This instrumental music also takes place and may be found in meters and in rhyming verses. Therefore we must know that the musical numbers and the proportions on which consonances depend occur not only in melodies and songs of our human voice [. . .], but occurs in words, [. . .]. And especially this music occurs in meters and in rhyming verses. Therefore we must consider that meters and rhyming verses are a kind of numbered speech measured by a certain measure [. . .].)[32]

This passage illustrates not only the continuity of such conceptions within the discourse of speculative music theory that subsumed metrical discourse under music (because its form can be described numerically) and conceived it as a manifestation of the numerically based cosmic order. The paragraph refers to syllabic, rhyming verse as *musica rhythmica*, which finds its true place in the French language:

> Et ne doit pas estre oublié que les mectres ont leur lieu seulement en latin, a parler proprement, car la langue latine est a certaines regles ramenee, et trop mieulx ordenee pour ce faire que la langue commune; et aussi est au contraire la rime mielx seant en la langue commune, et par especial en la langue françoise que ou latin, combien que elle y ait bien son lieu et y soit bien seant aucunesfois.

> (And it must not be forgotten that meters have their place only in Latin, properly speaking, because the Latin language is reduced to certain rules, and much better ordered for this than is the common language; and thus on the contrary rhyming verse is more appropriate in the common language, and especially in the French language, than in Latin, although it occurs there and is sometimes appropriate there.)[33]

The *measure* of the line, the cadencing of the verse according to its number of syllables, is opposed, as *droite musique*, to the "music" of what is clearly song or instrumental accompaniment.[34] This opposition must be clearly stressed with respect to Deschamps:

> Nous devons oultre considerer que, combien qu'il y ait en la proporcion des mettres et des rymes aussy comme une maniere de chant et que aucun legier chant y soit aucunefois, si comme Aristote mesmes dit des tragedies et d'aucunes hystoires, toutesfois, la musique principal qui est trouvee es rymes et es mettres doit estre rapportee au nombre des sillabes plus que a son ne a chant qui y puist estre. Briefment, c'est la droite musique qui y est et doit estre. Et ce peut apparoir particulierement es rymes.

> (We must also consider the fact that although in the proportion of meters and rhymes there is also a kind of singability, and that there is some subtle melody in them, just as Aristotle himself says of tragedies and certain works of historiography, nonetheless the principal music that is found in rhymes and meters is in the number of syllables more than in the sound or song that may be involved. In short, it is in the number of syllables that genuine music [*droite musique*] is and should be found. And this can appear particularly in rhymed verses.)[35]

The following definition combines the formal criteria of the number of syllables, the symmetrical division of the verse, and rhyme under the concept of equivalence:

> Quant est aussi des rimes, il convient qu'il y ait certain nombre de sillebes, maiz il ne convient ja qu'il y ait observance de longue ne de brieve, ainz suffit que elles soient proferees indifferemment, sauf tant qu'il est assés appartenant en bien seant en la prolacion des rimes qu'il y ait pauses et aucune demeure legiere en certains lieux, aussi comme *pour comparer une partie a l'autre musicaument.* Il convient oultre aussi secondement que tous les vers et les bastons des rimes qui ont regard ensemble et qui se *correspondent* ly uns a l'aultre soient d'une semblable terminacion et d'un accord en son.

> (As for rhyming verses, they should have a certain number of syllables, though there need be no observance of long and short [syllables], it suffices that they be recited without scansion, except that it is appropriate and suitable that in the enunciation of rhymed verses there be pauses and short rests in certain places in order *to relate one part to another musically.* Secondly, all the verses and rhymed lines that are related and *correspond* to each other should have a similar ending and agree in sound.)[36]

Caesuras and cadencing (*pauses et aucune demeure legiere en certains lieux*) bring out the "consonance" of the parts of the verse, the "musicality" of the rhyming verse lines and correspondingly rise to become central elements of versification: through the *rhythmical structure* of the discourse the *equal measure* of the rhymed lines becomes audible. The insistence on measure leads back to the theory of musical consonances, to the Pythagorean harmonics derived from the *divisio monochordi.* From our point of view, what is striking and instructive in this is the way in which the theory of proportions is taken for granted and related to the speculative conception of music: "All this is clearly and distinctly expressed, in part [presupposed] as something generally known and taken for granted:"[37]

> Car se nous soubtillement les [les vers] considerons bien et nous les voulons bien prononcier a leur droit, nous trouverons qu'il les convient partir et comparer ensemble les parties par les proporcions musicaulx dessus dictes et la faire sa pose et son arrest aucun aussy comme pour mettre difference entre les deux parties, comme l'oÿe fait entre les deux sons qui se accordent ensamble. Car par ce peut on mieulx leur bon accord entendre et leur consonancie. Et se les deux parties ou plusieurs dessus dictes en tout sont comparables musicaument, tant vauldra mieulx la chose. Car

lors sera la ryme plaisant a prononcier et de bonne mesure, et se rap-
portera celle dessus dicte comparoison des parties ensamble et a leur tout
aussy comme ce qui est dit par devant de la division du monocorde.

(For if we consider them [the verses] very carefully and try to pronounce
them correctly, we will find that it is fitting to divide them and compare
the parts in accord with the musical proportions mentioned above and
to make the pause and the rest as well, in order to make a difference between the two parts, as the ear does between two sounds that harmonize
with each other. For in this way one can hear their good accord and their
consonance better. And if the two or more parts mentioned above are in
every way comparable musically, the thing will be even better. For in this
case, the rhyming verse will be pleasing to utter and properly measured,
and in the way previously discussed, the relation of the parts to each
other and the relation of the parts to the whole will be comparable to the
relations previously described with regard to the division of the monochord.)[38]

Thus the caesura is supposed to divide the verse line in accord with the
proportions of the *divisio monochordi*. For example, the five-syllable verse
is divided after the second (2/3) or third (3/2) syllable, and thus corresponds
to the quint. The six-syllable verse is divided after the second or the fourth
syllable; this partition, corresponding to the proportions 2/4 or 4/2, identifies it as equivalent to the octave. If it is divided 3/3, the verse corresponds
to the interval of the prime, to perfect consonance, or, in accord with the
proportional relationship between the hemistich and the whole verse (1/2),
the octave. In the ten-syllable verse (4/6 or 6/4), we encounter the fifth
again; the Alexandrine (8/4, 9/3; 6/6) is here considered the ideal verse—it
can be divided in accord with all the harmonic proportions that can be
derived from the first *tetraktys*. The *tetraktys* allows to discern those verse
types that are in conformity with the system. This explains the relative rar-
ity of nine- and eleven-syllable verses, too: Since the *Glose* assumes no more
than one caesura per verse, they cannot be divided in accord with harmonic
proportions.[39]

The consistent "formalism" of this argumentation has little in common
with Dragonetti's modernizing interpretation based on the "autonomy"
of poetic art or with Febel's modernistic projections. It is the *similitudo*
of metrical discourse and the order of Being and Creation manifested in
numerical orders that guarantees the "musicality" of the verse and also
its dignity and relevance, awakens the "aesthetic" pleasure of the listener,
and thus is still the precondition and ontological ground of any profane

entertainment function of "musical" art. Without the presupposition of this relationship of similarity, the development of rhythmic verse, the artist's "work" is simply inconceivable under the conditions of the analogical *episteme*. The *Échecs amoureux* and the *Glose* devoted to it display the central determinants of the discourse of the speculative conception of music. They strengthen the conclusion that our reconstruction up to this point has suggested: when music theory contexts are invoked or classifications of *musica* are introduced, when their *effectus* is reflected upon, then the relevant statements of the discourse of speculative music theory in the Neoplatonic tradition are to be presumed as their conceptual foundation. This holds as long as a given text does not explicitly distance itself from the discourse of speculative music theory. The conception of metrical discourse as *musica* has its place in this discourse, and it is precisely the latter that hands down the distinction between *musica naturalis* and *musica artificialis musica* as well. It connects the quoted music theorists with the treatise literature on "literary" rhythmics, with Johannes de Garlandia's *Parisian poetria*, the *Échecs amoureux,* and the *Glose* on it. Thus our second working hypothesis can be considered proven. The connection of metapoetic reflection with the speculative conception of music is common and well documented. Since late Antiquity, it had been handed down in the speculative branch of disciplinary music theory. Originating from the Pythagorean-Neoplatonic substrate of Christian theology and being closely related to the Christian order of discourse's most central elements, this connection bears witness to the latter's world model.

Part III

CHAPTER TEN

Eustache Deschamps's
L'Art de Dictier Revisited

New Connections

THE RESULTS at which we arrived in part II thus confirm our working hypothesis. Research on Eustache Deschamps since Roger Dragonetti had agreed in asserting that after about 1300 there was a decline of speculative music theory and in concluding that a different, newer, "Aristotelian" or "nominalistic" frame of reference must be assumed for Deschamps's *Art de dictier*. It is these assumptions and the conception of the intellectual history of the Late Middle Ages underlying them that had given an appearance of historical plausibility to the claims regarding the "formalistic" verses of the *rhétoriqueurs* summarized in part I above. Our results put these assumptions and claims in question. At the same time, they provide new interpretive approaches in both areas.

The assumptions made by the scholarship on Deschamps presented in my second chapter will be reviewed in four stages. First, we must recognize that in the Late Middle Ages, opting for music theory as a discursive frame of reference for reflecting on the theory of poetry implies deciding *against* other frames of reference. It is highly significant that the *Art de dictier* does *not* discuss verse within the discursive context of rhetoric, to which the formation reconstructed in part II is to be seen, with regard to its importance for poetics, as a parallel, though secondary in its influence and productivity. The implications of this will be determined in the framework of a re-reading of the *Art de dictier* (chapter 11). We must also show that interpreting the text on the basis of its historical presuppositions in the discourse of medieval music theory can produce a complete and consistent reading of the *Art de dictier* and avoid the interpretive difficulties that Dragonetti and interpreters following his lead had to acknowledge. The continuity thesis underlying our argument must then suggest the question of Deschamps's direct sources. Two hypotheses will be developed to provide at least a tentative answer to this question. A few brief remarks on the possible consequences of the interpretive option developed here for assessing in particular the *balades de moralitez* conclude the chapter devoted to Deschamps.

Finally, moving beyond the relevance of our results to Deschamps, we will return to the poetry of the *rhétoriqueurs*. Scholarly descriptive interpretation of their works is on the whole satisfactory, and allows us to develop perspectives on the *rhétoriqueurs'* poetics by using examples selected for the purposes of a typology, chiefly from the work of Jean Molinet. The starting point for our reflections is Molinet's previously cited definition of verse as "une espèce de musique appellee richemique laquele contient certain nombre de sillabes avec aucune suavité de equisonance" ("a kind of music called *richemique,* which contains a certain number of syllables with some sweetness of consonance"): In the eleventh chapter, we will raise the question whether this definition can be interpreted on the basis of the same discursive presuppositions as Deschamps's conception of metrical discourse as *musique naturele.* In conclusion, we will offer an outlook on how this provenance hypothesis might contribute to the development of genuinely medieval perspectives on the "formalism" of the *Grands rhétoriqueurs.*

Changing the Discursive Frame of Reference: The Displacement of *noble rethorique*

In 1993 Michel Zink still felt compelled to note that the distinction between the high Middle Ages and the late Middle Ages as "a different world"[1] was premature. Crises of a sociopolitical, economic, religious, and also "epistemic" kind may have shaped the late fourteenth and fifteenth centuries. However, this does not tell us how literary production reacted to these crises: "It is often too easily said that this group of crises led to a decadence in literature. In reality, letters can be nourished by crises as well as suffer from them."[2] Crises can be dealt with productively in various ways. On the basis of the postulated break in the tradition and the liberation from the discursive restraints it had imposed, the scholarship summarized in part I not only inferred that literature made emphatic use of its newly acquired possibilities, but claimed that the ensuing, "liberated" semiotic practice was pursued to a degree of formal differenciation where convergences with modern and modernistic paradigms of the poetic become apparent. However, a reaction that tries to cope with a given historical context by drawing on established conceptual frameworks and, as as the case may be, variegating them is a possibility that must be taken into account as well.

In the tradition established since Dragonetti, Eustache Deschamps's description of verse as *musique naturele* was seen as a break with poetic reflection in the discursive context of speculative music theory in the Middle

Ages—as a symptom of its decline, as a sign heralding the modernistic rapprochement of poetic language and absolute music, and thus the focusing of poetic discourse on autonomy and deliberate transgression of the primary linguistic code. The continuities and implications of the discourse of speculative music theory discussed in part II suggest a different assessment. Seen in terms of its discursive premises, Deschamps's conception of metrical discourse as music is first of all a decision *against* the discursive frame of reference available in disciplinary rhetoric, a decision made in favor of music theory. It seems at first to be a shift from one long established discursive frame of reference for theoretical reflection on poetry to another. In order to pursue the question regarding the function and implications of this change around 1400, we will remain true to the principle of interpreting the given body of texts on the basis of its discursive presuppositions. However, to provide a gradual approach to the text, we will move first from the macrostructural level of the analogical epistéme and speculative music theory as a discursive formation to the mesostructural level of genetical or conceptual relations between concrete œuvres.

Jacqueline Cerquiglini argued that by expanding the thematic dyad "arms and love" by a third component "arts and writing," Guillaume de Machaut had already developed a "self-reflexive écriture";[3] according to Dragonetti, in the *Art de dictier* Deschamps announced first the emancipation of lyric poetry from instrumental accompaniment, and then the "autonomy of the poem"[4] in general. For Paul Zumthor and his followers, the formalism of the late fifteenth century develops this into a protomodern if not "modernistic" outline of poetic discourse. Machaut and Deschamps seem to mark (early) stages of a linear development leading from the verse of the high Middle Ages, integrated into the courtly milieu and connected with instrumental accompaniment, to the self-referential play of the autonomous signifier in the poetry of the *rhétoriqueurs*.[5] This construction seems to be supported by reference to the actual relation between Machaut and Deschamps. The biographical substrate that underlies the personal references in Deschamps's ballads 123, 124, and 447 and that led the anonymous fifteenth-century author of *Regles de seconde rhetorique* to speak of "Eustace Morel, nephew of master Guillaume de Machaut" may be unclear with regard to its significance in detail.[6] It is nonetheless undeniable that Deschamps shows reverence for Machaut. Ballads 123 and 124 mourn Machaut's death in 1377; they contain—and this is rare in Deschamps's work as a whole—passages relevant to poetic theory. The ballads present, as Jean-Claude Mühlethaler's detailed analysis of the ballads suggests, Machaut's positions concerning literary aesthetics: "By their content, the two funeral elegies occupy a special place in Deschamps's works; they reflect the aesthetics of Guillaume de Machaut."[7] The argumentative framework of this section will be based on these ballads:

Balade CXXIII

1 Armes, Amours, Dames, Chevalerie,
  Clers, musicans, faititres en françois,
  Tous sophistes, toute poeterie,
  Tous ceuls qui ont melodieuse voix,
5 Ceuls qui chantent en orgue aucune fois
  Et qui ont chier le doulz art de musique,
  Demenez dueil, plourez, car c'est bien drois,
  La mort Machaut le noble rethorique.

  Onques d'amours ne parla en folie,
10 Ains a esté en tous ses diz courtois,
  Aussi a moult pleu sa chanterie
  Aux grans seigneurs, a Dames et bourgeois.
  Hé! Orpheus, assez lamenter dois Las!
  Et regreter d'un regart autentique,
15 Arethusa et Alpheus, tous trois,
  La mort Machaut le noble rethorique.

  Priez pour lui si que nul ne l'oublie:
  Ce vous requiert le bailli de Valoys,
  Car il n'en est au jour d'ui nul en vie
20 Tel comme il fut, ne ne sera des mois.
  Complains sera de princes et de Roys,
  Jusqu'a longtemps pour sa bonne replique,
  Vestez vous noir, plourez tous, Champenois,
  La mort Machaut, le noble rethorique.

Ballad CXXIII

Arms, Loves, Ladies, Chivalry,
Clerics, musicians, writers
All sophists, all versifiers,
All who have a melodious voice,
Those who sometimes sing to instruments
And who cherish the sweet art of relic,
Mourn and weep, it is right and

Balade CXXIV

O fleur des fleurs de toute melodie,
Tresdoulz maistres qui tant fustes adrois,
O Guillaume, mondains dieux d'armonie,
Aprez vos faiz, qui obtendra le chois
Sur tous faiseurs? Certes, ne le congnoys.
Vo noms sera precieuse relique,
Car l'en plourra en France et en Artois
La mort Machaut le noble rethorique.

La fons Circé et la fontaine Helie
Dont vous estiez le ruissel et les dois,
Ou poetes mistrent leur estudie
Convient taire, dont je suis moult destrois.
C'est par vous qui mort gisez tous frois,
Qui de tous chans avez esté cantique.
Plourez, harpes et cors sarrazinois,
La mort Machaut, le noble rethorique.

Rubebes, leuths, vielles, syphonie,
Psalterions, trestous instruments coys,
Rothes, guiterne, flaustes, chalemie,
Traversaines, et vous, nymphes de boys,
Tympanne aussi, mettez en euvre dois,
Et le choro n'y ait nul qui pratique;
Faictes devoir, plourez, gentils Galois,
La mort Machaut le noble rethorique.

Ballad CCXXIV

O flower of the flowers of every melody,
Sweet master who was so skilled,
O Guillaume, earthly god of harmony,
After your deeds, who will be chosen
above all poets? Surely, I do not know.
Your name will be a precious music,
For France and Artois will bemoan

The death of Machaut the noble
  rhetorician.

He never spoke of love in madness,
But was ever courtly in all his poems,

And so his singing greatly pleased
Great lords, ladies and bourgeois.
Alas! Orpheus, you should lament
And weep with genuine respect,
Arethusa and Alpheus, all three,
The death of Machault the noble
  rhetorician.

Pray for him so no one will forget him
The bailiff of Valois demands it of you,
For there is no one alive today
Like him, nor will be in our time.
He will be missed by princes and kings
Many years for his good practice;
Dress in black, all mourn, Champenois,
The death of Machault the noble
  rhetorician.

The death of Machaut the noble
  rhetorician.

Font of Circé and spring of Helikon,
Of which you were the stream and
  channel,
To which poets devoted their study
Should fall silent, which devastates me.
Alas! It's because you're dead and cold,
You, the singer of all songs.
Weep, harps and Moorish horns, for
The death of Machaut the noble
  rhetorician.

Rubebes, lutes, vielles, viols,
Psalteries, all gentle instruments,
Rothes, guiternes, flutes, chalemies,
Traversaines, and you, wood nymphs,
Drum also, begin to play,
And the choron, as no one objects
Do your duty, weep, gentle Gauls,
The death of Machault the noble
  rhetorician.[8]

This is a *double ballade*, presumably written for parallel recitation.[9] In content, it follows the genre conventions of the simplest form of the funeral elegy, which Brunetto Latini's *Livre dou tresor* calls the fourth of the *colores rhetorici*: the *clamor* (lament).[10] Claude Thiry has traced the history of the subgenre. In the Middle Latin *planctus*, the central element of *deploratio* already appears in combination with elements of *consolatio*; in the course of the following centuries, the weight of the defunct's future *fama* gradually increases until the accent has shifted entirely from the fact of mortality to the triumph of worldly reputation after death. In this form, the funeral elegy remains largely stable down to the seventeenth and eighteenth centuries.[11] Deschamps's ballads fit with Thiry's description, and are as much songs of praise as songs of lament. However, his lament is the first in the French language to be devoted to a poet. The genre pragmatics had reserved the form for the aristocracy; even in its transgression in Deschamps's work, the limitation is still clearly marked. The term *noble rethorique* most prominently displayed in the last line of the refrain combines the predicate of nobility with a noun referring to the *clergie* and thus suspends the difference in rank.[12]

For the detailed analysis of the *double balade* we can refer to Mühletaler's previously mentioned work. For our further argument, an important indication is the basis for Machaut's fame according to Deschamps. Here two aspects are distinguished. The artists mentioned in the second verse of Ballad 123 are introduced in complementary pairs. To the cleric using Latin corresponds the *faititre* in French, whom the ballads also call *faiseur* and, in the identical refrain of both ballads, *rethorique*. Both are distinguished from the *poete*, a term that Deschamps generally reserves for the ancient poets.[13] From the writer of verse are distinguished "ceuls [. . .] qui ont chier le doulz art de musique" ("those [. . .] who cherish the sweet art of music") (Ballad 123, v. 5–6). The "chanterie" (v. 11) is contrasted with the "diz Courtois" (v. 10): in the first stanza of the ballad Machaut is praised as the author of "diz courtois," and as a poet in the second stanza of this ballad. Both oppositions recur in ballad 124. To "melodie" and "dieux d'armonie" correspond the "faiz" of the poet, the enjambment with verse 5 also accentuating the *faiseurs*. The mythological reference to the Hippocrene fountain and the "poetes" correspond to "chans" and "cantique." The consistently maintained distinction is decisive in our context. *As a poet*, Machaut is not a musician, but rather, as the refrain emphasizes, a rhetorician. The distinction itself and the disciplinary anchoring of verse is explained by the work of the person mourned.

Machaut's oeuvre includes about four hundred works in verse and twelve *dits*. As an introduction to his work as a whole (and not to the early *Dit dou Vergier*, which follows it in the collection), he produced a *Prologue*: "a resume of the poet's whole work, as much in its form as in its content,"[14] a text that "reflects the work and is a reflection of the work."[15] The *Prologue*, the most important source for the study of Machaut's poetics, includes four ballads, embedded in 184 octosyllabic verses rhyming in pairs. The ballads consist of two complementary thematic groups in a relationship of 2:2. In the first group, an allegorical *Nature* brings her three children *Scens, Retorique*, and *Musique* (Sense, Rhetoric, and Music) to Guillaume the character, so that they might teach him "nouviaus dis amoureus plaisans" ("pleasing new love poems"); in the second group, *Amours* brings him his three children *Dous Penser, Plaisance*, and *Esperance* (Sweet Thought, Pleasure, and Hope) to provide the content for these works.

The rhymed couplets enclose the ballads in a frame story that develops the allegories as a didactic text. After an inventory of the genres elaborated (v. 11–18), the positive ethical value of poetry is emphasized (v. 26–84), and the powers of music are presented by means of Biblical and pagan mythological references (v. 85–146). Finally, Retorique explains the finesses of rhyme (v. 147–158). The summary already reveals what is essential in our context. Determinants of form are distinguished from determinants of content; the latter stem from the topical inventory of courtly love, while the former are gifts of nature. Both rhetoric and music bear on the *form* of the poem. "Nature is on the side of the form of poetry, Love [is on the side of] content; and we see that in Machaut's thought form is primary."[16] Courtly love as subject matter moves into the background in comparison to the detailed discussion of the formal determinants of the lyric work: Machaut sketches out "a theory of poetic creation in which the notions of form and composition are fundamental."[17]

A distinction is carefully drawn between two kinds of formal determinants: metrical structure and rhyme, on the one hand, and musical accompaniment on the other. To the successful work, Musique contributes what accounts for the poem's singability, especially melody, that is, an interval structure; the contribution of Retorique is limited to metrical structure and rhyme:

> Retorique n'ara riens enfermé
> Que ne t'envoit en metre et en rimer.
> Et Musique en donra chans,
> Tant que vorras, divers et deduisans.
>
> (Rhetoric will not have concealed anything
> That she does not send you in meter and rhyme.
> And Music will give you songs
> As many as you want, diverse and pleasing.)[18]

Scens, Nature's third child, has been discussed as an element of the pair *matere-scens* (content-sense) with respect to the works of Chrétien de Troyes.[19] In the latter's writings, Jean Rychner observed, the two terms still form an "occasional couple."[20] Jacqueline Cerquiglini has shown that in contrast to that, in Machaut's works the pair has become firmly established:[21] "Par Scens aras ton engin enfourmé/De tout ce que tu vourras confourmer [. . .]" ("By Sens your mind will be informed/Of everything you will want compose").[22] Scens encourages composition, chooses the form, and conducts the *ars*—that is, the semantic niches occupied, according to Godefroy, by the verb *enfourmer*.[23] Thus Scens coordinates Retorique and Musique as well, as is emphasized, with respect to both *plaisance* (pleasure) and *sagesse* (wisdom): "Et il aourne en son langage/Par maniere plaisant et sage./Car Scens y est qui tout gouverne [. . .]" ("And he orders in his language/ Pleasantly and wisely./For Scens is there and governs all [. . .]").[24] Practically speaking—that is, with respect to the coordination of metrical discourse and the melody accompanying the poem—Scens's achievement is limited, as John Stevens has proposed, to numerical homology, the common measure, a common "structure."[25] The intrinsic right that this structuring can claim is narrowly limited. For Machaut, the poet is merely an "instrument" of Nature. The construction using the expression *faire faire quelque chose* is unambiguous here:

> Je, Nature, par qui tous est fourmé
> Quanqu'a ça jus et seur terre et en mer,
> Viens ci a toy, Guillaume, qui fourmé
> T'ay a part, *pour faire par toy fourmer*
> Nouviaus dis amoureus plaisans.
>
> (I, Nature, by whom all is formed
> down here on both land and sea,
> I come to you, Guillaume, who have formed
> On your own, *to cause you to form*
> New pleasant love poems.)[26]

Though the poet is also seen as singled out by Nature, artistic creation remains a matter of executing and completing what is inherent in the natural order. This is to be underscored, since Machaut also establishes relationships with the "holistic" concept of music—and not despite but rather, as has been shown, in a way complementary to the often cited verses "Et musique est une science/Qui vuet qu'on rie et chante et dance" ("And music is a science/That wants us to laugh and sing and dance").[27] However, in accord with the subsumption of metrical structure and rhyme under rhetoric, the relationships must be limited to music in the narrow sense. The latter is related to the order of Creation and conceived first of all as a song praising God:

> Puet on penser chose plus digne
> Ne faire plus gracieus signe
> Com essaucier Dieu et sa gloire,
> Loer, servir, amer et croire,
> Et sa douce mere, en chantant,
> Qui de grace et de bien a tant
> Que le ciel et toute la terre
> Et quanque li mondes enserre,

Grant, petit, moien et mensu
En sont gardé et soustenu?

(Can one imagine anything more worthy
Or make a more gracious sign
Than to exalt God and his glory,
To praise, serve, love, and believe,
And his sweet mother, by singing,
Who has so much grace and goodness
That heaven and all the earth
And however much the world contains,
Great, small, medium and measured,
Are protected and sustained by her?)[28]

Machaut knows about the choir of angels and saints that sing to God in the beyond, he knows about the ethos doctrine, and also reports about the power of the mythical Orpheus and the miracle-working powers of music.[29] Finally, as we can see in reading the following passage against the background of our reconstruction in part II, Machaut knows about the analogical relation between the one music, the musical *principium*, and the order that constitutes it, on the one hand, and its manifestation in melody, on the other hand. Whereas the allegorical Music introduced as Nature's child is always provided with a capital letter, the reference to the abstract principle fractures the concrete quality of the personification. The difference is marked by the lower-case letter:

N'instrument n'a en tout le monde
Qui seur musique ne se fonde,
Ne qui ait souffle ou touche ou corde
Qui par musique ne s'acorde.
Tous ses fais plus a point mesure
Que ne fait nulle autre mesure.

(There is no instrument in all the world
That is not based on music,
Nor any that has breath or key or string
That is not tuned by music.
All its acts [music's] measures more suitably
Than any other measure.)[30]

We have mentioned the reservations about the *ars nova* practiced by Machaut that were formulated by Pope John XXII in his extravagantis

Docta sanctorum patrum of 1323/24. The connection with the "holistic" concept of music can be situated in this context. For Machaut, the formal organization of language in poetry is anchored in the discipline of rhetoric. Thus, it displays only indirectly, via the structural homology of the musical phrase and metrical discourse, relationships with the speculative concept of music. Machaut thus argues "formalistically," but nonetheless does not emphasize the musicality intrinsic to metrical discourse in the sense of the tradition reconstructed in part II. The special significance of this finding with regard to Deschamps becomes evident when selected examples illustrate the practice of formal shaping in Machaut's work. In accord with the *Prologue*, research has given special attention to formal structure in his work. Summarizing observations and a few significant examples allow us to limit the excursus.

Machaut's rondeaux, which can serve as our first example, are commonly constructed isometrically, are for the most part based on the decasyllable,[31] and mostly consist of eight lines. In addition, there are three double rondeaux and a further elaborate form of twenty-four lines. The tendency to extend the basic form points to the future. Deschamps already preferred the form of the *rondeau double*, usually with thirteen verses rather than the simpler eight-line form. In the fifteenth century, a variety of more and more complex rondeau forms appear: the *rondeau layé, double layé, double rondeau demi-lai, rondeau jumeau, rondeau double redoublé*, etc.[32] The complex stages of development retain the circular structure constitutive of the rondeau: Machaut's poem "Ma fin est mon commencement" ("My End is My Beginning"), commonly called his "crab rondeau," is paradigmatic for the form in general. Its rhyme schemes are usually simple, although Machaut's rondeaux in particular provide a wide variety of rhyme types and schemes thoroughly inventoried by the *Arts de seconde rhetorique* of the fifteenth century,[33] including the *rime équivoque* so common in the work of the *rhétoriqueurs*.[34] The rondeau "Quant j'ay l'espart,"[35] for instance, which is composed of twenty-four tetrasyllabic lines, rhymes as follows: aabaab aabaab aabaabaabaab. In highly informative and at his time groundbreaking studies, Gilbert Reaney investigated the rondeaux's rhythmic-metrical and rhyme structure and summarized his results this way: "the varying combinations of rhymes show a definite search for variety, yet the poet always ends up with remarkable symmetry in a sort of compromise between fantasy and order."[36] Analogously, Daniel Calvez considers the suitability of the form for "a kind of roundness that harmonizes perfectly with the overall stanza structure, since the poem as a whole turns around on itself" responsible for the spread of the *rondeau quatrain* and sees the aim to create "a balance of rhymes harmonized with the structural equilibrium of the poem"[37] as the principle of the form's evolution up to 1500.

This finding can be extended to Machaut's ballads,[38] in which the isometric structure is an exception. Here the principle of isometricality is developed into the repetition of more complex metrical-rhythmical units, but it continues to be the principle of construction. The formal structure of two ballads can be given as an example. The ballad "Dous amis, oy mon complaint"[39] consists of forty-two verses in three stanzas. Each stanza is constructed in accord with the following rhyme and metrical scheme:

a	a	a	b	a	a	a	b	b	b	a	b	b	a
7	4	3	7	7	4	3	7	4	3	7	4	3	7

A form that consists of two halves, each symmetrical in itself, is repeated three times: the first half-stanza, lines 1 to 8, repeats the metrical form 7-4-3-7 with the rhyme scheme aaab, while the second half-stanza, lines 9–14, repeats the metrical form 4-3-7 with the rhyme scheme bba. The possibility that the form could be seen as *vers brisés*, as a metrical variation of isometrically sequenced heptasyllables, is suggested by Reaney's conclusion: "Unity through diversity is the key to Machaut's constructional genius."[40] At the same time, it should be emphasized that the rhythmic-metrical structure of the work is far more complex than the rhyme structure. This may confirm the conclusion drawn by John Stevens, who saw the predominance of the rhythmic as characteristic of verse set to instrumental music up to 1350 and related it to the numerical order: "[T]he aesthetics of 'number' predominated not only in the theory but in the practice [. . .] [T]his predominance bears directly upon the relationship of music and poetry."[41] The rhythmic-metrical connection integrates verbal art (here conceived on the basis of rhetoric) and the musical phrase into a whole: "Rhythm, often in most complex forms, could be far more important than the melody which went with it, [. . .]. [R]hythm in Machaut is a formal principle which binds his musical works together."[42]

It might be objected that this conclusion is hardly surprising and has little specific significance if it concerns the *formes fixes*, forms derived from folkdance songs whose characteristic feature is that they "are composed in accord with a set schema that covers the whole poem."[43] However, recent research stresses that the findings of Reaney and Stevens extend as far as the forms for which metrical *variety* is generally considered constitutive, such as the *virelai* or, to use Machaut's term, the *chanson baladée*.[44] None of Machaut's *virelais*, with the exception of *Comment qu'à moy lonteinne* and *Liement me deport*,[45] written in hexasyllables, is consistently isometric in structure. The length of the lines varies from two to nine syllables; the heptasyllable is most common, appearing in thirty-one of thirty-nine *virelais*. Each *virelai* is written in such a singular way that separate studies would be required to decipher its formal characteristics. But if such studies were undertaken, the objection could soon be refuted. For example, *Dame, vostre doux viaire*,[46] a poem consisting of forty-five lines, has the following structure in meter, rhyme, and musical phrasing:[47]

73	7	73	7	73	7	73	7	73	7	73	7	73	7	73	7	...
aa	b	aa	b	aa	b	aa	b	aa	b	aa	b	aa	b	aa	b	...
I	II	I	III	IV	V	IV	V	I	II	I	III	I	II	I	III	...

To represent the schema graphically, one would have to—following Robert L. Gieber—draw a horizontal spiral consisting of a total of eight loops connected through the syntagmatic axis. Comparable results could be formulated for any other *virelai*. For instance, in *Comment qu'à moy lonteinne*,[48] the refrain has four lines, and each of the three stanzas has eight lines. The refrain corresponds in the number of verses and syllables, but also in rhyme, with *frons* and *cauda*: the same cross-rhyme, abab, is repeated every four lines. A form this complex can hardly be structured symmetrically, and with regard to these *virelais* it is hard to avoid agreeing with Gieber that "writing down the metric scheme with the rhyme and musical scheme, one has the impression of writing down an algebraic formula or cabalistic ratio."[49] Structural (including rhythmic) variety seems to put Machaut's works firmly within the aesthetics of the *ars nova* as it has been outlined by Dorit Tanay.[50] Still, as David Maw has shown using the example of the coordination of mensuration and meter in Machaut's polyphonic songs, these complex variations are to be seen as "deformations of music conceived within a regular meter,"[51] as variations sublated in equivalence on higher levels of formal organization. Analogously, Poirion describes the principle underpinning the formal registers of Machaut's poetic works as "arithmetic abstraction."[52]

The poems by Machaut cited here bespeak a sophisticated *sense of form* that—if we take into account the fact that these poems were usually recited with instrumental accompaniment in public or semipublic spaces, and that the *virelai* was even sung while dancing—modern recipients presumably have lost. We may well raise the question whether the complex system of equivalences that underlies Machaut's formal art is invested semantically. However, the scholarship cited up to this point has made it clear that the genuine accent of this lyrical poetry falls not on this possible semantic dimension, but rather on the syntagmatic organization of equivalences as such. The crucial point is to recognize these equivalences as structural elements of a given *form*. Each equivalence creates reference points that make the formal framework of a complex structure "audible." Perceiving form thus means perceiving specific redundancies in a sequence of stimuli: redundancy and interruption, repetition and variation.[53]

In the narrower context of Machaut's work, this concept of form makes it possible to take into account the structural relationship between the musical phrase and the text. Regarding Machaut's music, Reaney has noted that "[t]here were points of rest, often at a considerable distance from each other, where all parts were in perfect consonance, but between these nodes dissonance of all kinds could occur."[54] Analogously, Michel Zink has formulated this, not accidentally in "musical" metaphors, using as his example the refrain in *formes fixes*: "The aesthetics of the refrain thus very naturally leads to repetition, which does not, however, define it at the origin. It plays [. . .] on dissonance and consonance, on rupture and familiarity."[55] Marie-Louise Göllner has extrapolated from both findings and suggested that we see Machaut's musical works and his lyrical poems as complementary insofar as both are built on the elementary distinction between contrast and repetition.[56] In the context of our investigation, the stimulating power of the examples cited here lies in the fact that the operationalization of these concepts led in practice to works for which a homologous *numerical* order combining verbal art and musical phrase, a *numerositas* equally appropriated by both, can be seen as constitutive. Machaut's poems can be viewed as *musica* in the sense reconstructed in part II of this study—but the reflection on poetics in the *Prologue* anchors metrics and rhyme in rhetoric. Among the lyrical poems, the group that can be conceptualized on the basis of disciplinary rhetoric and the group that can be conceptualized on the basis of disciplinary music seem in practice to be identical. Which conception of lyrical poetry stands behind a given work, the rhetorical or the "musical," cannot be determined from the work itself, and seems to have little practical relevance around 1370. *For precisely that reason*, Deschamps's deviation from Machaut's guidelines is significant. With regard to lyrical poetry, disciplinary rhetoric and music constitute two independent and independently established reflective discourses. As reflective discourses, they are *coextensive* in respect of their *objects*, but open up completely different *horizons of thought* concerning the legitimacy and relevance of poetry and the founding concepts of artistic creation and the work of art.

Although the concept of poetry set forth in Machaut's *Prologue* allowed, with certain restrictions, metrical discourse to be separated from instrumental accompaniment and understood as a rhetorical practice in its own right, Deschamps's *Art de dictier* did not make use of this option. Instead, he opted for the conception of metrical discourse as music. In distinguishing on the semantic level between Machaut the *rethorique* and Machaut the musician or composer, Deschamps's *double ballade* on the death of Machaut takes into account the view that the latter himself formulated in the *Prologue*. The *Art de dictier* thus deviates from Machaut through its recourse to the classificatory inventory handed down in the discourse of speculative music theory and through the appeal to a fundamentally different discursive horizon for reflection on lyrical poetry. The concept of form to which this discursive restitution leads is to be taken into account, for example, when we assess the formal elaboration of Deschamps's *double ballade* on Machaut's death, to which we return in the conclusion to this section.

In the analysis already cited, Jean-Claude Mühlethaler observes that the *Art de dictier* distinguishes itself from Machaut and formulates hypotheses regarding the reasons for this. These hypotheses are based on Dragonetti's studies:

> The "art poétique" that defines the double funereal elegy is not—this must be emphasized—the one provided by the *Art de dictier* written by Deschamps in 1392, that is, fifteen years later. The two ballads, a final homage paid to the dead poet, echo Machaut's conceptions. In the chapter "De musique," the *Art de dictier* connects poetry with music and not with rhetoric, and this is quite unusual at the time. [. . .] This is a profession of faith in the autonomy of the poem, Roger Dragonetti remarks, and the *Art de dictier* marks a double rupture: first with the earlier lyric tradition, and second with the Boethian tradition in music. In our view, the rupture is emphasized by the negative valorization of music: the *Art de dictier* takes a position opposite to the funeral elegies and their exaltation of song, of the melody of Machaut's work.[57]

The breaks outlined here once again have been refuted by our reconstruction in part II, insofar as the tradition of medieval music theory is concerned. Mühlethaler adopts Dragonetti's sweeping interpretations and sharpens them in the specific context: the depreciation of *musique artificiele* as opposed to *musique naturele* is supposed to correspond to the distancing from the musician and composer Machaut. If Deschamps's conception of metrical discourse as *musique naturele* were to be understood not as a break with an "earlier lyric tradition," but, in the suggested sense, as a shift in the discursive frame of reference for reflection on the theory of poetry, then what is presented in the *Art de dictier* in the mode of meta-poetic reflection could already be illustrated in the *double ballade* by a closely focused examination of its formal structure.

The two ballads, pragmatically *discours* of a weakly defined authorial *I*-*Origo*,[58] each consist of twenty-four conventional decasyllables, with a caesura after the fourth syllable. Compared with Machaut's work in ballads, we are dealing here with a long and complex form; this is exponentially true for the double ballad intended for parallel recitation. The syntagmatic organization of the ballads corresponds to this view, and displays symmetries and complex phenomena of redundancy on all structural levels of the text. It is these formal aspects that are of primary interest in the framework of our investigation. Both ballads share not only the decasyllable but also the refrain, the rhyme scheme, which is identical in all stanzas (abab/bcbc), and the rhymes themselves. Each of the six stanzas of the *double ballade* is in itself symmetrically constructed. The rhyme scheme is dominated by soft vowels, verses rhyming in [~wa], joined in cross-rhyme with verses rhyming in [~i] in the first half-stanza, which is devoted to praising Machaut, and with the unvoiced plosive [~ik] in the second half-stanza, which is devoted to the complaint. These variations in rhyme remain the same in each stanza. The half-stanzas are constructed in inverse symmetry, as the rhyme scheme shows; each stanza closes, to use Michel Zink's formulation, "in a circle":[59]

```
10  10  10  10  10  10  10  10  10  10  10  10  10  10  10  10  10  10  10  10  10  10  10  10
a   b   a   b   b   c   b   C   a   b   a   b   b   c   b   C   a   b   A   b   b   c   b   C
a   b   a   b   b   c   b   C   a   b   a   b   b   c   b   C   a   b   A   b   b   c   b   C
```

The schema appears as a triple repetition of the whole of a form, rhythmically structured by the refrain and doubled by a second "voice." Assuming roughly equal syllable lengths, the two recitations join together after every eight syllables, and after every seven verses in the refrain. The rhythmical structure is—here we make use of musical metaphors for lack of more convincing alternatives—to be understood as "voice leading": The "voices" separate, are led in parallel after equal periods of time in each case, then separate again, coincide again, separate, until the conclusion especially orchestrates the final merger through the expansion of the equivalence: in the twenty-third verse of each ballad, the rhyme *noir-devoir* in the fourth syllable heralds the "premature" coincidence of the two "voices" in the word *plourez* in the fifth and sixth syllables after the caesura; the rhyming toponyms *Champenois* and *Galois* at the end of the line complement the refrain and underscore the imperative *plourez*. The variations, for instance the cross rhyme between the first and second half-stanzas, respectively, are

embedded in a system of redundancies constituted by repetitions of a syn-
chronic (by different "voices") and diachronic (stanza for stanza) type—a
system that *sublates all differences in a system of equivalences*. The text
displays *the play of the same in the different*. We can point to counterparts
in text semantics, especially the isotopies and oppositions that structure
the text and present the universality of the grief manifested, significantly,
in "musical" terms.[60] However, this would lead away from the formal aspects that are primarily relevant here. The *double ballade* may convey how
Machaut saw himself, and it may lend expression to his thinking about
poetry. The *form* of the *double ballade*, the intricate "rhythmic"-prosodic
structure of the long, isometric ballad form displays what the *Art de dictier*
was to provide, a decade and a half later, with its own accent, though not
necessarily in opposition to Machaut's poetic concepts. What it displays is
the intrinsic and specific "musicality" of metrical discourse, but not in the
sense that the register of possible euphonies was exhausted. The "musicality" of metrical discourse does not imply, primarily or even necessarily,
statements regarding the euphonic quality of this discourse. "Musical" is
a *form*, manifest in metrical constraint, rhythmical structure, and circular
closure, that is, a form being a "whole" due to a determined relationality
of its components characterizable in terms of *aequalitas* or *similitudo*. Its
balance, attraction, and effects are due to the form's "wholeness" alone:
to the sublation of variety into equivalence—into the principle of *the One
and the Same*. It is this concept of form that relates the *Art de dictier* to the
discourse of speculative music theory.

Re-reading the *Art de dictier*

Deschamps discusses music in the disciplinary context whose appropriation
for the analogical order of discourse we were able to trace in Augustine's
De ordine. The discussion of music in the framework of the *septem artes
liberales* fundamentally distinguishes the *Art de dictier* from the Aristotelian
ordo scientiarum.

Like the fifteenth-century *Arts de seconde rhetorique*,[61] the *Art de dictier*
was conceived as a handbook; Deschamps dedicated it to his "tresgrant
et especial seigneur" ("very great and special lord").[62] This may explain
the strikingly low degree of elaboration noted by the last editor of the *Art
de dictier* in view of the complexity of the theoretical elements touched
upon.[63] Whereas the section on music is distinguished by its length, mode
of argumentation, and conceptual emphasis from the brief sections devoted
to the other arts, the latter are more strongly outlined practically. The arts
appear as a means of organizing the earthly world: "les vij arts et sciences

par lesquelles ce present monde est gouverne [. . .]" ("the seven arts and sciences by which this world of ours is governed").[64]

Just as in the section on geometry the stonemason shapes the rough block of stone, so the poet shapes language. As was shown in the survey of scholarship, attempts have been made to see in the transforming consciousness and developing self-esteem of "work" an important proof of the proto-modern character of the poetry of the fifteenth century in general and of the *rhétoriqueurs* in particular.[65] We began by reconstructing, on the basis of Augustine's *De musica*, the concept of work and artistry which functions in the horizon of the concept of *ordo* and the "holistic" concept of music. We saw that the discourse of speculative music theory and thus also the subsumption of poetic art under music imply a *positive* assessment of work on verbal form with regard to the exceptional power of its products. But this positive assessment of work for the sake of its product was necessarily accompanied by the devaluation of the artist with respect to his originary creativity. Still more, this devaluation was the presupposition for the positive assessment of artistic work, insofar as the anagogic relevance of the product of this work depended on the latter's exclusively "imitative" and "actualizing" character.[66]

The abstract nature of this devaluation of human work must be noted: the preceding creation *ex nihilo* includes *all possible forms*. Everything that can exist exists qua originary creation by God, and every actual creation is thus an imitation of an originary divine model. To be sure, we can repeatedly find emphatic assertions of the value of human work in Antiquity and the Middle Ages. There was never any lack of pride in craftsmanship, including that of the poet. What is crucial is the basis for this pride. If it is connected with the mastery of the *ars*, it is either (within limits) legitimate or undetermined in worth. In contrast, from the point of view of the doctrine reconstructed in part II, originary creation is simply impossible for the artist or craftsman. An appreciation of human work on the basis of its "creative" implications would be deemed condemnable, an act of hubris, and moreover: an epistemological misunderstanding, an error in ontology. According to Hans Blumenberg's studies, which carefully evaluate the sources, this conception remains dominant far into the fifteenth century. It is explicitly opposed for the first time in the work of Nicolas of Cusa (1401–1464), whose spoon-carver marked an epochal change with the lapidary phrase "Coclear extra mentis nostrae ideam aliud non habet exemplar" ("Other than the idea in our mind, the spoon has no model").[67] In French poetic theory, the consequences of this change await to be drawn until the work of Jacques Peletier du Mans (1517–1582).[68]

The traditional abstract argument was connected with a simple distinction in "artistic" practice. "Imitation" in the sense defined above can be carried out in a theoretically informed way and accordingly with an awareness of the relative inferiority of the activity. Generally, this does not occur: someone who has looked into the order of creation will not waste his time producing contingent goods. As a rule, the "imitator" is not aware of his models—he creates out of instinct, as Augustine says in *De musica* I.4.7, seconded by Boethius. To quote the latter's often-cited words about the poet: "The second category of those who concern themselves with music is that of the poets [*genus poetarum*], who are led to music not so much by speculation and reason [*non speculatione ac ratione*], but by some natural instinct [*quam naturali quodam instinctu fertur ad carmen*]."[69] The use of the passive voice must be emphasized here. The *instinctus naturalis* is the agent in accord with which the *poeta* creates "musical," that is, metrical, discourse. He may be aware of the value of his work, he may be as self-conscious as any other craftsmen. Insofar as it arises from instinct, his work goes in no way beyond the Creator's originary *creatio*. If we read them using the proper philological tools, this is the argument Deschamps's passages on *musique naturele* convey.

After an introductory passage on the *effectus musicae*, which appeared in the same position and with the same function in the work of Boethius and then became conventional in medieval treatises on the theory of music, Deschamps classifies music according to the established distinction between *musique naturele* and *musique artificiele. Musique naturele* presupposes (as the conditional structure of the sentence suggests) a previous mastery of the *ars*, but "elle ne puet estre aprinse a nul, se son propre couraige naturelment ne s'i applique."[70] The noun *couraige* is open to different readings. Greimas's reference work on Middle French affirms the intentional connotation that the modern reader will be inclined to discern, paraphrasing the noun as "détermination intérieure, volonté, énergie, zèle" ("inner determination, will, energy, zeal"). Nevertheless, Greimas retains as the primary meaning the unspecific "dispositions de l'âme, [. . .] l'ensemble des sentiments et attitudes" ("mental dispositions, [. . .] the whole of feelings and attitudes").[71] The verb *s'appliquer* emphasizes the intentional component, this may have provided part of the basis for the interpretive approaches summarized in part I. The agent behind the intention is determined by the adverb *naturelement*, which in the late fourteenth century occupied a semantic niche different from the one it occupies in modern French. Greimas defines this—*nota bene*—as "instinctivement, conformément aux lois de la nature" ("instinctively, in conformity with the laws of nature").[72] The philologically secured reading of the short passage thus brings it close to the conception of the poet in chapter I.34 of Boethius's *Institutio musica*. The use of the adverb *naturelement* is plausible as a paraphrase of Boethius's reference to *instinctus naturalis*. It occupies the same semantic niche as the Latin term, whereas both the adjective *instinctif* and the adverbial derivative *instinctivement* are not attested before 1801.[73]

In view of the wide distribution of the passage this finding does not prove that Deschamps drew on Boethius directly. However, it offers further evidence for what remains of Dragonetti's thesis, namely that the *Art de dictier* was inscribed in the discourse reconstructed in part II. The passage at the same time provides important evidence for the conception of poetry that Deschamps's *Art de dictier* formulates. The person who creates *musique naturele* creates "out of instinct" (in Boethius's sense) what is, by effect at least, in accord with *musica scientia*. Neither the valorization of work, of the *technique* of versification, above and beyond the one described in detail in chapters five and six above, nor in particular the "inspiration" of the poet that Sinnreich-Levy wanted to see in this passage,[74] can be extracted from the quoted phrase.

The "musicality" of metrical discourse consists, in accord with the originally Varronian definition of *musica scientia* as *scientia bene modulandi*, in the specific *numerositas* of the line, in its *measure*. Augustine's *De musica* had related the Neopythagorean and Neoplatonic ontology of number to the Biblical phrase from the *Liber scientiae* 11.21 and thus acquired a concept of *ordo entium* in accord with the Christian doctrine of original creation: a concept of order conceived as an inventory of forms, comprising the *measure* of metrical discourse. The depreciation of metrical discourse with respect to the "originality" of its form was the counterpart of its valorization as a manifestation of the *ordo entium* particularly well suited to the human cognitive faculty, as anagogically relevant, as a "sign of truth." The relation established between numerical form in metrical discourse and the order of creation was preserved in Thomism and survived in music theory down to the late Middle Ages. For the understanding of reflection on versification on the model of medieval music theory, this complex turned out to be crucial: it is not if or because it is "musical" in nature that the work makes the order of Creation manifest; rather, *it is only because it makes the order of Creation manifest that the concrete work is music at all. As musica,* the poetic discourse produced qua *instinctus naturalis* is a sensible concretization of the *ordo entium*, a "concretization of the whole of reality."[75] The reference to the "musicality" of metrical discourse correspondingly accentuates, as its essential quality, its specific *numerositas*, its measure, and indirectly a specific conception of form that refers to a relationality determined by *aequalitas* or *similitudo*. If we read Deschamps's statements in the horizon of the discourse of speculative music theory in the Middle Ages,[76] the text becomes completely comprehensible.

The introductory passage on the *effectus musicae* invokes the genre conventions of treatises on music theory. The distinction of *partes* or *genera musicae* complies with these conventions as well. It is in this context that Deschamps makes use of the classification of music established since Regino of Prüm: "Et est a scavoir que nous avons deux musiques, dont l'une est artificiele et l'autre est naturele" ("It must be recognized that we have two musics, one of which is artificial and the other natural").[77] We should note the use of the first person plural, and the verb *avoir*. Two kinds of music "are peculiar to humans," "humans can produce two kinds of music"— that is how this passage can be understood. *Both interpretations* emphasize humans' *instrumentum naturalis*, the voice.[78] *Musique artificiele* refers to the singing of the tones of the scale, and presupposes an acquired technical ability. In this passage Deschamps argues in a way similar to that of Aribo Scholasticus: "L'artificiele [. . .] est appellee artificiele de son art, car par ses vj notes, [. . .], l'en puet aprandre a chanter, acorder, doubler, quintoier, tiercoier, tenir, deschanter, par figure de notes, par clefs et par lignes, le plus rude homme du monde" ("Artificial [music] is called artificial in kind because with its six notes, [. . .] one can teach the least cultivated person in the world to sing, harmonize, sing seconds, fifths, and thirds, to sing the tenor or descant parts, using notes, clefs, and lines").[79] *Musique naturele* is defined as "musique de bouche" (vocal music) as well, but is not distinguished from *musique artificiele* in this respect. Its specific feature is that the measure that constitutes its "musicality" is not manifested in measured intervals, but rather in a formal determinant of discourse, as a measured number of syllables: "L'autre musique est appellee naturele [. . .] et est une musique de bouche en proferant paroules metrifiees [. . .]" ("The other music is called natural [. . .] and is a vocal music that utters measured words").[80] *Numerositas*, manifested in ways that are specific to each case but nonetheless "holistically" homologous, constitutes both singing in intervals and metrical discourse as music.

The structural homology of *musique artificiele* and *musique naturele*, which follows from the fact that both are founded on a numerical order, is characterized by Deschamps with the remark that "ces deux musiques sont si consonans l'une aveques l'autre" ("these two musics are thus consonant with one another").[81] In *De institutione arithmetica*, Boethius had conceived "consonant" proportions not as *specific* elements of the numerical order, not as elements of the numerical order among others, but as elements inherent in the numerical order *as such*: a "mixture" of *natura eiusdem* and *natura alterius*, of identity and difference, unity and plurality, immobility and movement, merged in *amicitia*. Insofar as both *musiques* are to be conceived as variants of *modulatio* and every *modulatio* presupposes a numerical measure, the "consonance" of *musique naturele* and *musique artificiele* designates nothing more or else than the foundation of both *musiques* in the numerical order. Deschamps's use of the term "consonance" is thus consistent with the Boethian concept.[82]

Dragonetti had argued that Deschamps's reference to the "consonance" of metrical discourse and the sung interval presupposed his having "forgotten" the concept's original context in the speculative conception of music, "[the] forgetting of what used to constitute the truth of all music"[83] and provided the basis for the new self-sufficiency of metrical discourse. Deschamps is supposed to have derived from Boethius's music theory the concept of a possible consonance of *musique naturele* and *musique artificiele*, though his formulations remained unclear with regard to the concept of consonance involved.[84] At the same time, Dragonetti was sure about Deschamps limiting himself to music perceptible through the senses: "Eustache Deschamps's conception moves almost entirely in the domain of a music that exists only at the phenomenal level."[85] The opposite is the case. Against the background of the reconstructed tradition of speculative music theory, it is precisely the presupposition of Deschamps's argument that the principle of every kind of "musicality" remains located beyond phenomenal existence. In addition, the distinction between *musique naturele* and *musique artificiele* as such does not fundamentally dissociate recitation from instrumental practice, but instead conceives *both* as a music, insofar as a specific measure, a specific *numerositas* underlies both of them. Observations on performative practice and arguments of the type "musical accompaniment and recitation separate at this or that point in time" remain unaffected by this result, but are irrelevant for the assessment of Deschamps's argument.[86] Moreover, preferring metrical discourse to *musique artificiele* is not innovative as such. For example, the gloss on the *Échecs amoureux,* which adheres closely to Boethius, contrasts lines "measured" by the number of syllables, presented as "droicte musique" ("genuine music"), with the "music" of what is clearly the sung word or instrumental accompaniment: "[L]a musique principal qui est trouvee es rymes et es mettres doit estre rapportee au nombre des sillabes plus que a son ne a chant qui y puist estre. Briefment, c'est la droite musique qui y est" ("The principal music which is found in rhymes and meters must be related to the number of syllables more than to the sound or song that may be in it. In short, it is the genuine music that is in them [in rhymes and meters]").[87]

Once again, relating the text to the discourse of speculative music theory makes the "formalistic" emphasis of the *Art de dictier* central, but suggests an understanding of this emphasis that differs from the one that Deschamps scholarship has presented up to this point. The reading proposed here is able to come to an understanding of the following difficult paragraph, which deals with this formalism:

> Et ja soit ce que ceste musique naturele se face de volunte amoureuse a
> la louenge des dames, et en autres manieres, selon les materes et le sente-
> ment de ceuls qui en cest musique s'appliquent, et que les faiseurs d'icelle
> ne saichent pas communement la musique artificiele ne donner chant par
> art de notes a ce qu'ilz font, toutesvoies est appellee musique ceste science
> naturele pour ce que les diz et chansons par eulx fait ou les livres metrifiez
> se lisent de bouche, et proferent par voix non pas chantable, tant que les
> douces paroles ainsis faictes et recordees par voix plaisant aux escoutans
> qui les oyent, [. . .].

> (And even if this natural music is made out of amorous desire in praise
> of ladies and in other ways, according to the subjects and the feeling of
> those who apply themselves to this music, and even if those who make it
> usually do not know *musique artificiele* or how to give by means of notes
> a song to what they make, nevertheless this natural science is called mu-
> sic because the *dits* and songs they make or the versified books are read
> aloud, and speak with a voice that does not sing, as long as the sweet
> words [are] made in this way and recalled in a pleasing voice to the audi-
> ence that hears them, [. . .].)[88]

The expression *ja soit que* and the conjunction *toutesvoies* organize the paragraph: Even if courtly love or another cause owing to the poet's feeling, his "instinctive impulse," influenced the production of *musique naturele*, and even if the poet knows only about "his" music, metrical discourse, and not about *musica melica*, *musique naturele* is nonetheless music, insofar as it is on the one hand a discourse, sound of the *instrumentum naturalis*, and on the other hand metrical, "measured," and as such provides enjoyment. The criterion for the "musicality" of verse is the measure of the verse line, a purely formal criterion, and therefore it remains free of all aspects going be-yond the latter, for example those concerning the writer's disposition or the-matic questions. Thus a concept of form is established that can be grasped systematically on the basis of Augustine: "[F]ormas habent, quia numeros habent: adime illis haec, nihil erunt" ("They have forms because they have numbers; separate them and there will be nothing").[89] Deschamps's paragraph is based on separating the lyrical form from its pragmatic "filling." With respect to the latter, lyrical form is prior and constitutive for the specific "musicality" of metrical discourse.

This concept of lyrical form includes by definition every form of equivalence and thus the bases for taking pleasure in the work: "Nihil [. . .] est horum sensibilium, quod nobis non aequalitate aut similitudine placeat. Ubi autem aequalitas aut similitudo, ibi numerositas" ("For there is nothing [. . .] in these sensible things that does not please us with equality and similarity. Where there is equality or similarity, however, there is harmony of numbers"):[90] that is how Augustine viewed the connection. Insofar as in Creation every form of relationality to be qualified as *aequalitas* refers to unity and equality in God himself and the "musical" phenomenon is *musica* insofar as it displays such relationality in a sensible form, poetic equivalence constitutes a dimension of meaning that may at times supplement the primary text semantics,[91] but on the whole cannot be reduced to that function. The conception of metrical discourse as music, the recourse to the terminology and theoretical elements of the discourse of speculative music theory, and the clear demarcation from Guillaume de Machaut's model indicates which discursive horizon this dimension of meaning opens up.

The "formalism" that can be derived from this conception of form is of a kind entirely different from the one summarized in part I, which tends to project modernistic positions. At the same time it is completely different in kind from the formalism that has been derived from courtly love poetry ever since the publication of Robert Guiette's standard work, "D'une poésie formelle en France au Moyen Age."[92] Neither does the formalism reflected in the connection of metrical discourse with the "holistic" conception of music constitute a poetic "autonomy" that would "playfully disassemble" the primary linguistic code, nor is the corresponding concept of poetry located in a necessary genetic relationship with the courtly love lyric that Guiette thinks can be described by means of an inventory of fixed topoi and a set of rules of usage,[93] even if homologies result and the boundaries of the strands of meta-poetic reflection are permeable.[94] Guiette himself indicated the starting point for possible homologies:

The poet plays. His work is an abstraction, a number that signifies on the level of this vocal music of the articulated and sung word. There is a poetry that emanates from this number, and it is essential. [. . .] poetry, in courtly songs, is situated entirely in the form, in the realized, existing object, whose usage is known. Style is everything and the ideological argument is no more than a "material." [. . .] The poetry of the courtly songs can exist only on a level opposed to that on which the poetry of Romanticism is located. We have to read these songs as we read musical forms [. . .].[95]

This methodological imperative also holds for poetry conceptualized in accord with the model of the discourse of speculative music theory, but it presupposes a clarification of the question as to *how* a "musical form" is to be read in the historical context. As music in Deschamps's sense, as metrical discourse, versification manifests synecdochally forms that make available to the senses the order of Creation structured by "measure, number, and weight." The conception of metrical discourse as music constitutes form as a *signum* that refers to the *unum principium* of everything created, and in this respect testifies to the continuity of the Christian order of discourse beyond the nominalist challenge to its theological basis. John Stevens noted this connection in his studies on poetry and music between 1050 and 1350 and was able to situate it in its disciplinary horizon, though unspecifically, for lack of a substantial analysis of writing on music theory:

> Needless to say, so far from diminishing, depreciating, the art of poetry by classing it as music, this conception, a commonplace of medieval theory, gives it the highest praise. Poetry is seen as one of the works of the Divine Mind that creates all things, by number, weight, and measure. It is for this reason that Deschamps insists that the speech-music of poetry is indeed music. [. . .] Deschamps's theory does not break with the past in any fundamental respect.[96]

It is no accident that Stevens clearly distanced himself from Dragonetti's break-hypotheses and assertions regarding discontinuities.[97] The "triumphant movement of musical naturalism"[98] asserted by Dragonetti is a chimera, insofar as it implies that the "holistic" conception of music lost its function or that its world-shaping quality became petrified across the board. The result of our research thus strictly opposes the conception of the text as a protomodern claim of autonomy for which, in addition to Dragonetti, especially Kenneth Varty and Sylvia Huot have argued. The *Art de dictier* presupposes theoretical elements that refer to the analogical order of discourse. The conception of lyrical poetry as music exploits a scope of legitimacy that had remained open for metrical discourse since the colonization of Neopythagorean and Neoplatonic ontology of number, and refers back to Plotinus.[99] Refraining from any claims to "poetic autonomy" is the price this conception pays for this.

The results of our research can integrate those aspects of Eustache Deschamps's work that encouraged the formulation of the autonomy hypothesis, and first of all the marked practical-ethical profile of his *balades de moralitez*. If the *lyrical form* as "musical" ensures relevance and legitimacy, its *pragmatic "filling"* opens up a broad subject area delimited only unspecifically by the general rules of Christian morals and practical ethics. These rules are also integrated into and present within the discourse of speculative music theory. We have proven the continuous claim of music theory from Christian late Antiquity down to the late Middle Ages in France that the perception of musical form encourages the activity of the *intellectus* and is salutary for body and mind, is at the same time pleasing to the senses, and has a positive value in Christian ethics. We have tracked the corresponding argument in detail in Augustine's *De musica*. We must accordingly recognize that Deschamps's concentration on formal determinants and the thematic scope of his lyrics are *complementary*, without this complementarity proving or even presupposing that poetic discourse has any form of "autonomy." How this complementarity is to be understood in detail is shown by the possible sources for the thematic register of Deschamps's poetry that research has identified.

Possible Sources: Two Hypotheses

The attempt to identify the precise sources from which Deschamps drew the conceptual tools for his recourse to music theory is inevitably defeated by the extremely small body of biographical sources, on the one hand, and the extensive number of texts from which the theoretical elements on which the *Art de dictier* is based could have been taken on the other. Here, the hegemony of the "holistic" concept of music down to the late Middle Ages makes things more difficult. Nonetheless, on the basis of the given sources, two hypotheses may be formulated. The first hypothesis follows from the few biographical sources we know. The second hypothesis can tap the current results of Deschamps philology for our interpretative approach and, substantiated by a possible source, suggest that the "musical" concept of poetry and the broadening of the thematic register since Deschamps should be seen, *on the basis of the "holistic" concept of music*, as complementary.

The *Art de dictier* situates music in the curricular context that had been made obsolescent by the transformation of the *ordo scientiarum* since the twelfth century: the older canon of the *artes liberales* preserved in the faculties of arts corresponds to the one developed in Augustine's *De ordine*. The theoretical profile of the section on music in the *Art de dictier* suggests the possibility of more closely defining Deschamps's sources on the basis of this curricular anchorage. Whereas sources are largely lacking for the famed elementary education in Champagne in the fourteenth and fifteenth centuries,[100] the history of the University of Orléans is well documented. The *collegia* of the city, which had been centers for ecclesiastical and secular studies since the ninth century, and in the early thirteenth century were still famous for the *ars dictaminis* and chancellery training, were gradually decaying. They "fell into decadence before the end of the thirteenth century, and [. . .] were eclipsed by the schools of law,"[101] whose foundation had been authorized by Gregory IX on 17 January 1235.[102] The University of Orléans, founded as an educational institution for canon law in 1306 by Pope Clement V with the bull *Inter Cetera*, called *Ordinatio Studii Aurelianensis*,[103] became in the fifteenth century one of the most famous universities in France. Guillaume Budé, Jean Calvin, Étienne de la Boétie, Agrippa d'Aubigné, and later Molière and Jean de la Bruyère are among its alumni. Deschamps, born in 1340, also studied law there between 1358 and 1366,[104] but cannot have completed the whole course of study in that length of time.

Scholarly contributions to the history of the University of Orléans and its statutes suggest that there are important gaps in Deschamps's biography. To be enrolled in the course of study in law at the University of Orléans, one had to have already completed the program in *artes*.[105] This explains the advanced age, by medieval standards, of most of the students. Whereas the University of Paris allowed students to take the baccalaureate examination when they were only fourteen, as late as 1528 the Venetian ambassador, after visiting Orléans, noted that students there, in contrast to what was usual elsewhere in France, were already adults: "tutti uomini, e non come negli altri studii di Franza, garzoni" ("all grown men, and not, as in other schools in France, boys").[106] If Deschamps studied in Orléans between 1358 and 1362, then he was about eighteen when he enrolled there, and twenty-two when he left the university prematurely, an unusually advanced age by medieval standards[107] that corresponds to the Venetian ambassador's observation.

Charles Vulliez's studies on the history of the University of Orléans in the late Middle Ages draw our attention to a detail that is crucial in our context. As already noted, enrollment for the study of law at the University of Orléans presupposed completion of propaedeutic studies in the *artes liberales*. If we are willing to allow the extrapolation of biographical data from Deschamps's extensive occasional poetry, his ballad 225 suggests that he too completed the study of the *artes*, including the quadrivial disciplines: "Tous les .vii. ars oy en ma retentive" ("I have in my memory all the seven arts").[108] However, this preparatory study could not have been done in Orléans. In the fourteenth century, the university did not have its own faculty of arts in which a knowledge of the quadrivial disciplines could be obtained: "In Orléans there was no faculty of arts, but only grammar schools (and perhaps schools of logic—we leave aside here the teaching of theology in the Dominican monastery)."[109] Information concerning the textbooks used in these extramural colleges or even the library holdings in Orléans is not to be had. Neither the extant statutes from 1288–1296 nor the papal bull on the founding of the university in 1305 indicate the prescribed or recommended *textus*.[110] A copy of Boethius's *Institutio musica* made in the tenth century has been preserved in Orléans,[111] while a central, catalogued library for study, whose catalog allows us to draw conclusions about the teaching, first appeared in Orléans "at the beginning of the fifteenth century," as Jarry's studies on the history of the library and its collection prove.[112] Discoveries regarding the possible sources of the section on music thus seem unlikely to emerge from the university context. As well, we must note that the first extant catalog of the reference library at the University of Orléans, which dates from 8 February 1419, lists exclusively legal textbooks and commentaries.[113] This tends to confirm the nonexistence of university study of the *artes* in Orléans. Accordingly, concerning any student who came to the city on the Loire to study law, we must ask where the examination required for enrollment in the course of studies in law was taken. Biographical studies on Deschamps have thus far left this question unanswered.

Carpenter assumed that the *artes* were taught in Orléans by *magistri regentes* who supported themselves by "tuition fees" they themselves charged, but she offered no evidence, not to mention proofs, for this assumption.[114] On the other hand, Vulliez proved, by means of a comparison of the student registration lists (*rotuli*), that most of those enrolled in Orléans had completed these propaedeutic studies in Paris.[115] Documents from the registrar's office and the university administration—for instance, a letter from the University of Paris to the rector of the University of Orléans asking the latter to check carefully the authenticity of examination results that were presented there and were allegedly taken in Paris, in order to determine whether the *studiosus* had in fact fulfilled the study requirements[116]—suggest that Vulliez is describing a widespread practice.

It must be admitted that corresponding proofs for Eustache Deschamps are not available. Still, on the basis of the generally not very extensive biographical data on the decades preceding 1370 we cannot flatly reject the hypothesis that he was familiar with the Parisian milieu. Accordingly, this possibility and its implications must be briefly considered here. Since 1323 the quadrivial studies offered at the Sorbonne had once again included, as we have shown, *lectiones* on *musica scientia*; we can assume that the *textus* was Johannes de Muris's *Musica speculativa secundum Boethium*, a text by the teacher whose *Summa musicae* divided music, following Regino of Prüm, into *naturalis* and *artificialis*. The *libraria communis*, the Sorbonne's study library whose collection on music is documented in the catalog of 1338, made available not only two copies of Boethius's *Institutio musica*, Augustine's *De musica,* and two volumes of commentaries, presumably on Boethius's work on music, but also Jerome of Moravia's *Tractatus de musica*, written in Paris between 1272 and 1304. This text, which exploits the work of Johannes Cotto, as we have shown, and may be the source of the *musica naturalis/musica artificialis* distinction, is a plausible stimulus for the emphasis on the *instrumentum naturalis*, and moreover discusses lyrical poetry as *musica*. The hypothesis that Deschamps studied at the University of Paris's faculty of arts could thus make it possible to consider Johannes de Muris or Jerome of Moravia sources for the section on music in the *Art de dictier*. Both references would substantiate the text's connection with the discourse of speculative music theory reconstructed in part II of this study. However, this hypothesis cannot be carried beyond conjectures of the most cautious kind: we would still have to ask not only why the time spent studying in Paris is not reflected in Deschamps's work, but also why he did not "remember" his knowledge of music theory until 1392.

A second hypothesis regarding sources is connected with this last question. It arises from discoveries made by recent research on Deschamps's *ballades de moralitez*. Mühlethaler has seen the "autonomy" allegedly claimed by the *Art de dictier* as the precondition for ethical-moral and political-social commitment, and attributed to Deschamps a conception of the art of poetry that goes back to Aristotle's *Rhetoric*:

> The self-sufficiency of the poetic text claimed by the *Art de dictier* is
> the presupposition for what represents, in Deschamps's work, political
> commitment. [. . .] The ballads in question [the *ballades de moralitez*]
> illustrate a function of the poetic text that corresponds to a conception of
> rhetoric that is Aristotelian in origin.[117]

Mühlethaler's thesis raises a simple question: why derive the concept and function of poetic discourse from Aristotelian *rhetoric*, when Deschamps himself conceives it most emphatically as a form of *music*?

The reference to rhetoric is also proposed by recent Deschamps scholarship. Ludmilla Evdokimova has sought to prove, using Deschamps's *Miroir de Mariage*, that he had taken cognizance of Aristotle's *Politics*, a pseudo-

Aristotelian *Economics*, the *Nicomachean Ethics*, and the *Rhetoric* in the translations by Nicolas Oresme (1325–1382), and made use of them for his concerns.[118] At first, we might be inclined, like Mühlethaler, to consider this a view regarding Deschamps's conception of poetry that points in a direction entirely different from the one suggested by our studies. The significance and scope of our reconstruction would be reduced to a few, comparatively abstract theses. If one assesses the texts Evdokimova sees as Deschamps's sources against the background that our studies have developed, then it can be seen that the reception relationships she demonstrates not only do not contradict our working hypotheses but once again confirm our account.

The annotated translations of Aristotle produced by Nicolas Oresme, whose significance for erudition in the fourteenth century requires no emphasis,[119] were produced between 1370 and 1377 at the behest of Charles V of France. These translations were present in the latter's court library, to which Evdokimova presumes Deschamps had access,[120] and which, with 965 volumes, was in the late fourteenth century the second-largest library in Christendom after Avignon and before even the Sorbonne. They included a *Livre des Ethiques*, an annotated translation of the *Nicomachean Ethics* from 1370, *Le Livre de Politiques et Yconomiques* in one volume, which contained the translation of the *Politics* and an *Economics* attributed to Aristotle, produced in 1372,[121] and also an annotated translation of *De caelo*.[122] Evdokimova argues that the misogynistic caricature of marriage depicted in Deschamps's *Miroir de mariage*[123] could be a reworking of material taken from Oresme's translation of the *Economics*. Critical passages on the vice-ridden wife and on faulty housekeeping flank here the representation of the condition of the family and the household striven for—the family as a "cell" of the body politic. Whereas the man has to go outside the household, engage in physical labor, and yield to his tendencies to activity and occupation, the woman, who is less inclined to physical effort, is to move within the limits of her own household.[124] It is worth noting the way this text praises the complementarity of the tasks of the married couple, seen as an ideal order:

> Et donques le homme est plus chaut, plus fort et plus actif et la femme
> plus froide, plus fieble et plus passive. Et ceste contrarieté ou varieté les
> ont enclinés a diverses operations, lesquelles leur sunt profictables et con-
> venables pour conserver ensemble. Et pour ce, quant ceste contrarieté ou
> dissimilitude est naturelment et selon meurs bien proporcionee, elle est
> douce et delectable. Et selon ce disoit le Sage que homme et femme qui

sunt consentans ou en concorde ensemble, ce est une chose pleiseinte a
son esperit, approvee et loee de Dieu et des hommes. Et me semble que
ce est aussi comme en musique: la dissimilitude et inequalité des sons fait
bon acort et bonne consonance, car elle est deuement proporcionee.

(And so the man is the warmer, stronger, and more active one, and the
woman the cooler, weaker, and more passive one. And this contrariness
or variety have inclined them to diverse kinds of activities, which are beneficial to them and suited to keep them together. And that is why, when
this contrariness or dissimilitude is naturally proportioned in accord with
manners, it is sweet and delightful. And accordingly the Sage says that a
man and woman who are consenting or in harmony with each other is a
thing pleasing to his mind, approved and praised by God and men. And it
seems to me that the same is true in music: the dissimilitude and inequality of sounds makes a good harmony and a good consonance, for it is
rightly proportioned.)[125]

If the couple's *contrariété* or *dissimilitude* is joined together rightly, "in a
natural way," *naturelement,* and duly proportioned in accord with manners,
with *meurs,* as Oresme puts it, probably drawing on the expression *debita
proportio* that occurs so often in Thomas Aquinas's work, then it is "harmonic," as in music, in accord with God's commandments, and pleasing
to humans. Oresme's commentary may have been inspired by the concept
of harmony in Aristotle's *Politics*, but it immediately makes the transition
to music as the order of proportions—and thus to the concept of *ordo* that
Thomas had reconceived as an order of proportion not solely numerical in
nature. Thus the connection of the argument with the "holistic" concept of
music is prepared. The concept of a *harmonia* pervading world and man
in accord with God's good Creation itself remains functional even in the
commentaries on Aristotle and the concerns of practical ethics and economics. This is proven by Oresme's other commentaries and translations.
The anticipated mediation between Aristotelian thinking about harmony
in politics and practical ethics and the "holistic" concept of music is here
executed and spelled out in accord with Boethian teaching.

This is shown first by Oresme's annotated translation of Aristotle's *Politics*. The passages devoted to music in Book VIII of this work make us expect
elaborations of what is only hinted at in the translation of the *Economics*,
and in fact Oresme's commentary deals with music at great length. Here,
too, the results of our studies in part II are confirmed. The commentary
holds fast, in opposition to Aristotle's text, to the speculative goal of disciplinary music: "Pythagoras [. . .] trouva les proportions des sons acordables.

Et pour ce, musique est mise entre les sciences mathématiques, et est speculative et appartenant a felicité speculative ou contemplative [. . .]" ("Pythagoras [. . .] discovered the proportions of sounds that can be harmonized. And for that reason music is placed among the mathematical sciences, and it is speculative and suitable for speculative or contemplative felicity [. . .]").[126] In the framework of the *artes liberales*, music as a discipline is connected with both "musique speculative" and "musique sensible."[127] The objects of "musique sensible" are defined as follows: "[E]n musique sunt .iii. choses: Metrum, melos, gestus. Metrum, le mettre, ce est la mesure. Melos, la melodie, ce sunt les acors. Gestus, le port, ce est le mouvement du corps ou des membres" ("In music there are three things: *metrum, melos, gestus. Metrum*, the meter, is the measure. *Melos*, the melody, is the harmonies. *Gestus*, the bearing, is the movement of the body or the limbs").[128] Oresme notes: "tous mettres sunt rimes" ("all meters are rhymes"), rhyme is defined as "toute mesure convenable de sillebes ou de sons en probation ou prononciation ou semblable" ("any suitable measure of syllables or sounds being uttered or pronounced or the like").[129] Thus metrical, "measured" discourse falls under music according to Oresme as well. In addition, "musique speculative" and "sensible" remain related to each other in the familiar way. The speculative point of convergence of *both* forms of music, the anagogical potential and the "signifying" or "pointing" character of "sensible" music, which includes verse as *metrum* or *mettre*, remain, and this should be emphasized, a core thesis of Oresme's commentary: "Or savons donques comment musique speculative et intellectuele est cause de delectation et de consolation. Et la musique sensible donne occasion de considerer de la speculative. Et ovecques ce, elle prepare l'ame a la speculation" ("Now therefore we know how speculative and intellectual music is the cause of delight and consolation. And sensible music provides an occasion for considering the speculative. And with this, it prepares the soul for speculation").[130]

The speculative accent of music theory, the aforementioned delight and the ethos doctrine are, for Oresme as well, part of a functional complex. First, the ethos doctrine is commented upon at length. It is adequately summarized and, as should be emphasized with respect to the introduction to the section on music in Deschamps's *Art de dictier*, extended to *rimes*. Thus Oresme first translates Aristotle:

Or est ainsi que les similitude [*sic*] des meurs sunt meismement vers les vrayes natures qui sunt es rimes et es melodies, si comme sunt les similitudes de mansuetude ou debonnaireté et de fortitude et de attrempance et de toutes les choses contraires a cestes et de toutes autres choses morales.

(Now it is so that the similiarities of manners exist in the same way
within the true natures that are in rhymes and in melodies, just as the
similarities of leniency or clemency and of fortitude and temperament and
all things contrary to these and all other moral affairs.)[131]

Then his commentary follows Boethius. Whereas Aristotle saw the diversity
of *modi* as a consequence and a document of the diversity of peoples and
temperaments, Oresme infers, with Boethius, the possibility of inducing affective dispositions through the corresponding music:

> Or avons donques par cest texte que rimes et melodies moevent les gens a
> compassion et refrenent leur fureur. Et a cest propos Boece en sa Musique
> recite pluseurs beauz exemples. [. . .] Et se delecte plus chescun en la mu-
> sique qui a plus de similitude a ses meurs, si comme delcare [*sic*] Boëce en
> sa Musique.
>
> (Now we therefore learn by this text that rhymes and melodies move
> people to compassion and restrain their madness. And on this subject Bo-
> ethius gives several fine examples in his *Music*. [. . .] And everyone takes
> delight in the music which has the most similarity to his manners, as Bo-
> ethius declares in his *Music*.)[132]

"Well-composed" music is thus the kind that works affectively: "de sa nature elle [musique] reduist et ramaine chescune passion immoderee ou excessive au moien, selon ce que la musique est composee" ("by its nature it
reduces and restrains every immoderate or excessive passion to the measure,
in accord with which the music is composed").[133] Oresme reads into Aristotle's text the sympathetic principle, which must be accepted as the condition
for the plausibility of the attested effects of "well-measured" music. His
commentary reveals the genuinely Platonic provenance of the concept, as
two short translations (T) and the associated commentaries (G) show:

> T.: Et semble que de nature humaine as armonies et as rimes soit une
> cognation ou cousinage et affinité.
> G.: Et pour ce, quant les ames se delectent et la [musique] scevent cog-
> noistre, ce est signe que elles sunt bien disposees. Et est jouxte ce que
> dit le Prophete: Beatus populus qui scit jubilationem. Le peuple est
> beneuré qui scet haut chant.
> T.: Et pour ce, grande multitude de sages dient les uns que l'ame est une
> armonie, les autres qu'elle a en soi armonie.
> G.: Ce est a dire chose bien attrempee et proporcionee selon les proportions
> des acors de musique. Et cest opinion tenoit Platon et pluseurs autres.

(T.:   And it seems that between human nature and harmonies and rhymes
       there is a relationship or kinship and affinity.
G.:   And for that reason when souls take pleasure and are able to under-
       stand it [music], that is a sign that they are well disposed. And added
       to this is what the Prophet says: Blessed is the people that knows
       sublime song.
T.:   And for that reason the great multitude of sages say some of them
       that the soul is a harmony, and others that it has harmony in itself.
G.:   That is to say, something well tempered and proportioned in accord
       with the proportions of the harmonies of music. And Plato and sev-
       eral others held this opinion.)[134]

It is obvious how the annotated translation merges heterogeneous material—in a synthetic interest, for the purpose of preserving the theoretical
elements handed down in the discourse of speculative music theory and the
analytical and descriptive, world-modeling power of the speculative concept
of music. The annexation of the concept of music and harmony implied by
the relationship of music (including metrical discourse) and the "harmony
of the soul" to the concept of *ordo* remains crucial. Boethius's concept of
musica mundana is cited, and we should note the express emphasis put on
the pleasure that speculation provides:

> [M]usique speculative [. . .] considere les proportions armoniques des
> sons et est une des .iiii. sciences mathematiques selon ce que dit Boëce en
> sa Musique. Et est une speculation tres grandement delectable en tant que
> ceulz qui bien l'entendent se tiennent a peine de retourner a elle, et tant
> plus y pensent et plus leur plaist. [. . .] Item, selon les anciens philosophes
> les quantités, les qualités des mixtions des elemens du monde et des corps
> du ciel aunt faites et disposees selon proportions armoniques, ce est as-
> savoir que selon celles meismes esqueles sont les corps de musique. Et
> ce appellent Saint Augustin et Boëce musique mondaine, pource que les
> parties et choses du monde sunt aussi comme concordablement conso-
> nans selon les proportions de musique. Item, Pythagoras, Plato, Boëce, et
> pluseurs autres tenoient que les corps du ciel par leurs mouvemens funt
> une melodie.

> (Speculative music [considers] the harmonic proportions of sounds and is
> one of the four mathematical sciences, according to what Boethius says in
> his *Music*. And it is a greatly delightful speculation insofar as those who
> understand it well can hardly wait to return to it, and the more they think
> about it the more it pleases them. [. . .] Item, according to the ancient phi-

losophers quantities, qualities of the mixtures of elements of the world, and heavenly bodies are made and arranged in accord with harmonic proportions, that is, in accord with the very ones in which musical bodies exist. And this is called cosmic music by Saint Augustine and Boethius, because the parts of the world and worldly things are as well harmoniously joined according to musical proportions. Item, Pythagoras, Plato, Boethius, and several others held that the heavenly bodies make a melody by their movements.)[135]

Oresme's glosses stay closest to Aristotle's statements about music when the subject is the problem of the sound made by the harmony of the spheres. Oresme touches on this in his commentary on *De caelo*. The controversial question as to whether the harmony of the spheres produces an actual sound is the subject of a lengthy excursus that recapitulates the Boethian doctrine in a modified but clearly recognizable form. The central argument is that the movement of the stars is based on a "proportional" order, which is to that extent musical. Once again we encounter the Thomistic concept of *proportio*, extended to the relationship among qualities: "[O]u ciel est une maniere de musique laquelle est es proporcions des quantités et des qualités et des mouvemens et des vertus et des influences des corps du ciel" ("where heaven is a kind of music that consists of proportions of quantities and of qualities and of the movements and virtues and influences of the heavenly bodies").[136] In order to reconcile the Boethian position with the Aristotelian one, Oresme assumes that there are two kinds of sound, one sensible and one intelligible:

> [S]elon ce l'en pourroit dire que aussi comme les sens naturelz des honmes et des bestes sont d'autre raison et d'autre maniere que l'entendement des intelligences ou des honmes, samblablement les sons sensibles sont d'autre guise et d'autre maniere que ne sont les sons celestielz lesquielz sont insensibles.

> (According to this one could say that just as the natural senses of men and beasts are of another kind and another manner than the understanding of intelligences or of men, so in a similar way sensible sounds are of an appearance and a manner different from heavenly sounds, which are not sensible.)[137]

In fact, the distinction should be untenable in either the Aristotelian or the Neoplatonic-Boethian frame of reference, but it fulfills its goal in terms of argumentative pragmatics. Now it can be maintained that "[L]es proporcions des sons celestielz sont armoniques" ("the proportions of celestial sounds are harmonic").[138] The core of the analogical world-shaping discourse is thereby preserved: the relationship between the *mundus sensibilis* and the *mundus intelligibilis* is still conceived as a hierarchically structured continuum of "proportional" orders corresponding to the figural relationship of "this-worldly" to "other-worldly" music. Everything existing can be viewed as being situated in a hierarchical-analogical order of "musical" phenomena, in detail sometimes disposed for the better, sometimes for the worse, but on the whole always, as must be emphasized with respect to Deschamps as well, "harmonic":

> [S]amblablement selon la variacion de la musique insensible du ciel les choses de cibas sont une fois en meilleur disposicion que en autre, et selon ce une fois est pais, autre guerre, si comme dit l'Escripture: Tempus belli, et tempus pacis; une fois sterilité, autre fois fertilité et ainsi des autres mutacions. Item, par aventure pourroit l'en dire que le ciel est aussi comme celui qui chante ou fait melodie et, avecques ce, dance et fait double musique: cantu et gestu, en chant et en deport. Et le monde de cibas fait seulement musique de deport, aussi comme celui qui dance et ensuit la mesure du chant que il escoute. Et peut estre ce que entendirent saint Augustin et Boëce et autres qui parlent de musique mondaine laquelle il [*sic*] appellassent celestiele, ne fust ce que elle se estent aus corps de cibas en la maniere dessus dite.

> (Apparently according to the variation of the insensible music of the heavens, things in this world are sometimes in a better disposition than at others, and accordingly there is sometimes peace and sometimes war, as Scripture says: *tempus belli*, and *tempus pacis*; sometimes sterility, sometimes fertility, and the same for other changes. Item, perhaps one could say that the heavens are also like someone who sings or makes a melody and, with it, dances and makes twofold music: *cantu* et *gestu*, in song and in movement. And this earthly world makes only music of movement, like someone who dances and follows the measure of the song that he hears. And perhaps what was heard by Augustine and Boethius and others who speak about *musica mundana*, which he [*sic*] called celestial, was not what it is in worldly bodies in the manner said above.)[139]

Accordingly, Oresme is able to introduce a hierarchical classification of the kinds of music that is modeled on Boethius. He emphasizes the speculative component, as did the extension of the Boethian triad to include *musica coelestis* since Johannes Aegidius Zamorensis, though Oresme's emphasis on this component is still stronger.[140] *Musica humana* and *instrumentalis* are consolidated in *musique humaine*:

Et doncques par ce que dit est et par ce qu'ensuit, nous povons raison-
nablement dire que de musique sont .iii. manieres: une est humaine, autre
mondaine et la tierce est divine. La premiere est sensible as oreilles et les
autres non, mes de la seconde l'en vient en cognoissance par raison humaine, et de la tierce ont experience des angelz et les ames beneurees.

(And thus by what is said and by what follows, we can reasonably say
that there are three manners of music: one is human, another worldly,
and the third divine. The first is sensible by the ears and the others are
not, but the second is known through human reason, and the third is experienced by angels and blessed souls.)[141]

The briefer distinction, whose surplus value with regard to the traditional
classification remains unclear, sticks to the point that is central for the whole
tradition to whose reconstruction we have devoted ourselves here. Chapter
II.18, which deals with this connection, closes with the reference to the relationship of subordination in which every kind of earthly music stands with
respect to other-worldly music and thus to God's act of creation:

Or appert doncques que les proporcions qui sont entre les regars du ciel
sont toutes armoniques et non pas seulement armoniques, mais conso-
nantes ou parties de consonances. Et doncques est ce bien signe que ou
ciel est musique et que entre elle et musique humaine de laquelle elle est
cause sous Dieu est colligacion. Et elle est causee et depent sanz moien de
la tierce musique divine et de Dieu, duquel dist l'Escripture que il fait concorde en ses choses hauteines.

(Thus it appears that the proportions that exist between the aspects of the
heavens are all harmonic and not only harmonic but consonant or parts
of consonances. And hence this is really a sign that there is music in the
heavens and that there is an affinity between it and the human music of
which it is the cause. And it is caused by and depends without mediation
on the third divine music and on God, of whom the Scripture says that he
produces concord in his lofty matters.)[142]

Thus if Evdokimova's hypothesis that Deschamps's familiarity with Aristotle in general and with rhetoric and ethics in particular is drawn from
the annotated translations that Oresme made before 1372 is correct, then
we have to note first of all that Oresme systematically incorporated the
Aristotelian doctrine into the world model of the Christian order of discourse, set forth in accord with the speculative concept of music. Here too
the discourse of speculative music theory maintains itself. This is true particularly, as should now be stressed, for the *practical-ethical emphasis* that

has been seen as typical of Deschamps's *balades de moralitez* and that has been generally related to the reception of Aristotle's *Ethics* and *Rhetoric*. In Oresme's commentaries, this emphasis is derived, in accord with the concept of *ordo* functioning in music theory, directly from the "holistic" concept of music and is viewed as an *effectus musicae*: "Et donques sont .iii. fins pourquoy musique peut estre. Une est gieu et oster solicitude, l'autre est deduction, et la tierce est *preparer et disposer l'ame a bonnes pensees de vie active*" ("And thus music exists for three purposes. One is play and to banish care, another is deduction, and the third is to *prepare and dispose the soul to good thoughts of active life*").[143] The connection between the *Art de dictier* and the discourse of speculative music theory can incorporate the results of research on the significance of Aristotle's *Ethics* and *Rhetoric* for Deschamps's work and at the same time explain why in the *Art de dictier* one single sentence is devoted to rhetoric, whereas verse is considered to be music and discussed at length.

Preparer et disposer l'ame a bonnes pensees de vie active: The "Holistic" Concept of Music and Deschamps's *Balades de moralitez*

The emphasis that Oresme puts on "musical" form as being simultaneously pleasing and of practical and ethical value in terms of Christian ethics had been an essential element of music theory since Augustine. Regarding the body, Augustine had observed: "For bodies [*corpora*] are so much better to the extent that they are more harmonious [*numerosiora*] through such numbers").[144] For the soul, "musical" *numeri* are an occasion to turn toward the "divine numbers of wisdom": "Indeed, the soul becomes better by lacking those numbers that it receives through the body, when it turns away from the carnal senses and is transformed by the divine numbers of Wisdom [*divinis sapientiae numeris*]."[145] Here the ethical and religious existence of man is consummated: "After delight has been restored to the numbers associated with reason [*rationis numeros*], our whole life is turned toward God, giving the numbers associated with health to the body [*corpori numeros sanitatis*], while not receiving happiness from the body; this will happen after the exterior man has been destroyed and his alteration for the better has taken place."[146] The conception of metrical discourse as music involves first of all a potential for legitimation and relevance that applies wholly to the lyrical form. It also involves an ethical emphasis that can be followed in the pragmatic "filling" of this form.

Deschamps's work avails itself of the possibilities opened up by the purely formal concept of poetry: a great bandwidth of poetic subjects. Groupings according to thematic points of view provide no more than a provisional approach to his extensive production; quantitative emphases can nonetheless be discerned. The narrative ballads constitute a comparatively small group; among them are the fable ballads, the mythological ballads (*De Céix et Alconne* XXXV), and historical reports (*Comment Alicandre le Grant* MCLV). Reflection on the art of poetry is extremely rare in Deschamps's many ballads (*Balade sur poeterie* CXXIX); the texts devoted to it could be added tentatively to the pieces devoted to witty linguistic play (e.g., the *balades à double entendement*; *Jeu d'esprit* LXXIII, *Tour de force poétique* IX) to form a small group. The ballads on love or friendship are thematically clear; a very large group is constituted by the ballads of an appellative character, elaborated as praise for the prince (e.g., *Sur Charles VI et son fils* MCXLII), as praise for God (*Il faut servir Dieu avant tout* XIV), as an invocation (*A X saints et saintes* MCCXXXVIII) or insult (DCCLXXVII). By far the largest group is devoted to questions of practical ethics and ranges from the almost topical complaint *Contre les vices du temps* (XII) to the formulation of worldly wisdom, counsels, and practical advice.

The topically recurring diagnosis of the time, which many of the pieces of an ethical nature take as their starting point, is characteristically somber. The dominant perspective involves the distinction of the "right order" from chaos and the topos of upside-down world: "du désordre, de l'instabilité, de l'émiettement" ("from disorder, instability, and disintegration").[147] The father betrays the son (ballad 375), the mother the daughter (ballad 245), and the serf fights with the lord (ballad 60). "Au jour d'ui double loy regne" ("Today there is a double standard"), we read in ballad 151, and worse yet: to the breaking of the right orders corresponds the ruling duplicity that Deschamps castigates in the most various contexts. For instance, in ballad 1180 we read that one must avoid "two tongues ["II langues"], sweet words and a tongue that bites." The distinction between mouth and heart has a topical quality: "Le cuer est aux levres variables" ("the heart varies with respect to the lips"), ballad 962 notes, and ballad 91 argues that "Se le cuer ment, la bouche se doit taire" ("If the heart lies, the mouth must keep silent"). Duplicitous speech is also the speech of false gods who have let the right order go off the tracks: "Que les paiens crurent en vain/En aourant telz faulx ydoles,/Ou les diables par paraboles /Leur donnoient doubles respons" ("The pagans believed in vain/adoring such false idols,/in which devils through parables/Gave them duplicitous replies") (ballad 1489). The Antichrist is coming; it seems, ballad 152 says, that the apocalypse is upon us. The order of values that speaks out of Deschamps's complaint against his time is Christian ethics, as for instance Murray L. Brown has shown using the example of ballad 288, *Pourquoi nous ne pouvons jamais avoir de paix* and its typological interpretation of Moses and the conception of the Hundred Years' War as punishment for the break with God.[148] The same holds for the social ideal that can be extrapolated from Deschamps's critical invectives. "Chacun doit rester à sa place" ("Everyone must stay in place"), he says very clearly in ballad 377.

> Deschamps is first of all a very good observer and witness to his time, who opposes above all the decadence of values at the court, in the broad sense of the term, implying the whole apparatus necessary for the successful conduct of the reign. Contesting neither the monarchical system nor courtly values, he criticizes everything that endangers these pillars of the society.[149]

The model of society Deschamps's work speaks in favor of remains the tripartite one: "Peuple, clergé, noblesce, clers et lais" ("People, clergy, and nobility, both clerics and laymen") (*Chant royal* 1171). Its motto was *Caritas Dei*: to God's love for humans, to the king's love for his subjects, correspond humility and obedience (ballads 14 and 252). The "harmonic" principle of the "natural order" is the principle of *unitas*, the principle of the *ordo entium*, of the order of Creation and thus also of the stratified social order. Sobzcyk put it well: "Of course, Deschamps's ideal is unity. Unity in society, the unity of mind and body, the unity of the truth. Unity and stability."[150] In accord with the Christian basis for Deschamps's invectives against his time, the latter argue for an eternal, "natural," and God-given order: "Selon la loy naturele et divine,/Il est un Dieu" ("According to the natural and divine law,/There is one God") (ballad 361). The concept of *ordo* based on the relationship between Creator and Creation is brought to bear on the trials and tribulations of the time: If it can be said that "Eustache Deschamps is chiefly a moralizer,"[151] then this describes a very conservative impulse that presupposes the existence of an analogical relation between individual morality, the political-moral, and the order of Creation.[152] In the conception of metrical discourse as *musique naturele* and the playing out of the ethical potential of such music in the service of a "harmonic" model of the social order, Deschamps stands in a tradition that goes back as far as Augustine's *De Civitate Dei*. Just as the lyre, the flute, and the voice must sound together, Augustine writes, citing Cicero's *De republica*, so a "harmonic" order must be obtained between ranks in society:

> Toward the end of the second book Scipio said: "As with lyres, flutes, song, and sound, harmony must be maintained [*concentus est tenendus*]

among the distinct sounds, which the ears of the learned are not able to bear if they are unchanged or out of tune; nevertheless, harmony can be made agreeable and accordant by moderation of even quite dissimilar sounds. Thus, as with sounds, reason's moderation can cause the state to be in harmony with the agreement of quite dissimilar interests among the highest, lowest, and middle ranks of society. What music calls harmony in song is concord in the state [*quae harmonia a musicis dicitur in cantu, eam esse in civitate concordiam*]."[153]

Jean Batany has underscored the validity of the model even for the late Middle Ages;[154] Daniel Poirion has concluded, with reference to the *envois* of Deschamps's *balades de moralitez*, that

> These *envois* enlighten us regarding the reading the author hoped for. He does not hope that we will take his invectives literally; he wishes that we should take them as figures to reform ourselves, especially if we are the prince. What the poetry offers is an anachronistic lesson in morals [. . .].[155]

Poirion's observation corresponds to the "individuality" or even the "subjective" nature of the lyrical "I" in Deschamps's ballads. In part, it may perform what Poirion calls the "the comedy of the self": the afflictions, cares, and hardships of an authorially shaped *I-origo*.[156] On the other hand, Deschamps systematically refrained from signing the "politically committed" *balades de moralitez*.[157] They are to be seen as the *discours* of a largely typified, apersonal *I-origo* in the tradition of medieval lyric, "which in most cases," as Judson Boyce Allen noted in a path-breaking study, "utters the position of a definite but unspecified ego whose position the audience is invited to occupy."[158] The "humanistic or intellectual characteristic"[159] that Susanna Bliggenstorfer, for instance, tried to discern in Deschamps's lyric poetry lacks the historically specific character of Christian ethics in the Middle Ages. The *I-origo*, at least that of the *balades de moralitez*, is not to be regarded as an early figuration of a modern "subject," but instead is absorbed into the role models of the narrator-prophet, the narrator-philosopher, the sage, the tutor of the prince and a multitude of others—and affects the potential recipient surveying Deschamps's work precisely because, as Catherine Attwood has concluded, it is "fragmented" into a plurality of "roles" the recipient can identify with.[160] To this approach corresponds the "typism" that was conceptualized by Karl Gotthart Lamprecht in his debate with Ranke and was in principle continued in the late Middle Ages.[161] It defines a register of speaker roles that opposes to the social dislocations the old ideal of a "harmonic" social order in terms of God's good Creation. Deschamps's statements regarding free will and the power of *Fortuna*, which scholars have often commented upon,[162] and the strongly personalized occasional poems are not fundamentally opposed to this. To speak for the traditional concept of *ordo* is to speak for God—a speaker's position that has not by any means been dissipated in pluralization and relativization, as Poirion stresses:

> The end of the Middle Ages thus casts a rather harsh eye on humanity in general, that of the sage and Christian who becomes even more severe when he considers the court. But we are far from Saint-Simon's way of seeing things. The eye that judges and condemns is still God's, the imperious and rigid Super-ego that censures any infraction of the moral law.[163]

The theocentric structure of Deschamps's ethical discourse and the apersonal profiling of the *I-origo* that corresponds to it are absorbed into the conception of the Christian *ordo* just as much as is Dechamps's concept of metrical discourse as music. In view of its *effectus*, the lyrical form, as an analogical manifestation of the *ordo entium* in which the sensory order, the cognitive order, and the ethical order coincide, already has an inherent positive ethical value, and in Deschamps's work it inclines toward the pragmatic "filling" of this form by practical-ethical subjects. The reception of Aristotle's *Ethics* may have contributed to this "harmonism"; however, a reference to the reception of Aristotle alone that does not take into account the fundamentally synthetic practice of reception in the case of Oresme is inadequate. The dominance of ethical subjects in Deschamps's work can also be seen—possibly complemented by conceptually suitable material—as an elaboration on the practical-ethical emphasis of the "holistic" conception of music, an emphasis inherent in the discourse of speculative music theory since its beginning. "Ordo autem sine harmonia esse non potest" ("Order cannot exist without harmony"),[164] as Calcidius put it, and Boethius noted in the same vein that "everything that is composed of opposites can be put together and conjoined with harmony. For harmony is the unity of the many, and the consent of the dissenting [*plurimorum adunatio et dissidentium consensio*]."[165] The "holistic" conception of music explains the conceptual rigor and unity of the *Art of dictier*, on the one hand, and the practical-ethical accent in Deschamps's work, on the other.

The Speculative Conception of Music and the "Formalist" Poetics of the *Grands Rhétoriqueurs*

J EAN MOLINET, who was born in Desvres in the Boulonnais in 1435 and died in 1507 in Varennes,[1] is considered the central representative of the group of poets who are still commonly called the *Grands rhétoriqueurs*. His *Art de rhetorique* is held to be one of the most important works on the theory of poetry written in the last third of the fifteenth century: Zumthor calls it "with due allowances, a major work,"[2] Patterson describes it as "the keystone in the arch of French poetic theory before the Renaissance *Arts poétiques*."[3] The text, which is datable only roughly to the years between March 1482 and 1492, and whose attribution to Molinet was at first controversial,[4] is extant in two manuscripts. In the manuscript from Louis de Bruges's collection, produced before 1492, Paris BNF f. fr. 2159, the text consists of 32 pages;[5] the manuscript Paris BNF f. fr.2375 is a copy dating from the sixteenth century.[6] The dissemination of the treatise is proven by several early printings. Antoine Vérard published his in Paris, on 10 May 1493; Jean Trepperel produced two more, at least one of which can be dated to 1499. Jean de Guerlins printed the text in Toulouse after 1491, and Jean and Enguilbert de Marnef printed it in Poitiers.[7] Several comparable treatises published between 1490 and 1525 borrowed heavily from Molinet, including Infortuné's *Instructif de la seconde rhetorique* and Pierre Fabri's *Grant et vrai art de pleine Rhetorique*.

The passages in the text that were summarized in part I above and that led both to "modernist" interpretive approaches and indirectly to the comparison of Eustache Deschamps with Jean Molinet, immediately follow a long dedication presented as a verbose *captatio benevolentiae*. Molinet begins his textbook with the definition of its subject: "Rhétorique vulgaire est une espece de musique appellée richemique laquele contient certain nombre de sillabes avec aucune suavité de equisonance, et ne se puet faire sans diction, ne diction sans sillabes, ne sillabe sans lettres" ("Vernacular rhetoric is a kind of music called rhythmic, which contains a certain number of syllables with some suaveness of equisonance, and cannot be composed without words, any more than words without syllables, or syllables without letters").[8]

Zumthor saw that Molinet's definition drew on models borrowed from music theory, but in the framework of his theses regarding the poetics of the *rhétoriqueurs* he could conceive this only as the "rediscovery" of ancient sources. Zumthor is unaware of the continuity and vitality of reflection on the theory of poetry in the discourse of speculative music theory, and thus his discussion of Molinet's approach ends up with theses comparable to those that Dragonetti defended with regard to Deschamps's *Art de dictier*:

> The appearance around 1500 of an adjective borrowed from the Greek
> ῥυθμικος reveals the emergence of new needs: [. . .] The recourse to the
> Greek source; the rediscovery, at least virtual, of connections between
> music and poetry: [. . .] Insofar as traditional rhetoric and versification
> survived, they were reduced to the level of mechanical techniques, while
> their aesthetic and properly poetic content groped toward an expression
> more musical in nature.[9]

Zumthor thus presupposed an earlier forgetting of the link between poetry and music ("rediscovery"). Once again, the connection with music appears as an epiphenomenon of the decline of genuinely medieval concepts of the art of poetry, as an element inherently heterogenuous in poetic theory, imported into poetics from the body of learned thought, and whose implications explode the boundaries of what can be explained on the basis of the conceptual resources of the late Middle Ages itself. Our studies suggest other theses, which shall be sketched out in this outlook. Molinet's text raises the question first whether the definition cited can be analyzed on the basis of the same discursive presuppositions as Deschamps's concept of poetry, and then, whether out of such a situation of the text new perspectives on the "formalism" of the *Grands rhétoriqueurs* can be developed.

Molinet's initially not very clear definition of *seconde rethorique* or *rethorique vulgaire* as *musique* is explained through the narrowed concept of rhetoric with which reflection on the theory of poetry has operated ever since Machaut. John Stevens succinctly sums up this concept: "For Machaut and his French contemporaries rhetoric is, essentially, not the traditional art of persuasion, nor even a broadly based system of figures of speech; it

is metre and rhyme [. . .]."[10] Jean Lemaire de Belges's well-known equation
of rhetoric and music—"Rhetorique et Musique sont une même chose"
("Rhetoric and music are the same thing")[11] must be understood in this
sense. The same still holds for Gratien du Pont, whose *Art et science de
rhetorique metrifiee* of 1539 notes: "[I]l y a deux manieres de rhetoricque
vulgaire. L'une est dicte rhetoricque prosaïque, l'aultre rhetoricque metrifiée, c'est a dire rithme, laquelle se faict par vers et mettres" ("There are
two kinds of vernacular rhetoric. One is called prosaic rhetoric, the other
measured, that is, rhythmical, rhetoric, and it is made with verses and
meters").[12] In this context, *Rethorique seconde* means nothing more than
"metrical discourse" or "writing in verse."[13]

A classification makes itself heard in the expression *une espece de musique*: in order to define verse as a *species musicae*, music as *genus proximum* is joined with the manifestation of a *numerositas* as syllable-counting
(*certain nombre de sillabes*) and rhyme (*aucune suavité de equisonance*) as
the *differentia specifica*. By its form, the definition suggests a connection
with the treatise literature on literary rhythmics and its reception in poetics that we have analyzed in chapter 8 above. As a prominent reference for
the link between literary rhythmics with speculative music theory, we have
discussed Johannes de Garlandia's *Parisiana poetria*. Langlois proposed this
work as Molinet's source; Dupire considered the same possibility.[14] There
is much to be said for this hypothesis. "Rhythmics is a branch of the art of
music [*species artis musice*],"[15] Johannes de Garlandia wrote locating this
species in a classification that took the speculative concept of music into account: "It is divided into the cosmic [*mundanam*], which consists in proportion within the conditions of the elements; the human [*humanam*], which
consists in proportion and concord within the humors; and instrumental
[*instrumentalem*], which consists in instrumental concord [*in concordia
instrumentali*]."[16] There is evidence of a direct reception. After Molinet's
death on 24 August 1507, his body was buried in the Count of Charolais's
chapel Salle le Comte. The tomb bears this inscription:

> Me Molinet peperit Divernia Boloniensis,
> Parisius docuit, aluit Vallis Cycnorum:
> Et qumvis magna fuerit mea fama per orbem,
> Haec mihi pro cunctis fructibus aula fuit.

Philip August Becker has shown the right way to read this:[17]

> Desvres near Boulogne bore me, Molinet,
> Paris educated me, and Valenciennes supported me:

Although my fame was great in the world,
My only reward was this tomb in the chapel.

In the chapel (*aula*) means, as Dupire has suggested,[18] in the chapel Salle le Comte. The verses, a pair of hexameters and an elegiac distich with a short syllable at the caesura in the second and third verses, allude to Molinet's study at the University of Paris in the years preceding 1461/62, where he took a Master's degree,[19] and where Johannes de Garlandia's textbook was still in use in the fifteenth century.

Thus our reconstruction confirms first of all the connection between Eustache Deschamps's *Art de dictier* and Jean Molinet's *Art de rhetorique vulgaire* on the basis of sources that are comparable with respect to the concept of poetry they convey. This outcome suggests the possibility of interpreting Molinet's work as well on the basis of the concept of poetry that was developed and handed down by the discourse of speculative music theory.

Unlike Deschamps's *Art de dictier*, which argues using well-established terminology in a comprehensive, sophisticated way and in accord with the model of the discourse of speculative music theory, Molinet limits himself to an expressive, but brief definition, though its provenance at least is discernible. To substantiate the connection between this definition and the discourse reconstructed in part II, we will first seek to define more precisely the concept of music applicable to Molinet.

First, this approach avoids pitting a concept of music reduced to phenomenal existence and practice against the speculative conception of music of the tradition reconstructed in part II, especially since musical compositions by Molinet have come down to us,[20] and contacts with the composers Johannes Ockeghem and Josquin Desprez, among others, have been proven. Molinet's contemporaries admired him not only as a poet but also as a composer.[21] His work testifies in every regard to musical sensibility and a profound knowledge of music and music theory.[22] The evidence of about eighty familiar songs in the *Oraison à Nostre Dame*, the *Collaudation à Madame Marguerite* and the *Débat du gendarme et le vieil amoureux* proves this, as do the rhymed letters to the Franco-Flemish composer Loyset Compère (c. 1440–1518), the composer and singer Antoine Busnoys (c. 1432–1492) or scattered evidence such as the use of the syllables employed in solmization in the rhymes of the *Recommendation à Jehan de Ranchicourt*.[23] Molinet's *Trosne d'honneur* (1467), in the first of two stanzas pertinent in this context, makes use of sophisticated rhyming and prosodic techniques, enumerates birds and their songs, and concludes with an allusion to a song of Busnoy's, *Doeul angoisseux*. In the second of these two stanzas, it enumerates musical instruments and concludes with a reference to *proportions, prolations,* and the distinction between *longs* and *breves,* concepts drawn from general music theory and the theory of composition. Since a translation would unquestionably prove incapable of rendering the poem's formal and semantic sophistication, this example of *rhétoriqueurs* poetry will be left untranslated:

> Oyseaux des champs, chantans chans et deschans,
> Changiés vos chans, mués vos gargonnés,
> Les tenebres de nos coeurs annoyans
> Noians, fondans, fendans et desplaisans:
> Plaisans montans, rossignols, cardonnés,
> Nets sansonnés, sonans sus buissonés,
> Sons et sonnets, sonnés sans soneries
> Doeul angoisseux en vos sansonneries
>
> Tubes, tambours, timpanes et trompettes,
> Leutz, orguetes, harpes, psalterions,
> Bedons, clarons, clocquettes, et sonnettes,
> Cors, musettes, simphonies doulcettes,
> Chansonettes de manicordions,
> Proportions, doulces prolations,
> Perfections de longues et de briefves,
> mettés vos tons en dissonances griefves.[24]

Study of the numerous elements in Molinet's chronicles and poems that are informed by music theory in this way has benefited from the results of musicological research devoted to the analysis of late medieval conventions regarding the classification of musical instruments and the description of musical styles and performances. For example, Edmund A. Bowles has shown, using Molinet as his example, how irritating older conventions concerning the description and analysis of musical works may appear to modern readers—as when instruments are classified not according to the way sound is produced, but rather according to the loudness, timbre, and penetrating power of the tones produced, according to the distinction of loud, high-pitched (*haut*) sounds from muted, deep, or soft (*bas*) ones.[25] On the basis of such results, in 1959 Carol MacClintock demonstrated the well-foundedness and conceptual coherence of the remarks on music and music theory in Molinet's *Faicts et Dictz*–as well as their proximity to Deschamps.[26]

Molinet's *Ballade appelée chant roial*[27]—probably an *aemulatio* of Guillaume de Machaut's *Dit de la Harpe*—allows us to outline his concept of music, which on the basis of these findings can be assumed to be theoretically founded. The stanza offers an episode that functions as a *descriptio* or *historia* and that Boethius had similarly presented in his *De institutione musica* I.27. Terpander strings his lyre—in Molinet a harp—with seven strings, in accord with the image of the seven planets, and tunes each of the strings at an interval of a second. Thus the instrument allows all the intervals of the heptatonic scale—designated by their Greek names—to sound. In Boethius, the image illustrates the analogical relation between *musica mundana* and *musica instrumentalis*; according to Molinet, correspondingly, the sound of this harp is the sensible manifestation of the *souveraine harmonie*:

> Quant Terpendreus sa harpe prepara
> De sept cordons, selonc les sept planettes,
> A Jupiter Ypaté compara,
> Sol a Mesé, et fit par ses sonnettes
> 5   Paripaté resambler Saturnus,
> Licanos Mars, Paramesé Venus,
> Neté Luna, Paraneté Mercure;
> Et quand ces sept cordons, sur son arcure
> Concave a point, saudee et bien vernie,
> 10   Furent assis, il eut par art et cure
> Harpe rendant souveraine armonie.

> (When Terpander prepared his harp
> Of seven strings, according to the seven planets,
> He compared the hypate to Jupiter,
> The mese to the Sun, and made by his sounds
> 5   Paripatae resemble Saturn,
> Licanos Mars, Paramese Venus,
> Neté the Moon, Paraneté Mercury;
> And when these seven strings [were] set properly
> Upon its concave, composite, varnished arch,
> 10   He had by art and care
> A harp producing a sovereign harmony.)

In a way that remained standard for a thousand years of reflection on music theory, Boethius had inferred from the analogical relation between *musica munda* and *instrumentalis* the positive ethical potential of the latter. Analogously, Molinet here invests the seven strings of the harp with seven values that may allude to the cardinal virtues. The Christian background is shown by the reference to *Foy* (faith), and especially the relationship of the instrument to the Mother of God. This relationship reveals as well the ballad's pious theme:

> Cette harpe, qui si belle forme a,
> Puis figurer par vives raisons nettes
> A Marie, vierge que Dieu forma
> 15 Du tronc Jessé et de ses racinettes.
> La seiche Anne dont on faisoit refus
> Porta le bois roial et le bel fustz,
> Dont ceste harpe eut humaine facture.
> Prudence, Force, Attrempance, Droiture,
> 20 Foy, Esperance et Charite unie
> Sept cordes sont, qui la font sans fracture,
> Harpe rendant souveraine armonie.

> (This harp, which has such a fair form,
> I can relate figurally by clear, vivid reasons
> To Mary, the Virgin who gave birth to God
> 15 From the tree of Jesse and its rootlets.
> The barren Anne who was rejected
> Bore the royal wood and the fine trunk
> From which this harp was made by men.
> Prudence, Strength, Moderation, and Righteousness,
> 20 Faith, Hope and Charity combined:
> Seven strings that make it without fault
> A harp producing sovereign harmony.)

In the third stanza, the relation between the harp and the Virgin Mary is developed and founded narratively:

> Au temple fut presentee et sonna
> Si hault que Dieu oÿst ses chansonnettes;
> 25 Rice salut Gabriel lui donna
> Et lui dict: "Vierge, entens mes chans honnestes:
> Le fils de Dieu concepveras, Jhesus."
> Sur ce teneur respondit au dessus:
> "Je ne cognois virile creature;
> 30 Nientmains selonc ta parolle ou lecture
> Il ne soit faict." Lors fut elle garnie
> D'art, de musique et fut, par conjecture,
> Harpe rendant souveraine armonie.

(It was presented in the temple and sounded
So highly that God heard its songs;
25   Gabriel greeted her sumptuously
And said to her: "Virgin, hear my courteous songs:
You shall conceive the Son of God, Jesus."
Over this tenor, she sang the following discant in response:
"I know no manly creature;
30   Nonetheless according to your word or lecture
Let it be so." Then she was adorned
By art, by music, and was, by conjecture,
A harp making sovereign harmony.)

The harp is taken into the Temple; its *souveraine harmonie*, which the lyrical text orchestrates in the first half-stanza, constructing it phonically in extended *rime croisée*, is pleasing to God. The archangel Gabriel *sings* "to her or it"—the pronoun *lui*, whose grammatical connection remains ambiguous throughout, plays with the *similitudo* between the harp and the Mother of God—about the imminent conception of the Son of God. This conception itself, the incarnation of God, provides the harp with *art* and *musique*. The redemption rings out, as it were, in the *souveraine harmonie* of the *musica mundana*.

The parallel between music and the act of redemption, which may have a historical correlate in Philip the Fair's inclusion of harp-players in chapel orchestras or in the addition of instruments of all kinds in mystery plays,[28] is further developed in the following stanza.

Car a ce mot deité s'accord
35   Au gendre humain marchant sus espinettes:
Si doulx accord sa harpe recorda
Qu'elle endormit serpenteaux et rainettes:
Sy tres doulx mos sont de sa bouche issus
Que les haulx cieulx de Dieu fais et tissus,
40   Jadis fermés, luy ont faict ouverture
Et ont brisiet infernale clausture,
Pour retirer humaine progenie:
Si dis qu'elle est, plus que dessus nature,
Harpe rendant souveraine armonie.

(For at this word the deity attunes itself
35   To humankind playing on its spinets:
Such sweet harmony its harp played

That it benumbs the serpents and the frogs:
Such very sweet words have issued from its mouth
That the lofty heavens God made and created,
40 Formerly closed, have been opened by them,
And they have broken the gate of Hell
To remove the progeny of man:
So I say that it is, more than above nature,
A harp producing sovereign harmony.)

In response to Mary's word, "the divinity attunes itself to the human key." The following present participle *marchant* is not derived from *marcher*, "to walk or march," but rather from *la marche*, from Latin *modus*, the key; the *espinette* is a late fifteenth-century predecessor of the spinet; it came from Italy. The harmony that now rings out benumbs the serpent, the image of the desire associated with original sin, and the frog. The latter, whose massive emergence as mentioned in Exodus 8.2 heralds the second of the Old Testament plagues, had been considered since Origen as the symbol of noisy garrulity and also heresy.[29] The *souveraine harmonie* that makes the order of Being and Creation resound breaks open the gates of Hell and relieves human beings of original sin. The conceptualization of the act of redemption as the ringing out of the *souveraine harmonie* appears as the *significatio per consequentiam* of the original identification of Mary with the harp. The "music" produced by the "Harp of Mary" resounds forever in Christ's act of redemption:

45 Pan oncques ne baritonisa
Diapason au son de ses musettes,
Pictagoras oncques n'organisa
Diapanté de si doulces busettes;
Par sept accors qui sont les sept vertus,
50 Sept planetes, dont sept cieulx sont vestus,
A surmonté sans villaine morsure;
Devant son fils, qui endura mort sure,
Est assumptee et en gloire infinie
Resonne et est, par compas et mesure,
55 Harpe rendant souveraine armonie.

45 (Pan never sang in baritone
A diapason to the sound of his pipes,
Pythagoras never organized
A fifth with such sweet flutes;
By the seven harmonies that are the seven virtues,

50   Seven planets, with which the seven heavens are adorned,
      It has surmounted without an evil bite;
      Before her son, who endured a certain death,
      Was raised and in infinite glory
      resounds and is, by compass and measure,
55   A harp making sovereign harmony.

In the *envoi* that concludes the ballad, to be read rhetorically as a *sententia*, the poet asks for singing and making music to honor the Virgin, and this request shows not only that Molinet is a devout Catholic, but also that he regards making music as a practice pleasing to God. The recourse to the Terpander episode borrowed from Boethius's *De institutione musica*, the reference to the given analogical relationships—on the one hand, those between the cosmic order of *musica mundana* manifested to the senses in the movements of the planets and the acoustic music of *musica instrumentalis*, and, on the other, between the instrument and the Mother of God and thus *per consequentiam* between the Redeemer and the *souveraine harmonie*—closes with the call not to sing *d'aventure, figuraliter*: to "attune" to Christian music, and to reap as one's future reward the *souveraine harmonie*:

> Prince du puy, qui chantés d'aventure
> Donnés accord, plain chant et floriture
> A l'humble fleur des vierges espanie,
> Et vous orrés, en la gloire future,
> 60   Harpe rendant souveraine armonie.
>
> (Prince of the *puy*, who sings according to circumstance,
> Give harmony, plain song, and flourishes
> To the humble blooming flower of the Virgin,
> And you shall hear, in the future glory,
> 60   The harp making sovereign harmony.)

The wealth of musical terminology worked out by Carol MacClintock-Terpander, Pan, and Pythagoras mark out the tradition of music theory; the expressions *baritonisa, organisa, diapason, diapente, resonne, compas, mesure, plain chant, accord, floriture, teneur*, and *dessus* are all of musical provenance[30]—is absorbed into the coherently developed isotopy of making the *souveraine harmonie* ring out, on the one hand, and the conception of the Redeemer on the other. The veneration of Mary, a frequent motif in Molinet's religious poetry,[31] and the motif of the harp, which is also used in Molinet's *Petit traictiet de la harpe* to explain Augustine's doctrine of the Trinity,[32] is reconciled with the concept of a "musical" *ordo* of Being and morality. The rhyme orchestrates the merger. This holds in particular for verses 23 to 26. The rhyme *chanconnettes/chans honnestes*, whose length contrasts with those in the rest of the poem—it is one of the *rimes équivoques* generally regarded as the emblem of the poetics of the *rhétoriqueurs*—orchestrates the playing of the harp, perceived even by God himself. Similarly, the rhyming element *mes chans honnestes (méchants—honnestes)* in line 26, to be read as a rhetorical *contentio* or antithesis, is sublated in the *équivoque* and illustrates the underlying concept of *harmonia* as the reconciliation of opposites, as the sublation of differences in unity (*discordia concors*).[33] The number of verses—sixty, which is equivalent to the first perfect even number, two, multiplied by the first perfect uneven number, three, and the "sacred" number, ten, which is the sum of the numbers one through four—can be connected with this. The conceptual foundation for the isotopy within the framework of the analogical episteme is the principle of a "musical" order that governs all existence. Molinet himself names it, in a passage in his *Chronique* on the siege of Neuss in 1474: "[C]ar musicque est la resonance des ciels, la voix des angelz, la joye de paradis, l'esperit de l'aer, l'organe de l'Eglise, le chant des oyselets, la persecution des deables et la recreation de tous coeurs tristes et desoléz" ("For music is the resonance of the heavens, the voice of the angels, the joy of Paradise, the spirit of the air, the organ of the Church, birdsong, the torment of the devils and comfort for all whose hearts are sad and desolate").[34]

Musique est la resonance des cieulx—it now remains to ask how this apparently "holistically" framed concept of music can be reconciled with Molinet's similarly "musical" definition of poetry as "une espece de musique appellée richemique." Molinet's textbook itself allows the formulation of a hypothesis. Following the introduction and the definition cited, Molinet distinguishes between vowels and consonants, syllable and word, and then between "masculine" or "complete" words, which end with an accented syllable, and "feminine" or "incomplete" words, which end with an unaccented syllable or *e muet*. If the initial sound of the following word is a vowel, an elision occurs. A feminine syllable at the end of the line will not be counted, so that isometric verses ending in feminine rhymes will have one phonetic syllable more than those ending in masculine rhymes. After these fundamental definitions, Molinet presents the rhyming couplet, and then the six- and seven-verse stanza types, as well as the possibilities of deriving from these further forms, such as the eight-verse and twelve-verse stanzas. There follow sections on various types of rhyme, *rime batelée, rime enchaînée, rime à double queue,* and *rime couronnée.* Molinet then presents different forms of the *rondeau,* ordered according to the number of verses they comprise, followed by *rondeaux jumeaux, doubles,* and *doubles à chanson,* or *virelai.* Then come *doubles virelais, virelais à la taille palinode,* which are repeated *in toto* in the verse, then *fatras,* then *ballade commune, ballade balladant, fatrisée* or *jumelle,* then *simple lay, lay renforcé, chant royal, serventois,* and finally playful forms such as *ricqueracque* and *baguenaude.* The *Art de rhétorique* recommends using *rime riche* or *rime equivocque* whenever possible, and offers examples. The material is strongly modularized and takes the form of *rules of construction;* stanzas and larger forms appear, as in Deschamps's *Art de dictier,* as sets of elements and their relations bound together by a *numerical order:*

> The constitutive units [of the poem], which must be enumerated for didactic reasons, are described only from outside, in arithmetical terms (so many syllables, so many lines, so many couplets): they are given no name that would identify them intrinsically, in an unequivocal way, and confer on them a fictive autonomous existence.[35]

Gisela Febel has accordingly conceived the *rhétoriqueurs'* poetics as a "combinatory,"[36] and seen the characteristic thus described as an "element of a modern procedural poetics."[37] In fact, the constructive option that Febel finds first in Molinet's sophisticated segmentation of the signifying material, and then in the abstract and formalistic description of lyrical forms, was inherent in precisely the concept of poetry in accord with which Molinet defined poetry as such: the concept that speculative music theory had handed down over the centuries.

The systematic reconstruction and inventory of the system of quantitative metrics undertaken in Augustine's *De musica* is, according to the result of our studies in chapter 5 above, to be seen in connection with the all-encompassing, because ontologically founded, claim of Augustinian music theory. The definition of the relation of a long to a short syllable in accord with the *proportio* 2:1, the establishment of the total number of the quantities of a prosodic foot, the description of the distribution of quantities within the metrical foot, and finally the determination of the minimum and maximum lengths of the units of the metrical order, *membrum, versus, metrum, rithmus,* and their conception as sequences of a certain number of *pedes* all define a manageable set of building blocks (metrical feet, possibly including *semi-pedes* and *silentiae*) and extremely elementary rules of combination. Sequences consist of a minimum of x and a maximum of y elements, and depending on the form of construction certain parts, at least the *arsis* and the *thesis,* have to correspond with respect to the extent of their quantities. Beyond that, the distribution of the quantities is not regulated.

A *membrum* defined by the kind of verse and the requirement of symmetry can be—this is the conclusion drawn—realized by a great number of combinations of *different* metrical feet. Deviations, the "extension" of redundancy by manifesting a certain amount of quantities in different metrical feet or different combinations of feet, do not erode the principle, but rather underline its validity. The verse establishes a rhythmical-metrical "framework" that accepts and indeed encourages varying contents. The tension between variations on the level of the lower units of order, and redundancy on the higher levels, between redundancy and its extension has "aesthetic" implicatures insofar as this tension is dissolved in the *whole* of the *form*: in the *sublation (Aufhebung)* of given variations under equivalences on higher orders. In this sense, Beierwaltes was able to emphasize that "equality" is "not to be identified with a 'uniformity' that fosters boredom, but is instead a rationality integrated into a unity as equivalent, rationally constructed and rationally conceivable 'magnitude.' "[38]

References to the "musicality" of poetry in the late Middle Ages in France in general and in the *rhétoriqueurs* in particular have generally been connected with rhyme. This connection involves risks inherent in the historical distance that separates us from this period. It leads to error, when euphony is applied as a *tertium comparationis* in an uncritical way; it is apt when the *specific redundancy* is recognized as such in precisely the sense summarized and related to the aforementioned sense of form. In this connection we have emphasized the "modular" arrangement of Augustine's work on music and later underscored that the switch from quantitative to syllable-counting metrics with end-rhyme did not limit the validity of the theoretical elements presented by Augustine: if "rhyme [*is*] characterized as phonetic repetition that plays a rhythmical role"[39] (Lotman), then the form manifest in rhyme is structurally isomorphic with the forms discerned by Augustine in the system of quantitative metrics. Systematically, Molinet's definition of lyrical poetry is to be read as a reference to this isomorphism. Isometric verse construction produces a form that is inherently less complex in comparison to quantitative metrics, but nonetheless can be repeated "rhythmically." Rhyme, which Lotman not accidentally defines as intersections of equivalences determined by sound and position,[40] sets the "rhythmical" accent, in a way comparable to the χρόνος πρῶτος or, if a somewhat catachrestic image is acceptable, the "rhythmical One." It was not for nothing that the Romance tradition initially clung to the prominence of the *penultima* in the Latin poetic tradition and positioned homophonies under the final accent of the verse. Zumthor's summary of the use of *formes fixes* in the poetics of the *rhétoriqueurs* is framed accordingly:

Rhythm, at its level, bears meaning [. . .]. That is probably the reason for the great favor enjoyed, even after 1500, by so-called *formes "fixes,"* or rather "round" forms (because they include a recurrent element that closes them in on themselves rhythmically). Forms of writing in which brevity and the recurrence of accents and rhymes impose a constraint that excludes any exhaustive utterance: fixed, but not rigid, these forms divide poetic discourse into metrical units that do not necessarily coincide with linguistic units.[41]

This division (*découpage*) results from the "musical" measure and sets the "rhythmical"-metrical form. Zumthor's remark to the effect that metrical units do not necessarily coincide with linguistic units underscores the absolute priority of this form, which follows logically from the conception of lyrical poetry in accord with the discourse reconstructed in part II. For the *rhétoriqueurs'* art of rhyming, the tendency to a more and more complex development of this form, especially through the expansion of the rhyme, has been emphasized as characteristic. Claude Thiry has spoken succinctly of the "search for complexity."[42] The results of part II of our study raise the question as to whether the concept of form reconstructed might be able to explain and to clarify this "search for complexity" on the basis of its historical presuppositions: on the basis of the conceptual relation between Molinet's definition of lyrical poetry, on the one hand, and the speculative concept of music, on the other. In view of the generally good descriptive analyses of the works of the *rhétoriqueurs*, we can limit ourselves to a few examples to substantiate the following remarks.

In the course of the fifteenth century, assonance declined to the rank of a supplementary embellishment; *rime pauvre* (not accidentally also called *rime rurale*) became unusual. Poets worked on the basis of rhyming syllables. In addition, *monorimie* was depreciated in favor of more varied groups of three or four rhyming verses.[43] Within such isometric, "rhythmically" stable groups, we can discern first the quantitative extension of end-rhyme. The easiest way to produce such extensive rhymes is *rime grammaticale*,[44] as in the *Lyon coronné*, where the same root is combined with changing suffixes. Here and in the following, we refrain from providing translations where examples are given to illustrate formal features of *rhétoriqueurs* poetry alone:

> Tous ses moyens sont félons et pervers,
> Ses manières, despites et perverses,
> Ses doulx attrayts dangereux et divers,
> . . . Pleins jusqu'à l'oeil d'acointances diverses.[45]

For the sake of extensive rhyme, the bending of the still not very settled[46] code, variations in spelling and phonetic norm were accepted, as in the following verses by Pierre Gringore, which use *pastour* instead of the correct *pasteur* (shepherd):[47]

> Lors que Cayn occist son frère Abel,
> Dieu s'en coursa; le jeu ne print a bel,
> Et n'est requis que quelque pastour rie,
> Quant luy souvient de ceste pastourie.
>
> (When Cain killed his brother Abel,
> God was angry; he didn't like the play,
> And no shepherd [*pastour*] has to laugh,
> When he recalls this tale of shepherds [*pastourie*].)[48]

The quantititave extension of end-rhyme can be structured more complexly. The path taken leads to the repetition of the rhyming syllable at the end of the line, as in Molinet's paean to the *hypericum perforatum*, the common St. John's wort:

> Tu es, pour ta bonté exquise, quise,
> En champ, en pré et en patente tente:
> Tu es, en ta gente pourprise, prise
> Pour rebouter, mieulx que la bise bise,
> Nostre ennemy qui, sans attente tente
> Du corps humain es la regente gente.
> Et de l'ame garde et nourice riche.[49]

This form, known as *rime à double queue* or *rime couronnée*, can be further developed. The triple repetition of the rhyming syllable is found in Guillaume Cretin:

> Quant du gay brut d'Amour souvent vent vente,
> Et l'amant, qui son cueur savant vend, vante
> S'amour, lors font telz cas, venuz nuz, nue
> Trouble, donc en plaisir Vénus n'euz nue.[50]

The form can also add a corresponding construction at the beginning of the line. This extension begins as a repetition of the rhyming syllables at the beginning of the following line, as a *rime enchaînée*, as here, in Jean Meschinot's *Lunette des princes*:

> Par ceste mort je sens guerre mortelle,
> Mort telle fut desonques très rebelle;
> Belle n'est pas, gente de avenante;

Venante à coup et voulentiers se cèle.
Celle fait tant que tout haut bien chancelle:
Ancelle est donc dommageuse et meschante.
Chante qui veut.[51]

The rhythmical base-form for the verse provided by the principle of iso-morphism can be "filled" more flexibly than by simple repetition, as, for example, in the "leonine" verse, where the end-rhyme is supplemented by an internal rhyme preceding the caesura. A popular form emerged, the *rime batelée*. Here is an example taken from the *Naufrage de la pucelle*:

Bonté divine, essence incompa*rable*,
Lume [*sic*] admi*rable*, infinie alt*itude*,
Pere ami*able*, eternel, verit*able*,
Inestim*able*, excellent, ineff*able*,
Doux, carit*able*, espoir de sainct*itude*,
Par larg*itude* ottroie plen*itude*
De fort*itude* a ta dolente an*celle*
Et prens pitié d'une povre pu*celle*.[52]

We find a similar example in Jean Lemaire de Belges:

Nostre eaige est brief ainsi comme les *fleurs*
dont les cou*leurs* reluisent peu d'es*passe*.
Le temps est court et tout remply de p*leurs*
et de dou*leurs*, qui tout voit et com*passe*. [53]

The resulting form, which now has two accents, can be further devel-oped by interweaving simple repetitions again, as already in Molinet's *Com-plainte de Grèce*:

Que feray je de ma laidure dure?
M'ardure dure et ma foiblesse blesse;
Mon corps s'encline a corrompure pure:
Mercure cure et n'y procure cure;
Morsure sure a moy l'adresse dresse;
Richesse cesse, et trop m'oppresse presse
Leesse laisse en la presente sente,
Car mort me mort, la tres pullente lente.[54]

Similar, but once again more complex and extremely finely constructed with respect to the rhythmical structure and the phonemes used, is this poem by Cretin:

> Par dis*cors cors* jà pris en re*cordz corps*,
> creux gar*niz nidz* où as mes a*mys mys*,
> en con*sors sortz* tant que en res*sors sors*
> hors jo*liz litz* non sentant de*litz lis*.[55]

Hardly any limits are set to the enrichment of the complex *rime batelée* by means of assonances. The following passage from Molinet's *Complainte des trepasses* can serve as an example:

> Le temps s'en *va*, la m*ort* qui ne d*ort pas*
> Vient *pas à pas*, pour r*ompre* gens à *tas*;
> P*ompes*, es*tas*, Tables, *banqués* et *bancs*,
> *Rubis, rubans, robbes* a larges *pans*,
> Luis*ans* que *pans*, ne sont que vieux juppeaux [. . .].[56]

The tendency that can be discerned in these examples ends up in astonishing accumulations, to be understood as increasingly more complex investments of simple metrical forms with elements bound in relations—relations of two or more elements to be described as *aequalitas* or *similitudo*. An example of such a cumulation is provided by Molinet's *Hault Siège d'amours*, in which the various types of rhyme are combined with alliterations, as well as by the twofold echo *mort-fors* and *darde-dard*, which "round out" the whole form. The use of italics for emphasis here reaches its limits:

> Mort, se tu as *darde, darde*
> Arc tur*qu*ois, bom*barde barde,*
> Ou quel*que* tai*llarde, larde*
> Et esc*arde*
> Mon c*oeur* de ta *dure perche,*
> Or*de, d*esplaisant lais*arde,*
> Viens av*ant, musant, musarde,*
> *Pappelotant pappelarde,*
> Je n'esg*arde*
> Fors *que* ton *d*ard me trans*perche*.[57]

The limit of this kind of accumulation is instructive with regard to this tendency's vanishing point: the *simplest, most easily perceptible,* and thus—in accord with the "aesthetic" implications of music theory in the Augustinian and Boethian tradition—the *perfect equivalence*. Guillaume Cretin's epistle to Charbonnier, consisting of 120 *decasyllabes*, extends end-rhyme and rhyme at the beginning of the line in such a way that in each pair of successive verses six to seven of the ten syllables are homophonic:

A celle fin qu'en mes ditz *contrefasse*
Assez le fin, pour face *contre face*
Vers et respons accorder, *plume ay prise,*
Vers serrés pontz, où beaucoup *plus mesprise*
L'accès de court, que se visse *mes sens*
Lassez de court, plaisir n'y ay, *mais sens*
Deuil et despris [. . .]
Quant cessera mautemps? *Incontinent*
Qu'en cepz sera désir *incontinent,*
Désir entends coeur de vain *et lasche homme*
Désirant temps qu'heure vienne, *et la chomme* [. . .].[58]

Perfect equivalence is attained in *vers-rime*. Chamard has found two lines by Marc Monnier that reach this pinnacle:

Gal, amant de la Reine, alla, tour magnanime,
Galamment de l'Arène à la Tour Magne, à Nîme.[59]

Cretin offers a less successful example:

Tournay, entour sa folle outrecuydance
Tournaye: entour s'affole outre, qui danse.[60]

For understandable reasons, *vers-rime* cannot be sustained over many verses. Two possibilities for its further development remain. The sequencing of hard sounds, expressly allowed for in the Boethian tradition,[61] becomes interesting. For example, the unvoiced plosives in the following verses by Roger de Collerye:

Qu'y vault le songer? Pas le truc.
Tant au soir, la nuyt, qu'au desjuc,
Prompt, prest, preux d'attendre le chox,
Bon pied, bon oeil, frès comme ung suc,
Acoustré comme ung petit duc,
Asseuré, plus ferme qu'ung roc,
Donnez du taillant, de l'estoc;
Gardez vous d'estre prins au bric;
Baillez, comptez, payez en bloc;
Toujours joyeulx, franc comme ung coq,
Aussi éveillé qu'ung aspic,
S'on vous menasse, dictes: pic!
A tous propos ayez bon bec,
Ne soyez longuement au nic,

> Mais poursuivez moy ric a ric
> Vos amourettes chault et sec.[62]

Another possibility is the extension of the indicated techniques beyond the boundaries of the French vernacular. Mixing French with Latin becomes interesting. Here Molinet stands out:

> [. . .] Si de meo statu petis,
> Perdus sommes grans et petis:
> Habuimus multa bella
> Depuis qu'Amiens se rebella . . .
> Si queras aliqua nova
> Pour sçavoir comment il nous va,
> Mortuus est papa Paulus.
> Qui estoit grans et espaulus . . .
> Si vis vivere honeste,
> Tant en yver comme en esté
> Fuge fatuos cum quibus
> On te prendra pour coquibus;
> Quere deum qui durabit
> Plus que de fer ung dur habit . . .[63]

This allows the evolution of form we have summarized to be repeated on a new, French-Latin basis. The verse arrives at the next limit, only seldom attained, when it can be read as both Latin and French. Henry Guy identifies two verses by Jean d'Auton in which this task is more or less achieved: "Ora per duces consors ter regens et posses Syon/Ludo vicia fui de milana Germanie . . ." can also be read as: "Or a perdu ces consors, terre, gens et possession /Ludovic ja fui de Melan a Germanie. . . ."[64]

One might ask whether the "evolution of form" that these examples are supposed to demonstrate owes more to the grouping of the examples than to the latter themselves. In fact, Molinet's work itself repeatedly shows the cumulative principle of the evolution of form, as in the following verses, which begin with a simple rhyming couplet and proceed through *rime batelée* and internal rhyme to a verse with nearly equivalent hemistiches:

> Tres haulte fleur de noblesse,
> En ce trosne de haultesse,
> De largesse respandue,
> De richesse qui ne cesse,
> De leesse qu'on ne lesse

Tu seras bien maintenue,
Main tenue, main tendue [. . .].[65]

The tendency that the examples offered here have illustrated by the shortest forms, consisting for the most part of two to four verses, can also be demonstrated at the higher and highest levels of organization. A single example will suffice in the interest of the outlook for further study intended here. Molinet's *Ressource du petit peuple*, "a clever orchestration of prose and verse,"[66] consists of 386 lines in prose and 355 in verse, in twelve parts, each of which has four short sections (3, 5, 8, and 10) and four long sections (1, 4, and 9) in prose, in the following indicated as "sp" and "lp," respectively, and four more in verse (2, 6, 11, and 12), indicated as "v." Section 6 in verse and section 7 in prose are located at the center of the work; a longer section in prose introduces the work, and a section in verse concludes it. Between the bipartite center and the framing sections, two complexes can be discerned (put between parentheses in the following schema), constructed in inverted parallelism, that is, parallel when seen from the center: A short section in prose is followed by a long section in prose, another short section in prose and a section in verse. The work can thus be represented by the following schema: lp – (v – sp – lp – sp) – v | lp – (sp – lp – sp – v) – v. Redundancy and symmetry, as types of equivalence on higher levels of organization, are here merged in a single form.

The tendency toward an increasingly complex structuring of the system of equivalences that our examples have illustrated has been summarized by Zumthor under the term *équivoque généralisée*. Despite his systematic reference to the "formalism" of the *rhétoriqueurs*, Zumthor did not inquire into the *concept of form* to be used, but understood the *équivoque* as a phenomenon of *meaning*: "For the *Rhétoriqueur* it is less a question of constituting in this way a structure than of eliciting, on the basis of an overall formalizing intention, shimmering and, as it were, aleatory effects."[67] And again:

These games of equivocation, whatever their form and point of impact, constitute the most pertinent common characteristic of this poetry. What is an equivocation, after all, if not the magnified, incongruous, delectable manifestation of the hidden place where language and meaning are connected [. . .] Through equivocation, the *Rhétoriqueur* escapes social rites and asserts the central value of the exceptional, which he forces us to consume, drowned in the sauce of hackneyed phrases, striving, in order to survive, to sanction his own form as different, impossible to discover in anything else. [. . .] Reading does not consist in locating convergences that establish unity, but instead points of diffraction. The equivocal question [. . .] denies principle and origin, but it does not substitute a different notion for them. Where then is the literal, primordial meaning, the initial given, to be found? No answer.[68]

Zumthor's basic thesis, which Febel in particular has elaborated and radicalized, presupposes the conception of rhyme and the forms of its extension that Lotman developed with respect to modern lyric. For Lotman, the "nature of rhyme" is the "convergence of the different" and the "discovery of difference in the similar."[69] The "springing up of differences," the exhibition of *points of diffraction*, which Zumthor sees as the characteristic effect of *rime équivoque*, corresponds to this conception. However, it is not for nothing that Roman Jakobson, in an article on Futurism that appeared in 1919, described the dissolution of formal conventions as a "dissolution of the static, an expulsion of the absolute," and the latter as the "chief tendency of *modern* times."[70] Thus, Lotman found himself compelled to distinguish very clearly his conception of rhyme (cited above) from the one that would have to be applied in the realm of the validity of an "aesthetics of identity" such as the one established by the Christian order of discourse.[71] With respect to a time of transition like the late Middle Ages, the decision as to which of these models is to be used for the analysis of the poetics of the *rhétoriqueurs* cannot be made solely by contextualization in terms of the history of discourses. It requires a criterion that can be applied to the structure of the text.

The predominantly polysyllabic inventory of lexemes and the analytic inflection of French lead to rhyme regularly falling, in its less ample stages of development, on derived or inflected suffixes. The latter unquestionably have grammatical but negligible lexical meaning. The realization of equivalence as the recurrence of semantically poor elements may thus give the impression that the signifier is freeing itself from its connection to the signified. Thus James Wimsatt emphasizes that "[t]his repetition of almost empty words—that is, words which because of their predictability and grammatical status bear little lexical import—has the effect of emphasizing sound values over sense."[72] To this argument, one might object that the poetry of the *rhétoriqueurs* practices precisely the extension of rhyme *beyond* such semantically poor elements, although this objection does not hold for the successive and intentional extension of rhyming phonemes right up to the *vers-rime*, which is characteristic of the poetics of the *rhétoriqueurs*. This extension does lead to the effect described by Wimsatt—it is not for nothing that Hugo Friedrich, discussing a general definition of "mannerism," connected the "hypertrophy of artistic means" with the "atrophy of the content."[73] Now these effects do not have per se the offensive-transgressive quality that Febel wanted to see in them. Already according to Augustine, most signs are subject to human arbitrariness.[74] Thus the grammarian's claim to metrics is rejected with the argument that his terms are no more than words, mere names, noise, and fumes, compared with *numerositas* and form, which are the subjects of *musica scientia*. The rhythmical-metrical as a *musical* order is from the outset deliberately placed in opposition to the arbitrariness of linguistic signs.[75] It is precisely this arbitrariness that makes it possible for speculative music theory to plausibly disregard text semantics in favor of the specific *numerositas* of metrical discourse. The historical difference lies in the assumption that *in addition* to the sign *ad libitum hominum* there exist truth signs (*signa sacra*), on the basis of which those arbitrary signs are to be interpreted. The *numerositates*, the numerical measures, are truth signs in this sense: they point to an order that man has not erected for his own convenience, but that he has rather "discovered" and "found out": "For it is obvious to the slowest among us that the discipline of numbers [*numeri disciplina*] was not created by men, but rather was explored and discovered by them [*indagata et inventa*]."[76] We must start out from a modern conception of signs based on arbitrariness and thus on difference in general, which then suggests a decision in favor of Lotman's "modern" conception of rhyme, only when *all* signs are considered arbitrary. This difference provides the criterion of decision sought.

In a recent article Jacqueline Cerquiglini has suggested that *rime équivocque* should be considered "a metaphysical tool that does not dissolve language, but reconstructs a world of splendors in which colors and sounds respond to one another."[77] This remark points in the right direction if this *response* is recognized as an "activation" of the *concept of form* handed down by the discourse of speculative music theory—if the "splendor" is recognized as *splendor formae*, as the splendor of form. In the fourteenth epistle of the *Douze dames de rhétorique*, the poetic correspondence between Jean de Montferrant and Georges Chastellain consisting of seventeen épîtres, partly in prose, partly in poetry, Chastellain conceived the poet's role as discovering, disclosing: "Mais suis celui qui à tous eux déprive/Beauté, vertu conjoint emprès leur forme" ("But I am the one who discloses to them all/Beauty, a virtue conjoined with their form").[78] In the realm influenced by the creationist ontology of the Christian Middle Ages, every "creation" of a form is only an "uncovering" or "disclosing." In *precisely this sense*, the poetics of the *rhétoriqueurs* relies, to adopt a distinction suggested by Winn, on "constructive principles," not "expressive principles."[79] In the framework of the rhythmical-metrical order provided by the principle of isometry, this poetics strives to realize perfect equivalence, complete congruence. "Equivalence" and "congruence" describe relational orders consisting of two or more members that are functionally equivalent to *aequalitas, similitudo, congruentia,* or *convenientia* in the terminology of the discourse of speculative music theory. Both terms affect statements concerning the relation of individual components constitutive of the given form: only the relationality of its parts that can be qualified with the aforementioned concepts constitutes form as a whole. For the "holistic" theory of music and its connection with the ontology of the beautiful and the concept of *ordo,* it was central that this relationality constitutive of form and thus of beauty was conceived as a *numerical relationship,* as a relationship of natural numbers: "[F]ormas habent, quia numeros habent: adime illis haec, nihil erunt" ("They have forms that have numbers: take these away, and they will be nothing"),[80] as Augustine put it. Correspondingly, the "ontologically conceived identity and difference [of numbers] constitute the qualitative identity and difference of the existent itself."[81] Laurence James's remarks concerning the *constructive principles* of the poetry of the *rhétoriqueurs,* which include the one inferred from the examples given, are directly applicable here:

1. One must arrange the regular recurrence of certain elements. [. . .]
2. A relationship of resemblance must be established between elements of a different nature. [. . .]
3. A clear relationship must be established between the beginning and the end of the text. [. . .]
4. One will seek to bring together certain elements that are parallel both in form and in content. [. . .] For the *Grands rhétoriqueurs,* the latter [a certain ideology of the poetic work] is defined by its form, in which the rhythmic and melodic elements as well as sonorities properly so called have a function that is simultaneously musical and constitutive, while satisfying the ear, they establish the unity of the whole by a complex network of identities and similarities.[82]

Not only the principle of isometry and the elaboration of a complex rhyme structure remains connectable with the concept of form as relationality qualified by *aequalitas* or *similitudo,* but also, ultimately and wholly in line with the all-encompassing construction of the Augustinian theory, *absolutely every* form of equivalence. As *form,* the system of equivalences has priority over its linguistic "filling." In the extreme case, the poetry of the *rhétoriqueurs* hardly requires a substrate of content, because the form itself is a priori "meaning-full," because according to music theory, the figural reading takes as its point of departure form alone. Choosing the point of departure of figural reading selectively is introduced as a procedure and legitimated through the tradition of distinguishing several *res significantes* in one (possibly literary) text that can be, independently of one another, the object of interpretation. Every rhythm, every "harmony" in the range of the concept's meanings, and especially each equivalence as a relationality qualifiable by *aequalitas* or *similitudo*, refers to God the Creator, and is to that extent perfect *as form*: "Riens n'est parfait, se Dieu ne le patronne" ("Nothing is perfect, if God does not provide its measure")[83]—and in this sense it is a *signum Dei*.

The conception of form as a truth sign constituted by metrical structure and rhyme taught by speculative music theory shows which concept of rhyme is relevant. The explanation of the *rhétoriqueurs'* art of rhyming on the basis of a display of differences of a semantic kind fails to grasp the historical profile of their verse defined as "une espece de musique appellée richemique." One can see in the *rhétoriqueurs'* advanced poetic technique, which may seem modern in view of the complexity of the generative programs worked out, a very sophisticated handling of the rhetorical *ars*. However, the principle underlying it is, as the explicit connection with music indicates, the concept of a "musical" *ordo*, which remained vital until the sixteenth century. The display of form is the "metaphysical tool" about which Cerquiglini wrote: it produces the relation to the concept of *ordo*, it is a truth sign, and represents *figuraliter* the "musical"-harmonic order of Creation.

As an interpretative hypothesis possible in the framework of the system of references given in Molinet's *Art de rhétorique* and in line with our argument, this finding is suggested by the structure of the *rhétoriqueurs'* text.[84] At the same time, it sheds new light on scholarly theses that have up to now been marginalized because they were at odds with the dominant interpretation of the *rhétoriqueurs'* poetry. Whereas modernistic interpretations of the poetics of the *rhétoriqueurs* rely on seeing their dominant formalism as arising from a deliberate transgression of the primary linguistic code, which itself derived from the creation of a radically personalized system of expression,[85] Beverly Evans has proposed a contrary thesis that supports our suggested interpretation: "Their itinerary [that of the *rhétoriqueurs*] leads to an exploration of the world of language as a reflection of an impersonal, universal harmony."[86] In one of his early studies on the poetics of the *rhétoriqueurs,* Paul Zumthor himself also saw this historically adequate interpretive option and by using it showed relations between Molinet and Deschamps. The later success of his book *Le Masque et la lumière*, the sweeping success of the semiologically inspired "modernistic" interpretation of the *rhétoriqueurs*, and the continuing absence of work on the sources seems to have generally hindered the reception of this early approach:

> According to Deschamps, "natural music" is based on "the same," *natura eiusdem*, that is, number, the metaphysical principle in action, collecting and structuring the units of the real. In this vocabulary, *numerus* is the Latin equivalent of the "Hellenism" *rhythmus*. *Numerorum ratione* the universe exists, and analogically the poetic word, insofar as the number that sub-tends it transcends and organizes the sensible. [. . .] Prosody, numbered harmoniously (that is, in "reason"), constitutes the energy that supports discourse and guarantees its coherence. [. . .] Neoplatonic influences, disseminated in the first stage of humanism, are concentrated by the *Grands Rhétoriqueurs* in their conception of versified form.[87]

The allegorical procedure, an "essential procedure of the Rhétoriqueur,"[88] is said to be located in a "vaguely Platonic perspective"[89] and to be seen in the horizon of a "diffuse Pythagoreanism of the fifteenth and sixteenth centuries."[90] The deprecating epithets used by Zumthor can be explained by his lack of awareness of the continuity that we have reconstructed in part II above. On all levels of the structuring and ordering of poetry, the *rhétoriqueurs'* poetics posits a system of equivalences that is "rhythmical" in nature, as Hans Ulrich Gumbrecht's handy definition still suggests ("Rhythm is the achievement of form under the [complicating] condition of temporality").[91] Down to the late fifteenth century, it seems to be taken for granted that this "rhythmical" ordering is an ordering in *time* related to musicality in general and to the Pythagorean-Neoplatonic concept of musicality in particular.[92] The study of this continuity leads to an amendment quickly expressed but—as the gap between the statements taken from Zumthor's early works and his later conclusions shows—wide-ranging in its consequences. It can be formulated in dialogue with Zumthor himself. His discovery of a "subordination of laboriously inventoried techniques to a general intention, which is to force language into the infinite plays of number"[93] goes wrong only in an adjective: the "plays of number" are constitutively *definite*. If the doctrine we have studied in part II and its continuity down to the late fifteenth century is uncovered and known, then all the rest follows by itself.

Many observations on the work of the *rhétoriqueurs* that complement our conclusion could be adduced. One could refer to the speculative etymology that often marks Molinet's supposedly purely "playful" handling of the signifier. According to Marbod of Rennes's precept, "Nomen commendat res nomine significata. / Ergo debemus naturam quaerere rerum, / Ex quo possimus de nomine cernere verum" ("The thing recommends its name when its name has been made known. / Therefore, we must seek out the nature of things, / And in doing so we may discern truth about the name"),[94] work on the signifier seeks to uncover the analogical order of the signifieds. This procedure underlies Molinet's *Oraison à Madame Saincte Anne*:

> Ton nom est Anne et en latin Anna;
> Dieu tout puissant, qui justement t'anna
> Veult qu'a l'anne tu soys comparee;
> Quatre quartiers une tres juste anne a
> Quatre lectres en ton nom amena
> Par quoy tu es juste et bien mesurée;
> Quatre vertus sont, dont tu es paree,
> Cardinalles et de haut artifice:
> Prudence, Force, Attrempance, Justice.
> Tu es droicte Anne, Anna ainsy l'approuve;
> S'on le retourne, Anna tousjours on trouve;
> Tu es l'arbre foeullu et le verd anne,
> Ou on trouva la Vierge sans reprouve
> Du juste anneur qui les bons anneurs anne.[95]

Jean R. Scheidegger summarized the main thrust of the procedure with regard to Molinet's work:

> The letter, the syllable, the word—everything is glossed in accord with the
> directions given by the signifier. The etymological gloss is the justification
> for the signifying relationships that link the words; it traces and rejoins
> this reason of the signifier in order to transform it into a *reasonable* dis-
> course, a discourse that gives meaning to the arbitrariness of the signifier.[96]

Here too the *motivation* of the signifier, its interpretation in terms of potential signs of truth, is central. Something similar can be said about the particularly marked formal structuration of Molinet's poems that deal with a theological subject.[97] The veneration of Mary predominates here, and we can thus cite his *Oroison sur Maria* as an example:

> Marie, mère merveilleuse,
> Marguerite mundifiée,
> Mère miséricordieuse,
> Mansion moult magnifiée,

Ma maistresse mirifiée,
Mon mesfait maculeux me matte.[98]

Sometimes the alliteration, known in the Middle Ages as *paronomeon*, is dominant; sometimes Molinet begins each verse of a poem with a word from the Latin *Pater Noster*, sometimes with a word from the French *Ave Maria*.[99] To celebrate the mother of God's five holy days, there is a ballad with five stanzas of ten verses apiece. The first syllables of each stanza are grouped together in the following invocation, repeated in each stanza: O/Ma/Ter/De/I/Me/Men/To/Me/I.[100] The same effort to produce an increasingly intense *motivation* by work on the lyric form is also shown in the "graphic" structure of Molinet's work, for which Gisela Febel has collected a large number of proofs. Thus Molinet's motto, "Vous seulement Dieu le sait" ("You alone, God knows"), is inscribed in the *Oraison de saint Ipolite*:

> Je *vous* tiens pour ma guide, s'il *vous* plait
> En vous *seul* est ma *seul*lette esperance,
> Pour voir *le* ciel, *le* noble gardinet
> Fort cler et net, et com*ment* il fut fet,
> Du tres parfaict *Dieu* nostre ramembrance;
> Par fol*le* oultrance eust horrib*le* souffrance;
> Dieu le *scet*, France et plus de *sept* roialmes;
> Par roix trop roix nos parois desroiames.[101]

The motto forms a cross, the Greek *chi*, the initial letter of the word Χριϛτός, God's anointed, the Redeemer. The echo *scet/sept* relates knowledge with the invocational power of the number seven: the sum of the first perfect uneven number, three, and the first perfect even number, four.

Such complements to the form, "musical" per se, accentuate its character as *signum Dei*. The idea of poetry based on the "holistic" concept of music continues to take into account, if not the "saying," then at least the "manifestation" of the highest truth that alone promises legitimacy. In this special respect it corresponds to the developmental stages of analogical discourse in which Dante's *Commedia* should also be situated.[102] With the connection between legitimacy and a formal quality, a space of play opens up that can be euphorically greeted as "freedom." The continuing currency of the formally closed *formes fixes*,[103] the formal flowers of the *rhétoriqueurs'* poetry, their "playful" character, and also the self-conscious *fere* ("making") of the poets in which Wolfzettel discerned the specific difference of the *rhétoriqueurs'* poetics, can be seen in this context.[104] However, none of these findings can be pitted against the genuinely medieval nature of this poetry. The artist's self-consciousness and the exhaustion of his "artistic" possibilities, including the "playful" and sensible components of the *rhétoriqueurs*' poetry, have a solid place precisely *within* the reconstructed discursive context. To this also corresponds their *social* role, which Zumthor has persuasively emphasized. In opposition to Zumthor's own radical emphasis, the *compensatory* function of the poetry of the *rhétoriqueurs* must be taken seriously:

> The role whose function is to keep the poet on the curial stage is, by delegation, that of the prince himself: a delegation that can be revoked at any moment but which, so long as it lasts, clothes him in ceremonial garb under which no one inquires about his body. The garb of language, cut in the fabric of the protocol produced by ancient, exhausted feudal traditions. At once song and discourse, giving rise, on the surface of real relations, to the figure of other relations that are homologous with it, to be sure, but without time or place. Every discourse thus built on the imaginary is orchestrated by virtue of a harmony that is exemplary, internal, and so gratuitous that in it the ornament merges with the substance [. . .].[105]

The *internal harmony*, the "old mythology of unity," which Zumthor discusses in another passage,[106] carries further, is more abstract and thus more adaptable than Zumthor's analyses suggest. The alleged "deconstruction" of the "process of signification" is no more than the suspension of the referential dimension of language—a suspension in favor of the display of a concept of order whose level of abstraction it largely immunizes, *from the perspective of the analogical order of discourse*, against attempts at "ludic ambiguization." This ambiguization could do no more than approach the differential dynamics of linguistic signs *ad libitum hominum*. The analogical order, which may already be collapsing in other passages, still holds in the relation between *musica* and the *ordo entium*.[107]

To assess the consequences, we have to recognize as *world-modeling* even the abstract concept of order that underlies the connection of the poetics of the *rhétoriqueurs* with the discourse of speculative music theory. "Musical form" at least claims to make possible to experience the *whole* of the *ordo entium*. In its performance, musical form confirms and affirms the concept of *ordo*, which comprehends and thus legitimates the feudal, tripartite, stratified order in an analogical relationship to the hierarchically organized cosmos of the order of Creation.[108] Thus here as well the relation of the *rhétoriqueurs*' poetic practice with the political-ethical profile of their works that Zumthor discerned is to be derived:

The "didactic" tendency that thus animates the discourse of the *Rhétoriqueurs* in their function as heralds of the court is sometimes manifested
in a different but closely related form: like this tendency, it magnifies an
order, claims an extratemporal guarantee within the vicissitudes of existence. [. . .] A vast religious schema includes virtually the narrative political model, but in an imprecise way, by virtue of the accepted coincidence
of what the court considers good and what God considers good, the latter
conferring on the former its ethical value.[109]

The political and practical-ethical discourse of the *rhétoriqueurs*, on the
one hand, and their "formalism," on the other, complement one another
to form, by recourse to the foundations of the analogical discourse, a *conservative position* in the crisis situation diagnosed by Michel Zink (see the
beginning of this chapter). Between Deschamps and Molinet, "musical"
poetry does in fact oppose to the crisis-ridden, "chaotic" world a compensatory order of signs, but this order is not "self-sufficient." The reference
to music and to the discourse of speculative music theory indicates that the
anagogic power of form as sign had not been forgotten. In their works, the
doctrine reconstituted in its continuity may lack transparency, but in its central statements it remained *uninterruptedly* available in the late Middle Ages
and beyond. Aspects of the Renaissance love of music, as well as concrete
connections with the "holistic" conception of music are found everywhere.
Guy le Fèvre de la Boderie's *Galliade* (1576) may be cited as an example
that in its *Cercle IV* not only summarizes Boethius's music theory, including the triad *musica mundana/humana/instrumentalis*, but also recalls, on
the basis of common conceptual sources, Molinet's *Ballade appellée chant
roial*.[110] The explicit recourse to Pythagoreanism and music theory in Johannes Kepler's epochal *Harmonices Mundi Libri V*, Mersenne's *Traité de
l'Harmonie universelle*, and Leibniz's use of the infinitesimal calculus to begin the mathematical restructuration of the natural sciences, all draw on the
same theoretical foundation. The music of Josquin Desprez moved Luther
to say that God had also preached the Gospel through it,[111] and even when
the Protestant Johann Sebastian Bach, to mention only the most obvious
example, chose in 1725 the uncommon term "musica formalis"[112] to define
his art conceptually, the reference was situated in the continuum developed
here for the Middle Ages, though in his time it gradually disintegrated and
finally broke off. Martin Geck has emphasized its role in the *Art of the
Fugue*: "[It is a question of] finding the essence of a mode of composition
that expresses the hidden order of nature with the greatest possible clarity.
Above all stands the motto: 'All out of one' [. . .]."[113]

The alterity of the concept of music to be used in arriving at a historically adequate understanding of statements on the theory of poetry made during the late Middle Ages in France must be strongly emphasized.[114] Thus the poetry of the *rhétoriqueurs* may be a "lustful" practice, as Zumthor and his followers have repeatedly stressed. *Delectatio* and *gaudium* have always been essential aspects of the speculative conception of music. Thus the poetry of the *rhétoriqueurs* may have a "ludic" component. Thomas Aquinas had granted proper play its justification. What is crucial is that the speculative concept of music claims that the latter is neither more nor less than a manifestation, in accord with its means, of *one* truth, on which the theologically authorized order of discourse bases its claim to supremacy. The dynamics that the poetics of the *rhétoriqueurs* follows does not put this in question. Instead, it exploits the means provided in the framework of a "musical" conception of poetry, exploits the maximally abstract claim of the discourse of speculative music theory to be able to motivate absolutely *every* form as a truth sign. Thus poetry has its place in the "house of Truth," and this place is, as Molinet's *Trosne d'honneur* unmistakably observes, the Church: "la maison de Vérité, c'est a savoir, l'Eglise."[115] The modern reader may tend to perceive in *rhétoriqueurs'* poetry an apparently indissoluble tension between contents that are partly banal, in any case topically conventionalized, on the one hand, and an extreme formal complexity on the other. Seen with its historical presuppositions and the abstract nature of the applicable concept of poetic form in mind, the poetry of the *rhétoriqueurs* provides an example of the "theoretical theologization of art"[116] that became one precondition of the developments to summarize as "Renaissance" today. To that extent the work of the *rhétoriqueurs* has a genuinely late medieval character and our suggested interpretation develops a genuinely medieval perspective on this work. It may be possible to discern in individual works by the *rhétoriqueurs* the element described as "discrepancy," which allows the *existence* of disciplinary discourses ultimately to break out into the *disjunctive plurality* of such discourses and truth claims.[117] It cannot be found in the principles of their poetics or in their reflections on theory of poetry.

Regnaud de Queux's *Instructif de la Seconde Rhetorique* (1501) notes that "de sapience on ordonne / Sa loquence en fait de practique" ("on the basis of wisdom one orders / one's words in matters of practice").[118] According to *Liber proverbium* 8, 22 sqq. wisdom *plays* in front of the eyes of God, before he founds the forms.[119] The poetry of the *rhétoriqueurs* may have a playful element. But here, the wisdom of the Creator is still at play. In the *musique naturele* of the late Middle Ages, the play of divinely created form still resounds in the poet's words.

Chapter One: **Trends in Recent Research on the Late Middle Ages**

1. On the initially merely heuristic profile of the distinction between late Middle Ages/Renaissance/Early Modern, see Kuhn 1980 and Schulz-Buschhaus 1984.

2. Since Poirion 1965.

3. In another connection, Schulz-Buschhaus 1985 has pointed out that courtly literature can dominate the literary discourse of a period without this making it possible to distinguish it from other periods that are also dominated by courtly codes: as a "social style" the "courtly" runs through literature regardless of period distinctions.

4. Huizinga 1939.

5. Stempel 1995 states this point programmatically.

6. Cerquiglini 2001, p. 7.

7. See, for example, Kendrick 1983 on Eustache Deschamps, Zink 1995 on Jean Froissart, Zink 1985 on René d'Anjou, Wolfzettel 1984 on Christine de Pizan, Schulz-Buschhaus 1995 on Villon. Cf. the summarizing presentations of this "subjectivization thesis" in Calin 1987, esp. pp. 13–39, and also in Gumbrecht 1995. Dissenting voices, such as Sobczyk 1999, are marginalized.

8. For a problematization of this view, see Gumbrecht 1983.

9. Gumbrecht 1988. Cf. Wolfzettel 1997.

10. Thus for example in Wolfzettel's thesis of subjectivity developed in relation to the problem of the unity of the "I" in evanescent time can be recognized a figure of argument that lead Foucault to the conception of the subject as an "empirical-transcendental doublet." See Foucault, 1966, pp. 314–354. Much the same can be said about the following summary conceptualization of the "literary" discourse of the fifteenth century, whose contour in research on the late Middle Ages seems to be similar to the one Foucault limits to lyric after Mallarmé: a "literary" discourse that seeks to transgress the linguistic code as such. See Foucault, 2001b, esp. p. 447f.

11. Castor 1964 remains the most concise presentation of the development in France, despite a large number of more recent investigations.

12. "Préface sur la Franciade, touchant le poëme heroïque" (1587), in Ronsard 1993–1994, vol. I, pp. 1161–1180, here p. 1164. Nevertheless, Ronsard occasionally took his inspiration from the poetry of the *rhétoriqueurs*, as Mayer 1964 shows in his commentary on Ronsard's ode "Bel aubespin verdissant."

13. Massieu 1739, p. 284; Goujet 1745.

14. Crépet 1861–1863, vol. 1, p. XXI.

15. Montaiglon 1861, p. 370.

16. Guy 1910; Champion 1923; Bossuat 1951.

17. Doumic 1916, p. 82.

18. For example, Küpper 1999 makes this argument, using the example of Petrarch.

19. Wiley 1948, Jodogne 1970. See as well Shapley 1970 and Jung 1971.

20. Schmidt 1967, esp. p. 187f.

21. Zumthor 1974, 1975a, 1976, 1978b, 1979, 1981.

22. Zumthor 1978a.

23. Ibid., p. 42f.

24. Poirion 1965, p. 23.

25. Ibid.

26. Ibid., p. 74f.

27. Ibid.

28. In the 1970s already, this thesis must have been considered outmoded. Poirion's reasoning seems to presuppose a preceding period of time in which there was at least a fundamental coincidence of the experienced world and the chivalric system of norms, whose dissolution left behind forms of staging of the old ideal that were not covered any more by the real and insofar may be seen as "empty" or "theatrical." For the high Middle Ages, Brunner 1948 already pointed to the "contradiction between ideal and reality" and emphasized that "chivalric poetry did not reflect the 'social reality' of the nobility, but was rather an expression of its ethos" (p. 88). Cf. Köhler 1956 and, on the "decline of the hypothesis of decline," Hempfer 1987, esp. pp. 350–355.

29. Zumthor 1978a, p. 38.

30. Luhmann 1997, vol. 2, p. 866f.

31. Zumthor 1978a, p. 31f.

32. Ibid., p. 50.

33. Ibid.

34. Ibid.

35. Ibid., p. 51.

36. Ibid., p. 52.

37. Ibid., p. 269.

38. Ibid., p. 55.

39. Ibid., p. 195.

40. Ibid., p. 264.

41. Ibid., p. 209.

42. Ibid.

43. Zumthor 1978a, p. 278.

44. For a larger number of reservations, see Thiry 1980.

45. Weber 1988 writes in the context of his theory of ideal types: "the more sharply and clearly the ideal types are constructed, the more unworldly they are, the better they perform their task, terminologically and classificatorily as well

as heuristically." Schulz-Buschhaus 1985, p. 222 puts it trenchantly: "The more closely one tries to adhere purely descriptively to the phenomena, the less one will arrive at distinctions of sufficient conceptual clarity."

46. Langlois 1974.

47. Zumthor 1978a, p. 281.

48. Ibid., pp. 180–243.

49. Ibid., p. 205.

50. *L'Art de rhetorique*, in Langlois 1978, pp. 214–252, here p. 216.

51. Zumthor 1978a, pp. 198, 208.

52. Ibid., p. 205.

53. Ibid., p. 206.

54. Ibid., p. 199.

55. See Stimpson 1984; Bernard 1959.

56. Cerquiglini-Toulet 1993, p. 125, citing Kris/Kurz 1987, p. 24f. in support.

57. Cerquiglini-Toulet 1993, pp. 89–95.

58. Cerquiglini 2001, p. 25f. Cf. Ingenschay 1982.

59. Wolfzettel 1995, p. 93. Cf., with similar conclusions, Wolfzettel 1992, Kelly 1978, Cerquiglini 1993, p. 103f., Cowling 2004.

60. The probable hypotheses are discussed in Lubienski-Bodenham 1979.

61. Harvey 1991, p. 79.

62. Ingenschay 1986, p. 50.

63. Wolfzettel 1995, p. 100.

64. Mühlethaler 1983, p. 63.

65. Wolfzettel 1995, p. 103f.

66. Febel 2001.

67. See the contributions to the special issue "Grands rhétoriqueurs" in the *Cahiers V.-L. Saulnier* 14 (1997), esp. Cerquiglini 1997 and Cornilliat 1994.

68. Febel 2001, p. 20.

69. Ibid., p. 16.

70. Ibid., p. 19.

71. Ibid., p. 26.

72. Ibid., p. 28.

73. Ibid., p. 28f.

74. Ibid.

75. Ibid.

76. Ibid., p. 32.

77. Ibid., p. 33.

78. Ibid., p. 32.

79. Ibid., p. 33.

Chapter Two: Eustache Deschamps, *L'Art de Dictier,* 1392

1. The biographical studies on Deschamps begin with Crapelet 1832; Pinon 1846–1847, and Sarradin 1878. They tend to read at least parts of his oeuvre as a literary autobiography and to extrapolate rather uncritically biographical

data from it. The problematic nature of this method is accentuated by the fact that Deschamps's work was published only in partial editions. This changed with Raynaud's edition of the Œuvres complètes (Deschamps 1878–1903), which was accompanied by a detailed biographical essay that examined Deschamps's works as a whole and supplementary sources (vol. 11, pp. 9–99). Along with Hoepffner 1903, Raynaud's overview was the main biographical survey until Laurie 1962 analyzed all the new sources discovered since the end of the nineteenth century. Laurie's account remains standard. Following Laurie, we can briefly summarize the biographical data on which there appears to be agreement: Eustache Morel was born in Vertus around 1340, as a member of the "local middle classes" (Laurie 1962, pp. 14–19). In the 1350s Deschamps met Guillaume de Machaut in Rheims; a long-lasting literary correspondence between them continued until Machaut's death in 1377. The assumption that the two men were related by family ties, which is found in some older biographical sketches and is based on a single source. The anonymous author of a *Règles de seconde rhétorique*, BNF nouv. acq. fr. 4237, fol. 1v, notes that "afterward came Eustace Morel, the nephew of Mr. Guillaume de Machaut, who was bailiff of Senlis and was very talented in verses and ballads and other things." This account is now considered refuted (Laurie 1962, pp. 19–28). Between 1358 and 1366 Deschamps was a student. The biographies mention that he studied law in Orléans. Between 1366 and c. 1370 Deschamps served as a juryman in the county of Vertus; in 1366 he entered the service of Isabelle of France; in 1369 he became an écuyer in the service of the king. In 1372 he became a *chevaucheur* and a year later appears as the *bailli* of the Valois. Around 1379 Deschamps accompanied Charles V as a *huissier d'armes* (sergeant-at-arms) in Vermandois and remained in the service of the king until the latter's death. Under Charles VI he was granted the Tower of Fisme as his residence. During the eventful 1380s Deschamps remained in the service of the royal house, participated in campaigns against the English and the Flemish, made trips as far as Hungary, and consolidated his status with titles. With the reforms of February 5, 1389, Deschamps became the provincial governor of Senlis, took the title of *Seigneur de Barbonval*, an estate near Fismes, and was made a *noble homme* on 2 October of the same year. In 1393 he was appointed *maître des eaux et des forêts* in Brie and Champagne for the house of Orléans. After 1400 Deschamps resigned his post as the king's *huissier d'armes* and in 1404 lost his post as provincial governor to Louis d'Orléans's former *maître d'hôtel*, Pierre de Précy. Deschamps died in the second half of 1404.

2. According to the editor of the Œuvres complètes, Deschamps 1878–1903, vol. 11, p. 155f. Here and in the following pages quotations of Deschamps's works refer to this edition; the *Art de dictier* will be cited according to the critical edition Deschamps 1994, which replaces the text in volume 7 of the Œuvres complètes as well as the partial edition of the section on music in Page 1977.

3. At some unknown time in the past, the manuscript had been divided into three parts, which were then put back together. The parts bear the signatures

3291–3293. The manuscript tradition of other works by Deschamps has been compiled by Becker 1996, pp. 22–31.

4. The text of this manuscript is the basis for the Deschamps 1994 edition.

5. Deschamps 1994, p. 54.

6. Zumthor 2000, pp. 232–247, here p. 234: "It is perhaps at the syntactical level that the system of the *chanson* manifests the greatest homogeneity: an extreme looseness in the relations of subordination, the predominance of parataxis, the rejection of almost all logical relations in favor of contextual associations."

7. See Cerquiglini 1988, Heger 1988.

8. Reaney 1959, p. 25; see as well Dömling 1970.

9. Deschamps 1994, p. 54 [capital letters in the original].

10. *De temporum ratione*, in Beda Venerabilis 1955–2001, vol. 6.2, pp. 263–544. The passage on the ages of the world, drawing on Augustine and Isidore of Seville, is in chap. LVI–LXXI, pp. 461–541.

11. See, to begin with, the overview in Dolch 1965, p. 135ff.

12. See the analysis of the *Miroir de mariage* in Evdokimova 2005.

13. Deschamps 1994, p. 54.

14. Ibid., pp. 54–56.

15. Ibid., p. 56.

16. Ibid.: "Geometrie est science de mesurer et faire par proporcion la taille des pierres et des merriens, et la perfection des tours rondes et quarrees; de faire et edifier les chasteaulx, salles et maisons pour habiter, les clochiers et autres difices en ront, en triangle et en quarrure, et les mener droit sans boce jusques a leur perfection; faire tonneaulx et autres vaisseaulx de certaines pieces, longueur et grosseur, [. . .]. Et cest art s'applique aux fevres, charpentiers et macons, auxquelz, se ilz sont bons ouvriers de leurs mestiers, il faut comprandre et avoir en ymaginacion de leur pensee toute la forme et la perfection d'un chastel, d'une maison, d'un grant vaissel et des circonstances, [. . .]" ("Geometry is the science of measuring and determining in proportion the size of stones and lumber, and constructing round and square towers; of making and building castles, halls, and dwellings, bell-towers and other edifices that are round, triangular, and rectangular, and making them perfectly straight and smooth; making barrels and other vessels with certain pieces, lengths and thickness. [. . .] And this art is applied to smiths, carpenters, and masons, who, if they are good workers in their trades, must understand and imagine in their thought every form and perfection of a castle, a house, a great vessel and circumstances [. . .].")

17. Ibid, p. 58: "Arismetique est science de getter et compter par le nombre de augorisme et autre nombre commun, et de mesurer et arpenter les terres; les boys et choses semblables, pour scavoir la haulteur des choses en alant vers le ciel; [. . .]; de scavoir les heures, les temps, les minutes et les moments; pour scavoir le commencement des jours et des nuis, des sepmaines, des moys et des ans pour venir au grant miliaire et scavoir par ce nombre, en querculant, la revolucion des temps et congnoistre le cours du soleil et de la lune, et du zodiaque;

scavoir la maniere du poys et de la loy des monnoiyes, tant en or comme en ar-
gent, les dragmes, caras, demi dragmes et les empirances; et a venir par gettes et
compter en montant et multipliant son nombre de la plus petite somme jusques a
la plus grande et haulte; [. . .] Et cest art appartient assez scavoir aux monnoyers
et changeurs, et si fait il bien aux astronomiens pour les jugemens de leur science" ("Arithmetic is the science of calculating with counters and by numerical
algorithms and other common numbers, and of measuring and surveying land;
woods and like things, in order to know the height of things in rising toward the
sky [. . .]; of knowing the hours, times, minutes, and moments; of knowing the
beginning of days and nights, of weeks, months, and years to arrive at the great
millennium and to know by this number, by further calculation, the revolution of
time and the course of the sun and the moon, and of the zodiac; of knowing the
kind of weight and the law of coinage, both in gold and in silver, the drachmas,
carats, demi-drachmas and bad coins; and by calculating and counting to increase
and multiply one's number from the smallest sum to the largest and highest. [. . .]
And coiners and money-changes have to know this art well enough, and so do
astronomers for judgments in their branch of knowledge").

   18. Ibid., pp. 58–60: "Astronomy is a science of the knowledge of the stars
and the seven and principal wandering planets, [. . .]; of their influences and dispositions according to their qualities and conjunctions in various signs and their
oppositions, to assess the natural inclinations of men according to their birth-
dates, and also the fertilities or sterilities of lands and crops, [. . .]."

   19. Ibid., in the preface, p. 11: "*L'Art de dictier* seems to be a set of notes for
a longer treatise."

   20. Ibid., p. 60.

   21. Ibid.

   22. Ibid., pp. 60–62.

   23. Ibid., p. 62.

   24. Ibid., p. 60–62.

   25. Ibid., p. 64.

   26. Ibid.

   27. See, e.g., the remarks on *sotes balades* and *pastourelles*, ibid., p. 94.

   28. Ibid., p. 70.

   29. Ibid., pp. 74–76.

   30. Ibid., p. 102.

   31. Patterson 1966, vol. 1, p. 87ff.

   32. Ibid., p. 87 with reference to Langlois 1978, p. LXVf.

   33. Lote 1949, p. 366f. summarizes his assessment as follows: "Let us be frank:
the metricians of the fourteenth and fifteenth centuries are very bad professors and
do not know how to teach. They manifest in this regard a remarkable impotence.
[. . .] Confusion, obscurity, disorder in their ideas and their way of presenting
them, such are the defects that we encounter in all the didactic works of this period. The author of the *Art de dictier* escapes this no more than the others, [. . .]."

34. Dragonetti 1961.

35. Ibid., p. 49.

36. Ibid.

37. Riethmüller 1990, p. 172.

38. Dragonetti 1961, pp. 50–52.

39. Ibid., p. 52 [emphasis and capitalization in the original].

40. Ibid., p. 54.

41. Ibid., p. 55.

42. Ibid.

43. Ibid.

44. Ibid.

45. Ibid., p. 58.

46. Ibid., p. 56.

47. Ibid., p. 62.

48. Ibid.

49. Ibid.

50. Ibid.

51. Pietzsch 1968.

52. Dragonetti 1961, p. 62.

53. Ibid.

54. Ibid., p. 63.

55. Ibid.

56. Ibid., p. 64.

57. See the detailed reconstruction in my seventh chapter.

58. London, Brit. Mus., Ms. Harl. 281 and Darmstadt, Landesbibliothek, 2663, fol. 56r–69r.

59. Varty 1965, p. 166.

60. Ibid., p. 164.

61. Ibid.

62. Ibid. Here Varty is following Laurie 1964, p. 568.

63. Heger 1967; Martineau-Genieys 1978, pp. 122–144; Martineau-Genieys 1981; Michon 1982; Magnan 1985; Planche 1984; Cropp 1989; Lassabatère 1994; Cerquiglini-Toulet 1992; Becker 1995; Becker 1998; Olson 1986, p. 147ff.

64. In addition to the early work by Olson 1973, see especially the pages devoted to the *Art de dictier* in Huot 1982 and Méchoulan 1989–1990.

65. Sinnreich 1987; her critical edition is Deschamps 1994.

66. Jewers 1998, Lacassagne 1998, Gally 2000, Denizot-Ghil 2000, Hüe 2000, Bliggenstorfer 2005. Dragonetti's theses are refuted on the basis of texts that will be discussed later in this book in Heller-Roazen 2010, a study that was published after this study came out in German in 2008.

67. Febel 2001, p. 499f.

68. Ibid., p. 502.

69. Ibid., p. 489, with reference to Schlager 1982.

70. Pietzsch 1968, pp. 57–66.

71. Ibid., p. 65f.: "Thus in his [Regino's] classification of music, what is at stake is not at all a distinction between forms of the practical execution of music, alongside which the inevitable harmony of the spheres is (still) accorded great importance, but rather a speculative consideration of the different kinds of music."

72. Bernhard 1979, p. 67ff.

73. Zaminer (ed.) 1985ff.

74. Bernhard 1990b; Bernhard 1990c.

75. Bernhard 1990b, p. 31.

76. Dahlhaus 1985.

77. Riethmüller 1985.

78. Riethmüller 1989a.

79. Bower 1971, p. 22: "Music exists on two levels: the natural, which embraces the music of the spheres, the harmony of the human body and the soul, and music sung to the praise of God in the eight tones; and the artificial, music created by man, instrumental music consisting of five tones and two semitones. [. . .] There is a clear implication that these two levels of music are links in a chain of being, that the lower is analogous to the higher, that the invisible is manifested in the visible."

80. Wellesz 1954, p. 1022.

81. Bower 1971, p. 32.

82. Beierwaltes 1991.

Chapter Three: Desiderata in Research

1. Febel 2001, p. 26.

2. Ibid., p. 16.

3. Ibid., p. 33.

4. Ibid., p. 33f.

5. Dragonetti 1961, p. 56.

6. Ibid., p. 55.

7. According to Hempfer 1983, p. 17.

8. *Vom Nutzen und Nachtheil der Historie für das Leben*, in Nietzsche 1999, vol. 3.1, p. 239f.

9. Gadamer 1975, p. 451 [emphasis in the original].

10. See in particular the distinction from a "hermeneutic nihilism" that would claim for "every encounter with [a given] work the rank and right of a new production" (ibid., p. 90): "Thus we can emphasize what is truly common to all forms of hermeneutics, [namely that] the meaning to be understood is first given concrete form and completed in interpretation, but that at the same time this interpretive activity remains completely bound to the meaning of the text" (ibid., p. 315).

11. See Jauß 1970, esp. p. 242, 64n, as well as the explicit replacement of Gadamer's concept of the "merging of horizons" by the "active performance of mediating between horizons" in Jauß 1994c, p. 381f.

12. Jauß 1977a, p. 25. On the consequences for medieval studies in particular, see the now historic positions taken by Vance 1973; Badel 1977; Gumbrecht 1979; and finally the contributions to the discussion begun by Jauß in the special issue of *New Literary History* 10, no. 2 (1979).

13. Küpper 2002a, p. 438, 32n.

14. Ibid., p. 431.

15. See in detail ibid., pp. 432–435, here p. 432: "Gadamer distanced himself from Hegel insofar as he refuses to adopt the latter's metaphysical assumptions. [He accepts] them in their undisputed pastness as a coherent relation to tradition [. . .], but without conceiving the present as an element of a teleology that is also prospective. Ultimately he maintains that the present in question to be, if not the 'objective,' the legitimately assumed goal of history, and it is primarily this idea that provides the basis for the model of universal understanding: If the material contained by the past were not organized as 'history,' that is, as meaningful development, there would be no 'understanding,' one could only note the absence of meaning."

16. Thus Jauß's late work also made concessions to deconstruction. See Jauß 1994a.

17. Küpper 2002a, p. 436f. The following examples are taken from Küpper's argument.

18. Jauß 1977b; in opposition to Friedrich 1942.

19. Küpper 2002a, p. 440.

20. Gadamer 1975, p. 246 "[. . .] it remains, however, that *all such understanding is ultimately a self-understanding.*"

21. Lotman 1972, pp. 410, 412.

22. Jauß 1994b.

23. Ibid., p. 320f.

24. Ranke 1867–1890, vol. 33, here p. VIII.

25. Küpper 2002a, p. 448.

26. Ibid., p 449.

27. See in particular Foucault 1969, chaps. II–VII, pp. 44–101, and also, on the concept of discourse and the distinction between discursive practices operating in the framework of discourse (énoncés) and the actualized events (énonciations), pp. 98–134 and on p. 250, the most concise definition of the concept of *episteme* developed throughout. A survey of Foucault's evolving theses arguing in the horizon of the debate with hermeneutics is offered in Frank 1984, pp. 135–243.

28. Riethmüller 1990, p. 172.

29. Pizzani 2003.

30. Foucault 2001c, p. 832: "These authors have the particularity of being not solely the authors of their works. They produced something more: the possibility and the rule for forming other texts."

31. Foucault 1969, p. 38f.

32. The existing studies are limited for the most part to individual texts and are cited in context. For an overview with respect to verse and music in practice, see Stevens 1986 and Page 1993, and in still more summary form, Winn 1981. Butterfield 2002 and Leach 2009 also deal with the relation between verse and musical practice, but focus especially on France. Medieval music theory is not dealt with systematically in these studies. Schueller 1988 and Bayreuther 2009 offer a concise overall account of ancient and medieval aesthetics of music, but without relating it to the theory of poetry.

Chapter Four: **From Pagan Late Antiquity to the Christian Middle Ages**

1. For an introduction, see Grabmann 1956, vol. 1, pp. 76–92; the following account is based largely on Blumenberg 1996 as well as on the abbreviated version emphasizing what is most relevant to literary scholarship provided in Küpper 1989, pp. 230–263. Whereas Foucault limited himself to describing the unbounded analogism of the Renaissance (see Foucault 1969, pp. 32–59), Küpper offers here an authoritative sketch of the stages in the development of analogic discourse from its constitution to its decline.

2. This expression is taken from the account in Nestle 1975.

3. Blumenberg 1996, p. 378.

4. Rom. 5:14–17. Cf. the analogous arguments in 1 Cor. 5:7 (pascal lamb/Christ); Gal. 3:16 (Abraham/Christ); Gal. 4:21–31 (Hagar and Sarah/undiscerning Jews and those who converted to Christ). On the following, see fundamentally Auerbach 1938.

5. According to Studer 1978, p. 85, "the terminology that was later to be used to rewrite Christ's work of salvation as *satisfactio* and *meritum*" is first found in Tertullian.

6. Evidence summarized in Hall 2002.

7. See Auerbach 1938, pp. 464–474.

8. Traces of the debate culture of the *polis* have been demonstrated in logic, using terminological traces, for instance by Kapp 1965 and Lloyd 1979, p. 246ff.

9. Beierwaltes 1998, p. 8: "Theology needs philosophy as a form of conceptual reflection and as an objective foundation and implication of its central intellectual content; and philosophy needs theology insofar as it does *not* seek simply to avoid, through irresponsible negligence, ignorance, or systematic denial, the question of the absolute, of Being in itself, of God as the plenitude of Being and thinking that has been central to it since its beginnings. [. . .] Theology had not only to come to terms with the Greeks *defensively* but also to achieve, precisely on the basis of this [Greek] metaphysics, its own understanding and development of theoretical elements in order to *conceptualize* its ideas determined by the Christian revelation: a *reflexive* grasp on faith." [Emphasis in the original.]

10. Küpper 1989, p. 234.

11. On this concept, see Koselleck 1989.

12. Cf. the contrast between conceptions of history in Blumenberg 1996, p. 36.

13. See Origen 1976, IV.3, pp. 730–780; Augustine, *De genesi ad litteram*, XI.1.2. Unless otherwise indicated, all quotations from the works of Augustine follow the Maurist text, cited in the edition Augustinus 1841–1849 in accord with the organizing structure of each work.

14. See Helmich 1976, p. 2f. with further literature listed in 11n.

15. These verses are found in every medieval textbook on the subject. On the theory of fourfold meaning, see the standard account in Lubac 1959–1964.

16. Rom. 1:19: "Because that which may be known of God is manifest in them; for God hath shewed it unto them."

17. Rom. 1:20. On the interpretation of this passage, see Kertelge 1987, especially pp. 86–90, and Theobald 1989. Paul leaves no doubt as to his view of those who do not respond to the message or who were cut off from the act of redemption because they were born too soon and had to rely on the "Book of Nature" alone, as Alain de Lille sums up a common Scholastic thesis ("Omnis mundi creatura / quasi liber, et picture / nobis est et speculum": Alanus ab Insulis 1855, col. 579ff.): "Professing themselves to be wise, they became fools" (Rom. 1:22). What is crucial is that the condition of this rebuff is the possibility of knowing God through his creation. Thus in Honnefelder 1992, p. 58f. we read: "If God Jesus Christ is at the same time the God of Creation and the God of Revelation, then on the assumption that he is the universal truth and the salvation of all men, [. . .] pagans must be capable of 'perceiving through reason the invisible truth in Creation,' as Paul puts it in Rom. 1:20. Only on this condition is it inexcusable if they fail to use the wisdom possible for them to conclude that they must worship God, that is, if they become 'fools.'"

18. See details in Auerbach 1938, pp. 450–464.

19. See Curtius 1993, pp. 49–52, 218, 443f., 447, 533f.; also, on the genesis of this thesis of priority, Honnefelder 1992, pp. 60–73.

20. Hieronymus 1845–1846, vol. 2, col. 665f.

21. On this, cf. Cumont 1977, pp. 14–18.

22. Lutz-Bachmann 1992 offers an overview of the discussion—which goes back to Adolf von Harnack—regarding the initially "Hellenic" profile of early Christianity.

23. Quintilian 1977, 8.6.44, vol. 3, p. 450. Isidor of Seville 1957–1962, I.37.22 offers a standard medieval definition: "Allegoria est alieniloquium. Aliud enim sonat, et aliud intellegitur."

24. Quoted in Küpper 1989, p. 242.

25. See Bultmann 1950, esp. col. 205f.

26. See Blumenberg 1996, pp. 46–63.

27. Augustine, *De diversis quaestionibus ad Simplicianum* II.II.2. Cf. the commentary in Auerbach 1953, p. 21f.

28. Augustine, *De civitate Dei* XV.1.

29. Cf. ibid., XIV.16 and 18 passim.

30. Küpper 1989, p. 243. Cf. Koselleck 1989, p. 140: "Augustine provides,

to put it in modern terms, formal categories that are incorporated as a set of conditions for possible historical movement. He provides enduring structural statements whose substantial determinations always aim at the finitude of historical configurations and thus at their temporality, but the reproduction of these configurations under comparable circumstances is posited as probable."

31. Küpper 1989, p. 231.

32. *Confessiones* VII.9.13. The debate as to precisely which texts are referred to here is still open. Investigations concentrate on Plotinus and Marius Victorinus's translation of Porphyry, whose pre-Christian work was not known to Augustine. O'Meara 1958 summarizes the discussions of the reception of Plato down to 1958; more recent discussions are summarized in Geerlings 1997. Augustine's *Epistulae* prove that he had contact with a Platonic group that included Hermogianus (see *Epistulae* I.3 b), Zenobius (*Epistulae* 2.3–4 and *De ordine* I.1.1), and Mallius Theodorus (*De beata vita* I.4), one of the most important Christian Platonists of his time. It has been claimed that he was the source of the Platonic influence on the young Augustine, for example in Courcelle 1948, pp. 125–128 and Courcelle 1968, pp. 153–156; Theiler 1953, p. 117 and O'Meara 1954, p. 152 argue against this claim. On Augustine's knowledge of Plotinus, see Pépin 1977; on Porphyry, see Dörrie 1976. Courcelle 1948, p. 167 argues that Augustine must have known at least the Latin translation of a text by Porphyry entitled *De regressu animae*, pointing to traces of the latter in *Contra academicos* and *De beata vita*; Hadot 1984, pp. 101–136 has been able to extend these observations to *De ordine*.

33. Ritter 1937, p. 9f. For further situating, see Ivánka 1964, pp. 189–223.

34. *De Moribus Ecclesiae et de Moribus Manichaeorum* VI.8; cf. the summarizing passages in *De Moribus Ecclesiae et de Moribus Manichaeorum* I.1; *Confessiones* VII.11.17; *De Genesi ad Litteram* I.8.14.

35. *Epistulae* II.1; *Soliloquia* I.1.4.

36. *Quaestiones* LXXXIII, qu. 19; cf. also. *De Genesi ad Litteram* IV.1.1.

37. *De natura Boni contra Manichaeos* XXXIX.

38. *Contra Epistulam Manichaei quam vocant Fundamenti* XL.46; *De Moribus Ecclesiae et de Moribus Manichaeorum* VI.8.

39. Ibid., II.2.

40. *Ennarationes in Psalmos* VII.19; *De natura Boni contra Manichaeos* III.18; *Quaestiones* LXXXIII qu. 6.

41. *De Genesi contra Manichaeos* I.12.18; cf. *De vera religione* XVIII.35 and *De libero arbitrio* II.16.44.

42. Ibid., II.16.42. In *De civitate Dei* XII.19 Plato is introduced for the doctrine of creation through the institution of a numerical order. On the Pythagorean-Platonic presuppositions of this appropriation, see the summary in Gaiser 1963, pp. 8–15. Here we can only note the Stoicizing character of this Christian appropriation of Platonic teachings.

43. See Eissfeldt 1956, p. 744.

44. On Patristic appropriation in general, see Peri 1983; on Augustine, see Beierwaltes 1969. Radke 2003 describes the connection between neopythagorean number theory and the Platonic tradition in relation to the history of science.

45. On the bases of this figure of argument, see, along with further literature, Lilla 1990.

46. *Retractationes* I.3.4.

47. Mayer 1969, vol. 1, p. 338.

48. For instance, in dealing with Origen's *De principiis*, Lubac 1959–1964, vol. 1, pp. 203–207.

49. Mayer 1969, vol. 1, p. 339.

50. Ritter 1937, p. 34.

51. *Commedia, Paradiso* II, pp. 123–138.

52. Rom. 1:20.

Chapter Five: **Augustine, *De musica***

1. Curtius 1993, p. 145f.

2. With reservations, this holds for medieval music theory in general: "The key element in medieval speculative music theory is harmony based on numbers and proportions, insofar as this harmony, taken as a principle, prevails in the whole, that is, in the macrocosm as well as in the microcosm. This key element derives from Greek philosophy and music theory, chiefly Pythagorean in orientation. It was transmitted by men such as Boethius, but also more generally by Patristic literature, Neoplatonism, and Neopythagoreanism. Essentially, medieval speculative music theory consists in a continuation and Christian reformulation or interpretation of ancient and late antique music theory." Riethmüller 1990, p. 175.

3. Hammerstein 1962, p. 120.

4. The text will be cited in the edition by Guy Finaert and F. J. Thonnard (Paris, 1947), which follows, with a few emendations, the text of the *Patrologia latina*.

5. Augustine, *Retractationes* I.6.

6. See ibid., I.6 and I.11, as well as the detailed discussion of the dating in Keller 1993, pp. 149–157, which contests earlier accounts that situate the conclusion of the work in the years preceding 388.

7. Scholars began to pay increased attention to Augustine's early work only at the end of the nineteenth century. The fundamental works here were Boissier 1987 (1891), pp. 339–379 and Harnack 1888. At first, this research seemed to contradict the image of the Church Fathers that had been acquired from Augustine's late work and especially the *Confessiones* (Harnack 1888, p. 16f.; Boissier 1987, p. 376f.). This led to the assumption that there was a "biographical break," which in turn led to more weight being given to the "experience of conversion," though at first no consensus regarding the "why and wherefore" of the conversion could be achieved: the early commentators consistently saw in it a "conversion

to philosophy" or to Platonism and then to Christianity. For instance, see Thimme 1908, p. 226: Augustine is said to be a Platonist whose sole effort was "to pursue truth by rational means through philosophical speculation"; Alfaric 1918, p. 399, goes even further: "Morally and intellectually, he was converted to Neoplatonism rather than to the Gospels." In each case, the interpretations presupposed a distinction between Neoplatonism and Christianity or between philosophy and Christian theology whose untenability was later demonstrated by Kamlah 1951, p. 191ff., initially with reference to *De Civitate Dei*. At least since Courcelle 1968 scholarship has assumed a continuous identification of philosophy and theology and sought to describe this identification as an integration and absorption of pagan philosophical materials as part of Christian apologetics. Cf. the summary of research in König 1970, pp. 9–15 and Hadot 1984, pp. 101–136.

8. Cf. *Epistolae* 101.4, and on it Keller 1993, p. 157.

9. In addition, we should consider the desire to take into account its importance for the path to faith, which at least the retrospective, conciliatory report in the *Confessiones* attributes to psalmody. See *Confessiones* IX.6.14 and IX.7.15, and also the praise of psalmody as an "antidote to Manichaeism," ibid., IX.4.8.

10. Cf. *Contra Academicos, De beata vita, De ordine, Soliloquia, De quantitate animae*. The dialogue form is abandoned only with *De magistro*, Book I of which was written in 388 in Rome, while Books II to VI were written in 395 in Hippo. In comparison to these works from Cassicacum, which might in fact be based on actual conversations (Marrou, 1982, pp. 263–268), the dialogic structure of *De musica* is less "lively" and more attributable to genre conventions such as those of the diatribe (Keller 1993, p. 70). The function is not the Platonic one, based on "recollection," but rather one that has been reshaped by Christianity. "Reason," which is said in *De musica* V.9 to reveal secrets itself, is Christ: "De universis autem, quae intellegimus, non loquentem, qui personat foris, sed intus ipsi menti praesidentem consulimus veritatem, verbis fortasse ut consulamus admoniti. Ille autem, qui consulitur, docet, qui in interiore homine habitare dictus est Christus" (*De magistro* XI.38). Cf. Voss 1970, p. 268f.

11. Augustinus, *Epistolae* 101.3.

12. See Plato's comments on the parts of the song in *Republic* 398d. All references to Plato are to the "Berlin edition" (Heidelberg, 1982); for quotations, the Stephanus pagination is given. On the Platonic provenance of the distinction, cf. Riethmüller 1989b, p. 226; on classification, see Castillo 1968 and Crocker 1958.

13. Aristides Quintilianus's compilation Περί Μουσικῆς can serve as an example. We know practically nothing about the author; dating is limited to the observation that Aristides's work on music used Martianus Capella as a model and is cited by Cicero. For an introduction to Aristides, see Vetter 2001; for details, see the editor's account in Aristides Quintilianus 1937, pp. 47–58. For the classification cited, ibid., p. 167: in music, a theoretical (θεωρητικόν) part is distinguished from a practical (πρακτικόν) part; metrics (μετρικόν), rhythmics (ῥυθμικόν), and harmonics (ἁρμονικόν), the doctrine of musical tempo (ἀριθμετικόν) and ontology (φυσικόν)

belong to the theoretical part, while melodical structure (μέλοποιία), rhythmical structure (ῥυθμοποιία), poetry (ποίησις), the theory of song (ᾠδικόν), organology (ὀργανικόν), and the art of acting (ὑποκριτικόν) belong to the practical part.

14. Frequent references to this textbook allow a tentative reconstruction of its comments on music. Aulus Gellius's *Noctes Atticae* (c. 170) suggest that Varro also presupposed the tripartite classification: "Pars quaedam geometria (ὀπτική) appellatur, quae ad oculos pertinet, pars altera, quae ad auris, (κανονική) uocatur, qua musici ut fundamento artis suae utuntur. Utraque harum spatiis et interuallis linearum et ratione numerorum constat. [. . .] *Κανονική* autem longitudines et altitudines uocis emetitur. Longior mensura uocis ῥυθμός dicitur, altior μέλος. Est et alia species, quae appellatur μετρική per quam syllabarum longarum et breuium et mediocrium iunctura et modus congruens cum principiis geometria aurium mensura examinatur. 'Sed haec,' inquit M. Varro 'aut omnino non discimus aut prius desistimus, quam intellegamus, cur discenda sint.'" Aulus Gellius 1968, XVI.18.1–5.

15. As Keller 1993, p. 197 conjectures, the simplification may go back to sources in Aristoxenos of Tarentum that Augustine might have known through older Latin theoreticians. It is certain that the accentuation of *musica rhythmica*, which is accompanied by a reduction of the original tripartite form to a binary form, offered Augustine, as a trained rhetorician and Christian, a way of taking advantage of the word to develop the points of his conception of music. It is also certain that he made use of the opportunity to formulate his own position within the old controversy as to whether music belonged to metrics or grammar. The short paragraph in *De musica* II.1.1–2.2, which seeks both to qualify and to justify the distinction, makes the clash with divergent opinions explicit. On this controversy, see Westphal 1861, p. 90ff. and Schäfke 1982, pp. 141–156. Finally, it is conceivable that the bipartite distinction accounts for the conception of *metra* as *rhythmi* or *numeri*, which will be discussed further below.

16. Forkel 1967, vol. 2, p. 134.

17. Fétis 1837, p. 44; similar remarks in Fétis 1869–1876, vol. 3, p. 576.

18. Scherer 1909, p. 63.

19. Huré 1924, p. 10: "Everyone concerned with musical art should meditate on these lines: they contain incontestable truths that are too often neglected. To-day, still more than in St. Augustine's time, there is a tendency to call musicians only those who execute music or have it executed, or compose it. Most of the time, they do not know what they are doing. I know a multitude of composers who do not understand even their own works; countless orchestra conductors and virtuosos who are completely ignorant of musical art, who have neither talents nor instinct, not the slightest sensitivity, no knowledge of harmony, counterpoint, rhythmical forms, structure, etc., what remains to them? A little professional skill? [. . .] In reality a *vague* knowledge of theory and the ability to clearly beat out the measure; not much" [emphasis in the original].

20. Meyer-Baer 1930, p. 41: "Just as practical music is a fusion of ancient

theory and oriental practice, in Augustine music theory is based on an interpen-
etration of these heterogeneous elements."

21. Grande 1930; Borghezio 1930.

22. Anonymous 1942.

23. Hüschen 2001b.

24. Hammerstein 1962, p. 120.

25. Wille 1967.

26. Vincent 1849.

27. Westphal 1861.

28. Weil 1862.

29. Ambros 1968, vol. 2, p. 69.

30. Crozals 1894.

31. Amerio 1929.

32. Edelstein 1929. Clop 1924 had previously been accorded little attention.

33. Edelstein 1929, p. 8f.

34. Ibid., p. 45.

35. Ibid., p. 46.

36. Hoffmann 1931.

37. Marrou 1938.

38. Hüschen 1957; Corbin 1962.

39. Hadot 1984.

40. Scharnagel 1954.

41. Amerio 1954.

42. Ibid., p. 1051f.

43. Ibid., p. 1056.

44. Ibid., p. 1058.

45. Perl 1955.

46. Fellerer 1959.

47. Dehnert 1967.

48. Nowak 1975.

49. Manferdini 1969.

50. Keller 1993.

51. Rief 1962 is already pertinent on this point.

52. See in particular de Bruyne 1946, Assunto 1963, Tatarkiewicz 1970; Eco
2004 reads in large measure like an abridged version of de Bruynes; here too
there is further and more recent literature. Contributions to scholarship on the
"aesthetic" position of Augustine's *De musica* will be discussed in the following sections; here I mention only Beierwaltes 1975. On the sources, Le Bœuf
1975 is particularly relevant, with remarks on the influence of Augustine's theory
of proportion and number theory in architecture. Hellgardt 1973 explores the
literary-aesthetic implications of *De musica* with regard to deliberate "numerical
composition," but not with regard to the poetry-music nexus that is our central
concern in the following pages. Here we can only mention the recent debate as

to whether with respect to Neoplatonism and its consequences we can speak of a regular "aesthetics." On this, cf., with references to further literature, Haug 2007.

53. Augustine 1947, I.1, p. 22.

54. Ibid.

55. Ibid.

56. On naming as the task of disciplinary grammar, cf. *De ordine* II.12.

57. Augustine 1947, I.1, pp. 22–24.

58. See Keller 1993, pp. 185–193; Wille 1967, p. 604. At the end of the nineteenth century Holzer 1890, pp. 6–9 had already pointed out that the definition had to come from the *Disciplinae*. All later studies draw on him, for instance Schmidt 1899, p. 32; Edelstein 1929, p. 69; Pietzsch 1968, p. 51; Svoboda 1933, p. 67; Marrou 1982, p. 172. Cf., in a broader framework, Simon 1966 and Richter 1965, p. 90.

59. Augustine 1947, I.2.2, p. 26. We translate *modulor, modulatus, modulatio*, etc. following the Oxford English Dictionary definition of "modulation": "The action of forming, regulating, or varying according to due measure and proportion," not the technical musical sense of the word: "a change in pitch."

60. Augustine 1947, I.2.2, p. 26: "I say this so that you should understand that modulation [*modulatio*] concerns music alone, since it derives from measure [*modus*], which can exist in other things as well; diction is properly attributed to orators, although everyone who speaks says something, and diction takes its name from speaking [*a dicendo dictio nominata sit*]."

61. Ibid., I.3.4, p. 30 [emphasis supplied].

62. The development of this conception of number, as Augustine interprets it for the purpose of connecting it with Christian creationism, is the ultimate goal and object of this chapter. However, cf. Becker 1960, Martin 1956, p. 74f., and also, in great detail, Radke 2003, esp. p. 427.

63. On this doctrine, see Abert 1968. Augustine addresses it, to give only one example, in *Confessiones* X.33: "For their variety, all the moods of our soul have their own modes in voice and song by whose secret familiarity they are excited in some way."

64. Augustine 1947, I.3.4, p. 30ff.

65. For a detailed discussion, see below, chap. 6.

66. In the *magister*'s view, this is mere aping: see Augustine 1947, I.4.5, p. 34. Cf. also *De ordine* II.19: "If reason is found in proportioned measurements, are the nests of birds less aptly and appropriately measured? Indeed, they are most harmoniously [*numerosissimum*] constructed. I am better than the birds, then, because I understand numbers, not because I make harmonious things. And so? Are birds, though they do not understand numbers, able to make harmonious things? They surely are. How is that? Because, we, too, adapt the tongue to the teeth and palate by certain measurements, so that letters and words come out of the mouth, yet when we speak we do not think about the movement of the mouth that produces speech. Then, what talented singer, even though he is not skilled at

music, does not maintain by a natural sense in singing both rhythm and melody as they are perceived by memory? The unlearned man does not know this, yet he performs by nature's prompting [*facit operante natura*]. But why is he considered better than the beasts? Because he knows what he is doing. And I am only ranked above the beasts because I am a rational animal." Cf. Riethmüller 2001.

67. Augustine 1947, I.4.7, p. 40. Cf. Keller 1993, p. 187: "[It becomes] clear that for him music is a *scientia*, a musical knowledge, a science that appears without any relation to practice. Thus from the outset Augustine rejects such an understanding of music, which derives from its practical use, and describes it as τέχνη as opposed to ἐπιστέμη." On the distinction, see Hüschen 1957, p. 121: "In contrast to the concept of *scientia*, which always refers solely to epistemology in music, the concept *ars* refers either simultaneously to epistemology and to the practice of the arts or else simply to the practice of the arts"; see also Marrou 1982, p. 465.

68. See Augustine 1947, I.4.9–I.6.11, pp. 44–48. Marrou 1938, p. 204: "If one wanted it to have a certain nobility, that it be worthy of entering into culture, there remained only solution: it had to be reduced to intelligence alone, to the reason through which man is essentially man; it had to become a rational science, a mathematical science, and then reduced to theory [. . .]."

69. Augustine 1947, I.4.8, p. 42.

70. Ibid., I.3.3, p. 30.

71. Rief 1962, p. 208.

72. Augustine 1947, I.7.13, p. 54.

73. Not the absolute duration, but rather the relative duration of a temporal unit is thus described, corresponding to the χρόνος πρῶτος of the Greek tradition, according, for instance, to Aristeides Quintilianus 1937, p. 212f.: "The first temporal unit or duration is thus the indivisible smallest one, also called a point. By that I mean the one that is for us (relatively) the smallest, the one that first becomes perceptible to the senses. It is called a point because it is indivisible; [. . .] This indivisible (duration) has the position of the unit (μονάς). Within the linguistic expression it is perceived in the syllable, within tonality in the tone or in a particular interval, within the movement of the body in a particular position or figure." Georgiades 1958, p. 22 calls this the "minimal, no longer divisible temporal value"; Riethmüller 1989b, p. 278 calls the problem raised in this way the "search for a unit with regard to the temporal course of speech, music, and dance and its definition, but not as a unit of time as such, but rather as the 'rhythmical one,' so to speak."

74. Augustine 1947 I.8.14, p. 56.

75. Plato, *Sophist*, esp. 236c ff.

76. Augustine 1947, I.9.15, p. 58.

77. Ibid.

78. See Marrou 1938, pp. 251–262, further details in Schmitt 1930, esp. p. 366.

79. Augustine 1947, I.11.18, pp. 64–66: "Do you understand that all those rational movements that bear some numerical relationship to each other can continue to infinity through numbers, unless some reason [*ratio*] keeps them back and recalls them to some measure and form?"

80. Ibid., I.12.20, pp. 66–68: "Since we are talking about movements governed by numbers [*de numerosis motibus*], I ask you first whether we ought to consider numbers themselves, so that the fixed and certain laws [*leges fixas certasque*] they have shown to us in those movements should be judged worthy of consideration and observation."

81. Ibid., p. 68.

82. Ibid.

83. Ibid., I.12.21, p. 70.

84. Ibid., p. 72.

85. Ibid.

86. Ibid., pp. 72–74.

87. Ibid., I.12.22, p. 74.

88. Ibid.

89. Ibid.

90. Ibid., pp. 74–76.

91. Ibid., p. 76.

92. Ibid., I.13.26, p. 82.

93. Ibid.

94. Ibid., I.12.22, p. 76.

95. Ibid., I.12.23, p. 76.

96. Ibid., I.12.24, pp. 78–80.

97. On the foundation (also terminological) of arithmetic, geometric, and harmonic proportion in music, which is encountered again in Boethius, see the Archytas fragment transmitted by Porphyry in Diels/Kranz (eds.) 1956, vol. 1, Archytas-Fragment (47) B 2, p. 435f.; for its cosmological use in Plato, see esp. *Timaeus* 32a ff., and on its further development in Neoplatonism see Baltes 1976–1978 and Phillips 1997. The ancient prehistory of the concept in the function incipient here is also traced in Kluxen 1971. On its roots outside music theory, see Lohmann 1970d, esp. p. 110ff.

98. Augustine 1947, I.12.23, p. 76.

99. Ibid., I.12.24, p. 78.

100. Ibid., p. 78: "amicissime copulata."

101. On the relationship between arithmetic and geometry, which deal with their objects (number and magnitude) "for themselves" or "related to themselves," and on music theory and astronomy, which deal with them "related to something other," cf. Radke 2003, p. 250ff., and also, specifically on music theory, p. 231: "[T]his new perspective, which is directed to relationships, is just as little an 'excursion into music theory' as the numbers that figure in it are an 'excursion into geometry.' Instead, it is part of an essential definition of number in itself [. . .]."

102. Augustine 1947, I.11.19, p. 68.

103. On the Platonic horizon of the relationship between kosmos and number, see Radke 2003, p. 341ff.

104. Augustine 1947, I.12.24, p. 78.

105. Ibid., I.12.25, p. 80.

106. Ibid., I.13.27, p. 84.

107. Ibid., I.13.28, p. 84.

108. Ibid., pp. 84–86.

109. Ibid., II.1.1, p. 94.

110. Pizzani 2003, p. 366. Cf. the detailed analysis of Books II–V in the editor's commentary in Augustine 1990, pp. 41–61.

111. Augustine 1947, II.1.1, p. 94.

112. Ibid., II.1.1, p. 94–96: "the grammarian, the particular custodian of history [*custos historiae*], disapproves of your pronunciation, but does not assert why a given syllable should be short, except that those who came before us, and whose books exist and are studied by grammarians, employed them as short, not long. And so, on this topic, whatever rules, authority rules."

113. Comparing syllable quantities means comparing sounds, and comparing sounds means comparing movements: "For everything that makes a sound is in movement; and syllables surely make sounds: [. . .]. When, therefore, syllables are compared to one another, movements are compared to one another, in which numbers can be found by the measures of the length of time" (ibid., II.3.3, p. 100). Whether syllable quantities or intervals, both are movements, *motus*, that can be measured.

114. Ibid., p. 96.

115. Ibid., II.2.2, p. 98.

116. See Störmer-Caysa 1996 and, on the consequences for poetics, Vance 1986, pp. 34–50.

117. Augustine 1947, II.2.2, p. 102.

118. On the provenance of this distinction, which stems from rhythmics, not from metrics, see Mathiesen 1985, p. 165ff.

119. Augustine 1947, II.4.4, p. 102.

120. On related number genuses, see ibid., I.9.15.

121. Ibid., II.5.5, p. 106.

122. Ibid.

123. Ibid., II.4.4–II.7.14.

124. Ibid., II.9.16–II.14.26.

125. Ibid., II.7.14, p. 122: "Have you sufficiently considered that the progression to the number four, which has been shown in numbers, is present also in feet? D.: Indeed, I accept that the reason [*ratio*] of progression is found in both."

126. Ibid.

127. See II.9.16, p. 130: "D.: [. . .] Say now, what feet are joined to one another. M.: You will judge this easily if you judge that equality and similarity are superior to inequality and dissimilarity."

128. Ibid.

129. Ibid.

130. Ibid., pp. 130–132: "M.: Well, then, are they not to be deemed of equal measure when they last the same amount of time? D.: That is true. M.: You will put together without offending the ears, therefore, feet lasting the same amount of time. D.: I see that, and it follows." However, cf. the remarks on Amphibrachus as an exception, in II.10.17 and on *levatio* and *positio* in II.10.18.

131. On the most important sources, see Crocker 1958, on Aristoxenos in particular Rowell 1979, here on the relation between Aristoxenos and Aristides Quintilianus pp. 64–66. Rowell also offers an annotated translation of the *Elementa rhythmica*, pp. 70–76.

132. Augustine 1947, III.1.1, p. 160: "I ask this of you, whether feet which properly go together can be joined together to create a perpetual number [*perpetuum numerum creare*], where no certain end appears, as when chorus-boys beat castanets and cymbals with their feet in certain numbers, which when combined together give pleasure to the ear but nevertheless in a perpetual tone, so that if you do not hear the flutes, you can in no way tell how far the combination of feet runs, and when it comes back to the beginning. It is as if you wanted a hundred pyrrhic or other feet, as many as you want, and feet that go together, run with continuous combination."

133. Augustine 1947, III.1.2, p. 162: "Sed quoniam haec apud nos nomina late patent, et cavendum est ne ambigue loquamur, commodius utimur graecis." Cf. Castillo 1968, S. 288: "The Greek texts cited manifestly posit that: a) the notion of 'order in movement' was in the Greek ῥυθμός, starting with Plato, as Benveniste shows; b) in Greek literature there is a convergence of ἀριθμός and ῥυθμός that can explain the fact that Latin combines the meanings of both terms in a single one: *numerus*; c) the semantic evolution of ῥυθμός seems to have followed a path similar to that followed by *numerus*: it is applied first to the movements of the dance—Plato, Isocrates, Lucretius—and later to the rhythm of discourse: Aristotle, Dionysius of Halicarnasus, Cicero."

134. Augustine 1947, III.1.2, p. 162. Mathiesen 1985 situates this argument in the context of ancient theories of rhythm; see esp. p. 167f.

135. Augustine 1947, III.2.3, p. 162.

136. Ibid., V.1.1, p. 294.

137. Ibid., V.22, pp. 296–298. The requirement of symmetry risks making the *membra* interchangeable, which would contradict the principle of a strictly sequential order ("In everything that we measure with a portion of time, one thing comes before, and another follows, one begins, and another ends; [. . .]," ibid., V.3.3, p. 298). Thus the parts of the verse must be both symmetrical, the same in one respect, and also ordered, noninterchangeable, and thus different in one respect. The consequence is the requirement that the *membra* of a verse be able to display the same number of half-feet (*semi-pedes*), but the second *membrum* must in principle end with a short syllable: ibid., V.3.4, p. 300.

138. Ibid., III.9.21, p. 206.

139. Ibid.

140. Ibid. In Book IV the discussion of meter is pursued farther with questions on practice: the lack of importance of the length of the last syllable (IV.1.1, rules for dealing with pauses and incomplete feet (IV.13.16, IV.15.26), the difference between unavoidable and voluntary "rests" (IV.15.27.29), rules for the correct combination of feet and the connection of meters (IV.16.30.34) are examined in detail.

141. Ibid., III.8.17, p. 198.

142. Ibid., III.8.17, p. 198.

143. Ibid., V.5.10, p. 312: "The people are not easily swayed by these truths. So great is the force of custom that if it arises out of false opinion and becomes entrenched, nothing is a greater enemy of truth."

144. Ibid.

145. Ibid., p. 314.

146. Ibid., V.12.25, V.13.27. On the *senarius*, ibid., V.11.24.

147. Ibid., V.13.26, p. 346. On the concept of equality functioning here as "identity of measure," see Radke 2003, p. 796, with proofs from Proclus.

148. See Theiler 1966, p. 174 and p. 200ff.; also Hentschel 1994, esp. p. 197.

149. Augustine 1947, V.13.28, p. 348.

150. Ibid., VI.2.2, p. 360. On the anagogical method in the Platonic tradition, see Radke 2003, p. 262–319; on the anagogic in Augustine, see König 1970, pp. 27–86, 99–103.

151. Pizzani 2003, p. 369.

152. Eichhorn 1996, p. 320. On the history of this tension far beyond Antiquity and the Middle Ages, cf. Eggebrecht 1995.

153. Augustine 1947, VI.1.1, p. 356.

154. Cf. Ritter 1937, p. 32ff.; Lilla 1990.

155. Augustine 1947, VI.1.1, pp. 356–358.

156. Ibid., p. 358.

157. Ibid., the verse from Ambrose, Hymni I.2.1, for instance in Bulst (ed.) 1956, p. 42. See the commentary on this text, which is presumably a vespers hymn, in Beyenka 1957, p. 134.

158. Augustine 1947, VI.1.1, p. 358.

159. Ibid., VI.2.3, p. 362.

160. Ibid.

161. Ibid., VI.3.4, p. 366.

162. Ibid.

163. Ibid.

164. Ibid., VI.2.3, p. 364. See also VI.3.4, p. 368: "If it is one thing to produce sound, which has to do with the body, another to hear, which is the soul experiencing sound in the body, another to bring about numbers, either at greater length or more briefly, another to remember those things, and yet another to pass judgment on all these things as by natural law by approving or rejecting them."

165. Ibid., VI.3.4, p. 368: "I do not know where the fifth kind came from; it exists in the very natural judgment of perception [*in ipso naturali judicio sentiendi*], when we are delighted by the equality of numbers [*parilitate numerorum*], or when we are offended by error in them. I do not scorn what you have seen, that without certain numbers hiding in it, our sense is in no way able to bring this about."

166. Nowak 1975, p. 202. Cf. also Beierwaltes 1998, pp. 174, 187.

167. On this in context, Gundert 1971, and on the other sources, Schmitt 1974, p. 207ff.

168. Augustine 1947, VI.4.7, p. 372.

169. Ibid.

170. Ibid., p. 372.

171. Ibid., pp. 372–374.

172. Ibid., p. 374.

173. Ibid.

174. Ibid.

175. Ibid.

176. Ibid., pp. 374–376.

177. Creuzer 1977, p. 7ff., esp. p. 11: "Plato shows the [. . .] second path to the highest good precisely in his work on the beautiful. As a whole, this work has [. . .] an ethical theme. This means [*sic*] that in this treatise Plotinus sets out to show how through contemplation of the beautiful, man is gradually led back to God, to the creator of this beauty, or to the highest good."

178. Augustine 1947, VI.11.33, p. 432. Cf. Beierwaltes 1981, p. 36ff.

179. Augustine 1947, VI.4.7, p. 374ff. Eccles. 7:26 of the Vulgate (7:25 in modern translations) is given as the source in both the edition published in the *Patrologia latina* series and the Benedictine edition by Guy Finaert and F. J. Thonnard, which is cited here. Augustine is therefore paraphrasing; the text of the Vulgate reads: "Lustravi universa animo meo ut scirem et considerarem et quaererem sapientiam et rationem."

180. Augustine 1947, VI.5.8, VI.5.11, pp. 376–384, the quotation VI.5.11, p. 384. The theory of perception as an active operation of the soul has proven controversial. Nash 1969, p. 43 still defends the then still dominant view that Augustine might have borrowed this concept from Plotinus, where it is first attested. This view can now be considered as refuted. On this, see Bernard 1988, who discerns in Plato and Aristotle models of the corresponding conceptions of the process of perception. Further sources are proposed in Gannon 1965; O'Daly 1987, pp. 84–87; Brittain 2002.

181. Augustine 1947, VI.5.12, p. 386. Cf. Keller 1993, p. 228ff.

182. Augustine 1947, VI.5.12, p. 386.

183. Blumenberg 1996, p. 362: "He [Augustine] sees the fundamental character of the world in its *utilitas* as the instrumentality *ad salutem*, whereas a fulfilled and fulfilling relation to Being can only be expected in the *fruitio* directed toward

God. The ordering principle of human life, which can be explicated in the ethical virtues, is found in the maxim that one must rightfully distinguish between the utility of things and the worthiness of taking pleasure in them." On this, see also Küpper 2002b.

184. On the execution of the anagoge according to Augustine's *De trinitate*, see Brachtendorf 2000.

185. Augustine 1947, VI.6.16, p. 394.

186. Ibid., VI.7.18, p. 396; cf. as well ibid., I.13.28.

187. Ibid., VI.7.19, p. 400.

188. Ibid., VI.8.20, pp. 400–402.

189. Ibid., VI.9.23, p. 410.

190. Ibid., pp. 410–412.

191. Ibid., VI.9.24, p. 412: "You should not trouble yourself over words, the subject is under control: words are imposed by opinion, not by nature."

192. Ibid., VI.9.24, p. 414.

193. Ibid., VI.10.25, p. 416.

194. Ibid.

195. Ibid., VI.10.26, p. 418 [emphasis supplied].

196. Ibid., VI.13.38, p. 442 [emphasis supplied].

197. Ibid., VI.17.56, p. 470.

198. Ibid., VI.17.57, p. 474.

199. Ibid., VI.11.33, p. 430. Cf. Plato's *Timaeus*, where it is explained that the demiurge introduced order into chaos through "forms of time, which imitates eternity and revolves according to a law of number" (38a), and "in a parallel way the muses gave humans harmony and rhythm" in order to "correct any discord which may have arisen in the courses of the soul, and to be our ally in bringing her into harmony and agreement with herself" (47d f.). The Christian interpretation of this source in Augustine is commented upon in Gérold 1973, p. 81ff.

200. Augustine 1947, VI.13.39, p. 444: "Finally, love of the vain knowledge of such things diverts the soul; it does so with sensual numbers, wherein reside, like rules of art, those who rejoice in imitation; out of these is born curiosity, whose very name implies care. Curiosity is an enemy to security, and is void of truth because of its vanity."

201. Ibid., VI.13.40, p. 444: "Indeed, the general love of action, which diverts the soul from truth, comes from pride [*superbia*], the vice by which the soul preferred to imitate God rather than to serve Him. [. . .] For this reason, to puff with pride is to go to extremes, and as I might put it, to become void, which is to be less and less."

202. Ibid., VI.14.45, pp. 452–454.

203. On the sources of the concept of *harmonia*, which is here colonized by Christianity, since the pre-Socratics, see Lippmann 1963.

204. Augustine 1947, VI.14.46, pp. 454–456.

205. Ibid., VI.14.48, p. 460.

206. Ibid., VI.17.56, p. 470.

207. Ibid., VI.17.58, p. 476.

208. Ibid., VI.12.35, p. 434.

209. Ibid., p. 424.

210. Augustine 1947, VI.11.29, pp. 422–424 [emphasis supplied]. The formulation "delectatio ergo ordinat animam" ("therefore, pleasure regulates the soul") is universally seen by scholars as a quotation from the corpus of Neoplatonic philosophy, but they disagree about the precise source. O'Daly 1986 argues for Iamblichus as the source; on the other hand, Theiler 1966, p. 215, argues for Proclus. On the general Platonic foundation of the argument, cf. details in Burnyeat 1999.

211. On the contextualization and on the polemics in other Church Fathers, cf. Gérold 1973, pp. 88–100.

212. Through this "holistic" conception skeptical questions regarding the existence of such an *ordo* reflect deficiencies of the person who asks the question rather than inconsistencies of the theory. If the person does not recognize it, then this results from the limited perspective of the observer, who is himself included in this order. Like the soldier in the line of battle who knows nothing of the wise decision made by the general and has no overall view of the army's movement, a human being recognizes only the slice of the great whole available to him. The reason for the limitation of this slice is our first ancestor's sin. Adam lost his privileged place in Creation; the original *peccatum* subjected human beings to the Law. See Augustine 1947, VI.11.30, p. 426: "In this way God established sinful man as shameful, but not shamefully. Man was made shameful by his own will, and by losing the universe that he possessed when he obeyed the commands of God. It was established in part that whoever chose not to pursue the law would be pursued by the law."

213. Augustine, *Retractationes* I.6. In addition to the six books on *musica rhythmica*, Augustine also completed a work on grammar; the *Ars breviata* traditionally ascribed to Augustine probably consisted of a summary of this work, which is otherwise presumably lost. Cf. Law 1984; Pizzani 1985. The rest did not go beyond formulating *principia*; the work on dialectics ascribed to Augustine is probably such a sketch; see Augustine 1975.

214. Augustine refers to this canon as *disciplinae*, sometimes as *disciplinae liberales*, and less often as *artes liberales*. For example, he speaks of *disciplinae* in *Contra Academicos* II.7.17: "eruditio autem disciplinarumque"; *De ordine* I.7.20: "eruditione disciplinarum"; ibid., I.8.24: "disciplinis"; ibid., II.12.35: "in disciplinis"; ibid., II.13.38: "disciplinam disciplinarum, quam dialecticam vocant"; ibid., II.16.44: "disciplinarum ordinem"; of *disciplinae liberales* in *De ordine* I.8.24: "eruditio disciplinarum liberalium," ibid., II.9.26: "disciplinis liberalibus atque optimis erudiri"; ibid., II.13.38: "studiis liberalibus disciplinisque"; and of *disciplinae liberales* in *De ordine* I.8.24: "eruditio disciplinarum liberalium," ibid., II.9.26: "disciplinis liberalibus atque optimis erudiri"; ibid.,

II.13.38: "studiis liberalibus disciplinisque." The term *artes liberales* is found, for instance, in *De ordine* I.16.44: "artes illae omnes liberals" and in *Confessiones* IV.16.30: "omnes libros artium, quas liberales uocant."

215. Contrary to the older conception—represented, for instance, by Friedländer/Wissowa 1919–1921, vol. 2, p. 161: "There never was a Roman history of music insofar as this is taken to mean an art in the higher sense of the word, but only a Greek history transplanted onto Roman soil"—there is now no longer any doubt that early Roman musical life was in no way inferior to that of other cultural groups and was cultivated in religious, military, public, and private life. It was continuously exposed to Greek influences, but despite them preserved its own contour until late antiquity. The available sources have been assessed in Wille 1967. The context in which Varro's lost work as well as Augustine's work on music are to be understood is nonetheless the Hellenistic-influenced music *theory* in the Latin language. It begins in the decades when Roman supremacy over the Greek empire was being established, at first west of the Bosphorus. Here we can consider Scipio Asiaticus's victory over the Seleucid king Antiochos III in 189 BCE, the incorporation of the four remaining Macedonian provinces in 148 BCE, and the fall of Corinth in 146 BCE as marking the most important stages in this process. Refugees and enslaved people brought to Rome "the musical knowledge, capabilities, and habits" (Wille 1967, p. 24) of Greek tradition. Cf. also Marrou 1957, p. 361. The Roman censors' prohibition of the Greek *ars ludicra* in 115 BCE testifies to the rapid establishment of Greek music practice. However, its legal curtailment remained without effect, as Wille is able to show by reference to representations on coins (Wille 1967, p. 219). Moreover, the reception of Hellenistic music theory went hand-in-hand with the appropriation of the Greek ἐγκύκλιος παιδεία, within which the complex of musical practice and music theory had been an essential component since the Persian Wars (492–479 BCE). Thus at least the "canonization" of music theory was begun (Wessely 2001). For an account that concentrates on the connection between music and poetry in the educational program, which is supposed to have originally included not only the playing of musical instruments and dance, but also aspects of religious practice, training in the use of the hoplites's weapons, the art of poetry and other "literary" education, as well as mathematics and pedagogy, see Koller 1962; more broadly Merlan 1953, p. 78ff.; Kühnert 1961 and Fuchs 1962.

216. On the reasons for this restructuration of the canon, and especially on the pagan symbolics of the number seven in Martianus Capella (3 + 4 = Mercury + *philologia*) as well as on the meaning of the number nine, the number of the books of *De nuptiis Philologiae et Mercurii*, see Lemoine 1972, p. 77ff.

217. Hadot 1984, p. 101: "As we have said, it is in Augustine that we encounter for the first time the idea of a cycle, closed in on itself, of the seven liberal arts"; on Varro's question, see the review of older research, ibid., pp. 156–190, with the summary and conclusion, p. 311: "Another part of this chapter examines in depth the question of the hypothetical influence of Varro's *Disciplines* on the

two works by Augustine and Martianus Capella that have just been discussed, and concludes that there is none."

218. For a wide-ranging account that reviews the sources and systematic contexts of Augustine's argumentation, see Rief 1962.

219. Dyroff 1930, p. 20.

220. Augustine, *De ordine* I.1.1: "Nor is there anything that the best minds seek out more avidly, and those who look at the rocks and storms of this life with heads raised as much as possible desire to hear and learn than how it is that God cares for human kind, and yet perversity in human affairs is so great and widespread, that it seems to be due not to divine management, nor even to some servile management, if such great power could be entrusted to it. For this reason, those concerned with such matters dismiss a conclusion that might seem necessary: either that divine providence does not reach these outermost and lowest places, or that all evils are committed by divine will. Both positions are wicked, but especially the latter." We complete the proof in the following presentation.

221. Ibid., I.6.15. Cf. also II.1.2: "For good things alone are not ruled by order, but good and evil together. When we say: Everything that exists, surely we do not speak only of good things. In such a way it comes about that everything together that God governs is governed by order [*omnia simul, quae Deus administrat, ordine administrentur*]."

222. Edelstein 1929, p. 47: "Thus the task of justifying evil becomes the task of grasping the order of the universe established by God. The term *perversio*, which is later equated with the theological *corruptio*, is expressly understood as the opposite of *ordinatio*. Augustine's first solution of the problem of evil thus maintains that the disorder of human life is included in the order of the divine universe, and that this order, and thus divine justice, would be incomplete without human disorder. God's justice consists in the fact that he allots to each existent what belongs to it; this just allotment is possible, however, only if the existent is structured and differentiated; and this structuring differentiation is impossible if every existent is good."

223. Augustine, *De ordine* I.6.18 [emphasis supplied]. Cf. the illustration of the concept using the image of the cockfight, ibid., I.8.25–26.

224. Ibid., I.1.2.

225. Ibid.

226. Ibid., I.2.3.

227. Ibid., I.4.14: "Who can deny, Great God, he said, that you govern all things with order? Look how all things hold themselves together! How they are compelled in unalterable succession towards their bonds! How many and how great are the facts that cause us to speak of these things! How many things are made so that we might find Thee!" The wise man sees, as it were, "the face of God": "What is the face of God but that truth for which we long and for the love of which we yield ourselves cleansed and beautiful?" (Ibid., I.8.23).

228. These are the Christian wise, as opposed to the pagan philosophers:

De ordine I.11.32. While Augustine's early work seems to strive for the appropriation of the βίος θεωρητικός as the ideal of Christian life (see in detail Ritter 1937, pp. 121–155), in *Retractationes* I.2 Augustine says: "to a learned man I said that the blessed life inhabits only the mind of the wise man during the time of this life, whatever the condition of his body, while the Apostle hopes for a perfect understanding of God [. . .] in the future life, which alone should be termed the blessed life"—a sentence that is one of the reasons for the decline of philosophy over the following centuries.

229. Augustine, *De ordine* I.8.24.

230. Ibid., I.1.2 and I.2.4.

231. Ibid., I.1.3: "The main cause of this error is that man does not know himself."

232. *Sermo* 43.7; *Epistola* 120.3; *De trinitate* I.1.1.

233. *De ordine* I.1.3.

234. The cultivation of the relation to oneself does not reveal precisely an individual "core identity," but rather again promises the individual God in his "innermost being": "Tu autem eras interior intimo meo" ("You were within my inmost self"), as the *Confessions* put it: III.7.11. On the difference invoked here, see the chapter devoted to a comparison of Augustine and Rousseau in Fritz 2007.

235. On the Neoplatonic roots and implications of this concept, see Beierwaltes 2001.

236. Anyone who does not recognize order is stupid, sick, or both; false opinions must be "cauterized" or "healed" through education in the disciplines: "Only those succeed at this who through solitude cauterize the injuries of opinion, which the course of everyday life inflicts, or who through the liberal disciplines cure those injuries" (*De ordine* I.2.3). The healed person, the healthy and completely self-composed person recognizes the "beautiful order": "Thus, when the mind has come back to itself, it recognizes what the beauty of the universe is [. . .]" (ibid.). On the sources in Porphyry, see Theiler 1966, pp. 188–191.

237. Augustine, *De ordine* II.9.26.27. On the problematics of *auctoritas/ ratio*, see the authoritative discussion in Lütcke 1968, esp. pp. 34–46, 182–195.

238. A concept borrowed from Foucault 1984, pp. 53–94.

239. Foucault 2001e, 1550f.: "Christianity gradually established a change with regard to ancient morality, which was essentially a practice, a style of freedom. Naturally, there were also certain behavioral norms that governed each individual's conduct. But in antiquity the desire to be a moral subject and the search for an ethics of existence were chiefly an effort to assert one's freedom and to give one's own life a certain form in which one could recognize oneself, be recognized by others, and even serve as an example for posterity. It seems to me that this elaboration of one's own life as a personal work of art, even if it was governed by collective rules, was central to moral experience to the moral will in antiquity, whereas in Christianity, with the religion of the text, the idea of a divine will and the principle of obedience, morality took far more the form of a body of rules

[. . .]. In passing from antiquity to Christianity, one passes from morality as essentially a quest for a personal ethics to morality as obedience to a system of rules."

240. Augustine, *De ordine* I.2.4.

241. Ibid., I.9.27.

242. Ibid., II.8.25 [emphasis supplied].

243. Ibid., II.9.16.

244. Ibid., II.9.26–27.

245. See the detailed account of the doctrine of signatures in Mayer 1969, vol. 1, pp. 222–247. This doctrine was first developed in *De doctrina christiana* and was Stoic in origin, but was reworked Platonically and gnoseologically. On the "detour" via the symbolic existent and the spirit's movement through *sensibilia* and *intelligibilia* to *rationabilia*, see esp. pp. 185–210.

246. Augustine, *De ordine* II.11.33: "As far as we have been able to investigate, we maintain that there are certain vestiges of reason in the senses, and as for what concerns sight and hearing, even in pleasure itself. Other senses usually require this name, not for the pleasure they give, but for something else: it is the nature of a rational animal to act with a goal in mind."

247. Ibid.

248. Ibid.

249. Ibid., II.11.34.

250. Ibid., with quotation from Virgil, *Georgica* II.V.480–481.

251. Ibid., II.12.35.

252. Ibid.

253. It now appears as an analytic-synthetic faculty: "Reason is a motion of the mind, which is able to distinguish and connect things it has learned" (ibid., II.11.30). On the theoretical premises guiding the reconstruction, see Radke 2003, p. 616ff.

254. Augustine, *De ordine* II.30: "What is rational in us, that is, what uses reason, and either makes or seeks rational things, since it was held by a natural bond in the society of those among whom reason was common, man could not be firmly associated with another man unless they spoke together and poured out, as it were, their minds and thoughts to one another; he saw that words, that is, sounds that signify, needed to be imposed on things so that, while men could not hear one another's minds, they used sense as a mediator, so to speak, to put things together for one another. But the words of people who were absent could not be heard; therefore, reason gave rise to letters, after having noted and categorized all the sounds of the mouth and the tongue. [. . .] Then reason reached a point where it noticed the sounds of the mouth by which we speak, and which it had already marked out with letters; it noticed that that there were some sounds which by a varied modulation of the mouth flowed from the throat freely and plainly without interference, and that others held a certain sound with a different pressure of the mouth, and that a last group was unable to utter sound unless it joined itself to the first two. Thus, in the order in which they were just presented, reason named

these: vocal, semi-vocal, and mute sounds. Then, it took note of syllables, and next it sorted words out into eight kinds and forms, and every motion, uniformity and combination was categorized cleverly and subtly."

255. Ibid.

256. Ibid.

257. It calls itself *litteratura*, absorbs everything written into itself, and for that reason burdens itself with historiography as well: "Grammar could have been perfect now, but since it declares by its very name that it teaches letters—hence it is called literature in Latin—it happened that whatever was set down in letters as worth remembering pertained to it by necessity. And thus, to this discipline history added itself, one in name, yet infinite and various in subject matter, full of cares more than of happiness or truth, burdensome more to grammarians than to historians themselves" (ibid., II.12.37). Obviously Augustine conceives historiography as an activity that does not require any conceptual work: as simple notation, whose difficulty is limited to achieving linguistic correctness.

258. Ibid., II.13.38: "When grammar had been perfected and established, reason was urged to seek and consider the power by which it produced art: for by defining, arranging and weighing it, not only had it explained and set it in order, but had even defended it against every assault of falsehood. How could it, therefore, pass on to making other objects, unless it first distinguished, noted and explained its own powers, as though they were machines and instruments, and produced that very discipline of disciplines, which they call dialectic? Dialectic teaches us how to teach and how to learn. In dialectic reason reveals itself, and discloses what it is, what it wants, and what its strength is. It knows what it is to know; it alone not only wants, but can make learned men."

259. Ibid.: "Since many foolish men in pursuing goals that are rightly, usefully and deservedly commended—for they do not see the purest truth as the exceptional man does—follow their own senses and habits, it is right that they be taught not only what they are capable of, but often and especially that they be moved emotionally. The part which accomplishes this is called rhetoric; filled more with need than with purity, it disburses to the people from its lap overflowing with delights so that people will deign to be led to what is useful for them."

260. Wolter 1969, p. 55.

261. Augustine, *De ordine* II.12.35.

262. Marrou 1938, p. 4.

263. Augustine, *De ordine* II.14.39.

264. Ibid.

265. Three kinds of sounds are distinguished on the basis of the ways they are produced: "Reason knew that sound only concerned the judgment of the ears, and that there were three kinds of sound: in the voice of living beings, in what breath produces in musical instruments, or in what is produced by percussion. The first concerns tragedies or comedies or a troop of any kind and everyone who sings with his own voice; the second is limited to flutes and similar instruments;

and the third concerns citharas, lyres, cymbals and all melodies produced by percussion" (ibid.).

266. Ibid., II.14.40: "Reason saw that this material was of a very low sort unless the sounds were arranged by a sure measure of time, and a well-regulated variety of high and low pitch."

267. Ibid.

268. Ibid.

269. Ibid., II.14.41. The works of the "musical arts" thus play "as large a role as reason." Therefore they are assigned a median position whose essence poets themselves are said to have conceived in an "image": because the numerical order viewed by ratio is eternal and immutable, while numerically measured sounds and verses pass away and at best have a certain permanence in the memory, the Muses were called the daughters of Jupiter and Memoria. Thus "And now reason very sadly accepted that the splendor and serenity of those things should be stained by the corporeal material of the voice. And because what the mind sees is always present and is taken as immortal, numbers appeared to be of this nature, while sound, since it is a thing of the senses, flowed out into the past, and was impressed on the memory by a rational lie; now that reason was favoring them, a story was made up that the Muses were the daughters of Jove and Memory. Need one ask what existed similarly in the offspring? Then that discipline, a partaker of sense and intellect, received the name of music" (ibid.). In *Retractationes* I.3.4 it is said to be displeasing when the Muses—even if only in jest—are treated as if they were goddesses; cf. also the—crushing—criticism of the myth of the Muses in *De doctrina christiana* II.17.27 f.

270. Augustine, *De ordine* II.16.44.

271. Radke 2003, p. 761 speaks of the "twofold nature" of mathematical objects and concepts, their "median status between the exclusively (conceptual) general and the exclusively (imaginable) particular."

272. Augustine, *De ordine* II.15.43.

273. Ibid.

274. Ibid., II.5.16.

275. Tertullian 1957, VII.9.13: "What does Athens have to do with Jerusalem? What agreement is there between the Academy and the Church? Between heretics and Christians? Our education comes from the porch of Solomon, who himself had taught that the Lord should be sought in the simplicity of the heart. Away with all attempts to produce a Stoic, Platonic, and dialectic Christianity. After Christ Jesus our concern is not with such a curiosity, nor with such inquiry after the gospel! When we believe, we desire nothing beyond believing. For we first believe this: there is nothing that we ought to believe beyond this." On the importance of "philosophical" conceptions in Tertullian, see Braun 1977.

276. Augustine, *De ordine* II.5.14. On the Pythagorean models transmitted by Iamblichus, see Staab 2002, pp. 462–472.

277. Augustine, *De ordine* II.19.50.

278. Augustine, *Confessiones* III.4.7: "The book was entitled *Hortensius*, and it contained an exhortation to study philosophy. That book changed my desires, and turned my prayers to you, Lord, and altered my hopes and desires. My every vain hope suddenly became worthless, and I began to desire the immortality of wisdom with an incredible fire in my heart, and I began to rise up so that I might return to you." Several attempts have been made to reconstruct the *Hortensius*, the latest being Cicero 1962 and Cicero 1990. To judge by the reconstructions, one must assume that the theme of beatitude was central to the text. However, Cicero's paganism at first leaves the searcher unsatisfied: "But this alone held me back from breaking into great flames: that the name of Christ was not found there, since this name *through your mercy, Lord,* this name of my savior, your Son, my tender heart drank in with the milk of my pious mother. And it held that name deep within it, and without it nothing captivated me entirely, no matter how learned, polished and true it was" (Augustine, *Confessiones* III.4.8; emphasis supplied). But Augustine's attempt to answer the question concerning the possibility and the paths to *beatitudo* on the basis of the Bible itself fails because his language is so flat in comparison to that of Cicero (ibid., III.5.9). There follows the Manichaean phase (Flasch 2003, pp. 28–36). Finally, contact with Neoplatonic teaching coincides with Augustine's residence in Milan. The concept of *beatitudo* that emerged from it corresponds to that propounded by Cicero, but is now inserted into the context of a Christian theology built upon Neoplatonic foundations.

279. See Beierwaltes 1981, p. 16ff. and Flasch 2003, p. 39f.: "According to Augustine, happiness must be defined as the possession of what cannot be lost. We can recognize happiness as such only if it is certain (*certum*)—from his earliest writings on, this is a constant in Augustine's thought."

280. This specification is necessary because the future world of salvation will also be a sensible one, but it will be immutable, according to *Retractationes* I.4.3: "I did not say 'all' sensible things, but *those* corruptible ones. I should have said this: such things will not be the sensible things of the future, in *the new heaven and the new earth* of the world to come."

281. See *De ordine* II.8.25.

282. See the detailed account in Staab 2002.

283. Augustine, *De ordine* II.20.53.

284. Ibid., II.20.54. We should note the distancing carried out by the *Retractationes*, especially since it emphasizes the decided currency of the Pythagorean tradition in Augustine's early theology. While working on *De ordine* he could see no flaw in the Pythagorean doctrine: "Nor am I pleased that I bestowed such great praise on the philosopher Pythagoras that whoever heard or read my words would think that I believed that there were no errors in Pythagorean teaching, whereas there are many and serious ones" (*Retractationes* III.3). Even in the *Retractationes*, the potential of the *artes* to lead to a vision of God is not rejected: "I wanted to attain, or to lead others to attain, by sure steps the non-corporeal through the corporeal" (*Retractationes* I.6).

285. Keller 1993, p. 274: "Beauty in Augustine's sense is not a matter of subjective taste and individual inclination, but rather [exists] independently of any objective property of things and therefore exists unaffected by human observation. [. . .] Beauty is an objective fact that necessarily produces an intersubjective, similar effect on every perceiving observer or—especially in music—listener." In addition to the standard works on "aesthetic" theory in the Middle Ages, let us mention Beierwaltes 1975, Horn 1979, and, because of the reworking of the materials, Svoboda 1933. O'Connell 1978 is not free of anachronistic value judgments, while Ellsmere 1988 concentrates entirely on the music theory context. Balthasar 1961–1962, vol. 2.1, pp. 97–143 offers supplementary references.

286. Beierwaltes 1975, p. 143 [emphasis in original].

287. Augustine, *De diversis quaestionibus octaginta tribus liber uno,* LXXXIII.26.

288. Cf. *De libero arbitrio* II.17.45.

289. *De diversis quaestionibus* LXXXIII.6; *Epistolae* XI.3; *De immortalitate animae* VIII.15.

290. *De vera religione* 18.35; *De immortalitate animae* 8.13; *Soliloquiae* II.18.32.

291. See in detail *De vera religione* 43.81 and *De libero arbitrio* II.16.44 ff.

292. See for instance *De immortalitate animae* VIII.13 in 1 *John* 9:9; *De vera religione* 18.35, 52–101.

293. Cf. Du Roy 1966.

294. See, in addition to *De musica* VI, esp. *De vera religione* 3.3; 30.55; 31.57; 32.59; 33.61; 36.66; 39.72; 41.77; 43.81; 55.113; *De ordine* I.18; *De diversis quaestionibus* LXXXIII.18; *De Civitate Dei* XXII.24; the proofs presuppose the Platonic connection of *pulchrum, verum,* and *bonum.* The restriction in the case of *aequalitas* emerges from the relative ineffability of *aequalitas* in relation to the existent, which will be discussed in detail further below.

295. See Radke 2003, pp. 785–801.

296. *Confessiones* VII.10.16.

297. Ibid., VII.10.17.

298. Radke 2003, p. 576: "Everything that is not only a unity is a compound of unity and plurality, or more precisely the unity of a plurality."

299. Ibid., p. 699.

300. *Epistolae* 3.4; *De ordine* II.11.33; *De quantitate animae* VIII.13f.; *De Civitate Dei* XXII.19.

301. See the review in Horn 1994. The complexes "Gewißheitssicherung," "Ordnungsleistung," "Zahlenästhetik," "Zahlenethik," "Zahlenbildung," and "Zahlensymbolik" (p. 389f.) are shown in *De ordine, Epistolae, De immortalitate animae, De moribus ecclesiae catholicae et de moribus Manichaeorum, De libero arbitrio, De genesi contra Manichaeos, De musica* (p. 401ff.), *De vera religione, Enarrationes in Psalmos, De Genesi ad litteram, Confessiones, De Trinitate* and *De civitate Dei.* The study proves the coherence of the concept of number

and its implication throughout Augustine's creative period.

302. Augustine, *De libero arbitrio* II.16.42.

303. Beierwaltes 1975, p. 147.

304. Radke 2003, p. 328.

305. Ibid., p. 427, cf. in detail ibid., pp. 432–575. In addition to Radke's study the survey in Klein 1936, pp. 18–105, 122–235, remains valuable; for the epistemological implications of the concept of number compared in different periods, see also Schmitt 1989.

306. See again Marrou 1938, pp. 251–262, the following according to Martin 1956. Nicomachus's work is extant in the Greek original; the first printed version appeared in Paris in 1536, the first scholarly edition is Nicomachus of Gerasa 1866. This work is central to the exposition in Radke 2003.

307. Commentaries were written in the fourth century by Iamblichus, Asclepios of Tralles, et al.; in the sixth century Philoponous produced an extensive commentary. A commentary by Proclus who saw himself as the reincarnation of Nicomachus, as Marinus of Neapolis reports in his *Vita Procli* (485) (Marinus of Neapolis 1960, p. 28), has not been preserved; and Boethius's *Institutio arithmetica*, was from the ninth century on a standard textbook of arithmetic, is a reworking that stays close to its model. On this see Robbins's comment on p. 132 in Nicomachus of Gerasa 1938: "A comparison of the two books [Nicomachus's and Boethius's textbooks] will convince the reader that Boethius follows Nicomachus from first to last, expanding here and condensing there, as he says in his preface that he will do, but never adding anything essential, either original or derived from other sources, that departs from his model."

308. Two independent sources confirm the existence of this work. The patriarch Photius provides a brief and hostile summary of the work in his *Bibliotheca* (c. 187); Iamblichus's *Theologoumena Arithmeticae* (Iamblichus 1922), a compilation of Neopythagorean writings on arithmetic proceeding from the entourage of Iamblichus's or Proclus's schools, sums up the work.

309. Nestle 1975. The following survey, which is extremely condensed because of the requirements of my exposition, draws on Burkert 1962; Martin 1956; Stenzel 1959; Horn 1995; Radke 2003.

310. A detailed account is found in Münxelhaus 1976, pp. 26–55, esp. p. 50ff. on the representation of the physical impossibility of what is reported in the "smithy" legend and the question why this was nonetheless handed down unchanged as late as the sixteenth century. Questions of attribution remain fundamental and are especially speculative for the Pythagorean tradition because the "tendency to ascribe all the knowledge acquired over time to Pythagoras himself and to guarantee it by his authority" has to be taken into account: Röd 1988, p. 55.

311. Zimmermann 1976, p. 83.

312. Lohmann 1970d, p. 106f.

313. Aristotle, *Metaphysics* 985b f. Trans. W.D. Ross. [In this English ver-

sion, unless otherwise indicated all references to Aristotle's works will be to *The Basic Works of Aristotle*, ed. Richard Mckeon; the standard Bekker pagination will be used.] Aristotle's presentation allows us to conclude that the Pythagorean school had described at least the number one and presumably the first ten natural numbers as substances, because Aristotle distances himself from the Pythagorean substantialization of numbers by arguing that numbers contain in undifferentiated form both the meaning of material and the meaning of accidents: "Evidently, then, these thinkers also consider that number is the principle both as matter for things and as forming both their modifications and their permanent states" (986a). Accordingly, Martin 1956, p. 14 comments: "The Pythagorean definition thus comes before the division of the concepts into form and matter and quality."

314. Martin 1956, p. 14.

315. See Staab 2002, pp. 454–461.

316. This is the term used for the type according to Pythagorean realism in Lenk 1995, p. 27.

317. Plato, *Statesman*, 287c; cf. also *Philebus* 16d f. Aristotle, *Metaphysics* 987b reports the partial identification of the Pythagorean concept of number and the Idea, and so does Plotinus, *Enneads* VI.6.9. Mathematicians hunt numbers/ideas: in the *Euthydemus* (290b) geometers, astronomers, and masters of calculation are compared with hunters. Just as the latter capture game and leave its preparation to the cooks, mathematicians hunt in their own way: "for these are a sort of hunters too, since they are not mere makers of diagrams, but they try to discover what is already there—so because they do not know how to use them, but only how to hunt, they hand over their discoveries, I take it, to the dialecticians to use up, at least all of them hand over who are not quite without sense" [trans. W. H. D. Rouse, modified]. The doctrine of Ideas resonates with the assessment that numbers correspond to what "is already there" and it is unmistakable that "true" concern with numbers is a matter for the philosopher.

318. Plato, *Phaedo*, 99d ff.

319. Ibid., 74a, 100c ff., 104b ff. Cf. Martin 1953, pp. 191–203, esp. p. 195.

320. Plato, *Phaedo* 74a ff.; cf. *Meno* 81e ff. and 85c ff.; *Sophist* 244d ff.; *Timaeus* 32a ff.; *Philebus* 15b ff.

321. Plotinus, *Enneads* VI.6.9, p. 59. Quoted from the edition Plotinus 1956–1971. On the quotation, see Martin 1956, pp. 51–56 and Creuzer 1977, p. 4ff.

322. Martin 1956, p. 54: "He [Plotinus] has to defend them against a standpoint that seeks to relocate the existence of numbers exclusively in thought, ideas, and the numbers of human beings, and he has to defend them against the teaching of Aristotle, according to which the true existence of numbers consists in their being accidents of the real, material, and sensible world."

323. Nicomachus of Gerasa, *Harmonicum Enchiridium* II.7, in Jan (ed.) 1966, vol. I, p. 279.

324. See Plotinus, *Enneads* VI.6.10; VI.6.11; VI.6.14; VI.6.16.

325. Ibid., VI.6.9 and depending on the subject, VI.6.4; VI.6.11; VI.6.16; VI.6.9.

326. Martin 1956, p. 51 on Plotinus, *Enneads* VI.6.2.

327. Ibid., VI.6.12, 79.

328. Ibid., VI.6.16.

329. Cf. Zintzen 1977, p. VIII: "It is debatable to what extent Plotinus opened up to Eastern ideas; it is undeniable that they exercised a great attraction on him and his successors. Plotinus and all the later Neoplatonists absorbed such stimulyses. A direct consequence was that philosophy turned into theology, which expressly equates the highest ontological level with God. In such a view, Pythagoras and Orpheus become authorities, and the rational way of seeing things soon follows the theological dogma." It is no accident that Pythagoras and Orpheus are named here; down to the early modern period they are emblematic advocates for music and inspired poetry. On the same aspect, cf. Cumont 1977 and Bernard 1990, pp. 107–164.

330. Cf. Augustine, *De civitate Dei* XII.19.

331. Plato, *Phaedrus* 249d f. Cf. the analogous argument in Plotinus, *Enneads* II.9.16.

332. Cf. Henry 1934, p. 122ff.; Solignac 1957; Rief 1962, pp. 66–73; Ziegenaus 1972, pp. 11–25; Keller 1993, pp. 236–246; Schmitt 2007, p. 69ff. In *Enneads* V.8, p. 1, Plotinus argues that if the arts "imitate" nature, then they do so not in the sense of a "doubling" of the real that is superfluous and even "conceals" its object; instead, they "rise to the rational forms (*lógoi*) from which Nature itself proceeds." They sense, as it were, what nature itself, as a being inherently moved by *geosía*, "imitates" or what constitutes Nature itself; they do not find enough in the purely factual or sensible, but instead realize the rational referential character of their object and are capable of putting the recipient at least on the path to the universal principle. In each case, "beautiful" art makes it evident that beauty is founded on the inner, intelligible form, and ultimately in the absolute *nous*, as the real and true being of the beautiful, and that beauty is therefore in the creative *techné* of the artist to a greater degree than in the work created. However, the latter refers to the former, and also to its absolute ground of possibility. Beauty is also knowable in Plotinus's sense in the thinking soul's return to itself (*epistrophé*), to the beginning of the transformation of thought into the integrative unity of Being and thinking in the spirit. Only through thought's insight into spirit, which is present in the soul and is permanently bound up with the intelligible that transcends it, is it possible to fulfill the presupposition that the Good or One reveals itself to thought, which has still to rise above its prereflexive basis, as the origin of every appearing beauty. These philosophemes, which are characteristic of Plotinus and based on the theory of the three divine hypostases in *Enneads* V.4.1, are the objective foundation for Augustine's ontology of the beautiful, no matter how much we must assume, with Dorrie 1969, that Augustine had access to Plotinus's philosophy through Porphyry's mediation and translation. On this, see Hadot 1977. The same still holds for the foundations of medieval theories of the beautiful through John Scotus Eriugena, for Suger of St. Denis,

and especially for the musical understanding of the Middle Ages. What Plotinus formulated in *Enneads* V.9.11.42 is still valid: "Furthermore, all music, which is directed by its ideas toward harmony and rhythm, is analogous to the music that contemplates the rhythm of the spiritual in the upper world."

333. See Küpper 2002b.

334. Augustine 1947, VI.13, p. 38 [emphasis supplied].

335. Ibid.

336. Beierwaltes 1991, p. 7.

337. Schmitt 1990, p. 234.

338. Cohen 1976. On the facets that the concept of equivalence has shown in the discussion since Jakobson 1970, see Küper 1988, pp. 10–71; on recurrence as a classeme of possible equivalences, esp. pp. 30–32, and the supplementary remarks in Rimmon-Kenan 1980, pp. 151–159.

339. Schmitt 1990, p. 236.

340. Beierwaltes 1975, p. 145. In this passage, see also Beierwaltes's commentary on the Plotinian sources of the concept in particular. Cf. further Keller 1993, p. 276: "The apparent symmetry in the outer form of things and—with the focus more on audible music—the harmony in sound stand in a mutual relationship with the inner unity of things. Through its own ontological connection with absolute unity, *aequalitas numerosa* lends not only a relative unity and thus a sensible beauty to physical shape, but at the same time points to the inner, absolute unity. This means: if unity in number gives concrete form and number provides the basis for beauty, then the unity constitutive of numbers (unity as the principle of numbers) is ultimately the ontological condition of beauty."

341. Lotman 1972, p. 176.

342. Ibid., p. 177.

343. Mediating between the historical concept of "form" and the cybernetic concept of "structure" according to Klaus 1971, vol. 2, s.v.

344. In the background stands the Aristotelian concept of *ars* or τέχνη. In the *Physics*, II.8.199a, Aristotle says that "generally art [*techné*] partly completes what nature cannot bring to a finish, and partly imitates her." The first element seems to indicate a certain independence of *techné* with respect to Nature, but this involves reading the passage precisely against its point: even that which *techné* can complete is inconceivable without the design already present in nature. Human work in no way goes beyond what is laid out in the teleological order of Nature, the limits of what is producible at all are set in the latter and by the latter. For Aristotle, Nature and Being ultimately coincide with the quintessence of everything possible insofar as the imitation of Nature is always an imitation of a teleological sequence of events or their result. The human mind is predisposed to adequation, and does not conceive what is not at least already inherent in Nature: "It is absurd to suppose that purpose is not present because we do not observe the agent deliberating. Art does not deliberate. If the ship-building art were in the wood, it would produce the same results *by nature*. If, therefore, purpose is present in

art, it is present also in nature. The best illustration is a doctor doctoring himself: nature is like that. It is plain then that nature is a cause, a cause that operates for a purpose" (ibid., 199b). On the thematic complex as a whole, see Ulmer 1953.

345. Augustine 1947, VI.12.35, p. 434.

346. Ibid.

347. Ibid., pp. 434–436.

348. Ibid., p. 439.

349. Keller 1993, p. 232f.

350. The corresponding *scientia* takes these forms themselves as its object. The connection is perhaps most strikingly formulated in Cassiodorus 2003, II.3.20, vol. 2, p. 384: "Plato and Aristotle, the accepted masters of secular letters, maintained that there was this difference between art and discipline: art is concerned with contingent things that can occur in different ways, whereas discipline is concerned with things that cannot happen in any other way."

351. Augustine 1947, II.9.16, p. 130.

352. Mayer 1969, p. 276. *De Civitate Dei* XII.2 offers a striking formulation: "He gave a more ample existence to some, a less ample existence to others, and thus he organized the natures of beings into gradations."

353. The following draws on Rief 1962, pp. 212–214; Mayer 1969, pp. 275–277.

354. Augustine, *De vera religione* XXX.55.

355. Rief 1962, p. 214.

356. See, in the "aesthetic" horizon, Küpper 2002b.

357. Augustine, *De musica* VI.17.57.

358. In the development of the concept of order laid out in *Liber sapientiae* 11.21 with precisely this point, Krings 1941 saw the characteristic feature of the Western concept of order itself; the consequences for art are further elaborated in Horn 1979, esp. p. 5.

359. For a summary of the grounds for this depreciation, see Ferrari 1989 and Gadamer 1968.

360. The verses from Virgil used as examples in *De musica* illustrate this, but on the whole they are not very instructive regarding the scope of the argument. A verse that presented something heterodox in a well-formed way, in which therefore the caveat regarding legitimacy concerned the content of the verse, necessarily led to a confrontation of the two attitudes toward poetry. It is crucial for all the arguments presented here that the apparent condemnation of blasphemous verse in this case leaves unaffected its specific musicality, and therefore its place in the harmony of Creation and its quality as a sensible manifestation of this "harmonious" order.

361. This confrontation takes place elsewhere. Cf. for instance the detailed argument in *De civitate Dei* I.30.33, II.4 and II.8 against dramatic art, the songs of pagan cults, and the Kybele cult and its songs, which repeatedly addresses specific deviant functions and contexts of musical practice.

362. Keller 1993, p. 288f. However, in this context Keller seems to exaggerate the definitely conciliatory positive assessment of art and to disregard Augustine's view that the *artifex* created mostly out of instinct, and mostly not out of *scientia*: "Thus the claim to represent reality is enacted in art. This does not mean copying and imitating another form in a way as true to the original as possible; [. . .] The artist is thus a perceiver who penetrates with his spiritual eye into the innermost grounds of all existence, to the principles of order and beauty, and thus to the creative ideas of God. However, the artist is also a creator who is capable of giving expression to his spiritual vision in a work of art. In him, seeing and creating merge."

363. It is not for nothing that Koch 1983 argued that they should be regarded as "the smallest unit" of the paradigm of poetic units, a repetitive structure, a relation composed of two identical or almost identical elements.

364. Keller 1993, p. 177.

365. Oberleitner et al. (eds.) 1969ff. In Italy, thirty-four manuscripts have been attested in Assisi, Cesena, Florence, Ivrea, Mantua, Milan, Naples, Padua, Rome, Todi, in the Vatican, in Venice and Vercelli; one of these copies dates from the tenth and eleventh centuries, six from the thirteenth century, three from the transition from the thirteenth to the fourteenth centuries, seven from the fourteenth century, and fifteen from the fifteenth century alone. See vol. 1.1, ed. Manfred Oberleitner, p. 124f. On the Iberian peninusula only two manuscripts from the fourteenth century are attested, both of them in Valencia. See vol. 4, ed. Johaness Divjak, p. 55. In the area of the Benelux countries there still exist five manuscripts, three in Brussels, and one in Bruges dating from the thirteenth and fourteenth centuries, along with a fifteenth-century manuscript in Utrecht. See vol. 8.1, ed. Marie Therese Wieser, p. 118. In Great Britain and Ireland there are eighteen copies extant, including three in Cambridge, one each in Durham, Glasgow, and Lincoln, four in London, and eight in Oxford. One of these manuscripts dates from the tenth or eleventh century, one from the twelfth, five from the thirteenth, six from the fourteenth, and four from the fifteenth century. See vol. 2.1, ed. Franz Römer, p. 131f.

366. Le Bœuf 1986, the following survey of the manuscripts is based on pp. 273–280: the manuscript Tours, Bib. mun. 286 (166) was produced in the first half of the ninth century and attested in the Saint-Martin de Tours monastery over the following centuries. The manuscript preserved in the abbey of Saint-Pierre in Corbie, Paris, BNF lat. 13375, was also produced in the first half of the ninth century. Valenciennes Bib. mun. 384, also from the ninth century, presumably copied in Rheims, is attested between 1150 and 1168 in Saint-Amand-en-Pévèle (now in Nord-Pas-de-Calais). Metz 288, from the tenth century, appears always to have been preserved in the library of Saint-Arnould de Metz; Paris BNF lat. 7200, possibly copied in the Laon-Soissons region, is already attested in the eleventh century in Fleury-sur-Loire. Paris, BNF lat. 6184, also from the tenth century, is attested in the convent of Carmes-Déchaussées in Clermont-

Ferrand; the provenance of the manuscript is not clear. In the eleventh century Angers 486, attested in Saint-Aubin d'Angers after 1153, as well as Paris, BNF lat. 7231, presumably in Saint-Martial de Limoges after 1034, are produced. In the twelfth century Paris, BNF lat. 17161, an extract from *De musica* preserved in the convent of the Feuillants, was produced; Paris, BNF lat. 16662, a personal study copy later chained in the Sorbonne, was produced in the early thirteenth century, as was Troyes 801 and Saint-Omer 85, attested in Clairmarais. Paris, BNF lat. 14477, which contains only Book VI of *De musica*, was produced in the thirteenth century and has been shown to have been in the Bibliothèque Saint-Victor as late as 1516, while Paris, BNF 17398 comes from the holdings of the Collège de Navarre. In France, the currency of the text, which can be measured by the production of new copies, extends beyond the thirteenth century into the late Middle Ages: in the fourteenth and fifteenth centuries, Paris, Mazarine 3472, Paris, BNF lat. 14294, and Paris, Arsenal 350, a manuscript including only Books I to V for the abbey of St. Victor, a copy of Book VI for the abbey of Notre-Dame-des-Dunes in Bruges (Bruge 151) and two copies of Book VI for the Collège de Navarre in Paris (Paris, Arsenal 307, and Paris, Mazarine 1639) are produced. Paris, BNF lat. 1974, also a copy of Book VI, is attested in 1369 in Avignon. So far as I know, there is no more complete survey of what we know about the manuscript tradition of *De musica* in France.

367. Le Bœuf 1986, pp. 185–187 bis.

368. Le Bœuf 1986, pp. 281–298, with detailed evidence. The oldest proof stems from the Reichenau monastery's library catalog, around 822–823, which lists *De musica* among Augustine's works; another catalog from the second half of the ninth century no longer mentions it there, but under the *classici* and textbooks of the *artes liberales*. A catalog from Saint-Riquier in Picardy dating from 831 mentions *De musica*. From the middle of the ninth century on, catalogs prove that copies of *De musica* existed in the abbeys of Lorsch in sourthern Hesse, Murbach in southern Alsace, and in Sankt Gallen. Two copies of the work are attested in the tenth century in the library of the famous scriptorium of San Colombano in Bobbio, in the Italian province of Piacenza, including one bound together with Priscian's textbook on grammar, the Venerable Bede's metrics and Boethius's *De institutione arithmetica*. A catalog drawn up toward the end of the tenth century at the abbey of Sankt Emmeran in Regensburg lists Augustine's *De musica* together with Boethius's *De institutione musica*. A catalog from the Benedictine abbey of St. Michael in Trier, dating from the eleventh or twelfth century, lists *De musica*; in Lobbes, which is now in Belgium, the work is attested at the beginning of the twelfth century; Cluny attests a complete copy of *De musica* as well as a *florilegium* that is bound together with Cassiodorus's *Institutiones*; the abbey of Bec-Hellouin in Normandy mentions the work in a catalog from the second half of the twelfth century; it is also attested in Saint-Germain-des-Prés and in Pontigny in Burgundy, the third Cistercian abbey founded after Fontenay and Cîteau. *De musica* is attested in Michelsberg in Bamberg between 1172 and 1201.

Around the turn of the fourteenth century, catalogs of the library in Christ Church in Canterbury alone mention three copies; in 1372 the catalog of the Augustinian canon in York lists it. The catalog of the library of the Florentine Cardinal Pierro Corsini, dating from 1405, mentions the text; the index of the Great Library of the Castle in Peñiscola, dating from 1409, lists one copy; in 1412, a copy comes from the private library of Amplonius Ratinck von Berkas to a Collegium in Erfurt; in 1437 a catalog of the Collège du Trésorier in Paris documents two copies of Book VI; in 1492 a copy of the work is attested in the abbey of Saint-Claude in the Juras; although as we might expect, no scholarly treatises or textbooks are found in the catalogs of the Grande Chartreuse, the motherhouse of the Carthusian order, a catalog from the fifteenth century nonetheless lists a copy of Augustine's *De musica*.

369. Here we should mention Florence, Laur. Ashb. 1051, and the abbreviations transmitted in the Parisinus lat. 7200 and in Ivrea LXXXIV (52) with Boethius and the ninth book of Martianus Capella's *De nuptiis Philologiae et Mercurii*, in Florence, Laur. Plut. XXIV.16 with Jacob of Liege's *Speculum musicae* and in the Parisinus lat. 16662 with excerpts from Isidore of Seville and the *Tonale Sancti Bernardi*.

370. Rome, Vat. lat. 4929, fol. 35r–50r (ninth century); Paris, BNF lat. 13955, fol. 158v–165v (ninth century); Malibu, CA, Getty-Museum, Philipps 16278 (ninth century); Florence, Laur. Ashb. 1051, fol. 42r–49v (twelfth century); Florence, Cod. Aedil. Flor. eccles. 168, fol. 86v–90v (fifteenth century). It could not be determined whether the same text is given by the thirteenth-century *Exce[r]ptiones de musica s. Augustini* extant in the London Codex Royal 4. B. X, fol. 69v–74v. A critical edition of the epitome is provided by Vecchi 1950a.

371. Le Bœuf 1986, pp. 361–365.

372. An extract from Book VI under the title *Genera numerorum in sensibus* contains, for instance, a manuscript from St. Gallen, also dating from the eleventh century. On this and other copies of Book VI alone, cf. Bernhard 1990b, p. 14f.

373. For instance, Tours 286, from the early ninth century (see Rand 1929, vol. 1.2, no. 18, table 30), and Paris, BNF lat. 7231, also with abundant interlinear glosses in Tironian notes.

374. For example, in Bamberg (Class. 36, fol. 50–87) there is a collection of glosses on *De musica* entitled *Expositiunculae in libros beati Augustini de musica* that was copied in the eleventh century and was strongly influenced by John Scotus Eriugena's *Periphyseon*. This collection of glosses is edited in Vecchi 1950. Le Bœuf 1986 re-edits and comments on them, apparently without being aware of this older edition.

375. This is the generic term chosen in Eco 2004, pp. 49–66.

376. On the influence of Augustinian music theory, see, with an assessment of earlier literature, Bernhard 1990b, pp. 7–35, as well as Handschin 1964, p. 113ff.; Nowak 1999, esp. p. 58ff.; Bowen 1988; Föllmi 1994.

377. Gérold 1973, p. 83ff.; on Clement in particular, cf. Irwin 1982.

378. Gérold 1973, p. 74ff., p. 83ff.

379. Examples in Bernhard 1990b, p. 16f.

380. Aldhelmus Schireburnensis 2001, p. 81.

381. Richenhagen 1989, pp. 40–93, esp. p. 43.

382. Phillips/Huglo 1985, p. 121.

383. Guido of Arezzo 1955.

384. Petrus de Sancto Dionysio 1972, p. 148: "Nam secundum Augustinum, secundo musicae libro: 'In motu etiam est omne quod sonat.'"

385. On these concepts, see below, chapter 6.

386. Ugolino of Orvieto 1959–1962; the direct reference to Augustine's *De musica* is in V.3.13.

387. In *Confessiones* IV.4.8 reference is made to singing psalters; the psalms are said to be songs of faith (*cantica fidelia*) that work against the (gnostic) arrogance of humanity. Bishop Athanasius of Alexandria (295–373) is supposed to have had the psalm reader recite rather than sing, a practice that leads Augustine to ask about the sense of melismatic solo psalmody: sung "with flowing voice and most fitting modulation [*modulatione*]" (ibid., XI.33.50), as he has heard done in Milan, the holy word has greater effect, since between the movements of the mind corresponding to it and the movements of the voice in song there is a "secret relationship [*occulta familiaritas*]" (ibid., IX.33.49). With *De musica* in mind, this *familiaritas* ought not really to be called *occulta*. On the passages in Augustine's work that can be read as documentary with respect to the experience of music, see Brennan 1988.

388. See Nowak 1999, pp. 60–63.

389. *Liber de natura et proprietate tonorum*, in Johannes Tinctoris 1975, vol. 1, pp. 65–108, here p. 69 with the quotation of *Confessiones* X.33; *Complexus effectuum musicae*, ibid., vol. 2, pp. 161–177, here p. 170, also with a quotation from *Confessiones* X.33.

390. Adam of Fulda 1963, p. 333a, with quotation from Augustine, *Epistola* 166: "Augustine said to Jerome: 'Music is the science of sense or of sense well modulated, and was granted by the generosity of God in order to remind mortals having rational souls about great things.'"

391. Kresteff 1962, p. 19.

392. Waite 1954, esp. pp. 8, 29, 35–39.

393. The core of Waite's thesis has survived: It is considered established that the constitution of the three *ordines* as coordinate groups of *longae* and *breves* in a ligature is based on the number theory developed in *De musica*. On this, see the critical discussion of Waite in Phillips/Huglo 1985.

394. Augustine, *De doctrina christiana* II.37.55 and II.38.56.

395. *De libero arbitrio* II.8.22–25; the lengthy speech given by the *magister* Augustine ends with an allusion to Eccles. 7:26: "I turned my heart that I might know, and consider, and seek wisdom and number [*sapientiam et numerum*]"; cf. ibid., II.9.108, II.11.123, and II.11.127. This equation is drawn from Iamblichus,

as Peck 1980, p. 30 shows. Cf. Cilleruelo 1968, and especially, on the sources of Augustine's arithmology, Most 1951.

396. Augustine, *De doctrina christiana* II.16.26: "Indeed, we find both number and music treated favorably in many places in the Holy Scriptures."

397. Hopper 1938.

398. Grossmann 1954, p. 21.

399. Ibid., pp. 45–51f.

400. Meyer 1975, on Augustine esp. pp. 26–34, and on the "Augustinianism" of Hugo of St. Victor, Odo of Morimond, Theobald of Langres, and William of Auberives, see pp. 46–52.

401. Amith 1908, on Pacioli p. 54.

402. Hellgardt 1973, on Augustine in particular, pp. 157–252, 256; Langosch 1970, on Goliardic poetry, using the example of the Archpoet, pp. 134–145; cf. also Haubrichs 1969.

403. On number symbolism in the Eulalia sequence, see Süpek 1993.

404. Simson 1956, p. 20.

405. See the detailed discussion in Bruyne 1946, vol. 1, p. 334ff., vol. 3, p. 189ff.

406. Ibid., vol. 2, p. 108.

407. Ibid., p. 203.

408. Ibid., p. 301 [italicized in the original].

409. Ibid., pp. 211ff., 220ff. The interpretations of the *Timaeus* to be gleaned from Macrobius, Calcidus, and Boethius are here unified under Augustinian auspices. See ibid., p. 301.

410. Ibid., vol. 3, p. 88–117; on the arithmetical foundation, see esp. p. 102.

411. Ibid., pp. 102, 142, 146.

412. Quoted in ibid., p. 126 from the Erfurt manuscript, Ampl. O.30. Cf. also ibid., p. 134f.: "The beauty of light derives from its simplicity and homogeneity; now, what is homogenious is what is most one, that is, what is the most equal to itself. Moreover, equality is the simplest relationship. What is in the closest harmony with itself, what realizes the maximum of agreement with itself, is what is the most beautiful [. . .]: light, in fact, is equal to itself, and equality expresses the first of the proportions."

413. Ibid., p. 131.

414. Quoted from ibid., p. 128.

415. Quoted from ibid., p. 129: "So that all things should remain delightedly in this association and unification [*congregatione et unificatione*]."

416. Ibid., p. 128, 4n.

417. Ibid., p. 139 [emphasis in the original].

418. Ibid., p. 142.

419. Ibid., p. 152.

420. Ibid., p. 199. The following draws on Bruyne 1946 and Peter 1964.

421. *Itinerarium mentis in Deum* II.10, quoted from the edition Bonaventura

1938, p. 311: "This speculation, however, *broadens* according to the consideration of seven differences of *numbers*, by which one rises up toward God as though by seven steps, as Augustine has shown in his book On True Religion and in the sixth book of On Music. In those places he marks off differences of numbers step by step rising up from sense impressions to the Maker of all things, so that God is seen in all things. Augustine says that numbers are in bodies, and especially in sounds and voices. He calls these *sounding* [*sonantes*] numbers. The numbers taken from these and received in our senses he calls *meters* [*occursores*]; numbers coming forth from the soul to the body, as in gestures and dancing he calls *advancing* [*progressores*] numbers; numbers for the delight of sense from the conversion of intention over the form received he calls *sensual*; numbers retained in memory he calls *memorial*; numbers through which we judge all these things he calls *judicial*, which exist necessarily above the mind as infallible and irrefutable. From these, however, *artificial* numbers are impressed on our minds, but Augustine does not list these among the steps because they have been associated with the *judicial* numbers. From these flow the advancing numbers from which are created the numerous forms of the *artisans*, so that a descent is established from the highest through the middle down to the lowest. We rise up step by step to the highest from *sounding* numbers through *meters*, *sensual*, and *memorial* numbers" [Emphases in the original]. On the *numeri artificiales*, see in detail Peter 1964, p. 86ff.

422. *Commentarium in quatuor libros sententiarum Magistri Petri Lombardi* a.2.3, quoted in the edition Bonaventura 1882–1902, vol. 2, p. 34: "All being has a certain form; and everything that has a certain form possesses beauty."

423. Ibid., p. 9: "That accord [*convenientia*] seeks unity and equality, therefore, where there is perfect beauty, there is accord and equality [. . .]."

424. *Itinerarium mentis in Deum* II.10, quoted in the edition Bonaventura 1938, p. 311f.

425. Ibid., II.5, p. 306.

426. Ibid., I.11, p. 299f.

427. *Commentarium in quatuor libros sententiarum Magistri Petri Lombardi* I, art. un. 3, concl. Bonaventura 1882–1902, vol. 1, p. 43: "God can only create a thing that is regulated in relation to Himself. Since order presupposes number, and number presupposes measure—because things are not regulated in relation to anything if they are not numbered, and they are not numbered unless they are delimited—it was necessary, therefore, that God create all things with number, weight, and measure."

428. Bonaventura, *Itinerarium mentis in Deum* II.11, Bonaventura 1938, p. 312f.

429. Ibid., II.8, p. 309: "If, therefore, 'delight is the conjunction of suitable with suitable,' and the likeness of God alone explains best what is lovely, mild and healthy, and is united according to truth, depth, and fullness filling every capacity, it can be seen clearly that in God alone is the wellspring of true delight, and that from all delightful things we are led by the hand to seek it."

430. Ibid., II.5, p. 306f.: "Delight follows this apprehension, if it concerns a suitable object. Sense delights in an object perceived through an abstract likeness, or, to express it properly, by reason of its beauty, as in sight, or by reason of its pleasantness, as in its odor or its sound, or by reason of its wholesomeness as in its taste and feel. Every delight exists by reason of proportionality [*ratione proportionalitatis*] [. . .], 'beauty is nothing but numerical equality' ['*pulcritudo nihil aliud est quam aequalitas numerosa*']."

431. *Commentarium in quatuor libros sententiarum Magistri Petri Lombardi* II, d. 9, art. unic. q. 6, Bonaventura 1882–1902, vol. 2, p. 252 [emphasis in original].

432. Bruyne 1946, vol. 3, pp. 153–188.

433. Hüschen 1970, esp. p. 210f. with many examples.

434. Bruyne 1946, vol. 3, p. 262.

435. See esp. ibid., pp. 269–271, here p. 270: "Ulrich remains faithful to his deep-seated objectivism. His theory recalls the Pythagorean-Platonic tradition [. . .]."

436. Föllmi 1994, p. 135ff.

Chapter Six: Boethius, *De institutione arithmetica* and
De institutione musica

1. Augustine, *Retractationes* I.6 and *Epistulae* 101.3.

2. This is not contradicted by the evidence that the incomplete nature of the *Insitutio musica*—the text breaks off in mid-sentence—is attributable to corruption in the course of its transmission. Cf. Bower 1978, esp. pp. 43–45, with the reconstruction of the originally seven books of the *Institutio musica*.

3. Boethius 1867, I.34, p. 225. All future quotations from Boethius's *De institutione musica* and *De institutione arithmetica* cite this edition.

4. Pizzani 2003, p. 361: "Deliberately, he simply did not discuss rhythm and metrics."

5. Cf. the summary, ibid., p. 376f.: "The hypothesis according to which Boethius borrowed from Augustine the ideas developed in the last chapter of the first book of *De institutione musica* becomes more probable. It is confirmed still more if we recall the particular place of this passage, which does not borrow from the work's main source, namely Nichomachus. Thus it is not unlikely that Boethius voluntarily limited himelf to dealing with the harmonic section of music, in order to complete Augustine's work."

6. Ibid., p. 377: "In the Middle Ages, scholars considered the two texts [. . .] to be the two parts of a single work."

7. For instance, in the Florence manuscript, Laur. Ashburn. 1051. For further examples, see Bernhard 1990b, p. 28f.

8. Bowen 1988, p. 35.

9. Among the late antique sources for the reconstruction of Boethius's life history are first of all the parts of the *Consolatio philosophiae* that can be read as

autobiographical (esp. I.4); in addition, the testimonies in the letters collected by
Cassiodorus, who had served as Theodoric's secretary (Cassiodorus 1973, I.10,
pp. 20–22; I.45, pp. 49–51; II.40, pp. 87–88); the *Anecdoton Holderi*, discovered
in 1860 in Karlsruhe; Ennodius's letters (*Epistulae* VII.13, VIII.1, VIII.31, and
VIII.37), a sixth-century chronicle known as *Anonymus Valesianus* that was first
published by Henri de Valois in 1636 as an appendix to Ammianus Marcellinus's
history, and republished in modern times in Mommsen 1892, pp. 322–328, and
finally Procopius of Caesarea's historical work *De bello Gothico*. In Carolingian
times six lives of Boethius were produced; these were handed down in the form
of introductions or appendices to medieval manuscripts, mostly copies of the
Consolatio. Rudolf Peiper included a few of these in his edition of the *Consolatio*
(Boethius 1871). An assessment of the available sources is undertaken in Patch
1970, pp. 8–19; the results of recent research are included in Kranz 2005, Matthews 1981, and Marenbon 2003, esp. pp. 7–16.

10. It is regularly speculated, on quickly comprehensible grounds, that Boethius studied under the first successors to Proclus (410–485) at the Neoplatonic
school in Athens. These speculations are based chiefly on the apocryphal text *De
disciplina scholarium*, which raises doubts. On this, cf. already Bonnaud 1929,
esp. p. 200; the text in Boethius 1847, vol. 2, col. 1223–1239. Unless otherwise
indicated, all quotations from the works of Boethius cite this edition and follow
the divisions in the work itself.

11. Boethius 1871, p. XXXV.

12. Although Boethius's writings were read in northwestern Europe from the
eighth century on, his name is found under the *auctoritates*, not under the *sancti*.

13. *Acta Sanctorum*, vol. I.5 (Rome 1680), pp. 702–710.

14. *Acta Sanctae Sedis* 16 (1883), p. 302f.

15. Carton 1930, p. 650f.

16. For an introduction, see Patch 1970, pp. 46–113.

17. Sassen 1984, p. 108.

18. Carton 1930, p. 577.

19. Sassen 1984, p. 109.

20. See the inquiry in Gibson/Smith (eds.) 1995–2001, which also allows us
to make inferences regarding geographical dissemination.

21. Cf. Glauche 1970, p. 61.

22. On the commentary tradition, which regularly produced references to Boethius's music theory, see the surveys in Courcelle 1939 and Silk 1935. Individual
commentaries and their references to Boethius's music theory are investigated in
Silk 1954, Terbille 1972, Crespo 1973, Bolton 1977, Brown 1978, D'Onofrio
1981, Nauta 1997a, Nauta 1997b.

23. Courcelle 1967 is pertinent; for supplementary information, see Burdach
1933 and Auer 1928, pp. 233–253.

24. Sedgefield 1968.

25. Kaylor 1992, p. 107.

26. An inventory and comparative analysis of French translations, each with additional literature, is offered by Cropp 1997. Thomas/Roques 1938 presents and classifies individual translations. Since Atherton/Atkinson 1992, p. 222ff., the translation reproduced here as Text XIII has been considered a compilation of earlier translations.

27. Chamberlain 1970, p. 80.

28. Boethius 1981, II.1, p. 43: "But it is time for you to drink and taste something mild and pleasant, which when taken within you will prepare the way for stronger draughts. Let us use Rhetoric's sweet persuasion, which only proceeds along the right way when our laws are not lacking; when this has been done, let Music, the servant girl of our house, sing her songs, now light and now serious." Unless otherwise indicated, quotations from the *Consolatio* cite this edition.

29. When Philosophia "sings," she herself makes use of metrical discourse, for its "musicality" indicates a mode of representation that is "easier" compared to logical deduction presented in prose. Thus Philosophia announces a *carmen*, which concludes a lengthy development on the relationship between Providence and free will, with the words: "But I see that for some time you have been weighted down by the seriousness of the question, and fatigued by the extent of my discourse, and that you long for the sweetness of song. Therefore, take a draught, so that when you have been made stronger, you may forge ahead" (IV.6, p. 216). However, the resulting effect cannot be reduced to simple catchiness: "She had finished her song, and yet its agreeableness left me, ears still alert, amazed and eager to hear more. Shortly thereafter: O, I said, great solace of weary minds, how you have refreshed me with the gravity of your teachings or the joyfulness of your singing, so that I no longer think myself unprepared for the blows of fortune. Therefore, I no longer fear the remedies that you just said were bitter, but I am eager to hear and earnestly request them" (III.1, p. 90). This "refreshing" effect of the musical, which is indebted to form, is a commonplace of both ancient and medieval music theory.

30. On the etiological-nosological statement, see Schmid 1956; on the symbolic implications of the choice of this image of illness in particular, see pp. 127–133.

31. As examples we can name, among others, Boethius 1981, I.m.5, p. 26ff.: The manifestations of the order of Creation opposed to the experience of contingency, the course of the stars and the seasons, are conceived in *De institutione musica* I.2 as *musica mundana*. The sufferer, according to Philosophia's diagnosis in I.m.2, p. 6f., has forgotten how to recognize the numerical order of Creation in the paths of the stars: "This man, once free beneath the open skies,/And used to run along heavenly pathways,/Saw the beams of the rosy sun,/And looked upon the heaven of the frigid moon./And any star that followed a wandering path,/bent through various spheres,/Like a conqueror, he apprehended with numbers [*Comprensam numeris victor habebat*]." Further examples suggest themselves, for instance II.m.8, where the God's guidance of worlds is exemplified

by the manifestations of *musica mundana*, or by the verse "Tu numeris elementa ligas" ("You who bind together the elements with numbers") in III.m.9 *O qui perpetua*, the poem in the *Consolatio* most often commented upon during the following centuries.

32. Chadwick 1981, p. 101ff.

33. Boethius, *Commentaria in Porphyrium V*, col. 137c.

34. See Marrou 1938.

35. In the middle of the fourth century, the Church Father Jerome had been one of the pupils who had studied under Aelius Donatus (late fourth century); Priscian (Priscianus Caesariensis), his contemporary, taught in Constantinople. In rhetoric, Cicero was still considered the model, Quintilian the authority. The fourth century had a prominent orator in Marius Victorinus, a teacher from the province of Africa who taught aristocrats' children in Rome and, as Augustine's *Confessiones* report citing Simplician, attracted a great deal of attention by converting to Christianity. His textbooks were still in use in Boethius's time.

36. Theon of Smyrna 1878.

37. The dating of individual texts remains a matter of debate. The attempt made by Brandt 1903 remains standard; the challenge to Brandt's chronology proposed by McKinlay 1907 has not been adopted by scholars.

38. Grabmann 1956. For recent scholarship on this subject, see Marenbon 2003, esp. pp. 17–42.

39. For the following, cf. Minio-Paluello 1972; Obertello 1974; Marenbon 2003, p. 17f.

40. *Dialogi in Porphyrium a Victorino translati und Commentaria in Porphyrium*, in Boethius 1847, vol. 2, col. 9.158. Brandt 1903, p. XXII, XXVI, LXXVIII, and LXXIX, recognized as a source, in addition to Alexander of Aphrodisias (c. 200 CE) and Boethos of Sidon (middle of the second century BCE), who are mentioned by name in Boethius's commentary, Ammonius Hermiae (fifth century CE).

41. *In librum Aristotelis de interpretatione Commentaria minor und Commentaria maior*, in Boethius 1847, vol. 2, col. 293–392 and 393–638.

42. *In Categorias Aristotelis libri quatuor*, in Boethius 1847, vol. 2, col. 159–292. The probative appendices are so distinctive that in the 1920s Joseph Bidez was able to use Boethius's commentary to reconstruct Porphyrys text, which had earlier been thought lost. See the report in Bidez 1923. A detailed analysis is undertaken in Asztalos 1993, pp. 372–377.

43. *De differentiis topicis*, in Boethius 1847, vol. 2, col. 1173–1217, here col. 1173c, col. 1184d f., col. 1216d. A translation of the *Analyticxa poseriora* made by Boethius appears to have been in circulation as late as the twelfth century. For proofs, see Wulf 1934–1947, vol. 1, p. 112.

44. In Boethius 1847, vol. II, col. 761–793, col. 1173–1217, col. 793–831, col. 831–875, col. 875–891. The treatise *De definitione*, long held to also be a work by Boethius, was produced by Marius Victorinus, according to Grabmann

1956, vol. 1, p. 152. *De unitate,* another work that used to be attributed to Boethius, is much later. Its author is now thought to be Dominicus Gundissalinus; see Correns 1891.

45. Chartularium Universitatis Parisiensis, vol. 1, p. 276. On the genesis of the text, its acceptance, and criticism, cf. Grabmann 1939.

46. The translations of the texts collected under the title *logica nova* are attributed to Jacob of Venice and dated to 1128: Glorieux 1968.

47. Thus Mandonnet 1911, p. 7, calls Boethius the "true introducer of Aristotle in the West." In fact, the dissemination of translations of Aristotle by Boethius and others beyond the texts mentioned remains unclear. If we read about an *antiquior translatio super eosdem libros* (Ueberweg 1956, p. 146), and if furthermore there is proof that Peter Abelard made use of the *Sophistici elenchi* and the *Analytica priora* (Geyer 1917), then this allows us to infer translations that are now lost and unknown. Here it is crucial, however, that in the High Middle Ages these translations were considered *littera Boethii.* See Grabmann 1956, vol. 1, p. 69, 42n; vol. 2, pp. 25–58, 112.

48. See the studies cited in the respective notes.

49. *De interpretatione,* in Boethius 1847, vol. 2, col. 433c f. Cf. Augustine, *Contra Academicos* III.29.42: a fundamental difference between the works of Plato and Aristotle could be seen only by "ignorant and inattentive readers." It is significant that Augustine does not seek at all to prove this by means of concepts, but rather in the framework of the brief history of philosophy that is developed in Book III of *Contra academicos:* The philosophy of Plato, of "the wisest and most learned man of his time" (III.17.37), spans all ages; but in the course of time it became necessary to protect this "true" doctrine from misuse by the "unworthy." The latter included, in his view, the Stoics Zeno and Chrysippus, the Cynics, and especially Epicurus (ibid., III.16.35ff.). The doctrine was handed down as "secret doctrine" and entrusted only to "initiates": ibid., III.17.38. Even the more recent Academicians were ultimately Platonists, but the secret was so well kept that they themselves did not realize it. . . . (ibid., III.17.37–39; cf. ibid., II.10.24; II.13.29 and III.7.14).

50. Usener 1969. The fragment in question is a tenth-century manuscript that comes from Reichenau and is now preserved in Karlsruhe. See Vijver 1931. The treatise *de fide catholica,* whose attribution to Boethius at first remained an open question or was challenged because of obvious stylistic differences (Rand 1901), is now considered authentic. Cf., with a summary of the discussion and the most recent research, Galonnier 1997 and Lambert 2003.

51. In the following we cite the edition Boethius 2005, the *Opuscula* here pp. 163–241.

52. Manitius 1911–1931, vol. 1, p. 36.

53. Boethius, *Contra Eutychen et Nestorium* 3, in Boethius 2005, p. 214. On the broader context, with the standard secondary literature in the footnotes, see Wald 1996.

54. Sassen 1984, p. 99. For details, cf. Carton 1930, and also, with the same result, especially regarding the *Opuscula sacra*, Bruder 1928.

55. Boethius, *De sancta trinitate* 4, in Boethius 2005, p. 173.

56. Ibid.,2, p. 170: "The divine substance is form without matter, and therefore is one, and it is what it is; other things are not what they are"; ibid., 4, p. 174: "God is nothing other than what he is, and for this reason He is God"; ibid: "man is not entirely man, and for this reason he is not substance"; *De hebdomadibus* II, p. 187: "Being is different from that which is; that is not yet being, but what is. Once its form of being has been accepted, it is and remains."

57. Boethius, *De sancta trinitate*, in Boethius 2005, p. 166f.

58. For an introduction, see Schrimpf 1966 and Grabmann 1956, vol. I, passim.

59. Boethius, *De hebdomadibus*, proem, in Boethius 2005, p. 187.

60. Grabmann 1956, vol. 1, p. 173. On methodology and the relation to Boethius in Alain, see Châtillon 1980 and Jolivet 1980.

61. Leinsle 1995, p. 95ff.

62. Sassen 1984, p. 106.

63. Diels/Kranz (eds.) 1956, vol. I, Archytas-Fragment (47) B1, p. 431f. On the systematic foundation of the quadrivial canon in Platonism, see Radke 2003, pp. 242–261 passim.

64. Cassiodorus 1973, I.45.4, p. 49f.

65. Cassiodorus 2003, II.6.3, vol. 2, p. 436. A few Latin fragments attributed to Euclid were long considered parts of a work by Boethius on geometry. They were published as such in the edition Boethius 1970. Pingree 1981 casts doubt on this attribution. A detailed presentation and discussion of the testimonies to this lost work is provided by Obertello 1974, pp. 173–196. In the Middle Ages, geometry had a low status as an ancillary science, especially in the form of geodesy, and the academic subject of *geometria* was accordingly arranged. However, Patch 1970, p. 37, has found echoes of Boethius's treatise in Alcuin and Gerbert of Aurillac.

66. Schrade 1947, p. 191: "[T]he pre-philosophic task of mathematics is clearly specified. The mathematical studies have no purpose of their own; they are instrumental in whetting man's appetite for investigating the true Being." Boethius follows the scientific concept developed by Nicomachus of Gerasa 1866, I.1.4, p. 3.

67. Boethius, *De institutione arithmetica* I.1, p. 9f.

68. Boethius, *De trinitate* 2, in Boethius 2005, p. 168f.: "There are three speculative parts. Physics is in motion and is nonabstract, ἀνυπεξαίρετος. Physics is concerned with the forms of bodies with matter, and which cannot be separated from bodies in motion. As bodies that are in motion—the earth tends downward, fire upward—form takes its motion according to its association with matter. Mathematics is without motion and is nonabstract. Mathematics investigates forms of bodies without matter, and therefore, without motion. Since these forms

are within matter, they cannot be separated from matter. Theology is without motion, and is abstract, but is also separable, for the substance of God lacks both matter and motion." See also *Commentaria in Porphyrium* I, col. 74a. On the general conception of the *quadruvium*, its presuppositions in the Platonist and Neuplatonist theory of science, and the systematic place assigned to *musica scientia* within that conception, see Radke 2003 and, focusing on Boethius in particular, Heilmann 2007.

69. Aristotle, *Metaphysics* 1026a.

70. Boethius, *De institutione musica* I.1, p. 179.

71. Schrade 1932, p. 368.

72. Brandt 1903.

73. "A comparison of the two books [Nicomachus's and Boethius's textbooks on arithmetic] will convince the reader that Boethius follows Nicomachus from first to last, expanding here and condensing there, as he says in his preface that he will do, but never adding anything essential, either original or derived from other sources, that departs from his model." This is the view of the editor of Nicomachus of Gerasa 1938, p. 132. A comparison of the two works is provided by Jean-Yves Guillaumin in his edition of Boethius's work, Boethius 1995, p. XXXIX–XLIV. Boethius develops his conceptions of arithmetic and music largely without taking Aristotelian philosophy into account. Leo Schrade has made a thorough effort to prove this; see for instance Schrade 1930; 1932; and 1947, p. 193: "The music Boethius described at the beginning of his literary activity is of Platonic-Pythagorean origin. It has no direct contact with the Aristotelian system of philosophy."

74. Boethius, *De institutione arithmetica* I.1, p. 7ff.: "Among all men of ancient authority who have flourished in the purer reason of the mind, with Pythagoras as their leader, it is obvious that hardly anyone ascended to the height of perfection in the philosophical disciplines unless he examined the nobility of such sagacity through a sort of quadrivium [*quadruvium*], as it were, which will not stay hidden from one who admires expertise. This is the wisdom of things that are, and as the comprehension of truth, it imparts immutable substance."

75. Ibid., p. 9.

76. For the definition, ibid., p. 9f.

77. See, also for subsequent references to Plato's late dialogue, Bakhouche 2003, esp. p. 9ff.

78. Cf. Nobis 1969, esp. p. 35f.

79. Boethius, *De institutione arithmetica*, I.2, p. 12.

80. Ibid., I.1, p. 10.

81. Ibid., I.2, p. 12. In view of Boethius's theory of music, the examples should be emphasized: "You bind the elements with numbers," we read in a similar passage in *Consolatio philosophiae* III.m.9, p. 128, "so that cold with flames / And dry with moist conjoins, lest the purer fire / Should fly away or weight cause the earth to sink."

82. Boethius, *De institutione arithmetica* I.2, p. 13.

83. Ibid., I.3, p. 13. Cf. Illmer 1990, here p. 222f. This definition could only seldom satisfy Scholasticism's desire for precision; cf. Illmer 1984, pp. 44–47.

84. Boethius, *De institutione musica* II.7, p. 232; cf. *De institutione arithmetica* I.7, p. 16: "For this reason, it is accepted as the unity of all numbers which are in natural order [*in naturali dispositione*], and that it is rightly acknowledged as the generator of all extended plurality [*prolixae genitricem pluralitatis*]." Cf. the commentary in Illmer 1990, pp. 242–252.

85. Plato, *Sophist*, passim., esp. 36c ff.; see Chadwick 1981, p. 75: "The insistence on the 'definite' character of goodness is to mark a contrast with the indefinite dyad, which for the Pythagoreans symbolizes evil because it marks the beginning of multiplicity over against the One. The knowable and therefore limited is prior to the unlimited and therefore unknowable. Whatever is undeterminate is without identity and is in permanent flux." Plato and Philolaus are mentioned together in *De institutione arithmetica* II.38, p. 126.

86. Ibid., II.31, p. 122f. On the background, see Gericke 1970, p. 29ff.

87. Both Philolaos (Diels/Kranz 1956, Philolaus fragment (44) B2, vol. 1, p. 407ff.) and Plato's *Timaeus* 35a take this as their starting point. On the passage in Philolaus, see the commentary in Burkert 1962, p. 250ff.; on the Platonic horizon, Radke 2003, p. 322ff.

88. Boethius, *De institutione arithmetica* II.54, p. 169.

89. Ibid., II.28, p. 118.

90. Ibid.

91. Ibid., II.33, p. 128.

92. Ibid., II.34, p. 131. Cf. Bruyne 1946, vol. 1, p. 18 [italicized in the original]: "The forms being mathematical in nature, all of them will be a harmonious mixture of the same and the different, of stability and movement, of unity and multiplicity, depending on the initial proportions."

93. Boethius, *De institutione arithmetica* II.33, p. 126 [emphasis supplied].

94. Ibid., II.40, p. 137.

95. Foucault 1966, here the chapter "La prose du monde," pp. 32–59.

96. For the rationale of the idea of an original language in which God is supposed to have spoken to humans and of which historical languages are considered corrupt derivatives that emerged after the confusion of languages connected with the Tower of Babel, see Augustine, *De doctrina christiana* II.4.5; a parallel is found in Plato, *Cratylus* 383d.

97. Ibid., II.1, p. 77. The context emphasizes opposition to Plato, who sees the ordering One as unrestrictedly primary, and the play of the unification and separation of opposites as mechanical and secondary; see *Laws* 889b. If it is a question of a conjunction of opposites, for instance of the elements of earth and fire in Timaeus's cosmogonic speculation (*Timaeus* 31b ff.), then this is also based in Plato on the unifying power of number: the demiurge forges between them a mathematical "bond" of two medial proportions that have the property, because

of the interchangeability of the terms, of making all the members "one" and "the same." For these categories in context, see *Sophist* 36c ff.

98. Boethius, *De institutione arithmetica* I.32, p. 66.

99. *Consolatio philosophiae*, III.9, S. 124.

100. Gerbert of Aurillac 1963.

101. Bower 1978, p. 8: "The work is, in fact, such an integral part of the *De institutione arithmetica* that the musical work appears to be a direct continuation of the arithmetical treatise."

102. Boethius, *De institutione arithmetica* II.42, p. 138f. Cf. Diels/Kranz (eds.) 1956, vol. 1, Archytas Fragment (47) B2, p. 435f.

103. Boethius, *De institutione arithmetica* II.42, p. 139.

104. For an annotated list of the manuscripts, see Masi 1983.

105. Evans 1978a; Evans 1978b and Bernhard 1988 also come to this conclusion.

106. S. Patch 1970, p. 37.

107. Kibre 1981, p. 72. Cf. the detailed account in Glorieux 1971, pp. 33–38; Patch 1970, p. 39ff.; Gilson 1952, p. 439ff.

108. Cf. Pedersen 1985.

109. Quoted in Thorndike 1948, App. II, p. 451.

110. Masi 1981, p. 81.

111. Bower 1978, p. 39f. On the sources of the work on music, see also Mickley 1898 and the editor's introduction in Boethius 1990. The summary in Edmiston 1974 is brief but useful.

112. Bower 1978, p. 40ff. Cf. the additional remarks in Caldwell 1981, esp. p. 140ff., and compare Solomon 1990.

113. Bower 1978, p. 41: "This document represents not only the Latin text which served as the essential textbook of musical theory for over a millennium but it likewise preserves the major musical treatise of Nicomachus. As such it is the only extant complete document representing the Pythagorean school of musical thought apart from the *Sectio canonis* and the all too brief *Enchiridion*."

114. See the previously cited account of the legend of the smithy, on the one hand, and on the other, that of the work on the monochord in Münxelhaus 1976, pp. 26–55. For the thesis that Pythagoras took a triangular harp as his starting point for his discoveries, see Schmidt 1966, pp. 70ff., 83ff. It remains to note that attributions in the Pythagorean tradition remain speculative because of the "tendency to attribute to Pythagoras himself all the discoveries made over time and [. . .] to establish them on the basis of his authority" (Röd 1988, p. 55). On the theory of consonance, see in particular Waerden 1943, esp. p. 178ff. Antiquity and the Middle Ages retained the Pythagorean theory of consonance, with the addition of the double octave (1/4), the duodecim, the octave of the fifth (1/3), and the complements to these intervals: the fifth and the fourth complement each other to form an octave (2/3 × 3/4 = 1/2), while the fifth, which also extends the octave, is complemented by the fourth to form a double octave (1/3 × 3/4 = 1/4).

An overall survey of Pythagorean thought on numbers, outstandingly illustrated, is provided in Heninger 1974, pp. 71–145; Radke 2003 is relevant for the reception history of this thought in the Platonic theory of knowledge.

115. Nicomachos of Gerasa, *Harmonicum Enchiridium* II.7, in: Jan (ed.) 1966, vol. 1, p. 279; the description and derivation of the intervals from the first *tetraktys* according to Nicomachus is found in Boethius, *De institutione musica* II.20.31, pp. 104–125. *De institutione musica* uses Latin and Greek terms in parallel: *tonus/sesquioctava, diapason/proportio dupla, diatessaron/sesquitertia, diapente/sesquialtera.*

116. See details, with a schematic representation, in Münxelhaus 1976, pp. 18–24. The modes of Greek harmonics—enharmonic, diatonic, chromatic—are represented as different ways of dividing up the two tetrachords. The sequence half-tone/whole-tone/whole-tone defines the diatonic mode, the sequence half-tone/half-tone/one and a half-tone defines the chromatic mode, and the sequence quarter-tone/quarter-tone/two whole-tones defines the enharmonic mode. The derivation of the modes is found in Boethius in *De institutione musica*, I.21, p. 104ff.

117. The following greatly abbreviates Fritz 1960 and Waerden 1943, pp. 179–181.

118. See Frobenius 1989, esp. p. 255f.

119. Koller 1962, p. 183.

120. See in particular Koller 1955; Koller 1958, 1960; in addition to these, see Lohmann 1970a, 1970b, 1970c, 1970d.

121. This has been discussed in detail with respect to its Pythagorean substrate: "[A]t *Philebus* 16b4–20a8 Plato is borrowing not just Philolaus' basic metaphysical principles, limiters and unlimiteds, but also his central insight that there is no knowledge without numbers [. . .]" (Huffmann 2001, p. 69). See also Barker 1996 and Meinwald 2002, with further literature.

122. Plato, *Philebus* 17c ff.

123. Zimmermann 1976, p. 83.

124. Cicero 1923–2005, vol. 44, V.3, p. 407.

125. Boethius, *De institutione arithmetica* I.1, p. 7ff.

126. *De institutione musica* II.2, p. 227.

127. *Laws*, 967 d f.; cf. *Republic* 531a ff.

128. For evidence of this, see Koller 1962, pp. 112–149 passim.

129. See Röd 1988, pp. 59–61.

130. For detailed proof, see Barker 1994.

131. Aristotle, *Metaphysics* 1053a: "The measure is always homogeneous with the thing measured; the measure of spatial magnitudes is a spatial magnitude, and in particular that of length is a length, that of breadth is a breadth, that of articulate sound is an articulate sound, that of a weight a weight, that of units a unit," with a cautiously approving reference to Protagoras.

132. Walter 1998, p. 69.

133. See the contributions in Beck/Bol (eds.) 1993.

134. The construction of a building according to the proportions of the human body allows it to be in harmony with the numerical-harmonic order of the cosmos. For example, temples have to correspond to these proportions, as is stated in Book III. See Vitruvius 1847, III.1, vol. 1, p. 242. Cf. Koch 1951, p. 15f. passim.

135. Thus in the tenth-century Selestat 17 manuscript an organ-pipe measure is noted right after Vitruvius's text: see Sachs 1970–1980, vol. 1, p. 39. An important manuscript of the *Musica enchiriadis*, Valenciennes 337, contains Faventius's epitome of Vitruvius in its first part; however, closer examination of the manuscript has shown that in this case two originally separate fascicles were bound together: Müller 1884, p. 11ff. The anonymous author of the eleventh-century *Alia musica* shows that he knows Vitruvius; he cites *De architectura* I.6 regarding the classification of the winds and relates it to tones and half-tones. See Alia Musica 1962, 154, p. 95.

136. Boethius, *De institutione arithmetica* I.1, p. 9.

137. Ibid., I.3, p. 189: "If everything remains immobile, one thing cannot rush to meet another, so that one thing might be set in motion by another, but with all things remaining still and lacking motion, by necessity no sound can come about. For this reason, sound is defined as the percussion of the air that remains unbroken all the way to the ear."

138. Ibid., I.3, p. 190. It is crucial for the understanding of the context of the (Platonic) doctrine to recognize as the basis for comparing the two phenomena not their quantifiability but rather their numerical nature: "According to the Platonic conception, in their primarily conceptual meaning number and magnitude are not kinds of quantity, but rather kinds of being as such. [. . .] From this it follows that number and magnitude must be constitutive principles of every existent and that it must be possible ultimately to trace the recognizable determination of *every* individual back to either number or magnitude." Radke 2003, p. 246 [emphasis in original].

139. Accordingly, for Boethius the prime does not count as an interval.

140. Boethius, *De institutione musica* I.8, p. 195.

141. Ibid., p. 191.

142. Ibid., II.7, p. 232.

143. Walter 1998, p. 72 [my emphasis]; on the sources, cf. West 1992, p. 160ff.

144. Boethius, *De institutione musica* I.1, p. 187. Cf. Plato, *Timaeus* 80b, and Aristotle, *De anima* 426b, *De sensu* 447a f.

145. For a detailed presentation, see Schrade 1930; Schrade 1932, p. 400: "The musical form of knowledge is thus, as we have seen, primarily 'disciplinaliter,' equal in sense to the method mathematics represents, as it were, the 'disciplina disciplinarum.' As a result of the high esteem for the *numerus* that makes itself known therein, music, along with the whole number theory, moves

beyond a certain second-class ontic status and becomes the norm and example for the scientific method of knowledge and demonstration (*demonstratio*). [. . .] In general, *ratio* in music is located on the same level of valid and normative methods of knowledge. It seeks to show that the concepts in musical knowledge are irrefutable and true; as reason, it is the guideline of knowledge. In both characteristics, *disciplinaliter* and *ratio*, the goal is only to indicate how one arrives at insight into music at all. Only *intelligentia* as a form of knowledge includes both the ontic nature and the status of music."

146. Boethius, *De institutione musica* I.34, p. 224. It may be noted that Boethius connects this music theoretician with *ratio*, not with *intellectus*. Nonetheless: "It seems that Boethius understood *ratio* and *regulae* as eternal verities, just as Augustine did his *aeternae rationes*." Schrade 1932, p. 399.

147. Boethius, *De institutione musica* I.2, p. 187.

148. For instance, in Plato (*Timaeus* 32c, 35–36; *Laws* 889 b–c; *Symposium* 188a), Cicero (*De re publica* VI.18.18), Macrobius (*Commentarii in Somnium Scipionis* II.1.2f.), Censorinus (*De die natali* XII), Ps.-Plutarch (*De musica* 1147) or Ptolemy (*Harmoniae* III.10.16, 104.111). References to Aristides Quintilianus are given in the continuous text, see Mathiesen 1990, esp. pp. 50–63.

149. Bower 1978, p. 44. Cf. also Pizzani 1965, p. 34 and Wille 1967, pp. 661–663.

150. Bruyne 1946, vol. 1, p. 310 [emphasis in original].

151. Macrobius 1994, II.3.11, p. 106: "We have said before that the causes of music are contained in the world-soul, into which they have been woven. The world-soul gives life to all living things: From this source come the race of men and beasts, the lives of flying creatures, and the monsters that the sea holds beneath its shining water [Virgil, *Aeneid* 6.728–29]. Justly, therefore, does music capture everything that lives, since the heavenly soul, by which the universe is animated, took its beginning from music."

152. Favonius Eulogius 1957, II.III, p. 15: "I think that we must consider first that Pythagoras, the founder of Italic wisdom, judged that nature is governed by numbers, that the whole world moves with harmonious modulation [*consona modulatione*] to the music of the spheres [*musicam caeli*], according to fixed and correct intervals, and that one number applies to different things, [. . .]. Therefore, number is the eternal, knowable, and uncorrupted thing, which gathers everything under its sway [*totumque sub numerum uenit quicquid aut sensibus aut animi cogitatione comprehenditur*]." "Harmonia mundana" is discussed in chap. XXV (p. 43).

153. Aristeides Quintilianus 1937, p. 41.

154. Boethius, *De institutione musica* I.2, p. 187.

155. Ibid., p. 187f. The restriction is covered by the sources. Nicomachus of Gerasa had represented this view, and Cicero's *Somnium Scipionis* also argued this way.

156. Aristeides Quintilianus 1937, p. 41.

157. Boethius, *De institutione musica* I.2, p. 187.

158. Reckow 1975, p. 59. Fischer 1981, p. 235 and Haas 1982, p. 344, 86n follow Reckow.

159. Boethius, *De institutione musica* I.27, p. 219.

160. Ibid., I.20, p. 206.

161. Ibid.

162. Bukofzer 1942, p. 167f.: "[M]usic was located in the shadow of a greater whole. Actual music had no independent existence, but borrowed its meaning from the *musica mundana*. [. . .] Very revealing in this connection is the manner in which Boethius justified the very existence of the *musica instrumentalis*. It is the only music in which man can create, but would be meaningless, were it not connected with the universal harmony. Boethius regards such music as man's imitation of the *musica mundana*. [. . .] [M]an may reflect the image of God in music as well as in other respects. This interpretation of earthly music is the basic allegory: *musica instrumentalis* stands in its entirety for the nonperceptible *musica mundana*. Other interpretations of the special aspects of music are only subsidiary allegories."

163. Bruyne 1846, vol. 1, p. 21.

164. Ibid., p. 4.

165. Boethius, *De institutione musica* I.34, p. 224.

166. I.34, p. 225.

167. See Eichhorn 1996, p. 320, and Eggebrecht 1995.

168. Aristeides Quintilianus 1937, p. 41.

169. Boethius, *De institutione musica* I.2, p. 188f.

170. Aristotle discusses the ethical dimension of the relation between the rational and the irrational parts of the soul in the *Nicomachean Ethics* I.12; in *De anima* III.9, 432a–432, the distinction is rejected as too little differentiated for the physical-psychological investigation announced here. The analysis carried out in Plato's *Timaeus* is differentiated. It proceeds "physically" insofar as the soul is conceived as composed of the two primary substances that also constitute the world-soul, complemented by a third that is produced from the first two (35a, 41d). It touches on "mathematical" aspects insofar as it notes that the "sound" of the soul corresponds harmonically with that of the world-soul, and this is based on an identity of the numerical relationships underlying them (35–36, 43d, 44d, cf. Handschin 1950a). It proceeds "psychologically" insofar as it investigates the conditions under which, out of the two basal principles of the "same" and the "different" that the soul shares with the world-soul, either true knowledge or mere opinion is produced (37a–c, 44a–c). Finally, the analysis touches on "moral" aspects insofar as the soul will have to suffer in Hades (42b–c, 44c) if the rational part of the soul (41c–d), which is created by the highest god, does not rise as ruler over the mortal part of the soul associated with the body (41c, 42b), which is created by the lower gods, and lives righteously (42b, 47b–c). Regarding Boethius, Chamberlain 1970, p. 83 concludes: "In fact, the whole of

Boethius's human music is essentially an adaptation of Plato's treatment of man in the 'Timaeus.'" Sulovski 1957–1961 sheds light on Calcidius's interpretation of the *Timaeus*; on the conceptualization of the soul and its activity as "numerical" in the Platonic horizon, see Radke 2003, pp. 492–496.

171. Boethius, *De institutione musica* I.1, p. 186.

172. Ibid., p. 180f.: "On this evidence, what Plato correctly said can be understood, that the world-soul was arranged according to musical harmony [*musica convenientia*]. When we hear what has been conjoined aptly and suitably in sound based on what has been joined and suitably fit together within us, and take delight in this, we also recognize that we ourselves have been composed in the same likeness. [. . .] Therefore, when rhythms and modes have come down into the mind through the ears, there can be no doubt that they affect and shape the mind in the same way." The remarkable equation of *musica mundana* and the Platonic world-soul is already found in Macrobius 1994, II.3.11, p. 106.

173. We have already cited the formulation of this interest: "Just as in seeing it is not enough for learned men to see colors and forms, unless they investigate also what their nature is, so it is not enough for songs to be enjoyed unless we also learn the ratio of voices by which they have been brought together," ibid., p. 187. Cf. Schrade 1932, p. 381 [emphasis in the original]: "But we must note above all that the upward-directed striving of music is aimed at *philosophy*, that the intelligible world of music is subordinate to *true Being*, to *form apprehensible by the intellect*, no matter whether it is a matter of *musica mundana*, *humana*, or *instrumentalis*. Therein we can see a foundation of the medieval view of music [. . .]."

174. Augustine, *De libero arbitrio* II.16.41.

175. Boethius, *De institutione musica* I.1, p. 179.

176. Ibid., p. 184.

177. Ibid., V.2, pp. 352–354.

178. Ibid., V.3, p. 354f.

179. Ibid., p. 352: "Harmonics is the faculty of weighing the differences between high and low sounds by the use of sense and reason. For sense and reason are the instruments of the faculty of harmonics."

180. Ibid., V.2, p. 352.

181. Ibid., I.1, p. 180.

182. Ibid.

183. Ibid. Boethius alludes to the old terminology of the *modi*, the later church modes or *toni ecclesiastici*, using the Greek terms (Ionic, Doric, Phrygian, Lydian, Mixolydian, Aeolian, Locrian). The argument presented already underlies Plato's and Aristotle's well-known fears that changes in the musical culture of a community might put the latter itself in question. See for instance Plato, *Republic* 424b ff.: "[the overseers of our state] must throughout be watchful against innovations in music and gymnastics counter to the established order, and to the best of their power guard against them, [. . .]. For a change to a new type of music is something to beware of as a hazard of all our fortunes. For the modes of music

are never disturbed without unsettling the most fundamental political and social conventions [. . .]"; cf. Aristotle, *Politics* 1339a–1342b.

184. Boethius, *De institutione musica* I.1, p. 186f.

185. Ibid., p. 181.

186. Payen 1980.

187. Boethius, *De institutione musica* II.18, p. 249f.

188. Ibid., II.18, p. 249.

189. Ibid., I.7, p. 194. Cf. ibid., II.18, p. 249.

190. Dümmler (ed.) 1978–1997, vol. 1, p. 96. Bischoff 1965, p. 46 discerns in this sentence "a lost circular dating from about 780" calling for the remission of copies.

191. Bower 1981, p. 167f. with further literature.

192. Bernhard 1990a, p. 142f. and Bernhard 2003, pp. 601–603.

193. Ibid., p. 604: "The concentration of ninth-century documents, heretofore little known, testifying to the spread of the *Institutio musica* over a very narrowly limited area strengthens the assumption that the reception of the text began from the court school. It is particularly remarkable that we have not a single reference to the *Institutio musica* from Italy, England, or Ireland that dates before the year 1000."

194. That is the conclusion drawn by the detailed study of Bower 1998, p. 169f.: "Music [is thus] not only a propaedeutic discipline for the study of philosophy, but also in fact part of the *philosophia naturalis*. Hence the *artes liberales* are then called *artes naturales*, and music is viewed within philosophy, not merely as a stage preliminary to philosophical speculation or even outside philosophy." Cf. also Heller 1939.

195. The earliest manuscript tradition already points to the western part of the empire. There is strong evidence to suggest that the monastery of Corbie in the Somme valley, the site of the momentous transition to the Carolingian miniscule around 780, acquired especially the classical manuscripts from Charlemagne's court library after his death. See Bischoff 1965, p. 61 and Bischoff 1966a. Against this background, it is noteworthy that of the eleven ninth-century codices of the *Insitutio musica* extant (cf. in detail Bower 1988), it is certain that three, namely Paris BNF lat. 13020, BNF lat. 13955, and BNF lat. 14080, come from Corbie. This is shown by Ganz 1990, pp. 150–153. Bernhard 2003, p. 603 hypothesizes: "The seven other ninth-century codices extant came, with a single exception, from northern France and may have their common archetype in the court library's copy [. . .]."

196. Bischoff 1965.

197. Bower 1981, p. 171.

198. Mittelalterliche Bibliothekskataloge 1918–1979, vol. 1, p. 258. The ninth-century library catalog of the monastery of Gorze in Lorraine lists "Boetii duo de arte musica." See Morin 1905, p. 10. A letter from the middle of the ninth century records the request made by an unknown monk to his lord "B" to send him a copy of Boethius's "musica": Dümmler (ed.) 1978–1993, vol. 1, p. 197ff.

199. In addition to Bower 1988, which is based on commentaries, proofs of provenance, datings, and evidence of the relations among manuscripts, Masi 1971 offers an overview. Moreover, Gibson/Smith (eds.) 1995 now discusses successively the transmission of Boethius's complete works. Volume 1 describes the manuscripts in Great Britain and Northern Ireland, volume 2 those in Austria, Belgium, Denmark, Luxemburg, the Netherlands, Sweden, and Switzerland, volume 3 those in Italy and the Vatican.

200. Orléans, Bibl. Mun. 293. More detailed knowledge about the holdings in Orléans are not available. The university did not have a firm and catalogued library collection until "the beginning of the fifteenth century," according to Jarry 1873, p. 11.

201. Bower 1988, No. 101, p. 236.

202. An inventory of the independently transmitted excerpts is found in Bower 1988, pp. 244–246; ninth-century glosses refer to the manuscripts Orléans 293b, Paris, BNF 720 and 13908, as well as Rome, Vat. Reg. 1638. These glosses became the foundation for an extensive corpus that was copied and multiplied up to the twelfth century. Pizzani 1980, pp. 329–357 edited some of these glosses; the *Glossa maior* is now available in Bernhard/Bower 1993–1996. The codices from the eleventh and twelfth centuries are particularly richly glossed, Paris, BNF 10275, Milan, C 128 inf., Vienna 2269, Autun 46 and Rome, Vat. Reg. lat. 1005. Independent glosses are offered above all by late medieval manuscripts such as Paris, BNF 16201 and 18514, Oxford, Bodleian Library, Ashb. 1524 and Corpus Christi College 118, as well as Milan Q 9 sup.

203. With the incipit "Primo videndum est, quid sit musica," a 37-page text was produced in the priory of St. Florian in Upper Austria that refers to Boethius's text in brief keywords. Oxford, Bodl. 77 contains a further commentary with which Oxford, All Souls Coll. XC in part coinicides. The commentaries in Siena L. V. 30, from the fifteenth-century, and Paris, BNF 18514 are very summary. Moreover, the most important elements of Boethius's teachings are summarized in the *Tractatus de musica collectus ex his quae dicta sunt a Boetio supra atque declaratio musicae practica* in the manuscript Paris, BNF 18514. Finally, Johannes de Muris's treatment of Boethius under the title *Musica speculativa*, which played a central role in university teaching in the late Middle Ages, was the most widespread. We will return to this text.

204. Duchez 1980; opposed by Bernhard 1990b, p. 28f.

205. The following is based on Schmidt 1967, p. 8off. and also on the investigation in Englisch 1994, which concentrates on the quadrivial sciences.

206. Isidore of Seville 1957–1962 I.1.3: "Plato and Aristotle maintained that there was this difference between art and discipline: art is concerned with things that can embrace themselves and other things, whereas discipline is concerned with things that cannot exist in any other way."

207. The classifications handed down in parallel are summarized in Weisheipl 1965.

208. Curtius 1993, p. 48f.

209. Gibson 1982.

210. The view that was at first dominant, namely that the commentary edited by Cora E. Lutz under the name of Dunchad (Lutz 1944) is a work by the Irishman Martin of Laon, has been challenged by J. Contreni. The authorship has subsequently been regarded as unclear.

211. On further commentary literature, see Lutz 1971.

212. See Leonardi 1959 and 1960. Whether this organizational grid fulfills essentially an ordering or at least at the same time a legitimating function that allows it to be fitted into the Christian order of discourse with Prov. 9:1 "Wisdom has built her house, she has set up her seven pillars," is debatable.

213. The text of Martianus Capella, fol. 1r–7r, Augustine's *De musica* fol. 7v–40v, Boethius's *De institutione musica* fol. 41r–86r. See Leonardi 1960, p. 55.

214. Bower 1981, p. 160.

215. Schrade 1947, p. 188.

216. Bernhard 1990b, p. 9. The importance of the work is elaborated by Phillips 1990.

217. See Caldwell 1986, p. 201.

218. Bernhard 1996, p. 16.

219. Bernhard 2003, p. 611.

220. Carpenter 1972, p. 11.

221. Ibid., p. 18. See also Haas 1982, p. 337: "In the Middle Ages it [*De institutione musica*] was not only repeatedly the central source for discussions of *musica speculativa*, that is, of music theory, but also the textbook of the discipline *musica*, at first within the *septem artes liberales*, and then also in the domain of university teaching."

222. Beaujouan 1954–1956.

223. Clagett 1953; Goldat 1957.

224. Thorndike 1948.

225. Haas 1984, p. 114.

226. Haas 1998, 1999. For supplementary information, see Sachs 1999 and the older investigation of the relation between music and grammar in elementary education in Gurlitt 1944, esp. p. 72ff.

227. Haas 1999, p. 26. On elementary music education, cf. Carpenter 1972, pp. 17–32.

228. On the *Institutio musica* in this function, see Bower 1981.

229. Carpenter 1972, p. 21f.

230. Haas 1982, p. 353f. Cf. also Carpenter 1972, pp. 46–69. See my discussion of this collection of *quaestiones* in my seventh chapter.

231. See Meyer 2003, esp. p. 669; White 1981, esp. p. 182ff., and in general on the status of quadrivial studies around 1300, Kibre 1969, esp. p. 191: "the mathematical or quadrivial arts, although no longer in their traditional framework, did continue into the thirteenth century to constitute an integral part of the

university arts curriculum." For a different view, see Dyer 2009.

232. Carpenter 1972, p. 63. On its situation in context, cf. Rohloff 1943.

233. Hirtler 1995, p. 84.

234. S. Lafleur 1988, p. 328. To this corresponded the uninterrupted presence of the textbook on arithmetic. See Evans 1978a and Evans 1978b.

235. Beaujouan 1987, p. 15. See also Meyer 2003, p. 676.

236. Carpenter 1972, p. 68. See also Bernhard 1996, p. 26f.: "The success of Boethius's writings continued down to the late Middle Ages. [. . .] Johannes de Sacrobosco, with his practically oriented *Algorismus*, and Johannes de Muris, with his textbooks *Arithmetica speculativa* and *Musica speculativa*, which were expressly presented as abridgments of Boethius, became Boethius's heirs." For a different view, see again Dyer 2009, esp. pp. 179 and 202ff.

237. Carpenter 1972, p. 63.

238. Ibid., p. 68.

239. Bernhard 1990b, p. 31.

240. See Répertoire International des Sources Musicales, vol. 2, pp. 36–43, 47f., 81f., 89ff., 120–123.

Chapter Seven: **Speculative Music Theory in the Boethian Tradition, 500–1500**

1. On its distribution and influence in the Middle Ages, see Lehmann 1959. Down to Poggio Bracciolini's rediscovery of a complete copy made in 1416, the text was known only in fragments. On the "rediscovery" and its consequences, see the account in context in Murphy 1974, S. 357ff.

2. See Müller 1969.

3. Censorinus 1983. On this work, which draws on the "traditonal teachings of the Pythagoreans," see Richter 1965, here p. 71, and Richter 1968.

4. Dombibl. 166. The codex is dated to the eighth century and was produced, according to Lowe, under insular influence, but in a continental center. See *Codices Latini Antiquiores*, vol. 8, s.v. Two other manuscripts, Vaticanus 4929, in which Censorinus's work is bound together with an excerpt from Augustine's *De musica* and other texts, and Vaticanus Pal. Lat. 1588, from Lorsch, are copies of the Cologne manuscript. The use of Censorinus's work in the oldest document on European organum, the *Musica enchiriadis*, also goes back, as Bernhard 1990b, p. 12, suggests, to the oldest manuscript of the *Musica Enchiriadis* from Werden, not far from Cologne. On this, see the editor's introduction in *Musica et Scolica enchiriadis* 1981, pp. 1–7 as well as *Musica enchiriadis* 1999.

5. The commentary is extant in a manuscript miscellany on music theory that was written in the Gembloux monastery in the eleventh century: Brussels 10078–95.

6. Medieval library catalogs list the text, which was produced in North Africa in the second half of the fifth century, in numerous copies (Manitius 1935, p. 301ff.), but its influence was limited to transmitting mythical accounts of the

origin and effects of music. Thus a Florentine codex from the twelfth century (Ashb. 1051, fol. 145v–146v; a copy of this codex is Rome, Reg. lat. 1315, fol. 78v–80v) collects, under the title *Incipit sentencia Fulgencii quam scripsit de musica*, the chapters "De novem musis" (I.15), "Apollo et Marsyas" (III.9), and "Orpheus et Euridice" (III.10). A twelfth-century copy of the *Mitologiae* is bound together with a music theory miscellany in a codex in the Bibliotheca Vallicelliana (B 81). The Orpheus legend is mentioned in the *Musica enchiriadis*, Regino of Prüm's *Epistola de armonica institutione*, John Scotus Eriugena's *Annotationes in Marcianum* Remigius of Auxerre's commentary on Martianus Capella, and other works. "The Middle Ages did not come to terms with Fulgentius' remarks that really concern music theory," according to Bernhard 1990b, p. 23. The following overview generally follows Bernhard's investigation.

7. The relatively limited information at our disposal regarding the author is assembled by the editor of Calcidius 1962, p. IX–XVII; on the systematic context of the commentary, cf. Gersh 1986, vol. 2, pp. 421–492.

8. See the research report on Calcidius's sources in the previously cited edition of his commentary, pp. XXXV–XXXVIII.

9. See ibid., pp. CVII–CXXXI with the stemma, p. CXLVIII.

10. *Musica et scolica enchiriadis* 1981, pp. 224–232.

11. Sachs 1970–1980, vol. 1, p. 59ff.

12. Aribo Scholasticus 1951, p. 47: "Moreover, Plato showed the morality of music, saying 'We used to establish peace of mind in the design and amiability of music.'" The quotation is taken from Calcidius's translation of the *Timaeus* (18a); the paraphrase of Plato on p. 46 could be traced back to Calcidius's commentary, chapter XL or L, or else to Macrobius's *Commentarii in somnium Scipionis*, II.2.

13. Engelbert of Admont 1998, p. 167.

14. On the manuscript tradition, including the commentaires and excerpts, see Barker-Benfield 1975. Among the commentators there are many influential authorities, for example William of Conches: Jeauneau 1960. In addition, the commentaries of an anonymous author are well known (Munich, clm 14708) and fragments of such a commentary are extant on the flyleaf of the Parisinus 2794. On its contributions to music theory, see Peden 1998.

15. Préaux 1953.

16. See Schedler 1916; cf. also, with regard to the genesis of the Scholastic system, Duhem 1954–1958, vol. 3, pp. 62–87.

17. Bernhard 1979, p. 34ff.

18. Aribo Scholasticus 1951, p. 45.

19. Ramos de Pareja 1901, p. 24.

20. John Wylde 1982, p. 57, p. 92ff.

21. Marchettus of Padua 1963, p. 65a.

22. *Liber de arte contrapuncti* II.1.2, in Johannes Tinctoris 1975, vol. 2, pp. 90–93.

23. Engelbert von Admont 1998, p. 167; Ugolino von Orvieto 1959–1962, V.31, vol. 3, p. 185; Johannes Hothby 1964, pp. 61–76, here pp. 62, 75.

24. On this, see details in Deiters 1881b and the summary of this work in Deiters 1881a. A survey of more recent research is provided by Grebe 1999; on the part on music in particular, see Grebe 1993.

25. Martianus Capella 1983, IX.930, p. 356.

26. Ibid., IX.936, p. 360.

27. Martianus Capella 1983, VII.736f., p. 265f. On the ontology of number, see esp. VII.742ff., p. 269ff.

28. Ibid., VIII.803, p. 302.

29. Ibid., IX.970ff., p. 356ff.

30. Ibid., IX.974ff., p. 375ff.

31. On the whole complex, see Sundermeyer 1910.

32. On this, see once again Leonardi 1959 and Leonardi 1960.

33. The previously mentioned ninth-century codex Paris, BNF lat. 7200 still presents Martianus Capella's remarks on music (fol. 208v–218v) alongside Boethius's *De institutione musica* and Augustine's *De musica*, and the tenth-century Bamberg manuscript Class. 9 (Hj. IV.19) presents it alongside the *Musica enchiriadis*, *Scolica enchiriadis*, and Boethius. The eleventh-century Ivrea 84 codex binds Book IX alone with Boethius, Augustine, and the scholia of Remigius of Auxerre. Furthermore, Leonardi 1959–1960, p. 468, records a note on an eleventh-century library catalog from Corbie: "Boetii Musica et in eodem glosae de Martiano." Fragments of the ninth-century book are contained in the Parisinus 7211, from the eleventh or twelfth century (fol. 133r–134r); here they are presented alongside excerpts from Cassiodorus and Aurelianus. In the codex Bern, Stadtbibl. B 56, from the tenth or eleventh century, seven pipe measures precede a complete Martianus Capella.

34. Remigius of Auxerre 1962–1965, vol. 2, p. 329.

35. Hucbald of Saint-Amand 1963, p. 117a. Hereafter Hucbald is quoted from Gerbert's edition; the newer edition in Chartier 1973 was not available to me.

36. Regino of Prüm 1989, p. 69ff. (Regino of Prüm 1963a, p. 245a f.).

37. Engelbert of Admont 1998, p. 167.

38. Born into an old provincial family of nobles of Syrian ancestry who had settled in the province of Calabria, Cassiodorus had family connections with the Roman urban nobility, with the family of the Anitii and the Symmachi, among others. Around the year 501 he entered politics as the *consiliarius* of his father, who was at that time serving as *praefectus praetoria*. On 1 September 506 he rose to the office of *quaestor* after producing a eulogy of Theodoric, and from then on wrote his king's letters. The *Variae* are a selection from these letters. In 514 he was made *consul ordinarius* or *corrector* of Lukania and Bruttium, an office that allowed him the leisure to write a history of his family. The previously mentioned *Anecdoton Holderi* transmits fragments of this history. In 523 he succeeded Bo-

ethius in the office of *magister officiorum* in Ravenna. In 527 he left politics, but served as *praefectus praetoriae* again from 533 to 537. The decline of the Goth's reign, with which his political career was closely connected, led him to withdraw from public offices. A number of years between 540 and 554, he lived in Constantinople; at some point after his return, and precisely in the years of the dramatic struggles between the Eastern Romans and the Goths, Cassiodorus founded on one of his estates near Syllacium the monastery of Vivarium, which was named after a nearby fishpond, and is now called Stalleti. On this, see Vyver 1931, 1941; Löwe 1948; Ludwig 1967; Hafner 2002.

39. Cassiodorus 1973, pp. 87–91, here p. 87.

40. Ibid., p. 89f. On the whole excerpt, cf. Fridh 1988.

41. Ibid., p. 88.

42. Ibid., p. 89.

43. Pietzsch 1968, p. 89.

44. Riethmüller 1989a.

45. Aristides Quintilianus 1983, I.2, p. 72.

46. Ibid., I.5, p. 76f.

47. On this inventory, see Aristeides Quintilianus 1937, pp. XXXVII–XLIV, as well as Hofmeister 1931, esp. the stemma on p. 38.

48. Cassiodorus 1973, II.40, p. 71.

49. Cassiodorus 2003, I.1.1, vol. 1, p. 91f. On the historical context, cf. Illmer 1971, p. 57 and Bardy 1945; on Agapetus's role in the planning of higher education, see Caspar 1930–1933, vol. 2, p. 312f.; also Curtius 1993, pp. 444–446.

50. Cassiodorus 2003, II.5.2, vol. 2, p. 414.

51. Ibid., II.5.9f., vol. 2, p. 428.

52. Cassiodorus 2003, II.5.5, vol. 2, p. 416.

53. Ibid.

54. Ibid. Cf. the definition taken from Donatus's *Ars maior* 4.367, ibid., II.1.2, vol. 2, p. 304: "Vocal articulation is air struck [*aer percussus*] so that however much is in it can be heard"; on this, see the detailed presentation in Borinski 1965, vol. 1, p. 140.

55. Ibid. Seen as objects and function of grammar are, in accord with tradition, the prose stylistics and metrics learned from authorities, on the one hand, and vigilance regarding linguistic correctness on the other: Cassiodorus 2003, II.1.1, vol. 2, p. 302.

56. See Borinski 1965, vol. 1, p. 13ff.

57. Cassiodorus 2003, II.3.21, vol. 2, p. 388.

58. Bower 1981, p. 160f.

59. Grabmann 1961, pp. 25–29.

60. The rich manuscript tradition is documented in Roger Mynor's older edition: Cassiodorus 1937. The preface also documents several layers of interpolation that affected especially the second book, which deals with the secular sciences.

61. For instance, St. Gallen 270 from the ninth century, the excerpt in fol. 35–45; Chartres 130 from the eleventh century contains the chapter on music— without incipit or an indication of the writer—after *Musica enchiriadis*, *Scolica enchiriadis*, and Pseudo-Bernelinus in fol. 29v–31r. The composite manuscript Monte Cassino 318 from the eleventh century gives the text as chapter 31 in fol. 55–58; Monte Cassino 10078.95 also contains, in a corpus of early medieval treatises on music, the Cassiodorus excerpt. In a *Liber officiorum* from around 1142 (Piacenza 65), Cassiodorus, supplemented with explanatory miniatures, is placed at the end of the codex. Excerpts are found in Paris, BNF 7211, a manuscript produced around 1100, together with Martianus Capella and Aurelianus Reomensis. In Oxford, Balliol Coll. 173, fol. 79, Cassiodorus figures along with Isidore of Seville's chapter on music; in the illustrated codex Paris, BNF lat. 8500, fol 39v–41r, a manuscript from the fourteenth century, we find a later proof of the study of Cassiodorus.

62. Hüschen 2001c.

63. See the reproduction in Hörmann 1965, table 13.

64. Bernhard 1990b, p. 32f. concludes that Aurelianus Reomensis had direct knowledge of Cassiodorus's work from the fact that he lists transposition scales following Cassiodorus.

65. Regino of Prüm 1989, p. 57 (Regino of Prüm 1963a, p. 239b). Regino borrows the genera of the instruments from Cassiodorus, and possibly also the story of David. See ibid., pp. 49–51 (235b, 236b); for details and further examples suggesting direct knowledge, see Bernhard 1979, p. 36.

66. Federhofer-Königs 1960, p. 19f.

67. Walter Odington 1970, pp. 61, 87.

68. Schmidt 1899, p. 31ff.

69. See the inventory in Bischoff 1966b.

70. See Fontaine 1983.

71. Martin Gerbert used such an excerpt on the theory of music (Vienna Cpv 2503) in vol. 1, pp. 20–24 of his *Scriptores*. Further excerpts are listed in Bernhard 1990b, p. 33f. For an introduction to Isidore's influence in music theory contexts, see Hüschen 1958–1961 and León Tello 1952.

72. In the *Etymologiae*, the sections *De officiis* (VI.19) and *De ecclesia* (VII.2) are informative; see also, in *De ecclesiasticis officiis*, the sections *De canticis* (I.4), *De Psalmis* (I.5), *De hymnis* (I.6), *De antiphonis* (I.7), *De responsoriis* (I.9), *De horis* (I.19–23), and *De psalmistis* (II.12), along with *Regula monachorum*, chap. 6.

73. See Fontaine 1983, vol. 1, pp. 373–383.

74. Isidore of Seville 1957–1962, III.15 (unpaginated edition).

75. Ibid., II.14.

76. Ibid., III.17.

77. On this, which is conceived just as it is in Augustine, see also the section "De metris," ibid., I.39.

78. Ibid., III.18.

79. Ibid., III.19. Cf. Augustine, *Enarratio in psalmos* 150; *De ordine* II.14; *De doctrina christiana* II.17.

80. Isidore of Seville 1957–1962, III.20.

81. Ibid., III.21.

82. Ibid., III.16. On the Old Testament figures of Iubal or Tubal as possible founders of *muscia scientia*, see McKinnon 1978.

83. Isidore of Seville 1957–1962, IV.13.

84. See Kümmel 1977; on the pulse, esp. pp. 23–62; on Cassiodorus und Isidore, esp. p. 26ff.

85. Isidore of Seville 1957–1962, III.17.

86. Ibid.

87. See León Tello 1952, p. 24.

88. *De universo* XVIII.4, in Hrabanus Maurus 1851, col. 495.

89. Pseudo-Aristotle 1963, p. 253.

90. Marchettus of Padua 1963, p. 66.

91. *De universo* XVIII.4, in Hrabanus Maurus 1852, col. 495.

92. Giraldus Cambrensis 1867, III.11–15.

93. Göller 1959 edited and commented on the passages on music in the *Speculum doctrinale* in the context of his study.

94. Pseudo-Aristotle 1963, p. 253.

95. Simon Tunstede 1963, p. 205.

96. See Ellinwood 1945.

97. Walter Odington 1970, p. 100.

98. Ugolino of Orvieto 1959–1962, I.1 and I.64, vol. I, pp. 16, 103.

99. *Complexus effectuum musices*, in Johannes Tinctoris 1975, vol. 2, p. 173f.

100. Abert 1905, p. 126.

101. Ibid.

102. Bernhard 2003, p. 609.

103. On this, see ibid., pp. 609–612 and Phillips 1990.

104. Duchez 1981, p. 562f., summarizes as follows: "A first period, pre-theoretical and empirical, that corresponds to a phenomenological knowledge proceeding from the musical practice of the cantor of the service, and provides an intuitive verbal description of music as it is perceived, executed, and taught. This description, which is both qualitative and comprehensive, is concerned above all with the concrete conditions of the production of music to guide its direct, immediate reproduction [. . .]. It is carried out by the sole means of language [. . .]. Linking music with the chant that it supports and that supports it, the verbal knowledge of music connects music with language and with the discipline that studies it in the framework of the Trivium: grammar. [. . .] A second period of elaborating an operative knowledge of music takes shape in the middle of the ninth century [. . .]. It is an arithmetical description that, using specific notions and signs, describes music in terms of number and measure. Cultural in origin, it borrows its arithmo-musical concepts from ancient music theory, of which the

musicus is the learned depository. In accord with the Pythagorean-Platonic tradition, this numerical knowledge integrates music into the cosmology of number and, like arithmetic, from which it is inseparable, makes it a mathematical science taught in the Quadrivium."

105. See Richenhagen 1989.

106. See the editor's introduction in Hrabanus Maurus 1900, p. 16ff.; also in Hrabanus Maurus 1996 the editor's "studies," pp. 3–139, which show the close connection between the work completed in 819 and the Aachen reforms of 816–819.

107. See examples in Klopsch (ed.) 1985, pp. 124–143.

108. See the selection in Godman (ed.) 1985, pp. 215–229.

109. Heito/Walahfrid Strabo 1984. A more recent, annotated edition is Heito/Walahfrid Strabo 2004.

110. According to Corbin 1977, esp. pp. 21–41.

111. Cf. Gennrich 1932, p. 107ff.

112. In the following, the critical edition Aurelianus Reomensis 1975 is cited. This edition is the published version of the editor's dissertation (Aurelianus Reomensis 1963b), an edition in 2 vols. with an extensive critical commentary greatly abridged for publication.

113. Bernhard 1986 provides detailed proof. From this point on, it is futile to track down every quotation: "With the beginning of medieval literature on music theory in the ninth century, the text of the *Institutio musica* becomes common knowledge and is henceforth cited by almost all authors, whenever speculative music theory is discussed in any form." Bernhard 1990b, p. 29.

114. According to the editor in Aurelianus Reomensis 1975, p. 12.

115. Ibid., p. 58: "The great authority of the ancients, the gentiles, and especially the saints affirms that the discipline of music is not to be scorned."

116. Ibid., p. 61: "Music is the science of modulating sound and song properly [*sciencia recte modulandi sono cantuque congrua*]."

117. See the detailed account in Handschin 1950b.

118. See in particular chapters I, III, VII, VIII, and XX. Thus what Grabmann said about the status of the sciences shortly after the Carolingian reform holds true at least for this text: "The chief signature of academic activities in the Carolingian age and subsequently, down to early Scholasticism, is *receptivity, traditionalism*. Prescholasticism is a time of collecting and excerpting, of reproduction and compilation. The decisive respect for *auctoritas* and the dependency on the statements and views of the great teachers of the Patristic age is characteristic of early medieval education. *Ratio*, the rational working out, the penetration and independent understanding of the material transmitted by tradition, retreat behind this unconditional acceptance of the authority of the Fathers, behind this cult of *auctoritas*." Grabmann 1956, vol. 1, p. 179f. [emphasis in the original].

119. Aurelianus Reomensis 1975, p. 64.

120. Ibid., p. 64f.

121. Ibid., p. 65f. [emphasis in the original], with quotation from Mark 16:15.

122. Ibid., p. 66.

123. Ibid.

124. Ibid., p. 66f.

125. Pietzsch 1968, p. 61.

126. Aurelianus Reomensis 1963a.

127. See the description of the two manuscripts in the edition Aurelianus Reomensis 1975, pp. 47f., 49.

128. For proofs, see Curtius 1993, pp. 467–469.

129. Aurelianus Reomensis 1975, p. 63. Cf. Walter 1998, p. 74.

130. Aurelianus Reomensis 1975, p. 80f.

131. Ibid., p. 59.

132. Ibid., p. 59f.

133. Ibid., p. 67.

134. Ibid.

135. Beda Venerabilis 1991, XXIV, p. 160ff. Bede himself borrows the content of the passage from Marius Victorinus and Audax. The relationship is investigated in Crocker 1958, p. 8ff. and Fassler 1987, p. 168ff. Kunz 1955 provides a summary that is still useful.

136. To those whose curiosity makes them ask for more, Bede recommends the study of Donatus: Beda Venerabilis 1991, p. 92.

137. Ibid., II, pp. 43–46.

138. Ibid., IX, p. 93.

139. Ibid., XXI, p. 154.

140. Ibid., XXIIII, p. 160.

141. Crocker 1958, p. 9.

142. See Meyer 1905, esp. pp. 108–118; for details, cf. my chapter 8.

143. Beda Venerabilis 1991, pp. 160–163.

144. Beda Venerabilis 1991, p. 160. The first verse of Jerome cited as an example consists of only seven syllables. This irregularity remains occasional and is neither noted nor commented upon in the text.

145. An overview of the historical context, Regino's biography, the works mentioned, and the state of the sources is found in the already cited works and in the following: Hüschen 1962, Chartier 1965, Bower 1971, Bernhard 1979.

146. In contrast to the *Tonarius*, for which a reliable edition has been available since 1867, for a long time there was no comparable edition of the *Epistola*. For more than two hundred years the only edition was the one provided by Martin Gerbert in his *Scriptores ecclesiastici de musica sacra potissimum* (Regino of Prüm 1963a). The validity of the bases of Gerbert's text has regularly been questioned, and in addition, additional manuscripts have recently been discovered. The edition produced by Mary Protase LeRoux (Regino of Prüm 1965) offered hardly any progress in this regard, since it not only failed to take into account parts of the manuscript tradition, but also, as Bernhard 1979 has shown, repeats

old errors. These were first corrected by Bernhard's new edition in his *Clavis Gerberti* (Regino of Prüm 1989). This edition will be cited here. References to Gerbert's collection will be given as well, taking into account the latter's wide diffusion down to the present. On the state of the sources for the *Epistola* and on the stemma, see Bernhard 1979, pp. 3–33.

147. Ibid., p. 67.

148. Regino of Prüm 1989, p. 39 (Regino of Prüm 1963a, 230a f.).

149. Preparatory studies on the identification of Regino's sources have been provided in Brambach 1883, p. 8ff. and Pietzsch 1968, p. 63ff.; then more detailed in Bernhard 1979, pp. 34–42.

150. Ibid., p. 37ff.; here possible quotations are identified and discussed.

151. Regino of Prüm 1989, p. 42 (Regino of Prüm 1963a, p. 232a).

152. Ibid., p. 45 (Regino of Prüm 1963a, p. 233a).

153. Ibid., passim, e.g., p. 55f. (Regino of Prüm 1963a p. 239a).

154. Ibid., p. 53 (Regino of Prüm 1963a, S. 237a f.). The definiton quotes verbatim Boethius, *De institutione musica*, II.7, p. 191.

155. Regino of Prüm 1989, p. 57 (Regino of Prüm 1963a, p. 239b).

156. Ibid., p. 45f. (Regino of Prüm 1963a, p. 233b f.).

157. Ibid., p. 46 (Regino of Prüm 1963a, p. 234a).

158. Ibid., p. 48 (Regino of Prüm 1963a, p. 235a).

159. The translation to be found in research, "divinely inspired" (Bernhard 1979, p. 49) is misleading. Such an interpretation might be made plausible at least for Christian choral music, but hardly for the *bestiae* whose sounds Regino considers to be a form of *musica naturalis*. The created body is the reference point for Reginio's formulation, which rather seems to be modeled on Gen. 2:7: "The Lord God, therefore, formed man from the slime of the earth and breathed into his face the breath of life, and man was made into a living being." Cf. Bernhard 1979, p. 67: "His [Regino's] main concern is a problem of his time: bringing ancient theory into agreement with Church musical practice. This idea is shown most clearly in Regino's altered conception of the division of music, a mindset that basically does not move far beyond Boethius so far as the filling out of the invididual genera is concerned, but whose approach shows a Christian tendency insofar as it opposes music inspired by God to that conceived by humans and therefore can subsume *musica mundana* and *musica humana*, both of which are influenced by God, under a single principle."

160. Regino of Prüm 1989, p. 50f. (Regino of Prüm 1963a, p. 236b).

161. Hüschen 1962, S. 216.

162. Regino of Prüm 1989, p. 51 (Regino of Prüm 1963a, p. 236b).

163. Bower 1971, p. 21. In addition to that, Regino distinguishes among the three genera of instruments according to Cassiodorus: "Similarly, artificial music is divided into three kinds, concerned with stretching, blowing, and striking [*tensibile, inflatile, & percussibile*]." Regino of Prüm 1989, p. 51 (Regino of Prüm 1963a, p. 236b).

164. Ibid.

165. Wellesz 1954, p. 1022.

166. See Wellesz 1961, p. 57–60 passim.

167. Bower 1971, p. 25.

168. See Remigius of Auxerre 1962–1965, chap. 73.16, vol. 1, p. 198; John Scotus Eriugena 1939, chap. 60.5, p. 65.

169. Remigius of Auxerre 1962–1965, vol. 2, chap. 476.15, p. 304f.

170. The two oldest manuscripts of Regino's work share with John Scotus Eriugena's commentary on Martianus Capella and with Remigius of Auxerre an idiosyncratic spelling, *artificalis* rather than *artificialis*: Bower 1971, p. 26, 40n, with proofs.

171. *Expositiones in ierarchiam coelestem*, in John Scotus Eriugena 1853, col. 139.

172. Ibid., col. 139f.

173. Bower 1971, p. 27.

174. Silk 1935, p. 157. On the editor's argument regarding John Scotus Eriugena's authorship, see p. xviii f.

175. Bower 1971, p. 28.

176. *De divisione naturae*, in John Scotus Eriugena 1853, III.6, col. 637f.

177. Handschin 1927; on Riemann's thesis p. 320, 3n.

178. Waeltner 1977; on this passage in the commentary, p. 3ff.

179. Ibid., p. 3: "John Scotus compares the universe with the *organicum melos*, whose *dulcedo naturalis* corresponds to the harmony of the universe: although they are composed of different individual elements, both nonetheless constitute a unity." More precisely, p. 25: "To clarify his Neoplatonic idea of the harmonia universitatis, John Scotus chose the *organicum melos*, the instrumental sound in the sense of the aforementioned analogy. In doing so he appeals not only to a specific musical or instrumental practice, but also to the natural phenomenon of the consonance of different notes in general."

180. For example, Ansorge 1996 investigates this integration in John Scotus Eriugena.

181. On this "eschatological view of harmony," see Niemöller 1998.

182. Beierwaltes 1991.

183. Ibid., p. 12 [emphasis in the original]. For details see also Vrin 1980, pp. 85–97.

184. Beierwaltes 1991, p. 13 [emphasis in the original]. Cf. Handschin 1927, p. 329.

185. John Scotus Eriugena 1853, col. 475.

186. Bower 1971, p. 30; on John Scotus Eriugena 1853, col. 472f.

187. Ibid., col. 866.

188. Ibid., col. 869f.

189. Ibid.

190. Regino of Prüm 1989, p. 45 (Regino of Prüm 1963a, p. 233a).

191. See Hüschen 2001d.

192. Hammerstein 1962, p. 126f.

193. Regino of Prüm 1989, p. 48 (Regino of Prüm 1963a, p. 235a).

194. Ibid.

195. See Oberti 1960, esp. p. 343ff.; also Pietzsch 1968, p. 65: "By putting the accent on this [the acoustic reality of the different kinds of music], in his classification he foregrounds, as it were, the final result of 'musica humana'; because only a human being who is shaped by its laws will be able to make music well, that is, numerically and beautifully."

196. Regino of Prüm 1989, p. 48f. (Regino of Prüm 1963a, p. 235b).

197. See Ernstbrunner 2002, esp. p. 74ff.

198. See the discussion in Abert 1905, p. 166f.

199. Deschamps 1994, p. 62.

200. Johannes Cotto 1950, chap. III.1 and IV.1.

201. Johannes de Muris 1963a, pp. 193b ff., 195a ff., 199a ff.

202. Bernhard 1979, p. 3.12, lists as manuscripts from the twelfth-century Paris, BNF lat. 10509 and Oxford, Bodleian Library, Bodley 613.

203. Adam of Fulda 1963, pp. 333a ff., 337b ff., 355a ff.

204. The necessity of using the plural here with reference to the twelfth century has already been strongly emphasized by Chenu 1956; a survey of research is offered by Marenbon 1997.

205. See the overview in Vignaux 1931, esp. col. 738–752 on the *recusatio* of the Thomistic theory of individuation. On the effect of nominalist arguments on music theory and compositional theory, see the detailed account in Tanay 1989, esp. pp. 149–219.

206. William of Conches 1965, pp. 58–61.

207. Ibid., p. 60.

208. Ibid., p. 61.

209. Ibid.

210. See presentation and summary in Clerval 1977, p. 220ff.

211. Jeauneau 1954 offers an edition of the prologue, with studies; reprinted in Jeauneau 1973, pp. 87–91.

212. See Evans 1982.

213. Alanus ab Insulis 1955, III.416ff., p. 101.

214. See Grabmann 1956, vol. 2 passim, esp. pp. 64–81 and, especially on the consequences for the systematic place of *musica scientia*, Dyer 2007.

215. Weisheipl 1965, p. 65ff. situates them in their precise context.

216. Grabmann 1956, vol. 2, p. 235.

217. Weisheipl 1965, p. 66.

218. *Didascalion* I.1.2.3, in Hugo of St. Victor 1854, vol. 2, col. 741, 743.

219. Dyer 2007, p. 20.

220. Hugo of St. Victor 1854, vol. 2, col. 752–763.

221. Schmidt 1967, p. 97.

222. Hugo of St. Victor 1854, vol. 2, col. 756b–757a.

223. Ibid., col. 757.

224. Johannes Cotto 1963.

225. See esp. chap. XVIII: *Praecepta de cantu componere*, ibid., p. 253a ff.

226. See Hirschmann 2000.

227. Johannes Cotto 1963, p. 234a f.

228. Ibid.

229. Thus for Cotto, whether or not the accent of his presentation is on acoustic phenomena, only the "sonus discretus" is the object of music: ibid., p. 234b.

230. Ibid., p. 253a.

231. Jerome of Moravia 1935. We know nothing about the author other than that he lived in the thirteenth century and resided around 1250 in the Rue St. Jacques monastery. The treatise and its author are discussed in detail in Cserba 1934.

232. Jerome of Moravia 1935, p. 7f.; p. 10: "Music is defined as follows: music is the knowledge of number as it relates to sound [*scientia de numero relato ad sonos*]"; pp. 75–103. Number is conceived Neoplatonically as the principle of unity of a discrete multitude: "Number is a collection of unities [*unitatum collectio*], or number is a multitude composed of units [*multitudo ex unitatibus aggregata*]" (p. 77).

233. See ibid., pp. 16–35; the detailed presentation of Boethius's triad is found in chap. VI, pp. 23–25.

234. Ibid., p. 41.

235. Ibid., p. 43.

236. Meyer 2001, p. 308.

237. Aribo received his education in the monastery of St. Emmeran near Regensburg, died as the principal (*scholasticus*) of the cathedral school in Freising, and dedicated his treatise on music to Bishop Ellenhard of Freising (1052–1078); we have no other dates concerning his life. On these, the state of the sources, and the stemma of his *De musica*, see Rawski 1962 and Ilnitchi 1997, which provides a detailed description and discussion of the manuscript tradition (pp. 20–85).

238. Hüschen 2001a.

239. Ibid., pp. 197–220. On Aribo's treatise as a whole, see the concise analysis in Ilnitchi 1997, esp. the chapter "Aribo's Technical Model and his Concept of 'Natura,'" pp. 179–234.

240. Ibid., pp. 20–85.

241. Boethius, *De institutione musica*, I.34, p. 225.

242. Regino of Prüm 1989, p. 45 (Regino of Prüm 1963a, p. 233b): "Thus, natural music is that which produces sound with no musical instrument, [. . .], but breathed upon by God [*sed divinus adspirata*] and with nature alone as teacher [*sola natura docente*], it measures out [*modulatur*] sweet modes. This music comes about in the motion of the heavens or in the human voice. Some add a third kind that is made by irrational creatures with sound or voice."

243. Aribo Scholasticus 1951, p. 46. Cf. Regino of Prüm 1989, p. 44 (Regino of Prüm 1963a, p. 233a).

244. Ibid., p. 51 (p. 236b).

245. Aribo Scholasticus 1951, p. 47.

246. Aribo Scholasticus 1951, p. 56, the section "De Nobilitate & ignobilitate consonantiarum"; on the proportions functioning here, see p. 58f.

247. Ibid., p. 28.

248. Ibid., p. 41.

249. For details, see Bernhard 1979, p. 46f.

250. For instance by Fischer 1981, p. 236, who argues that Aribo distances himself from Regino.

251. Ilnitchi 1997, p. 179ff. discusses in detail the relations with *ordo naturalis* in Aribo, and juxtaposes them with evidence drawn from the works of Hermann of Reichenau and William of Hirsau.

252. Zumthor 1978a, p. 264.

253. See esp. Zumthor 1975b.

254. Ibid., p. 36.

255. BNF lat. 796, fol. 212v.

256. Waesberghe 1967. In the subsequent discussion we follow his commentary.

257. Stockmann 1985.

258. We continue to follow the account in Blumenberg 1996, here pp. 159–233 passim, as well as Gilson 1952, pp. 525–550.

259. On the bases in Aristotle, see Cassirer 1932, esp. pp. 1–47.

260. The decree, which was not directed against the Scholastic will to systematization in general, but rather against Siger of Brabant in particular, *Opiniones ducentae undeviginti Sigeri de Barbantia, Boetii de Dacia aliorumque, a Stephano episcopo Parisiensi de consilio doctorum sacrae scripturae condemnatae* is found in Chartularium Universitatis Parisiensis, vol. 1, pp. 543–558. With the incrimination of the statement "That God is not able to be the cause of any new thing, nor can He bring forth anything completely new," attention is drawn to the weak point of the Scholastic construction of reality, whose assumptions immediately become the subject: "That God is not able to move anything irregularly, that is, in any way other than the way He moves, because in Him there is no alteration of the will. [. . .] That it is necessary that God make whatever comes to be immediately by Himself.—This is error, as can be discerned either from the necessity of joint-action, which takes away freedom, or from the necessity of immutability, because it imposes the inability of doing otherwise" (nn 48, 50, 53). Cf. the commentary in Blumenberg 1996, p. 178ff.

261. See details in Geenen 1946.

262. All quotations from Aquinas's work follow the text given in Thomas von Aquin 1882.

263. See the presentation in I, qu. 45, 48, 75, 95, and 105, along with the

commentary in Gilson 1952, pp. 532–538; for details on the theory of individuation, Klinger 1964, and on the historical presuppositions, Santeller 1939, pp. 254–269; on the concept of analogy, Montagnes 1963, passim, esp. pp. 60–63.

264. Cf. details in Blumenberg 1996, p. 384ff.

265. Küpper 1989, p. 254.

266. See the edition Dominicus Gundissalinus 1903, pp. 162–164, as well as the study, pp. 164–314. The work, "a cleverly fabricated collection of materials from Arabic (Al-Kindi, Al-Farabi, Avicenna, An-Nairizi, Al-Gazel, and other unknown authors) and Latin (Boethius, Isidore, Bede) sources," is already based "entirely on an Aristotelian foundation" (p. 314). On the systematic place of music, see details in Dyer 2007, pp. 32–37.

267. Chartularium Universitatis Parisiensis, vol. 1, p. 276. On the genesis, establishment, and criticism of the text, see Grabmann 1939.

268. Cf. Glorieux 1968.

269. Grabmann described the manuscript on several occasions, for instance in Grabmann 1928, pp. 51–63; Grabmann 1934 and Grabmann 1941, pp. 113–125. Furthermore, Grabmann drew attention to three additional manuscripts that are related to Barcelona, Ripoll 109 (Grabmann 1934, p. 226f.): Vienna, Nationalbibliothek, ms. lat. 2373, fol. 66b–75; Kassel, Murhardsche Bibliothek, 2° philos. 30.4, fol. 44b–50, and Munich, Bayerische Staatsbibliothek 14460, fol. 28b–32a. Haas 1982 collates passages on quadrivial music from the manuscripts in Barcelona and Munich and publishes them in the framework of a comprehensive study. In the following, the manuscript will be cited in this edition.

270. Ibid., p. 354.

271. Ibid., p. 354f.

272. Cf. the inventory of passages in the *corpus aristotelicum* that are relevant to music theory in Haas 1982, p. 342f.; on the *Problemata*, see Ventura 2004.

273. The following presentation but not the conclusions drawn from Hirtler 1995, pp. 53–65.

274. Haas 1982, p. 354.

275. Ibid., p. 360.

276. See Boethius, *De institutione arithmetica* I.1, p. 10f.

277. See Boethius, *De institutione musica* I.3, p. 189f.

278. Haas 1982, p. 354.

279. Hirtler 1995, p. 55.

280. Ibid., p. 358.

281. The theory of subordination is presented and discussed in Köpf 1974, pp. 145–149.

282. Haas 1982, p. 358. Whether the two specifications are viewed as distinct and thus hiearchically equal in rank or sound is viewed as subordinate to *numerus* remains an open question.

283. Ibid.

284. Ibid., p. 359.

285. That is how it is seen in Hirtler 1995, p. 59.

286. Haas 1982, p. 359.

287. See Burnyeat 1987.

288. Haas 1982, p. 358.

289. See Burnyeat 1987.

290. Beaujouan 1954–1956, p. 15; likewise Meyer 2003, p. 676.

291. Haas 1982, p. 359 [emphasis supplied].

292. On musical practice we can mention the commentary on Psalm 32 in his *Psalmos Davids expositio*, the sections "Utrum Deus sit ore laudandus," "Utrum in divinis laudibus sint cantus assumendi" (II-II.91, 1.2), the commentaries on the musical structure of the Mass (III.81.4c), the annotations on the singers in the commentary on Isa. 23:16, the corresponding passages in the commentary on Aristotle, and, with respect to the beautiful, above all the commentary on Pseudo-Dionysius the Areopagite's *De divinis nominibus*. The treatise *De musica* attributed to Thomas in older scholarly literature, was edited by Ambrogio M. Amelli on the basis of the codex Pavia, Bibl. univ. 130 D.18, under the title *Thomae Aquinatis de arte musica nunc primum ex codice bibliothecae Universitatis Ticinensis edidit et illustravit* (Amelli 1880), and attributed on the ground of an alleged allusion to it in a work by Johannes de Muris and certain stylistic features. Since Grabmann's concise refutation of this claim (Grabmann 1949, p. 416ff.), the work has no longer been attributed to Aquinas.

293. The following remarks draw on Burbach 1966; Kovach 1961; Czapiewski 1964; Gässler 1994; Bruyne 1946, vol. 3, p. 282ff. passim. I refer in particular to the older but still noteworthy essay Dyroff 1929, with the supplements provided by Koch 1931.

294. Thomas Aquinas, *Sententia libri Metaphysicae* I. l.16, 4n [emphasis in the original].

295. Haas 1982, p. 393.

296. Thomas Aquinas, *Super Boetium de Trinitate* III, qu. 5, a. 3 ad 4: "Mathematics is not abstracted from just any matter, but only from sensible matter. The parts of quantity, however, from which the cited demonstration in some way appears to be selected by means of a material cause, are not sensible matter, but pertain to intelligible matter, which is found even in mathematics, as is clear from the seventh book of the Metaphysics."

297. Ibid., III, qu. 5, a. 3 ad 5.

298. Ibid., III, qu. 5, a. 3 ad 6. On the argument in a wider context, see Gagné 1967 and on the narrow context of music theory, Dyer 2007, pp. 67–69.

299. Pertinent here is Faucon 1975, a work that concentrates on the relation between Aquinas and Pseudo-Dionysius the Areopagite; on ontology, also see especially Kremer 1966.

300. Thomas Aquinas, *Super De Trinitate* I, qu. 1, a. 2 ad 3.

301. Schütz 2006, s.v.

302. Thomas Aquinas, *Super De Trinitate* I, qu. 1, a. 2, ad 3.

303. Thomas Aquinas, *In libros Physicorum* II.l. 5, 4n.

304. Thomas Aquinas, *Summa theologiae* I, qu. 22, a. 2 co. See details in Gässler 1994, pp. 72–78; for the Aristotelian bases, see Aristotle's *Physics* II.3 and *Metaphysics* V.3.

305. Also according to Gässler 1994, p. 73.

306. This connection is developed in Meyer 1938, pp. 319–570.

307. Krings 1941, p. 111: "Thus if relation corresponded only to Being in the mind, it would have no place among the Aristotelian categories"; in this connection, cf. Kring's annotations on the "pointing function," p. 166ff. On this, see also Dyroff 1929, p. 179, according to whom Thomas tried "to bring Aristotle's categories into Dionysius's list [of the proportions]."

308. Bruyne 1946, vol. 3, p. 306.

309. See, with proofs, Burbach 1966, p. 25.

310. Thomas Aquinas, *Summa theologiae* I, q. 39, a. 8 co.

311. Thomas Aquinas, *In libros Physicorum* I.l.19, 4n.

312. Thomas Aquinas, *Summa theologiae* I-II, qu. 29, a. 1 co.

313. Ibid., I, qu. 39, a. 2, arg. 1 [emphasis in the original].

314. Thomas Aquinas, *In librum beati Dionysii De divinis nominibus expositio*, cap. 11.l. 2. [emphasis in the original]. On this passage, see the commentary in Dyroff 1929, pp. 168, 174 passim.

315. Thomas Aquinas, *In librum beati Dionysii De divinis nominibus expositio*, cap. 4.l.6.

316. Ibid., cap. 7.l.4.

317. Ibid., cap. 11.l.2 [emphasis in the original].

318. See Henle 1956, pp. 176–183 and details in Durantel 1919, esp. pp. 62–68 and 218–234; also Czapiewski 1964, pp. 80–86.

319. Ibid. p. 75 [emphasis in the original]. See also Dyroff 1929, p. 166ff. with the systematic commentary on *De divinis nominibus* and the concluding assessement: "Thomas contradicts nowhere. He only perhaps reorganizes here and there [. . .]."

320. Thomas Aquinas, *In librum beati Dionysii De divinis nominibus expositio*, chap. 4.l.8.

321. Thomas Aquinas, *Summa theologiae* II-II, qu. 141, a. 2 ad 3: "a measured and fitting proportion [*moderata et conveniens proportio*], in which the nature of beauty consists."

322. See the survey, with selected bibliography, in Schneider 1998; the "subjective" component is made conspicuously strong by Eco 1970.

323. Thomas Aquinas, *Summa theologiae* I-II, q. 27, a. 1 ad 3; Bruyne 1946, vol. 3, p. 282f.

324. Ibid., p. 297: "Neither pure knowledge based on the senses, nor abstract scientific knowledge, it assumes the immanence of the mind to sensibility: the total intuition resulsts from the 'application' of reason to perception and, in its aesthetic character, from mental detachment with regard to vital necessities."

The purposelessness of contemplation limits the latter to human beings: Thomas Aquinas, *Summa theologiae* II–II, qu. 141 a. 4 ad 3.

325. Ibid., I, qu. 91, a. 4; cf. also ibid. II–II, qu. 141, a. 4 ad 3m.

326. Thomas Aquinas, *In librum beati Dionysii De divinis nominibus expositio*, chap. 4.l.10.

327. Dyroff 1929, p. 195.

328. On the following, in addition to the analysis in Czapiewski 1964, pp. 25–34, esp. p. 32, cf. Pouillon 1946, on Aquinas pp. 305–311, along with the critical qualification in Schneider 1998, p. 777.

329. Czapiewski 1964, p. 34.

330. Thomas Aquinas, *In librum beati Dionysii De divinis nominibus expositio* chap. 4.l.5 [emphasis in the original].

331. Ibid.

332. Thomas Aquinas, *Summa theologiae* I, qu. 39, a. 8. On this passage and the following, cf. Kovach 1961, pp. 106–144.

333. See for instance *Scriptum super Sententiis* I, dist. 31.2.1, sol.

334. Thomas Aquinas, *Summa theologiae* I, qu. 4, a. 1 c. On the metaphysical relationships, see Bruyne 1946, vol. 3, p. 301, who argues that the supplement of *perfectio* connects the "completeness" formulated with *integritas* to its metaphysical principle: the beautiful is completeness developed in terms of entelechy. See also Kovach 1961, p. 108f.

335. Suger of St. Denis 1979, XXXIII, p. 62. On Suger's indirect references to Pseudo-Dionysius the Areopagite, see Panofsky 2002, esp. p. 146ff.

336. See the brief survey in Eco 2004, pp. 67–79.

337. Kovach 1961, p. 131ff.

338. Thomas Aquinas, *In librum beati Dionysii De divinis nominibus expositio*, c. 4.l.5 [emphasis in the original].

339. Bruyne 1946, vol. 3, p. 307.

340. Lotman 1972, pp. 410, 412. On the obviously Platonic roots of the concept, of which Thomas was aware as such and which he defended, along with Augustine and Pseudo-Dionysius the Areopagite, against Aristotle, see Faucon 1975, pp. 181–326.

341. Bruyne 1946, vol. 3, p. 298.

342. *Summa contra Gentiles* III.c. 139, 5n; likewise, under the superior category of *species*, in the early *Expositio super Isaiam ad litteram*, c. 53: "species properly respects beauty in so far as it respects the symmetry of parts." On this, see Koch 1931, p. 267.

343. Thomas Aquinas, *Summa theologiae* I–II, qu. 54 a.1 corpus. Cf. also Thomas Aquinas, *In librum beati Dionysii De divinis nominibus expositio* c. 4.l.22: "Beauty [is] symmetry of parts."

344. Ibid. [emphasis in original]. On the connection between "proportional" *ordo* and *proportio* as an "objective" condition of the beautiful, see Kovach 1961, pp. 113–125. However, Kovach does not recognize the relations with the Neoplatonic tradition's "musical" concept of *ordo*.

345. Thomas Aquinas, *Summa theologiae* I, qu. 1, a. 1 co.: "It was necessary for human salvation that there be learning according to divine revelation, and apart from philosophical learning, which is approached through human reason."

346. Thomas Aquinas, *In De anima* I.l.7, 97n. Cf. also the detailed discussion of *delectatio* in *Scriptum super sententiis* IV, dist. 49, qu. 3, a. 5.

347. Thomas Aquinas, *Summa theologiae* I, qu. 5, a. 4 ad 1.

348. Ibid.: "Appetite is a kind of motion toward a thing."

349. Ibid. I–II, qu. 27, a. 1 ad 3. On this, see Kovach 1961, pp. 242–256 and Dyroff 1929, pp. 183ff., 192.

350. Aristotle, *Nicomachean Ethics* 1094a; quoted in Thomas Aquinas, *Summa theologiae* I, qu. 5, a. 1 co; cf. also ibid., qu. 5, a. 1 ad 1.

351. Thomas Aquinas, *In librum beati Dionysii De divinis nominibus expositio* chap. 4.l.9.

352. Dyroff 1929, p. 196.

353. Thomas Aquinas, *Summa theologiae* I, qu. 5, a. 4 ad 1; cf. *Scriptum super Sententiis* I, dist. 31, qu. 2, a 4.

354. Bruyne 1946, vol. 3, p. 302 [emphasis supplied].

355. On the discussion and attribution of the completion to Peter, see Grabmann 1949, p. 284. Grabmann bases his attribution on an annotation in the codex Vienna, Bibl. Rossiana IX.259, which is found in identical form in Vat. lat. 777 and 7778, and also in Paris, BNF lat. 6457 and 6612.

356. Thomas Aquinas, *Sententia libri Politicorum, Continuatio a Petro de Alvernia* VII.l.2.2n.

357. Ibid., VII.l.2.23n.

358. Thomas Aquinas, *Summa theologiae* I, qu. 1, a. 9 co.

359. Ibid. II–II, qu. 180, a. 2 ad 3. The comment made in Dyroff 1929, p. 176, is noteworthy: "For him, discursive knowledge (*discurrere per diversa*), with its possibilities of error and multiplicities, obviously ranks lower than absolutely uniform contemplation, which receives its uniformity from its uniform principle, God."

360. Ibid. II–II, qu. 169, a. 2 ad 4; II–II, qu. 91, a. 2c.

361. Ibid., II–II, qu. 169, a. 2 ad 1.

362. Ibid., II–II, qu. 169, a. 2 ad 2.

363. Ibid., II–II, qu. 168, a. 3 ad 3.

364. Ibid., II–II, qu. 168, a. 2 co.

365. Ibid.

366. Ibid.

367. Ibid.

368. Ibid.

369. See Augustine 1947, I.3.4, p. 30ff.

370. Thomas Aquinas, *Summa theologiae* II–II, qu. 168, a. 2 s.c.

371. Ibid. qu. 168, a. 1 co.; likewise, ibid. qu. 168, a. 2 co.: "One must pay attention, as one does in all other human activities, that play is suitable to person, time, and place, and that it be arranged dutifully in accord with other circumstances, in particular, that it be worthy of the time and the individual."

372. Thomas Aquinas, *Super De Trinitate* I, qu. 1, a. 2, ad 3.

373. Gässler 1994, pp. 73–79, 82–86.

374. Thomas Aquinas, *Summa theologiae* II–II, qu. 168, a. 4 ad 3.

375. Ibid., II–II, qu. 168, a. 3 ad 3.

376. Ibid., I, qu. 39, a. 8 co.

377. Ibid., II–II, qu. 91, a. 2 co. Cf. as well Thomas Aquinas, *In psalmos Davidis expositio* 32, 2n.

378. Thomas Aquinas, *Summa theologiae* I, qu. 1, a. 9 ad 1: As for the occasional use of metaphor in the Bible, which explains the need for allegorical interpretation, see Augustine, *De Civitate Dei* XI.18, *De doctrina christiana* II.6.7–8, and IV.11.26, as well as Thomas Aquinas, *Summa theologiae* I, qu. I, a. 9 co. ff. and I–II, qu. 101, a. 2 co. ff.

379. Thomas Aquinas, *Quaestiones de quolibet* VII, qu. 6, a. 3 arg 2.

380. Here we can only refer to the debate regarding the authenticity of this letter. See the report on the positions in Lieberknecht 1999, p. 4ff.

381. Dante 1965; the letter to Cangrande della Scala, pp. 860–872, here par. 7ff., p. 862f. Without going into the possible difference between the text of the Bible and that of the *Commedia*, the letter presents the allegorical reading of Scripture in order to show how the same procedure can be used to read the *Commedia*. The literal subject of the work is said to be the "the state of souls after death," while the allegorical subject is man as subject and object of salvation: "the subject is man, and whether he is worthy of reward or punishment according to justice, and earns merit or does not earn merit through the exercise of free will." The levels of interpretation in the theory of fourfold meaning are also found in the following, and the purpose and outcome of the interpretation seem to correspond exactly to that of the allegorical interpretation of the Bible. Nonetheless, shortly afterward the author calls the *Commedia* a "poetica narratio," the ensuing *modus tractandi* "fictivus." Cf. the detailed discussion of these passages in Küpper 2007, pp. 51–59.

382. *De vulgari eloquentia* II.4.2, in Dante 1965, pp. 653–692, here p. 677: "Looking back, therefore, at what has been said, we recall that we have often called poets those who make verses in the vernacular; and doubtlessly we have presumed to speak with reason, since they are certainly poets, if we think correctly about poetry, which is nothing other than fiction established by rhetoric and music [*fictio rethorica musicaque poita*]."

383. Thomas Aquinas, *In librum beati Dionysii De divinis nominibus expositio*, cap. 4.l.5.

384. Ibid., cap. 11.l.2 [emphasis in the original].

385. S. Harrison 1963; Montagnes 1963, pp. 115–158; also McInerny 1961 on *analogia* and *proportio*, esp. p. 11f.

386. Hentschel 2000 has traced this adaptation in detail, and drawn the conclusion, which corresponds to our working hypotheses, that medieval *musica theorica* should be conceived as "an institutionalized strategy for harmonizing the

self and the world" (p. 224), and that it continued to function in this way down to the late Middle Ages.

387. Riethmüller 1990, p. 173: "The history of music theory is marked by the fact that music theory as 'scientia practica' moves increasingly into the foreground at the expense of music theory as 'scientia theorica.' " Tanay 1989 has described the development surveying closely music theory, on the one hand, and writings on philosophical-theological Aristotelianism and nominalism on the other.

388. Riethmüller 1990, p. 177.

389. Corpus Iuris Canonici, the extravagantis in vol. 2, col. 1255–1257, here col. 1256. Although this text strongly influenced music theory, its relevance for compositional practice remained minimal: "It had hardly any effect," concludes Machabey 1953–1954, p. 35. This does not mean that polyphony intentionally opposes the theologically motivated reservation, but rather, as Machabey (p. 42) shows, that the polyphonic technique of composition was used for religious pieces and quickly penetrated the liturgical canon: "This *Ars nova*, in parallel with the orientation of classical gothic toward the flamboyant, continued to evolve, monopolizing not only religious texts but the liturgy itelf, transforming into *conduits*, motets, and canons the *Kyrie*, the *Gloria*, even the *Credo*, the *Agnus* and the *Sanctus* [. . .]."

390. See Delisle 1969, vol. 2, p. 182; also Rouse 1967.

391. See Delisle 1969, vol. 2, pp. 8–72, as well as the assessment of the holdings relevant to music and the collection of available information regarding the manuscripts in Hentschel 2000, pp. 271–280.

392. See again Haas 1999, p. 26.

393. Anonymous 1988, p. 204f.

394. Roger Bacon 1965, p. 229.

395. Ibid., p. 230.

396. A current example of this view of Bacon is provided by Clegg 2003; for an overview of recent research, which tends to qualify this view, see the essays in Hackett (ed.) 1997 and Uhl (ed.) 2001–2002. The tendency in Bacon's work that is oriented toward the stability of the Christian order of discourse in general and the hegemony of theology in particular is elaborated in Lértora-Mendoza 1989.

397. Roger Bacon 1965, p. 232.

398. Ibid., p. 267.

399. Ibid.

400. Bruyne 1946, vol. 3, p. 227.

401. Roger Bacon 1965, p. 232 [emphasis supplied].

402. Ibid., p. 232. Cf. Aristotle, *Metaphysics* 1026a.

403. Roger Bacon 1897–1900, vol. 1, p. 103; on logic's dependency on mathematics, see p. 102.

404. See the detailed account in this connection in Crombie 1971; on Bacon in particular, see esp. pp. 139–162, 204–218, 278ff., and Fisher/Unguru 1971.

405. See my chapter 4.

406. Roger Bacon 1897–1900, vol. 1, p. 6.

407. Ibid., vol. 1, p. 42.

408. For instance, by Englisch 1999, p. 66f.

409. Weisheipl 1965, p. 79.

410. See Foucault 1965, pp. 60–91, esp. pp. 64–72.

411. Roger Bacon 1897–1900, vol. 1, p. 97. Cf. Easton 1952 and Tonna 1992.

412. Weisheipl 1965, p. 72.

413. Ibid., p. 81. Cf. Ehrle 1970.

414. Roger Bacon 1897–1900, vol. 2, p. 49, and vol. 1, p. 151. Cf. Schramm 1981.

415. Adank 1978, p. 52.

416. Ibid., p. 35.

417. Roger Bacon 1897–1900, vol. 1, p. 99.

418. Roger Bacon 1965, p. 308. As Weisheipl 1965, p. 70 notes, the distinction may have been borrowed from Al-Farabi via Gundissalinus.

419. Roger Bacon 1965, p. 308.

420. Roger Bacon 1897–1900, pars VII passim.

421. In discussing this distinction, Bacon uses the example of the theologian: "Although it is not required for knowledge of the scriptures that a theologian know how to sing, or that he be acquainted with instruments, and other things related to music, nevertheless, he ought to know the theory of all these things, so that he might know the nature and properties of these things, and of the works [. . .]." Ibid., vol. 1, p. 237.

422. Ibid., vol. 1, p. 99.

423. Adank 1978, p. 36.

424. Roger Bacon 1897–1900, vol. 1, p. 100.

425. Roger Bacon 1965, p. 303. Here Bacon may be taking into account the new *artes praedicandi* that were emerging in the twelfth and thirteenth century and that contrasted with the view of preaching developed in Book IV of Augustine's *De doctrina christiana*. See Murphy 1974, pp. 269–356.

426. Roger Bacon 1965, p. 307.

427. Bruyne 1946, vol. 3, p. 234.

428. Roger Bacon 1897–1900, vol. 1, p. 101.

429. Ibid., p. 100.

430. Ibid., p. 102f.

431. For an analysis, see Hirtler 1995, pp. 67–86 and Dyer 2007, pp. 37–44.

432. Engelbert von Admont 1998.

433. For an introduction, see Fowler 1947 and the editor's detailed discussion in Engelbert of Admont 1998, pp. 5–26.

434. Engelbert of Admont 1998, p. 167.

435. Ibid., p. 288b.

436. An overview of Pythagorean elements in Arab music theory is provided in Godwin 1993, pp. 112–126.

437. For his important work in the context of music theory, see Farmer 1934 and Randel 1976.

438. Haas 1984, p. 120; examples of the defects in the translation are given in no. 129.

439. Ibid.

440. Johannes Aegidius Zamorensis 1963, p. 370b.

441. Ibid., p. 376b f.

442. Ibid., p. 377b f.

443. Ibid.

444. Ibid., p. 378a f.

445. For an introduction, see Pirrotta 1955.

446. Marchettus of Padua 1963. On the dating, see Strunk 1974.

447. Marchettus of Padua 1963, p. 67a.

448. Herlinger 1993, p. 371.

449. Herlinger 1993 presents the corresponding proofs.

450. Marchettus of Padua 1963, p. 66b.

451. Ibid., p. 76 a.

452. Ibid., p. 83b f. [emphasis supplied].

453. Ibid., p. 84a.

454. Ibid., p. 66a f.

455. In Marchettus of Padua 1963, p. 76b ff., see esp. the explicit "expositio secundum Pythagoricos," p. 86b.

456. See Vecchi 1968.

457. Herlinger 1990, p. 253.

458. Besseler 2001.

459. See the presentation and commentary in Busard 1971.

460. See Gushee 1969 and Michels 1970.

461. Johannes de Muris 1963a, here both versions (the shorter pp. 249–255, the longer pp. 255–283). On the dating, analysis and state of the manuscripts see Michels 1970, pp. 17–24.

462. Haas 1982, pp. 338, 414.

463. See Falkenroth 1992, pp. 40–64.

464. For textual evidence, see Haas 1982, p. 338.

465. See Werner 1956; Meyer/Wicker 2000. An account of Johannes de Muris's music theory that is focused on the *Notitia artis musicae*, strongly emphasizes its trend-setting element, and takes into account the mathematical as well as the theological horizons is offered in Tanay 1993.

466. Johannes de Muris 1963a, p. 256a.

467. Ibid.

468. Ibid., p. 257a. On the Pythagorean nature of the structure as a whole and its compositional-practical relevance in and after Johannes de Muris, see Witkowska-Zaremba 1993.

469. Johannes de Muris 1963a, p. 257a–258b.

470. This is discussed in detail by Hirtler 1995, pp. 119–135.

471. Johannes de Muris 1963a, p. 258a ff.

472. Ibid., p. 259a f.

473. Ibid., p. 260a.

474. Ibid.

475. Johannes de Muris 1963b, p. 303a. On the compendium, cf. Michels 1970, p. 26.

476. Johannes de Muris 1963c.

477. Ibid., p. 199a.

478. Ibid., p. 199a f.

479. See the edition Jacob of Liège 1955–1973, the commentary in Smith 1966–1983, and the detailed presentation of the manuscript tradition and the work itself in Bragard 1953–1954. For further information about the author see Desmond 2000.

480. Pietzsch 1968, p. 69.

481. Bragard 1953–1954, p. 97.

482. Aertsen 1998, p. 318. Aertsen's interpretation presupposes the theses set forth in Aertsen 1996 and Aertsen 1994, which see Thomism as a reconstitution of theology as a disciplinary-metaphysical science of Being.

483. Jacob of Liège 1955–1973, II.56, vol. 2, p. 135f. Cf. Smith 1963.

484. Jacob of Liège 1955–1973, VI.113, vol. 6, p. 311.

485. Ibid., I.12, vol. 1, p. 43f.

486. Aertsen 1998, p. 306.

487. On the theological points of the *Speculum musicae*, see Slocum 1987.

488. Jacob of Liège 1955–1973, I.1, vol. 1, p. 11.

489. On the *Speculum musicae* in particular, see Slocum 1993 and Smith 1967.

490. Jacob of Liège 1955–1973, I.2, vol. 1, p. 16.

491. Ibid., I.11, vol. 1, p. 37f.

492. Ibid., I.10, vol. 1, p. 36 [emphasis supplied].

493. In each case the starting point is basically the Boethian conception, for instance regarding *musica mundana*, ibid. I.11–13, vol. 1, pp. 37–50, esp. p. 49; on *musica humana*, ibid. I.14, vol. 1, pp. 50–52, esp. p. 50.

494. Ibid., I.10, vol. 1, p. 37. On *musica coelestis* in the *Speculum musicae*, see Slocum 1991.

495. Jacob of Liège 1955–1973, I.8, vol. 1, p. 28f.

496. Ibid., I.11, vol. 1, p. 38.

497. Ibid., p. 38f.

498. For an example, see the concise argument in Honnefelder 1987.

499. Thomas Aquinas, *Summa theologiae* I, qu. 1, a. 3 ad 2.

500. Hirtler 1995, p. 138. The question as to whether Jacob of Liège's guiding theological concept should itself be seen as nominalistic is investigated in Tanay 1989, pp. 113–148.

501. Thus *musica instrumentalis* is introduced with the comment: "haec est

musica proprie dicta" ("this is music properly so called") (Jacob of Liège 1955–1973, I.15, vol. 1, p. 54); Boethius's harsh polemic against those who turn to *musica scientia* for the sake of creating works is thus weakened. In the *Speculum musicae*, he is considered the (ideal) *musicus*, who is proficient in music theory as well as in practice. See ibid., I.3, vol. 1, pp. 17–19.

502. Ibid., I.15, p. 54.

503. Ibid., I.16, p. 55.

504. Ibid., I.17, p. 57.

505. Ibid.

506. For an introduction, see Seay 1955.

507. Ugolino of Orvieto 1959–1962, vol. 1, p. 13f.

508. Ibid., p. 14.

509. "Man's good consists in recognition of the truth; the highest good of man, however, does not consist in recognition of any truth [*cuiuslibet veri*], but in recognition of the highest truth [*summae veritatis*]": Thomas Aquinas, *Summa theologiae* II–II, qu. 167, a. 1 ad 1. Cf. the commentary in Blumenberg 1996, p. 387f.: "The Augustinian idea of the inquiry that does not maintain the proper religious aim, the *non religiose quaerere*, finds in Thomas a very characteristic modification and Aristotelianizing correction. [. . .] Curiosity is superficial dwelling on the object, on the prospect of the phenomena, a dissolution into the breadth of arbitrary obective variations, which represses the cognitive claim by resting content with truths while giving up all claim to *the* truth." English trans., *The Legitimacy of the Modern Age*, trans. Robert M. Wallace (Cambridge, MA: MIT Press, 1983), pp. 332–333.

510. Ugolino of Orvieto 1959–1962, I.1, vol. 1, p. 15f.

511. Ibid., I.1, vol. 1, p. 16. Cf. also ibid., V.3, vol. 3, p. 96f.

512. Ibid., I.1, vol. 1, p. 16. Cf. also V.2, vol. 3, p. 94f.

513. Ibid., I.2, vol. 1, p. 19.

514. Adam of Fulda 1963.

515. Ibid., p. 350b.

516. Ibid., p. 334b.

517. Ibid., p. 348a.

518. Ibid., p. 332b.

519. Ibid.

520. Ibid., p. 337b.

521. Ibid., p. 333a.

522. Ibid.

523. Ibid., p. 333b f.

524. Ibid., 333a.

525. Ibid., p. 347b.

526. Ibid.

527. Cf. on commercial arithmetics in particular Busse Berger 1990.

528. Kreyszig 1993, with further literature. Cf. also Palisca 1990.

529. Sandresky 1979.

530. The studies of Yudkin 1990 bear indirectly on this.

531. Although Nan Cooke Carpenter's account of the history of music theory is generally considered outdated, parts of the conclusions presented in Carpenter 1971 endure. This holds true for the following, p. 30: "If all other evidence were lacking, the musical treatises would make it abundantly clear that although instruction in music in the medieval schools followed two trends—*musica theoretica* and *musica practica*—the two were generally quite closely connected."

532. The tendency to semanticize redundant "natural" phenomena and to make them the point of departure for spiritualistic speculation has continued uninterrupted down to the present. It is not for nothing that Pythagoreanism is still alive today in the various versions of esotericism. But the musicological description of rhythm also refers to cyclically repeated phenomena in the lifeworld: "Human beings, who strive to understand and integrate continuous time as articulated duration, perceive the effects of a rhythmical principle in their whole environment, and especially in constructions whose articulation is presented *as a constant repetition of a similar event at similar times.*" Dürr/Gerstenberg 2001 [emphasis in the original].

533. If for the purpose of a thought-experiment we wanted to take into account the nominalistic argument, then we would have to note that it is precisely nominalism's pessimistic assessment of the ability of scientific discourse to attain "absolute" truth regarding Creation that allows the continuation of the discourse of speculative music theory as a world-modeling discourse—though at the price of having to suspend a decision concerning the "truth" of such a discourse. Even if Pietzsch points out that the discourse of speculative music theory transmits a "reservoir" of Platonic views down to the late Middle Ages (Pietzsch 1968, p. 18), it becomes clear that *in its consequences* nominalism testifies not against but rather *for* our continuity thesis. For "renaissances of Platonism" such as were stimulated in the late thirteenth and early fourteenth centuries by the spread of Latin translations of the works of Plotinus and Proclus (on this generally less well-known "renaissance of Platonism," see Steel 1997), after the arrival of the Platonic corpus from Constantinople around the middle of the fifteenth century, after the reception in France of Ficino's translations in the sixteenth century, and, as research on music theory has emphasized (see for instance Riethmüller 1990, p. 173f. with further literature), as late as Kepler and Leibniz, we can prove a continuity of speculative music theory that always cultivates close relationships with Pythagorean and Platonizing arguments. On the other hand, the Ockhamite perspective leads to nothing more than the final reduction of *musica scientia* to a *scientia physica*, as Panti 1990 shows—and otherwise to extensive shifts in composition theory and stylistics that must be noted (on this, see once again the outstanding study by Tanay 1989), but need not affect the core of the speculative music theory pursued here.

Chapter Eight: Speculative Music Theory and Poetics

1. See Klopsch 1980, p. 64ff.

2. See Norden 1958, vol. 2, p. 889f.; Curtius 1993, pp. 155–158.

3. Klopsch 1980, p. 65: "The late antique inclusion of poetics among the *artes* [. . .] works out in theory in such a way that in scientific systems in general poetics appears in the wake of grammar, but its rules are those of rhetoric, supplemented by metrics." Klopsch is unaware of thought on metrics within the framework of music theory.

4. Faral 1924 offers key passages along with an analysis of them that has, furthermore, not been superseded or continued in this form by an almost overwhelming multitude of contributions on individual authors; see in addition the complements in Sedgwick 1927 and Sedgwick 1928.

5. Kelly 1966, p. 273.

6. Murphy 1974, p. 135. The following draws on Murphy's account, p. 144ff.

7. Alexander de Villadei 1893. On situating this text, see the editor's comments in Alexander de Villadei 1958, p. 9ff.; the work is described in Murphy 1974, pp. 146–153.

8. Ibid., p. 144f.: "What seems to have happened is that the monolithic *ars grammatica* of Donatus and Priscian, even when buttressed by centuries of approving commentary, simply broke up into its constituent parts around the year 1200. The philosophical tensions inherent within it finally proved unbearable to a great many intelligent students of language. [. . .] The thirteenth century *ars grammatica* is a multi-faceted array of varied sub-arts radically different from the traditional *ars grammatica* of the early twelfth century." A precise account of the new textbooks is offered by Abelson 1965, p. 43ff.

9. Daly 1961, p. 84; also Thurot 1965.

10. See the detailed account in Hunt 1941–1950. Hunt's study pursues in particular the discussion of logical questions in the relevant commentaries (for instance, Petrus Helias's *Summa super Priscianum maior*), which in many respects lay the foundations for the later *grammatica speculativa*.

11. See Grabmann 1951, vol. 2, pp. 421–433, which takes earlier scholarship into account; for details, see Pinborg 1967 and Rosier-Catach 1983. Robins 1971, pp. 77–89, provides a precise summary.

12. A few of the work's chapter titles can provide examples of the subjects that now dominated disciplinary grammar: *De subdivisione nominis proprii* (21), *De modis accidentalibus nominis in communi* (22), *De modo significandi accidentali qui facit speciem* (23), *De modo significandi qui facit genus* (24), *De modo significandi accidentali qui facit figuram* (25), *De modo significandi qui facit numeram* (26), *De modo significandi accidentali qui facit casum* (27), *De modo significandi accidentali qui facit personam* (28), *Quomodo pronomen dividitur in modum relationis et demonstrationis* (29).

13. Robins 1971, p. 155f.

14. Bursill-Hall 1971, p. 32, points out that the editions available hardly make sufficiently probing studies possible. Despite his own edition of one of the *modistae*'s key texts, Thomas of Erfurt's *Grammatica speculativa* (London, s.d.), this seems still to be the case.

15. Thurot 1965, p. 41f. identifies Michael of Marbais as the writer sharply attacked in Erasmus of Rotterdam's *Confluctus Thaliae et barbarei*.

16. *Didascalion* II.30, in Hugo of St. Victor 1854, col. 765.

17. Murphy 1974, p. 156.

18. Ibid., p. 161: "We have seen, then, that the once unitary traditional grammar of Donatus and Priscian had begun to fragment into several parallel movements as a result of probing investigations in the twelfth century. One result was an updated traditional grammar, [. . .]. Meanwhile dialectical analysis led off in a different direction, which was to result in the late thirteenth-century grammar of the *modistae*. In a third and parallel development, grammarians studied the nature of rhythmical language. It was in this climate that the six preceptive grammars of the *ars poetriae* were composed."

19. Quoted from Keil (ed.) 2002, p. 206.

20. Borinski 1912, p. 141.

21. Quantitative verse did not die out, but its composition now presupposed more education: "Obviously, quantitative verse continued to be written at the end of Antiquity and throughout the Middle Ages, but knowledge of the quantity of syllables was acquired through laborious technical study. Quantitative verse thus no longer had a natural basis in the spoken language [. . .]." Norberg 1958, p. 87.

22. Ibid., p. 64ff.

23. Meyer 1905, esp. pp. 110, 137ff.

24. Norden 1958, vol. 2, pp. 810–908; comparable theses also in Polheim 1963.

25. Kuhn 1977, p. 24.

26. Dihle 1954.

27. Norden 1958, vol. 2, p. 810ff.

28. Raby 1957, p. 23ff.

29. Norberg 1958, p. 125; in addition, see the richly documented study Brinkmann 1977.

30. Bede 1991, p. 160.

31. Lausberg 1955.

32. Norberg 1958, pp. 87–135.

33. Meyer 1905 and the further studies collected in the same volume had sought to prove that "rhythmical" verse became increasingly differentiated and autonomous with regard to metrical-quantitative poetics; Norberg 1958 arrives at the opposed conclusion, namely that "rhythmical" poetry remained guided by the "metrical" tradition in different, but systematically reconstructable ways.

34. Norberg 1958, p. 92f.

35. A detailed account of the process of transition is offered by Fuller 1969,

see esp. the summary pp. 11–14. Iverson 1980, pp. 293–302, is able to make the change clear by comparing Agnus Dei tropes from the abbey of St. Gall in Carolingian times with a later repertory of rhymical texts from the same abbey.

36. The oldest sources are offered in Zaminer 1959; see also Treitler 1983.

37. Mari 1899, p. 2f.

38. Norberg 1958, p. 136.

39. This is the strategy pursued by Fassler 1987, by which our subsequent remarks are also guided.

40. See the annotated edition by Hugh H. Davis based on the manuscript Leningrad, Publichnaja Biblioteka O. v. XVI 3, which was probably produced in northern Italy in the twelfth century: Alberic of Monte-Cassino 1966. See in addition Blum 1956.

41. Alberic of Monte-Cassino 1966, p. 204.

42. See examples in Norberg 1958, p. 92ff.

43. Alberic of Monte-Cassino 1966, p. 208. Alberic von Monte Cassino thus provides what Crocker 1958, p. 13, identifies, with reference to Bede, as a systematic desideratum: "An analogy between poetry and music would not be necessary if only rhythmics were to be applied, since rhythmics, *musica rhythmica*, was the division most akin to harmonics in its underlying mathematical method."

44. Alberic of Monte-Cassino 1966, p. 211. Cf. Fassler 1987, p. 171: "It was merely clear to him [Alberic] that many 'rithmi' borrowed patterns found in metrical schemata. But when they did so, they reflected them through accent rather than through duration and used them at cadences." On the quantitative *ictus* and cadencing, see Norberg 1958, p. 90f.

45. Fassler 1987, p. 172.

46. Murphy 1974, p. 159.

47. Zumthor 1975c, p. 128.

48. See Phillips/Huglo 1985.

49. Fassler 1987, p. 173 [emphasis supplied]. On the connection between music and grammar in questions of metrics, cf. Haas 1984, pp. 132–135. Extensive evidence will also be found in Duchez 1981.

50. Stevens 1986, here on the Augustinian foundation p. 14 ff., and also on the relation between syllable-counting, *numerus*, and the speculative conception of music, pp. 372–412.

51. Thomas of Capua 1929, p. 13. On the schema, cf. Klopsch 1972, p. 32f.

52. Ibid. [emphasis supplied]. On *rima/rithmus* and the (ultimately unresolved) question of the etymological connection between the two, see Toernquist 1935.

53. On dating the other texts, see Fassler 1987, p. 174f.

54. Mari 1899, p. 11.

55. Ibid., p. 11f.

56. Ibid., p. 17.

57. Ibid., p. 23.

58. Zarncke 1871, pp. 40–41.

59. Mari 1899, p. 28.

60. Ibid., p. 91f.

61. Fassler 1987, p. 175: "Rhyme has become an essential part of the definition of a 'rithmus.'"

62. Latini 1963, p. 481.

63. Seitenstetten CVII, fol. 42a–47b; first published in Dreves (ed.) 1889–1896, vol. 1, p. 13ff. Mari 1899 lists the treatise under number VIII, p. 97ff.

64. Ibid., p. 97.

65. Ibid.

66. Ibid.

67. Borinski 1912, p. 145. The omnipresence of the reference to *musica* in the theories of poetry of the High and Late Middle Ages has been pointed out by Schaller 1981, p. 256f.

68. Mari 1899, p. 9.

69. Borinski 1912, p. 148.

70. Dossat 1970. In 1229, Raymond VII of Toulouse founded a university and appointed Johannes de Garlandia and Roland of Cremona to the chairs of grammar and rhetoric.

71. The most detailed biographical information is provided by Paetow 1927 and Bursill-Hall 1976. The small amount of available literature on the author is presented in Storck 1992.

72. Grabmann 1956, vol. 2, p. 116ff., and Grabmann 1975, vol. 1, esp. pp. 104–146. The writings of Johannes de Garlandia are presented in Habel 1909. A few of Habel's attributions must be revised. On this and on influence see the editor's introduction in Johannes de Garlandia 1927.

73. Johannes de Garlandia 1974, p. xi–xv.

74. Hugo of Trimberg 1969, V, p. 355ff.

75. See the survey in Bursill-Hall 1976.

76. For an overview of the work and the manuscript tradition, along with a compilation of the discussions regarding the controversial attributions, see ibid.

77. Waite 1960, p. 180; on the situation of the work in the music theory discourse of the time, see Sanders 1980 and Pinegar 1991.

78. Coussemaker 1963, vol. 1, pp. 157–175.

79. Ibid., pp. 175–182. Stanley H. Birnbaum has published a new edition with a translation: Johannes de Garlandia 1978.

80. Waite 1960, p. 183.

81. See Jerome of Moravia 1963, the summary of Johannes de Garlandia's text on p. 194ff. A critical edition of both of Johannes de Garlandia's treatises is available in the edition Johannes de Garlandia 1996.

82. Waite 1960.

83. Johannes de Garlandia 1972, esp. pp. 1–17.

84. Rasch 1969.

85. Johannes de Garlandia 1856, p. 100f. The edition quoted makes the seventh-to-last line end with "cubis." Waite 1960, p. 185, 30n, recommends that the meaningless "cubis" be emended to read "tubis," a recommendation we have followed here.

86. *Commentaria in Porphyrium*, in Boethius 1847, vol. 2, col. 73f.

87. See Johannes de Garlandia 1927, p. 101, 87n.

88. Pietzsch 1968, p. 73. With regard to the questionable identity of the grammarian and the music theorist, we might point out the disparity between the treatment of music, which is differentiated up to the third level, and that of disciplines that are merely mentioned, including grammar.

89. Johannes de Garlandia 1974, p. 4.

90. For details, see Wetherbee 1967, p. 74ff., p. 235.

91. Brüssels, Bibliothèque publique, Ms. 546, fol. 145v, 148v–174v, an extensively glossed manuscript from the second half of the thirteenth century; Cambridge, University Library, Ms. Ll. 1.14, fol. 55r–69r, an incomplete copy from the late thirteenth or early fourteenth century; Munich, Bayerische Staatsbibliothek, Ms. lat. 6911, fol. 1r–22r, also from the late thirteenth or early fourteenth century; Oxford, Bodleian Library, Ms. lat. misc. d 66, fol. 1r–40r, from the late fourteenth or fifteenth century, a manuscript originally preserved in the Admont monastery; Paris, BNF lat. 11867, fol. 46r–57v, from the late thirteenth century; Vienna, Österreichische Nationalbibliothek, Ms. lat. 3121, fol. 154v–158v, a summary of the part on rhythmics from the fifteenth century. Traugott Lawler, the editor, discusses the manuscripts in the previously cited edition Johannes de Garlandia 1974, p. xix–xxi.

92. Ibid., p. xvi.

93. Both texts are in Faral 1924, pp. 194–263, 263–321.

94. Cf. the summarizing presentation of the whole work in Klopsch 1980, pp. 147–163.

95. Johannes de Garlandia 1974, p. 158. Scholarship is certainly not always aware of the provenance of this triad and the connection of rhymed verse with the speculative conception of music. For instance, Klopsch 1980, an introduction presenting an abundance of material, mentions only William of Conche's commentary on the *Timaeus* as a source for this triad and writes off the relation between the disposition of rhyming syllables and the musical doctrine of proporitions as "contrived": "Johannes sought in two ways to incorporate the theory of rhythmical poetry into the body of the sciences, of the *artes*. He did so by establishing a relation with music (469–474), making use of a classification of music that was first provided in this form by William of Conches [. . .] In addition, he connected the disposition of rhymes in the stanza with the musical doctrine of proportions in an excessively contrived way" (p. 162).

96. Johannes de Garlandia 1974, p. 158.

97. Ibid., p. 160 [emphasis supplied].

98. Ibid.

99. Ibid.: "Rhyme [*rithmus*] takes its origin, according to some, from a rhetorical embellishment called 'Ending Similarly [*similiter desinens*].'"

100. See Münxelhaus 1976, p. 61f.

101. Johannes de Garlandia 1974, p. 164.

102. See Waite 1960, p. 181f., who sees the mention of this concept as proof that the grammarian and the music theoretician may be the same person.

103. Johannes de Garlandia 1974, p. 170.

104. Ibid.

105. Ibid.

106. Hugo of St. Victor's *De scripturis et scriptoribus sacris* distinguishes six meaning-bearing categories: *res, persona, locus, tempus, gestum,* and *numerus* (Hugo of St. Victor 1854, vol. 1, col. 20f.), and puts particular emphasis on the last one with reference to the concept of *ordo.* As Meyer 1975, p. 40ff., has emphasized, for number allegory, but also for numerical composition, addressing instances of *numerositas* as *res significans* is almost the only relevant procedure. Johannes of Garlandia's work must not be considered a "refounding" of the relationship between musical and literary rhythmics, as Waite 1960, p. 190, implies by using the verb "restore": "Recognizing the original musical qualities of rhythm, and at the same time realizing the essential rôle that rhyme played in the contemporary conception of rhythm, he endeavored to restore mathematical proportions as a regulative force in poetic theory by correlating the incidence of rhyme with musical proportions [. . .]."

107. Fassler 1987, p. 170. The tendency, exemplified by research on works as early as *Scolica enchiriadis, Commemoratio brevis,* and Remigius of Auxerre's commentary on Martianus Capella's *De nuptiis philologiae et Mercurii* (Seidel 1985; Bruyne 1946, vol. 1, pp. 306–339, esp. p. 319ff.), to conceive *musica rhythmica* solely in relation to vocal practice, but no longer as a "bridge" to poetry and poetics, is not valid, as we have already argued. It is not for nothing that research has shown how much the previously standard reference for the differentiation of musical and "literary" rhythmics, Guido of Arezzo's eleventh-century *Micrologus,* continues to insist on their connection, which is in any case given under the speculative conception of music. On the contrary, the parallel is elaborated: if in music a peculiar "musical poetics" or *musica poëtica* is developed, then the latter depends on the theory of poetry and thus consolidates the relationship between the two rather than separating them. See the (fifteenth) chapter on rhythmics in Guido of Arezzo 1955, pp. 162–177; the passages on the parallels between musical and "poetic" rhythmics are on p. 170ff. In opposition to the discussion of this chapter as an example of the differentiation of the two areas in Crocker 1958, pp. 35–40, Fassler 1984, p. 170, has emphasized that it was only this parallel that allowed Guido to develop his points in the first place. Pirrotta 1976 and Hirschmann 1999 make the same argument.

108. Winkelmann 1878, here p. 487ff. The text is referred to in Klopsch 1980, p. 86ff.

1. Körting 1871, p. vii.

2. On Évrart de Conty's authorship of both the *Échecs amoureux* and the prose commentary, see the contributions by Guichard-Tesson 1980, Guichard-Tesson 1983, and Raimondi 1997, all of which argue on the basis of close textual relationships.

3. A description of both manuscripts is offered by Mettlich 1902, p. 4f. In the preface to their edition of the parts of the commentary devoted to astronomy and music, Reginald Hyatte and Maryse Ponchard-Hyatte list other parts of the commentary on the *Échecs amoureux* published independently: Échecs amoureux 1985, p. xii, 3n.

4. See ibid., p. xii, 2n. A description of the manuscript and a synopsis of its contents based on the Dresden manuscript is offered in Junker 1886/1887; on the sources used, see Sieper 1898 and Höfler 1905.

5. Abert 1904.

6. Ibid., pp. 917–925.

7. Ibid., p. 887 (fol. 131b).

8. See again Chamberlain 1970; on the influence in France, where "the influence of the poetic book of the world [grew] enormously," Burdach 1933, here p. 534.

9. Abert 1904, p. 888 (fol. 131c). Cf. Boethius, *De institutione musica* I.1, p. 180.

10. Ibid., p. 912 (fol. 136a): "Tiercement je dy que musique/vault a la vie politique /et ce puez assez savoir tu/pour ce qu'elle encline a vertu, /a bons meurs et a bonne oeuvre./car musique en l'ame humaine oeuvre/et y failt moult d'impressions/dont l'ame en ses effeccions /est a vertu mieulx ordonnee/et, quant elle est passionnee, /si la ramaint elle a mesure/et la garde de mespresure/et de mainte desordonnance" ("Thirdly I say that music/is valuable for political life/and you can see this clearly enough/because it inclines [people] to virtue,/to good morals and good works./for music works within the human soul/and makes many impressions there/by which the soul in its affections/is better commanded to virtue/and, when it [the soul] is in the grip of passions,/it [music] brings it back to moderation/and protects it from misprision and many disorders").

11. The old church rejected the warrior class. To resolve the gaping contradiction between the Germanic social structure, which was dominated by this class, and Christian ethics, from the ninth century on we find the first attempts to mediate between *militia Dei* and *militia saecularis*; a decisive turning point was reached with the Cluniac order. With the ecclesiastical reform of the eleventh century, lay knighthood was ideologically Christianized; from then on it was France "that provided the crucial further development of the idea of defending the Church, of the ecclesiastical symbolism of the military life, and the important connection with the cult of the saints" (Erdmann 1974, p. 84).

12. Abert 1904, p. 894 (fol. 132c).

13. Ibid., p. 907 (fol. 135a).

14. Ibid., p. 912 (fol. 136a). In this context, we come across an argument that Regino of Prüm's *Epistula de armonica institutione* had suggested. Only a person who is "balanced" in the sense of the *ethos* doctrine, the person with "harmonic" *musica humana*, can sing harmonically: "for sadness deprives the heart/of reason, so that no fine play/nor fine singing will take place" ("car la tristesse le cuer prive/de raison, siquez nul beau jeu/ne nul beau chanter n'y a lieu"). Ibid., p. 887 (fol. 131b); on *musica humana* see also ibid., p. 902 (fol. 134a f.).

15. Ibid., p. 889 (fol. 131c).

16. Ibid., p. 894f. (fol. 132c f.); cf. also ibid., p. 901f. (fol., 134a f.); on the four elements and the seasons, ibid., p. 903 (fol. 134b).

17. Ibid., p. 895 (fol. 132d).

18. Ibid., p. 898f. (fol. 133b) [emphasis supplied].

19. Ibid., p. 906 (fol. 134d).

20. Ibid., p. 898 (fol. 133b).

21. Ibid., p. 898 (fol. 133b).

22. Ibid: "aussy puet on dire, ce samble/des corps du ciel, qui se descordent /en nature et si s'accordent/si bien quant a faire les chosez/qui sont en ce bas monde enclosez,/que leur concorde et leur mesure/est tres aggreable a nature/et li dieu du ciel qui l'entendent/aussi comme j'ay ja dit, prendent/tres grande delectacion /en la consideracion/de leur merveilleuse concorde/et du prouffit qui s'i accorde" ("it can also be said, it seems/of the heavenly bodies, which are discordant/by nature and yet are harmonized/so well for making the things/that are included in this base world,/that their concord and their measure/is very agreeable to [our] nature/and the gods of heaven who hear it/also take, as I have said/very great delight /in the contemplation/of their marvelous concord/and the benefit associated with it").

23. See Guichard-Tesson 1983 and Gatherole 1965. On dating the text, see details in the editor's commentary in Échecs amoureux 1985, p. xxv f. The *terminus post quem* is the University of Paris's judgment of twenty-eight heretical theses in 1398, which is mentioned in the commentary; the *terminus ante quem* is the mention of the commentary in a list of manuscripts acquired by Geoffroy Malpoinre. A facsimile of the manuscript Paris, BNF f. fr. 9197 is provided by the edition Échecs amoureux 1991, and a detailed commentary will be found in Guichard-Tesson 1980.

24. Paris, BNF f. fr. 143, 1508, 9197, 19114, and 24295, as well as The Hague, Koninklijke Bibliotheek 129 A 15; on these see Hyatte 1982. The commentary has thus far been published only in excerpts; the seventh part, which will be relevant in the following discussion, is available in a critical edition based on the five Paris manuscripts: Échecs amoureux 1985. For further partial publications, cf. the editor's foreword, ibid., p. vi f.

25. Jung 1971, p. 61.

26. Paris, BNF f. fr. 1508, fol. 1r. To inquire whether the statement that the commentary is related to a "[livre] fait en rime nagueres et de nouvel venu a congnoissance" does not speak against Guichard-Tesson's assumption that the Échecs amoureux and the *Glose* should be attributed to the same writer, Évrard de Conty, or at least that the commentary was produced in his immediate entourage, would lead us too far away from our subject. But the question should nonetheless be raised.

27. On this, see Jeay 1985.

28. Échecs amoureux 1985, p. xvii.

29. Mettlich 1911, on the connections between the *Glose* and Johannes de Garlandia, see esp. p. 26f. In addition to a commentary, Mettlich offers an edition of the corresponding sections from the manuscript Paris, BNF f. fr. 9197, fol. 90v ff., with a German translation.

30. Ibid., p. 5.

31. The following passages are commented upon in Hüe 2000, pp. 32–35.

32. Échecs amoureux 1985, XXXII, p. 70.

33. Ibid., p. 71.

34. Thus the thesis put forward in Roy 1999, p. 30ff., which sees Évrart de Conty's commentary as a prolongation of High Scholastic Aristotelian positions, is hardly convincing.

35. Échecs amoureux 1985, XXXIII, p. 73.

36. Ibid., XXXIII, p. 71 [emphasis supplied].

37. Mettlich 1911, p. 6.

38. Échecs amoureux 1985, XXXIII, p. 71.

39. Ibid.: "Finablement, les rymes composeez en telz nombres de sillabes que on ne les peut ainsy musicaument partir ne sont pas dignes d'estre oÿes. Les rymes doncques requierent certains nombres de sillabes et tel que la parole soit bien seant en la bouche et plaisant a oïr" ("Finally, rhymes composed in such numbers of syllables as cannot be thus divided up musically are not worthy of being heard. Rhymes thus require certain numbers of syllables and such that the word is suitable in the mouth and pleasant to hear").

Chapter Ten: Eustache Deschamps's *L'Art de Dictier* Revisited

1. Zink 1993, p. 121.

2. Ibid. Cf. the problematization in Zimmermann 1991.

3. Cerquiglini-Toulet 1993, p. 125.

4. Dragonetti 1961, p. 64; similarly but more pointedly, Huot 1982, pp. 101–131.

5. Zumthor 1978a, p. 264.

6. Laurie 1962, pp. 19–28.

7. Mühlethaler 1990, p. 403.

8. Ballads 123 and 124 in the edition Deschamps 1878–1903, vol. 1, pp. 243–246.

9. The evolution of the subgenre is described following Kooijman 1982.

10. Latini 1963, p. 487f.

11. Thiry 1985.

12. On the context, see Cerquiglini 2001, chap. II.1: "Le clerc-écrivain," pp. 107–138.

13. The exceptions are Chaucer and, later, Machaut.

14. Machaut 1908–1921, editor's introduction, vol. 1, p. LIV. For the text of the *Prologue,* see ibid., pp. 1–12.

15. Cerquiglini 2001, p. 17.

16. Ibid., p. 17.

17. Ibid., p. 20.

18. Machaut 1908–1921, vol. 1, p. 2 (v. 12–14). Cf. ibid., p. 10 (v. 147–153): "Retorique versifier/Fait l'amant et metrefier,/Et si fait faire jolis vers,/Noviaus et de metre divers: [. . .]" ("Rhetoric makes the lover versify and metrify, and thus makes lovely verses, new and in diverse meters: [. . .]"). The reading of the *Prologue* presented in Wolfzettel 1994 seems to give too little weight to the narrow conception of rhetoric to be applied here, which is limited to metrical structure and rhyme. Cf. Kelly 1978, pp. 7–12 and Stevens 1984, p. 120.

19. The most important contributions to this debate, which took place around 1970, are Rychner 1967 and the replies to this article by Lecoy 1968, Rychner 1969, Frappier 1972, Rychner 1972.

20. Rychner 1967, p. 16, 55n: "Concerning this occasional couple, I note in passing that in the traditional interpretation 'matter' and 'sense' are one and the same, and in no way resemble familiar couples such as arms and legs, mother and father, heaven and earth, bodies and souls, form and content, etc., since unless I am mistaken they are nowhere else attested together. If the idea of a couple sense/matter nonetheless haunts our minds, that is only because everything said about the matter and the sense of Chrétien's romances has finally impressed it there, in the slot already made by the couple matter and form, as if it had already been made to order for it."

21. Cerquiglini 2001, p. 18f.

22. Machaut 1908–1921, vol. 1, p. 2 (v. 10–11).

23. Godefroy 1881–1902, s.v.

24. Machaut 1908–1921, vol. 1, p. 11 (v. 157–160).

25. Stevens 1984, p. 119: "It is not easy to find a good word other than 'structured' to describe the relationship between the words and the music."

26. Machaut 1908–1921, vol. 1, p. 1 (v. 1–9) [emphasis supplied].

27. Ibid., p. 9 (v. 85–86). The connection between the Prologue and the speculative concept of music in the Augustinian-Boethian tradition is elaborated in Lukitsch 1983, pp. 266–268.

28. Machaut 1908–1921, vol. 1, p. 9 (v. 105–114).

29. Ibid., p. 9f. (v. 85ff., 115–122 and 135–146).

30. Ibid., p. 9 (v. 95–100). The presence of the "holistic" concept of music in

Machaut's work is pursued expressly and with a multitude of proofs in Lanoue 1981, pp. 36–83.

31. Reaney 1959, here p. 34: "Every one of Machaut's Rondeaux is isometric, though a variety of line lengths is to be found in the Rondeaux as a whole."

32. See, with examples, Calvez 1982.

33. See for example Jacques Legrand's treatise in Langlois 1974, p. 4ff.

34. For example in the rondeau *Tant doucement me sens emprisonnées* (Machaut 1973, p. 571f.), in the rondeau *Merci vous pri, ma douce dame chiere* (ibid., p. 569f.), and in the rondeaux *Cinc, trese, huit, nuef d'amour fine* and *Se vous n'estes pour mon guerredon née* (ibid., p. 571).

35. Ibid., p. 570.

36. Reaney 1959, p. 36.

37. Calvez 1982, p. 466.

38. Reaney 1959, esp. the analytical table on pp. 39–41.

39. Machaut 1973, p. 540.

40. Reaney 1955, p. 53.

41. Stevens 1986, p. 492.

42. Reaney 1955, p. 40.

43. Elwert 1965, p. 169. Cf. at greater length Zink 1992, p. 181f.

44. See especially Maw 2004.

45. Machaut 1973, p. 585f. and 618f.

46. Ibid., p. 600ff.

47. The analysis of the musical phrasing is taken from Gieber 1982, p. 9.

48. Machaut 1973, p. 585f.

49. Gieber 1982, p. 9.

50. Tanay 1996, see especially pp. 257–275.

51. Maw 2004, p. 98; cf. the examples and detailed analysis in Maw 1996.

52. Poirion 1961, p. 452.

53. Zumthor 1984a, p. 83: "Discursive recurrence constitutes the most effective way to verbalize a spatio-temporal experience and make the listener participate in it. Then, in the space created by the sound, the image sensorially experienced is objectified: from rhythm knowledge is born, and legitimated."

54. Reaney 1953, p. 129.

55. Zink 1992, p. 182. On Machaut, cf., with comparable results, Wilkins 1972, pp. 19–21.

56. Göllner 1995. Similar results, particularly concerning Machaut's musical work, are arrived at by Dömling 1971, and Reichert 1956, who wants to understand the "strict periodicity" of the motet not only as a genre characteristic but also, decidedly, as an "expression of a constructive will to order" (p. 210). For Reichert, the possibility of experiencing this order through the senses is central for comprehending the work: "With their conspicuous structure, the hockets [represent] precisely the prototype of a rhythmical pattern that is easy to recognize despite the changing sound material, so that its return at the exactly corresponding

points of the individual *taleae* seems absolutely appropriate to make the periodic nature of the work perceptible to the hearer as well" (p. 211, brackets in the original). On this see also Butterfield 2002, pp. 273–290.

57. Mühlethaler 1990, p. 402f.

58. On the concept of the *I-origo*, see originally Bühler 1965, pp. 102–120 passim; the distinction between *histoire* and *discours* is borrowed here from Benveniste 1966, p. 238ff. The personal character is limited to text-external references in Ballade 123, v. 18 and 23: "bailli de Valoys" is the office held by Deschamps, while "Champenois" refers to his ancestry.

59. Zink 1992.

60. The respective first half-stanzas, phrased in a past tense, praise Machaut's achievements and elaborate the *fama* of the deceased, while the respective second half-stanzas, harking back to the *hic et nunc* of the utterance and phrased in the present tense, goes back to the *deploratio* of the bereavement, which the refrain prominently displays. In lines 1 through 4 the focus is on the achievements of the deceased, and *histoire* and the tenses of *récit* come into play; in lines 5 to 8 the present is the dominant tense, the discourse of the *hic et nunc* and thus the expression of grief dominates. This symmetry, present in stanzas II and III of ballad 123 and II of ballad 124, is once again an inverse one. Ballad 123 begins with an *enumeratio*, while ballad 124 concludes with one; the structure of the enumeration breaks with the syntactical division that marks the other stanzas, and emphasizes it by contrast. The inversion is confirmed and motivated by the tenses of the verbs: in stanza II of ballad 123 the future tense "complains sera" (v. 21) appears before the imperative "plourez tous, Champenois." The future form heralds pain as the performance of mourning for which the funeral elegy calls, and thus the success of the imperative. The poem moves from the staged utterance to the narrated statement of its effect. The same structure, but once again in inverted form, is found in ballad 124. Here the future form "vo noms sera precieuse relique / Car l'en plourra en France [. . .]" (v. 6–7) begins the poem; what was the result in ballad 123 becomes here the point of departure; the conviction that what was foretold has now come to pass motivates the following summons to lament. The shaping of a "universal" mourning is the dominant motif of the *double ballade*. This universality is translated in literary form by the merging of opposites in the lament. The *enumeratio* at the beginning of ballad 123 shows this in an exemplary way. On the semantic level the first line is organized chiastically. The third and fourth items of the *enumeratio*, *Dames* and *Chevalerie*, correspond in reverse order to *Armes* and *Amour*. The semantic complex *Dames/Amour* on the one hand, and *Chevalerie/Armes* on the other are perceived as opposites and thus as complementary with regard to the intended statement. This *enumeratio* replies, at the beginning of the enumeration of instruments in ballad 124, to line 15, "Plourez, harpes et corrs sarrazinois" ("Weep, harps and Moorish horns"). The harp, a stringed instrument, is the instrument of Orpheus and David, and "it refers to the celestial harmonies" (Mühlethaler 1990, p. 391), to music as a

"holistic" principle in the Greek-Pagan and Judeo-Christian tradition of the West. The Moorish horn, a wind instrument resembling a trumpet, refers to the pagan Orient. The connection in binary oppositions implies no evaluation of any kind; it measures out the existent, like the triad "grands seigneurs, Dames et bourgeois" in line 12 of ballad 123. The merging of the opposite parts of the funeral elegy opens up an all-inclusive dimension. Thus in the *enumeratio* of the instruments with which ballad 124 closes: Five "instruments coys," five stringed instruments, are followed by *rothe* and *guiterne*, once again stringed instruments, and then come *flauste* and *chalemie*, wind instruments, followed finally by *tympanne* and *choros*, percussion instruments.

61. On this, see Jung 1971, p. 45: "The *arts de seconde rhétorique* were not able to make any contribution to the theory of poetry, or rather they did not seek to make any. Instead they sought, as was fitting for a medieval *ars*, to teach the versifier his craft and to introduce him to the labyrinth of poetic forms that are sometimes infinitely complicated." See also Zumthor 1978a, p. 207: "All these texts, so far as one can judge, were written for aristocratic amateurs; and rather than setting forth a general theory for them, the authors limited themselves to a display of the latter's external framework, by formulating recipes."

62. Deschamps 1994, p. 102.

63. Ibid., p. 11: "*L'Art de dictier* seems to be a set of notes for a longer treatise."

64. Ibid., p. 54.

65. See esp. Wolfzettel 1995.

66. See my chapter 5, especially the summary.

67. Here is the quotation in context: "The unlearned man [*idiota*], having picked up the spoon in his hand, said: Outside of the idea in our mind, the spoon has no model [*Coclear extra mentis nostrae ideam aliud non habet exemplar*]. For even if the sculptor or the painter takes his models from things that he wants to portray, I do not do so, for I make spoons from wood, and trays and bowls from clay. In doing so, I do not imitate the figure of any natural thing [*Non enim in hoc imitor figuram cuiuscumque rei naturalis*]. The forms of the spoons, trays and bowls are made by human art alone [*sola humana arte perficiuntur*].". *Idiota de mente* II, n. 62ff., in Nicholas of Cusa 2002, vol. 2, p. 15f. The quotation illustrates the new interpretation of the idea of man being created in God's image—this quality no longer consists primarily in the immortality of the soul or the capacities of the *intellectus*, but rather in humans' creative power. On this, cf. in detail Thomas 1996. In Blumenberg 1996, p. 435ff., this passage is set in the context of the early modern project of mastering the world; the argument is repeated, but with a different emphasis in Blumenberg 2001b, p. 13f.: "The forms of spoons, pots, and plates produced by 'laymen' are purely technical forms, and no leap is now required to move from the joy taken in this fact to its accentuation with regard to the product itself as an essential feature of modern industrial design. To determine their rank in existence, humans no longer look to nature, the

cosmos, but rather to the world of things, which has emerged *sola humana arte*." The consequences for the theory of poetry have been evaluated by Haug 1986.

68. See Staub 1967.

69. Boethius, *De institutione musica* I.34, p. 225.

70. Deschamps 1994, p. 62.

71. Greimas/Keane 2001, s.v.

72. Ibid., s.v. The etymological part of the corresponding lemma in TLF, s.v. adds "according to the principles of nature," "in conformity with the peculiar nature of something," "in a way imitating nature exactly."

73. Ibid., s.v.

74. Deschamps 1994, p. 1: "He [Deschamps] redefined natural music as stemming from inspiration and redefined lyricism as the expression of the poet in his own right."

75. Keller 1993, p. 288f.

76. In the sense of Foucault 1969, p. 115: "It [the utterance] is not at all a unit in itself, but rather a function that crosses a domain of possible structures and units and makes them appear, with concrete contents, in time and space."

77. Deschamps 1994, p. 60.

78. This should be compared with the hypothesis put forward apodictically by Carpenter 1972, pp. 74–75, who proposes Al-Farabi's *De scientiis* as a source for Deschamps's distinction between *musique naturele* and *musique artificiele*. The study of the text in Orléans cannot be proven, its dissemination provides no evidence for the claim, and the proof Carpenter offers for the presence of the distinction in Al-Farabi is not pertinent. Carpenter cites the English translation of the text in Farmer 1934, p. 29: "And as for practical music, its concern is the production of the various kinds of perceptible melodies in the instruments adapted for them either by nature or by artifice. And as for the natural instrument[s], they are the larynx and the uvula, and what is in them, and then the nose. And the artificial instrument[s] are like the reedpipes and the lutes and such like." Deschamps views both *musique naturele* and *music artificiele* as products of the voice. Their difference lies, as might be expected, in the ways measure (*modus*) manifests itself respectively—about which Al-Farabi says nothing at all.

79. Deschamps 1994, pp. 60–62.

80. Ibid., p. 82.

81. Deschamps 1994, p. 64.

82. Boethius, *De institutione musica* I.3, p. 189. See, in addition to part II above, Stumpf 1901.

83. Dragonetti 1961, p. 64.

84. Ibid., p. 62.

85. Ibid.

86. Instead, the frame of reference is set by the findings of the history of metrics, which tells us about the increasing establishment of the isometric form of construction in all lyrical genres. See Gieber 1982, p. 7; Reaney 1962, esp. p. 426; also Jung 2001, table p. 291.

87. Échecs amoureux 1985, XXXIII, p. 73.

88. Deschamps 1994, pp. 60–62.

89. Augustine, *De libero arbitrio* II.16.42.

90. Augustine 1947, VI.13.38.

91. Bliggenstorfer 2005 is devoted specially to such cases.

92. Guiette 1972.

93. See ibid., passim; there is a brief summary of the central thesis on p. 66.

94. It is not for nothing that Guiette notes (ibid., p. 35) that: "Poetry was never more rigorous, more totally and more consciously calculation, mathematics, and harmony."

95. Ibid., p. 36f., p. 42.

96. Stevens 1984, p. 123f. On Deschamps in particular, see also Wimsatt 1991b, p. 134f.

97. Stevens 1984, p. 124: "It will be evident that I believe the view of Deschamps's *L'Art du Dictier* [*sic*] and its relationship to the past as formulated by Roger Dragonetti in an influential article is the reverse of the truth."

98. Dragonetti 1961, p. 56.

99. After the original German edition of this study was published in 2008, Heller-Roazen 2010 came to the same conclusions, partly arguing on the basis of the same sources in Medieval music theory.

100. See Guilbert 1982.

101. Delisle 1869, p. 148.

102. The document is in Fournier 1970a, vol. 1, p. 2, no. 2.

103. The document is in ibid., p. 11ff., no. 19; cf. Fournier 1970b, p. 98ff.

104. See once again the biographical overview in Laurie 1962, pp. 1–152.

105. Feenstra 1962; the corresponding document, date 17 July 1312, is found in Fournier 1970a, vol. 1, p. 36, no. 37.

106. Quoted in Vulliez 1982, p. 162, 33n.

107. Feilzler 1971, pp. 120–123.

108. Deschamps 1878–1903, vol. 2, ballad 225, p. 52.

109. Vulliez 1982, p. 161. An examination of the extant university adminstration documents that Fournier published confirms this. At no point, even when explicit reading and study assignments were handed out, is there any mention of a study of the *artes*. See, for example, the reading assignments made by the rector of the university on 24 August 1324: Fournier 1970a, vol. 1, p. 64, no. 72. Carpenter 1972, pp. 69–76, tried to reconstruct the courses on quadrivial music offered in Orléans; an effort that is bemusing when seen against the background of Vulliez's (later) studies. Carpenter, who argues among other things that the theorists we have discussed, Aribo Scholasticus and Engelbert of Admont, taught in Orléans toward the end of the twelfth or at the beginning of the thirteenth century, draws her theses from Waesberghe 1938. Carpenter was unaware of the refutations of Smits van Waesberghe's thesis that there was an alleged "Liège school" of music theory—refutations that were formulated in the late 1940s and 1950s, first and most acutely in Kreps 1948.

110. Fournier 1970a, vol. 1, p. 2, no. 2. The statutes published in this volume
are explained and commented upon in Jullien de Pommerolle 1978.

111. Orléans, Bibl. Mun. 293.

112. Jarry 1873, p. 11. The contract for the erection of the library building
signed by the library and the master mason Jean Bacon on 20 April 1411, is extant and has been published in Fournier 1970a, vol. 1, p. 194, no. 262.

113. Ibid., vol. 1, p. 199f., no. 268.

114. Carpenter 1972, pp. 69–76.

115. Vulliez 1982, p. 162.

116. Fournier 1970a, vol. 1, p. 242, no. 327.

117. Mühlethaler 1990, p. 403.

118. Evdokimova 2005; on Oresme, esp. p. 62ff.

119. See Taschow 2003.

120. Evdokimova 2005 argues this point on p. 65.

121. On the library, see Avril/Lafaurie 1968, as well as the studies in Delisle
1967. The extant manuscripts of Oresme's translations have been collected in
the editions Oresme 1940, pp. 46–48; Oresme 1957, p. 5; Oresme 1970, p. 6.
On the question of the author of the pseudo-Aristotelian *Economics*, see the editor's foreword to the edition Aristotle 1968, p. XVIII–XXVI. The manuscripts
that were available in Charles V's library are The Hague, Museum Meermanno-
Westreenianum 10 D–1 (the *Ethics*) and Brussels, Bibliothèque royale 2904 (*Politics* and *Economics*).

122. In the inventory in Delisle 1967 these volumes bear the numbers 471,
484, and 485 (vol. 2, pp. 80, 82); an accurate description of the manuscripts is
provided in Delisle 1880, pp. 257–282.

123. On this, see Becker 1997.

124. Oresme 1957, p. 815 (332d).

125. Ibid., (332d–333a).

126. Oresme 1970, p. 341 (296d).

127. Ibid., p. 343 (298a).

128. Ibid., p. 349 (303b f.).

129. Ibid.

130. Ibid., p. 348 (302a).

131. Ibid., p. 349 (303c).

132. Ibid., p. 349f. (303b ff.).

133. Ibid., p. 355 (308c).

134. Ibid., p. 351 (305a).

135. Ibid., p. 347 (301c f.). In Augustine we know of no passage in which
musica mundana is discussed under that designation.

136. Oresme 1968, p. 478 (125b).

137. Ibid.

138. Ibid. (125c).

139. Ibid., p. 482 (126b f.).

140. On this classeme, see again Slocum 1991.

141. Oresme 1968, p. 482 (126c).

142. Ibid., pp. 484–486 (127b).

143. Oresme 1970, p. 346 (300c f.) [emphasis supplied].

144. Augustine 1947, VI.4.7, p. 374.

145. Ibid., pp. 374–376.

146. Ibid., VI.11.33, p. 432.

147. Sobczyk 2005, p. 234.

148. Brown 1985, pp. 231, 236ff.

149. Bliggenstorfer 2005, p. 259.

150. Sobczyk 2005, p. 240.

151. Boudet 1997, p. 51.

152. Poirion 1978, p. 104: "Between the moral and the political, the image of the natural world establishes an analogical relationship. Poetic invention consists first of all in grasping this analogy, and then exploiting it by means of a kind of lexical contiguity."

153. Augustine, *De Civitate Dei* II.21.

154. Batany 1980.

155. Poirion 1978, p. 97.

156. Poirion 1965, p. 334f.

157. Mühlethaler 1987.

158. Allen 1984, p. 208.

159. Bliggenstorfer 2005, p. 27.

160. Attwood 1998, p. 160.

161. Lamprecht 1974.

162. See Wolfzettel 1996, p. 121f.

163. Poirion 1978, p. 106.

164. Calcidius 1962, p. 304.

165. Boethius, *De institutione arithmetica* II.32, p. 126.

Chapter Eleven: The Speculative Conception of Music and the "Formalist" Poetics of the *Grands Rhétoriqueurs*

1. After studying in Paris before 1462/63, Molinet entered the service of the counts of Burgundy as *indiciaire* or chronicler and secretary to Georges Chastellains. In 1475 Molinet took over Chastellain's office as court historian, which he retained under the following potentates. His chronicles for the years 1474 to 1504 are extant: MOLINET 1935–1937, cf. Devaux 1996. After Charles the Bold's death on the battlefield at Nancy in 1477, Molinet entered the service of Mary of Burgundy, and in 1497 that of her son Philip the Fair. In 1485 Molinet had already received a canonry in Valenciennes; in 1501, having become a widower, Molinet was ordained as a priest. The available sources on his biography have been meticulously evaluated in Dupire 1932a, pp. 7–25.

2. Zumthor 1978a, p. 207.

3. Patterson 1966, vol. 1, p. 150.

4. The debate is summarized in Dupire 1932a, pp. 63–65, with a clear bias in favor of Molinet.

5. See the description of the manuscript in Deslisle 1969, vol. 1, p. 144.

6. See Dupire 1932b, pp. 56–66.

7. Dupire 1932a, p. 61.

8. Langlois 1974, p. 216.

9. Zumthor 1975, p. 141f.

10. Stevens 1984, p. 120; similarly, Kelly 1978, pp. 7–12 and Lukitsch 1983, p. 259.

11. In an undated letter addressed in 1513 "to Monsieur Maistre François Le Rouge," quoted from the edition Lemaire de Belges 1973, vol. 3, p. 197.

12. Gratien du Pont 1539, fol. 5r.

13. Cf. Saulnier 1964.

14. Langlois 1974, p. IIIf.; Dupire 1932a, p. 67ff.

15. Johannes de Garlandia 1974, p. 158.

16. Ibid.

17. Becker 1967, p. 541.

18. Dupire 1932a, p. 8.

19. Ibid.

20. The song *Tart ara mon cueur* is generally attributed to Molinet: see Dijon 517, Laborde and Kopenhagen, Königl. Bibl., Ms. Thott 291-8 (see Jeppesen [ed.] 1927, p. xxxiv f.); Eitner 1959, vol. 7, p. 20 notes a *Salve regina* written by Molinet in Munich, Staatsbibl. 88.7.

21. Jean Lemaire de Belges, for example, remarks that Molinet "s'est adonné au service de musique et de rhétorique" ("devoted himself to the service of music and rhetoric") from his childhood on (Lemaire de Belges 1881–1892, vol. 4, p. 522).

22. Dupire 1932a, p. 354. See also Ferrand 1980 passim.

23. Molinet 1934, vol. 2, p. 804f.

24. Molinet 1934, vol. 1, p. 39f. The dominent rhyme is *rime batelée*: the rhyming phonemic group is repeated not at the end of the following verse, but rather preceding the caesura of the latter. The first stanza supplements the *rime battelée* with a *rime enchainée*, the repetition of the rhyming phonemic group appearing at the end of the line at the beginning of the following line, which produces an echo-structure in the first hemistich of each verse. There is no need to point out the wealth of assonance in the verses quoted.

25. Bowles 1954.

26. MacClintock 1959; for the reference to Deschamps, p. 112f. Here MacClintock is able to correct earlier contributions to scholarship that did not read Molinet's statements on music on the basis of the music theory and practice of his time, and thus overlooked the plausibility of such a reading: Marix 1939, p. 153f., and Brenet 1927.

27. The text is in Molinet 1934, vol. 2, p. 447–449.

28. Doorslaer 1934, p. 159; Bowles 1954, p. 135ff.

29. Origen had developed the figural interpretation of the second plague into an extensive polemic against the *carmina poetarum*: "By the second plague, which produced frogs, I think that the songs of the poets are meant figuratively [*indicari figuraliter arbitror carmina poetarum*]. In senseless and inflated modulation, like the sounds and songs of frogs, the songs of the poets transmit foolish stories of deception [*deceptionis fabulas*] to this world. This is of no use to any other animal, beyond giving voice to wicked and churlish shrieking." These lines appear in *In Exodium homilia* IV.6, quoted from the edition Origen 1920.

30. MacClintock 1959.

31. Cf. Tetel 1979.

32. Molinet 1934, vol. 2, pp. 439–442.

33. See once again, in addition to the discussion in chapters 5 and 6 above, Lippmann 1963.

34. Molinet 1937, vol. 1, p. 74.

35. Zumthor 1978a, p. 208.

36. Febel 2001, p. 20.

37. Ibid., p. 28.

38. Beierwaltes 1975, p. 145.

39. Lotman 1972, p. 180.

40. Ibid., p. 179: "In verse, one can observe on the lowest level equivalences that are determined by position (rhythmical) and by euphony (acoustic). The intersection of these two classes of equivalents is defined as rhyme."

41. Zumthor 1978a, p. 229.

42. Thiry 1978, p. 87.

43. Châtelain 1975, pp. 244–248, 268.

44. Zumthor 1978a, p. 236.

45. Le Lyon coronné 1958, p. 60.

46. See the survey of the tendencies in orthographic and grammatical standardization around 1500 in Tilley 1959, vol. 1, pp. 30–34.

47. Greimas/Keane 2001, s.v. This loan word, attested since the eleventh century, is here assimilated to the relatively recent neologism *pastourie*.

48. Gringore 1858–1877, vol. 1, p. 72.

49. Molinet 1934, vol. 1, p. 96.

50. Cretin 1977, p. 320.

51. Meschinot 1972, p. 10.

52. Molinet 1934, vol. 1, p. 80.

53. Lemaire de Belges 1967, p. 196.

54. Molinet 1934, vol. 1, p. 12f.

55. Cretin 1977, p. 270.

56. Molinet 1934, vol. 2, p. 434. This ballad is analyzed in Gros 1981.

57. Molinet 1934, vol. 2, p. 576f.

58. Cretin 1977, p. 279.

59. Chamard 1920, p. 144, without reference to the source.

60. Cretin 1977, p. 276.

61. Bruyne 1946, vol. 1, p. 12f.

62. Collerye 1855, p. 59f.

63. Molinet 1934, vol. 1, p. 209.

64. Guy 1910, vol. 1, p. 96; further examples in Zumthor 1978a, p. 267ff.

65. Molinet 1934, vol. 1, p. 49.

66. Gordon 1989, p. 57.

67. Zumthor 1978a, p. 247.

68. Ibid., p. 275.

69. Lotman 1972, p. 186.

70. Cited here from Jakobson/Pomorska 1982, p. 53 [emphasis supplied].

71. Lotman 1972, p. 187.

72. Wimsatt 1991b, p. 139.

73. Friedrich 1964, p. 597.

74. Augustine 1947, I.1, p. 22ff.; cf. *De ordine* II.12.

75. For Augustine's conception of the arbitrariness of signs in the human world and the confusion of languages after the Tower of Babel (Gen. 11:1–9), see *De doctrina christiana* II.4.5ff.

76. Ibid., II.38.56.

77. Cerquiglini 1997, p. 82.

78. Quoted from Maurin 1959, p. 483. The text is printed in Chastellain 1971, vol. VII; a critical edition is now available in Chastellain/Robortet/Montferrant 2002.

79. Winn 1981, pp. 74–121.

80. Augustine, *De libero arbitrio* II.16.42.

81. Beierwaltes 1975, p. 147.

82. James 1984, p. 228.

83. Molinet 1934, vol. 1, p. 211.

84. On these possible criteria for the validity of an interpretive hypothesis, see once again Hempfer 1983.

85. Valéry 1957.

86. Evans 1995, p. 164.

87. Zumthor 1974, p. 96.

88. Gordon 1989, p. 65.

89. Zumthor 1975a, p. 117.

90. Zumthor 1978a, p. 225.

91. Gumbrecht 1995b, p. 717.

92. See Sandresky 1979.

93. Zumthor 1978a, p. 205.

94. Marbod of Rennes 1854, col. 1671C.

95. Molinet 1934, vol. 2, p. 504.

96. Scheidegger 1983, p. 205.

97. See Zumthor 1978a, pp. 74–76.

98. Molinet 1934, vol. 2, p. 455.

99. Ibid., pp. 491f., 483f.

100. Ibid., p. 450.

101. Ibid., p. 522 [emphasis in the original].

102. In the sense of Küpper 2007, p. 59: "In the stage of literature and the arts for which the *Commedia* stands, the claim to state the highest truth [was] apparently required if the text was to gain legitimacy."

103. Rahn 1980.

104. Wolfzettel 1995, p. 94f.

105. Zumthor 1978a, p. 48f.

106. Ibid., p. 29

107. Zumthor 1978a, p. 81: "Analogical thought, despite the linguistic order that kept up appearances, was growing weaker. In the sixteenth century a discursive procedure subsisted, almost unchanged, but Resemblance had crumbled and the Order that justified it had exploded: the Names by which it had always been designated remained, but no one quite knew any longer where this Order was."

108. Duby 1978, pp. 83–152.

109. Zumthor 1978a, pp. 72–74.

110. Fèvre de la Boderie 1578, Cercle IV, fol. 82r ff. Further examples taken from French Renaissance literature will be found in Dauphiné 1974.

111. Luther 1910–1921, vol. 1, p. 11.

112. Bach 1963–1972, vol. 1, p. 37.

113. Geck 2001, p. 261. Cf. Siegele 1978 on the ultimately Pythagorean origin of number theory in Bach's work.

114. See also Wegman 1995, esp. p. 311.

115. Molinet 1934, vol. 1, p. 54.

116. Küpper 2007, p. 71.

117. See Hempfer 1983, p. 29f.; cf. Hempfer 1987, esp. pp. 258–283, and Hempfer 1993.

118. Quoted from Griffin 1999, p. 157, 4n.

119. "The Lord created me, the beginning of his ways, before he made anything from the beginning./Out of eternity I was established, and from the ages before the earth came about./[. . .] when He weighed out the foundations of the earth, /I was with Him constructing everything. I rejoiced every day as I played before Him always,/playing on the earth, and my joy was to be with the sons of men."

Primary Sources

Acta Sanctorum: *Acta Sanctorum. Quotquot toto urbe coluntur, vel a catholicis scriptoribus celebrantur. Quae ex latinis & graecis, aliarvmque gentium antiquis monumentis collecta*, ed. Johannes Bollandus et al., 11 vols. in 64 fasc., Brussels et al. 1684–1940.

Adam of Fulda 1963: Adam of Fulda, *De musica*, in *Scriptores ecclesiastici de musica sacra potissimum*, ed. Martin Gerbert, 3 vols., St. Blasien 1784, rpt. Hildesheim 1963, vol. 3, pp. 329–381.

Adelard of Bath 1906: Adelard of Bath, *De eodem et diverso*, ed. Hans Willner, Münster 1906 [Beiträge zur Geschichte der Philosophie des Mittelalters 4.1].

Alain de Lille 1855: Alanus ab Insulis, *Opera omnia*, ed. Jacques-Paul Migne, Paris 1855 [Patrologia latina 210].

Alain de Lille 1955: Alanus ab Insulis, *Anticlaudianus*, ed. Robert Bossuat, Paris 1955 [Textes philosophiques du Moyen Age 1].

Alberic of Monte Cassino 1966: Davis, Hugh H., "The 'De rithmis' of Alberic of Monte Cassino: A Critical Edition," *Mediaeval Studies* 28 (1966), pp. 198–227.

Albert the Great 1890–1899: Albertus Magnus, *Opera omnia, ex editione Lugdunensi religiose castigata, et pro auctoritatibus ad fidem Vulgatae versionis accuratiorumque patrologiae textuum revocata, auctaque B. Alberti vita ac bibliographia operum a pp. Quétif et Echard exaratis, etiam revisa et locupletata*, ed. Auguste Borgnet, 39 vols., Paris 1890–1899.

Alcuin 1851: Flaccus Alcuinus, *B. Flacci Albini seu Alcuini abbatis et Caroli Magni Imperatoris magistri opera omnia*, ed. Jacques-Paul Migne, 2 vols., Paris 1851 [Patrologia latina 101].

Aldhelm 2001: Aldhelmus Schireburnensis, *Opera*, ed. Rudolf Ewald, Munich 2001 [Monumenta Germaniae Historica. Auctores antiquissimi XV].

Alexander de Villa Dei 1893: Alexander de Villa Dei, *Das Doctrinale*, ed. Dietrich Reichling, Berlin 1893 [Monumenta germaniae paedagogica 12].

Alexander de Villa Dei 1958: Alexander de Villa Dei, *Ecclesiale*, ed. and rev. Levi R. Lind, Lawrence KS 1958.

Alia musica 1962: *Alia musica. Édition critique commentée avec une introduction sur l'origine de la nomenclature modale pseudo-grecque au Moyen-Âge*, ed. Jacques Challey, Paris 1962 [Publications de l'Institut de Musicologie de l'Université de Paris 6].

Ammonius Hermiae 1891: Ammonius Hermiae, *Commentaria in Aristotelem Graeca*, ed. Adolf Busse, Berlin 1891.

Anonymus 1988: Anonymus, *Accessus philosophorum*, in *Quatre introductions à la philosophie du XIIIe siècle. Textes critiques et étude historique*, ed. Claude Lafleur, Montréal and Paris 1988 [Université de Montréal, Publications de l'Institut d'Études Médiévales 23], pp. 179–244.

Aribo Scholasticus 1951: *De musica*, ed. Joseph Smits van Waesberghe, Rome 1951 [Corpus scriptorum de musica 3].

Aribo Scholasticus 1963: Aribo Scholasticus, *De musica*, in *Scriptores ecclesiastici de musica sacra potissimum*, ed. Martin Gerbert, 3 vols., St. Blasien 1784, rpt. Hildesheim 1963, pp. 197–220.

Aristeides Quintilianus 1937: Quintilianus, Aristeides, *Von der Musik*, ed. and rev. Rudolf Schäfke, Berlin 1937.

Aristides Quintilianus 1983: Quintilianus, Aristides, *On Music. In Three Books*, ed. Thomas J. Mathiesen, New Haven 1983 [Music Theory Translation Series].

Aristotle 1961: Aristoteles, *Die Lehrschriften. Probleme*, ed. and rev. with commentary Paul Gohlke, Paderborn 1961.

Aristotle 1968: Aristotle, *Oeconomica*, ed. and rev. Bernhard A. van Groningen, Paris 1968.

Aristotle 1995: Aristotle, *Philosophische Schriften in sechs Bänden*, Hamburg 1995.

Aristoxenos of Tarentum 1883–1893: *Aristoxenus Tarentinus. Melik und Rhythmik des klassischen Hellenentum*, ed. Rudolf Westphal, 2 vols., Leipzig 1883–1893, rpt. Hildesheim 1965.

Aristoxenos of Tarentum 1954: Aristoxenos of Tarentum, *Elementa harmonica*, ed. Rosetta DaRios, Rome 1954 [Scriptores Graeci et Latini].

Augustine 1841–1849: Augustinus, *Sancti Aurelii Augustini Hipponensis episcopi opera omnia*, 11 vols. in 16 fasc., ed. Jacques-Paul Migne, Paris 1841–1849 [Patrologia latina 32–47].

Augustine 1947: Augustinus, *De musica. Œuvres de Saint Augustin, 1re série. Opuscules, vol. VII. Dialogues philosophiques IV*, ed. Guy Finaert and F. J. Thonnard, Paris 1947.

Augustine 1955–1984: Augustinus, *Opera*, 17 vols. in 20 fasc., Turnholt 1955–1984 [Corpus christianorum, series latina].

Augustine 1975: *Augustinus' De dialectica*, ed. Jan Pinborg, rev. with an introduction by B. Barrell Jackson, Dordrecht/Boston 1975.

Augustine 1990: Augustinus, *De musica*, ed. Ubaldo Pizzani and Gustavo Milanese, Palermo 1990 [Lectio Augustini 5].

Augustine 2002: Augustinus, *De musica Bücher I und VI. Vom ästhetischen Urteil zur metaphysischen Erkenntnis*, rev. with an introduction and commentary by Frank Hentschel, Hamburg 2002 [Philosophische Bibliothek 539].

Aulus Gellius 1968: Aulus Gellius, *Noctes Atticae*, 2 vols., ed. Peter K. Marshall, Oxford 1968 [Scriptorum classicorum bibliotheca Oxoniensis].

Aurelianus Reomensis 1963a: Aurelianus Reomensis, *Musica disciplina*, in *Scriptores ecclesiastici de musica sacra potissimum*, ed. Martin Gerbert, 3 vols., St. Blasien 1784, rpt. Hildesheim 1963, vol. 1, pp. 28–63.

Aurelianus Reomensis 1963b: Aurelianus Reomensis, *Musica disciplina*, ed. Lawrence Gushee, 2 vols., New Haven 1963.

Aurelianus Reomensis 1975: Aurelianus Reomensis, *Musica disciplina*, ed. Lawrence Gushee, Rome 1975 [Corpus Scriptorum de Musica 21].

Bach 1963–1972: *Bach-Dokumente*, ed. Bach-Archiv Leipzig, 3 vols., Leipzig 1963–1972.

Bede 1955–2001: Beda Venerabilis, *Opera*, 6 vols. in 11 fasc., Turnholt 1955–2001 [Corpus christianorum. Series latina 118–123].

Bede 1991: Beda Venerabilis, *Libri II de arte metrica et de schematibus et tropis. The Art of Poetry and Rhetoric*, ed. and rev. with commentary Calvin B. Kendall, Saarbrücken 1991.

Bernardus Silvestris 1964: Bernardus Silvestris, *De mundi universitate libri duo sive megacosmus et microcosmus*, ed. Carl Sigmund Barach and Johann Wrobel, Innsbruck 1876, rpt. Frankfurt a. M. 1964.

Boccaccio 1951: Boccaccio, Giovanni, *Genealogie deorum gentilium*, ed. Vincenzo Romano, Bari 1951.

Boethius 1847: Boethius, Anitius Manlius Severinus, *Opera omnia*, ed. Jacques-Paul Migne, 2 vols., Paris 1847 [Patrologia latina 63–64].

Boethius 1867: Boethius, Anitius Manlius Severinus, *De institutione arithmetica libri duo. De institutione musica libri quinque. Accedit geometria quae fertur Boethii*, ed. Gottfried Friedlein, Leipzig 1867 [Bibliotheca scriptorum graecorum et romanorum teubneriana].

Boethius 1871: Boethius, Anitius Manlius Severinus, *Philosophiae consolationis libri quinque. Accedunt eiusdem atque incertorum opuscula sacra*, ed. Rudolf Peiper, Leipzig 1871 [Bibliotheca scriptorum graecorum et romanorum teubneriana].

Boethius 1970: *Boethius's Geometrie II. Ein mathematisches Lehrbuch des Mittelalters*, ed. Menso Folkerts, Wiesbaden 1970 [Boethius. Texte und Abhandlungen zur Geschichte der exakten Wissenschaften 9].

Boethius 1981: Boethius, Anitius Manlius Severinus, *Consolatio philosophiae. Trost der Philosophie*, ed. and rev. Olof Gigon, Munich 1981 [dtv bibliothek].

Boethius 1990: Boethius, Anitius Manlius Severinus, *De institutione musica*, ed. Giovanni Mari, Rome 1990.

Boethius 1995: Boethius, Anitius Manlius Severinus, *De institutione arithmetica*, ed. Jean-Yves Guillaumin, Paris 1995.

Boethius 2005: Boethius, Anitius Manlius Severinus, *De consolatione philosophiae. Opuscula theologica*, ed. Claudio Moreschini, Munich/Leipzig 2005 [Bibliotheca scriptorum graecorum et romanorum teubneriana].

Bonaventura 1882–1902: Bonaventura, Johannes, *Doctoris Seraphici pp. Bonaventurae pp. R. E. Episcopi Cardinalis Opera Omnia*, 10 vols. and a supplementary vol., ed. Collegium pp. Bonaventura, Quaracchi/Florence 1882–1902.

Bonaventure 1938: Bonaventura, Johannes, *Tria opuscula seraphici doctoris p. Bonaventurae. Breviloquium, itinerarium mentis in Deum et de reductione artium ad theologiam*, ed. Collegium p. Bonaventura, Florence 1938.

Bulst (ed.) 1956: *Hymni latini antiquissimi LXXI. Psalmi III*, ed. Walther Bulst, Heidelberg 1956.

Calcidius 1962: Calcidius, *Timaeus a Calcidio translatus commentarioque instructus*, ed. Jan Hendrik Waszink et al., London/Leiden 1962 [Corpus Platonicum medii aevi. Plato Latinus 4].

Cassiodorus 1937: Cassiodorus, Flavius Magnus Aurelius, *Senatoris institutiones*, ed. Roger Aubrey Baskerville Mynors, Oxford 1937.

Cassiodorus 1847–1848: Cassiodorus, Flavius Magnus Aurelius, *Opera omnia*, ed. Jacques-Paul Migne, 2 vols., Paris 1847–1848 [Patrologia latina. Series latina 69–70].

Cassiodorus 1973: Cassiodorus, Flavius Magnus Aurelius, *Variarum libri XII. De anima*, ed. Å. J. Friedh and J. W. Halporn, Turnholt 1973 [Corpus christianorum. Series latina 96].

Cassiodorus 2003: Cassiodorus, Flavius Magnus Aurelius, *Institutiones divinarum et saecularium*, ed. Wolfgang Bürsgen, 2 vols., Freiburg i. Br. et al. 2003 [Fontes christiani 39].

Censorinus 1983: Censorinus, *De die natali liber*, ed. Klaus Sallmann, Leipzig 1983 [Bibliotheca scriptorum graecorum et romanorum teubneriana].

Chartularium Universitatis Parisiensis 1964: *Chartularium Universitatis Parisiensis*, ed. Heinrich Denifle and Émile Chatelain, 4 vols., Paris 1891–1899, rpt. Brussels 1964.

Chastellain 1971: Chastellain, Georges, *Œuvres*, ed. Joseph M. B. C. Kervyn de Lettenhove, 8 vols., Brussels 1863–1868, rpt. Geneva 1971.

Chastellain/Robortet/Montferran 2002: Georges Chastellain, Jean Robertet, Jean de Montferrant, *Les douze dames de rhétorique*, ed. David Cowling, Geneva 2002 [Textes littéraires français 549].

Cicero 1923–2005: Cicero, Marcus Tullius, *Scripta quae manserunt omnia*, ed. Max Polenz et al., 48 vols., Leipzig/Munich 1923–2005 [Bibliotheca scriptorum graecorum et romanorum teubneriana].

Cicero 1963: Cicero, Marcus Tullius, *Hortensius*, ed. Alberto Grilli, Varese/Milan 1962.

Cicero 1990: *Ciceros Hortensius*, ed. Laila Straume-Zimmermann, Bern/Frankfurt a. M. 1976 [Europäische Hochschulschriften Reihe XV, Serie XV.9], Neuausgaben Darmstadt 1990 und Munich/Zürich 1990.

Collerye 1855: Collerye, Roger de, *Œuvres*, ed. Charles d'Héricault, Paris 1855 [Bibliothèque elzévirienne].

Corpus iuris canonici: *Corpus iuris canonici*, ed. Emil Friedberg and Ludwig Richter, 2 vols., Leipzig 1879–1881, rpt. Graz 1955.

Coussemaker 1963: *Scriptorum de musica medii aevi novam seriem a Gerbertina alteram*, ed. Charles Edmond de Coussemaker, 4 vols., Paris 1864–1872, rpt. Hildesheim 1963.

Cretin 1977: Cretin, Guillaume, *Œuvres poétiques*, ed. Kathleen Chesney, Geneva 1977.

Dante 1965: Dante Alighieri, *Tutte le opere. Edizione del centenario*, ed. Fredi Chiappelli, Milan 1965.

Deschamps 1878–1903: Deschamps, Eustache, *Œuvres complètes*, ed. Gaston Raynaud and Auguste-Henry-Edouard, marquis de Queux de Saint-Hilaire, 11 vols., Paris 1878–1903 [Société des anciens textes français].

Deschamps 1994: Deschamps, Eustache, *L'Art de dicitier*, ed. Deborah M. Sinnreich-Levi, East Lansing 1994.

Diehl 1959: Diehl, Ernst (ed.), *Anthologia lyrica graeca*, Leipzig 1959.

Diels/Kranz (ed.) 1956: *Die Fragmente der Vorsokratiker. Griechisch und deutsch*, ed. Hermann Diels and Walter Kranz, 3 vols., Zürich et al. 1956.

Diogenes Laërtius 1850: Diogenes Laërtius, *De clarorum philosophorum vitis, dogmatibus et apophtegmatibus libri decem*, ed. Anton Westermann and Carel Gabriel Cobet, Paris 1850 [Scriptorum Graecorum bibliotheca 9].

Dominicus Gundissalinus 1903: Dominicus Gundissalinus, *De divisione philosophiae. Herausgegeben und philosophiegeschichtlich untersucht nebst einer Geschichte der philosophischen Einleitung bis zum Ende der Scholastik von Ludwig Baur*, Munich 1903 [Beiträge zur Geschichte der Philosophie des Mittelalters 4.2–3].

Dreves (ed.) 1889–1896: *Historiae Rhythmicae. Liturgische Reimoffizien des Mittelalters*, ed. Guido Maria Dreves, 8 vols., Leipzig 1889–1896 [Analecta hymnica medii aevi].

Dümmler (ed.) 1978–1997: *Monumenta Germaniae Historica. Poetae latini aevi Carolini*, ed. Ernst Dümmler, 2 vols., Berlin 1881–1884, rpt. Berlin 1978–1997.

Dunchad 1944: Dunchad, *Glossae in Martianum*, ed. Cora E. Lutz, Lancaster 1944 [American Philological Association, Philological Monographs 12].

Échecs amoureux 1904: Abert, Hermann, "Die Musikästhetik der Échecs amoureux," *Romanische Forschungen* 15 (1904), pp. 884–925.

Échecs amoureux 1985: *L'Harmonie des sphères. Encyclopédie d'astronomie et de musique extraite du commentaire sur Les Echecs amoureux (XVe s.) attribué à Evrart de Conty. Edition critique d'après les mss. de la Bibliothèque nationale de Paris*, ed. Reginald Hyatte and Maryse Ponchard-Hyatte, New York/Bern/Frankfurt a. M. 1985 [Studies in the Humanities 1].

Échecs amoureux 1991: *Le livre des échecs amoureux: Bibliothèque nationale, ms. fr. 9197*, ed. Anne-Marie Legaré, Paris 1991.

Engelbert of Admont 1963: Engelbert of Admont, *De musica*, in *Scriptores ecclesiastici de musica sacra potissimum*, ed. Martin Gerbert, 3 vols., St. Blasien 1784, rpt. Hildesheim 1963, vol. 2, pp. 287–369.

Faral 1924: Faral, Edmond, *Les Arts poétiques du XIIe et XIIIe siècles. Recherches et documents sur la technique littéraire du Moyen Âge*, Paris 1924 [Bibliothèque de l'École des hautes études 238].

Favonius Eulogius 1957: Favonius Eulogius, *Disputatio de somnio Scipionis*, ed. Roger E. van Weddingen, Brussels 1957 [Collection Latomus 27].

Federhofer-Königs 1960: Federhofer-Königs, Renate, "Ein unvollständiger Musiktraktat des 14. Jahrhunderts in Ms. 1201 der Universitätsbibliothek Graz," *Kirchenmusikalisches Jahrbuch* 44 (1960), pp. 14–27.

Fèvre de la Boderie 1578: Fèvre de la Boderie, Guy le, *La Galliade ou de la Révolution dans les arts et les sciences*, Paris 1578.

Fischer (ed.) 1968: *The Theory of Music from the Carolingian Era up to 1400 II: Italy*, ed. Peter Fischer, Munich/Duisburg 1968 [Répertoire International des Sources Musicales III.2].

Fournier 1970a: Fournier, Marcel, *Les Statuts et privilèges des universités françaises. Depuis leur fondation jusqu'en 1789*, 4 vols. in 5 fasc., Paris 1890–1894, rpt. Aalen 1970.

Gerald of Wales 1867: Giraldus Cambrensis, *Topographia Hibernica*, ed. James F. Dimock and John S. Brewer, London 1867.

Gerbert (ed.) 1963: *Scriptores ecclesiastici de musica sacra potissimum*, ed. Martin Gerbert, 3 vols., St. Blasien 1784, rpt. Hildesheim 1963.

Gerbert von Aurillac 1963: Gerbert von Aurillac, *Gerberti Opera mathematica*, ed. Nicolaus Bubnov, Berlin 1899, rpt. Hildesheim 1963.

Gottfried von St. Victor 1956: Godfrey of St. Victor, *Fons philosophiae*, ed. P. Michaud-Quentin, Louvain/Lille 1956 [Analecta Mediaevalia Namurcensia 8].

Gratien du Pont 1539: Gratien du Pont, *Art et science de rhetoricque metrifiée*, Paris 1539.

Gringore 1858–1877: Gringore, Pierre, *Œuvres complètes*, ed. Charles d'Héricault, 2 vols., Paris 1858–1877 [Bibliothèque elzévirienne].

Guido of Arezzo 1955: Guido of Arezzo, *Micrologus de musica*, ed. Joseph Smits van Waesberghe, Rome 1955 [Corpus Scriptorum de Musica 4].

Häring (ed.) 1971: *Commentaries on Boethius Thierry of Chartres and His School*, ed. Nikolaus M. Häring, Toronto 1971 [Studies and Texts. Pontifical Institute of Mediaeval Studies 20].

Heito/Walahfrid Strabo 1984: Heito, Walahfrid Strabo, *Visio Wettini*, in *Monumenta Germaniae Historia. Poetae II*, ed. Ernst Dümmler, Munich 1984, pp. 301–333.

Heito/Walahfrid Strabo 2004: Heito, Walahfrid Strabo, *Visio Wettini*, ed. Hermann Knittel, 2nd exp. ed., Heidelberg 2004 [Reichenauer Texte und Bilder 12].

Hermannus Contractus 1936: Hermann Contractus (Hermann of Reichenau), *De musica*, ed. Leonard Webster Ellinwood, Rochester 1936 [Eastman School of Music Studies 2].

Hieronymus 1845–1846: Hieronymus, Sophronius Eusebius, *Opera omnia*, ed. Jacques-Paul Migne, 11 vols. in 9 fasc., Paris 1845–1846 [Patrologia latina 22–30].

Hincmar of Reims 1852: Hincmarus Remensis, *Opera omnia*, ed. Jacques-Paul Migne, 2 vols., Paris 1852 [Patrologia latina 125–126].

Hrabanus Maurus 1852: Hrabanus Maurus, *Opera omnia*, ed. Jacques-Paul Migne, Paris 1852 [Patrologia latina 111].

Hrabanus Maurus 1900: Hrabanus Maurus, *De institutione clericorum*, ed. Aloysius Knoepfler, Munich 1900 [Veröffentlichungen aus dem kirchenhistorischen Seminar Munich 5].

Hrabanus Maurus 1996: Hrabanus Maurus, *De institutione clericorum libri tres*, ed. with studies by Detlev Zimpel, Frankfurt a. M. et al. 1996 [Freiburger Beiträge zur mittelalterlichen Geschichte 7].

Hucbald of Saint-Amand 1963: Hucbald of Saint-Amand, *De musica*, in *Scriptores ecclesiastici de musica sacra potissimum*, ed. Martin Gerbert, 3 vols., St. Blasien 1784, rpt. Hildesheim 1963, vol. 1, pp. 103–152.

Hugo of St. Victor 1854: Hugo of St. Victor, *Opera omnia*, ed. Jacques-Paul Migne, 3 vols., Paris 1854 [Patrologia latina 175–177].

Hugo of St. Victor 1939: Hugo of St. Victor, *Didascalicon*, ed. Charles H. Buttimer, Washington, DC, 1939 [Studies in Medieval and Renaissance Latin 10].

Hugo of Trimberg 1969: Langosch, Karl, *Das Registrum multorum auctorum des Hugo von Trimberg. Untersuchung und kommentierte Textausgabe*, Nedeln 1969.

Iamblichus 1922: Iamblichos, *Theologoumena artithmeticae*, ed. Vittorio de Falco, Leipzig 1922 [Bibliotheca scriptorum graecorum et romanorum teubneriana].

Isidore of Seville 1957–1962: *Isidorus Hispalensis Episcopi Etymologiarum sive originum libri XX*, ed. Wallace M. Lindsay, 2 vols., Oxford 1957–1962 [Scriptorum classicorum bibliotheca Oxoniensis].

Jacob of Liège 1955–1973: Jacobus Leodiensis, *Speculum musicae*, ed. Roger Bragard, 7 vols. in 9. fasc., Rome 1955–1973 [Corpus scriptorum de musica 3].

Jan (ed.) 1966: *Musici scriptores Graeci*, ed. Carl von Jan, 2 vols., Leipzig 1896–1899 [Bibliotheca scriptorum graecorum et romanorum teubneriana], rpt. Hildesheim 1966.

Jeppesen (ed.) 1927: *Der Kopenhagener Chansonnier. Das Ms. Thott 291 in der Kgl. Bibliothek Kopenhagen*, ed. Knud Jeppesen, Kopenhagen/Leipzig 1927.

Jerome of Moravia 1963: Jerome of Moravia, *Tractatus de musica*, in *Scriptorum de musica medii aevi novam seriem a Gerbertina alteram*, ed. Charles Edmond de Coussemaker, 4 vols., Paris 1864–1872, rpt. Hildesheim 1963, vol. 1, pp. 1–94.

Johannes Aegidius Zamorensis 1963: Johannes Aegidius Zamorensis, *Ars musica*, in *Scriptores ecclesiastici de musica sacra potissimum*, ed. Martin Gerbert, 3 vols., St. Blasien 1784, rpt. Hildesheim 1963, vol. 2, pp. 369–393.

Johannes Cotto 1950: Johannes Cotto (Affligemensis), *De musica cum tonario*, ed. Joseph Smits van Waesberghe, Rome 1950 [Corpus scriptorum de musica 1].

Johannes Cotto 1963: Johannes Cotto (Affligemensis), *De musica*, in *Scriptores ecclesiastici de musica sacra potissimum*, ed. Martin Gerbert, 3 vols., St. Blasien 1784, rpt. Hildesheim 1963, vol. 2, pp. 230–265.

Johannes de Garlandia 1856: Johannes de Garlandia, *De triumphis ecclesiae libri octo*, ed. Thomas Wright, London 1856.

Johannes de Garlandia 1927: Paetow, Louis J., "The *Morale Scolarium* of John of Garland (Johannes de Garlandia) with an Introduction on the Life and Works of the Author," *Memoirs of the University of California* IV.2 (1927), pp. 69–273.

Johannes de Garlandia 1972: Johannes de Garlandia, *De mensurabili musica*, ed. Erich Reimer, Wiesbaden 1972.

Johannes de Garlandia 1974: Johannes de Garlandia, *The Parisiana Poetria*, ed. Traugott Lawler, New Haven/London 1974.

Johannes de Garlandia 1978: Stanley H. Birnbaum, *Johannes de Garlandia—Concerning Measured Music (De mensurabili musica)*, Colorado Springs 1978.

Johannes de Garlandia 1996: Gwee, Nigel, *"De plana musica" and "Introductio musica": A Critical Edition and Translation with Commentary of Two Treatises Attributed to Johannes de Garlandia*, Diss., Baton Rouge 1996.

Johannes Hothby 1964: Johannes Hothby, *Dialogus in arte musica*, ed. Albert Seay, Rome 1964 [Corpus scriptorum de musica 10].

Johannes de Muris 1963a: Johannes de Muris, *Musica speculative secundum Boethium*, zwei Fassungen, in *Scriptores ecclesiastici de musica sacra potissimum*, ed. Martin Gerbert, 3 vols., St. Blasien 1784, rpt. Hildesheim 1963, vol. 3, pp. 249–283.

Johannes de Muris 1963b: Johannes de Muris, *Quaestiones super partes musicae*, in *Scriptores ecclesiastici de musica sacra potissimum*, ed. Martin Gerbert, 3 vols., St. Blasien 1784, rpt. Hildesheim 1963, vol. 3, pp. 301–304.

Johannes de Muris 1963c: Johannes de Muris, *Summa musicae*, in *Scriptores ecclesiastici de musica sacra potissimum*, ed. Martin Gerbert, 3 vols., St. Blasien 1784, rpt. Hildesheim 1963, vol. 3, pp. 190–248.

Johannes Tinctoris 1975: Johannes Tinctoris, *Opera theoretica*, ed. Albert Seay, 2 vols., Rome 1975 [Corpus scriptorum de musica 22].

John Scotus Eriugena 1853: Johannes Scotus Eriugena, *Opera omnia*, ed. Heinrich J. Floss, Paris 1853 [Patrologia latina 122].

John Scotus Eriugena 1939: Johannes Scotus Eriugena, *Annotationes in Marcianum*, ed. Cora E. Lutz, Cambridge 1939.

John Wylde 1982: John Wylde, *Musica manualis cum tonale*, ed. Cecily Sweeney, Neuhausen/Stuttgart 1982 [Corpus scriptorum de musica 28].

Keil (ed.) 1857–1880: *Grammatici latini*, ed. Heinrich Keil, 8 vols., Leipzig 1857–1880.

Keil (ed.) 2002: *Scriptores artes metricae. Marius Victorinus, Maximus Victorinus, Caesius Bassus, Atilius Fortunatianus, Terentius Maurus, Marius Plotius Sacerdos, Rufinus, Mallius Theodorus, Fragmenta et Excerpta metrica*, ed. Heinrich Keil, Leipzig 1874 [Grammatici latini 6], rpt. Hildesheim 2002.

Langlois 1974: Langlois, Ernest, *Recueil d'Arts de seconde rhétorique*, Paris 1902, rpt. Geneva 1974. Latini 1963: Latini, Brunetto, *Li Livres dou Tresor*, ed. Polycarpe Chabaille, Paris 1963 [Collection de documents inédits sur l'histoire de France. Première série: Histoire littéraire].

Lemaire de Belges 1881–1892: Lemaire de Belges, Jean, *Œuvres*, ed. Jean A. Stecher, 4 vols., Louvain 1881–1892.

Lemaire de Belges 1967: Jodogne, Pierre, "Un recueil poétique de Jean Lemaire de Belges en 1498 (le manuscrit de la Bibl. Nat. de Paris, Nouv. Acq. fr. no. 4061)," in *Miscellanea di studi e ricerche sul quattrocento francese*, ed. Franco Simone, Turin 1967, pp. 179–210.

Luther 1910–1921: Luther, Martin, *Werke. Weimarer Ausgabe. Abteilung II. Tischreden*, 6 vols., Weimar 1910–1921.

Lutz 1944: Lutz, Cora E., *Glossae in Martianum*, Lancaster 1944 [American Philological Association; Philological Monographs 12].

Lyon coronné 1958: *Le Lyon coronné (1467). Texte bourguignon inédit*, ed. Kenneth Urwin, Geneva 1958 [Textes littéraires français 81].

Machaut 1908–1921: Machaut, Guillaume de, *Œuvres*, ed. Ernest Hoepffner, 3 vols., Paris 1908–1921.

Machaut 1943: Karl Young, "Guillaume de Machaut: *Le Dit de la Harpe*," in *Essays in Honor of Albert Feuillerat*, ed. Henry M. Peyre, New Haven 1943 [Yale Romanic Studies 22], pp. 1–20.

Machaut 1973: Machaut, Guillaume de, *Poésies lyriques. Édition complète en deux parties, avec introduction, glossaire et fac-similés*, ed. Vladimir Chichmaref, 2 vols., Paris 1909, rpt. in one vol., Geneva 1973.

Macrobius 1994: Macrobius, Ambrosius Theodosius, *Commentarius in Somnium Scipionis*, ed. Jakob Willis, Stuttgart/Leipzig 1994 [Bibliotheca sciptorum graecorum et romanorum teubneriana].

Marbod von Rennes 1854: *Venerabilis Hildeberti primo Cenomanensis episcopi, deinde Turonensis archiepiscopi opera omnia tam edita quam inedita. Accesserunt Marbodi Redonensis episcopi, ipsius Hildeberti supparis opuscula. Quae hactenus edita, haec autem autem auctiora et plura nondum edita prodeunt, omniaque ad manuscriptos codices recensita, notis passim illustrantur*, ed. Jean-Jacques Bourassé, Paris 1854 [Patrologia latina 171].

Marchettus of Padua 1963: Marchettus of Padua, *Lucidarium musicae planae*, in *Scriptores ecclesiastici de musica sacra potissimum*, ed. Martin Gerbert, 3 vols., St. Blasien 1784, rpt. Hildesheim 1963, vol. 3, pp. 65–121.

Mari 1899: Mari, Giovanni, *I trattati medievali di ritmica latina*, Milan 1899 [Memorie del R. Istituto Lombardo di scienze e lettere 20].

Marinus of Naples 1960: Marinus Neapolitanus, *De vita Procli*, Frankfurt a. M. 1960.

Martianus Capella 1866: Martianus Capella, *De nuptiis Philologiae et Mercurii*, ed. Franz Eyssenhardt, Leipzig 1866.

Martianus Capella 1983: Martianus Capella, *De nuptiis Philologiae et Mercurii*, ed. James Willis, Leipzig 1983 [Bibliotheca scriptorum graecorum et romanorum teubneriana].

Meschinot 1972: Meschinot, Jean, *Les Lunettes des princes*, ed. Christine Martineau-Genieys, Geneva 1972.

Mittelalterliche Bibliothekskataloge 1918–1979: *Mittelalterliche Bibliothekskataloge Deutschlands und der Schweiz*, ed. der Bayerischen Akademie der Wissenschaften, 9 vols., Munich 1918–1979.

Molinet 1934: Molinet, Jean, *Les Faictz et dictz*, ed. Noël Dupire, 3 vols., Paris 1934 [Société des anciens textes français].

Molinet 1935–1937: Molinet, Jean, *Chroniques*, ed. Omer Jodogne and Georges Doutrepont, 3 vols., Brussels 1935–1937 [Collection des anciens auteurs belges].

Mommsen 1892: *Monumenta Germaniae Historia. Auctores antiquissimi IX. Chronica minora saec. IV-VII*, ed. Theodor Mommsen, Berlin 1892.

Musica enchiriadis 1963: *Musica enchiriadis*, in *Scriptores ecclesiastici de musica sacra potissimum*, ed. Martin Gerbert, 3 vols., St. Blasien 1784, rpt. Hildesheim 1963, vol. 1, pp. 153–211.

Musica enchiriadis 1999: *Musica enchririadis. Das älteste Dokument zur Entstehung der abendländischen Mehrstimmigkeit. Eine Handschrift aus Werden an der Ruhr. Das "Düsseldorfer Fragment,"* ed. Dieter Torkewitz, Stuttgart 1999 [Beihefte zum Archiv für Musikwissenschaft 44].

Musica et scolica enchiriadis 1981: *Musica et scolica enchiriadis. Una cum aliquibus tractatulis adiunctis*, ed. Hans Schmid, Munich 1981 [Veröffentlichungen der Musikhistorischen Kommission der Bayerischen Akademie der Wissenschaften 3].

Musica et scolica enchiriadis 1995: *Musica enchiriadis and Scolica enchiriadis*, ed. Raymond Erickson, New Haven/London 1995.

Nicolas of Cusa 2002: Nikolaus von Kues, *Philosophisch-theologische Werke. Lat./Dt.*, ed. Karl Bormann, Hamburg 2002.

Nicomachus of Gerasa 1866: *Nicomachi Geraseni Pythagorei introductionis Arithmeticae libri II*, ed. Richard Hoche, Leipzig 1866 [Bibliotheca scriptorum graecorum et romanorum teubneriana].

Nicomachus of Gerasa 1938: Nicomachos of Gerasa, *Introduction to Arithmetic, translated into English by Martin Luther d'Ooge, with studies in Greek arithmetic by Frank Eagleston Robbins and Louis Charles Karpinski*, Ann Arbor 1938.

Oresme 1940: Oresme, Nicole, *Le Livre de Ethiques d'Aristote*, ed. Albert D. Menut, New York 1940.

Oresme 1957: Oresme, Nicole, *Le Livre de Yconomique d'Aristote*, ed. Albert D. Menut, Philadelphia 1957 [Transactions of the American Philosophical Society 47.5].

Oresme 1968: Oresme, Nicole, *Le Livre du ciel et du monde*, ed. Albert D. Menut and Alexander J. Denomy, Madison/London 1968 [The University of Wisconsin Publications in Medieval Science 11].

Oresme 1970: Oresme, Nicole, *Le Livre de Politiques d'Aristote*, ed. Albert D. Menut, Philadelphia 1970 [Transactions of the American Philosophical Society 60.6].

Origen 1920: Origines, *Werke. Homilien zum Hexateuch in Rufins Übersetzung, Teil 1. Die Homilien zu Genesis, Exodus und Leviticus*, ed. Wilhelm A. Baehrens, Leipzig 1920 [Die griechischen christlichen Schriftsteller der ersten drei Jahrhunderte 29].

Origen 1976: Origines, *De principiis libri IV. Lat.-dt.*, ed. and rev. with critical and explanatory annotations, by Herwig Görgemanns and Heinrich Karpp, Darmstadt 1976.

Peter Lombard 1854–1855: Petrus Lombardus, *Opera omnia*, ed. Jacques-Paul Migne, 2 vols., Paris 1854–1855 [Patrologia latina 191–192].

Petrus Damiani 1853: Petrus Damiani, *Opera Omnia*, ed. Costantino Gaetani, 2 vols., Paris 1853 [Patrologia latina 144–145].

Petrus de Sancto Dionysio 1972: Petrus de Sancto Dionysio, *Tractatus de musica*, ed. Hans Ulrich Michels, Rome 1972 [Corpus Scriptorum de Musica 17].

Pisan 1886–1891: Pisan, Christine de, *Œuvres poétiques*, ed. Maurice Roy, 2 vols., Paris 1886–1891.

Plato 1982: Plato, *Sämtliche Werke*, 3 vols., Heidelberg 1982 [Berliner Ausgabe].

Plotinus 1956–1971: Plotinus, *Schriften*, rev. Richard Harder, with Greek text ed. Rudolf Beutler and Willy Theiler, 6 vols. in 12 fasc., Hamburg 1956–1971 [Philosophische Bibliothek 211–215, 276].

Ps.-Aristotle 1963: Ps.-Aristotle, *Tractatus de musica*, in *Scriptorum de musica medii aevi novam seriem a Gerbertina alteram*, ed. Charles Edmond de Coussemaker, 4 vols., Paris 1864–1872, rpt. Hildesheim 1963, vol. 1, pp. 251–281.

Quintilian 1977: Quintilianus, Marcus Fabius, *Institutiones oratoriae*, ed. H. E. Butler, 4 vols., Cambridge/London 1977 [Loeb Classical Library].

Regino of Prüm 1963a: Regino of Prüm, *Epistula de armonica institutione*, in *Scriptores ecclesiastici de musica sacra potissimum*, ed. Martin Gerbert, 3 vols., St. Blasien 1784, rpt. Hildesheim 1963, vol. 1, pp. 230–247.

Regino of Prüm 1963b: Regino of Prüm, *Tonarius*, in *Scriptorum de musica medii aevi novam seriem a Gerbertina alteram*, ed. Charles Edmond de Coussemaker, 4 vols., Paris 1864–1872, rpt. Hildesheim 1963, vol. 2, pp. 1–73.

Regino of Prüm 1965: *The "De harmonica institutione" and "Tonarius,"* ed. Mary Protase LeRoux, Diss., Washington, DC, 1965.

Regino of Prüm 1989: Regino of Prüm, *Epistula de armonica institutione*, in Michael Bernhard, *Clavis Gerberti. Eine Revision von Martin Gerberts Scriptores ecclesiastici de musica sacra potissimum (St.Blasien 1784)*, 1 vol., Munich 1989, pp. 37–73.

Ramos de Pareja 1901: Ramos de Pareja, Bartolomé, *Musica practica*, ed. Johannes Wolf, Leipzig 1901 [Publikationen der internationalen Musikgesellschaft, Beihefte 2].

Remigius of Auxerre 1962–1965: Remigius of Auxerre, *Commentum in Martianum Capellam*, ed. Cora E. Lutz, 2 vols., Leiden 1962–1965.

Richard of St. Victor 1958: Richard of St. Victor, *Liber exceptionum*, ed. Jean Châtillon, Paris 1958 [Textes philosophiques du Moyen Age 5].

Roger Bacon 1897–1900: Roger Bacon, *Opus maius*, ed. John Henry Bridges, 3 vols., Oxford 1897–1900.

Roger Bacon 1902: Roger Bacon, *Grammatica graeca*, ed. Edmond Nolan, Cambridge 1902.

Roger Bacon 1965: Roger Bacon, *Opus tertium*, in *Opera Fr. Baconis hactenus inedita*, ed. John P. Brewer, London 1859 [Rerum Britannicarum medii aevi scriptores 15], rpt. New York 1965.

Roman de la Rose: Guillaume de Lorris, Jean de Meun, *Le Roman de la Rose. Édition d'après les manuscrits BN 12786 et BN 378*, ed. Armand Strubel, Paris 1992.

Ronsard 1993–1994: Ronsard, Pierre de, *Œuvres complètes*, ed. Jean Céard, Daniel Ménager, and Michel Simonin, 2 vols., Paris 1993–1994 [Bibliothèque de la Pléiade].

Sedgefield (ed.) 1968: *King Alfred's Old English Version of Boethius de Consolatione Philosophiae*, ed. Walter J. Sedgefield, Darmstadt 1968.

Sedulius Scottus 1966: Sedulius Scottus, *Liber de rectoribus Christianis*, ed. Siegmund Hellmann, Munich 1906, rpt. Frankfurt a. M. 1966 [Quellen und Untersuchungen zur lateinischen Philologie des Mittelalters 1.1].

Sedulius Scottus 1968: Sedulius Scottus, *Seine Dichtungen*, ed. Reinhard Düchting, Munich 1968.

Silk 1935: Silk, Edmund Taite, *Saeculi noni auctoris in Boetii Consolationem philosophiae commentarius*, Rome 1935 [Papers and Monographs of the American Academy in Rome 9].

Simon Tunstede 1963: Simon Tunstede, *Quatuor principalia musicae*, in *Scriptorum de musica medii aevi novam seriem a Gerbertina alteram*, ed. Charles Edmond de Coussemaker, 4 vols., Paris 1864–1872, rpt. Hildesheim 1963, vol. 4, pp. 200–298.

Suger of St. Denis 1979: Suger of St. Denis, *Liber de rebus in administratione sua gestis. Abbot Suger on the Abbey Church of St. Denis*, ed., rev., and commentary by Erwin Panofsky, Princeton 1979.

Terence 1947–1978: *Térence*, ed. Jules Marouzeau, 9 vols., Paris 1947–1978.

Tertullian 1957: Tertullianus, Quintus Septimus Florens, *De praescriptione haereticorum*, ed. François Refoulé, Paris 1957 [Sources chrétiennes 46].

Theon von Smyrna 1878: Theon von Smyrna, *Expositio rerum mathematicarum ad legendum Platonem utilium*, ed. Edmund Hiller, Leipzig 1878.

Thomas Aquinas 1882: *Sancti Thomae Aquinatis doctoris angelici opera omnia*, 42 vols., Paris/Rome 1882ff.

Thomas of Capua 1929: Thomas of Capua, *Ars dictandi*, ed. Emmy Heller, Heidelberg 1929.

Thomas of Erfurt: *Grammatica speculativa*, ed. and rev. Geoffrey L. Bursill-Hall, London s.d.

Ugolino of Orvieto 1959–1962: Ugolino of Orvieto, *Declaratio musicae disciplinae*, ed. Albert Seay, 3 vols., Rome 1959–1962 [Corpus scriptorum de musica 7].

Vecchi 1950: Vecchi, G., "Praecepta artis musicae collecta ex libris sex Aurelii Augustini 'De musica.' Post A. Maium nouis collatis codicibus denuo edidit," *Memorie della Reale Accademia delle scienze dell'istituto di Bologna. Classe di scienze morali, serie V.1* (1950), pp. 91–153.

Victorinus 1967: Victorinus, Gaius Marius, *Ars grammatica*, ed. Italo Mariotti, Florenz 1967 [Serie dei classici Greci e Latini/Biblioteca nazionale 6].

Vincent von Beauvais 1959: Vincent von Beauvais, *De musica*, ed. Gottfried Goeller, Regensburg 1959.

Vitruvius 1847: Vitruvius Pollio, Marcus, *De architectura*, ed. Charles-Louis Maufras, 2 vols., Paris 1847 [Bibliothèque Latine-Française].

Vitruvius 1987: Vitruvius Pollio, Marcus, *De architectura libri decem. Zehn Bücher über Architektur*, ed. Curt Fensterbusch, Darmstadt 1987.

Walter Odington 1970: Walter Odington, *Summa de speculatione musicae*, ed. Frederick Hammond, Rome 1970 [Corpus scriptorum de musica 14].

Westphal 1861: Westphal, Rudolf, *Die Fragmente und Lehrsätze der griechischen Rhythmiker*, Leipzig 1861 [Metrik der griechischen Lyriker und Dramatiker, 1. Supplementband].

William of Conches 1965: Guillaume de Conches, *Glosae super Platonem*, ed. Edouard Jeauneau, Paris 1965 [Textes philosophiques du Moyen Âge 13].

Winkelmann 1878: Winkelmann, Eduard, "Reisefrüchte aus Italien und anderes zur deutsch-italienischen Geschichte, 8: Drei Gedichte Heinrichs von Avranche an Kaiser Friedrich II," *Forschungen zur deutschen Geschichte* 18 (1878), pp. 482–492.

Zaminer 1959: Zaminer, Frieder, *Der Vatikanische Organum-Traktat (Ottob. lat. 3025). Organum-Praxis der frühen Notre Dame-Schule und ihre Vorstufen*, Tutzing 1959 [Municher Veröffentlichungen zur Musikgeschichte 2].

Secondary Sources

Abelson 1965: Abelson, Paul, *The Seven Liberal Arts, a Study in Medieval Culture*, New York 1965 [Columbia University contributions to education 11].

Abert 1901–1902: Abert, Hermann, "Zu Cassiodor," *Sammelbände der internationalen Musikgesellschaft* 3 (1901–1902), pp. 439–453.

Abert 1905: Abert, Hermann, *Die Musikanschauung des Mittelalters und ihre Grundlagen*, Halle 1905.

Abert 1968: Abert, Hermann, *Die Lehre vom Ethos in der griechischen Musik: Ein Beitrag zur Musikästhetik des klassischen Altertums*, Tutzing 1968.

Adank 1978: Adank, Thomas, "Roger Bacons Auffassung der Musica," *Archiv für Musikwissenschaft* 1 (1978), pp. 33–56.

Aertsen 1994: Aertsen, Jan A., "Was heißt Metaphysik bei Thomas von Aquin?" in *Scientia und Ars im Hoch- und Spatmittelalter*, ed. Ingrid Cramer-Ruegenberg, Berlin/New York 1994 [Miscellanea Mediaevalia 22], pp. 217–239.

Aertsen 1996: Aertsen, Jan A., *Medieval Philosophy and the Transcendentals: The Case of Thomas Aquinas*, Leiden et al. 1996.

Aertsen 1998: Aertsen, Jan A., " 'Speculum musicale' als Spiegel der Philosophie," in *Musik—und die Geschichte der Philosophie und Naturwissenschaften im Mittelalter. Fragen zur Wechselwirkung von "Musica" und "Philosophia" im Mittelalter*, ed. Frank Hentschel, Leiden/Boston/Cologne 1998, pp. 305–321.

Alfaric 1918: Alfaric, Prosper, *L'Évolution intellectuelle de Saint Augustin*, Paris 1918.

Allen 1984: Allen, Judson Boyce, "Grammar, Poetic Form, and the Lyric Ego: A Medieval *A Priori*," in *Vernacular Poetics in the Middle Ages*, ed. Lois Ebin, Kalamazoo 1984 [Studies in Medieval Culture 16], pp. 199–226.

Ambros 1968: Ambros, August Wilhelm, *Geschichte der Musik*, 6 vols., 3rd rev. ed., Leipzig 1887–1911, rpt. Hildesheim 1968.

Amelli 1880: *Thomae Aquinatis de arte musica nunc primum ex codice bibliothecae Universitatis Ticinensis edidit et illustravit*, ed. Ambrogio M. Amelli, Milan 1880.

Amerio 1929: Amerio, Franco, *Il de Musica di pp. Agostino*, Turin 1929 [Didaskaleion 4].

Amerio 1954: Amerio, Franco, "Agostino e la musica," *Humanitas: Rivista mensile di cultura* 9 (1954), pp. 1050–1058.

Amith 1908: Amith, David Eugene, *Rara arithmetica: A Catalogue of the Arithmetics Written before the Year MDCI*, Boston 1908.

Anderson 1989: Anderson, Gordon, "La Ressource du Petit Peuple (1481). Essai de pleine rhétorique," *Travaux de littérature* 2 (1989), pp. 55–67.

Anonymus 1942: Anonymus, "Pensées de Saint Augustin sur la musique," *Dissonances. Revue musicale indépendante* 5–6 (1942), pp. 70–74.

Ansorge 1996: Ansorge, Dirk, *Johannes Scottus Eriugena. Wahrheit als Prozeß. Eine theologische Interpretation von "Peryphyseon,"* Innsbruck/Vienna 1996 [Innsbrucker theologische Studien 44].

Apfel 1989: Apfel, Ernst, *Die Lehre vom Organum, Diskant, Kontrapunkt und von der Komposition bis um 1480*, Saarbrücken 1989.

Assunto 1963: Assunto, Rosario, *Die Theorie des Schönen im Mittelalter*, Cologne 1963 [Geschichte der Ästhetik 2].

Asztalos 1993: Asztalos, M., "Boethius as a Transmitter of Greek Logic to the Latin West: The *Categories*," *Harvard Studies in Classical Philology* 95 (1993), pp. 367–407.

Atherton/Atkinson 1992: Atherton, Béatrice, Atkinson, J. Keith, "Les Manuscrits du Roman de Fortune et de Félicité," *Revue d'Histoire des Textes* 22 (1992), pp. 169–251.

Attwood 1998: Attwood, Catherine, *Dynamic Dichotomy: The Poetic "I" in Fourteenth- and Fifteenth-Century French Lyric Poetry*, Amsterdam/Atlanta 1998 [Faux titre 149].

Auer 1928: Auer, Albert, *Johannes von Dambach und die Trostbücher vom 11. bis zum 16. Jahrhundert*, Münster 1928.

Auerbach 1938: Auerbach, Erich, "Figura," *Archivum romanicum* 22 (1938), pp. 436–489.

Auerbach 1953: Auerbach, Erich, *Typologische Motive in der mittelalterlichen Literatur*, Krefeld 1953 [Schriften und Vorträge des Petrarca-Instituts 2].

Avril/Lafaurie 1968: Avril, François, Lafaurie, Jean, *La Bibliothèque de Charles V*, Paris 1968.

Badel 1977: Badel, Pierre-Yves, "Pourquoi une poétique médiévale?" *Poétique* 31 (1977), pp. 306–321.

Bakhouche 2003: Bakhouche, Béatrice, "Boèce et le Timée," in *Boèce ou la Chaîne des Savoirs*, ed. Alain Galonnier, Louvain/Paris/Dudley 2003 [Philosophes médiévaux XLIV], pp. 5–22.

Baltes 1976–1978: Baltes, Matthias, *Die Weltentstehung des platonischen Timaios nach den antiken Interpreten*, 2 vols., Leiden 1976–1978.

Balthasar 1961–1962: Balthasar, Hans Urs von, *Herrlichkeit. Eine theologische Ästhetik*, 2 vols. in 3 fasc., Einsiedeln 1961–1962.

Bardy 1945: Bardy, G., "Cassiodore et la fin du monde ancien," *L'année théologique* 6 (1945), pp. 383–425.

Barker 1994: Barker, Andrew, "Ptolemy's Pythagoreans, Archytas, and Plato's Conception of Mathematics," *Phronesis* 39 (1994), pp. 113–135.

Barker 1996: Barker, Andrew, "Plato's Philebus: The Numbering of a Unity," in *Dialogues with Plato*, ed. Eugenio Benitez, Edmonton 1996 [Apeiron 29.4], pp. 143–164.

Barker-Benfield 1975: Barker-Benfield, Bruce C., *The Manuscripts of Macrobius' Commentary on the "Somnium Scipionis,"* Diss., Oxford 1975.

Batany 1980: Batany, Jean, " 'Concordia'. Le Pluralisme organique dans la polyphonie et dans la théorie fonctionnelle de la société," in *Musique, littérature et société au Moyen Âge. Actes du colloque, 24–29 mars 1980*, ed. Danielle Buschinger and André Crépin, Paris 1980, pp. 5–10.

Bautz 1975–2005: *Biographisch-Bibliographisches Kirchenlexikon*, ed. Traugott Wilhelm Bautz, 25 vols., Hamm/Herzberg/Nordhausen 1975–2005.

Bayreuther 2009: Bayreuther, Rainer, *Untersuchungen zur Rationalität der Musik in Mittelalter und Früher Neuzeit*, Freiburg 2009.

Beaujouan 1954–1956: Beaujouan, Guy, "L'enseignement de l'arithmétique élémentaire à l'université de Paris au XIIIe et XIVe siècle, in *Homenáje a Millas-Vallicrosa*," 2 vols., Barcelona 1954-1956, vol. 2, pp. 93-124.

Beaujouan 1987: Beaujouan, Guy, "La Transformation du quadrivium au XIIe siècle," in *L'Enseignement de la musique au Moyen Âge et à la Renaissance*, Royaumont 1987 [Rencontres de Royaumont], pp. 11-16.

Beck/Bol (eds.) 1993: *Polykletforschungen*, ed. Herbert Beck and Peter C. Bol, Berlin 1993 [Schriften des Liebighauses].

Becker 1960: Becker, Oskar: "Die Aktualität des pythagoreischen Gedankens," in *Die Gegenwart der Griechen im neueren Denken. Festschrift für Hans-Georg Gadamer zum 60. Geburtstag*, ed. Dieter Henrich, Walter Schulz, and Karl-Heinz Volkmann-Schluck, Tübingen 1960, pp. 7-30.

Becker 1967: Becker, Philip August, "Jean Molinet 1435-1507," in *Zur romanischen Literaturgeschichte. Ausgewählte Studien und Aufsätze*, Munich 1967, pp. 541-557.

Becker 1993: Becker, Karin, "Les realia dans les poèmes de voyages d'Eustache Deschamps," in *Les "realia" dans la littérature de fiction du Moyen Age. Actes du Colloque du Centre d'Études Médiévales de l'Université de Picardie—Jules vernes, Chantilly 1-4 avril 1993*, ed. Danielle Buschinger, Greifswald 1993 [Wodan 25—Greifswalder Beiträge zum Mittelalter 10], pp. 11-21.

Becker 1995: Becker, Karin, "Kochkunst und Diätetik in der Dichtung Eustache Deschamps," *Zeitschrift für Romanische Philologie* 111 (1995), pp. 347-374.

Becker 1996: Becker, Karin, *Eustache Deschamps. L'État actuel de la recherche*, Orléans 1996 [Mediaevalia 21].

Becker 1997: Becker, Karin, "Textintention und Geschlechterprojektion in Eustache Deschamps' *Miroir de Mariage*," in *Text und Geschlecht. Mann und Frau in Eheschriften der frühen Neuzeit*, ed. Rüdiger Schnell, Frankfurt a. M. 1997, pp. 230-252.

Becker 1998: Becker, Karin, "Eustache Deschamps' Medical Poetry," in *Eustache Deschamps, French Courtier Poet: His Works and His World*, ed. Deborah M. Sinnreich-Levi, New York 1998 [AMS Studies in the Middle Ages 22], pp. 209-228.

Beierwaltes 1969: Beierwaltes, Werner, "Augustins Interpretation von Sapientia 11, 21," *Revue des Études Augustiniennes* 15 (1969), pp. 51-61.

Beierwaltes 1975: Beierwaltes, Werner, "Aequalitas numerosa. Zu Augustins Begriff des Schönen," *Wissenschaft und Weisheit* 38 (1975), pp. 140-157.

Beierwaltes 1979: Beierwaltes, Werner, *Proklos. Grundzüge seiner Metaphysik*, 2nd rev. ed., Frankfurt a. M. 1979 [Philosophische Abhandlungen 24].

Beierwaltes 1981: Beierwaltes, Werner, *Regio beatitudinis. Zu Augustins Begriff des glücklichen Lebens*, Heidelberg 1981 [Sitzungsberichte der Heidelberger Akademie der Wissenschaften. Philosophisch-Historische Klasse 6].

Beierwaltes 1991: Beierwaltes, Werner, "Der Harmonie-Gedanke im frühen Mittelalter," *Zeitschrift für philosophische Forschung* 45 (1991), pp. 1-21.

Beierwaltes 1998: Beierwaltes, Werner, *Platonismus im Christentum*, Frankfurt a. M. 1998 [Philosophische Abhandlungen 73].

Beierwaltes 2001: Beierwaltes, Werner, *Das wahre Selbst. Studien zu Plotins Begriff des Geistes und des Einen*, Frankfurt a. M. 2001.

Beinhauer 1990: Beinhauer, Ruth, *Untersuchungen zu philosophisch-theologischen Termini in Boethius De Trinitate*, Vienna 1990 [Dissertationen der Universität Wien 204].

Bent 1991: Bent, Margaret, "Deception, Exegesis and Sounding Number in Machaut's Motet 15 Amours Qui a le Pouoir/Faus Samblant/Vidi Dominum," *Early Music History* 10 (1991), pp. 15–27.

Benveniste 1966: Benveniste, Émile, *Problèmes de linguistique générale*, Paris 1966.

Bernard 1959: Bernard, Suzanne, *Mallarmé et la musique*, Paris 1959.

Bernard 1988: Bernhard, Wolfgang, *Rezeptivität und Spontaneität der Sinneswahrnehmung bei Aristoteles*, Baden-Baden 1988.

Bernard 1990: Bernard, Wolfgang, *Spätantike Dichtungstheorien. Untersuchungen zu Proklos, Herakleitos und Plutarch*, Stuttgart 1990 [Beiträge zur Altertumskunde 3].

Bernhard 1979: Bernhard, Michael, *Studien zur Epistola de armonica institutione des Regino von Prüm*, Munich 1979 [Bayerische Akademie der Wissenschaften. Veröffentlichungen der Musikhistorischen Kommission 5].

Bernhard 1986: Bernhard, Michael, "Textkritisches zu Aurelianus Reomensis," *Musica disciplina* 40 (1986), pp. 49–61.

Bernhard 1988: Bernhard, Michael, "Glossen zur Arithmetik des Boethius," in *Scire litteras. Forschungen zum mittelalterlichen Geistesleben*, ed. Michael Bernhard and Sigrid Krämer, Munich 1988 [Bayerische Akademie der Wissenschaften. Abhandlungen der philosophisch-historischen Klasse, Neue Folge 99], pp. 23–34.

Bernhard 1989: Bernhard, Michael, *Clavis Gerberti. Eine Revision von Martin Gerberts Scriptores ecclesiastici de musica sacra potissimum (St. Blasien 1784)*, Munich 1989.

Bernhard 1990a: Bernhard, Michael, "Glosses on Boethius's *De institutione musica*," in *Music Theory and its Sources: Antiquity and the Middle Ages*, ed. A. Barbera, Notre Dame 1990 [Notre Dame Conferences in Medieval Studies 1], pp. 136–149.

Bernhard 1990b: Bernhard, Michael, "Überlieferung und Fortleben der antiken lateinischen Musiktheorie im Mittelalter," in *Geschichte der Musiktheorie*, ed. Frieder Zaminer, 11 vols., Darmstadt 1984ff., vol. 3 (1990), ed. Michael Bernhard, pp. 7–35.

Bernhard 1990c: Bernhard, Michael, "Das musikalische Fachschrifttum im Mittelalter," in *Geschichte der Musiktheorie*, ed. Frieder Zaminer, 11 vols., Darmstadt 1984ff., vol. 3 (1990), ed. Michael Bernhard, pp. 37–104.

Bernhard/Bower 1993–1996: Bernhard, Michael, Bower, Calvin M., *Glossa maior in institutionem musicam Boethii*, 3 vols., Munich 1993–1996 [Bayerische Akademie der Wissenschaften. Veröffentlichungen der musikhistorischen Kommission 9–11].

Bernhard 1996: Bernhard, Michael, "Boethius im mittelalterlichen Schulunterricht," in *Schule und Schüler im Mittelalter. Beiträge zur europäischen Bildungsgeschichte des 9. bis 15. Jahrhunderts*, ed. Martin Kintzinger, Sönke Lorenz, and Michael Walter, Cologne/Weimar/Vienna 1996 [Beihefte zum Archiv für Kulturgeschichte 42], pp. 11–28.

Bernhard 2003: Bernhard, Michael, "Die Rezeption der *Institutio musica* des Boethius im frühen Mittelalter," in *Boèce ou la Chaîne des Savoirs*, ed. Alain Galonnier, Louvain/Paris/Dudley 2003 [Philosophes médiévaux XLIV], pp. 601–612.

Besseler 2001: Besseler, Heinrich, "Johannes de Muris," in *Die Musik in Geschichte und Gegenwart. Allgemeine Enzyklopädie der Musik*, ed. Friedrich Blume et al., digital version of the first ed. (1949–1986), Berlin 2001 [Digitale Bibliothek 60], s.v.

Beyenka 1957: Beyenka, Mary Melchior, "St. Augustine and the Hymns of St. Ambrose," *The American Benedictine Review* 2 (1957), pp. 121–132.

Bidez 1923: Bidez, Joseph, "Boèce et Porphyre," *Revue belge de philologie et d'histoire* 2 (1923), pp. 189–201.

Bischoff 1960: Bischoff, Bernhard, *Die südostdeutschen Schreibschulen und Bibliotheken in der Karolingerzeit. Teil I: Die bayrischen Diözesen*, Wiesbaden 1960.

Bischoff 1965: Bischoff, Bernhard, "Die Hofbibliothek Karls des Großen," in *Karl der Große. Lebenswerk und Nachleben*, ed. Bernhard Bischoff, Wolfgang Braunfels, and Hermann Schnitzler, 5 vols., Düsseldorf 1965, vol. 2, pp. 42–62.

Bischoff 1966a: Bischoff, Bernhard, "Hadoard und die Klassikerhandschriften aus Corbie," in *Mittelalterliche Studien. Ausgewählte Studien zur Schriftkunde und Literaturgeschichte*, 3 vols., Stuttgart 1966–1981, vol. 1 (1966), pp. 49–63.

Bischoff 1966b: Bischoff, Bernhard, "Die europäische Verbreitung der Werke Isidors von Sevilla," in *Mittelalterliche Studien. Ausgewählte Studien zur Schriftkunde und Literaturgeschichte*, 3 vols., Stuttgart 1966–1981, vol. 1 (1966), pp. 171–194.

Bliggenstorfer 2005: Bliggenstorfer, Susanna, *Eustache Deschamps. Aspects poétiques et satiriques*, Tübingen/Basel 2005 [Romanica Helvetica 125].

Blum 1956: Blum, Owen J., "Alberic of Monte Cassino and the Hymns and Rhythms Ascribed to Saint Peter Damian," *Traditio* 12 (1956), pp. 87–148.

Blumenberg 1996: Blumenberg, Hans, *Die Legitimität der Neuzeit. Erneuerte Ausgabe*, Frankfurt a. M. 1996.

Blumenberg 2001a: Blumenberg, Hans, "Anthropologische Annäherung an die Aktualität der Rhetorik," in *Ästhetische und metaphorologische Schriften*, ed. Anselm Haverkamp, Frankfurt a. M. 2001, pp. 406–434.

Blumenberg 2001b: Blumenberg, Hans, " 'Nachahmung der Natur.' Zur Vorgeschichte der Idee des schöpferischen Menschen," in *Ästhetische und metaphorologische Schriften*, ed. Anselm Haverkamp, Frankfurt a. M. 2001, pp. 9–46.

Boissier 1987: Boissier, Gaston, *La Fin du paganisme. Étude sur les derniéres luttes religieuses en occident au quatrième siècle*, Paris 1891, rpt. Hildesheim 1987.

Bolton 1977: Bolton, Diane K., "Remigian Commentaries on the *Consolation of Philosophy* and their Sources," *Traditio* 33 (1977), pp. 381–394.

Bonnaud 1929: Bonnaud, R., "L'éducation scientifique de Boèce," *Speculum* 4 (1929), pp. 199–206.

Borghezio 1930: Borghezio, Gino, *La musica in San Agostino*, Rome 1930.

Borinski 1912: Borinski, Karl, "Antike Versharmonik im Mittelalter und in der Renaissance," *Philologus* 71 (1912), pp. 139–159.

Borinski 1965: Borinski, Karl, *Die Antike in Poetik und Kunsttheorie. Vom Ausgang des klassischen Altertums bis auf Goethe und Wilhelm von Humboldt*, 2 vols., Leipzig 1914–1921, rpt. Darmstadt 1965.

Bossuat 1951: Bossuat, Robert, *Manuel bibliographique de la littérature du Moyen Âge*, Melun 1951.

Boudet 1997: Boudet, Jean-Patrice et al., *Eustache Deschamps en son temps*, Paris 1997.

Bowen 1988: Bowen, William R., "St. Augustine in Medieval and Renaissance Musical Science," in *Augustine on Music: An Interdisciplinary Collection of Essays*, ed. Richard R. La Croix, Lewiston/Queenston 1988 [Studies in the History and Interpretation of Music 6], pp. 29–43.

Bower 1971: Bower, Calvin M., "Natural and Artificial Music: The Origins and Development of an Aesthetic Concept," *Musica Disciplina* 25 (1971), pp. 17–33.

Bower 1978: Bower, Calvin M., "Boethius and Nicomachus: An Essay Concerning the Sources of *De institutione musica*," *Vivarium* 1 (1978), pp. 1–45.

Bower 1981: Bower, Calvin M., "The Role of Boethius' *De institutione musica* in the Speculative Tradition of Western Musical Thought," in *Boethius and the Liberal Arts: A Collection of Essays*, ed. Mario Masi, Bern et al. 1981 [Utah Studies in Literature and Linguistics], pp. 157–174.

Bower 1988: Bower, Calvin M., "Boethius' De institutione musica: A Handlist of Manuscripts," *Scriptorium* 42 (1988), pp. 205–251.

Bower 1998: Bower, Calvin M., "Die Wechselwirkung von philosophia, mathematica und musica in der karolingischen Rezeption der 'Institutio musica' von Boethius," in *Musik—und die Geschichte der Philosophie und Naturwissenschaften im Mittelalter. Fragen zur Wechselwirkung von "Musica" und "Philosophia" im Mittelalter*, ed. Frank Hentschel, Leiden/Boston/Cologne 1998, pp. 163–183.

Bowles 1954: Bowles, Edmund A., "Haut and Bas: The Grouping of Musical Instruments in the Middle Ages," *Musica Disciplina* 8 (1954), pp. 115–140.

Brachtendorf 2000: Brachtendorf, Johannes, *Die Struktur des menschlichen Geistes nach Augustinus. Selbstreflexion und Erkenntnis Gottes in "De trinitate,"* Hamburg 2000 [Paradeigmata 19].

Bragard 1929: Bragard, Roger, "L'Harmonie des sphères selon Boèce," *Speculum* 4 (1929), pp. 206–213.

Bragard 1953–1954: Bragard, Roger, "Le *Speculum musicae* du compilateur Jacques de Liège," *Musica disciplina* 7 (1953), pp. 59–104 and 8 (1954), pp. 1–17.

Brambach 1883: Brambach, Wilhelm, *Die Musiklitteratur des Mittelalters bis zur Blüthe der Reichenauer Sängerschule 500–1050 n. Chr.*, Karlsruhe 1883.

Brandt 1903: Brandt, P., "Entstehungszeit und zeitliche Folge der Werke des Boethius," *Philologus* 62 (1903), pp. 141–154, 234–275.

Braun 1977: Braun, René, *Deus Christianorum. Recherches sur le vocabulaire doctrinal de Tertullien*, Paris 1977.

Brenet 1927: Brenet, Michel, "Quelques passages concernant la musique dans les poésies de Jehan Molinet," *Bulletin de la Société Française de Musicologie* 1 (1927), pp. 21–27.

Brennan 1988: Brennan, Brian, "Augustine's *De musica*," *Vigiliae Christianae* 42 (1988), pp. 267–281.

Brinkmann 1977: Brinkmann, Hennig, "Der Reim im frühen Mittelalter," in *Die Genese der europäischen Endreimdichtung*, ed. Ulrich Ernst and Peter-Erich Neuser, Darmstadt 1977 [Wege der Forschung 144], pp. 149–176.

Brittain 2002: Brittain, Charles, "Non-Rational Perception in the Stoics and Augustine," *Oxford Studies in Ancient Philosophy* 22 (2002), pp. 253–308.

Brown 1978: Brown, Virginia, "Lupus of Ferrières on the Metres of Boethius," in *Latin Script and Letters, A.D. 400–900: Festschrift Presented to Ludwig Bieler on the Occasion of His 70th Birthday*, ed. John J. O'Meara and Bernd Naumann, Leiden 1978, pp. 63–79.

Brown 1985: Brown, Murray L., "The Order of the Passion of Jesus Christ: A Reconsideration of Eustache Deschamps's 'Ballade to Chaucer,' " *Mediaevalia* 11 (1985), pp. 219–244.

Brown 1987: Brown, Cynthia J., "Du nouveau sur le 'mistere' des *Douze Dames de Rhétorique*. Le rôle de Georges Chastellain," *Bulletin de la Commission royale d'histoire* 153 (1987), pp. 181–221.

Brownlee 1984: Brownlee, Kevin, *Poetic Identity in Guillaume de Machaut*, Madison 1984.

Bruder 1928: Bruder, Konrad, *Die philosophischen Elemente in den Opuscula sacra des Boethius*, Leipzig 1928 [Forschungen zur Geschichte der Philosophie und der Pädagogik 3.2].

Brunner 1948: Brunner, Otto, "Die ritterlich-höfische Kultur," in *Adeliges Landleben und europäischer Geist. Leben und Werk Wolf Helmhards von Hohberg (1612–1688)*, Salzburg 1948, pp. 74–102.

Bruyne 1946: Bruyne, Edgar de, *Études d'esthétique médiévale*, 3 vols., Bruges 1946 [Rijksuniversiteit te Gent. Werken uitgegeven door de Faculteit van de Wijsbegeerte en Letteren].

Bühler 1965: Bühler, Karl, *Sprachtheorie. Die Darstellungsfunktion der Sprache*, Stuttgart 1965.

Bukofzer 1942: Bukofzer, Manfred F., "Speculative Thinking in Medieval Music," *Speculum* 17 (1942), pp.165–180.

Bultmann 1950: Bultmann, Rudolf, "Ursprung und Sinn der Typologie als hermeneutischer Methode," *Theologische Literaturzeitung* 4/5 (1950), col. 205–212.

Burbach 1966: Burbach, Hermann-Josef, *Studien zur Musikauffassung des Thomas von Aquin*, Regensburg 1966 [Kölner Beiträge zur Musikforschung 34].

Burdach 1933: Burdach, Konrad, "Die humanistischen Wirkungen der Trostschrift des Boethius im Mittelalter und in der Renaissance," *Deutsche Vierteljahrsschrift für Literaturwissenschaft und Geistesgeschichte* 11 (1933), pp. 530–558.

Burkert 1962: Burkert, Walter, *Weisheit und Wissenschaft. Studien zu Pythagoras, Philolaos und Platon*, Nürnberg 1962 [Erlanger Beiträge zur Sprach- und Kunstwissenschaft 10].

Burnyeat 1987: Burnyeat, Myles F., "Platonism and Mathematics: A Prelude to Discussion," in *Mathematics and Metaphysics in Aristotle. Mathematik und Metaphysik bei Aristoteles. Akten des X. Symposium Aristotelicum Sigriswil, 6.–12. September 1984*, ed. Andreas Graeser, Bern/Stuttgart 1987, pp. 213–240.

Burnyeat 1999: Burnyeat, Myles F., "Plato on Why Mathematics is Good for the Soul," in *Mathematics and Necessity: Essays in the History of Philosophy*, ed. Timothy Smiley, Oxford 1999 [Proceedings of the British Academy 103], pp. 1–81.

Bursill-Hall 1971: Bursill-Hall, Geoffrey L., *Speculative Grammar of the Middle-Ages: The Doctrine of the Partes orationis of the Modistae*, The Hague/Paris 1971.

Bursill-Hall 1976: Bursill-Hall, Geoffrey L., "Jean de Garlande—Forgotten Grammarian and the Manuscript Tradition," *Historiographia Linguistica* 3 (1976), pp. 155–175.

Busard 1971: Busard, H. L. L., "Die 'Arithmetica speculativa' des Johannes de Muris," *Scientiarum historia* 13 (1971), pp. 103–132.

Busse Berger 1990: Busse Berger, Anna Maria, "Musical Proportions and Arithmetic in the Late Middle Ages and Renaissance," *Musica disciplina* 44 (1990), pp. 89–118.

Butterfield 2002: Butterfield, Ardis, *Poetry and Music in Medieval France: From Jean Renart to Guillaume de Machaut*, Cambridge 2002 [Cambridge Studies in Medieval Literature].

Caldwell 1981: Caldwell, John, "The De Institutione Arithmetica and the De Institutione Musica," in *Boethius: His Life, Thought, and Influence*, ed. Margaret Gibson, Oxford 1981, pp. 135–154.

Caldwell 1986: Caldwell, John, "Music in the Faculty of Arts," in *The History of the University of Oxford*, ed. T. H. Aston, 8 vols., Oxford 1984–2000, vol. 3 (1986), ed. James McConia, pp. 201–212.

Calin 1987: Calin, William, *In Defense of French Poetry—An Essay in Revaluation*, London/University Park 1987.

Calvez 1982: Calvez, Daniel, *"La Structure du rondeau. Mise au point,"* The *French Review* 55 (1982), pp. 461–470.

Carpenter 1972: Carpenter, Nan Cooke, *Music in the Medieval and Renaissance Universities*, Norman 1972.

Carton 1924: Carton, Raoul, *L'Expérience physique chez Roger Bacon. Contribution à l'étude de la méthode et de la science expérimentale au XIIIe siècle*, Paris 1924.

Carton 1930: Carton, Raoul, "Le christianisme et l'augustinisme de Boèce," *Revue de philosophie* 30 (1930), pp. 573–659.

Caspar 1930–1933: Caspar, Erich, *Geschichte des Papsttums. Von den Anfängen bis zur Höhe der Weltherrschaft*, 2 vols., Tübingen 1930–1933.

Cassirer 1932: Cassirer, Ernst, *Aristoteles' Schrift "Von der Seele" und ihre Stellung innerhalb der aristotelischen Philosophie*, Tübingen 1932 [Heidelberger Abhandlungen zur Philosophie und ihrer Geschichte 24].

Castillo 1968: Castillo, Carmen, " 'Numerus,' qui graece 'ῥυθμός' dicitur," *Emerita. Revista de linguistica y filologia clásica* 35 (1968), pp. 279–308.

Castor 1964: Castor, Grahame, *Pléiade Poetics: A Study in Sixteenth Century Thought and Terminology*, Cambridge 1964.

Cerquiglini 1988: Cerquiglini, Jacqueline, "Le Rondeau," in *Grundriß der romanischen Literaturen des Mittelalters*, in collaboration with Jean Frappier et al., ed. Hans-Robert Jauß and Erich Köhler, 11 vols. in 30 fasc., Heidelberg 1968ff., vol. 8.1 (1988), ed. Daniel Poirion, pp. 45–58.

Cerquiglini-Toulet 1993: Cerquiglini-Toulet, Jacqueline, *La Couleur de la mélancolie. La fréquentation des livres au XIVe siècle (1300–1415)*, Paris 1993 [Brèves littérature].

Cerquiglini 1997: Cerquiglini, Jacqueline, "L'éclat de la langue. Éléments d'une esthétique des Grands Rhétoriqueurs," *Cahiers V.-L. Saulnier* 14 (1997), pp. 75–82.

Cerquiglini 2001: Cerquiglini, Jacqueline, *"Un engin si soutil": Guillaume de Machaut et l'écriture au XIVe siècle*, Paris 2001 [Bibliothèque du XVe siècle 47].

Chadwick 1981: Chadwick, Henry, *Boethius: The Consolations of Music, Logic, Theology, and Philosophy*, Oxford 1981.

Chamard 1920: Chamard, Henri, *Origines de la poésie française de la Renaissance*, Paris 1920.

Chamberlain 1970: Chamberlain, David S., "Philosophy of Music in the 'Consolatio' of Boethius," *Speculum* 45 (1970), pp. 80–97.

Champion 1923: Champion, Pierre, *Histoire poétique du XVe siècle*, 2 vols., Paris 1923.

Chartier 1965: Chartier, Yves, *L'epistula de armonica institutione de Réginon de Prüm*, Diss., Ottawa 1965.

Châtelain 1975: Châtelain, Henri, *Recherches sur le vers français au XVe siècle*, Paris 1907, rpt. Geneva 1975.

Châtillon 1980: Châtillon, Jean, "La méthode théologique d'Alain de Lille," in *Alain de Lille, Gautier de Châtillon, Jakemart Giélée et leur temps*, ed. Henri Roussel and François Suard, Lille 1980, pp. 47–60.

Chenu 1956: Chenu, Marie-Dominique, "Les platonismes du XIIe siècle," in *La Théologie au douzième siècle*, Paris 1956 [Études de philosophie médiévale 45], pp. 108–141.

Cilleruelo 1968: Cilleruelo, P. L., "Numerus et sapientia," *Estudio Agustiniano* 3 (1968), pp. 109–121.

Clagett 1953: Clagett, Marshall, "The Medieval Latin Translations from the Arabic of the *Elements* of Euclid with Special Emphasis on the Versions of Adelard of Bath," *Isis* 44 (1953), pp. 16–42.

Clagett/Post (eds.) 1961: *Twelfth-century Europe and the Foundations of Modern Society*, ed. Marshall Clagett and Gaines Post, Madison 1961.

Clegg 2003: Clegg, Brian, *The First Scientist: A Life of Roger Bacon*, London/New York 2003.

Clerval 1977: Clerval, Alexandre, *Les Écoles de Chartres au moyen âge du Ve au XVIe siècle*, Paris 1895, rpt. Geneva 1977.

Clop 1924: Clop, E., *Du beau à Dieu par le nombre d'après Saint Augustin*, Mâcon 1924.

Codices latini antiquiores: *Codices Latini antiquiores: A Paleographic Guide to Latin Manuscripts Prior to the 9th Century*, ed. Elias Avery Lowe, 12 vols., Oxford 1934–1971.

Cohen 1976: Cohen, Jean, "Poésie et redondance," *Poétique* 28 (1976), pp. 413–422.

Corbin 1962: Corbin, Solange, "Musica spéculative et cantus pratique. Le rôle de saint Augustin dans la transmission des sciences musicales," *Cahiers de civilisation médiévale* 5 (1962), pp. 1–12.

Corbin 1977: Corbin, Solange, *Die Neumen*, Cologne 1977 [Palaeographie der Musik 1].

Cornilliat 1994: Cornilliat, François, *"Or ne mens." Les couleurs de l'éloge et du blâme chez les Grands Rhétoriqueurs*, Paris 1994 [Bibliothèque littéraire de la Renaissance 3.30].

Correns 1891: Correns, P., *Die dem Boethius fälschlich zugeschriebene Abhandlung des Dominicus Gundisalinus*, Münster 1891.

Courcelle 1939: Courcelle, Pierre, "Étude critique sur les commentaires de la Consolation de Boèce (IXe–XVe siècles)," *Archives d'histoire doctrinale littéraire du Moyen Âge* 14 (1939), pp. 5–140.

Courcelle 1948: Courcelle, Pierre, *Les Lettres grecques en occident. De Macrobe à Cassiodore*, Paris 1948.

Courcelle 1967: Courcelle, Pierre, *La Consolation de philosophie dans la tradition littéraire. Antécédents et postérité de Boèce*, Paris 1967 [Études augustiniennes].

Courcelle 1968: Courcelle, Pierre, *Recherches sur les Confessions de saint Augustin*, Paris 1968.

Cowling 2004: Cowling, David, "Les métaphores de l'auteur et de la création littéraire à la fin du Moyen Âge. Le cas des Grands Rhétoriqueurs," in "*Toutes choses sont faictes cleres par escripture.*" *Fonctions et figures d'auteurs du moyen âge à l'époque contemporaine*, ed. Virginie Minet-Mahy, Claude Thiry, and Tania Van Hemelryck, Louvain 2004 [Les Lettres romanes. Hors série 2004], pp. 99–112.

Crapelet 1832: Crapelet, Georges Adrien, *Précis historique et littéraire sur Eustache Deschamps*, Paris 1832.

Crépet et al. (eds.) 1861–1863: *Recueil de chefs-d'oeuvres de la poésie française depuis les origines jusqu'à nos jours avec une notice littéraire sur chaque poëte*, ed. Eugène Crépet et al., 4 vols., Paris 1861–1863.

Crespo 1973: Crespo, Roberto, "Il Prologo alla traduzione della Consolatio philosophiae di Jean de Meun e il commento di Guglielmo d'Aragonia," in *Romanitas et Christianitas. Studia Iano Henrico Waszink oblata*, ed. Willem den Boer, Amsterdam et al. 1973, pp. 55–70.

Creuzer 1977: Creuzer, Friedrich, "Skizze der Philosophie Plotins," in *Die Philosophie des Neuplatonismus*, ed. Clemens Zintzen, Darmstadt 1977 [Wege der Forschung 436], pp. 3–13.

Crocker 1958: Crocker, Richard L., "*Musica rhythmica* and *Musica metrica* in Antique and Medieval Theory," *Journal of Music Theory* 2 (1958), pp. 2–23.

Crombie 1971: Crombie, Alistair C., *Robert Grosseteste and the Origins of Experimental Science 1100–1700*, Oxford 1971.

Cropp 1981: Cropp, Glynnis M., "Boèce et Christine de Pizan," *Le Moyen Age* 87 (1981), pp. 397–417.

Cropp 1989: Cropp, Glynnis M., "Fortune and the Poet in Ballades of Eustache Deschamps, Charles d'Orléans and François Villon," *Medium Aevum* 1 (1989), pp. 125–132.

Cropp 1997: Cropp, Glynnis M., "The Medieval French Tradition," in *Boethius in the Middle Ages: Latin and Vernacular Traditions of the Consolatio philosophiae*, ed. Maarten J. F. M. Hoenen and Lodi Nauta, Leiden et al. 1997 [Studien und Texte zur Geistesgeschichte des Mittelalters 58], pp. 243–265.

Crozals 1894: Crozals, Jacques-M. de, "Quelques théories de St. Augustin sur la métrique. D'après son Traité 'de la musique'" *Annales de l'enseignement supérieur de Grenoble* VI.3 (1894), pp. 499–540.

Cserba 1934: Cserba, Simon M., *Der Musiktraktat des Hieronymus Moravia*, Diss., Freiburg 1934.

Cumont 1977: Cumont, Franz, "Plotin," in *Die Philosophie des Neuplatonismus*, ed. Clemens Zintzen, Darmstadt 1977 [Wege der Forschung 436], pp. 14–37.

Curtius 1993: Curtius, Ernst Robert, *Europäische Literatur und lateinisches Mittelalter*, Tübingen/Basel 1993.

Czapiewski 1964: Czapiewski, Winfried, *Das Schöne bei Thomas von Aquin*, Freiburg/Basel/Vienna 1964 [Freiburger Theologische Studien 82].

Dahlhaus 1985: Dahlhaus, Carl, "Was heißt 'Geschichte der Musiktheorie?'," in *Geschichte der Musiktheorie*, ed. Frieder Zaminer, 11 vols., Darmstadt 1985ff., vol. 1 (1985), pp. 8–39.

Daly 1961: Daly, Lowrie J., *The Medieval University, 1200–1400*, New York 1961.

Dauphiné 1974: Dauphiné, James, "L'Image musicale de l'homme et du monde dans quelques textes du XVIe siècle," *Annales de la faculté des lettres et sciences humaines de Nice* 22 (1974), pp. 53–68.

Dehnert 1967: Dehnert, Edmund John, "Music as Liberal in Augustine and Boethius," in *Arts libéraux et philosophie au Moyen Âge. Actes du Quatrième Congrès de International de Philosophie Médiévale. Université de Montréal, Canada, 27 août—2 septembre 1967*, Paris 1967, pp. 987–991.

Deiters 1881a: Deiters, Hermann, "Ueber das Verhältnis des Martianus Capella zu Aristides Quintilianus," in *Programm des Königlichen Marien-Gymnasiums in Posen für das Schuljahr 1880/81*, Posen 1881, pp. 1–28.

Deiters 1881b: Deiters, Hermann, *Studien zu den griechischen Musikern. Über das Verhältnis des Martianus Capella zu Aristides Quintilianus*, Posen 1881.

Delisle 1869: Delisle, Léopold, "Les Écoles d'Orléans, au douzième et treizième siècle," *Annuaire-Bulletin de la Société de France* 1869, pp. 139–154.

Delisle 1880: Delisle, Leópold, *Mélanges de paléographie et de bibliographie*, Paris 1880.

Delisle 1967: Delisle, Léopold, *Recherches sur la librairie de Charles V, roi de France, 1337–1380/81. Recherches sur la fondation de la librairie et description des manuscrits*, 2 vols., Paris 1907, rpt. 1967.

Delisle 1969: Delisle, Léopold, *Le Cabinet des manuscrits de la Bibliothèque Nationale*, 4 vols., Paris 1868–1881, rpt. Hildesheim/New York 1969.

Denizot-Ghil 2000: Denizot-Ghil, Michèle J., *Poétique de la Discontinuité dans l'oeuvre lyrique d'Eustache Deschamps*, Diss., New York 2000.

Desmond 2000: Desmond, Karen, "New Light on Jacobus, Author of *Speculum musicae*," *Plainsong and Medieval Music* 9 (2000), pp. 19–40.

Devaux 1996: Devaux, Jean, *Jean Molinet, indiciaire bourguignon*, Paris 1996 [Bibliothèque du XVe siècle].

Dihle 1954: Dihle, Albrecht, "Die Anfänge der griechischen akzentuierenden Verskunst," *Hermes* 82 (1954), pp. 182–199.

Dömling 1970: Dömling, Wolfgang, *Die mehrstimmigen Balladen, Rondeaux und Virelais Guillaume de Machauts*, Tutzing 1970 [Municher Veröffentlichungen zur Musikgeschichte 16].

Dömling 1971: Dömling, Wolfgang, "Isorhythmie und Variation. Über Kompositionstechniken in der Messe Guillaume de Machauts," *Archiv für Musikwissenschaften* 28 (1971), pp. 24–32.

Dörrie 1969: Dörrie, Heinrich, "Porphyrios als Mittler zwischen Plotin und Augustin," in *Platonismus in der Philosophie des Mittelalters*, ed. Werner Beierwaltes, Darmstadt 1969 [Wege der Forschung 197], pp. 410–439.

Dolch 1965: Dolch, Josef, *Lehrplan des Abendlandes. Zweieinhalb Jahrtausende seiner Geschichte*, Ratingen 1965.

D'Onofrio 1981: D'Onofrio, Giulio, "Giovanni Scoto e Remigio di Auxerre. A proposito di alcuni commenti altomedievali a Boezio," *Studi Medievali* 22 (1981), pp. 587–693.

Doorslaer 1934: Doorslaer, George van, "La Chapelle musicale de Philippe le Beau," *Revue belge d'archéologie et d'histoire d'art* 4 (1934), pp. 21–57, 139–165.

Dossat 1970: Dossat, Yves, "Les premiers maîtres à l'université de Toulouse. Jean de Garlande, Hélinand. Les universités du Languedoc au XIIIe siècle," *Cahiers de Fanjeaux* 5 (1970), pp. 179–203.

Doumic 1916: Doumic, René, *Histoire de la littérature française*, Paris 1916.

Dragonetti 1961: Dragonetti, Roger, " 'La Poesie . . . ceste musique naturele.' Essai d'exégèse d'un passage de l'*Art de Dictier* d'Eustache Deschamps," in *Fin du moyen âge et renaissance. Mélanges de philologie française offerts à Robert Guiette*, Anvers 1961, pp. 49–64.

Duby 1978: Duby, Georges, *Les trois ordres ou l'imaginaire du féodalisme*, Paris 1978 [Bibliothèque des histoires].

Duchez 1980: Duchez, Marie-Elizabeth, "Jean Scot Erigène premier lecteur du 'De institutione musica' de Boèce?," *Abhandlungen der Heidelberger Akademie der Wissenschaften. Philosophisch-historische Klasse* 3 (1980), pp. 165–187.

Duchez 1981: Duchez, Marie-Elisabeth, "Description grammaticale et description arithmétique des phénomènes musicaux. Le tournant du IXe siècle," in *Sprache und Erkenntnis im Mittelalter. Akten des VI. internationalen Kongresses für mittelalterliche Philosophie der Société internationale pour l'étude de la philosophie médiévale, 19. August—3. September 1977 in Bonn*, ed. Jan P. Beckmann, 2 vols., Berlin/New York 1981 [Miscellanea mediaevalia 13], vol. 2, pp. 561–579.

Dürr/Gerstenberg 2001: Dürr, Walther, and Walter Gerstenberg, "Rhythmus, Metrum, Takt," in *Die Musik in Geschichte und Gegenwart. Allgemeine Enzyklopädie der Musik*, ed. Friedrich Blume et al., digital version of the first edition (1949–1986), Berlin 2001 [Digitale Bibliothek 60], s.v.

Duhem 1954–1958: Duhem, Pierre, *Le système du monde. Histoire des doctrines cosmologiques de Platon à Copernic*, 8 vols., Paris 1954–1958.

Dupire 1932a: Dupire, Noël, *Jean Molinet. La vie, les oeuvres*, Paris 1932.

Dupire 1932b: Dupire, Noël, *Étude critique des manuscrits et éditions des poésies de Jean Molinet*, Paris 1932.

Durantel 1919: Durantel, Jean, *Saint Thomas et le Pseudo-Denys*, Paris 1919.

Du Roy 1966: Du Roy, Olivier, *L'intelligence de la foi en la trinité selon Saint Augustin. Genèse de sa théologie trinitaire jusqu'en 391*, Paris 1966 [Études Augustiniennes].

Dyroff 1929: Dyroff, Adolf, "Ueber die Entwicklung und den Wert der Aesthetik des Thomas von Aquino," in *Festgabe für Ludwig Stein zum 70. Geburtstag. Archiv für Systematische Philosophie und Soziologie* 32 (1929), pp. 157–215.

Dyroff 1930: Dyroff, Adolf, "Über Form und Begriffsgehalt der augustinischen

Schrift De ordine," in *Aurelius Augustinus. Die Festschrift der Görres-Gesellschaft zum 1500. Todestag des Heiligen Augustinus*, ed. Martin Grabmann and Joseph Mausbach, Cologne 1930, pp. 15–62.

Easton 1952: Easton, Stewart C., *Roger Bacon and His Search for a Universal Science: A Reconsideration of the Life and Works of Roger Bacon in the Light of His Own Purposes*, New York 1952.

Eco 1970: Eco, Umberto, *Il problema estetico in Tommaso d'Aquino*, Milan 1970 [Idee nuove 53].

Eco 2004: Eco, Umberto, *Kunst und Schönheit im Mittelalter*, rev. Günter Memmert, Munich, 2004.

Edelstein 1929: Edelstein, Heinz, *Die Musikanschauung Augustins nach seiner Schrift De musica*, Ohlau 1929.

Edmiston 1974: Edmiston, Jean, "Boethius on Pythagorean Music," *The Music Review* 35 (1974), pp. 179–184.

Eggebrecht 1995: Eggebrecht, Hans Heinrich. "Formsinn und Emotionsgehalt," in *Musik verstehen*, Munich/Zürich 1995, pp. 71–81.

Ehrle 1970: Ehrle, Franz, "Der Augustinismus und der Aristotelismus in der Scholastik gegen Ende des 13. Jahrhunderts," in *Gesammelte Aufsätze zur englischen Scholastik*, ed. Franz Pelster, Rom. 1970 [Storia e letteratura 50], pp. 3–57.

Eichhorn 1996: Eichhorn, Andreas, "Augustinus und die Musik," *Musica* 50 (1996), pp. 318–323.

Eissfeldt 1934: Eissfeldt, Otto, *Einleitung in das alte Testament unter Einschluss der Apokryphen und Pseudoepigraphen. Entstehungsgeschichte des Alten Testaments*, Tübingen 1934 [Neue theologische Grundrisse].

Ellinwood 1945: Ellinwood, Leonard, "Ars musica," *Speculum* 20 (1945), pp. 290–299.

Ellsmere 1988: Ellsmere, Patricia K., "Augustine on Beauty, Art and God," in *Augustine on Music: An Interdisciplinary Collection of Essays*, ed. Richard L. La Croix, Lewiston/Queenston 1988 [Studies in the History and Interpretation of Music 6], pp. 97–113.

Elwert 1965: Elwert, Wilhelm Theodor, *Traité de versification française*, Paris 1965 [Bibliothèque française et romane A 8].

Englisch 1994: Englisch, Brigitte, *Die artes liberales im frühen Mittelalter (5.–9. Jahrhundert). Das Quadrivium und der Komputus als Indikatoren für Kontinuität und Erneuerung der exakten Wissenschaften zwischen Antike und Mittelalter*, Stuttgart 1994 [Sudhoffs Archiv 33].

Englisch 1999: Englisch, Brigitte, "Artes und Weltsicht bei Roger Bacon," *Artes im Mittelalter*, ed. Ursula Schaefer, Berlin 1999, pp. 53–68.

Erdmann 1974: Erdmann, Carl, *Die Entstehung des Kreuzzugsgedankens*, Stuttgart 1935 [Forschungen zur Kirchen- und Geistesgeschichte 6], rpt. Darmstadt 1974.

Erickson 1992: Erickson, Raymond, "Eriugena, Boethius and the Neoplatonism of 'Musica' and 'Scolica enchiriadis,' " in *Musical Humanism and its Legacy: Essays in Honor of Claude V. Palisca*, Stuyvesant 1992, pp. 53–78.

Ernstbrunner 1998: Ernstbrunner, Pia, *Der Musiktraktat des Engelbert von Admont (ca. 1250–1331)*, Tutzing 1998 [Musica mediaevalis Europae occidentalis 2].

Ernstbrunner 2002: Ernstbrunner, Pia, "Vocis enim factor . . . ab anima movetur. Die menschliche Stimme im Fachschrifttum des Spätmittelalters," *Basler Jahrbuch für historische Musikpraxis* 26 (2002), pp. 59–78.

Evans 1978a: Evans, Gillian R., "Introductions to Boethius's Arithmetica of the Tenth to the Fourteenth Century," *History of Science* 16 (1978), pp. 22–41.

Evans 1978b: Evans, Gillian R., "A Commentary on Boethius's Arithmetica of the Twelfth or Thirteenth Century," *Annals of Science* 35 (1978), pp. 131–141.

Evans 1982: Evans, Gillian R., "Thierry of Chartres and the Unity of Boethius' Thought," *Studia Patristica* 17 (1982), pp. 440–445.

Evans 1995: Evans, Beverly, " 'Musique appellee richmique': Voyage de la découverte chez Jean Molinet," in *L'Hostellerie de pensée. Études sur l'art littéraire au Moyen Âge offertes à Daniel Poirion par ses anciens élèves*, ed. Danielle Bohler and Michel Zink, Paris 1995 [Cultures et civilisations médiévales XII], pp. 163–172.

Evdokimova 1999: Evdokimova, Ludmilla, "Rhétorique et poésie dans l'Art de dictier," in *Autour d'Eustache Deschamps. Actes du Colloque du Centre d'Études Médiévales de l'Université de Picardie-Jules Verne, Amiens, 5–8 Novembre 1998*, ed. Danielle Buschinger, Amiens 1999, pp. 93–102.

Evdokimova 2005: Evdokimova, Ludmilla, "Éthique, économie, politique, rhétorique. La Classification aristotélicienne des sciences et la poésie didactique de Deschamps," in *Les 'dictez vertueulx' d'Eustache Deschamps. Forme poétique et discours engagé à la fin du Moyen Âge*, ed. Miren Lacassagne and Thierry Lassabatère, Paris 2005, pp. 57–72.

Falkenroth 1992: Falkenroth, Christoph, *Die Musica speculativa des Johannes de Muris: Kommentar zur Überlieferung und kritische Edition*, Stuttgart 1992 [Beihefte zum Archiv für Musikwissenschaft 34].

Farmer 1934: Farmer, Henry George, *Al-Farabi's Arabic-Latin Writings on Music*, Glasgow 1934 [Collection of Oriental Writers on Music II].

Fassler 1987: Fassler, Margot E., "Accent, Meter, and Rhythm in Medieval Treatises 'De rithmis' " *The Journal of Musicology* 1 (1987), pp. 164–190.

Faucon 1975: Faucon, Pierre, *Aspects néoplatoniciens de la doctrine de Saint Thomas d'Aquin*, Paris/Lille 1975.

Febel 2001: Febel, Gisela, *Poesia ambigua oder Vom Alphabet zum Gedicht. Aspekte der Entwicklung der modernen französischen Lyrik bei den Grands Rhétoriqueurs*, Frankfurt a. M. 2001 [Analecta Romanica 62].

Feenstra 1962: Feenstra, Robert, "L'organisation de l'enseignement du droit civil à Orléans au Moyen Âge," *Bulletin de la Société archéologique et historique de l'Orléanais*, nouvelle série, 3 (1962), pp. 213–222.

Feilzler 1971: Feilzler, Heinrich, *Jugend in der mittelalterlichen Ständegesellschaft. Ein Beitrag zum Problem der Generationen*, Vienna 1971.

Fellerer 1959: Fellerer, Karl Gustav, "Die musica in den artes liberales," in *Artes liberales. Von der antiken Bildung zur Wissenschaft des Mittelalters*, ed. Josef Koch, Cologne/Leiden 1959 [Studien und Texte zur Geistesgeschichte des Mittelalters 5], pp. 33–49.

Ferrand 1980: Ferrand, François, "Le Grand Rhétoriqueur Jean Molinet et la chanson polyphonique à la Cour des Ducs de Bourgogne," in *Musique, littérature et société au Moyen Âge. Actes du colloque, 24–29 mars 1980*, ed. Danielle Buschinger and André Crépin, Paris 1980, pp. 395–407.

Ferrari 1989: Ferrari, G. R. F., "Plato and Poetry," in *The Cambridge History of Literary Criticism*, ed. Peter Brooks and Hugh Barr Nisbet, 9 vols., Cambridge/New York/Melbourne 1989–2001, vol. 1 (1989), ed. George E. Kennedy, pp. 92–148.

Fetis 1837: Fetis, François-Joseph, *Biographie universelle des musiciens et bibliographie générale de la musique*, Paris 1837.

Fetis 1869–1876: Fetis, François-Joseph, *Histoire générale de la musique. Depuis les temps les plus anciens jusqu'à nos jours*, 5 vols., Paris 1869–1876.

Fischer 1981: Fischer, Kurt von, "Musica," in *Die Renaissance der Wissenschaften im 12. Jahrhundert*, ed. Peter Weimar, Zürich 1981 [Zürcher Hochschulforum 2], pp. 233–248.

Fisher/Unguru 1971: Fisher, N. W., Unguru, S., "Experimental Sciences and Mathematics in Roger Bacon's Thought," *Traditio* 27 (1971), pp. 353–378.

Flasch 2003: Flasch, Kurt, *Augustin. Einführung in sein Denken*, 3rd ed. with bibliographical supplement, Stuttgart 2003.

Föllmi 1994: Föllmi, Beat A., *Das Weiterwirken der Musikanschauung Augustins im 16. Jahrhundert*, Bern et al. 1994 [Europäische Hochschulschriften, Reihe XXXVI, 116].

Fontaine 1983: Fontaine, Jacques, *Isidore de Seville et la culture classique dans l'Espagne wisigothique*, 3 vols., Paris 1983 [Études Augustiniennes].

Forkel 1967: Forkel, Johann Nicolaus, *Allgemeine Geschichte der Musik*, 2 vols., Leipzig 1788–1801, new ed., O. Wessely, Graz 1967 [Die großen Darstellungen der Musikgeschichte in Barock und Aufklärung].

Foucault 1966: Foucault, Michel, *Les Mots et les choses. Une archéologie des sciences humaines*, Paris 1966 [Bibliothèque des sciences humaines].

Foucault 1969: Foucault, Michel, *L'Archéologie du savoir*, Paris 1969 [Bibliothèque des sciences humaines].

Foucault 1984: Foucault, Michel, *Histoire de la sexualité III. Le souci de soi*, Paris 1984.

Foucault 2001a: Foucault, Michel, "Le Langage à l'infini," in *Dits et Écrits*, ed. Daniel Defert and François Ewald, 2 vols., Paris 2001 [Quarto], vol. 1, pp. 278–288.

Foucault 2001b: Foucault, Michel, "La Folie, l'absence d'œuvre," in *Dits et*

Écrits, ed. Daniel Defert and François Ewald, 2 vols., Paris 2001 [Quarto], vol. 1, pp. 440–449.

Foucault 2001c: Foucault, Michel, "Qu'est-ce qu'un auteur?," in *Dits et Écrits*, ed. Daniel Defert and François Ewald, 2 vols., Paris 2001 [Quarto], vol. 1, pp. 817–848.

Foucault 2001d: Foucault, Michel, "Nietzsche, la généalogie, l'histoire," in *Dits et écrits*, 2 vols., ed. Daniel Defert and François Ewald, Paris 2001 [Quarto], vol. 1, pp. 1004–1024.

Foucault 2001e: Foucault, Michel: "Une esthétique de l'existence," in *Dits et écrits*, ed. Daniel Defert and François Ewald, 2 vols., Paris 2001 [Quarto], vol. 2, pp. 1549–1554.

Fournier 1970b: Fournier, Marcel, *Histoire de la science de droit en France 3. Les universités françaises et l'enseignement du droit en France au moyen âge*, Paris 1892, rpt. Aalen 1970.

Fowler 1947: Fowler, George Bingham, *Intellectual Interests of Engelbert of Admont*, New York 1947 [Studies in History, Economics and Public Law 530].

Frank 1956–1957: Frank, Istvàn, *Répertoire métrique de la poésie des troubadours*, 2 vols., Paris 1956–1957 [Bibliothèque de l'École des Hautes Études].

Frank 1984: Frank, Manfred, *Was ist Neostrukturalismus?*, Frankfurt a. M. 1984.

Frappier 1972: Frappier, Jean, "Le prologue du *Chevalier de la Charrette* et son interprétation," *Romania* 93 (1972), pp. 337–377.

Fridh 1988: Fridh, Åke, "Cassiodorus' Digression on Music, Var. II 40," *Eranos* 86 (1988), pp. 43–51.

Friedländer/Wissowa 1919–1921: Friedländer, Ludwig, Wissowa, Georg, *Darstellungen aus der Sittengeschichte Roms*, 4 vols., Leipzig 1919–1921.

Friedrich 1942: Friedrich, Hugo, *Die Rechtsmetaphysik der göttlichen Komödie. Francesca da Rimini*, Frankfurt a. M. 1942.

Friedrich 1964: Friedrich, Hugo, *Epochen der italienischen Lyrik*, Frankfurt a. M. 1964.

Fritz 1960: Fritz, Kurt von, *Mathematiker und Akusmatiker bei den alten Pythagoreern*, Munich 1960 [Sitzungsberichte der Bayerischen Akademie der Wissenschaften. Philosophisch-historische Klasse, Heft 11].

Fritz 2007: Fritz, Jochen, *Ruinen des Selbst. Autobiographisches Schreiben bei Augustinus, Rousseau und Proust*, Munich 2007 [Forum europäische Literatur 11].

Frobenius 1989: Frobenius, Wolf, "Die Zahlen der Timaios-Skala in der Musiktheorie des 14. Jahrhunderts," in *Kontinuität und Transformation der Antike im Mittelalter. Veröffentlichung der Kongreßakten zum Freiburger Symposion des Mediävistenverbandes*, ed. Willi Erzgräber, Sigmaringen 1989, pp. 245–260.

Fuchs 1962: Fuchs, Harald, "Enkyklios Paideia," in *Reallexikon Antike und Christentum. Sachwörterbuch zur Auseinandersetzung des Christentums mit der antiken Welt*, ed. Georg Schöllgen et al., Stuttgart 1950ff., vol. 5 (1962), col. 365–398.

Fuchs 1999: Fuchs, Peter, "Moderne Identität—im Blick auf das europäische Mittelalter," in *Identität und Moderne*, ed. Herbert Willems and Alois Hahn, Frankfurt a. M. 1999, pp. 273-297.

Fuller 1969: Fuller, Sarah, *Aquitanian Polyphony of the Eleventh and Twelfth Century*, Diss., Berkeley 1969.

Gadamer 1968: Gadamer, Hans-Georg, "Plato und die Dichter," in *Platos dialektische Ethik*, Hamburg 1968, pp. 181-204.

Gadamer 1975: Gadamer, Hans-Georg, *Wahrheit und Methode. Grundzüge einer philosophischen Hermeneutik*, Tübingen 1975.

Gagné 1967: Gagné, Jean, "Du quadrivium aux scientiae mediae," in *Arts libéraux et philosophie au moyen âge. Actes du quatrième congrès international de philosophie médiévale, Montréal 27 août–2 septembre 1967*, Montréal/Paris 1967, pp. 975-986.

Gaiser 1963: Gaiser, Konrad, *Platons ungeschriebene Lehre. Studien zur systematischen und geschichtlichen Begründung der Wissenschaften in der platonischen Schule*, Stuttgart 1963.

Gally 2000: Gally, Michèle, "Archéologie des arts poétiques français," *Nouvelle Revue du XVIe Siècle* 1 (2000), pp. 9-23.

Galonnier 1997: Galonnier, Alain, *Anecdoton Holderi ou Ordo generis Cassiodorum. Éléments pour une étude de l'authenticité Boécienne des "Opuscula sacra*," Louvain/Paris 1997 [Philosophes médiévaux 35].

Gannon 1965: Gannon, M. A. I., "The Active Theory of Sensation in St. Augustine," in *The New Scholasticism* 39 (1965), pp. 154-180.

Ganz 1990: Ganz, David, *Corbie in the Carolingian Renaissance*, Sigmaringen 1990 [Beihefte der Francia 20].

Gässler 1994: Gässler, Gregor Fidelis, *Der Ordo-Gedanke unter besonderer Berücksichtigung von Augustinus und Thomas von Aquino*, St. Augustin 1994 [Academia-Hochschulschriften 5].

Gatherole 1965: Gatherole, Patricia M., "Medieval Science: Evrart de Conty," in *Romance Notes* 6 (1965), pp. 175-181.

Geck 2001: Geck, Martin, *Bach. Leben und Werk*, Reinbek bei Hamburg 2001.

Geenen 1946: Geenen, G., "Saint Thomas d'Aquin," in *Dictionnaire de théologie catholique contenant l'exposé des doctrines de la théologie catholique, de leurs preuves et leur histoire*, ed. Alfred Vacant et al., 15 vols. in 30 fasc. and 15 supplements., Paris 1899-1950, vol. 15.1 (1946), col. 618-761.

Geerlings 1997: Geerlings, Wilhelm, "*Libri platonicorum*. Die philosophische Bildung Augustins," in *Platon in der abendländischen Geistesgeschichte. Neue Forschungen zum Platonismus*, ed. Theo Kobusch and Burkhard Mojsisch, Darmstadt 1997, pp. 60-70.

Gennrich 1932: Gennrich, Friedrich, *Grundriß einer Formenlehre des mittelalterlichen Liedes*, Halle 1932.

Georgiades 1958: Georgiades, Thrasybulos, *Musik und Rhythmus bei den Griechen. Zum Ursprung der abendländischen Musik*, Hamburg 1958 [Rowohlts deutsche Enzyklopädie 61].

Gérold 1973: Gérold, Théodore, *Les Pères de l'église et la musique*, Paris 1931, rpt. Geneva 1973.

Gersh 1986: Gersh, Stephen, *Middle Platonism and Neoplatonism: The Latin Tradition*, 2 vols., Notre Dame 1986 [Publications in mediaeval studies 23].

Geyer 1911: Geyer, Bernhard, "Radulphus Ardens und das *Speculum universale,*" *Theologische Quartalsschrift* 93 (1911), pp. 63–89.

Geyer 1917: Geyer, Bernhard, "Die alten lateinischen Übersetzungen der aristotelischen Analytik, Topik und Elenchik," *Philosophisches Jahrbuch* 30 (1917), pp. 37–40.

Gibson (ed.) 1981: *Boethius: His Life, Thought, and Influence*, ed. Margaret T. Gibson, Oxford 1981.

Gibson 1982: Gibson, Margaret T. "Boethius in the Carolingian Schools," *Transactions of the Royal Historical Society, 5th series*, 32 (1982), pp. 43–56.

Gibson/Smith (eds.) 1995: *Codices Boethiani: A Conspectus of Manuscripts of the Works of Boethius*, ed. Margaret T. Gibson and Lesley Smith, 3 vols., London/Turin 1995 [Warburg Institute Surveys and Texts 25, 27, 28].

Gieber 1982: Gieber, Robert L., "Poetic Elements of Rhythm in the Ballades, Rondeaux and Virelais of Guillaume de Machaut," *Romanic Review* 1 (1982), pp. 1–12.

Gilson 1928: Gilson, Étienne, "La cosmogonie de Bernardus Silvestris," *Archives d'histoire doctrinale et littéraire du Moyen-Âge* 3 (1928), pp. 5–24.

Gilson 1952: Gilson, Étienne, *La Philosophie au moyen âge. Des origines patristiques à la fin de XIVe siècle*, Paris 1952.

Glauche 1970: Glauche, Günter, *Schullektüre im Mittelalter. Entstehung und Wandlungen des Lektürekanons bis 1200 nach den Quellen dargestellt*, Munich 1970 [Münchener Beiträge zur Mediävistik und Renaissance-Forschung 5].

Glorieux 1968: Glorieux, Palémon, "L'enseignement au Moyen Âge. Techniques et méthodes en usage à la faculté de théologie de Paris, au XIIIe siècle," *Archives d'histoire doctrinale et littéraire du Moyen Âge* 43 (1968), pp. 65–186.

Glorieux 1971: Glorieux, Palémon, *La Faculté des Arts et ses maîtres au XIIIe siècle*, Paris 1971 [Études de philosophie médiévale 59].

Godefroy 1881–1902: Godefroy, Frédéric, *Dictionnaire de l'ancienne langue française et de tous ses dialectes du IXe au XVe siècle*, 10 vols., Paris 1881–1902.

Godman (ed.) 1985: *Poetry of the Carolingian Renaissance*, ed. Peter Godman, London 1985 [Duckworth Classical, Medieval and Renaissance Editions].

Godwin 1993: Godwin, Joscelyn, *The Harmony of the Spheres. A Sourcebook of the Pythagorean Tradition in Music*, Rochester 1993.

Göller 1959: Göller, Gottfried, "Vinzenz von Beauvais O. P. (um 1194–1264) und sein Musiktraktat im Speculum doctrinale," *Kölner Beiträge zur Musikforschung* XV (1959), pp. 86–118.

Göllner 1995: Göllner, Marie-Louise, "Interrelationships between Text and Music in the Refrain Form of Guillaume de Machaut," in *Songs of the Dove and* the *Nightingale: Sacred and Secular Music c. 900–c. 1600*, ed. Greta Mary Hair and Robyn E. Smith, Basel 1995, pp. 105–123.

Goldat 1957: Goldat, George D., *The Early Medieval Tradition of Euclid's Elements*, Diss., Wisconsin 1957.

Gordon 1989: Gordon, Alex L., "La Ressource du petit peuple (1481): Essai de pleine rhétorique," *Travaux de littérature* 2 (1989), pp. 55–67.

Goujet 1745: Goujet, Claude-Pierre, *Bibliothèque françoise ou histoire de la littérature françoise*, Paris 1745.

Grabmann 1928: Grabmann, Martin, *Mittelalterliche lateinische Aristotelesübersetzungen und Aristoteleskommentare in spanischen Bibliotheken*, Munich 1928.

Grabmann 1934: Grabmann, Martin, "Eine für Examinazwecke abgefaßte Quaestionensammlung der Pariser Artistenfakultät aus der ersten Hälfte des 13. Jahrhunderts," *Revue néoscolastique de philosophie* 36 (1934), pp. 211–229.

Grabmann 1939: Grabmann, Martin, *Methoden und Hilfsmittel des Aristotelesstudiums im Mittelalter*, Munich 1939.

Grabmann 1941: Grabmann, Martin, *I divieti ecclesiastici di Aristotele sotto Innocenzo III e Gregorio IX*, Rome 1941 [Miscellanea Historiae Pontificiae V.7].

Grabmann 1949: Grabmann, Martin, *Die Werke des hl. Thomas von Aquin*, Münster 1949.

Grabmann 1951: Grabmann, Martin, "Die geschichtliche Entwicklung der mittelalterlichen Sprachphilosophie und Sprachlogik im Überblick," in *Mélanges Joseph de Ghellinck*, 2 vols., Gembloux 1951 [Museum Lessianum. Section historique], vol. 2, pp. 421–433.

Grabmann 1956: Grabmann, Martin, *Geschichte der scholastischen Methode*, 2 vols., Freiburg 1909, rpt. Berlin 1956.

Grabmann 1961: Grabmann, Martin, *Die Geschichte der katholischen Theologie seit dem Ausgang der Väterzeit*, Darmstadt 1961.

Grabmann 1975: Grabmann, Martin, *Mittelalterliches Geistesleben. Zur Geschichte der Scholastik und Mystik*, 3 vols., Munich 1926, rpt. Hildesheim/New York 1975.

Grande 1930: Grande, Carlo del, "S. Agostina e la musica," *La Rassegna Musicale* 8 (1930), pp. 269–276.

Grebe 1993: Grebe, Sabine, "Die Musiktheorie des Martianus Capella. Eine Betrachtung der in 9, 921–935 benutzten Quellen," *International Journal of Musicology* 2 (1993), pp. 23–60.

Grebe 1999: Grebe, Sabine, *Martianus Capella "De nuptiis Philologiae et Mercurii." Darstellung der sieben freien Künste und ihrer Beziehungen zueinander*, Stuttgart/Leipzig 1999.

Greimas/Keane 2001: Greimas, Algirdas Julien, and Teresa Mary Keane, *Dictionnaire du moyen français*, Paris 2001.

Griffin 1999: Griffin, Robert, "Second rhetoric and the *grands rhétoriqueurs*," in *The Cambridge History of Literary Criticism*, ed. Peter Brooks and Hugh Barr

Nisbet, 9 vols., Cambridge/New York/Melbourne 1989–2001, vol. 3 (1999), ed. Glyn PP. Norton, pp. 155–160.

Gröber 1933: Gröber, Gustav, *Geschichte der mittelfranzösischen Literatur*, 2 vols., new, rev. ed. Stefan Hofer, Berlin/Leipzig 1933.

Gros 1981: Gros, Gérard, "De la *Ballade des pendus* à la *Complainte des trepasses* de Jean Molinet. Permanence d'un thème," *Senefiance* 10 (1981), pp. 315–335.

Grossmann 1954: Grossmann, Ursula, "Studien zur Zahlensymbolik des Frühmittelalters," *Zeitschrift für Katholische Theologie* 76 (1954), pp. 19–54.

Guichard-Tesson 1980: Guichard-Tesson, Françoise, *La Glose des échecs amoureux d'Évart de Conty. Les idées et le genre de l'oeuvre d'après le commentaire du Verger de Déduit*, Diss., Montréal 1980.

Guichard-Tesson 1983: Guichard-Tesson, Françoise, "Evrart de Conty, auteur de la *Glose des Échecs amoureux*," *Le Moyen Français* 8–9 (1983), pp. 111–148.

Guiette 1972: Guiette, Robert, *D'une poésie formelle en France au Moyen Âge*, Paris 1972.

Guilbert 1982: Guilbert, Sylvette, "Les écoles rurales en Champagne au XVe siècle. Enseignement et promotion sociale," *Annales de l'Est* 1–2 (1982), pp. 127–148.

Gumbrecht 1979: Gumbrecht, Hans Ulrich, " 'Gegenwart des Mittelalters'—eine Aufgabe kultureller Vermittlung und ein Problem wissenschaftlicher Forschung," *Lendemains* 16 (1979), pp. 3–10.

Gumbrecht 1983: Gumbrecht, Hans Ulrich, "Rekurs/Distanznahme/Revision. Klio bei den Philologen," in *Der Diskurs der Literatur- und Sprachhistorie. Wissenschaftsgeschichte als Innovationsvorgabe*, ed. Bernard Cerquiglini and Hans Ulrich Gumbrecht, Frankfurt a. M. 1983, pp. 556–622.

Gumbrecht 1988: Gumbrecht, Hans Ulrich, "Complexification des Structures du Savoir. Esquisse d'une Société Nouvelle à la Fin du Moyen Age," in *Grundriß der romanischen Literaturen des Mittelalters*, in collaboration with Jean Frappier et al., ed. Hans-Robert Jauß and Erich Köhler, 11. vols. in 30 fasc., Heidelberg 1968ff., vol. 8.1 (1988), ed. Daniel Poirion, pp. 20–28.

Gumbrecht 1995a: Gumbrecht, Hans Ulrich, "Stimme als Form. Zur Topik lyrischer Selbstinszenierung im 14. und 15. Jahrhundert," in *Musique naturele. Interpretationen zur französischen Lyrik des Spätmittelalters*, ed. Wolf-Dieter Stempel, Munich 1995 [Romanistisches Kolloquium 7], pp. 15–39.

Gumbrecht 1995b: Gumbrecht, Hans Ulrich, "Rhythmus und Sinn," in *Materialität der Kommunikation*, ed. Hans Ulrich Gumbrecht and K. Ludwig Pfeiffer, Frankfurt a. M. 1995, pp. 714–729.

Gundert 1971: Gundert, Hermann, *Dialog und Dialektik. Zur Struktur des platonischen Dialogs*, Amsterdam 1971.

Gurlitt 1944: Gurlitt, Willibald, "Musik und Rhetorik. Hinweise auf ihre geschichtliche Grundlageneinheit," *Helicon* 5 (1944), pp. 67–87.

Gushee 1969: Gushee, Laurence, "New Sources for the Biography of Johannes de Muris," *Journal of the American Musicological Society* 22 (1969), pp. 3–26.

Guy 1910: Guy, Henry, *Histoire de la poésie française au XVIe siècle, tome. I: L'École des Rhétoriqueurs*, Paris 1910.

Haas 1982: Haas, Max, "Studien zur mittelalterlichen Musiklehre I. Eine Übersicht über die Musiklehre im Kontext der Philosophie des 13. und frühen 14. Jahrhunderts," in *Aktuelle Fragen der musikbezogenen Mittelalterforschung. Texte zu einem Basler Kolloquium des Jahres 1975*, ed. Hans Oesch and Wulf Arlt, Winterthur 1982 [Forum Musicologicum. Basler Beiträge zur Musikgeschichte 3], pp. 323–456.

Haas 1984: Haas, Max, "Die Musiklehre im 13. Jahrhundert von Johannes de Garlandia bis Franco," in *Geschichte der Musiktheorie*, ed. Frieder Zaminer, 11 vols., Darmstadt 1984ff., vol. 5 (1984), ed. Hans Heinrich Eggebrecht et al., Darmstadt 1984, pp. 89–160.

Haas 1998: Haas, Max, "Die 'Musica Enchiriadis' und ihr Umfeld. Elementare Musiklehre als Propädeutik zur Philosophie," in *Musik und die Geschichte der Philosophie und Naturwissenschaften im Mittelalter. Fragen zur Wechselwirkung von "musica" und "philosophia" im Mittelalter*, ed. Frank Hentschel, Leiden/Boston/Cologne 1998 [Studien und Texte zur Geistesgeschichte des Mittelalters 62], pp. 207–226.

Haas 1999: Haas, Max, "Funktionen der *ars musica* im Mittelalter," in *Artes im Mittelalter*, ed. Ursula Schaefer, Berlin 1999, pp. 13–33.

Habel 1909: Habel, Edwin, "Johannes de Garlandia, ein Schulmann des 13. Jahrhunderts," *Mitteilungen der Gesellschaft für deutsche Erziehungs- und Schulgeschichte* 19 (1909), pp. 1–34.

Hackett (ed.) 1997: *Roger Bacon and the Sciences: Commemorative Essays*, ed. Jeremiah Hackett, Leiden/New York/Cologne 1997 [Studien und Texte zur Geistesgeschichte des Mittelalters 57].

Hadot 1977: Hadot, Pierre: "Die Metaphysik des Porphyrios," in *Die Philosophie des Neuplatonismus*, ed. Clemens Zintzen, Darmstadt 1977 [Wege der Forschung 186], pp. 208–237.

Hadot 1984: Hadot, Ilsetraut, *Arts libéraux et philosophie dans la pensée antique*, Paris 1984 [Études Augustiniennes].

Hafner 2002: Hafner, German, *Cassiodor. Ein Leben für kommende Zeiten*, Stuttgart 2002.

Halfwassen 2004: Halfwassen, Jens, *Plotin und der Neuplatonismus*, Munich 2004.

Hall 2002: Hall, Stuart George, "Typologie," in *Theologische Realenzyklopädie*, ed. Gerhard Krause and Gerhard Müller, 42 vols., Berlin/New York 1976–2006, vol. 34 (2002), pp. 208–224.

Hammerstein 1962: Hammerstein, Reinhold, *Die Musik der Engel. Untersuchungen zur Musikanschauung des Mittelalters*, Bern/Munich 1962.

Handschin 1927: Handschin, Jacques, "Die Musikanschauung des Johannes Scotus (Eriugena)," *Deutsche Vierteljahrsschrift für Literaturwissenschaft und Geistesgeschichte* 5 (1927), pp. 316–341.

Handschin 1950a: Handschin, Jacques, "The *Timaeus* Scale," *Musica disciplina* 4 (1950), pp. 3–42.

Handschin 1950b: Handschin, Jacques, "Eine alte Neumenschrift," *Acta musicologica* 22 (1950), pp. 69–97.

Handschin 1964: Handschin, Jacques, *Musikgeschichte im Überblick*, Luzern/Stuttgart 1964.

Häring 1964: Häring, Nikolaus M., "Thierry de Chartres and Dominicus Gundissalinus," *Medieval Studies* 26 (1964), pp. 271–286.

Harnack 1888: Harnack, Adolf von, *Augustins Confessionen. Ein Vortrag*, Gießen 1888.

Harrison 1963: Harrison, Frank J., "The Cajetan Tradition of Analogy," *Franciscan Studies* 23 (1963), pp. 197–204.

Harvey 1991: Harvey, Carol J., "Rime et raison, sens et folie (Trois poèmes anglo-normands du ms. Corpus Christi College 450)," *Le Moyen Français* 29 (1991), pp. 69–79.

Haug 1986: Haug, Walter, "Das Kugelspiel des Nicolaus Cusanus und die Poetik der Renaissance," *Daphnis* 2–3 (1986), pp. 357–374.

Haug 2007: Haug, Walter, "Gab es eine mittelalterliche Ästhetik aus platonischer Tradition?," in *Neuplatonismus und Ästhetik. Zur Transformationsgeschichte des Schönen*, ed. Verena Olejniczak Lobsien and Claudia Olk, Berlin/New York 2007 [Transformationen der Antike 2], pp. 19–42.

Heger 1967: Heger, Henrik, *Die Melancholie bei den französischen Lyrikern des Spätmittelalters*, Bonn 1967 [Romanistische Versuche und Vorarbeiten 21].

Heger 1988: Heger, Henrik, "La ballade et le chant royal," in *Grundriß der romanischen Literaturen des Mittelalters*, in collaboration with Jean Frappier et al., ed. Hans-Robert Jauß and Erich Köhler, 11. vols. in 30 fasc., Heidelberg 1968ff., vol. 8.1 (1988), ed. Daniel Poirion, pp. 59–69.

Heilmann 2007: Heilmann, Anja, *Boethius' Musiktheorie und das Quadrivium. Eine Einführung in den neuplatonischen Hintergrund von De institutione musica*, Göttingen 2007.

Heller 1939: Heller, Bruno, *Boethius im Lichte der frühmittelalterlichen Musiktheorie*, Diss., Vienna 1939.

Heller-Roazen 2010: Heller-Roazen, Daniel, "Le gai savoir des vers vieillis," in *Livres anciens, lectures vivantes*, ed. Michel Zink, Paris 2010, pp. 37–50.

Hellgardt 1973: Hellgardt, Ernst, *Zum Problem symbolbestimmter und formalästhetischer Zahlenkomposition in mittelalterlicher Literatur. Mit Studien zum Quadrivium und zur Vorgeschichte des mittelalterlichen Zahlendenkens*, Munich 1973.

Helmich 1976: Helmich, Werner, *Die Allegorie im französischen Theater des 15. und 16. Jahrhunderts*, Tübingen 1976 [Beihefte zur Zeitschrift für französische Philologie 156].

Hempfer 1983: Hempfer, Klaus W., "Überlegungen zu einem Gültigkeitskriterium für Interpretationen und ein komplexer Fall. Die italienische Ritterepik der Renaissance," in *Interpretation. Das Paradigma der europäischen Renaissance-Literatur. Festschrift für Alfred Noyer-Weidner zum 60. Geburtstag*, ed. Klaus W. Hempfer and Gerhard Regn, Wiesbaden 1983, pp. 1–31.

Hempfer 1987a: Hempfer, Klaus W., "Ernst und Spiel oder die Ambivalenz des Rittertums um 1500," *Romanische Forschungen* 99 (1987), pp. 348–374.

Hempfer 1987b: Hempfer, Klaus W., *Diskrepante Lektüren—Die "Orlando Furioso"—Rezeption im Cinquecento. Historische Rezeptionsforschung als Heuristik der Interpretation*, Stuttgart 1987 [Text und Kontext 2].

Hempfer 1993: Hempfer, Klaus W., "Probleme traditioneller Bestimmungen des Renaissancebegriffs und die epistemologische 'Wende,'" in *Renaissance—Diskursstrukturen und epistemologische Voraussetzungen. Literatur, Philosophie, bildende Kunst*, ed. Klaus W. Hempfer, Stuttgart 1993 [Text und Kontext 10], pp. 9–45.

Heninger 1974: Heninger, Simeon K., *Touches of Sweet Harmony: Pythagorean Cosmology and Renaissance Poetics*, San Marino CA 1974.

Henle 1956: Henle, Robert John, *Saint Thomas and Platonism: A Study of the Plato and Platonici Texts in the Writings of Saint Thomas*, The Hague 1956.

Henry 1934: Henry, Paul, *Plotin et l'Occident. Firmicus Maternus, Marius Victorinus, Saint Augustin et Macrobe*, Louvain 1934 [Spicilegium sacrum Lovaniense 15].

Hentschel 1994: Hentschel, Frank, "Sinnlichkeit und Vernunft in Augustins 'De musica,'" *Wissenschaft und Weisheit* 57/1 (1994), pp. 189–200.

Hentschel 2000: Hentschel, Frank, *Sinnlichkeit und Vernunft in der mittelalterlichen Musiktheorie. Strategien der Konsonanzwertung und der Gegenstand der musica sonora um 1300*, Stuttgart 2000 [Beihefte zum Archiv für Musikwissenschaft 47].

Herlinger 1981: Herlinger, Jan F., "A Fifteenth-Century Italian Compilation of Music Theory," *Acta Musicologica* 53 (1981), pp. 90–105.

Herlinger 1990: Herlinger, Jan F., "Marchetto's Influence: The Manuscript Evidence," in *Music Theory and Its Sources: Antiquity and the Middle Ages*, ed. André Barbera, Notre Dame 1990 [Notre Dame Conferences in Medieval Studies 1], pp. 235–258.

Herlinger 1993: Herlinger, Jan, "Marchetto the Pythagorean," *Ars nova italiana del Trecento* 6 (1993), pp. 369–386.

Herzog 1987: Herzog, Reinhart, "Veritas Fucata. Hermeneutik und Poetik in der Frührenaissance," in *Die Pluralität der Welten. Aspekte der Renaissance in der Romania*, ed. Wolf-Dieter Stempel and Karlheinz Stierle, Munich 1987 [Romanistisches Kolloquium 4], pp. 107–126.

Hirschmann 1999: Hirschmann, Wolfgang, "Das Kompositionskapitel als Modell poietischer Reflexion. Zur pragmatischen Transformation der ars musica in der Musiktheorie des Hoch- und Spätmittelalters," in *Artes im Mittelalter*, ed. Ursula Schaefer, Berlin 1999, pp. 174–186.

Hirschmann 2000: Hirschmann, Wolfgang, "Kritische Aktualisierung eines Modells. Der Musiktraktat des Johannes als 'imitatio' von Guidos 'Micrologus,'" in *Florilegien, Kompilationen, Kollektionen*, ed. Kaspar Elm, Wiesbaden 2000 [Wolfenbütteler Mittelalter-Studien 15], pp. 209–241.

Hirtler 1995: Hirtler, Eva, *Die Musik als scientia mathematica von der Spätantike bis zum Barock*, Frankfurt a. M. et al. 1995 [Europäische Hochschulschriften 36.137].

Höfler 1905: Höfler, Hans, *Les Échecs Amoureux. Untersuchung über die Quellen des II. Teils*, Diss., Munich 1905.

Hoepffner 1903: Hoepffner, Ernst, *Eustache Deschamps. Leben und Werk*, Straßburg 1903.

Hörmann 1965: Hörmann, Wolfgang, "Probleme einer Aldersbacher Handschrift (Clm 2599)," in *Buch und Welt. Festschrift Gustav Hofmann zum 65. Geburtstag dargebracht*, ed. Hans Striedl, Wiesbaden 1965, pp. 335–389.

Hoffmann 1931: Hoffmann, Wilhelm, *Philosophische Interpretation der Augustinusschrift De arte musica*, Marburg 1931.

Hofmeister 1931: Hofmeister, Adolf, "Die Überlieferung von Cassiodors 'Variae,'" *Historische Vierteljahrsschrift* 26 (1931), pp. 13–46.

Holzer 1890: Holzer, Ernst, *Varroniana. Wissenschaftliche Beilage zum Programm des Kgl. Gymnasiums in Ulm*, Ulm 1890.

Honnefelder 1987: Honnefelder, Ludger, "Der zweite Anfang der Metaphysik. Voraussetzungen, Ansätze und Folgen der Wiederbegründung der Metapysik im 13./14. Jahrhundert," in *Philosophie im Mittelalter. Entwicklungslinien und Paradigmen*, ed. Jan P. Beckmann et al., Hamburg 1987, pp. 165–186.

Honnefelder 1992: Honnefelder, Ludger, "Christliche Theologie als 'wahre Philosophie,'" in *Spätantike und Christentum. Beiträge zur Religions- und Geistesgeschichte der griechisch-römischen Kultur und Zivilisation der Kaiserzeit*, ed. Carsten Colpe, Ludger Honnefelder, and Matthias Lutz-Bachmann Berlin 1992, pp. 55–76.

Hopper 1938: Hopper, Vincent Foster, *Medieval Number Symbolism*, New York 1938 [Columbia University Studies in English and Comparative Literature 132].

Horn 1979: Horn, Hans-Jürgen, "Lügt die Kunst? Ein kunsttheoretischer Gedankengang des Augustinus," *Jahrbuch für Antike und Christentum* 22 (1979), pp. 50–60.

Horn 1994: Horn, Christoph, "Augustins Philosophie der Zahlen," *Revue des Études Augustiniennes* 40 (1994), pp. 389–415.

Horn 1995: Horn, Christoph, *Plotin über Sein, Zahl und Einheit. Eine Studie zu den systematischen Grundlagen der Enneaden*, Stuttgart/Leipzig 1995.

Hüe 2000: Hüe, Denis, "Le vers et le nombre. Notes sur quelques théories poétiques," *Nouvelle Revue du Seizième Siècle* 18/1 (2000), pp. 25–40.

Hüschen 1957: Hüschen, Heinrich, "Die Musik im Kreise der artes liberales," *Bericht über den internationalen musikwissenschaftlichen Kongreß, Hamburg 1956*, Kassel/Basel 1957, pp. 117–123.

Hüschen 1961: Hüschen, Heinrich, "Der Einfluß Isidors von Sevilla auf die Musikanschauung des Mittelalters," in *Miscelánea en homenaje a Monseñor Higinio Anglés*, 2 vols., Barcelona 1961, vol. 1, pp. 397–406.

Hüschen 1962: Hüschen, Heinrich, "Regino von Prüm, Historiker, Kirchenrechtler und Musiktheoretiker," in *Festschrift Karl Gustav Fellerer. Zum 60. Geburtstag am 07. Juli 1962 überreicht von Freunden und Schülern*, ed. Heinrich Hüschen, Regensburg 1962, pp. 205–223.

Hüschen 1970: Hüschen, Heinrich, "Albertus Magnus und seine Musikanschauung," in *Speculum musicae artis. Festgabe für Heinrich Husmann zum 60. Geburtstag*, ed. Heinz Becker and Reinhard Gerlach, Munich 1970, pp. 205–218.

Hüschen 2001a: Hüschen, Heinrich, "Aribo, Scholasticus," in *Die Musik in Geschichte und Gegenwart. Allgemeine Enzyklopädie der Musik*, ed. Friedrich Blume et al., digital version of the first ed. (1949–1986), Berlin 2001 [Digitale Bibliothek 60], s.v.

Hüschen 2001b: Hüschen, Heinrich, "Augustinus," in *Die Musik in Geschichte und Gegenwart. Allgemeine Enzyklopädie der Musik*, ed. Friedrich Blume et al., digital version of the first ed. (1949–1986), Berlin 2001 [Digitale Bibliothek 60], s.v.

Hüschen 2001c: Hüschen, Heinrich, "Cassiodorus," in *Die Musik in Geschichte und Gegenwart. Allgemeine Enzyklopädie der Musik*, ed. Friedrich Blume et al., digital version of the first ed., (1949–1986), Berlin 2001 [Digitale Bibliothek 60], s.v.

Hüschen 2001d: Hüschen, Heinrich, "Modus," in *Die Musik in Geschichte und Gegenwart. Allgemeine Enzyklopädie der Musik*, ed. Friedrich Blume et al., digital version of the first ed. (1949–1986), Berlin 2001 [Digitale Bibliothek 60], s.v.

Huffman 1988: Huffman, Carl A., "The Role of Number in Philolaus' Philosophy," *Phronesis* 33 (1988), pp. 1–30.

Huffman 2001: Huffman, Carl, "The Philolaic Method: The Pythagoreanism behind the Philebus," *Essays in Ancient Greek Philosophy VI: Before Plato*, ed. Anthony Preus, Albany 2001, pp. 67–85.

Huffman 2003: Huffman, Carl, "Philolaus," in *The Stanford Encyclopedia of Philosophy (Fall 2003 Edition)*, ed. Edward N. Zalta, http://plato.stanford.edu/archives/fall2003/entries/philolaus/.

Huglo 1971: Huglo, Michel, *Les Tonaires. Inventaire, analyse, comparaison*, Paris 1971 [Publications de la Société Française de Musicologie 3.2].

Huglo 1992: Huglo, Michel, "Le 'De musica' des Etymologies de Saint Isidore de Séville d'apres le manuscrit de Silos (Paris, B.N., Nouv. acq. lat. 2169)," *Revista de musicología* 15 (1992), pp. 565–578.

Huizinga 1939: Huizinga, Johan, *Herbst des Mittelalters. Studien über Lebens- und Geistesformen des 14. und 15. Jahrhunderts in Frankreich und in den Niederlanden*, trans. T. Wolff-Mönckeberg, Stuttgart 1939.

Hunt 1941–1950: Hunt, Richard W., "Studies in Priscian in the Eleventh and Twelfth Centuries," in *Medieval and Renaissance Studies* 1 (1941), pp. 194–231 and 2 (1950), pp. 1–56.

Hunt 1948: Hunt, Richard W., "The Introduction to the 'Artes' in the Twelfth Century," in *Studia Mediaevalia in honorem admodum Reverend Patris Raymundi Josephi Martin*, Bruges 1948, pp. 85–112.

Huot 1982: Huot, Sylvia, *Lyric Poetics and the Art of Compilatio in the Forteenth Century*, Diss., Cambridge 1982.

Huot 1987: Huot, Sylvia, *From Song to Book: The Poetics of Writing in the Old French Lyric and Lyrical Narrative Poetry*, Ithaca/London 1987.

Huré 1924: Huré, Jean, *Saint Augustin musicien. D'après le De musica et différentes pages, de ses œuvres, consacrées à la musique*, Paris 1924.

Hyatte 1982: Hyatte, Reginald L., "The Manuscripts of the Prose Commentary (Fifteenth Century) on *Les Echecs Amoureux*," *Manuscripta* 26 (1982), pp. 24–30.

Illmer 1971: Illmer, Detlef, *Formen der Erziehung und Wissensvermittlung im frühen Mittelalter. Quellenstudien zur Frage der Kontinuität des abendländischen Erziehungswesens*, Munich 1971 [Municher Beiträge zur Mediävistik und Renaissance-Forschung 7].

Illmer 1984: Illmer, Detlef, "Arithmetik in der gelehrten Arbeitsweise des frühen Mittelalters. Eine Studie zum Grundsatz 'Nisi enim nomen scieris, cognitio rerum perit,' " in *Institutionen, Kultur und Gesellschaft im Mittelalter. Festschrift für Josef Fleckenstein zu seinem 65. Geburtstag*, ed. Lutz Fenske et al., Sigmaringen 1984, pp. 35–58.

Illmer 1990: Illmer, Detlef, "Die Zahlenlehre des Boethius," in *Geschichte der Musiktheorie*, ed. Frieder Zaminer, 10 vols., Darmstadt 1984ff., vol. 3 (1990), ed. Michael Bernhard, pp. 219–252.

Ilnitchi 1997: Ilnitchi, Gabriela, *Aribo's "De musica": Music Theory in the Cross-Current of Medieval Learning*, Diss., New York 1997.

Ingenschay 1980: Ingenschay, Dieter, "Pragmatische Form und lyrische Besetzung—Zur Konstitution von Ballade und Testament bei Deschamps und besonders Villon," in *Literatur in der Gesellschaft des Spätmittelalters*, ed. Hans Ulrich Gumbrecht, Heidelberg 1980 [Begleitreihe zum Grundriß der romanischen Literaturen des Mittelalters 1], pp. 169–190.

Ingenschay 1982: Ingenschay, Dieter, "La rhétorique et le 'monde quotidien' chez Eustache Deschamps," in *Du mot au texte. Actes du IIIe Colloque International sur le Moyen Francais, Düsseldorf, 17–19 septembre 1980*, ed. Peter Wunderli, Tübingen 1982, pp. 253–261.

Ingenschay 1986: Ingenschay, Dieter, *Alltagswelt und Selbsterfahrung. Ballade und Testament bei Deschamps und Villon*, Munich 1986 [Theorie und Geschichte der Literatur und der schönen Künste. Reihe B: Funktion, Wirkung, Rezeption 5].

Irwin 1982: Irwin, Eleanor, "The Songs of Orpheus and the New Song of Christ," in *Orpheus: Metamorphoses of a Myth*, ed. John Warden, Toronto/Buffalo/London 1982, pp. 51–62.

Ivánka 1964: Ivánka, Endre von, *Plato Christianus. Übernahme und Umgestaltung des Platonismus durch die Väter*, Einsiedeln 1964.

Iverson 1980: Iverson, Gunilla, *Tropes de l'Agnus Dei*, Stockholm 1980 [Corpus Troporum IV].

Jackson 1962: Jackson, William T. H., *The Literature of the Middle Ages*, New York/London 1962.

Jakobson 1979: Jakobson, Roman, "Linguistik und Poetik," in *Poetik. Ausgewählte Aufsätze 1921–1971*, ed. Elmar Holenstein and Tarcisius Schelbert, Frankfurt a. M. 1979, pp. 83–121.

Jakobson/Pomorska 1982: Jakobson, Roman, and Krystyna Pomorska, "Die Zeit als Faktor in Sprache und Literatur," in *Poesie und Grammatik. Dialoge*, Frankfurt a. M. 1982, pp. 53–72.

James 1984: James, Laurence, "'L'objet poétique' des Grands rhétoriqueurs," *Annales de la faculté des lettres et sciences humaines de Nice* 48 (1984), pp. 225–234.

Jarry 1873: Jarry, L., *La Librairie de l'Université d'Orléans*, Orléans 1873.

Jauß 1960: Jauß, Hans Robert, "Form und Auffassung der Allegorie in der Tradition der Psychomachia (von Prudentius bis zum ersten Roman de la Rose)," in *Medium aevum vivum. Festschrift für Walther Bulst*, ed. Hans Robert Jauß and Dieter Schaller, Heidelberg 1960, pp. 179–206.

Jauß 1970: Jauß, Hans Robert, "Geschichte der Kunst und Historie," in *Literaturgeschichte als Provokation*, Frankfurt a. M. 1970, pp. 208–251.

Jauß 1977a: Jauß, Hans Robert, "Alterität und Modernität der mittelalterlichen Dichtung," in *Alterität und Modernität der mittelalterlichen Dichtung. Gesammelte Aufsätze 1956–1976*, Munich 1977, pp. 9–47.

Jauß 1977b: Jauß, Hans Robert, "Die klassische und die christliche Rechtfertigung des Häßlichen in mittelalterlicher Literatur," in *Alterität und Modernität der mittelalterlichen Dichtung. Gesammelte Aufsätze 1956–1976*, Munich 1977, pp. 385–410.

Jauß 1994a: Jauß, Hans Robert, "Brief an Paul de Man," in *Wege des Verstehens*, Munich 1994, pp. 296–303.

Jauß 1994b: Jauß, Hans Robert, "Alter Wein in neuen Schläuchen?," in *Wege des Verstehens*, Munich 1994, pp. 304–323.

Jauß 1994c: Jauß, Hans Robert, "Salzburger Gespräch über musikalische und literarische Hermeneutik," in *Wege des Verstehens*, Munich 1994, pp. 378–401.

Jeauneau 1954: Jeauneau, Edouard, "Le Prologus in Eptateuchon de Thierry de Chartres," *Medieval Studies* 16 (1954), pp. 171–175.

Jeauneau 1960: Jeauneau, Edouard, "Gloses de Guillaume de Conches sur Macrobe. Note sur les manuscrits," *Archives d'histoire doctrinale et littéraire du moyen âge* 35 (1960), pp. 17–28.

Jeauneau 1973: Jeauneau, Edouard, *Lectio philosophorum. Recherches sur l'école de Chartres*, Amsterdam 1973.

Jeay 1985: Jeay, Madeleine, "La mythologie comme clé de mémorisation. La

Glose des Echecs amoureux," in *Jeux de mémoire. Aspects de la mnémotechnie médiévale*, ed. Bruno Roy and Paul Zumthor, Montréal/Paris 1985, pp. 157–166.

Jewers 1998: Jewers, Caroline A., "L'Art de musique et le gai sentiment: Guillaume de Machaut, Eustache Deschamps and the Medieval Poetic Tradition," in *Eustache Deschamps, French Courtier Poet: His Works and His World*, ed. Deborah M. Sinnreich-Levi, New York 1998 [AMS Studies in the Middle Ages 22], pp. 163–180.

Jodogne 1970: Jodogne, Pierre: "Les 'rhétoriqueurs' et l'humanisme: Problème d'histoire littéraire," in *Humanism in France at the end of the Middle Ages and in the early Renaissance*, ed. A. H. T. Levi, Manchester/New York 1970, pp. 150–175.

Johnson 1990: Johnson, Leonard W., *Poets as Players: Theme and Variation in Late Medieval French Poetry*, Stanford 1990.

Jolivet 1980: Jolivet, Jean, "Remarques sur les *Regulae Theologicae* d'Alain de Lille," in *Alain de Lille, Gautier de Châtillon, Jakemart Giélée et leur temps*, ed. Henri Roussel and François Suard, Lille 1980, pp. 83–99.

Jonsson/Treitler 1983: Jonsson, Ritva, and Leo Treitler, "Medieval Music and Language: A Reconsideration of the Relationship," *Studies in the History of Music* 1 (1983), pp. 1–23.

Jullien de Pommerolle 1978: Jullien de Pommerolle and Marie-Henriette, *Sources de l'histoire des universités françaises au Moyen Âge 1. L'Université d'Orléans*, Paris 1978.

Jung 1971: Jung, Marc-René, "Poetria. Zur Dichtungstheorie des ausgehenden Mittelalters in Frankreich," *Vox romanica* 30 (1971), pp. 44–64.

Jung 2001: Jung, Marc-René, "Les plus anciennes ballades de Machaut et la tradition antérieure de la ballade. Aspects métriques," in *Épopée, lyrique, roman. Mélanges offerts à Madeleine Tyssens*, ed. Nadine Henrard, Paolo Moreno, and Martine Thiry-Stassins, Brussels 2001, pp. 287–297.

Junker 1886–1887: Junker, H. P., "Les Échecs Amoureux," *Berichte des Freien Deutschen Hochstifts zu Frankfurt a. M.* 2 (1886/1887), pp. 28–39.

Kamlah 1951: Kamlah, Wilhelm, *Christentum und Geschichtlichkeit. Untersuchungen zur Entstehung des Christentums und zu Augustins "Bürgerschaft Gottes,"* 2nd rev. ed., Stuttgart/Cologne 1951.

Kapp 1965: Kapp, Ernst, *Der Ursprung der Logik bei den Griechen*, Göttingen 1965.

Kaylor 1992: Kaylor, Noel H., *The Medieval "Consolation of Philosophy": An Annotated Bibliography*, New York 1992 [Garland Reference Library of the Humanities 1215. Garland medieval bibliographies 7].

Keller 1993: Keller, Adalbert, *Aurelius Augustinus und die Musik. Untersuchungen zu "De musica" im Kontext seines Schrifttums*, Würzburg 1993 [Cassiciacum 44].

Kelly 1966: Kelly, Douglas, "The Scope of the Treatment of Composition in the

Twelfth- and Thirteenth-Century Arts of Poetry," *Speculum* 41 (1966), pp. 262–278.

Kelly 1978: Kelly, Douglas, *Medieval Imagination: Rhetoric and Poetry of Courtly Love*, Madison/London 1978.

Kendrick 1983: Kendrick, Laura, "Rhetoric and the Rise of Public Poetry: The Career of Eustache Deschamps," *Studies in Philology* 80.1 (1983), pp. 1–13.

Kertelge 1987: Kertelge, Karl, " 'Natürliche Theologie' und Rechtfertigung aus dem Glauben bei Paulus," in *Weisheit Gottes—Weisheit der Welt. Festschrift für Joseph Ratzinger zum 60. Geburtstag*, ed. Walter Baier, St. Ottilien 1987, pp. 83–95.

Kibre 1969: Kibre, Pearl, "The Quadrivium in the Thirteenth Century Universities (With Special Reference to Paris)," in *Arts libéraux et philosophie au moyen âge. Actes du quatrième congrès international de philosophie médiévale, Montréal 27 août–2 septembre 1967*, Montréal/Paris 1969, pp. 175–191.

Kibre 1981: Kibre, Pearl, "The Boethian *De institutione arithmetica* and the Quadrivium in the Thirteenth-Century University Milieu at Paris," in *Boethius and the Liberal Arts: A Collection of Essays*, ed. Mario Masi, Bern et al. 1981 [Utah Studies in Literature and Linguistics 18], pp. 67–80.

Klaus 1971: Klaus, Georg, *Wörterbuch der Kybernetik*, 2 vols., Frankfurt a. M. 1971.

Klein 1936: Klein, Jacob, *Die griechische Logistik und die Entstehung der Algebra*, Berlin 1936 [Quellen und Studien zur Geschichte der Mathematik, Astronomie und Physik. Abt. B: Studien, 3].

Klinger 1964: Klinger, Ingbert, *Das Problem der Individuationslehre bei Thomas von Aquin. Versuch einer Interpretation und Vergleich mit zwei umstrittenen Opuscula*, Muensterschwarzach 1964 [Muensterschwarzacher Studien 2].

Klopsch 1972: Klopsch, Paul, *Einführung in die mittellateinischen Verslehren*, Darmstadt 1972.

Klopsch 1980: Klopsch, Paul, *Einführung in die Dichtungslehren des lateinischen Mittelalters*, Darmstadt 1980 [Das lateinische Mittelalter. Einführungen in Gegenstand und Ergebnisse seiner Teilgebiete und Nachbarwissenschaften].

Klopsch (ed.) 1985: *Lateinische Lyrik des Mittelalters*, ed. Paul Klopsch, Stuttgart 1985.

Kluxen 1971: Kluxen, Wolfgang: "Analogie," in *Historisches Wörterbuch der Philosophie. Völlig neubearbeitete Ausgabe des "Wörterbuchs der philosophischen Begriffe" von Rudolf Eisler*, ed. Joachim Ritter, 9 vols., Basel 1971–1995, vol. 1 (1971), col. 214–227.

Knight 1948: Knight, William F. J., *Saint Augustine's De musica: A Synopsis*, London 1948.

Koch 1931: Koch, Josef, "Zur Ästhetik des Thomas von Aquin," *Zeitschrift für allgemeine Ästhetik und Kunstwissenschaft* 25 (1931), pp. 267–271.

Koch 1951: Koch, Herbert, *Vom Nachleben des Vitruv*, Baden-Baden 1951 [Deutsche Beiträge zur Altertumswissenschaft 1].

Koch 1983: Koch, Walter A., *Poetry and Science: Semiogenetical Twins; Towards an Integrated Correspondence Theory of Poetic Structures*, Tübingen 1983.

Köhler 1953: Köhler, Erich, "Scholastische Ästhetik und höfische Dichtung," *Neophilologus* 37.1 (1953), pp. 202–207.

Köhler 1956: Köhler, Erich, *Ideal und Wirklichkeit in der höfischen Epik. Studien zur Form der frühen Artus- und Graldichtung*, Tübingen 1956 [Beihefte zur Zeitschrift für romanische Philologie 97].

König 1970: König, Eckard, *Augustinus Philosophus. Christlicher Glauben und philosophisches Denken in den Frühschriften des Augustinus*, Munich 1970 [Studia et Testimonia Antiqua 11].

Köpf 1974: Köpf, Ulrich, *Die Anfänge der theologischen Wissenschaftstheorie im 13. Jahrhundert*, Tübingen 1974 [Beiträge zur historischen Theologie 49].

Körting 1871: Körting, Gustav, *Altfranzösische Übersetzung der "Remedia amoris" des Ovid (ein Theil des allegorisch-didactischen Epos "Les Echecs amoureux")*, Leipzig 1871.

Koller 1954–1955: Koller, Hermann, "Enkuklios paideia," *Glotta* 34 (1954–1955), pp. 174–189.

Koller 1955: Koller, Hermann, "Stoicheon," *Glotta* 3/4 (1955), pp. 6–24.

Koller 1958: Koller, Hermann, "Die Anfänge der griechischen Grammatik," *Glotta* 1/2 (1958), pp. 5–40.

Koller 1960: Koller, Hermann, "Die dihäretische Methode," *Glotta* 1/2 (1960), pp. 6–24.

Koller 1962: Koller, Hermann, *Musik und Dichtung im alten Griechenland*, Bern 1962.

Kooijman 1982: Kooijman, Jacques, "Une étrange duplicité. La double ballade au bas moyen âge," in *Le génie de la forme. Mélange de langue et littérature offerts à Jean Mourot*, Nancy 1982, pp. 41–49.

Koselleck 1989: Koselleck, Reinhart, "Geschichte, Geschichten und formale Zeitstrukturen," in *Vergangene Zukunft. Zur Semantik geschichtlicher Zeiten*, Frankfurt a. M. 1989, pp. 130–143.

Kovach 1961: Kovach, Francis J., *Die Ästhetik des Thomas von Aquin. Eine genetische und systematische Analyse*, Berlin 1961.

Kranz 2005: Kranz, Dirk Kurt, "Boethius, Anitius Manlius Severinus," in *Biographisch-Bibliographisches Kirchenlexikon*, ed. Traugott Bautz, 28 vols., Hamm/Herzberg 1975–2007, vol. 24 (2005), col. 259–310.

Kremer 1966: Kremer, Klaus, *Die neuplatonische Seinsphilosophie und ihre Wirkung auf Thomas von Aquin*, Leiden 1966 [Studien zur Problemgeschichte der antiken und mittelalterlichen Philosophie 1].

Kreps 1948: Kreps, Joseph, "Aribon de Liège. Une légende," *Revue belge de musicologie* 2 (1948), pp. 138–143.

Kresteff 1962: Kresteff, Assen D., "Musica Disciplina and Musica Sonora," *Journal of Research in Music Education* 10 (1962), pp. 13–29.

Kreyszig 1993: Kreyszig, Walter Kurt, "Franchino Gaffurio als Vermittler der Musiklehre des Altertums und des Mittelalters. Zur Identifizierung griechischer und lateinischer Quellen in der *Theorica musice* (1492)," *Acta musicologica* 2 (1993), pp. 134–150.

Krings 1941: Krings, Hermann, *Ordo. Philosophisch-historische Grundlegung einer abendländischen Idee*, Halle 1941.

Kris/Kurz 1987: Kris, Ernst, and Otto Kurz, *L'Image de l'artiste. Légende, mythe et magie*, trans. M. Hechter, Paris 1987.

Kristeva 1969: Kristeva, Julia, "Le Texte clos," in Σημειωτική: *Recherches pour une sémanalyse*, Paris 1969, pp. 113–142.

Kristeva 1974: Kristeva, Julia, *La Révolution du langage poétique. L'avant-garde à la fin du XIXe siècle. Lautréamont et Mallarmé*, Paris 1974.

Kühnert 1961: Kühnert, Friedmar, *Allgemeinbildung und Fachbildung in der Antike*, Berlin 1961 [Schriften der Sektion für Altertumswissenschaft 30].

Kümmel 1977: Kümmel, Werner Friedrich, *Musik und Medizin. Ihre Wechselbeziehung zwischen Theorie und Praxis von 800–1800*, Freiburg i.Br./Munich 1977 [Freiburger Beiträge zur Wissenschafts-und Universitätsgeschichte 2].

Küper 1988: Küper, Christoph, *Sprache und Metrum. Semiotik und Linguistik des Verses*, Tübingen 1988.

Küpper 1989: Küpper, Joachim, *Diskurs-Renovatio bei Lope de Vega und Calderón. Mit einer Skizze zur Evolution der Diskurse in Mittelalter, Renaissance und Manierismus*, Tübingen 1989 [Romanica Monacensia 32].

Küpper 1999: Küpper, Joachim, "(H)ER(E)OS. Petrarcas Canzoniere und der medizinische Diskurs seiner Zeit (Mit einer Nachbemerkung zur Kontingenz des Entstehens von Texten epochalen Rangs)," *Romanische Forschungen* 2 (1999), pp. 178–224.

Küpper 2002a: Küpper, Joachim, "Grenzen der Horizontverschmelzung. Überlegungen zu Hermeneutik und Archäologie," in *Poetologische Umbrüche. Romanistische Studien zu Ehren von Ulrich Schulz-Buschhaus*, ed. Werner Helmich, Helmut Meter and Astrid Poier-Bernhard, Munich 2002, pp. 428–451.

Küpper 2002b: Küpper, Joachim, "Uti und frui bei Augustinus und die Problematik des Genießens in der ästhetischen Theorie des Okzidents," in *Genuß und Egoismus. Zur Kritik ihrer geschichtlichen Verknüpfung*, ed. Wolfgang Klein and Ernst Müller, Berlin 2002, pp. 3–29.

Küpper 2007: Küpper, Joachim, "Zu einigen Aspekten der Dichtungstheorie in der Frührenaissance," in *Renaissance—Episteme und Agon. Für Klaus W. Hempfer anläßlich seines 60. Geburtstages*, ed. Andreas Kablitz and Gerhard Regn, Heidelberg 2007, pp. 47–72.

Kuhn 1976: Kuhn, Thomas P., *Die Struktur wissenschaftlicher Revolutionen*, Frankfurt a. M., 1976.

Kuhn 1977: Kuhn, Karl Georg, "Zur Geschichte des Reims," in *Die Genese der europäischen Endreimdichtung*, ed. Ulrich Ernst and Peter-Erich Neuser, Darmstadt 1977 [Wege der Forschung 144], pp. 22–33.

Kuhn 1980: Kuhn, Hugo, "Versuch über das fünfzehnte Jahrhundert in der deutschen Literatur," in *Literatur in der Gesellschaft des Spätmittelalters*, ed.

Hans Ulrich Gumbrecht, Heidelberg 1980 [Begleitreihe zum Grundriß der romanischen Literaturen des Mittelalters 1], pp. 19–38.

Kunz 1955: Kunz, L., "Beda über reinrhythmische und gemischtrhythmische Liedtexte," *Kirchenmusikalisches Jahrbuch* 39 (1955), pp. 3–9.

Lacassagne 1994: Lacassagne, Miren, *Eustache Deschamps. Discours et société*, Diss., St. Louis 1994.

Lacassagne 1998: Lacassagne, Miren, "*L'Art de dictier*: Poetics of a 'New' Time," in *Eustache Deschamps, French Courtier Poet: His Works and His World*, ed. Deborah M. Sinnreich-Levi, New York 1998 [AMS Studies in the Middle Ages 22], pp. 181–193.

Lafleur 1988: Lafleur, Claude, *Quatre introductions à la philosophie au XIIIe siècle*, Montréal 1988 [Publications de l'Institut d'Études Médiévales 23].

Lambert 2003: Lambert, Michael, "Nouveaux éléments pour une étude des *Opuscula sacra* de Boèce," in *Boèce ou la Chaîne des Savoirs*, ed. Alain Galonnier, Louvain/Paris/Dudley 2003 [Philosophes médiévaux XLIV], pp. 171–192.

Lamprecht 1974: Lamprecht, Karl Gotthart, "Über Individualität und Verständnis für dieselbe im deutschen Mittelalter," in *Ausgewählte Schriften zur Wirtschafts- und Kulturgeschichte und zur Theorie der Geschichtswissenschaft*, ed. Herbert Schönebaum, Aalen 1974, pp. 21–66.

Langosch 1970: Langosch, Karl, "Komposition und Zahlensymbolik in der mittellateinischen Dichtung," in *Methoden in Wissenschaft und Kunst des Mittelalters*, ed. Albert Zimmermann, Berlin 1970 [Miscellanea Mediaevalia. Veröffentlichungen des Thomas-Instituts zu Köln 7], pp. 106–151.

Lanoue 1981: Lanoue, David G., *Musical Imagery in the Poetry of Juan Ruiz, Guillaume de Machaut, and Chaucer: A Comparative Study*, Diss., Lincoln 1981.

Lassabatère 1994: Lassabatère, Thierry, *La Politique selon Eustache Deschamps. Sources, thèmes, diffusion*, Mémoire de DEA, Paris 1994.

Laurie 1962: Laurie, Ian P., *Eustache Deschamps: His Life and His Contribution to the Development of the Rondeau, the Virelai, and the Ballade*, Diss., Cambridge 1962.

Laurie 1964: Laurie, Ian S., "Deschamps and the Lyric as Natural Music," *Modern Language Review* 59 (1964), pp. 561–570.

Lausberg 1955: Lausberg, Heinrich, "Zur altfranzösischen Metrik," *Archiv für das Studium der neueren Sprachen* 191 (1955), pp. 183–217.

Law 1984: Law, V., "St. Augustine's *De grammatica*: Lost or Found?," *Recherches Augustiniennes* 19 (1984), pp. 155–183.

Leach (ed.) 2003: Leach, Elizabeth Eva (ed.), *Machaut's Music: New Interpretations*, Woodbridge 2003.

Leach 2009: Leach, Elizabeth Eva, *Sung Birds: Music, Nature, and Poetry in the Later Middle Ages*, Ithaca/London 2009.

Le Bœuf 1986a: Le Bœuf, Patrick, *La tradition manuscrite du "De musica" de*

Saint Augustin (et son influence sur la pensée et l'esthétique médiévale), 4 vols., thèse pour le diplôme d'archiviste-paléographe, École Nationale des Chartes, Paris 1986.

Le Bœuf 1986b: Le Bœuf, Patrick, "Un commentaire d'inspiration érigénienne du 'De musica' de Saint Augustin," *Recherches Augustiniennes* 21 (1986), pp. 243–316.

Lecoy 1968: Lecoy, F., [Reply to Rychner 1967], *Romania* 89 (1968), pp. 571–573.

Lehmann 1959: Lehmann, Paul, "Die Institutio oratoria des Quintilianus im Mittelalter," in *Erforschung des Mittelalters. Ausgewählte Abhandlungen und Aufsätze*, 5 vols., Leipzig/Stutttgart 1941–1962, vol. 2 (1959), pp. 1–28.

Leinsle 1995: Leinsle, Ulrich G., *Einführung in die scholastische Theologie*, Paderborn et al. 1995 [UTB 1865].

LeMoine 1972: LeMoine, Fanny, *Martianus Capella: A Literary Reevaluation*, Munich 1972 [Münchener Beiträge zur Mediävistik und Renaissance-Forschung 10].

León Tello 1952: León Tello, Francisco J., "La teoria de la musica en las obras de San Isidoro," *Música* 1–2 (1952), pp. 11–28.

Leonardi 1959: Leonardi, Claudio, "I codici di Marziano Capella," *Aevum* 33 (1959), pp. 443–489.

Leonardi 1960: Leonardi, Claudio, "I codici di Marziano Capella," *Aevum* 34 (1960), pp. 1–99, 411–524.

Lértora-Mendoza 1989: Lértora-Mendoza, Celine A., "Roger Bacon. Sus ideas exegéticas," *Naturaleza y gracia* 26.2 (1989), pp. 195–372.

Lieberknecht 1999: Lieberknecht, Otfried, *Allegorese und Philologie—Überlegungen zum Problem des vierfachen Schriftsinns in Dantes "Commedia,"* Stuttgart 1999 [Text und Kontext 14].

Lilla 1990: Lilla, Salvatore, "Die Lehre von den Ideen als den Gedanken Gottes im griechischen patristischen Denken," in *EPMHNEYMATA. Festschrift für Hadwig Hörner zum sechzigsten Geburtstag*, ed. Herbert Eisenberger, Heidelberg 1990, pp. 27–50.

Lippmann 1963: Lippmann, Edward A., "Hellenic Conceptions of Harmony," *Journal of the American Musicological Society* 1 (1963), pp. 3–35.

Lloyd 1979: Lloyd, Geoffrey E. R., *Magic, Reason, and Experience: Studies in the Origin and Development of Greek Science*, Cambridge 1979.

Lohmann 1970a: Lohmann, Johannes, "Musiké und Logos," in *Musiké und Logos. Aufsätze zur griechischen Philosophie und Musiktheorie. Zum 75. Geburtstag des Verfassers am 9. Juli 1970*, ed. Anastasios Giannarás, Stuttgart 1970, pp. 1–16.

Lohmann 1970b: Lohmann, Johannes, "Die griechische Musik als mathematische Form," in *Musiké und Logos. Aufsätze zur griechischen Philosophie und Musiktheorie. Zum 75. Geburtstag des Verfassers am 9. Juli 1970*, ed. Anastasios Giannarás, Stuttgart 1970, pp. 17–26.

Lohmann 1970c: Lohmann, Johannes, "Der Ursprung der Musik," in *Musiké* und *Logos. Aufsätze zur griechischen Philosophie und Musiktheorie. Zum 75. Geburtstag des Verfassers am 9. Juli 1970*, ed. Anastasios Giannarás, Stuttgart 1970, pp. 77–88.

Lohmann 1970d: Lohmann, Johannes: "Mythos und Logos," in *Musiké und Logos. Aufsätze zur griechischen Philosophie und Musiktheorie. Zum 75. Geburtstag des Verfassers am 9. Juli 1970*, ed. Anastasios Giannarás, Stuttgart 1970, pp. 105–113.

Lote 1949: Lote, Georges, "Quelques remarques sur L'Art de dictier d'Eustache Deschamps," in *Mélanges de philologie romane et de littérature médiévale offerts à Ernest Hoepffner*, Strasbourg 1949, pp. 361–367.

Lote 1949–1955: Lote, Georges, *Histoire du vers français. Partie I. Le moyen âge*, 3 vols., Paris 1949–1955.

Lotman 1972: Lotman, Juriij M., *Die Struktur literarischer Texte*, Munich 1972 [UTB 103].

Löwe 1948: Löwe, Heinz, "Cassiodor," *Romanische Forschungen* 60 (1948), pp. 420–446.

Lubac 1959–1964: Lubac, Henri de, *Exégèse médiévale. Les quatre Sens de l'Écriture*, 4 vols., Paris 1959–1964 [Théologie 41.1, 41.2, 42, 59].

Lubienski-Bodenham 1979: Lubienski-Bodenham, H., "The Origins of the Fifteenth Century View of Poetry as 'seconde rhétorique,'" *Modern Language Review* 74 (1979), pp. 26–38.

Ludwig 1967: Ludwig, Günter, *Cassiodor. Über den Ursprung der abendländischen Schule*, Frankfurt a. M. 1967.

Lütcke 1968: Lütcke, Karl-Heinrich, *"Auctoritas" bei Augustin*, Stuttgart 1968 [Tübinger Beiträge zur Altertumswissenschaft 44].

Luhmann 1993a: Luhmann, Niklas, "Gesellschaftliche Struktur und semantische Tradition," in *Gesellschaftsstruktur und Semantik. Studien zur Wissenssoziologie der modernen Gesellschaft Band 1*, Frankfurt a. M. 1993, pp. 9–70.

Luhmann 1993b: Luhmann, Niklas, "Individuum, Individualität, Individualismus," in *Gesellschaftsstruktur und Semantik. Studien zur Wissenssoziologie der modernen Gesellschaft Band 3*, Frankfurt a. M. 1993, pp. 149–258.

Lukitsch 1983: Lukitsch, Shirley, "The Poetics of the *Prologue*: Machaut's Conception of the Purpose of his Art," *Medium Aevum* 52 (1983), pp. 258–271.

Lutz 1956: Lutz, Cora E., "Remigius' Ideas on the Classification of the Seven Liberal Arts," *Traditio* 12 (1956), pp. 65–86.

Lutz 1971: Lutz, Cora E.: "Martianus Capella," in *Catalogus translationum et commentariorum: Mediaeval and Renaissance Translations and Commentaries. Annotated Lists and Guides*, ed. Paul Oskar Kristeller and Virginia Brown, 8 vols., Washington, DC, 1960ff., vol. 2 (1971), pp. 367–381.

Lutz-Bachmann 1992: Lutz-Bachmann, Matthias, "Hellenisierung des Christentums," in *Spätantike und Christentum. Beiträge zur Religions- und Geistesgeschichte der griechisch-römischen Kultur und Zivilisation der Kaiserzeit*, ed. Carsten Colpe, Ludger Honnefelder, and Matthias Lutz-Bachmann, Berlin 1992, pp. 77–98.

MacClintock 1959: MacClintock, Carol, "Molinet, Music, and Medieval Rhetoric," *Musica Disciplina* 13 (1959), pp. 109-121.

Machabey 1953-1954: Machabey, Armand: "La musique religieuse en France au XIVe siècle," *La Revue musicale* 1953-1954, pp. 30-43.

Magnan 1985: Magnan, Robert, *Aspects of Senescence in the Work of Eustache Deschamps*, Diss., Minneapolis 1985.

Mandonnet 1911: Mandonnet, Pierre, *Siger de Brabant et l'averroisme latin au XIIIe siècle*, Louvain 1911.

Manferdini 1969: Manferdini, Tina, *L'estetica religiosa in P. Agostino*, Bologna 1969 [Studi e Richerche 16].

Manitius 1911–1931: Manitius, Max, *Geschichte der lateinischen Literatur des Mittelalters*, 3 vols., Munich 1911–1931 [Handbuch der klassischen Altertums-Wissenschaft in systematischer Darstellung; vol. 9, sect. 2, parts 1–3].

Manitius 1935: Manitius, Max, *Handschriften antiker Autoren in mittelalterlichen Bibliothekskatalogen*, Leipzig 1935 [Beiheft zum Zentralblatt für Bibliothekswesen 67].

Marenbon 1997: Marenbon, John, "Platonismus im 12. Jahrhundert. Alte und neue Zugangsweisen," in *Platon in der abendländischen Geistesgeschichte. Neue Forschungen zum Platonismus*, ed. Theo Kobusch and Burkhard Mojsisch, Darmstadt 1997, pp. 101–119.

Marenbon 2003: Marenbon, John, *Boethius*, Oxford 2003 [Great Medieval Thinkers].

Marix 1939: Marix, Jeanne, *Histoire de la musique et des musiciens de la Cour de Bourgogne sous le règne de Philippe le Bon*, Strasbourg 1939 [Collection d'études musicologiques 29].

Marrou 1938: Marrou, Henri-Irénée, *Saint Augustin et la fin de la culture antique*, Paris 1938 [Bibliothèque des écoles françaises d'Athènes et de Rome].

Marrou 1957: Marrou, Henri-Irénée, *Geschichte der Erziehung im klassischen Altertum*, ed. R. Harder, rev. C. Beumann, Freiburg/Munich 1957.

Marrou 1969: Marrou, Henri-Irénée, "Les Arts libéraux dans l'antiquité classique," in *Arts libéraux et philosophie au moyen âge. Actes du quatrième congrès international de philosophie médiévale, Montréal 27 août–2 septembre 1967*, Montréal/Paris 1969, pp. 5–27.

Marrou 1982: Marrou, Henry-Irénée, *Augustinus und das Ende der antiken Bildung*, ed. J. Götte, rev. L. Wirth-Poelchau, Paderborn et al. 1982.

Martin 1953: Martin, Gottfried, "Platons Lehre von der Zahl und ihre Darstellung durch Aristoteles," *Zeitschrift für Philosophische Forschung* 7 (1953), pp. 191–203.

Martin 1956: Martin, Gottfried, *Klassische Ontologie der Zahl*, Cologne 1956 [Kantstudien-Ergänzungshefte 70].

Martineau-Genieys 1978: Martineau-Genieys, Christine, *Le Thème de la mort dans la poésie française de 1450 à 1550*, Paris 1978.

Martineau-Genieys 1981: Martineau-Genieys, Christine, "Corps chrétien, corps païen ou la dramatique du corps chez Eustache Deschamps," *Razo. Cahiers du Centre d'Etudes Médiévales de Nice* 2 (1981), pp. 51–70.

Masi 1971: Masi, Michael, "Manuscripts containing the 'De Musica' of Boethius," *Manuscripta* 15 (1971), pp. 88–97.

Masi 1981: Masi, Michael, "The Influence of Boethius' *De arithmetica* on Late Medieval Mathematics," in *Boethius and the Liberal Arts: A Collection of Essays*, ed. Mario Masi, Bern et al. 1981 [Utah Studies in Literature and Linguistics 18], pp. 81–96.

Masi 1983: Masi, Michael, *Boethian Number Theory: A Translation of the "De Institutione Arithmetica,"* Amsterdam 1983 [Studies in Classical Antiquity 6].

Massieu 1739: Massieu, Guillaume, *Histoire de la poësie française à partir du XVIe siècle*, Paris 1739.

Mathiesen 1985: Mathiesen, Thomas J., "Rhythm and Meter in Ancient Greek Music," *Music Theory Spectrum* 7 (1985), pp. 159–180.

Mathiesen 1990: Mathiesen, Thomas J., "Music, Aesthetics, and Cosmology in Early Neo-Platonism," in *Paradigms in Medieval Thought—Applications in Medieval Disciplines. A Symposion*, ed. Nancy van Deusen and Alvin E. Ford, Lewiston et al. 1990 [Mediaeval Studies 3], pp. 37–64.

Matthews 1981: Matthews, John, "Anicius Manlius Severinus Boethius," in *Boethius: His Life, Thought, and Influence*, ed. Margaret T. Gibson, Oxford 1981, pp. 15–43.

Maurin 1959: Maurin, Mario, "La poétique de Chastellain et la 'Grande Rhétorique.'" *Publications of the Modern Language Association of America* 74 (1959), pp. 482–484.

Maw 1996: Maw, David, *Words and Music in the Secular Songs of Guillaume de Machaut*, Phil. Diss., Oxford 1996.

Maw 2004: Maw, David, "Trespasser mesure: Meter in Machaut's Polyphonic Songs," *Journal of Musicology* 21.1 (2004), pp. 46–126.

Mayer 1964: Mayer, C. A., "Ronsard et Molinet," *Bibliothèque d'Humanisme et Renaissance* 26 (1964), pp. 417–418.

Mayer 1969: Mayer, Cornelius Petrus, *Die Zeichen in der geistigen Entwicklung und in der Theologie des jungen Augustinus*, 2 vols., Würzburg 1969 [Cassiciacum 24].

McInerny 1961: McInerny, Ralph M., *The Logic of Analogy: An Interpretation of St. Thomas*, The Hague 1961.

McKinlay 1907: McKinlay, A. P., "Stylistic Tests and the Chronology of the Works of Boethius," *Harvard Studies in Classical Philology* 18 (1907), pp. 123–156.

McKinnon 1978: McKinnon, James W., "Jubal vel Pythagoras, quis sit inventor musicae?," *The Musical Quarterly* 64 (1978), pp. 1–28.

Méchoulan 1989–1990: Méchoulan, Éric, "La Musique du vulgaire. Arts de seconde rhétorique et constitution de la littérature," *Études littéraires* 22 (1989–1990), pp. 13–22.

Meinwald 2002: Meinwald, Constance Chu, "Plato's Pythagoreanism," *Ancient Philosophy* 22.1 (2002), pp. 87–101.

Merlan 1953: Merlan, Philipp, *From Platonism to Neoplatonism*, The Hague 1953.

Mettlich 1902: Mettlich, Joseph, *Ein Kapitel über Erziehung aus einer altfranzösischen Dichtung des 14. Jahrhunderts*, Münster 1902.

Mettlich 1911: Mettlich, Josef, *Die Abhandlung über Rymes et mettres in der Prosabearbeitung der "Échecs amoureux,"* Münster 1911.

Meyer 1905: Meyer, Wilhelm, "Anfang und Ursprung der lateinischen und griechischen rhythmischen Dichtung," in *Gesammelte Abhandlungen zur mittellateinischen Rhythmik*, 2 vols., Berlin 1905, vol. 2, pp. 1–201.

Meyer 1938: Meyer, Hans, *Thomas von Aquin. Sein System und seine geistesgeschichtliche Stellung*, Bonn 1938.

Meyer 1975: Meyer, Heinz, *Die Zahlenallegorese im Mittelalter. Methode und Gebrauch*, Munich 1975 [Münstersche Mittelalter-Schriften 25].

Meyer 1977: Meyer, Christian, "La Tradition du *Micrologus* de Guy d'Arezzo: Une contribution à l'histoire de la réception du texte," *Revue de musicologie* 83 (1997), pp. 5–31.

Meyer 2001: Meyer, Christian, "L'Enseignement de la musique à Paris au XVe siècle," in *Quellen und Studien zur Musiktheorie des Mittelalters III*, ed. Michael Bernhard, Munich 2001, pp. 305–328.

Meyer 2003: Meyer, Christian, "Lectures et lecteurs du *De institutione musica* de Boèce au XIIIe siècle," in *Boèce ou la Chaîne des Savoirs*, ed. Alain Galonnier, Louvain/Paris/Dudley 2003 [Philosophes médiévaux XLIV], pp. 665–678.

Meyer/Wicker 2000: Meyer, Christian, and Jean-François Wicker, "Musique et mathématique au XIVe siècle. Le *De numeris harmonicis* de Leo Hebraeus," *Archives internationales d'histoire des sciences* 50 (2000), pp. 30–39.

Meyer-Baer 1930: Meyer-Baer, Kathi, *Bedeutung und Wesen der Musik*, Leipzig/Straßburg/Zürich 1930.

MGG 2001: *MGG: Die Musik in Geschichte und Gegenwart. Allgemeine Enzyklopädie der Musik*, ed. Friedrich Blume et al., digital version of the first ed. (1949–1986), Berlin 2001 [Digitale Bibliothek 60].

Michels 1970: Michels, Ulrich, *Die Musiktraktate des Johannes de Muris*, Wiesbaden 1970 [Beihefte zum Archiv für Musikwissenschaft 8].

Michon 1982: Michon, Patricia, *Le vocabulaire de l'affectivité dans l'oeuvre d'Eustache Deschamps. Inquiétudes, souffrances et bouleversements*, Diss., Paris 1982.

Mickley 1898: Mickley, W., *De Boethii libri primi de musica fontibus*, Jena 1898.

Minio-Paluello 1972: Minio-Paluello, Lorenzo, *Opuscula. The Latin Aristotle*, Amsterdam 1972.

Montagnes 1963: Montagnes, Bernard, *La Doctrine de l'analogie de l'être d'après Saint Thomas d'Aquin*, Louvain/Paris 1963.

Montaiglon 1861: Montaiglon, Anatole de: "Quinzième siècle," in *Recueil de chefs-d'oeuvres de la poésie française depuis les origines jusqu'à nos jours avec une notice littéraire sur chaque poëte*, ed. Eugène Crépet et al., 4 vols., Paris 1861–1863, vol. 1 (1861), pp. 1–3.

Most 1951: Most, W. G., "The Scriptural Basis of St. Augustine's Arithmology," *The Catholic Biblical Quarterly* 8 (1951), pp. 284–295.

Mühlethaler 1983: Mühlethaler, Jean-Claude, *Poétiques du quinzième siècle. Situation de François Villon et Michault Taillevent*, Paris 1983.

Mühlethaler 1990: Mühlethaler, Jean-Claude, "Un poète et son art face à la postérité. Lecture des deux ballades de Deschamps pour la mort de Machaut," *Studi francesi* 99 (1990), pp. 387–407.

Müller 1884: Müller, Hans, *Hucbalds echte und unechte Schriften über Musik*, Leipzig 1884.

Müller 1969: Müller, Ulrich, "Zur musikalischen Terminologie der antiken Rhetorik. Ausdrücke für Stimmlage und Stimmgebrauch bei Quintilian, Institutio oratoria 11.3," *Archiv für Musikwissenschaft* 1 (1969), pp. 29–49, 105–124.

Münxelhaus 1976: Münxelhaus, Barbara, *Pythagoras musicus. Zur Rezeption der pythagoreischen Musiktheorie als quadrivialer Wissenschaft im lateinischen Mittelalter*, Bonn-Bad Godesberg 1976 [Orpheus—Schriftenreihe zu Grundfragen der Musik 19].

Murphy 1974: Murphy, James J., *Rhetoric in the Middle Ages: A History of Rhetorical Theory from Saint Augustine to the Renaissance*, Los Angeles/Berkeley/London 1974.

Nash, 1969: Nash, R. H., *The Light of the Mind: St. Augustine's Theory of Knowledge*, Lexington 1969.

Nauta 1997a: Nauta, Lodi, "The 'Glosa' as Instrument for the Development of Natural Philosophy. William of Conches' Commentary on Boethius," in *Boethius in the Middle Ages: Latin and Vernacular Traditions of the Consolatio Philosophiae*, ed. Lodi Nauta and Maarten J. F. M. Hoenen, Leiden et al. 1997 [Studien und Texte zur Geistesgeschichte des Mittelalters 58], pp. 3–40.

Nauta 1997b: Nauta, Lodi, "The Scholastic Context of the Boethius Commentary by Nicholas Trevet," in *Boethius in the Middle Ages: Latin and Vernacular Traditions of the Consolatio Philosophiae*, ed. Lodi Nauta and Maarten J. F. M. Hoenen, Leiden et al. 1997 [Studien und Texte zur Geistesgeschichte des Mittelalters 58], pp. 41–68.

Nestle 1975: Nestle, Wilhelm, *Vom Mythos zum Logos: Die Selbstentfaltung des griechischen Denkens von Homer bis auf die Sophistik und Sokrates*, Stuttgart 1975.

Niemöller 1998: Niemöller, Klaus Wolfgang, "Musik im Weltbild des Johannes Scotus Eriugena," in *Musik—und die Geschichte der Philosophie und Naturwissenschaften im Mittelalter. Fragen zur Wechselwirkung von "Musica" und "Philosophia" im Mittelalter*, ed. Frank Hentschel, Leiden/Boston/Cologne 1998, pp. 293–304.

Nietzsche 1999: *Sämtliche Werke. Kritische Studienausgabe*, ed. Giorgio Colli and Mazzino Montinari, 15 vols., Berlin/New York/Munich 1999.

Nobis 1969: Nobis, Heribert M., "Die Umwandlung der mittelalterlichen Naturvorstellung. Ihre Ursachen und ihre wissenschaftsgeschichtlichen Folgen," in *Archiv für Begriffsgeschichte* 13 (1969), pp. 34–57.

Norberg 1958: Norberg, Dag, *Introduction à l'étude de la versification latine médiévale*, Stockholm 1958 [Acta Universitatis Stockholmiensis: Studia Latina Stockholmiensia 5].

Norden 1958: Norden, Eduard, *Die antike Kunstprosa vom VI. Jahrhundert nach Christus bis in die Zeit der Renaissance*, 2 vols., Darmstadt 1958.

Norton 1935: Norton, A. Edward, *The Amenities of Book-Collecting and Kindred Affections*, New York 1935.

Nowak 1975: Nowak, Adolf, "Die 'numeri judiciales' des Augustinus und ihre musiktheoretische Bedeutung," *Archiv für Musikwissenschaft* 32 (1975), pp. 196–207.

Nowak 1999: Nowak, Adolf, "Augustinus. Die Bedeutung Augustins in Geschichte, Theorie und Ästhetik der Musik," *Frankfurter Zeitschrift für Musikwissenschaft* 2 (1999), pp. 55–77.

Oberleitner (ed.) 1969: *Die handschriftliche Überlieferung der Werke des Heiligen Augustinus*, ed. Manfred Oberleitner, 17 vols., Vienna 1969ff. [Veröffentlichungen der Kommission zur Herausgabe des Corpus der lateinischen Kirchenväter].

Obertello 1974: Obertello, Luca, *Severino Boezio*, Genoa 1974 [Accademia Ligure di Scienze e lettere, Collana di monografie 1].

Oberti 1960: Oberti, Elisa, "L'estetica musicale di Reginone di Prüm e l'attualità dell'estetica medievale," *Rivista di filosofia neo-scolastica* 1 (1960), pp. 336–354.

O'Connell 1978: O'Connell, Robert J., *Art and the Christian Intelligence in St. Augustine*, Oxford 1978.

O'Daly 1986: O'Daly, Gerard J. P., "Anima, animus," in *Augustinus-Lexikon*, ed. Cornelius Petrus Mayer et al., 3 vols. in 7 fasc., Basel/Stuttgart 1986ff., vol. 1.1 (1986), s.v.

O'Daly 1987: O'Daly, Gerard J. P., *Augustine's Philosophy of Mind*, Berkeley 1987.

Ohly 1983: Ohly, Friedrich, "Synagoge und Ecclesia. Typologisches in mittelalterlicher Dichtung," in *Schriften zur mittelalterlichen Bedeutungsforschung*, Darmstadt 1983, pp. 312–337.

Olson 1973: Olson, Glending, "Deschamps' *Art de dictier* and Chaucer's Literary Environment," *Speculum* 48 (1973), pp. 714–723.

Olson 1986: Olson, Glending, *Literature as Recreation in the Later Middle Ages*, Ithaca 1986.

O'Meara 1954: O'Meara, John J., *The Young Augustine: The Growth of St. Augustine's Mind up to His Conversion*, London 1954.

O'Meara 1958: O'Meara, John J., "Augustine and Neo-platonism," *Recherches Augustiniennes* 1 (1958), pp. 91–103.

Paetow 1927: Paetow, Louis J., "The *Morale Scolarium* of John of Garland (Johannes de Garlandia) with an Introduction on the Life and Works of the Author," *Memoirs of the University of California* IV.2 (1927), pp. 69–273.

Page 1977: Page, Christopher, "Machaut's 'Pupil' Deschamps and the Performance of Music," *Early Music* 4 (1977), pp. 484-491.

Page 1993: Page, Christopher, *Discarding Images: Reflections on Music and Culture in Medieval France*, Oxford 1993.

Palisca 1990: Palisca, Claude V., "Boethius in the Renaissance," in *Music Theory and Its Sources: Antiquity and the Middle Ages*, ed. Andre Barbera, Notre Dame 1990 [Notre Dame Conferences in Medieval Studies 1], pp. 259-280.

Panofsky 2002: Panofsky, Erwin, "Abt Suger von St. Denis," in *Sinn und Deutung in der bildenden Kunst*, Cologne 2002, pp. 125-166.

Panti 1990: Panti, Cecilia, "La scienza musicale nella prospettiva 'occamista' di un anonimo *magister artium* del tardo medioevo," *Studi musicali* 19 (1990), pp. 3-32.

Patch 1970: Patch, Howard R., *The Tradition of Boethius: A Study of His Importance in Medieval Culture*, New York 1935, rpt. New York 1970.

Patterson 1966: Patterson, Warner Forrest, *Three Centuries of French Poetic Theory: A Critical History of the Chief Arts of Poetry in France (1328-1630)*, 3 vols., New York 1966 [University of Michigan Publications. Language and Literature].

Payen 1980: Payen, Jean-Charles, "L'Harmonie intérieure et l'harmonie cosmique dans les textes romans (Recherches sur l'esthétique musicale chez quelques moralistes et romanciers du Moyen Âge)," in *Musique, littérature et société au Moyen Âge. Actes du colloque, 24-29 mars 1980*, ed. Danielle Buschinger and André Crépin, Paris 1980, pp. 27-38.

Peck 1970: Peck, Russell A., "Theme and Number in Chaucer's *Book of the Duchess*," in *Silent Poetry: Essays in Numerological Analysis*, ed. Alastair Fowler, London 1970, pp. 73-115.

Peck 1980: Peck, Russel A., "Number as Cosmic Language," in *Essays in the Numerical Criticism of Medieval Literature*, ed. Caroline D. Eckhardt, Lewisburg/London 1980, pp. 15-64.

Peden 1998: Peden, Alison, "Music in Medieval Commentaries on Macrobius," in *Musik—und die Geschichte der Philosophie und Naturwissenschaften im Mittelalter*, ed. Frank Hentschel, Leiden et al. 1998 [Studien und Texte zur Geschichte des Mittelalters 62], pp. 151-161.

Pedersen 1985: Pedersen, Olaf: "In quest of Sacrobosco," *Journal for the History of Astronomy* 16 (1985), pp. 175-221.

Pépin 1977: Pépin, Jean: "Une curieuse déclaration idéaliste du *De Genesi ad litteram* (XII.10.21) de saint Augustin, et ses origines plotiniennes (*Ennéade* 5.3, 1-9 et 5.5, 1-2)," in *"Ex Platonicorum persona." Etudes sur les lectures philosophiques de saint Augustin*, Amsterdam 1977, pp. 183-210.

Peri 1983: Peri, Israel: "*Omnia in mensura et numero et pondere disposuisti*. Die Auslegung von Weish 11.21 in der lateinischen Patristik," in *Mensura. Maß, Zahl, Zahlensymbolik im Mittelalter*, ed. Albert Zimmermann, Berlin/New York 1983 [Miscellanea Mediaevalia 16], pp. 1-21.

Perl 1955: Perl, Carl Johann, "Augustinus und die Musik," in *Augustinus Magister. Actes du Congrès International Augustinien, Paris 21–24 septembre 1954*, Paris 1955 [Études Augustiniennes I.3], pp. 439-452.

Peter 1964: Peter, Karl, *Die Lehre von der Schönheit nach Bonaventura*, Werl 1964 [Franziskanische Forschungen 17].

Petit de Julleville 1896-1899: Petit de Julleville, Louis, *Histoire de la langue et de la littérature française des origines à 1900*, 8 vols., Paris 1896-1899.

Phillips 1990: Phillips, Nancy, "Classical and Late Latin Sources for Ninth-Century Treatises on Music," in *Music Theory and Its Sources: Antiquity and the Middle Ages*, ed. André Barbera, Notre Dame 1990 [Notre Dame Conferences in Medieval Studies 1], pp. 100-135.

Phillips 1997: Phillips, John F., "Neoplatonic Exegeses of Plato's Cosmology," *Journal of the History of Philosophy* 35 (1997), pp. 173-197.

Phillips/Huglo 1985: Phillips, Nancy, and Michel Huglo, "Le 'De musica' de saint Augustin et l'organisation de la durée musicale du IXe au XIIe siècles," *Recherches Augustiniennes* 20 (1985), pp. 117-131.

Pietzsch 1968: Pietzsch, Gerhard, *Die Klassifikation der Musik von Boetius bis Ugolino von Orvieto*, Halle 1928, rpt. Darmstadt 1968.

Pinborg 1967: Pinborg, Jan, *Die Entwicklung der Sprachtheorie im Mittelalter*, Münster/Kopenhagen 1967 [Beiträge zur Geschichte der Philosophie und Theologie des Mittelalters 42.2].

Pinegar 1991: Pinegar, Sandra, *Textual and Conceptual Relationships among Latin Theoretical Writings on Polyphony from Garlandia to Jacobus de Liège*, Diss., New York 1991.

Pingree 1986: Pingree, David, "Astrologia, Astronomia," in *Augustinus-Lexikon*, ed. Cornelius Petrus Mayer et al., 3 vols. in 7 fasc., Basel/Stuttgart 1986ff., vol. 1.1 (1986), s.v.

Pinon 1846-1847: Pinon, F., "Eustache Deschamps, poète champenois du XIVe siècle," *Séances et Travaux de l'Académie de Reims* 6 (1846-1847), pp. 259-271, 365-386, 423-445.

Pirrotta 1955: Pirrotta, Nino, "Marchettus de Padua and the Italian Ars nova," *Musica disciplina* 9 (1955), pp. 57-71.

Pirrotta 1976: Pirrotta, Nino, " 'Musica de sono humano' and the Musical Poetics of Guido of Arrezzo," *Medievalia et humanistica* 7 (1976), pp. 13-27.

Pizzani 1965: Pizzani, Ubaldo, "Studi sulle fonti del 'De institutione musica' di Boezio," *Sacris Erudiri* 16 (1965), pp. 5-164.

Pizzani 1980: Pizzani, Ubaldo, "Musica theorica sive Scholia in Boethii De institutione musica libros quinque," *Romanobarbarica* 5 (1980), pp. 329-357.

Pizzani 1985: Pizzani, Ubaldo, "Gli scritti grammaticali attribuiti a pp. Agostino," *Augustinianum* 1-2 (1985), pp. 361-383.

Pizzani 2003: Pizzani, Ubaldo, "Du rapport entre le *De musica* de p. Augustin et le *De institutione musica* de Boèce," in *Boèce ou la Chaîne des Savoirs*, ed. Alain Galonnier, Louvain/Paris/Dudley 2003 [Philosophes médiévaux XLIV], pp. 357-377.

Planche 1984: Planche, Alice, "Le corps en vieillesse. Regards sur la poésie du Moyen-Age tardif," *Razo. Cahiers du Centre d'Etudes Médiévales de Nice* 4 (1984), pp. 39–57.

Poirion 1965: Poirion, Daniel, *Le Poète et le Prince. L'Évolution du lyrisme courtois de Guillaume de Machaut à Charles d'Orléans*, Paris 1965 [Université de Grenoble. Publications de la faculté des lettres et sciences humaines 35].

Poirion 1978: Poirion, Daniel, "Eustache Deschamps et la société de cour," in *Littérature et société au Moyen Âge. Actes du colloque des 5 et 6 mai 1978*, ed. Danielle Buschinger, Paris 1978, pp. 89–109.

Polheim 1963: Polheim, Karl, *Die lateinische Reimprosa*, Berlin 1963.

Pouillon 1946: Pouillon, Henri, "La Beauté, propriété transcendentale, chez les Scolastiques (1220–1270)," *Archives d'histoire doctrinale et littéraire du Moyen Âge*, 1946, pp. 263–329.

Préaux 1953: Préaux, J., "Le commentaire de Martin de Laon sur l'oeuvre de Martianus Capella," *Latomus* 12 (1953), pp. 437–459.

Raby 1957: Raby, Frederic J. E., *A History of Secular Latin Poetry in the Middle Ages*, Oxford 1957.

Radke 2003: Radke, Gyburg, *Die Theorie der Zahl im Platonismus. Ein systematisches Lehrbuch*, Tübingen et al. 2003.

Rahn 1980: Rahn, Jay, " 'Fixed' and 'Free' Forms in French Monophonic Song, ca. 1480–1520," *Le Moyen Français* 5 (1980), pp. 130–158.

Raimondi 1997: Raimondi, Gianmario, "*Les eschés amoureux.*" *Studio preparatorio all'edizione dei vv. 1–16300*, Diss., Rome 1997.

Rand 1901: Rand, Edward K., "Der dem Boethius zugeschriebene Traktat De Fide Catholica," *Jahrbücher für Klassische Philologie. Supplementband* 26 (1901), pp. 407–461.

Rand 1904: Rand, Edward K., "On the Composition of Boethius' *Consolatio Philosophiae*," *Harvard Studies in Classical Philology* 15 (1904), pp. 1–28.

Rand 1906: Rand, Edward K., *Johannes Scottus*, Munich 1906 [Quellen und Untersuchungen zur lateinischen Philologie des Mittelalters vol. 1, H. 2].

Rand 1929a: Rand, Edward K., *Founders of the Middle Ages*, Cambridge 1929.

Rand 1929b: Rand, Edward K., *Studies in the Script of Tours*, 2 vols. in 3 fasc., Cambridge 1929.

Rand 1934: Rand, Edward K., "The Supposed Commentary of John the Scot on the 'Opuscula sacra' of Boethius," *Revue néoscolastique de philosophie* 36 (1934), pp. 67–77.

Randel 1976: Randel, Don M., "Al-Farabi and the Role of Arabic Music Theory in the Latin Middle Ages," *Journal of the American Musicological Society* 2 (1976), pp. 173–188.

Ranke 1857–1890: Ranke, Leopold von, *Sämmtliche Werke*, 54 vols., Leipzig 1867–1890.

Rasch 1969: Rasch, Rudolf, *Iohannes de Garlandia en de ontwikkeling van de voor-Franconische notatie*, Brooklyn 1969 [Institute of Mediaeval Music, Brooklyn, NY, Wissenschaftliche Abhandlungen 20].

Rawski 1962: Rawski, Conrad H., "Notes on Aribo Scholasticus," in *Natalica musicologica. Knud Jeppesen septuagenario collegis oblata*, ed. Björn Helmborg and Sören Sörensen, Oslo et al. 1962, pp. 19–29.

Reaney 1953: Reaney, Gilbert, "Fourteenth Century Harmony and the Ballades," *Musica Disciplina* 7 (1953), pp. 129–146.

Reaney 1955: Reaney, Gilbert, "The Ballades, Rondeaux and Virelais of Guillaume de Machaut: Melody, Rhythm and Form," *Acta Musicologica* 27 (1955), pp. 40–58.

Reaney 1959: Reaney, Gilbert, "The Poetic Form of Machaut's Musical Works I: The Ballades, Rondeaux and Virelais," *Musica Disciplina* 13 (1959), pp. 25–41.

Reckow 1975: Reckow, Fritz, "Organum-Begriff und frühe Mehrstimmigkeit. Zugleich ein Beitrag zur Bedeutung des 'Instrumentalen' in der spätantiken und mittelalterlichen Musiktheorie," *Forum musicologicum. Basler Studien zur Musikgeschichte* 1 (1975), pp. 31–167.

Reichert 1956: Reichert, Georg, "Das Verhältnis zwischen musikalischer und textlicher Struktur in den Motetten Machauts," *Archiv für Musikwissenschaft* 3/4 (1956), pp. 197–216.

Répertoire International des Sources Musicales: *Répertoire International des Sources Musicales*, ed. Société Internationale de Musicologie, Munich/Kassel 1960ff.

Richenhagen 1989: Richenhagen, Albert, *Studien zur Musikanschauung des Rabanus Maurus*, Regensburg 1989 [Kölner Beiträge zur Musikwissenschaft 162].

Richter 1965: Richter, Lukas, "Griechische Traditionen im Musikschrifttum der Römer. Censorinus, *De die natali*, Kapitel 10," *Archiv für Musikwissenschaft* 2 (1965), pp. 69–98.

Richter 1968: Richter, Lukas, "Die Geburtstagsschrift des Censorinus als musiktheoretische Quelle," in *Studien zur Geschichte und Philosophie des Altertums. Vorträge gehalten auf dem Kongreß für klassische Philologie der Ungarischen Akademie der Wissenschaften, Budapest, 1.–6. Nov. 1965*, ed. János Harmatta, Amsterdam 1968, pp. 215–223.

Richter 1999: Richter, Lukas, "Struktur und Rezeption antiker Planetenskalen," *Die Musikforschung* 52 (1999), pp. 289–306.

Rief 1962: Rief, Josef, *Der Ordobegriff des jungen Augustinus*, Paderborn 1962 [Abhandlungen der Moraltheologie 5].

Riethmüller 1985: Riethmüller, Albrecht, "Stationen des Begriffs Musik," in *Geschichte der Musiktheorie*, ed. Frieder Zaminer, 11 vols., Darmstadt 1985ff., vol. 1 (1985), ed. Frieder Zaminer, pp. 59–95.

Riethmüller 1989a: Riethmüller, Albrecht: "Musica naturalis," in *Kontinuität und Transformation der Antike im Mittelalter. Veröffentlichung der Kongreßakten zum Freiburger Symposion des Mediävistenverbandes*, ed. Willi Erzgräber, Sigmaringen 1989, pp. 221–230.

Riethmüller 1989b: Riethmüller, Albrecht: "Musik zwischen Hellenismus und Spätantike," in *Neues Handbuch der Musikwissenschaft*, ed. Carl Dahlhaus and Hermann Danuser, 13 vols. in 15. fasc., Laaber/Wiesbaden 1989–1992, vol. 1 (1989), in collaboration with Ellen Hickmann, ed. Albrecht Riethmüller and Frieder Zaminer, pp. 207–325.

Riethmüller 1990: Riethmüller, Albrecht: "Probleme der spekulativen Musiktheorie im Mittelalter," in *Geschichte der Musiktheorie*, ed. Frieder Zaminer, 11 vols., Darmstadt 1985ff., vol. 3 (1990), ed. Michael Bernhard, pp. 163–202.

Riethmüller 2001: Riethmüller, Albrecht: "Die Verdächtigung des Virtuosen—Zwischen Midas von Akragas und Herbert von Karajan," in *Virtuosen. Über die Eleganz der Meisterschaft*, ed. Herbert von Karajan, Centrum, Vienna 2001, pp. 100–124.

Rimmon-Kenan 1980: Rimmon-Kenan, Shlomith, "The Paradoxical Status of Repetition," *Poetics Today* 1/4 (1980), pp. 151–15.

Ritter 1937: Ritter, Joachim, *Mundus intelligibilis. Eine Untersuchung zur Aufnahme und Umwandlung der neuplatonischen Ontologie bei Augustinus*, Frankfurt a. M. 1937 [Philosophische Abhandlungen 6].

Robins 1971: Robins, Robert H., *Ancient and Medieval Grammatic Theory: With Particular Reference to Modern Linguistic Doctrine*, Port Washington/London 1971 [Classics Series], pp. 77–89.

Röd 1988: Röd, Wolfgang, *Geschichte der Philosophie I. Von Thales bis Demokrit*, 2nd rev. ed., Munich 1988.

Rohloff 1943: Rohloff, Ernst, *Studien zum Musiktraktat des Johannes de Grocheo*, Leipzig 1943 [Media latinitatis musica 1].

Rosier-Catach 1983: Irène Rosier-Catach, *La Grammaire spéculative des modistes*, Lille 1983.

Rouse 1967: Rouse, Richard H., "The Early Library of the Sorbonne," *Scriptorium* 21 (1967), pp. 42–71, 227–251.

Rowell 1979: Rowell, Lewis, "Aristoxenus on Rhythm," *Journal of Music Theory* 23.1 (1979), pp. 63–79.

Roy 1999: Roy, Bruno, "Eustache Deschamps et Évrart de Conty théoriciens de l'art poétique," in *Cy nous dient . . . Dialogues avec quelques auteurs médiévaux*, Orléans 1999, pp. 25–40.

Rychner 1967: Rychner, Jean, "Le prologue du *Chevalier de la Charrette*," *Vox romanica* 26 (1967), pp. 1–23.

Rychner 1969: Rychner, Jean, "Le prologue du Chevalier de la Charrette et l'interprétation du roman," in *Mélanges offerts à Madame Rita Lejeune à l'occasion du 30e anniveraire de son enseignement académique*, Gembloux 1969, pp. 1121–1135.

Rychner 1972: Rychner, Jean, "Encore le prologue du *Chevalier de la Charrette*," *Vox romanica* 31 (1972), pp. 263–271.

Sachs 1970-1980: Sachs, Klaus-Jürgen, *Mensura fistularum. Die Mensurierung der Orgelpfeifen im Mittelalter*, 2 vols., Stuttgart 1970–1980.

Sachs 1990: Sachs, Klaus-Jürgen, "Musikalische Elementarlehre im Mittelalter," in *Geschichte der Musiktheorie*, ed. Frieder Zaminer, 11 vols., Darmstadt 1985ff., vol. 3 (1990), ed. Michael Bernhard, pp. 105–161.

Sainte-Beuve 1828: Sainte-Beuve, Charles Augustin de, *Tableau historique et critique de la poésie française et du théâtre français au XVIe siècle*, Paris 1828.

Sanders 1980: Sanders, Ernest H., "Consonance and Rhythm in the Organum of the 12th and 13th Century," *Journal of the American Musicological Society* 33 (1980), pp. 264–286.

Sandresky 1979: Sandresky, Margaret Vardell, "The Continuing of the Platonic-Pythagorean System and Its Application to the Analysis of Fifteenth-Century Music," *Music Theory Spectrum* 1 (1979), pp. 107–120.

Sandy 1998: Sandy, John E., *A History of Classical Scholarship*, 3 vols., Bristol 1998.

Santeler 1939: Santeler, Josef, *Der Platonismus in der Erkenntnislehre des Heiligen Thomas von Aquin*, Innsbruck/Leipzig 1939 [Philosophie und Grenzwissenschaften 7.2–4].

Sarradin 1878: Sarradin, Amédée, *Étude sur Eustache des Champs, sa vie et ses oeuvres*, Versailles 1878.

Sassen 1936–1937: Sassen, Ferdinand, "De Middeleeuwsche bibliotheek der Abdij Kloosterrade," *Nederlands Archief voor Kerkgeschiedenis* 29 (1936/1937), pp. 19–76.

Sassen 1984: Sassen, Ferdinand, "Boethius—Lehrmeister des Mittelalters," in *Boethius*, ed. Manfred Fuhrmann, Darmstadt 1984 [Wege der Forschung 483], pp. 82–123.

Saulnier 1964: Saulnier, Verdun L., "Rhétoriqueurs," in *Dictionnaire des lettres françaises. Le Moyen-Âge*, ed. Geneviève Hasenohr, Paris 1964, pp. 634–635.

Schäfke 1982: Schäfke, Rudolf, *Geschichte der Musikästhetik in Umrissen*, Tutzing 1982.

Schaller 1981: Schaller, Hans Martin, "Dichtungslehren und Briefsteller," in *Die Renaissance der Wissenschaften im 12. Jahrhundert*, ed. Peter Weimar, Zürich 1981 [Zürcher Hochschulforum 2], pp. 249–272.

Scharnagel 1954: Scharnagel, August, "Aurelius Augustinus' De musica. Zur 1600sten Wiederkehr seines Geburtstages am 13. November," *Musica* 11 (1954), pp. 481–483.

Schedler 1916: Schedler, Matthaeus, *Die Philosophie des Macrobius und ihr Einfluß auf die Wissenschaft des christlichen Mittelalters*, Münster 1916 [Beiträge zur Geschichte der Philosophie des Mittelalters 13.1].

Scheidegger 1983: Scheidegger, Jean R., "La lettre du nom. L'Anthroponymie de Jean Molinet," *Le Moyen Français* 8–9 (1983), pp. 198–235.

Scherer 1909: Scherer, Wilhelm, "Des hl. Augustinus 6 Bücher 'De musica,'" *Kirchenmusikalisches Jahrbuch* 22 (1909), pp. 63–67.

Schlager 1982: Schlager, Karlheinz, "Aspekte der mittelalterlichen Musik," in *Propyläen Geschichte der Literatur. Literatur und Gesellschaft in der westlichen Welt*, ed. Erika Wischer, 6 vols., Frankfurt a. M. 1981–1984, vol. 3 (1982), pp. 401–413.

Schletterer 1885: Schletterer, Hans, *Geschichte der Spielmannskunst in Frankreich*, Berlin 1885 [Studien zur Geschichte der französischen Musik 2].

Schmid 1956: Schmid, Wolfgang, "Philosophisches und Medizinisches in der Consolatio des Boethius," in *Festschrift Bruno Snell. Zum 60. Geburtstag am 18. Juni 1956 von Freunden und Schülern überreicht*, Munich 1956, pp. 113–144.

Schmidt 1899: Schmidt, Karl, *Quaestiones de musicis scriptoribus Romanis imprimis de Cassiodoro et Isidoro*, Darmstadt 1899.

Schmidt 1967a: Schmidt, Albert-Marie, "L'âge des rhétoriqueurs (1450–1530)," in *Histoire des littératures*, ed. Raymond Queneau, 3 vols., Paris 1967 [Encyclopédie de la Pléiade], vol. 3, pp. 175–190.

Schmidt 1967b: Schmidt, Martin A., "Scholastik," in *Die Kirche in ihrer Geschichte: Ein Handbuch*, ed. Kurt Dietrich Schmidt, Ernst Wolf and Bernd Moeller, 4 vols. published in parts, Göttingen 1961ff., vol. 2, part G (1967), pp. 67–181.

Schmitt 1930: Schmitt, Alois, "Mathmatik und Zahlenmystik," in *Aurelius Augustinus. Die Festschrift der Görres-Gesellschaft zum 1500. Todestag des heiligen Augustinus*, ed. Martin Grabmann and Joseph Mausbach, Cologne 1930, pp. 353–366.

Schmitt 1974: Schmitt, Arbogast, *Die Bedeutung der sophistischen Logik für die mittlere Dialektik Platons*, Diss., Würzburg 1974.

Schmitt 1989: Schmitt, Arbogast, "Zur Erkenntnistheorie bei Platon und Descartes," *Antike & Abendland* 35 (1989), pp. 54–82.

Schmitt 1990: Schmitt, Arbogast, "Zahl und Schönheit in Augustins *De musica*, VI," *Würzburger Jahrbücher für die Altertumswissenschaft. Neue Folge* 16 (1990), pp. 221–237.

Schmitt 2007: Schmitt, Arbogast, "Symmetrie und Schönheit. Plotins Kritik an hellenistischen Proportionslehren und ihre unterschiedliche Wirkungsgeschichte in Mittelalter und Früher Neuzeit," in *Neuplatonismus und Ästhetik. Zur Transformationsgeschichte des Schönen*, ed. Verena Olejniczak Lobsien and Claudia Olk, Berlin/New York 2007 [Transformationen der Antike 2], pp. 59–84.

Schneider 1998: Schneider, Jakob H. J., "Thomas von Aquin," in *Ästhetik und Kunstphilosophie. Von der Antike bis zur Gegenwart in Einzeldarstellungen*, ed. Julian Nida-Rümelin and Monika Betzler, Stuttgart 1998, pp. 774–780.

Schrade 1930: Schrade, Leo, "Das propädeutische Ethos in der Musikanschauung des Boethius," *Zeitschrift für Geschichte der Erziehung und des Unterrichts* 20 (1930), pp. 179–215.

Schrade 1932: Schrade, Leo, "Die Stellung der Musik in der Philosophie des Boethius als Grundlage der ontologischen Musikerziehung," *Archiv für Geschichte der Philosophie* 3 (1932), pp. 368–400.

Schrade 1947: Schrade, Leo, "Music in the Philosophy of Boethius," *The Musical Quarterly* 33 (1947), pp. 188–200.

Schramm 1981: Schramm, Matthias, "Roger Bacons Begriff vom Naturgesetz," in *Die Renaissance der Wissenschaften im 12. Jahrhundert*, ed. Peter Weimar, Zürich 1981 [Zürcher Hochschulforum 2], pp. 197–209.

Schrimpf 1966: Schrimpf, Gangolf, *Die Axiomenschrift des Boethius (De Hebdomadibus) als philosophisches Lehrbuch des Mittelalters*, Leiden 1966.

Schueller 1988: Schueller, Herbert M., *The Idea of Music: An Introduction to Musical Aesthetics in Antiquity and the Middle Ages*, Kalamazoo 1988 [Early Drama, Art, and Music Monograph Series 9].

Schulz-Buschhaus 1984: Schulz-Buschhaus, Ulrich, "Überlegungen zur literarhistorischen Epochenschwelle zwischen Mittelalter und Renaissance," *Zeitschrift für Romanische Philologie* 100 (1984), pp. 112–129.

Schulz-Buschhaus 1985: Schulz-Buschhaus, Ulrich, "Gattungsmischung—Gattungskombination—Gattungsnivellierung. Überlegungen zum Gebrauch des literarhistorischen Epochenbegriffs 'Barock,'" in *Epochenschwellen und Epochenstrukturen im Diskurs der Literatur- und Sprachhistorie*, ed. Hans Ulrich Gumbrecht and Ursula Link-Heer, Frankfurt a. M. 1985, pp. 213–233.

Schulz-Buschhaus 1995: Schulz-Buschhaus, Ulrich, "Elegisches und Satirisches bei Villon," in *Musique naturele. Interpretationen zur französischen Lyrik des Spätmittelalters*, ed. Wolf-Dieter Stempel, Munich 1995 [Romanistisches Kolloquium 7], pp. 381–418.

Schütz 2006: Schütz, Ludwig, *Thomas-Lexikon. Sammlung, Übersetzung und Erklärung der in sämtlichen Werken des hl. Thomas von Aquin vorkommenden Kunstausdrücke und wissenschaftlichen Aussprüche*, 3rd ed., ed. Enrique Alarcón, Pamplona 2006.

Seay 1955: Seay, Albert, "Ugolino of Orvieto, Theorist and Composer," *Musica Disciplina* 9 (1955), pp. 111–166.

Sedgwick 1927: Sedgwick, Walter B., "Notes and Emendations on Faral's *Les arts poétiques*," *Speculum* 2 (1927), pp. 331–343.

Sedgwick 1928: Sedgwick, Walter B., "The Style and Vocabulary of the Latin Arts of Poetry," *Speculum* 3 (1928), pp. 349–381.

Seidel 1985: Seidel, Wilhelm: "Rhythmus/numerus," in *Handwörterbuch der musikalischen Terminologie*, ed. Hans Heinrich Eggebrecht, Wiesbaden 1972ff., vol. 5 (1985), s.v.

Shapley 1970: Shapley, C. S., *Studies in French Poetry of the Fifteenth Century*, The Hague 1970.

Siegele 1978: Siegele, Ulrich, *Bachs theologischer Formbegriff und das Duett F-Dur*, Neuhausen/Stuttgart 1978.

Sieper 1898: Sieper, E., *Les Échecs Amoureux. Eine altfranzösische Nachahmung des Rosenromans und ihre englische Uebertragung*, Weimar 1898 [Literarhistorische Forschungen 9].

Simon 1966: Simon, Manfred, "Zur Abhängigkeit spätrömischer Enzyklopädien der Artes liberales von Varros Disciplinarum libri," *Philologus. Zeitschrift für das Klassische Altertum* 110 (1966), pp. 88–101.

Simson 1956: Simson, Otto von, *The Gothic Cathedral: Origins of Gothic Architecture and the Medieval Concept of Order*, New York 1956.

Sinnreich 1987: Sinnreich, Deborah M., *Eustache Deschamps' L'Art de Dictier*, Diss., New York 1987.

Slocum 1987: Slocum, Kay B., *Speculum musicae: Jacques de Liège and the Medieval Vision of God*, Diss., Kent 1987.

Slocum 1991: Slocum, Kay B., "Musica coelestis: A Fourteenth Century Image of Cosmic Music," *Studia mystica* 1991, pp. 3–12.

Slocum 1993: Slocum, Kay B., "*Speculum musicae*: Jacques de Liège and the Art of Musical Number," in *Medieval Numerology: A Book of Essays*, ed. Robert R. Surles, New York et al. 1993 [Garland Reference Library of the Humanities 1640: Garland Medieval Casebooks 7], pp. 11–37.

Smith 1963: Smith, F. Joseph, "Jacques de Liège, an Anti-Modernist?," *Revue belge de Musicologie* 17 (1963), pp. 3–10.

Smith 1966–1983: Smith, F. Joseph, *Jacobi Leodiensis 'Speculum musicae': A Commentary*, 4 vols., Henryville et al. 1966–1983 [Musicological Studies 13, 22, 42, 43].

Smith 1967: Smith, F. Joseph, "A Medieval Philosophy of Number: Jacques de Liège and the 'Speculum musicae,'" in *Arts libéraux et philosophie au Moyen Âge. Actes du Quatrième Congrès de International de Philosophie Médiévale. Université de Montréal, Canada, 27 août–2 septembre 1967*, Paris 1967, pp. 1023–1039.

Sobczyk 1999: Sobczyk, Agata, "La place du Moi dans les poèmes d'Eustache Deschamps," in *Autour d'Eustache Deschamps. Actes du Colloque du Centre d'Études Médiévales de l'Université de Picardie-Jules Verne, Amiens, 5–8 Novembre 1998*, ed. Danielle Buschinger, Amiens 1999 [Médiévales 2], pp. 233–243.

Sobczyk 2005: Sobczyk, Agatha, "'Au jour d'ui partout double loy regne.' Eustache Deschamps dans un univers dédoublé," in *Les "dictez vertueulx" d'Eustache Deschamps. Forme poétique et discours engagé à la fin du Moyen Âge*, ed. Miren Lacassagne and Thierry Lassabatère, Paris 2005 [Cultures et civilisations médiévales], pp. 233–240.

Solignac 1957: Solignac, A., "Réminiscences Plotiniennes et Porphyriennes dans le début du 'De ordine' de Saint Augustin," *Archives de philosophie* 20 (1957), pp. 446–465.

Solomon 1990: Solomon, Jon, "A Preliminary Analysis of the Organization of Ptolemy's *Harmonics*," in *Music Theory and Its Sources: Antiquity and the Middle Ages*, ed. Andre Barbera, Notre Dame 1990 [Notre Dame Conferences in Medieval Studies 1], pp. 68–84.

Staab 2002: Staab, Gregor, *Pythagoras in der Spätantike. Studien zu De vita Pythagorica des Iamblichos von Chalkis*, Munich/Leipzig 2002 [Beiträge zur Altertumskunde 165].

Staub 1967: Staub, Hans, *Le Curieux désir. Scève et Peletier du Mans poètes de la connaissance*, Geneva 1967 [Travaux d'humanisme et renaissance 94].

Steel 1997: Steel, Carlos, "Das neue Interesse für den Platonismus am Ende des 13. Jahrhunderts," in *Platon in der abendländischen Geistesgeschichte. Neue Forschungen zum Platonismus*, ed. Theo Kobusch and Burkhard Mojsisch, Darmstadt 1997, pp. 120–133.

Stempel 1995: Stempel, Wolf-Dieter, "Einleitung," in *Musique naturele. Interpretationen zur französischen Lyrik des Spätmittelalters*, ed. Wolf-Dieter Stempel, Munich 1995 [Romanistisches Kolloquium 7], pp. 7–10.

Stempel (ed.) 1995: *Musique naturele. Interpretationen zur französischen Lyrik des Spätmittelalters*, ed. Wolf-Dieter Stempel, Munich 1995 [Romanistisches Kolloquium 7], pp. 7–10.

Stenzel 1959: Stenzel, Julius, *Zahl und Gestalt bei Platon und Aristoteles*, 3rd, rev. ed., Darmstadt 1959.

Stevens 1984: Stevens, John, "The 'Music' of the Lyric: Machaut, Deschamps, Chaucer," in *Medieval and Pseudo-Medieval Literature: The J. A. W. Bennett Memorial Lectures Perugia, 1982–1983*, ed. Piero Boitani and Anna Torti, Tübingen/Cambridge 1984, pp. 109–130.

Stevens 1986: Stevens, John, *Words and Music in the Middle Ages: Song, Narrative, Dance and Drama, 1050–1350*, Cambridge et al. 1986.

Stimpson 1984: Stimpson, Brian, *Paul Valéry and Music: A Study of the Techniques of Composition in Valéry's Poetry*, Cambridge 1984.

Stockmann 1985: Stockmann, Doris, "'Musica vulgaris' im französischen Hochmittelalter: Johannes de Grocheo in neuer Sicht," *Musikethnologische Sammelbände* 7 (1985), pp. 163–180.

Storck 1992: Storck, Hans-Walter, "Johannes de Garlandia," in *Biographisch-Bibliographisches Kirchenlexion*, ed. Traugott Bautz, 25 vols., Hamm/Herzberg/Nordhausen 1975–2005, vol. 3 (1992), col. 363–365.

Störmer-Caysa 1996: Störmer-Caysa, Uta, *Augustins philologischer Zeitbegriff. Ein Vorschlag zum Verständnis der distentio animi im Lichte von "De musica,"* Berlin 1996 [Abhandlungen der sächsischen Akademie der Wissenschaften zu Leipzig. Philologisch-historische Klasse 74.3].

Strosetzki 1982: Strosetzki, Christoph, "Réflexion moraliste chez les Rhétoriqueurs. Les actes du langage chez Deschamps," in *Du Mot au Texte. Actes du IIIème Colloque International sur le Moyen Français, Düsseldorf, 17–19 septembre 1980*, ed. Peter Wunderli, Tübingen 1982, pp. 241–252.

Strunk 1974: Strunk, William Oliver, "On the Date of Marchetto da Padova," in *Essays on Music in the Western World*, New York 1974, pp. 39–43.

Studer 1978: Studer, Basil, *Soteriologie in der Schrift und Patristik*, Freiburg/Basel/Vienna 1978 [Handbuch der Dogmengeschichte 3, Fasz. 2a].

Stumpf 1901: Stumpf, Carl, "Geschichte des Consonanzbegriffes," *Abhandlungen der philosophischphilologischen Classe der Königlich-Bayerischen Akademie der Wissenschaften* 21 (1901), pp. 1–78.

Sulovski 1957–1961: Sulovski, Jan, "Les sources du *De consolatione Philosophiae* de Boèce," *Sophia* 25 (1957), pp. 76–85 and 29 (1961), pp. 67–94.

Sundermeyer 1910: Sundermeyer, Albrecht, *De re metrica et rhythmica Martiani Capellae*, Marburg 1910.

Svoboda 1933: Svoboda, Karel, *L'Esthétique de Saint Augustin*, Brünn/Paris 1933.

Tanay 1989: Tanay, Dorit Esther, *Music in the Age of Ockham: The Interrelations Between Music, Mathematics, and Philosophy in the 14th Century*, Diss., Berkeley 1989.

Tanay 1993: Tanay, Dorit Esther, "Jehan de Meur's Musical Theory and the Mathematics of the Fourteenth Century," *Tractrix* 5 (1993), pp. 17–43.

Tanay 1996: Tanay, Dorit, *Noting Music, Marking Culture: The Intellectual Context of Rhythmic Notation, 1250–1400*, Holzgerlingen 1996 [Musicological studies and documents 49].

Taschow 2003: Taschow, Ulrich, *Nicole Oresme und der Frühling der Moderne: Die Ursprünge unserer modernen quantitativ-metrischen Weltaneignungsstrategien und neuzeitlichen Bewusstseins- und Wissenschaftskultur*, Halle 2003.

Tatarkiewicz 1970: Tatarkiewicz, Wladislaw, *History of Aesthetics II: Medieval Aesthetics*, The Hague/Paris 1970.

Tetel 1979: Telel, Marcel, "Mariolatry: From the Rhétoriqueurs to the Baroque," *Degré Second. Studies in French Litterature from the Renaissance to the Present* 3 (1979), pp. 1–12.

Theiler 1953: Theiler, Willy, "Review of P. Courcelle: Recherches sur les Confessions de Saint Augustin," *Gnomon* 25 (1953), pp. 117.

Theiler 1966: Theiler, Willy, *Forschungen zum Neuplatonismus*, Berlin 1966 [Quellen und Studien zur Geschichte der Philosophie 10].

Theobald 1989: Theobald, Michael, "Glaube und Vernunft. Zur Argumentation des Paulus im Römerbrief," *Theologische Quartalsschrift* 169 (1989), pp. 287–301.

Thimme 1908: Thimme, Wilhelm, *Augustins geistige Entwickelung nach seiner "Bekehrung," 386-391*, Berlin 1908 [Neue Studien zur Theologie und zur Kirche].

Thiry 1978: Thiry, Claude, "Lecture du texte de 'rhétoriqueur,' " *Cahiers d'analyse textuelle* 20 (1978), pp. 85–101.

Thiry 1980: Thiry, Claude, "La poétique des grands rhétoriqueurs. À propos d'un ouvrage récent," *Le Moyen Âge* 1 (1980), pp. 117–133.

Thiry 1982: Thiry, Claude, "Au carrefour des deux rhétoriques. Les prosimètres de Jean Molinet," in *Du Mot au Texte. Actes du IIIe Colloque International sur le Moyen Français*, Tübingen 1982, pp. 213–225.

Thiry 1985: Thiry, Claude, *La plainte funèbre*, aktualisierte Auflage, Paris 1985 [Typologie des sources du moyen âge occidental 30].

Thiry 1988: Thiry, Claude, "La poésie de circonstance," in *Grundriß der romanischen Literaturen des Mittelalters*, in collaboration with Jean Frappier et al., ed. Hans-Robert Jauß and Erich Köhler, 11. vols. in 30 fasc., Heidelberg 1968ff., vol. 8.1 (1988), ed. Daniel Poirion, pp. 111–138.

Thiry 2001: Thiry, Claude, "Eustache Deschamps, ou le changement dans la (fausse) continuité lyrique," in *Convergences médiévales. Épopée, lyrique, roman. Mélanges offerts à Madeleine Tyssens*, ed. Nadine Henrard, Paola Moreno, and Martine Thiry-Stassin, Brussels 2001 [Bibliothèque du Moyen Âge], pp. 511–526.

Thomas 1917: Thomas, Antoine, "Notice sur le Ms. 4788 du Vatican," in *Notices et extraits de MSS de la Bibliothèque Nationale* 41 (1917), pp. 29–90.

Thomas/Roques 1938: Thomas, A., Roques, M., "Traductions françaises de la *Consolatio philosophiae* de Boèce," *Histoire littéraire de la France* 37 (1938), pp. 419–488.

Thomas 1996: Thomas, Michael, *Der Teilhabegedanke in den Schriften und Predigten des Nikolaus von Kues (1430–1450)*, Münster 1996 [Buchreihe der Cusanus-Gesellschaft 12].

Thorndike 1948: Thorndike, Lynn, *The Sphere of Sacrobosco and its Commentators*, Chicago 1948.

Thurot 1965: Thurot, Charles M., *Notices et extraits de divers manuscrits latins pour servir à l'histoire des doctrines grammaticales au moyen âge*, 1868, rpt. Frankfurt a. M. 1965.

Tilley 1959: Tilley, A., *The Literature of the French Renaissance*, 2 vols., New York 1959.

TLF: *Trésor de la langue française. Dictionnaire de la langue française du XIXe et du XXe siècle (1789–1960)*, ed. Institut national de la langue française Nancy, 16 vols., Paris 1971–1994.

Toernquist 1935: Toernquist, Nils, *Zur Geschichte des Wortes Reim*, Lund 1935 [K. Humanistiska Vetenskapssamfundetsk á Lund Arsberättsele 3].

Tonna 1992: Tonna, Ivo, "La concezione del sapere in Ruggero Bacone (1214–1292)," *Antonianum* 67 (1992), pp. 461–471.

Touya de Marenne 2005: Touya de Marenne, Eric, *Musique et poétique à l'âge du symbolisme. Variations sur Wagner: Baudelaire, Mallarmé, Claudel, Valéry*, Paris 2005 [Littératures comparées].

Treitler 1983: Treitler, Leo, "Der Vatikanische Organumtraktat und das Organum von Notre Dame de Paris. Perspektiven der Entwicklung einer schriftlichen Musikkultur in Europa," *Basler Jahrbuch für historische Musikpraxis* 7 (1983), pp. 23–31.

Ueberweg 1915: Ueberweg, Friedrich, *Grundriß der Geschichte der Philosophie II: Die patristische und scholastische Zeit*, rev. Michael Baumgartner, Berlin 1915.

Uhl (ed.) 2001–2002: *Roger Bacon in der Diskussion*, ed. Florian Uhl, 2 vols., Frankfurt a. M. 2001–2002.

Ullmann 1974: Ullmann, Walter, *Individuum und Gesellschaft im Mittelalter*, Göttingen 1974 [Kleine Vandenhoeck-Reihe 1370].

Ulmer 1953: Ulmer, Karl, *Wahrheit, Kunst und Natur bei Aristoteles. Ein Beitrag zur Aufklärung der metaphysischen Herkunft der modernen Technik*, Tübingen 1953.

Usener 1969: Usener, Hermann, *Anecdoton Holderi. Ein Beitrag zur Geschichte Roms in ostgothischer Zeit*, Bonn 1877, rpt. Hildesheim 1969.

Valéry 1957: Valéry, Paul, "Questions de poésie," in *Œuvres*, 2 vols., ed. Jean Hytier, Paris 1957–1960 [Bibliothèque de la Pléiade], vol. 1, pp. 1280–1294.

Vance 1973: Vance, Eugene, "The Modernity of the Middle Ages in Future," *Romanic Review* 64 (1973), pp. 140–159.

Vance 1986: Vance, Eugene, *Marvelous Signals: Poetics and Sign Theory in the Middle Ages*, Lincoln/London 1986.

Varty 1965: Varty, Kenneth, "Deschamp's *Art de Dictier*," *French Review* 19 (1965), pp. 164–167.

Vecchi 1968: Vecchi, Giuseppe, "Primo annuncio del sistema proporzionale di Marchetto in un passo del *Lucidarium*," *Quadrivium* 9 (1968), pp. 83–93.

Ventura 2004: Ventura, Iolanda, "*Quaestiones* and Encyclopedias: Some Aspects of the Late Medieval Reception of the Pseudo-Aristotelian *Problemata* in Encyclopedic and Scientific Culture," in *Schooling and Society: The Ordering and Reordering of Knowledge in the Western Middle Ages*, ed. Alasdair MacDonald and Michael W. Twomey, Louvain/Paris/Dudley 2004, pp. 23–42.

Vetter 2001: Vetter, Walther, "Aristides Quintilianus," in *Die Musik in Geschichte und Gegenwart. Allgemeine Enzyklopädie der Musik*, ed. Friedrich Blume et al., digital version of the first ed. (1949–1986), Berlin 2001 [Digitale Bibliothek 60], s.v.

Vignaux 1931: Vignaux, P. et al., "Nominalisme," in *Dictionnaire de théologie catholique contenant l'exposé des doctrines de la théologie catholique, de leurs preuves et leur histoire*, ed. Alfred Vacant et al., 15 vols. in 30 fasc. and 15. supplements, Paris 1899–1950, vol. 11 (1931), col. 717–784.

Vijver 1931: Vijver, A. van de, "Cassiodore et son oeuvre," *Speculum* 6 (1931), pp. 244–292.

Vincent 1849: Vincent, Alexandre J. H., *Analyse du traité de métrique et de rhythmique de St. Augustin intitulé De musica. Nouvelles considérations sur la poésie lyrique*, Paris 1849.

Voss 1970: Voss, Bernd-Rainer, *Der Dialog in der frühchristlichen Literatur*, Munich 1970 [Studia et testimonia antiqua 9].

Vrin 1980: Vrin, Jacques, "Harmonie musicale et harmonie naturelle à l'époque carolingienne. Exégèse d'un passage de Jean Scot Erigène," in *Musique, littérature et société au Moyen Âge. Actes du colloque, 24–29 mars 1980*, ed. Danielle Buschinger and André Crépin, Paris 1980, pp. 85–97.

Vulliez 1982: Vulliez, Charles, "Une étape privilégiée de l'entrée dans la vie: Le temps des études universitaires à travers l'exemple orléanais des derniers siècles du Moyen Age," *Annales de l'Est* 1–2 (1982), pp. 149–182.

Vyver 1931: Vyver, A. van de, "Cassiodore et son oeuvre," *Speculum* 6 (1931), pp. 244–293.

Vyver 1941: Vyver, A. van de, "Les institutiones de Cassiodore et sa Fondation à Vivarium," *Revue Bénédictine* 53 (1941), pp. 59–88.

Waeltner 1977: Waeltner, Ernst Ludwig, *Organicum melos. Zur Musikanschauung des Iohannes Scottus (Eriugena)*, Munich 1977.

Waerden 1943: Waerden, B. L. van der, "Die Harmonielehre der Pythagoreer," *Hermes* 78 (1943), pp. 163–199.

Waesberghe 1938: Waesberghe, Joseph Smits van, *De Luiksche Muziekschool als Centrum van het Muziektheoretisch Onderricht in de Middeleeuwen*, Tillburg 1938.

Waesberghe 1967: Waesberghe, Joseph Smits van, "Eine merkwürdige Figur und ihr musik-geometrisches Geheimnis," in *Festschrift Bruno Stäblein zum 70. Geburtstag*, Kassel et al. 1967, pp. 234–238.

Waite 1954: Waite, William G., *The Rhythm of Twelfth-Century Polyphony: Its Theory and Practice*, New Haven 1954 [Yale Studies in the History of Music 2].

Waite 1960: Waite, William G., "Johannes de Garlandia, Poet and Musician," *Speculum* 2 (1960), pp. 179–195.

Wald 1996: Wald, Berthold: "'*Rationalis naturae individua substantia.*' Aristoteles, Boethius und der Begriff der Person im Mittelalter," in *Individuum und Individualität im Mittelalter*, ed. Jan A. Aertsen and Andreas Speer, Berlin/New York 1996 [Miscellanea Mediaevalia 24], pp. 371–388.

Walter 1998: Walter, Michael, "Über den musikalischen Begriff proportio," in *Musik—und die Geschichte der Philosophie und Naturwissenschaften im Mittelalter. Fragen zur Wechselwirkung von "Musica" und "Philosophia" im Mittelalter*, ed. Frank Hentschel, Leiden/Boston/Cologne 1998, pp. 69–95.

Weber 1988: Weber, Max, *Gesammelte Aufsätze zur Wissenschaftslehre*, Tübingen 1988 [UTB 1492].

Wegman 1995: Wegmann, Rob C., "Sense and Sensibility in Late-Medieval Music: Thoughts on Aesthetics and 'Authenticity,'" *Early Music* 23 (1995), pp. 299–312.

Weil 1862: Weil, H., "Augustinus, *De musica*," *Jahrbücher der classischen Philologie* 85 (1862), pp. 333–356.

Weisheipl 1965: Weisheipl, James, "Classifications of the Sciences in Medieval Thought," *Medieval Sciences* 27 (1965), pp. 24–90.

Wellesz 1954: Wellesz, Egon, "Musicology," in *Grove's Dictionary of Music and Musicians*, 5th ed., 5 vols., London 1954, vol. 5, s. v.

Wellesz 1961: Wellesz, Egon, *A History of Byzantine Music and Hymnography*, 2nd rev. ed., Oxford 1961.

Werner 1956: Werner, Eric, "The Mathematical Foundation of Philippe de Vitri's *Ars nova*," *Journal of the American Musicological Society* 2 (1956), pp. 126–132.

Wessely 2001: Wessely, Othmar, "Musikerziehung," in *Die Musik in Geschichte und Gegenwart. Allgemeine Enzyklopädie der Musik*, ed. Friedrich Blume et al., digital version of the first ed. (1949–1986), Berlin 2001 [Digitale Bibliothek 60], s.v.

West 1992: West, Martin L., *Ancient Greek Music*, Oxford 1992.

Wetherbee 1967: Wetherbee, Winthrop, *The School of Chartres and Medieval Poetry*, Diss., Berkeley 1967.

Wetherbee 1972: Wetherbee, Winthrop, *Platonism and Poetry in the Twelfth Century: The Literary Influence of the School of Chartres*, Princeton 1972.

White 1981: White, Alison, "Boethius in the Medieval Quadrivium," in *Boethius: His Life, Thought, and Influence*, ed. Margaret T. Gibson, Oxford 1981, pp. 162–205.

Wiley 1948: Wiley, William L., "Who named them *Rhétoriqueurs?*," in *Medieval Studies in Honor of Jeremiah Denis Matthias Ford*, ed. Alex J. Denomy and Urban T. Holmes, Cambridge 1948, pp. 333–352.

Wilkins 1972: Wilkins, Nigel, *La louange des dames by Guillaume de Machaut*, Edinburgh 1972.

Wille 1967: Wille, Günther, *Musica Romana. Die Bedeutung der Musik im Leben der Römer*, Amsterdam 1967.

Wimsatt 1991a: Wimsatt, James I., "Chaucer and Eustache Deschamps," in *Chaucer and His French Contemporaries: Natural Music in the Fourteenth Century*, Toronto/Buffalo/London 1991, pp. 242–272.

Wimsatt 1991b: Wimsatt, James I., "Chaucer and Deschamps' 'Natural Music,'" in *The Union of Words and Music in Medieval Poetry*, ed. Rebecca A. Baltzer, Thomas Cable, and James I. Wimsatt, Austin 1991, pp. 132–150.

Winn 1981: Winn, James Anderson, *Unsuspected Eloquence: A History of the Relations between Poetry and Music*, New Haven/London 1981.

Witkowska-Zaremba 1993: Witkowska-Zaremba, Elżbieta, "Some Aspects of Pythagorean Harmony in the Late Middle Ages: 'Figura circulorum' from the Treatise 'Musica speculativa' by Johannes de Muris," in *From Idea to Sound: Proceedings of the International Musicological Symposium Held at Castle Nieborów in Poland, September 4–5, 1985*, ed. Anna Czekanowska et al., Krakau 1993, pp. 44–55.

Wolfzettel 1984: Wolfzettel, Friedrich, "Zur Poetik der Subjektivität bei Christine de Pisan," *Chloe* 1 (1984), pp. 379–398.

Wolfzettel 1992: Wolfzettel, Friedrich, "Gattungstradition und Wertewandel: Zur Entdeckung der Arbeit in der französischen Literatur der Frührenaissance," in *Festschrift für Walter Haug und Burghart Wachinger*, ed. Johannes Janota et al., 2 vols., Tübingen 1992, vol. 1, pp. 103–121.

Wolfzettel 1994: Wolfzettel, Friedrich, "Guillaume de Machaut: Dichter und Welt im Zeichen der Dame Rhétorique," *Wolfram-Studien* 13 (1994), pp. 42–57.

Wolfzettel 1995: Wolfzettel, Friedrich, "Abundante Rhetorik. Selbstverständnis und historische Funktion lyrischer Sprache von Machaut zu den Grands Rhétoriqueurs," in *Musique naturele. Interpretationen zur französischen Lyrik des Spätmittelalters*, ed. Wolf-Dieter Stempel, Munich 1995 [Romanistisches Kolloquium 7], pp. 75–104.

Wolfzettel 1996: Wolfzettel, Friedrich, "Spätmittelalterliches Selbstverständnis des Dichters im Zeichen von Fortuna: Guillaume de Machaut und Christine de Pizan," *Das Mittelalter* 1 (1996), pp. 111–128.

Wolfzettel 1997: Wolfzettel, Friedrich, "Zeitangst, Geschichtskrise und Ich-Bewußtsein in der frühen Neuzeit: Petrarca—Charles d'Orléans—Montaigne," in *Zeit-

konzeptionen, Zeiterfahrung, Zeitmessung. Stationen ihres Wandels vom Mittelalter bis zur Moderne, ed. Trude Ehlert, Paderborn et al. 1997, pp. 309–324.

Wolter 1969: Wolter, Hans, "Geschichtliche Bildung im Rahmen der Artes Liberales," in *Artes Liberales. Von der antiken Bildung zur Wissenschaft des Mittelalters*, ed. Josef Koch, Leiden/Cologne 1969 [Studien und Texte zur Geistesgeschichte des Mittelalters 5], pp. 50–83.

Wulf 1934–1947: Wulf, Maurice de, *Histoire de la philosophie médiévale*, 3 vols., Louvain 1934–1947.

Yudkin 1990: Yudkin, Jeremy, "The Influence of Aristotle on French University Music Texts," in *Music Theory and Its Sources: Antiquity and the Middle Ages*, ed. Andre Barbera, Notre Dame 1990 [Notre Dame Conferences in Medieval Studies 1], pp. 173–189.

Zaminer (ed.) 1985ff.: Zaminer, Frieder (ed.), *Geschichte der Musiktheorie*, 11 vols., Darmstadt 1985ff.

Zarncke 1871: Zarncke, Friedrich, "Zwei mittelalterliche Abhandlungen über den Bau rhythmischer Verse," *Berichte über die Verhandlungen der Königlich Sächsischen Gesellschaft der Wissenschaften zu Leipzig. Philologisch-Historische Classe* 23 (1871), pp. 40–41.

Ziegenaus 1972: Ziegenaus, Anton, *Die trinitarische Ausprägung der göttlichen Seinsfülle nach Marius Victorinus*, Munich 1972 [Münchener Theologische Studien II, 41].

Zimmermann 1976: Zimmermann, Jörg, "Wandlungen des philosophischen Musikbegriffs," in *Musik und Zahl. Interdisziplinäre Beiträge zum Grenzbereich zwischen Musik und Mathematik*, ed. Günter Schnitzler, Bonn-Bad Godesberg 1976 [Orpheus—Schriftenreihe zu Grundfragen der Musik 17], pp. 81–136.

Zimmermann 1991: Zimmermann, Margarete, "La littérature française à la fin du Moyen Âge—une littérature de crise?," in *Actes du VIe Colloque International sur le Moyen Français 3. Recherches sur la littérature du XVe siècle*, ed. Sergio Cigada, Milan 1991 [Contributi del Centro Studi sulla Letteratura Medio-Francese e Medio-Inglese 9—Pubblicazioni dell'Università Cattolica del Sacro Cuore. Scienze filogogiche e letteratura 46], pp. 207–220.

Zink 1985: Zink, Michel, "La tristesse du coeur dans *Le Livre du Cuer d'Amours espris* de René d'Anjou," in *Le Récit amoureux*, ed. Didier Coste and Michel Zéraffa, Seyssel 1985 [L'Or d'Atalante], pp. 22–38.

Zink 1992: Zink, Michel, "Le Lyrisme en rond. Esthétique et séduction des poèmes à forme fixe au Moyen Âge," in *Les Voix de la conscience. Parole du poète et parole de Dieu dans la littérature médiévale*, Caen 1992, pp. 177–196.

Zink 1993: Zink, Michel, *Introduction à la littérature française du Moyen Âge*, Paris 1993 [Références].

Zink 1995: Zink, Michel, "L'amour en fuite—l'Espinette amoureuse et Le joli buisson de Jeannette de Froissart ou la poésie comme histoire sans objet," in *Musique naturele. Interpretationen zur französischen Lyrik des Spätmittelalters*, ed. Wolf-Dieter Stempel, Munich 1995 [Romanistisches Kolloquium 7], pp. 195–210.

Zintzen 1977: Zintzen, Clemens, "Einleitung," in *Die Philosophie des Neuplatonismus*, ed. Clemens Zintzen, Darmstadt 1977 [Wege der Forschung 186], pp. VII–XXIX.

Zumthor 1972: Zumthor, Paul, "Rhétorique et poétique latines et romanes," in *Grundriß der romanischen Literaturen des Mittelalters*, in collaboration with Jean Frappier et al., ed. Hans-Robert Jauß and Erich Köhler, 11. vols. in 30 fasc., Heidelberg 1968ff., vol. 1 (1968), ed. Hans-Robert Jauß, pp. 57–91.

Zumthor 1974: Zumthor, Paul, "Les Grands Rhétoriqueurs et le vers," *Langue française* 23 (1974), pp. 88–98.

Zumthor 1975a: Zumthor, Paul, "Le discours polyvalent de Jean Molinet (La Ressource du petit peuple)," in *Mélanges de linguistique et de littérature offerts à Lein Geschiere*, Amsterdam 1975, pp. 103–130.

Zumthor 1975b: Zumthor, Paul, "Jonglerie et langage," in *Langue—Texte—Énigme*, Paris 1975 [Poétique], pp. 36–54.

Zumthor 1975c: Zumthor, Paul, "Du rythme à la rime," in *Langue—Texte—Énigme*, Paris 1975 [Poétique], pp. 125–143.

Zumthor 1976: Zumthor, Paul, "Le carrefour des rhétoriqueurs. Intertextualité et rhétorique," *Poétique* 27 (1976), pp. 317–337.

Zumthor 1978a: Zumthor, Paul, *Le Masque et la lumière. La poétique des Grands rhétoriqueurs*, Paris 1978.

Zumthor 1978b: Zumthor, Paul, *Anthologie des grands rhétoriqueurs*, Paris 1978 [Coll. 10/18].

Zumthor 1979: Zumthor, Paul, "From Hi(story) to Poem, or the Paths of Pun: The Grands Rhétoriqueurs of Fifteenth-Century France," *New Literary History* 2 (1979), pp. 231–264.

Zumthor 1981: Zumthor, Paul, "The Great Game of Rhetoric," *New Literary History* 3 (1981), pp. 493–508.

Zumthor 1984a: Zumthor, Paul, *La poésie et la voix dans la civilisation médiévale*, Paris 1984 [Essais et conférences/Collège de France].

Zumthor 1984b: Zumthor, Paul, *La lettre et la voix. De la "littérature" médiévale*, Paris 1984 [Poétique].

Zumthor 2000: Zumthor, Paul, *Essai de poétique médiévale*, Paris 2000 [Points essais 433].

equivalence, 79–80, 103–105, 108,
144, 261, 262, 267, 287, 304, 305,
307, 308, 315, 346, 347–353, 354,
356–357, 358, 401, 469
Erasmus of Rotterdam, 255
ethics, Christian, 46–49, 51, 54, 55,
75, 76, 81, 83, 88–89, 94–95, 96,
125, 131, 141, 144–149, 160, 163,
173, 186, 190, 195, 214, 218–219,
220–222, 223, 239, 248, 264,
271–274, 298, 317, 320–322, 328,
329, 330–333, 339–340, 361–362,
392, 402, 427, 457, 467
ethos, doctrine of, in music theory, 17,
23, 26, 57, 58, 117, 120, 144–149,
161, 167, 186–187, 195, 222, 225,
239, 250, 271–274, 301, 312, 317,
323, 324, 422–423, 458
Euclid, 61, 97, 152
Eudemus of Rhodes, 98
Évrart de Conty, 270–289, 459

Fabri, Pierre, 334
Favonius Eulogius, 141, 156
Ficino, Marsilio, 116, 121, 450
fiction, 206, 222–223, 444
figura, 42–46, 49, 50, 80, 82, 86, 113,
222, 223, 327, 340, 343, 357
finiteness/infiniteness, 9, 60, 62, 63, 91,
104, 126, 136, 142, 199, 358, 416
fixed forms, 14, 20, 303–304, 305, 346,
360
foot in metrics, 57, 66, 67–72, 80, 103,
104, 159, 161, 174, 345
form
numerically determined, 21, 50, 57,
58, 59, 62, 67, 69, 77, 79, 81, 82,
90, 93, 96–101, 102, 112, 113,
114, 116, 126, 127, 130, 135, 138,
146, 149, 167, 179, 183, 195–196,
203, 204, 205, 206, 209, 213, 224,
227, 231, 259–269, 276, 285, 286,
287, 304, 308, 311–317, 344, 345,
356, 383, 399, 401
in ontology, 48, 49, 50, 62, 63, 65,
72, 80, 81, 82, 83, 95–101, 106–
107, 108, 114, 115, 116, 123, 126,
127, 130, 138, 140, 141, 142, 144,
146, 167, 179, 182, 183, 185, 196,

199, 203, 205, 206–207, 210, 211,
212, 213, 215–217, 218, 223, 224,
281, 309, 311, 333, 355, 356, 361,
362, 399, 401, 408, 414, 416, 463
as sign, 82, 108, 112, 196, 217, 223,
281, 323, 355, 356, 357, 360, 361,
362, 363, 403 (*see* anagoge)
of the work of art, as opposed to content or meaning, 20, 21, 67–72, 76,
79, 81, 83, 90, 92, 97, 102–108,
112, 114, 115, 116, 138, 139,
140, 144, 149, 206–207, 216, 217,
223, 227, 230, 259–269, 285, 287,
298–308, 309, 311–317, 329–330,
333, 335–363, 400, 402, 403, 411,
460, 464
formalism
in *Grands rhétoriqueurs* poetry, 10,
11, 12, 26, 31, 37, 113, 293, 294,
295, 335–363
as in the "musical" conception of poetry, 12, 83–84, 90, 102–107, 142–
143, 148–149, 288–289, 315–317,
329, 333, 335–363
Fourfold Meaning, Theory of, 11, 44,
51, 223, 269, 375, 444, 456. *See
also* hermeneutics
Fulgentius, 156, 177

Gafori, Franchino, 116, 154, 251
Geoffrey of Vinsauf, 253, 266
geometry, as liberal art, 15, 16, 71, 84,
94, 124, 125, 131, 138, 152, 185,
190, 202, 209, 309, 369, 383, 414
Gerbert of Aurillac, 131, 133, 144, 153,
157
Gervais of Melkley, 254
Giraldus Cambrensis, 167
Glareanus, 116
Gottfried of St. Victor, 157
Gottschalk of Orbais, 165
grammar, as liberal art, 12, 15, 16, 31,
57, 66, 72, 73, 91, 92, 121, 169,
184, 229, 230, 231, 233, 234, 253,
254–256, 264, 266, 355, 379, 384,
389, 394, 429, 431, 451, 452
Grands rhétoriqueurs, 4–13, 21, 27, 28,
31, 32, 35, 37, 196, 246, 293, 294,
295, 302, 309, 334–363

John Scotus Eriugena, 30, 111, 113,
     119, 150, 151, 157, 180–185
John XXII (Pope), 225, 301
Justin Martyr, 45

Kepler, Johannes, 362
Kircher, Athanasius, 116

lai, 18, 20
Latini, Brunetto, 261, 297
legitimacy of verbal art, 93, 101, 102,
     149, 224, 278, 305, 309, 316, 317,
     329, 360, 402, 469, 471
Leibniz, Gottfried Wilhelm, 362
Lemaire de Belges, Jean, 4, 336, 349
Levi ben Gerson (Leo Hebraeus, Ger-
     sonides), 237
Luther, Martin, 116, 362

Machaut, Guillaume de, 3, 4, 5, 6, 10,
     15, 112, 246, 295, 296, 298–308,
     315, 335, 338, 368, 462
Macrobius Ambrosius Theodosius, 121,
     141, 157–158, 159, 177, 179, 232,
     251, 271, 420
Mallarmé, Stéphane, 10
Mallius Theodorus, 253
mannerism, 5, 355
Marbod of Rennes, 359
Marchettus of Padua, 25, 157, 167,
     168, 188, 235–237
Martianus Capella, 30, 35, 84, 121,
     150, 151, 157, 158–159, 166, 177,
     180, 189, 232, 271
Martin of Dacia, 254
Martin of Laon, 157
Matthew (Evangelist), 42
Matthew of Vendôme, 253
Maximus Victorinus, 253
measure
   as constituent of form, 57–58, 59,
     62, 65, 66, 70, 79, 83, 89–90, 91,
     92, 96, 100–101, 102, 103, 108,
     114, 115, 137, 139, 178, 183, 191,
     195, 206, 215, 217, 232, 235, 259,
     262, 264, 278, 285, 286, 300, 301,
     311–312, 313, 347, 355, 381, 386,
     395, 437, 441, 464
   in discourse, 18, 21, 57–72, 68, 69,

82, 90, 130, 145, 162, 164, 166,
     174, 175, 191, 206, 230, 245,
     236–269, 285, 286, 287, 288, 300,
     311–312, 313, 314, 323, 336, 347,
     381
   in ontology, 48, 49, 60, 80, 82, 114,
     137, 138, 178, 183, 191, 232, 243,
     278, 280, 316, 357, 381, 395, 418
   in sound, 57, 66, 90, 281, 301, 312,
     327, 431
membrum (metrics), 69–72, 102, 104,
     174, 285, 345, 346, 385
Mersenne, Marin, 362
Meschniot, Jean, 348
metaphor, 222–223, 444
meter (metrics), 54, 66, 68–71, 80, 90,
     93, 102, 104, 107, 164, 166, 174,
     175, 206, 227, 230, 233, 245, 256,
     257, 258, 259, 260, 266, 269, 285,
     286, 299, 313–314, 323, 336, 345,
     386. *See also* measure
methexis, 95–97, 101, 106, 214–215
Methodios of Olympos, 110
metrics. *See also* measure
   quantifying, 60, 66–72, 174, 246,
     253, 258, 285, 345–346, 384, 452
   syllable-counting, 130, 159, 175, 245,
     246, 253, 256–269, 286, 287, 335,
     336, 345–346, 452
Michael of Marbais, 254, 255
Michael Scotus, 167
mode, 58, 117, 136, 148, 170, 176, 177,
     178, 185, 186, 235, 418, 422–423
modistae, 254–256, 452
Molinet, Jean, 4, 7, 9, 30, 35, 154, 196,
     248, 251, 294, 334–345, 347, 348,
     349, 350, 352, 353, 357, 358, 359,
     362, 363, 467
Monnier, Marc, 351
Montferrant, Jean de, 355
Morley, Thomas, 116
movement (*motus*), 58, 60, 61, 65, 66,
     70, 73, 79, 111, 137, 139, 158,
     178, 182, 184, 185, 191, 193, 199,
     200, 202, 208–209, 227, 233, 237,
     244, 252, 277, 278, 281–282, 313,
     326, 327, 343, 381, 383, 384, 385,
     406, 414–415, 416, 419
Murphy, James J., 254, 259

Remigius of Auxerre, 151, 159, 177, 180

repetition, as constituent of form, 70, 79–80, 103, 114, 144, 260, 278, 303, 304, 305, 308, 346, 450

rhetoric, as liberal art, 10, 12, 15, 16, 31, 51, 84, 91, 107, 120, 121, 156, 185, 186, 206, 223, 229–231, 233, 234, 253, 261, 264, 293, 295, 298, 299, 300, 320, 328, 329, 335–336, 357, 394, 411, 412, 444

Rhetorica ad Herennium, 266

rhyme, 9, 20, 31, 108, 175, 246, 256–269, 284–288, 299, 304, 305, 313–314, 323–325, 335–336, 344–345, 346–357, 459

rhythm, 9, 12, 23, 25, 26, 52, 58–59, 66, 67–72, 74, 75, 77, 79, 80, 84, 92, 93, 104, 105, 107, 117, 118, 137, 139, 144, 158, 159, 161, 162, 166, 167, 174, 175, 185, 189, 193, 230, 231, 233, 234, 235, 236, 245, 246, 253, 254, 256–269, 273, 287, 289, 303, 304, 335, 336, 346–347, 355, 356, 357, 358, 378–379, 382, 385, 388, 401. *See also* measure; *musica rhythmica*

Richard Kilwardby, 232

Richard of St. Victor, 113

rime équivoque, 345, 355

Robert Grosseteste, 113–114, 116, 133, 227, 229

Roger Bacon, 23, 26, 133, 167, 226–232

Roman de la Rose, 283

rondeau, 14, 18, 20, 302–303, 344, 345

Ronsard, Pierre de, 4

Salinas, Francisco, 116

scales, 21, 98, 135, 136, 137, 142, 185, 195, 262, 268, 312, 339

Scholasticism, 35, 113, 115, 121, 123–124, 131, 165, 170, 185, 187–188, 189, 190, 198–200, 207–210, 240, 252, 255, 280, 375, 432, 438

Sebillet, Thomas, 4

seconde rhetorique, 9, 11, 21, 261, 295, 302, 308, 334, 335, 336, 363

Seneca, Lucius Annaeus, 116

sense perception, 74–84, 386–387

Siger of Courtrai, 254, 255

signatures, doctrine of, 89–90, 393

similitude, as constituent of form, 79, 80, 96, 100, 102, 105–107, 144, 145, 195, 213, 218, 281, 282–283, 308, 312, 315, 350, 356, 357

Simon Tunstede, 167

song, 20, 24, 25, 36, 59, 83, 90, 114, 117, 140, 166, 167, 173, 175, 177, 186, 190, 191, 194, 201, 245, 250, 259, 273, 275, 285, 286, 297, 299, 303, 313–314, 315, 325, 327, 331–332, 361, 378, 379, 381, 402, 406, 411, 422, 432, 469

Suger of St. Denis, 215

symmetry, as constituent of form, 69–70, 71, 80, 86, 104, 174, 212, 285, 287, 302–303, 304, 307, 345, 346, 353, 385, 401, 442

sympathia, 130

Tempier, Etienne, 198

temporality, 46

tempus (metrics), 57, 60, 66–70, 92

Terentianus Maurus, 253

Tertullian, 51, 94

tetraktys, 63, 135, 136, 138, 139, 144, 192, 195, 198, 211, 212, 236, 238, 288, 418

Theodulf of Orléans, 169

Theon of Smyrna, 61, 121, 142

Thierry of Chartres, 15, 189

Thomas Cajetan, 224

Thomas of Capua, 259–260

Thomas of Erfurt, 254

Thomas of York, 227

Tubal, 167

typology in theology, 42–50, 375

Ugolino of Orvieto, 26, 29, 111, 154, 157, 168, 188, 246–248

Ulrich of Strasburg, 116

unity, in ontology and epistemology, 48, 49, 63–65, 67, 80, 83, 96, 97, 104, 106, 127–131, 138–140, 142, 145, 182, 184, 218, 232, 250, 259, 267, 313, 315, 333, 344, 346, 361, 363, 417–418

util/frui, 77, 106, 107, 387–388